MEMOIR

OF THE

LIFE, WORKS AND CORRESPONDENCE,

OF THE

REV. ROBERT ASPLAND,

OF HACKNEY.

BY

R. BROOK ASPLAND, M.A.

LONDON:
EDWARD T. WHITFIELD, 2, ESSEX STREET, STRAND.

M.DCCC.L.

PREFACE.

This Memoir, originally printed in successive Numbers of the "CHRISTIAN REFORMER," is now published in a separate form, in compliance with the wishes of many friends, and in the hope that it may promote the love of Scriptural Truth, and zeal for its diffusion, by exhibiting the example of one who sought it earnestly, and, when he believed he had found it, made it the business of his life to diffuse it.

CONTENTS.

CHAPTER I. 1782—1797.
Robert Aspland's birth and parentage, and school education 1

CHAPTER II. 1797.
Studies under Rev. Timothy Thomas, of Islington—Becomes acquainted with the Middleton family—Is admitted on Ward's Foundation 17

CHAPTER III. 1797, 1798.
Studies under Rev. Joseph Hughes, of Battersea—Begins to preach 31

CHAPTER IV. 1798, 1799.
Enters the Bristol Academy—His correspondence while there—Dr. F. A. Cox his companion there 47

CHAPTER V. 1799, 1800.
Vacation at Wicken—Goes to the University at Aberdeen—His orthodoxy is shaken 70

CHAPTER VI. 1800.
Returns to Wicken—His doubts respecting orthodoxy increase—Resigns the Ward Exhibition, and engages in trade 90

CHAPTER VII. 1800, 1801.
His disgust with trade—Preaches on probation at Newport, Isle of Wight—Is chosen minister—Marries—Is ordained—Opens a school 98

CHAPTER VIII. 1801—1804.
Happy and useful at Newport—Becomes acquainted with the Rev. Thomas Belsham 114

CHAPTER IX. 1804.
His first publication, a political sermon—Becomes a contributor to the Universal Theological Magazine—Is invited to remove to Norton, in Derbyshire—Death of his father 134

CHAPTER X. 1804, 1805.

Sermon on the Revolution of 1688—Accepts the invitation to Norton—Farewell sermon at Newport—Receives an invitation from the Gravel-Pit congregation, Hackney, to preach as a candidate 151

CHAPTER XI. 1805, 1806.

At Norton—Mr. Shore—Preaches at Hackney—Accepts an invitation to settle there—Initiatory sermon at Hackney—Difficulties of his position—Sermon on the death of Charles James Fox 168

CHAPTER XII. 1806.

Efforts to increase the organization and union of the Unitarians—Establishes the Monthly Repository—Founds the Unitarian Fund 183

CHAPTER XIII. 1807—1809.

Religious conferences at Hackney—Lectures to the young people—Death of Rev. Theophilus Lindsey—Persecution of Mr. Gisburne at Soham—Exposure of Andrew Fuller's bigotry 199

CHAPTER XIV. 1805—1809.

Miscellaneous extracts from the Diary 216

CHAPTER XV. 1809, 1810.

Letters from Dr. Toulmin, Mr. Benjamin Flower, Mr. William Christie and Mr. James Taylor—Christian Tract Society established............... 237

CHAPTER XVI. 1810, 1811.

Extracts from the Diary—New Gravel-Pit meeting opened—New Hymnbook—Lord Sidmouth's Bill successfully opposed—Correspondence with Mr. Belsham respecting the Bill 251

CHAPTER XVII. 1811—1813.

Repeal of persecuting statutes—Death of Mr. Perceval—Trinity Bill passed—Unitarian Fund and its proceedings—Richard Wright—Mr. Lyons—Mr. Winder 270

CHAPTER XVIII. 1812.

The Widows' Fund—Rev. Hugh Worthington—Correspondence with Rev. Samuel Webley, of Wedmore—Establishment of the Unitarian Academy—Rev. J. B. Dewhurst.. 293

CHAPTER XIX. 1812—1818.

Rev. Jeremiah Joyce—Rev. T. B. Broadbent—Dr. Morell—Plan of study at the Academy—Lectures on preaching—List of students—Rev. Benjamin Goodier—Rev. T. W. Horsfield 312

CHAPTER XX. 1812, 1813.

Sermon against Atheism—Mrs. Catherine Cappe—Mrs. Mary Hughes—Rev. Edward Harries—Publication of the Plea for Unitarian Dissenters 331

CHAPTER XXI. 1813, 1814.

Publication of "Three Sermons"—"British Pulpit Eloquence," and Haynes on the Attributes—Establishment of the Christian Reformer—Thanksgiving Sermon on the Peace—Death of his mother 351

CHAPTER XXII. 1816, 1817.

Death of Mr. Joyce and Mr. Vidler—Persecutions of the French Protestants—Thos. Hardy, the political reformer—Prosecution of Mr. John Wright at Liverpool—The Wolverhampton case—Sermons on Blasphemy—Letters of Sir Samuel Romilly—Three trials of William Hone 366

CHAPTER XXIII. 1817—1821.

Dr. Daniel Williams and his Trusts—List of Trustees—Dr. Thomas Rees's letter on Mr. Aspland's share in the administration of the Trust—Table talk at the Library—Mr. Aspland's conversational powers—Establishment of the Non-Con Club 389

CHAPTER XXIV. 1818—1821.

Correspondence with Mr. Belsham, Mr. Yates, &c.—Illness—Establishment of the Association for protecting the Civil Rights of Unitarians—Prosecution of unbelievers—Mr. Aspland's letters to the "Times"—Letters of Lord Holland—Queen Caroline 407

CHAPTER XXV. 1820—1823.

Brougham's Education Bill—Death of Dr. James Lindsay—Exertions to save Harris, a convict—The Christians' Petition—Dr. Channing—The Presbyterian Fund—Visit to Wales—Correspondence 424

CHAPTER XXVI. 1822—1826.

Serious illness—Rammohun Roy—Dr. Pett—Correspondence with Mr. Chas. Butler—Dr. Abraham Rees—Completion of the twentieth year of Mr. Aspland's ministry at Hackney—Ordination service at Chester 446

CHAPTER XXVII. 1825—1828.

Unitarian Association—Monthly Repository—Repeal of the Test and Corporation Acts—Commemorative banquet at Freemasons'—Mr. Aspland's speech—Correspondence with Mr. Charles Butler and Lord Holland .. 464

CHAPTER XXVIII. 1828, 1829.

Catholic Emancipation—Lord John Russell—Mr. Ivimey—Rev. James Holt—Death of Mr. Benjamin Flower—Mr. David Eaton and Mr. Isaac Aspland—Death of Rev. Thos. Belsham—Correspondence with Dr. Drummond—Unitarian Association—Visit to Paris 490

CHAPTER XXIX. 1830—1833.

Death of George IV.—Address to William IV.—Orthodox discontents at the *Socinian* representation at the Throne—French Revolution—Rammohun Roy's visit to England and death—Reform Bill—Sermon on Patriotism—Death of Mr. Christopher Richmond—Volume of Sermons—Correspondence with Mr. James Taylor—Death of Mr. John Emons 506

CHAPTER XXX. 1836, 1837.

Marriage Law and Dissenters' Marriages Act—Presbyterian Form of Marriage—Dissolution of the Three Denominations by the secession of the Presbyterian ministers and deputies—Letter to an eminent Independent minister—Reception of the Presbyterian ministers at the court of Queen Victoria 524

CHAPTER XXXI. 1834—1840.

Enlarged series of the Christian Reformer—Psalmody—Death of Richard Wright—Celebration of the Third Centenary of the English Reformation—Letter of Mr. James Taylor—Severe illness—Aggregate meeting of Unitarians—Death of Mr. William Sturch—Publication of Tracts for the People—Catechism and Prayers for the Young—Letter of reminiscences by Rev. Charles Wicksteed 546

CHAPTER XXXII. 1840.

Death of Lord Holland, of Mr. Frend, Mr. Dyer and Mr. Rutt—Visit to the Monastery of St. Bernard's—To Dukinfield—Great "turn-out"—Death of Dr. Channing—Proceedings in defence of Presbyterian endowments—Death of the Duke of Sussex—Visits in Devonshire 564

CHAPTER XXXIII. 1843—1845.

Death of Mr. G. W. Wood—Mr. Aspland's last sermon—Dissenters' Chapels Bill—Death of Mr. Benjamin Wood—Death of Mrs. Henry Ridge—Parting Address as editor of the Christian Reformer—Death and funeral—Tribute to his memory by Rev. John Kentish 585

APPENDIX.

List of his Publications 607
Letters omitted in the Memoir.................................... 612

MEMOIR OF REV. ROBERT ASPLAND.

CHAPTER I.

THE late Rev. ROBERT ASPLAND occupied for more than forty years a very prominent place amongst the Protestant Dissenters of England, and during that time his opinions and counsels had great weight with the religious denomination with which he more particularly united himself. A full and faithful memoir of his life is due alike to his memory and to the public. Happily, abundant materials for writing his life exist in his letters and journals, which, with a few slight interruptions, extend from the year 1793 to the close of his life,—in his extensive manuscript and printed works,—and in the recollections of his numerous surviving family and friends. From these materials, his eldest son, to whom he by will bequeathed his manuscript books and papers, trusts to be able to form a narrative which will be regarded as a not unworthy memorial of the labours and virtues of his revered Father, and a not unacceptable contribution to the history of liberal Dissent in England during the present century.

The family of Aspland has for more than a century been seated chiefly in the village of Wicken, in the county of Cambridge. The first of the family who settled there was Isaac, the son of Robert Aspland, of Downham, in the Isle of Ely. He successfully established himself as the proprietor of the village shop which supplied the various wants of all the inhabitants. For more than a hundred years have the premises which his successful industry enabled him to purchase been devoted to the same purpose, and been in the successive possession of members of the same family. It may be added as a proof of the primitive and unchanged character of this Cambridgeshire village, that when, in the beginning of the year 1846, the writer visited it, he found that the shop established by his ancestor was still the sole village store.

Isaac Aspland died in the year 1762, and was followed in a few months by his wife, whose maiden name was Mary Steadman. They left a young family, of which Robert, the eldest son, had not completed his 16th year at the time of his father's death. He was fortunately gifted with considerable vigour of character, and proved himself equal to the heavy responsibility thus early thrown upon him. He is still remembered by a few aged people, and spoken of with respect as a man of sterling sense, of simple manners, and possessed of a very kind heart. His name was never mentioned by his late son but with reverential affection.* He was twice married. His second marriage was the

---

* The following tribute to his father's memory was inserted by the Rev. Robert Aspland in the Universal Theological Magazine, Vol. II. pp. 340, 341. It shews some striking points of resemblance in the character of father and son.

"On Saturday, Nov. 3, (1804,) Mr. Robert Aspland, of Wicken, in the county of Cambridge, in the fifty-eighth year of his age. In him were united a rare assemblage of virtues, and his loss is deeply felt and sincerely deplored by all who knew him. In business he was distinguished for capacity, integrity, industry and punctuality. He was long known in his neighbourhood as the avowed enemy of parochial tyranny, and as the friend to humanity and the poor. In his family, he was uniformly tender, forbearing and kind; no man ever possessed more innate benevolence, or delighted more in exercising it, than himself; always serene and cheerful in his aspect, and mild and charitable in his deportment, he conciliated universal esteem, and died lamented by a whole village. With an uncommon and unaffected share of modesty, he was yet on most topics extremely well informed. He was a true patriot, and steady and open in his attachment to the cause of peace and freedom. He was a sincere Christian. Originally a zealous Churchman, he was for the last twenty years a Dissenter; and being such from the conviction of an honest and inquiring mind, he was bold and active, though not intemperate and obtrusive, in his religious profession. Till of late he continued among the Calvinists, and for a series of years opened his hand and house, and fitted up a place of worship, for preachers of that persuasion. He was disgusted, however, at length with their bitterness and bickerings, and in some instances their disregard of morality, and settled, upon investigation, in the Unitarian doctrine,—a doctrine which was congenial with the manly simplicity and ardent benevolence of his heart, and which, as the writer of this article witnessed with exultation, administered the warmest consolation to him in his last illness. Becoming an Unitarian, as at first a Dissenter, upon principle, he was never shaken in his opinions by the illiberal sneers or harsh judgment of his orthodox acquaintance. Not having within the vicinity of his residence any religious society whose views accorded with his own, he was under the necessity of late of carrying on worship himself, which, with the assistance of a few friends, he did to the last. On this occasion, his plan was to read select parts from Dod-

cause of an important change. Hannah Brook, of Isleham (a village in the neighbouring fen), his second wife, was a woman of strong religious convictions, which had been moulded in accordance with the definite views and strict discipline of an orthodox Dissenting church. Her husband had, like his forefathers, been accustomed to attend the parish church, and was not without zeal in the defence of the doctrines and usages of the Established Church. But her stronger convictions gradually wrought a change in his opinions, and in the course of a few years he became an avowed Dissenter. They had several children born to them, but the only one who survived infancy was Robert, the subject of this memoir, who was born January 23rd, 1782. It may perhaps be regarded as a presumption that his mother had been brought up amongst the Independents* rather than the Baptists, that her son, like the other children of her husband, was baptized at the parish church. The baptism is registered April 7, 1782. But about the year 1784, both his parents became regular attendants at the Baptist meeting at Soham, a town distant two miles from Wicken, on the road to Ely. It does not appear that they became members of *the church*, or underwent the rite of baptism. The Baptist society of Soham had been the means of calling into regular exercise the pulpit talents of the celebrated Andrew Fuller. He was born of parents engaged in husbandry at Padney, a farm in the parish of Wicken. Till he was twenty years of age, he followed the agricultural pursuits of his parents. He then, as his biographer says, "arose out of obscurity, propelled by the force of his own native genius," and accepted the call of the Baptist church at Soham to become their pastor. Mr. Fuller's ministry was exercised in this place for eight years. He drew up, and his church adopted, a covenant and articles of faith, subscrip-

---

dridge's Family Expositor and the works of Tillotson, Robinson, Price and Priestley; and he and those that associated with him have often expressed the pleasure and improvement which they derived from their small but harmonious and liberal meetings. * * * * On his death-bed, he was particularly affected and edified by the saint-like and apostolic death of the venerable Priestley, and lamented with tears of concern that that great and pious man should have been followed even to the grave with reproach and calumny."

* There is a confirmation of this conjecture in Mr. Robinson's "Present State of Nonconformity in Cambridgeshire, 1775," given in Dyer's Life of Robinson, p. 463. Opposite to "Isleham," the word "Independent" alone is placed, the pastor being Rev. Samuel Lambert. Of his church, therefore, it may be concluded that Hannah Brook was a member until her marriage and removal to Wicken.

tion to which was made a test of membership. Although Mr. Fuller left Soham for Kettering in 1782, we may well believe that his influence continued to be great, and assisted to direct the Nonconformity of both Wicken and Soham into a strictly Calvinistic channel. There was, indeed, at that time in Cambridgeshire another man who enjoyed amongst the Dissenters a high and well-deserved reputation, and whose spirit was far more bland and catholic, Robert Robinson. Fuller and Robinson had come into conflict a few years before this on the subject of the terms of communion, Robinson advocating open communion, and Fuller taking the opposite view. Between Cambridge and Wicken twelve tedious miles of fen intervened, and there is no tradition of this or other villages in the neighbourhood having been made the scene of Robinson's inimitable village preaching.

Of the childhood of Robert Aspland, only scanty recollections or traditions now survive. There lived in the village of Wicken, fourteen years ago, a venerable man, named John Emons, the owner of the village forge. He was "in some respects an extraordinary man,"[*] and exercised at some critical periods a not unimportant influence over his young neighbour. He possessed a strong and penetrating understanding, and had an eager thirst for knowledge. His countenance, when softened by age, bore a striking resemblance to the portraits of John Locke. In very early childhood, Robert Aspland felt the attraction of this thoughtful man's society, and was often seen near his forge. The old man used to detail with much interest the searching and perplexing questions which this child put to him, especially on theology. John Emons had been converted and baptized by Andrew Fuller, and was a member of the Soham church. He afterwards saw reason to adopt, with his youthful friend, a milder theology than Calvinism; and Mr. Fuller, who could appreciate the qualities of John Emons' understanding and felt a natural pride in his convert and disciple, strongly resented and never forgave his "backsliding."

Mr. Aspland remembered to the end of his life, and often spoke with pleasure of, his intercourse when a boy with the worthy blacksmith. He also spoke of the great delight which reading gave him even in early boyhood. He was a very precocious politician, and in his eighth year became the reader to the family of the weekly newspaper. As the

---

[*] See a pleasing tribute to his memory, by the Rev. W. Clack, of Soham, in Christian Reformer, 1st Series, Vol. XIX. pp. 375—377.

French Revolution proceeded, his thirst for political information became intense, and it is still remembered that, on his way from Soham, with the newspaper for which he had called on returning from school, he was often seen sitting by the road-side, or slowly walking, and eagerly devouring the news for which he could not wait till he became the reader to the home circle.

He was accustomed to speak of his early home as being cheerful and happy. Amongst his cherished recollections was that of his father's eager and fearless patriotism. He held in the strongest dislike the measures of Mr. Pitt, and both in private and public expressed hostility to that unscrupulous statesman. This circumstance gave Mrs. Aspland some uneasiness, when it became known that spies and informers were abroad in the country, ready to pounce on any imprudent opponent of the Government. Several times did the young Robert Aspland sit up with his mother long beyond his usual hour of rest, comforting her, in her husband's absence at market or a parish meeting, and allaying her apprehensions lest he had fallen, through his honest warmth, into the hands of the enemies of liberty. Joyful was the greeting when the kind husband and father returned in safety. But the recollection of those anxious hours never left the mind of this affectionate son, and served, twenty years afterwards, when, under the discreditable Administration of Lords Liverpool and Castlereagh, the Government again resorted to the base services of spies and informers, to whet his indignation against their proceedings.

A source of anxiety common to both his parents was the difficulty of obtaining for their son the means of educating those talents, of the existence of which they soon became conscious and proud. In this respect, Wicken furnished no advantages beyond the humblest dame-school. There were no educated Dissenting ministers, and there was no resident clergyman. The towns of Ely, Cambridge and Newmarket, were each distant about two hours' ride. The neighbouring villages were scarcely better off as respects teachers than Wicken. The only resource was the grammar-school at Soham, at which, twenty years before, Andrew Fuller had gained all that he ever had of school education. To this Robert Aspland was accordingly daily sent, with one or two young companions, as soon as he was old and strong enough to trudge across the huge, unenclosed field that lies between Wicken and Soham.

The master of the grammar-school at Soham at this time, and for many subsequent years—for he kept his post for half a century—was Mr. John Aspland, who, besides being a cousin of the family at Wicken, had married a sister of Robert Aspland, Sen. He was a self-taught man, of rough manners and eccentric habits. He had the reputation of being a superior mathematician, and there is this evidence that he deserved it, that he prepared his only son for the University of Cambridge, the Rev. Isaac Aspland, of Pembroke Hall, who successfully stood for a Fellowship, and afterwards obtained the living of Earl Stoneham, near Framlingham. To his mathematical reputation John Aspland added that of a musician, and, where required, taught the harpsichord, the fashionable instrument of that day. As a teacher of the languages and of general knowledge, he had no great skill. Of the art, so important to a schoolmaster, of winning the affections of his pupils, the master of Soham school was utterly deficient. One of his later pupils records of him that he was somewhat merciless in the use of a whip, the handle of which served him as a poker. A marked feature in his character was avarice. He was a man of some humour, and, after his fashion, a poet; and the following anecdote shews that he did not care to conceal from himself or others the peculiarity of his character. His housekeeper (for his wife was dead) having unsuccessfully applied to him for some articles necessary in housekeeping, remarked that his visitors would blame her for not keeping his house in proper order. "Well, madam," said he, "they shall not blame you: I will write your apology, and you may hang it up in self-defence!" He went to his desk and presently produced the following doggrel lines, which were hung up for the inspection of visitors:

> "Be it known to all those
> Who perhaps may suppose
> That this house is not kept very clean,
> Neither mop, brush nor plow
> Will its master allow—
> Such a niggard scarce ever was seen."

John Aspland was a High-Churchman in both religion and politics, and looked with no approving eye on the recent Nonconformity of his relations at Wicken, or on their liberal politics, which were very much in accordance with the views maintained by Mr. Benjamin Flower in his popular journal, "The Cambridge Intelligencer." He did not always restrain himself from expressions of dislike and contempt, and the words "Pogram" and "Jacobin," prevalent cant Tory terms to denote a Dissenter and a liberal politician, fell harshly on the ears of his young relative and pupil, who in consequence carried from the Soham school a burning sense of the indignity offered to his parents, and the injustice done to himself, by its master. It accords with the recollections of one who was Robert Aspland's daily companion from Wicken to the Soham school, that this sense of wrong was not without foundation; that, notwithstanding his quickness and desire of learning, his master treated him with neglect and harshness on account of the obnoxious opinions of his father. Certain it is that between the master and his pupil there was no sympathy. After about four years' instruction, the pupil began to be aware of wants which his master could not supply, and he panted for that rapid progress of which he felt himself capable, but for which Soham school furnished no facilities. His parents' judgment seconded his earnest entreaties, and it was at length resolved that he should go to some school in the neighbourhood of London. But here no slight difficulty was felt in making a selection. The only acquaintances his parents had in London were business correspondents and one or two relations, themselves engaged in trade, and not particularly qualified to recommend a school.

A school at Islington, conducted by a Mr. Gillyat, was at length fixed upon, and thither the young Robert Aspland proceeded when eleven years of age, i. e. in the beginning of 1793. His letters to his parents were frequent, and shew powers of observation, a strong desire of improvement, and the warmest feelings of filial affection. The bias to Nonconformity which his mind had received from parental example and instruction, soon evinces itself. He describes the wretchedness of the Sundays passed at school. When prevented, as was frequently the case, from going to church, the occupation of the pupils was to read aloud throughout the afternoon, one after another, the Church prayers. Another Sunday occupation, against which his taste from the first revolted, was the repeating the Church Catechism and Collects. But he was permitted to spend most of his Sundays with his friends in London, and was a regular and deeply-interested attendant at the various Dissenting chapels near to their residences. Frequently he was a hearer of Dr. Benjamin Davies, who was the Classical Tutor at Homerton, and preached to an Independent congregation in Fetter Lane. Towards the close of his first year's residence at Islington, he expresses in a confidential letter his satisfaction with the literary advantages afforded him at his school, and contrasts the ten hours' daily study with the four hours' which was all he had the benefit of at Soham school.

The year 1794 was characterized by much political animosity and popular tumults, and by Mr. Pitt's bold, but happily unsuccessful, attempt to destroy English liberty, and to take the lives of Horne Tooke, the Rev. Jeremiah Joyce, and other members of the "Society for Constitutional Information," under a false charge of High Treason. In the course of that summer, Robert Aspland accompanied some country friends to the Tower of London. The attendant who shewed them round pointed to a court connected with the prison, where some of the State prisoners were taking exercise. Young as he was, he looked at them with intense interest and compassion, and breathed a prayer for their deliverance. He little thought at the time that one at least of these patriotic sufferers would afterwards be his own intimate associate and friend. The public events of this year made a deep, and for a time injurious, impression on the mind of this ardent and high-spirited youth, who began to entertain the painful thought that Government was an engine of oppression, rather than a protection to the people. It required the more careful observation and the discriminating judgment of a riper age to correct this strong youthful impression.

During his frequent visits to London, he was a spectator of some of the riotous proceedings of the London mob. The following extract from a letter to his parents, dated Aug. 21, 1794, will at least serve to shew the excited and passionate state of feeling into which a harsh Administration had goaded the popular mind.

"There have been many riots in London about the recruiting offices. It is said they have trap-doors in some of the public-houses. When the people go for beer, the trap-doors sink down into the cellars. Then the men below take them and fasten them down with heavy irons. It is said that Government favours this plan, and the belief of it is likely to be attended with very bad consequences. Is this the way they get poor men against their will, torn from their wives and children (perhaps never to see each other more), to go and support this *glorious war?* The riot first began on Friday night, at Charing Cross. They had got a man up in a garret. They put soldiers' clothes on him and shaved his head. Rather than be kept by them, he resolved to venture his life; so he got out of the window, and, falling head foremost into the street, he was killed. A mob immediately assembled and pulled the house down. A gunner who lived next door fired at the people. Before they could get to him, the horse-guards arrived. But the people said it would not end so. On Monday night they went to a house in Wycombe Street and demolished it. The horse-guards drove the mob away. Then the mob collected in Shoe Lane. The Lord Mayor read the Riot Act three times before the mob dispersed. Isaac and I went to Shoe Lane on our way from Camberwell. There was a great number of persons there. I durst not go on, but stood a little way off; but the people increased so fast, I was soon surrounded. The constables could do no good till the soldiers came. All passage through the street was stopped, and the mob knocked down the constables. The soldiers drew their bayonets, and would have charged the mob, had they not retired. We called as we came back at Bride Lane, where the mob pulled a house down last night; another in Holborn; another at Clerkenwell; and another in Long Lane. It was said last night that Pitt's house would soon come down, as he was thought to favour the proceedings at the recruiting offices. I got up this morning at six o'clock, and saw the people breaking the furniture in Bride Lane. I have not forgot Mr. Fuller's book,* but I have not had time to get it, as it is only sold at particular places."

Towards the close of 1794, he saw reasons to wish to leave the school at Islington, where the personal comforts of the pupils were but little consulted. His indulgent parents consented to a change, and he put himself under the care of the Rev. Ed. Porter, of Highgate, minister of the Presbyterian chapel† in Southwood Lane. Here he was treated with the greatest kindness, and gratefully records the almost maternal attentions of Mrs. Porter. Mr. Porter conducted his school without the assistance of an usher, and admitted his new pupil to much confidential intercourse. A conversation with Mr. Porter developed his wish to devote himself to the Christian ministry, which he states with much modesty in a letter to his parents dated February, 1795. At Highgate he met with a daughter of the celebrated preacher, Mr. Romaine, who lent him various religious books and was otherwise kind to him.

But we find him in the course of this year making another and a final change in his school. What the reasons of the change were do not appear, but its results were in every respect satisfactory. In August, 1795, he entered the highly respectable school in Well Street,‡

---

* Probably Mr. Fuller's "Calvinistic and Socinian Systems examined and compared," which had been published the preceding year.

† Mr. Porter published, in 1792, a sermon on the death of a daughter of Captain Lewis, aged seven years and two months. The preacher, with more kindly feeling than judgment, details the death-bed scene and triumphant words of this juvenile disciple.

‡ The premises now belong to the Hackney Theological Seminary, over which the Rev. George Collison presides,—an institution which was liberally endowed by Mr. Townsend, formerly a member of Ram's chapel.

Hackney, of the Rev. John Eyre. This gentleman was the minister of a small Episcopalian chapel at Homerton, commonly known by the name of Ram's chapel.* He was also one of the early Editors of the Evangelical Magazine and Secretary to the Missionary Society. Some extracts from Robert Aspland's letters will best describe his new school.

"The terms are thirty pounds per annum, washing included. Mr. Eyre is a nice man; I like him very much. He asked Mr. Warren what I was intended for. He told him—'You had some thoughts of my being a minister.' He questioned me and warned me particularly against being a minister unless I had the grace of God. He kindly said he would give me all the advice that lay in his power."

In another letter, dated Aug. 26, 1795, he writes,

"I shall now, according to my mother's wishes, give you an account of Mr. Eyre's school. It is, in my opinion, a very good school. I like it much. We have family prayer twice a day. Mr. E. is a very zealous and religious man. He preaches twice a day at his chapel at Homerton. I like his preaching very much. You wished to know if he was of the Establishment. I suppose he is;† but his place of worship is a chapel. He reads some of the Church prayers. He very often preaches in churches, and very often in meetings of all denominations. I don't think he has the least bigotry. He preached on Sunday at Mr. Thomas's, the Baptist. Mr. Pearce, the Baptist minister of Birmingham, will, I expect, preach for Mr. E. on Sunday."

Mr. Eyre's school enjoyed, and not without deserving it, considerable reputation. The second master in the establishment was Mr. Wells,‡ an amiable and intelligent man, who, as well as his principal, appears to have secured the confidence and affections of the pupils. Some not undistinguished men were pupils of Mr. E. Daniel Wilson, afterwards Vicar of Islington, and now Bishop of Calcutta, left the school a little before Robert Aspland came to it. The residence of the latter at Hackney continued for nearly two years. He appears to have been allowed

---

* The chapel was originally built, in 1723, by Stephen Ram, Esq.

† Mr. Eyre was previously curate under Rev. Mr. Cadogan, at Chelsea. A great change has taken place in fifty years in the stringency of ecclesiastical discipline in the Church of England. But even the amiable Prelate who in 1796 presided over the Metropolitan see (Dr. Porteus) must have been scandalized at the ecclesiastical irregularities of Mr. Eyre, who not only exchanged pulpits with Dissenters and omitted portions of the Liturgy, but often preached alternately with Rowland Hill in London Fields. Mr. Eyre died in 1803, and his funeral sermon was preached at Ram's chapel to a most crowded audience by Rowland Hill.

‡ Mr. Wells afterwards established a school at Leominster.

much liberty, and to have spent nearly all his Sundays in London, where he resorted to various "orthodox" Dissenting chapels. He had become tolerably skilled in short-hand, and was accustomed to take copious notes of the sermons which he heard. It was probably about this time that the following incident occurred.* He was occasionally a hearer of William Huntingdon, who appended to his name S.S., *Sinner Saved*. Huntingdon at this time rented on Tuesday evenings the meeting-house occupied on Sundays by the Presbyterian congregation under the charge of Mr. (afterwards Dr.) James Lindsay in Monkwell Street. As a stranger, he sat at the end of the table-pew, immediately facing the preacher; and being used to make short-hand notes of curious passages uttered from the pulpit, he was in the act of writing down something startling, when there was a sudden pause, and on looking up he saw the orator's keen eyes fastened upon him, and the fore-finger of his right hand pointed at him: there followed immediately these words, which continued to ring in his ears after the lapse of half a century:—"What is that young man there scribbling? Does he want to learn to be a parson? Be swift to hear and slow to speak, young man!" Huntingdon sometimes preached sermons well worthy of being recollected, and notes of one on the *books* and *parchments* mentioned in 2 Tim. iv. 13, on the Fast-day, March 9, 1796, exist in the hand-writing of the "young man" thus strangely rebuked. For this a place may hereafter be found in the C. R. Other preachers whom he heard about this time were, Timothy Priestley, Dr. Rippon, Rev. Abraham Austin, Rowland Hill, Mr. Booth, and Mr. Smith, of Eagle-Street chapel. His predilection for the services of the Baptists became, in 1796 and 1797, confirmed. In a letter to his father, he states that he had in the first instance been induced to resort to their preaching, and to listen to the arguments adduced in favour of their system, by the frequent invectives he had heard against them. The reader will already have observed traces of the independence of his mind and his mental courage. Of the latter quality he gave a proof by purchasing and attentively reading, in August, 1796, Paine's "Age of Reason." He at the same time read Bishop Watson's "Apology for the Bible," and thus reports to his parents the judgment he formed on this controversy:—"Paine is utterly unable to cope with the Bishop. Like the feeble javelin of aged Priam, his attack on Christianity has scarcely reached the mark. It has fallen

---

* See Christian Reformer, N. S., I. 351, note.

to the ground without a stroke." It is not often that youths of fourteen are prepared to read without injury Paine's caustic and unscrupulous appeals to the ignorance of his readers. In this case, happily, the mind of the student was prepared and protected, not only by familiar acquaintance with the Scriptures, but by deep and habitual piety.

In a letter to his father, April, 1796, he gives a remarkable account of the way in which he had spent his Easter holidays. On the morning of Good Friday, he heard "an aged and very able preacher" (whose name is not given) "discourse from Hebrews ii. 9, in refutation of the Arminians and Socinians." The young hearer, little thinking what his own after-views would be, gave his mind and heart to the strong Calvinism of the preacher. In the evening of that day, not knowing where he could hear "gospel preaching," he went with some relatives to Mr. Thelwall's Forum. Though not insensible to the speaker's talent, and feeling some sympathy with him as a man who had been persecuted for his free politics, he perceived and resented the "Deism" of his remarks. On Easter Sunday, he rose early and hastened through the snow to hear a sermon before breakfast from "a good old man who preached at Mr. Reynolds's meeting in Camomile Street." After breakfast, he heard Mr. Booth, whose discourse, on Matt. xiii. 47, was "awful." In the afternoon, he heard from Dr. Rippon "a very elaborate discourse" on baptism. In the evening, he was a hearer, at the Baptist chapel in Broad Street, of an "excellent discourse" from Mr. Smith, in defence of the justice of God in decreeing the damnation of his creatures. In a round of services, much in the same strain, including a public baptism at Devonshire Square, the whole of the holiday week was spent. The preaching appears to have been acceptable to him in proportion to the amount of Calvinism which it contained. It is somewhat curious, and may be regarded as an indication of his theological taste at that time, that during his two years' residence in Hackney, notwithstanding his discursive Sunday wanderings, no trace whatever exists of his having entered the Gravel-Pit meeting-house. It would have been interesting to observe the effect produced on his mind by the simple and earnest preaching, the clear elucidation of Scripture, the bold enunciation of theological doctrine, and the close logic of the discourses which he might there have heard, from ministers whose society and friendship he, ten years afterwards, greatly valued.*

---

* The Rev. Thomas Belsham became, in 1794, morning preacher at the Gravel-

During his youth, his health was not robust. Ague (then the common penalty of having been brought up in the fens—now, happily, through a better system of drainage, little known) followed him to Hackney. We find him in 1796 writing anxiously to his parents concerning his health, and fearing that the weakness of his lungs may prevent the fulfilment of his desire to become a minister.

Soon after he had entered on his sixteenth year, his mind became deeply impressed with the importance of "the ordinances of Christ," Baptism and the Lord's Supper, and he was uneasy at the reflection that he had not yet openly "dedicated himself to God by associating himself with some body of Christians." He hesitated, however, for a time, to take any step towards being admitted to "a church," from the feeling of uncertainty as to his continuance in the neighbourhood of London, and from a dislike of asking, immediately after becoming a member, for his dismission to another church. His wishes were directed towards the Baptist Academy at Bristol. He was in the first instance given to understand that, in order to admission into the Academy, it was necessary not only that the candidate should be a church-member, but that he should receive from the church testimonials of his possessing ministerial graces. His feelings naturally revolted from making the acquirement of church-membership a stepping-stone to his own personal advancement, and he anxiously inquired if he might not postpone his admission into the Baptist church until after his entrance into the Academy. In this difficulty he consulted the Rev. Timothy Thomas, the very worthy and amiable pastor of the society of Particular Baptists worshiping at Devonshire Square.* In him he had already found an instructive pastor, and he now found a judicious adviser.

Mr. Thomas interested himself warmly in the views and hopes of his young hearer, and wrote in his behalf both to Dr. Ryland and Mr. Fuller. Application had in the mean time been made direct from

---

Pit, succeeding Dr. Priestley on his departure for America. In the spring of the following year, the Rev. John Kentish was associated with him as the afternoon preacher.

* This is said to have been the earliest Baptist church formed in London. Its first minister was the celebrated William Kiffin. The predecessor of Mr. Thomas was John Macgowan, one of Dr. Priestley's coarsest assailants. The second title of his "Socinianism brought to the Test," was, "Christ proved to be the Adorable God, or a notorious Impostor." See Wilson's Dissenting Churches, I. 408—454, and "Remarkable Passages in the Life of William Kiffin," by Orme, p. 101.

Wicken to Mr. Fuller, to which, as the result shews, he paid immediate and respectful attention. He probably felt considerable gratification in promoting the studies and religious welfare of a native of his own village. The following letters, now transcribed from the original autographs, were probably given by Mr. Thomas to him whom they chiefly concerned. The first letter is from Dr. Ryland to Mr. Fuller.

"Dear Brother,—We have two new students from Rippon's, and are as full as we can hold—sixteen of them in all, including Flint and Page. But I suppose Ward will settle at Melksham next vacation, and Daniel will probably go to Ireland; Coles also is going to Scotland; so there will be three vacancies on the Bristol Fund. Mr. Webb, Mrs. Steadman's brother, will, I hope, be admitted for one; and I think there would be no great fear but young Mr. Aspland would be accepted for another, if recommended by you and Mr. Timothy Thomas; but he should be a church-member, though he need not on *that* foundation* to have been formally tried and recommended by the church. I should think he might as well join Mr. Thomas's church, as he is already well known there; he might then be dismissed to us. I know not how we could squeeze him into our house before the vacation; we have no spare bed nor half-bed. Or, if it were absolutely necessary, I could baptize him, and he might have been here at his own expense for a quarter of a year, though that would seem more hurrying and forcing things forward than for him to join Mr. Thomas's. If a young man at his years gives pretty strong evidences of piety, I think such are the best persons to send to Scotland, if any, as it would not be so safe either for body or mind for them to become constant and popular preachers so early.

"I should think it would be no bad plan for him to spend from this time to the first week in August at Kettering; then you might baptize him and send him here. In that case, an application should be made 'To the Managers of the Bristol Baptist Fund,' and directed to Mr. Harris, the sooner after the young man is baptized, the better, that so he may not have others apply before him, though I have already spoken for him to Mr. Harris. * * * *

Yours cordially,

"13 April, 1797." JOHN RYLAND.

The next letter, written on the same sheet of paper, is from Mr. Fuller to Mr. Thomas.

"My dear Brother,—I suppose brother R. intended this to get to Birmingham time enough for me to take to the Arnsby meeting; but it was somehow delayed, so that I did not receive it till a day or two after I returned.

---

* *Note by Mr. Fuller—*"By 'that foundation,' I suppose is meant the foundation of the Bristol Fund."

But judging the case of young Aspland of some consequence, I was unwilling to detain this letter till I sent you a parcel, and shall send it by post.

"The occasion of this letter was a letter which A. F. received from Mr. Aspland, Sen., since his return from London,* concerning his son, wishing to know whether he could *at the vacation* go to Bristol, and whether it was necessary that he should be a member of a church, as the young man seemed to feel it unpleasant to join (suppose Mr. Thomas's church) under such circumstances, as it would have the appearance of his doing it merely with a view to the ministry. A. F. sent Mr. Aspland's letter to Bristol, and this is the answer. But brother Ryland mistakes the request, supposing that the young man wants to go *immediately*. He only wishes to know if he may depend on going at the vacation. By this letter, however, it should seem that brother R. would recommend his joining Mr. Thomas's church; and I wish so too; and perhaps the sooner the better, if agreeable to Mr. Thomas and the church at Devonshire Square and the young man himself. I suppose when he leaves Mr. Eyre he would wish to go home awhile. If it be settled for his going to Bristol, and he wishes to call at Kettering by the way, I should be glad to see him.

"Kettering, April 29, '97."   A. F.

He had, however, by the advice of his father, anticipated Mr. Fuller's counsel, and been proposed, a few days before this letter arrived, as a member of Mr. Thomas's church. He thus writes to his parents, April 18, 1797:

"I attended at Devonshire Square last sabbath afternoon, and the members being desired to stay while the rest of the congregation withdrew, I related to them my past experience, and Mr. Thomas proposed to me several simple questions, which I answered, and the members agreed upon admitting me, after having been baptized into full communion. I was very comfortable, and less intimidated than it was natural to expect. Mr. T. and the members acted in a manner which deserves my highest gratitude and esteem. They seemed happy to see me willing to follow the path of duty."

On the following Sunday, April 23rd, he was publicly baptized at Devonshire Square by Mr. Thomas.

One friend alone disapproved of this important step and remonstrated with him. This was his kind master, Mr. Eyre, who endeavoured to convince him of the necessity and scriptural claims of infant baptism.

---

* Mr. Fuller had visited Mr. Thomas the previous month and preached at Devonshire Square, where, and at Mr. Thomas's house, R. A. "had much agreeable conversation with him." (MS. letter of March 22, 1797.) After interviews with this distinguished man were not always agreeable.

In the warmth of the discussion that ensued, Mr. E. asserted, that "without infant baptism there would be no religion in the world,"—a declaration from which, his pupil remarked, he would in his cooler moments recoil.

The difference of sentiment on the subject of baptism did not, however, diminish Mr. Eyre's habitual kindness. He appreciated the deep religious feelings and the natural talents of his pupil, and not unfrequently asked his assistance in preparing documents for the Missionary Society. Illness soon after this withdrew Mr. Eyre from Hackney, and when he was enabled to resume his duties as a teacher, Robert Aspland was no longer his pupil. His school-boy days terminated at Midsummer, 1797.

CHAPTER II.

The early education of Robert Aspland, it has been shewn, was not without its difficulties. Had his relative at Soham proved a painstaking and kind teacher, he would certainly have secured the affections of his kinsman, and gratitude might have made the pupil blind to the deficiencies of the master. The mortifications endured at Soham, however, brought about a change of plan, and in his new residence a variety of circumstances conspired to call into exercise those religious tastes which his parents had planted and fostered in his mind. If his youthful days had all been spent in his native village, his intellectual powers might have been blunted; still more probable is it that, seeing little that was attractive or impressive in the ministerial character, he would have shewn neither aptitude nor desire himself to assume it. He might then have become an energetic farmer and been the oracle of the weekly market-table, or at best a shrewd attorney, fearless of the bench at petty sessions, and more acute than half the lawyers at the assize. It was a happy circumstance that those whose instructions he most valued in his youth inspired him with deep respect for the office of a teacher of religion. The influence of his school-days in his case certainly affected the whole current of his life.

Notwithstanding the apparent facilities for his entrance on academic life, detailed at the close of the first Chapter, the commencement of that important epoch in his history was in fact attended with some obstacles and many anxieties. He was not elected to fill one of the "three vacancies on the Bristol Fund" spoken of by Dr. Ryland. The reason of this, though nowhere stated, probably was the existence of another foundation, of which mention will hereafter be made, and election on which was commonly reserved for youths of the best promise in the Baptist communion. For this distinction the Bristol managers probably deemed him not unworthy.

Thinking it undesirable to be long absent from London while any obscurity hung over his future destination, he accepted an invitation to pass a few days or weeks, as his convenience might require, at the house of his kind and hospitable pastor.

The Rev. Timothy Thomas resided at Islington, where he conducted a boarding-school. The visit was unexpectedly protracted from June till November, with the exception of a portion of July, which he spent at home. Mr. Thomas entered most warmly into the views and wishes of his young friend, and gave him the advantage of personal introductions to the leading men among the London Baptists. The following extracts are from a letter to his parents, dated June 24, 1797:

"I came to Islington on Monday evening home with Mr. Thomas from the exhortation. On Tuesday evening I met Mr. T. at the Jamaica Coffee-house, Sun Court, Cornhill, where the Baptist ministers meet in a room by themselves every week to converse. Mr. T. there spoke to some persons concerning me, but nothing particular resulted. On Thursday morning I went with Mr. T. to the monthly meeting of the Baptists at Dr. Stennett's meeting, Wild Street. I dined with the ministers at the King's Head, Poultry. Mr. Booth and several other principal men proposed having a day of humiliation among the Dissenters on account of the state of the nation, which was carried. * * * There was a great deal of fruitless disputation on the subject, which I did by no means like. I believe most of the Baptist ministers were present, and many deacons. I will now mention what surprised me, viz., *that I am not to go to Bristol.* Mr. Hughes, late assistant Tutor at Bristol, having left, the Committee have ordered that the young men on Dr. Ward's foundation should be with him. He is a learned and a very able preacher. He lives at Battersea, about five miles from Town. There are many disadvantages in this plan, and doubtless some advantages. Upon the whole, I am very sorry. * * * I saw Mr. Hughes at the Jamaica Coffee-house. He is a free, affable man, as far as I can judge not thirty. I sat next to him at the dinner at the King's Head, and was much pleased with him. * * * Mr. Thomas and his family have been exceedingly kind to me. I owe him (and I hope I shall never be forgetful of it) my warmest thanks."

"Ward's foundation" spoken of in this letter was a Trust established by the will of Dr. John Ward,* the Gresham Professor of Rhetoric,

---

* Dr. John Ward was no common man. He was the son of a Baptist minister, and was born in London, 1679. He was so passionately fond of knowledge, that in the year 1710 he gave up a Government office to become a teacher of youth, preferring, as he expressed himself in a letter to a friend, "converse even with boys upon subjects of literature, than to transact the ordinary affairs of

for the instruction of candidates for the Christian ministry, two to be on the institution at a time. The term of study prescribed by the will is six years, of which two are to be spent in England in the acquisition of grammar learning, and four in one of the Scottish Universities, the places in both cases to be determined by the Trustees. None are to be admitted under fourteen or above eighteen years of age. The other qualification of students is descent of parents, one or other or both of whom are by profession Baptists, and also communion with some church of the same persuasion. But the will specifies, that if a regular succession of young men of the Baptist denomination are not found to enjoy the benefits of the Trust, then those of the Presbyterian denomination shall be eligible to it.* The destination of the student educated on this foundation might be either that of a preacher or a tutor. The trust also provides for the continuance of the bursary to the students for one year immediately following the completion of their studies.† By the aid of this foundation some eminent men were educated for the Christian ministry, amongst whom were Dr. Joseph Jenkins, Rev. Robert Hall, Dr. John Evans and Rev. Joseph Hughes.

The recommendation of Robert Aspland to the Ward Trustees was attested by Andrew Fuller and Robert Hall. Their recommendation was sought, in preference to that of London ministers, not only on account of their great reputation amongst the Baptist churches, but also because they were connected with the county in which the family of the young candidate resided. Notwithstanding the weight of his testimonials, he was kept for some months in a state of harassing un-

---

life among men." In 1720, he was elected Professor of Rhetoric in the Gresham College. He died October 17, 1758, in the 80th year of his age. He was in early life a member of the church in Devonshire Square. Mr. Ivimey states in his History of the Baptists, Vol. IV. 610, that he belonged to the congregation in Little Wild Street. Dr. Toulmin, however, states (Univ. Theol. Mag. I. 235) that he became, on withdrawing from Devonshire Square, a constant worshiper with the congregation in the Old Jewry, under the ministry of the learned Dr. Chandler. It is certain that Dr. Chandler composed the epitaph on Dr. Ward. See Mem. of Thomas Hollis, p. 792. Mr. Hollis had been a pupil of Dr. Ward. He designates him his "old excellent master and much-honoured friend." Dr. Ward was an accomplished theologian. Dr. Lardner styled him his "learned and ingenious friend," and commends his "intimate acquaintance with antiquity, his uncommon skill in all parts of literature, his sincere piety and respect for the sacred Scriptures."

* See Universal Theol. Mag. for Sept. 1804, p. 127, a letter to the Editor from Robert Aspland, under the signature *Episcopus*.

† Leifchild's "Memoir of the late Rev. Joseph Hughes," p. 35.

certainty as to the success of his application. The acting Trustees in 1797 were the Rev. Josiah Thompson, a retired Baptist minister living on his fortune at Clapham, and a Mr. Smith, of Colebrook Row, Islington, a deacon of the Baptist church in Little Wild Street. The latter was a kind-hearted man, and offered frequent civilities to his young neighbour. But Mr. Thompson was a man of considerable eccentricity, somewhat rugged in his disposition, hard to please, and not soon reconciled if offended. He was a strong loyalist, and a devoted supporter of Mr. Pitt's Government. Of this he gave a somewhat remarkable proof, considering that he was the minister of a religion of peace, by contributing a hundred pounds towards the carrying on of the French war. Against the Baptist Academy at Bristol he had some strong objections: one was, that the students educated there came out, as he considered, too much tinctured with revolutionary principles. This was a mere prejudice. An objection better founded may be stated in his own words, taken from a letter to Mr. Hughes,* then Classical Tutor at Bristol:

"I perceive the Seminary at Bristol still continues to go on in the old absurd method; first send the young fellows into the pulpit and then instruct them for it. If it was an Irish seminary, it might not appear so wonderful; but continuing the custom at Bristol must ever reflect a disgrace and reproach on the institution, and it is astonishing that the directors and managers of it do not see the absurdity. You have once or twice favoured me with a sketch of a discourse for my remarks; I could wish you would send me some thoughts on Proverbs viii. the first part of the 12th verse" [*I, Wisdom, dwell with Prudence*].

Mr. Thompson was in this matter of good Richard Baxter's way of thinking, who said,† "Nor should men turn preachers, as the river Nilus breeds frogs (saith Herodotus), where one half *moveth* before the other is *made*, and while it is yet but *plain mud*."

It may well be imagined that a high-spirited youth of fifteen, whose mind glowed with a love of liberty in all its righteous forms,‡ and who

---

* See Leifchild's Memoir, p. 128.

† This saying was applied by Robert Hall to his own case, when telling how he was called upon, at eleven years of age, to preach to a company one-half of whom wore wigs.

‡ His political feelings were not at this period materially different from those which have been described as influencing him in 1794. An anecdote, illustrating the strength of his patriotic sympathies at that time, has been just commu-

was utterly incapable of dissimulation, could not easily pass muster with a prejudiced politician and a straitlaced disciplinarian of the old school, such as Mr. Thompson, then in his seventy-fourth year, was.* Nor could his kind host and pastor aid him. Mr. Thomas had incurred the displeasure of the great man at Clapham.

The months during which Robert Aspland was kept in suspense were not, however, lost. He made what return he could to Mr. Thomas for his friendly and zealous services by assisting him in his school; and when his friend was summoned to Leominster by the death of his father,† he undertook, to the great relief and satisfaction of Mr. Thomas,

---

nicated by the Rev. J. C. Means, who received it from Mr. Aspland himself. During his first residence at Islington, he had an illness in the month of November, and was directed, for the benefit of his health, to take an airing in a carriage. The place to which this invalid boy of not thirteen years of age instructed the driver to take him was *the Old Bailey, where the memorable State Trials were going on*, in order that he might hear something of their progress or result.

* The Rev. Josiah Thompson was pastor of the Particular Baptist church at Unicorn Yard, Tooley Street, 1746—1761. He was during a part of this time afternoon preacher to Dr. Savage's congregation in Bury Street. Though not popular as a preacher, he appears to have possessed considerable influence amongst the Dissenters. He was on three occasions employed to present addresses to the Throne on behalf of the Protestant Dissenting Ministers. (Wilson's Diss. Chur. IV. 236.) He died in June 1806, aged 82. Ivimey, in his History of the Eng. Baptists (IV. 429), speaks of him as "an educated man," but adds, he was not "very laborious in his Master's work," and did not "do much good as a minister." He accounts for the low condition in which Mr. T. left his church, by his having "the habits and feelings of a gentleman,"—a severe, and it is to be hoped unjust, censure of Baptist churches. Amongst the English Presbyterians there have happily been many laborious and useful ministers who have been distinguished by their possession of the manners and feelings of gentlemen. Mr. Thompson appears to have felt a very sincere interest in the history of Protestant Dissent. Of this he has left a laborious monument in a series of folio MS. volumes now deposited in Dr. Williams's Library. The title of these volumes is, "A Collection of Papers, containing an Account of some Hundred Protestant Dissenting Congregations, the Succession of their Pastors and remarkable Providences and Transactions which have happened amongst them to the Present Time, taken from their Church Books, the Testimony and Report of Old People, Private Papers and other Authentic Records. Begun to be collected in the Year 1772, with a view to assist any one who may be disposed to pursue the Inquiry and to draw up a more perfect and accurate Account."

† The Rev. Joshua Thomas was a much-respected Baptist minister at Leominster. He was particularly active, and had much to do with the churches of the Baptists in Wales. He died in the 79th year of his age. He preached three times, however, the Sunday preceding his death. At the ordination of his son Timothy, Mr. Thomas delivered the charge, and with questionable taste took as his text, *O Timothy, keep that which is committed to thy trust.*

for three weeks, the whole conduct of the school. That he ever formally undertook the office of "an usher," as has been publicly stated and printed, does not accord with the knowledge of his family. If he had been a paid usher, no false pride would have prevented his mentioning it; for he held the office of instructor of the young in great respect, and often talked with animation of a later period of his life when he received pupils into his house.

The performance of his duties in Mr. Thomas's school-room was, to one of the pupils at least, as gratifying as it was to the principal of the school. The circumstance is mentioned, as it was the occasion of an intimacy which Robert Aspland soon after this time formed, and which gave a colour to his whole subsequent personal history. One of the pupils was Joshua Middleton, a very young lad, who, partly from bad health, partly from deficient ability, and perhaps in part from his habitual instructor's want of skill, (for, excellent as he was as a man and a pastor, Timothy Thomas was not "apt to teach" little boys,) was painfully backward in school-learning. This sickly boy, nevertheless, sometimes shewed glimpses of peculiar and almost precocious intellect. Sympathy and curiosity combined to interest Robert Aspland in this young pupil; for throughout life it was his habit to study human nature; and intellectual eccentricity often in his view imparted an interest to characters in which common observers could see nothing worthy of regard. Poor Joshua was by the mere force of gratitude immediately attracted to his new teacher, and when he went home spoke of his "friend Aspland" in such terms as induced his family to seek his acquaintance.

John Middleton* (the father of Joshua) was an opulent tradesman, residing in Westminster, whose character and opinions were sufficiently marked to entitle him (independently of his subsequent relationship to the subject of this Memoir) to respectful notice. He sprung from a respectable family engaged in trade in the town of Horncastle,

---

* The Rev. Erasmus Middleton, the Vicar of Turvey, in Bedfordshire, and the author of the *Biographia Evangelica* (4 vols. octavo, Lond. 1779), was his brother. He was a protegée of Selina, Countess of Huntingdon, in whose Memoirs are many notices of his early career. He was one of the pious young Oxonians who were expelled from the University for "preaching and praying" in a manner unauthorized by the Book of Common Prayer or the Statutes of the University. Erasmus was a kind and good man, but was much shocked at the heresies which sprung up in his brother John's family. His anxious warnings on this head sometimes defeated their object, and led to inquiry and the adoption of "heresy" by others.

Lincolnshire. His father was a kind and good parent, except where his religious prejudices were concerned. He was a High-churchman, and partook of all the bigotry which belongs to the character. His son John soon aroused his anxiety by a very manifest tendency to examine every subject independently of paternal authority, and to form his own opinions. Anxiety was deepened into grief and resentment when, during his apprenticeship, John avowed himself a Methodist or *Culemite*, as a Methodist was then termed in Lincolnshire, from John Cule, a noted preacher of that persuasion. At the expiration of his apprenticeship, John Middleton resolved to proceed to London; but his incensed father, fearing he would become a Methodist preacher, refused for a time to render him any assistance. John, however, followed out his plan, procured an engagement as a commercial traveller, and ultimately, by his probity, intelligence and industry, assisted in the end by his father, became the sole proprietor of a valuable business in St. Martin's Lane, for the manufacture and supply of colours, &c., for the use of artists. His religious opinions underwent many changes, but ultimately settled into a very singular system of his own. In respect to the Object of worship and to the person of Christ, his views were strictly Unitarian; in respect to most other disputed theological questions, they tended to a modified Calvinism. Thus he received the doctrine of election, but for the terrific dogma of the eternal torments of the non-elect, he substituted the doctrine of their annihilation at the close of life. He regarded the death of Christ as the means appointed for man's salvation by the love of God, but rejected the doctrine that it satisfied the justice and appeased the wrath of God. Notwithstanding the deviations of his creed from the straight line of "orthodoxy," he habitually frequented Calvinistic preaching and worship.

Mr. Middleton was a very generous contributor to Dissenting institutions and chapels, and to public charities. When, in 1781, the Baptists of London united their means to enable Mr. Robinson to devote his time and attention to a History of Baptism, Mr. Middleton was appointed Treasurer* of the fund, and, in conjunction with another

---

* Dyer's Life of Robinson, pp. 214—216.—Mr. Robinson was Mr. Middleton's frequent guest, and great delight did his visits give to every member of the family, but especially to the children. On one occasion he stayed at St. Martin's Lane for several weeks in consequence of an accident. The house was besieged by a constant succession of admirers and friends. Mr. R. had the art of fascinating people of all descriptions. Among the visitors who had the entrée was

gentleman, general manager of the business. His house was always open to Dissenting ministers from the country.* In his intercourse with them, he spoke without reserve of his religious views, and so friendly were his manners and so liberal his gifts, that even the least tolerant of them heard him without impatience or resentment. In his case it was seen that good effects may result from some conscientious men's going but half-way in their reasoning. A simple-minded country minister once said to him, after an hour or two of discussion on the Trinity and the person of Christ,—"Well, Mr. Middleton, I shall go home and read the New Testament with quite new views; but if one of the gentlemen called *Socinians* had said all this to me, I should not have paid any attention to him."

For several years during the latter period of his life, Mr. Middleton himself became a preacher, being led to this step, not by any idea of his possessing peculiar fitness for the office, but by a charitable motive. He had joined himself to a little congregation of Particular Baptists. The chief support of the minister was an endowment, the proceeds of which were divided between the minister and the poor of the flock. On the occasion of a vacancy in the pulpit, great difficulty was experienced in finding a minister. A friend advised Mr. Middleton to preach to the good people himself. He did so, and divided the whole endowment amongst the indigent of the congregation. The writer once attended the service, which was held in a large room near St. Luke's church. The scene was, to a youthful observer, very extraordinary, from the great age and the singular dress—nearly half a century behind the fashion of the day—of the persons present. The preacher, a dignified and very handsome man, whose every look and word became the gentleman, was a striking contrast to many of his flock. Once a month, some of the little flock were assembled around their kind pastor's table to dinner. The interval between dinner and tea was spent in devotional exercises and the exposition of Scripture.

But Mr. Middleton's house was visited not merely by country minis-

---

a dull-looking carpenter, who came daily, took his seat in a corner of the room, and, having listened and gazed in perfect silence at the great speaker, took his departure.

* So habitual was Mr. Middleton's hospitality, that the person whose business it was to conduct country ministers with begging cases, was accustomed to recommend them so to time their visit to St. Martin's Lane, that they might secure not only a subscription, but a welcome to the dinner-table.

ters and town oddities, but was also resorted to by persons of education and talent and agreeable manners. Amongst these were the admirable writer (whose genius, as it kindled with "Thaddeus of Warsaw" and "The Scottish Chiefs," first taught us the value of the historical novel), Jane Porter and her fascinating sister (now, alas! no more) Anna Maria, Mr. Nasmyth and other artists.

The society which Robert Aspland enjoyed at Mr. Middleton's house was, according to the recollections of a friend who often saw him there, in no small degree enlivened by the frank manners and great conversational talents of Joshua Middleton's "friend." His appearance and manners were striking, but not entirely without a dash of oddity. He was plain almost to singularity in his dress. "Who," said Miss Porter, the first time she saw him, "is that *Quaker-looking* young man?" He had in childhood gained, probably from books, some interesting associations with the "Friends," and wished to be like them; accordingly, when the time came that he could gratify his own taste in dress, he clad himself in a suit of dark brown, of somewhat strait cut, and did not give up this unbecoming fashion until he put on professional black. As a youth, he was by no means so handsome as he became in middle life; but his countenance was full of mind, of penetration and vivacity, not without something of that constitutional irritability which on *unimportant* occasions would through life betray itself. His expression of countenance sometimes reminded his friends of the line,

"A scattered frown exalts his matchless air."

To his young friends his conversation was very striking, characterized by knowledge much beyond his years, and giving utterance to sentiments that were noble and liberal. When he was in the society of familiar friends, he was fond of drawing out every thing those about him had to say on any subject that interested him. This sometimes induced him to take the *opposing* side to that espoused by others, a habit which puzzled persons devoid of penetration, who knew not whether to regard him as an inconsistent thinker, or as one who carried into society the practices of the debating club. In vivacity he was surpassed by no one; and a close observer has stated he was rarely seen to give way in company to reverie. The exception was at a time of *tender* anxiety, when his friends smiled to observe him so wrapped in the luxury of his own thoughts, that he continued to stir the cup of tea just handed to him so long and so eagerly, that a large portion of it was spilled on the carpet.

He devoted much of his time during his second residence in Islington to theological study. He mentions with great delight that he had "a pleasant garden to walk in, and *plenty of books*." From the library of his pastor he selected the "Body of Divinity, Doctrinal and Practical," by Dr. John Gill,* "the most rabbinical Doctor of his age." Though greatly interested in reading this crabbed book, the reflections it excited by no means strengthened his "orthodoxy." Doubts and difficulties perpetually arose in his mind. These he communicated without the least reserve to Mr. Thomas, who, though he could not always re-establish his young friend in "orthodoxy," won his admiration and gratitude by his patience and candour. Sometimes, in the long conversations he held with Mr. Thomas, he was astonished to find his pastor not far short of his own degree of heterodoxy. But this statement, which rests upon a letter to his parents, need not be regarded as any impeachment of Mr. Thomas's sincerity as an "orthodox" preacher; for, however heterodox in spirit, Robert Aspland continued for some time to be on most points "orthodox" in his interpretations of Scripture.

The following letter to Andrew Fuller was written a little before Robert Aspland took up his temporary abode with Mr. Thomas. It is interesting as containing a reference to his early doubts and fears in respect to speculative theology:

"Rev. Sir,—Your kind letter was forwarded to me by Mr. Thomas on Sabbath week, and I know not how to express my gratitude for it better than by sending you these few lines, agreeably to your request.

"Though I received a material shock by reading the *Age of Reason*, yet I have reason to bless God that I have been led to see the fallacy of the author's arguments, and obliged to fly to Revelation in order to enjoy any true comfort. I trust it has been productive of good to my soul. At least it has stirred me up to greater watchfulness. I sometimes fear that I shall one day or other fall by that monster, Deism. But that the Lord may preserve and strengthen me in the right way, and prohibit me from wandering in erroneous and destructive paths, is my frequent and I hope earnest prayer.

"I can safely say respecting those principles you mention, and which are commonly called Calvinistic, that no material change has taken place since I wrote to you last, though I have had many inward struggles concerning them. * * * But though these appear to me at present to be the only sentiments

---

* Dr. Gill was the favourite preacher of Robert Robinson during his apprenticeship in London.—Dyer's Life of Robinson, p. 17.

which the word of God authorizes, yet as I have never so investigated the subject as to be acquainted and conversant with the arguments that are brought by those of contrary opinions, mostly through fear of being carried away, having seen so many sad examples of the kind, I have deferred it, perhaps irrationally and unscripturally, till my reasoning powers may be more expanded and my judgment more solid, and am almost afraid positively to determine on any thing. Therefore I must cast myself on your candour, and solicit those instructions on the subject, whenever opportunity offers, which my youthfulness and limited experience stand in need of."

A few extracts from his letters, written from Islington, to his parents, to whom he habitually unbosomed all his conflicting thoughts, and to some of his friends, will sufficiently indicate the change going on in his mind. The comparative repose and freedom from excitement which he here enjoyed, were friendly to mental discipline of the best kind, and trains of thought promptly arose which were previously unknown, but which produced in a few years very important results.

"August, 1797.

"I have heard Mr. Thomas but once since I left you. And, indeed, his preaching is not quite so pleasing, after hearing Mr. Hall. Mr. H. is a man of astonishing abilities, an ornament to the cause he espouses. Never attend to the low and groundless accusations of his adversaries. I believe him to be a truly pious man, though too conscientious, too free from enthusiasm for *some—many*. * * *

"Some of the old women [of Devonshire Square] have accused me very violently of wandering. But I would wish to remember they are only *old women*. I am a friend to religious liberty, and, as such, think any person has a right to attend where he pleases, now and then, provided he in the main associates with the people to whom he is united. I like not such narrow, despotic principles. But they will not be fully eradicated at present, though they have received a violent shock from the spread of principles which inculcate freedom in every shape. * * * I have been very low-spirited at times for a day or two. It arises, I believe, in part, from a view of the miseries, temporal and spiritual, of mankind; in part, from a reflection on the ignorance of man and the mystery of every thing around him; and, perhaps, most of all from the corruptions of my own heart."

"Islington, Sept. 22, 1797.

"With respect to my going to Battersea, I am not certain, neither am I anxious about it. If I go, I go; if not, I shall be contented. If an admission on such a foundation is denied, I doubt not but I could obtain one at Bristol, where I should prefer going. * * * I should not wonder, from what has lately passed in my own mind, if my religious sentiments were in some measure to be diverted into a different channel from what they are at present. But so uncertain are all human affairs, that I must leave it undecided. I conceive an increasing disgust to some enthusiastic, irrational proceedings of the age, and cannot say where it will end. May it end well! I am determined to seek after and embrace the Truth as far as I am able, and to explode and reject every thing that is in the least tinctured with error. *Reason*, however spoken against, shall be my attendant in all my researches, the standard of my faith and practice. Perhaps what I have said may need some explanation. When I use the term *Reason*, I would be understood to mean Reason *aided and assisted by the simple and sublime truths of Revelation.* * * * I trust my good parents will not be frightened or distressed at any thing I have advanced, but will allow me to think and act for myself. I need not say, keep these things secret, because you know as well as myself that of late the word *heterodoxy* has been more execrated and detested in the Calvinistic world than that of *parricide*. I hope to see better days, but patience is requisite here."

Under the date of September, 1797, in a letter to the Rev. Thomas Niclin, of Burwell, Cambridgeshire, anxiety is again expressed with regard to "some generally-received opinions."

"Dear Sir,—If I mistake not, I promised when we were last together to write to you. I now sit down to perform that promise. * * * I have been frequently harassed in my mind since I saw you respecting some generally-received opinions. May the Lord preserve me from deviating from the way of truth, from wandering in the paths of error and delusion! It is my sincere desire, and I trust my chief aim, to explode and reject every thing that is in the least tinctured with falsehood. May my desire be completed—may my ends be obtained! May I, after having proved all things, hold fast that which is good! * * * I long to hear from you. Let me have this pleasure soon, and let your letter be as long as possible. What health do you enjoy? How do you like Burwell? What success in your ministry? Any additions to the church? Do you ever preach at any of the villages around you? I hope you have not forgot Wicken. My dear friend, consider the ignorant, the deplorably ignorant condition of its inhabitants, and pray go over and help them as opportunity presents."

He appears to have in part regained his theological composure before he left Islington; but that a great change had taken place in his taste is apparent from the commendation he gives to such preachers as Mr. Pearce, of Birmingham, and Mr. Evans, of Worship Street. The name of the latter gentleman is mentioned pleasantly in a letter of the date of November 4, 1797.

"Though I have heard nothing from Battersea since my father left town, yet, as I promised, I write. I *hope* you are all well; but were I inclined to pay attention to *dreams*, two serious ones, which disturbed my repose two successive nights this week, would rob me of this pleasure. I heed them not. They undoubtedly proceeded from some anxiety which lay upon my mind in the course of each day. I am persuaded that God speaks not now by visions or dreams. Christianity forbids the idea. On Monday afternoon, I was at the performance of the ordinance of baptism at Mr. Dore's meeting, Maze Pond, Southwark. There were four baptized, two males and two females. The service was conducted with great propriety, and the sermon was very forcible. I almost wish you had been there. One of the men who were baptized was the son of Mr. Beddome, Baptist minister, deceased.* Upon his coming down into the water, Mr. D. exclaimed, "Here is the child of many prayers!" Upon which there seemed to be a general stir among the people present (the number of whom was great), and many could not refrain from weeping. It was a very comfortable opportunity to most present. The path of duty is the path of comfort.

"Yesterday afternoon, I was at Wild-Street meeting, where I saw Mr. Flint (that amiable young preacher) baptize for the first time two ladies. They went through the service with the greatest fortitude and cheerfulness. The Baptist churches in Town have experienced, I think, a great revival lately. Many have already been baptized, and many are now eager to follow their Divine Master in that despised ordinance. Some seem to think baptism a hardship, and either entirely refrain from it, or do it with the greatest reluctance. Let such remember that the Son of God himself descended the banks of Jordan and was buried beneath its waves. Surely, then, instead of being disgraceful, it is quite the reverse. It confers the highest honour upon man, and gives him a right to dignified privileges. Oh, that the professors of the gospel would more attend to the apostolic commission, Matt. xxviii. 19! Oh, that men would consider on what authority the ordinance is founded! On that of God himself. * * * I went this afternoon to the Sabbatarian Baptist meeting in London Wall, Cripplegate, and heard Mr. Burnside. There were only *eight* hearers—6 women, 1 girl and 1 man—beside myself. Yet they don't despair. You must never complain of non-attendance at Wicken, but persevere in well-doing, and in due time ye shall reap, if ye faint not.

"How few preachers can rank with an *Evans!* His name will ever be remembered by me with pleasure. His sermons will never be forgotten. I anticipate to-morrow evening's lecture, and often take a retrospective view of that of last Lord's-day. I hope his sermon then on "The Folly of Atheism" has made such impressions on your mind, that whenever you hear or read

---

* The Rev. Benjamin Beddome, minister to the Baptist church at Bourton for fifty-five years, died Sept. 3, 1797, aged 79 years. He left behind him, besides sermons, a volume of devotional poetry, afterwards published.

the xivth Psalm, the ideas he then advanced will crowd upon your memory and warm your heart. I expect Mr. Hughes will be somewhat like him. I wish he may."

It was not till the 19th of November that he was enabled to inform his parents that the Trustees had voted him admission to Mr. Ward's foundation,* and had directed that he should, in the first instance, put himself under the care of Mr. Hughes.† To both of the Trustees this gentleman had been known from his childhood upwards.‡

---

* The first year's allowance was only £27, which did not meet three-fourths of Mr. Hughes's moderate charge of £40. The pecuniary arrangements of the Baptist managers at that time seem to have been on a very humble scale. Thus Mr. Hughes received at Bristol, as a salary for the two offices of Assistant Minister at Broadmead chapel and Classical Tutor at the Academy, "the annual stipend of £120, and that when he had established a home for himself, with the prospect of a rising family."

† In communicating the good news, he writes, "I ought to be highly grateful for the mercies of God already received, and for those in prospect."

‡ Leifchild's Memoir, p. 31, note.

CHAPTER III.

The Rev. Joseph Hughes, afterwards so well known to all denominations of the religious world as the founder of the Bible Society, and for many years its gratuitous Secretary, was at this time a young man not twenty-nine years of age. He had recently [July, 1796] removed from Bristol to undertake the pastoral office at Battersea to a congregation "dwindled into insignificance." He had gathered his school learning first under Rev. Robert Smalley, the Presbyterian minister of Darwen, in Lancashire, and next under Mr. Norcross, master of the free school at Rivington, in the same county. He afterwards entered the Bristol Academy, then conducted by Dr. Caleb Evans. Hence he removed to Aberdeen, where he had the privilege of attending the divinity lectures of Drs. Gerard and Campbell. He graduated M. A. at King's College, March, 1790, and at the close of that year removed to the University of Edinburgh. In 1791, he was appointed Classical Tutor and temporary President of the Bristol Academy; and in that city he continued for five years to discharge the arduous duties both of tutor and preacher. One of his first pupils at the Academy was the afterwards celebrated John Foster. The foundations were then laid for a friendship which lasted to the very close of Mr. Hughes's life.*

Mr. Hughes's removal from Bristol to Battersea was occasioned by some little jealousies which had sprung up between himself and Mr.

---

* There are in Mr. Foster's "Correspondence," recently published by Mr. J. E. Ryland, numerous letters and references to Mr. Hughes, which it cannot be doubted will prove the most lasting and honourable memorial of his talents and character. Leifchild's Memoir of Hughes is a very unsatisfactory performance, prepared for "the religious world" alone, and having most of the deficiencies and faults which belong to that class of publications. They make their subjects mere *platform* heroes, and teach about as much of human nature as the stage does of real life.

(afterwards Dr.) Ryland, the Pastor of Broadmead and the President of the Academy.

In selecting Mr. Hughes as their English Tutor, the Ward Trustees exercised a sound discretion. Foster* described Mr. Hughes as " free, sprightly and communicative," possessing " great energy of mind, a variety and originality of thought," and " a vivid imagination, which without effort supplied an endless train of ideas and images." At a later period of his life, Mr. Foster stated that the company of Mr. Hughes was always " the highest excitement of his faculties." He was moderately learned; his classical attainments were respectable; in general literature he was tolerably versed; and in polemics was well read.

That Robert Aspland's residence and studies at Battersea, though not long continued, were very serviceable to him, in expanding his knowledge and refining his taste, is more than probable. His letters at this period indicate both greater facilities of expression and the widening grasp of his mind. His brief diary records his daily studies, and the amount of his reading is of itself a proof of his steady application. Amongst his papers there was found a card, on which was written the following scheme for the allotment of his time at Battersea:

" Sabbath—Devotional Works. To go regularly through some author before breakfast. Greek and Latin till dinner. All writing immediately after dinner. Ecclesiastical History every afternoon. Monday afternoon—French. Tuesday—Grammar, &c. Thursday—Mathematics. Every evening some modern [author?]. Saturday—Short-hand.

" Battersea." "R. A. Jan. 18, '98."

During the greater part of his residence at Battersea, he had for the companion of his studies Mr. Samuel Saunders, who, like himself, was

---

* Letter to Dr. Fawcett, I. 15.

These were some of Foster's reminiscences of his friend after his death:—
" He had great mental activity, quickness of apprehension, and discriminate [discriminating?] perception. He had considerable ambition of intellectual superiority, but less, I think, for any purpose of ostentation than for the pleasure of mental liberty and power. He was apt, like other young men, to be somewhat dazzled by the magniloquent style in writing; but at the same time always justly appreciated plain, strong, good sense, whether in books, sermons, or conversation. * * * His preaching, as a young man, was often very animated, rather unmethodical and diffuse, and extremely rapid; in this last respect, in perfect contrast to his pulpit exercises towards the close of life. His temperament was what is called mercurial—lively, hasty, earnest, versatile and variable."
II. 250.

destined for the ministry amongst the Baptists, and who fulfilled his destination with considerable usefulness, being minister for many years of the oldest Baptist church at Liverpool.*

At Mr. Hughes's he had the advantage of mixing in a circle of society of which that gentleman was the centre. If the frequent tea parties often interfered with his evening's study they familiarized him with the world and extended his knowledge of human nature. Here he formed an acquaintance with Mr. Foster, and listened with delight both to his conversation and his original and profound discourses.†

He still continued to gratify his religious taste and curiosity by attending the services of all the most eminent Dissenting ministers of London and the vicinity. In addition to his tutor and Mr. Thomas, whom he continued to regard as his pastor, he heard Rowland Hill, Mr. Hinton, of Oxford, Dr. Winter, Mr. Romaine, Mr. Urwick, of Clapham, Mr. John Evans, and Hugh Worthington.

He now not merely attended the prayer meetings at Devonshire Square and occasionally at Battersea, but, as the phrase was, "engaged" therein. This duty inured him by degrees to addressing public audiences, and encouraged him to increase his Scripture vocabulary. Several persons are living who remember with interest his fervid devotional addresses in the communion-pew of Devonshire Square. His prayer was once censured by a very worthy and intelligent member of the church, a female in humble life, named Morris. She possessed a most liberal mind,‡ and resented what she thought "the presumption of so very young a man praying against the errors of Christians." He

---

* He published a volume of Sermons on the Lord's Prayer.

† Mr. Foster was not at this period generally listened to with much favour by the Baptists of London. Some resented his disregard of clerical costume, and few of them could appreciate his philosophical addresses, which were "vastly removed from Methodistic violence." Some suspected (and with reason) that he was not in the right "parallels of latitude with respect to orthodoxy." The patience of the lady of the house where Foster was wont to sojourn at Battersea was somewhat tried by the eccentricities of this son of genius. At the hour of meals he would often be wandering miles away, wrapt in some excursion of fancy, and return, thoughtful but half famished, hours after the cloth was withdrawn.

‡ This vigorous-minded woman had been for many years a member of the church, and under the ministry of Mr. Thomas's predecessor, M'Gowan, in no slight degree annoyed that theological firebrand by writing and sending to him, after each of his lectures, an exposure of his self-contradictory arguments and his intolerant, unchristian spirit. The race of M'Gowans survives—I fear that of Mrs. Morris is extinct.

proved to her satisfaction that they were one in spirit, by telling her, with a smile, that she had "misunderstood him, for he was in fact praying against the little bigotries of some of their good folks."

It has been already intimated that Robert Aspland had in a great measure recovered his mental composure as to theological doctrines before his removal to Battersea. His spirit, however, became increasingly catholic, and his mind more fearless; and it is probable that Mr. Hughes observed the heretical tendencies of his pupil, and that his anticipation of the actual result diminished his interest in the after welfare of one whose talents and character he must in other respects have appreciated. It is certain that there were discordances of sentiment and feeling, never indeed expressed, which in after-life prevented intercourse beyond that of formal civility. It is somewhat singular that within twelve months Mr. Hughes should have had residing under his roof two men of no ordinary character, like Robert Aspland and John Foster, both of them, in his view, manifesting dangerous spiritual symptoms, and both labouring under the same disease. It is made matter of congratulation amongst "orthodox" people that, in the latter case, Mr. Hughes proved a successful spiritual physician, and saved his distinguished patient.* It may be equally matter of con-

---

* How sharp and painful the remedies were in Mr. Foster's case, sufficiently appears from his deeply affecting letters preserved in the Correspondence (I. 93 and 108) of the date, Chichester, February 15 and April 29, 1799. In the former letter he speaks of Mr. Hughes's "remonstrances, accusations and regrets." Of what nature the accusations were, we gather clearly enough from the second letter: "Enmity against God" (p. 109), affection alienated from the Saviour (p. 110), indifference to him as "a deliverer from the miseries of *sin*" (p. 111), "a vain self-sufficiency" (p. 112), "deceptions of imagination" (p. 113), and neglect of Scripture diction (p. 115). Well might Foster feel that he was in the hands of a "sharp inquisitor" (p. 109), that he was "repelled from every point of religious confraternity, and doomed, still doomed, a melancholy monad, a weeping solitaire." What anguish it was that extorted from him the cry, "Oh world! how from thy *every* quarter blows a gale, wintry, cold and bleak, to the heart that would expand!" Appeal appears to have been made equally to the fears and the affections of the patient. The apostolic felicities of such a man as Pearce are represented to him, that he may become like him in spirit and action. Foster is evidently made to feel that his doubts and disbelief are shutting him out from "the Messiah's kingdom." This was a mordent application to a mind like Foster's, teeming with the "irresistible conviction that 'the truth as it is in Jesus' is incomparably the best thing that could be administered to his fellow-mortals, and that he is the noblest of men who administers this with the most fidelity and zeal." No lover of mental freedom can read these touching letters without feeling that the Protestant *inquisition* is sometimes more skilful and not less unscrupulous than that of any disciple of Ignatius Loyola. Assuredly it has its *tortures*.

gratulation, with persons of a different stamp, that in the former case Mr. Hughes's treatment was ineffectual in staying the onward course of a free and generous mind.

But we must return to Robert Aspland's first impressions of Battersea and his tutor. Several of his letters at this period, though not of any great importance, contain references to passing events which make them worth preserving.

"Battersea, Saturday, Dec. 2, '97.

"Dear Parents,—With extreme pleasure I inform you that I am at length settled. I came here on Monday, and began my studies on the Tuesday. Mr. Hughes appears to be a very amiable man; but I must for the present suspend my judgment. He is very studious, and preaches excellent discourses. This is a very pleasant village, about four miles from London. The Thames washes our garden, which is of a good size. We sit in the study and see the boats sailing upon it. My room is very agreeable; it also looks out upon the garden and the Thames. * * * I was at Mr. Poole's meeting, Chelsea, last night, and heard Mr. Medley.* I cannot recollect his sermon without disdain and disgust. His chief aim seemed to be to create laughter and mirth. Is *this* preaching the word of life? Did the Saviour of the world so preach?"

"Dec. 16, 1797.

"I went to Devonshire Square last Sabbath-day, and heard Mr. Winterbotham† preach his first sermon since his liberation from Newgate. I had formed too high an opinion of the preacher, and was much disappointed. He was very plain, and far from eloquent. * * * I have hitherto spent the Sundays

---

* Rev. Samuel Medley was for twenty-seven years pastor of a Baptist church in Liverpool. He was greatly followed as a popular preacher, both at home and in his annual visit to London, where he supplied at the Tabernacle. He began life as a sailor, being a midshipman on board the ships Buckingham and Intrepid. In a sickness consequent on a wound received in action, he was converted. He delighted to introduce sea terms and naval illustrations into his sermons. The sermon so abhorrent to the taste of his young hearer was probably set forth with nautical illustrations, suggested to him by his being close to the great river of the Metropolis.

† Rev. William Winterbotham, an amiable Baptist minister of Plymouth, was the much-pitied victim of a Government prosecution. He was indicted for preaching two seditious sermons, was found guilty, and received the cruel sentence of *four years' imprisonment and a fine of* £200. In those evil days of Tory rule, truth was sedition! This righteous man solaced himself during his long imprisonment in Newgate by writing his *Historical View of the United States*. Mr. Lindsey proved a most kind and generous friend of Mr. Winterbotham, who ever afterwards expressed unbounded gratitude to Mr. Lindsey, and named a son after him. See Belsham's Life of Lindsey, p. 358; C. R. (1839), p. 375, and C. R. (1846), p. 486.

in London, but shall in general after Christmas spend them at Battersea. I like Mr. Hughes's preaching much. He studies his sermons thoroughly. They are quite free from the enthusiastic rant which so much prevails, and are distinguished by sober thought and manly sense. He is more practical than doctrinal. * * * How does the triple assessment* affect you and the other inhabitants of Wicken? All grumble here. Mr. Pitt is the greatest revolutionist in the kingdom. Are you prepared to join in the formal mockery of * * * [the MS. is here defective] on Tuesday next? I shall endeavour to get a sight, if I can.† Mr. Pitt, we understand, has excused himself from attending on account of business."

"Battersea, Jan. 12, '98.

"I do not know what to say about *Pitt's day*, as you call it. I saw him. He was received with hisses and other signs of disapprobation. I did not see Fox or Tierney. The sailors who preceded with the flags were generally well received. The Royal Family concluded the procession. The King did not care to be seen. He leaned back in his carriage. Here and there, hats were pulled off, and some few shouts of applause were heard; but they often closed in groans.‡ The windows of the principal streets were well attended, but there was nothing like joy. Every thing assumed the appearance of melancholy and dejection.§

"Mr. Fuller has been up in Town lately. I was with him at Mr. Thomas's the last evening he spent in Town. We were engaged in political discussion most of the time. He is acquainted with Wilberforce, and attempted to vindicate his political conduct. Thence he proceeded to vindicate a monarchical form of government. His chief argument was, 'that there is in Majesty

---

* This alludes to Pitt's newly-adopted financial project for raising money to carry on the war. This unpopular burthen lost none of its odiousness when it was afterwards converted into an *income* and property tax.

† At the close of the year 1797, the King, attended by both Houses of Parliament and the great officers of State, went in procession to St. Paul's to offer up public thanksgiving for the victories obtained by the British navy in several parts of the world. The flags and colours taken from the French, Spanish and Dutch, were borne with much pomp to the Cathedral and placed on the altar!

‡ In R. A.'s pocket-book for this year, entitled "The Patriot's Pocket Companion," it is stated that one Kydd Wake, a journeyman printer, was tried Feb. 19, 1796, for hissing at the King. He was found guilty and sentenced to five years' imprisonment, with hard labour, in Gloucester gaol, and to be once put into the pillory, and to give security for his good behaviour in £1000 for ten years, his imprisonment to continue until the security was given.

§ Mr. Foster, in a letter dated July 13, 1798 (Vol. I. p. 88), thus sums up the events of the neighbourhood of Chichester: "The parade of soldiers, and arms, and drums, and loyalty, and fashion, contrasted with complaints of declining trade, an enormous pressure of taxes, the wan and hopeless looks of poverty, *execration of the government and governors, and sighs for a revolution.*"

a certain something which adds stability to a government and keeps the multitude in awe.' See to what shifts an able man is driven in support of a miserable cause! Mr. T. was his principal opposer in the fore part of the controversy; I in the latter."

"February 3, 1798.

"Through the mercy of God, I have now completed my sixteenth year. May gratitude accompany all His favours! May I spend this year in the fear of God! * * * In the evening (of Jan. 25) Mr. and Mrs. H. and I went to the *Westminster Forum*, a debating society. The question was, 'Are there not abundant reasons to support the belief that the Pope is Antichrist, and that the French are the means appointed by Providence for his destruction?' In these assemblies any one is permitted to speak. Five spoke there; three who opposed the question were professed infidels. They dare not admit the truth of the question, because it would also establish the truth of the gospel prophecy. They used much declamation, but no serious argument. J. G. Jones, 'the martyr of freedom,' who is about to receive sentence for *sedition*, concluded the debate. He attacked political and religious systems together. He is a very fluent speaker, and has a very sonorous voice. All eyes were fixed upon him. He took farewell of his fellow-citizens in a very pathetic manner. * * * I mentioned to you something unpleasant with Mr. Fuller. I have written to him and received an answer. My letter was as respectful as reason could make it. But he does not appear to be satisfied, though he wishes the matter to rest where it is. He concludes in a very grave, priestly manner, lamenting the fallacy, or rather the violence, of my political principles. He is not angry that I know of, but that I do not devote myself to *Wilberforce* and others of his pious patrons! I shall let it remain in silence.

"I have had repeated requests to begin preaching. Perhaps I may soon. But I would be cautious. If I do, it will only be before auditors similar to those of Soham and Wicken. * * * Considering the state of my mind some time ago, I have great reason for thankfulness. I hope I am more free from doubts of any kind than ever."

But although, for a time, free from the doubts which had previously harassed him, it will appear from the following letter that the Calvinistic form of religion into which his mind had once more subsided did not inspire him with cheerful views of human nature. It was addressed immediately after his settlement at Battersea to his friend Robert Fyson, a skilful and successful farmer residing at Fordham, in Cambridgeshire. Mr. Fyson was a man of vigorous understanding and habitual piety. For many years he preached occasionally at Fordham in an humble chapel built by himself, and occasionally at Wicken and other places. His spirit was enlarged and catholic, and he was a great lover of mental freedom, as may be gathered from his warm admiration of the preaching and writings of Robert Robinson. Mr. Fyson earned, even in the days of his orthodoxy, the suspicion and dislike of Andrew Fuller. These feelings were once freely communicated to Robert Aspland by Mr. Fuller, and did not increase his respect for that gentleman's judgment and temper.

"It is impossible for me to communicate to you the sensations which a reflection on *man* sometimes produces within me. Who can contemplate his natural situation without tears of pity and regret? Who can view his moral condition without the most painful feelings and the most alarming apprehensions? Born to trouble as the sparks fly upwards, he is the heir of misery and woe. No sooner is he born than he begins to sigh. His health is assailed by a thousand ills, and his life is in constant danger. Well may Young exclaim,

'He that is born is listed; life is war,
Eternal war with woe.'

"And if we view the other side, what a melancholy picture does it present! *Subject to oppression*, and harassed with a constant fear of his fellow-creatures! Overwhelmed by anxious cares, and despairing under an accumulated burthen of sorrow! Tormented by the fear of death and an unknown something beyond it! Enveloped with ignorance, and desirous of freeing himself from its painful servitude! Perplexed by systems of religion without number, and doubtful which to choose! Is this the glory of the creation, the image of his Maker? This the peculiar favourite of Deity? * * *

"But let us drop a scene too mysterious for our comprehension, and anticipate that happy era which Revelation authorizes us to expect, when man shall exhibit in his own person an assemblage of every virtue, when human misery shall no longer be known, when philosophy and science shall advance in a continued accelerated progression,

'And Benevolence,
Her open arms unfolding as to clasp creation,
Will then extend her universal empire;'

And when the earth shall be full of the glory of the Lord; when all shall know him from the least to the greatest.

"Are you not eager to forward this desirable epoch by every means in your power? If so, why do you not go to Wicken, and exhilarate the minds of its inhabitants by the glad-tidings of salvation? * * * Send me word how you go on in the *evangelizing* way at Fordham, how often you preach, and what number of hearers."

Robert Aspland valued and improved the opportunities he enjoyed during his residence at Battersea of "an introduction to the religious world." Early in the year (1798), he accompanied his tutor on a pedestrian journey to Northampton (walking thirty miles on each of two successive days). The pleasure of this excursion was greatly heightened by a series of introductions to Baptist and Independent ministers who resided in the villages and towns through which they passed. He was also introduced to Dr. Crombie, who was then the proprietor of a large boarding-school at Highgate. At St. Alban's they visited Mr. Burder, the Independent, and Mr. Gill (nephew of the learned Dr. of that name), the Baptist minister. At Daventry they were the guests of Mr. Robins, formerly tutor of the Academy, and minister of the Dissenting congregation there. At the house of this kind and excellent man they passed the day, in company with Mr. Morell, the Independent minister.

Mr. Hughes appears to have habitually made the young men residing in his house his companions in his visits as well as his studies. One who lived with him as a private pupil about this time, thus describes the routine of his avocations:—" We were accustomed to spend some hours in study in the morning, in classics, theology and general literature; and afterwards to take extensive walks around and in London,—dining in one family, taking tea in another, and supping in another,—usually returning home the same evening. Those were indeed walks of combined pleasure and usefulness."*

The spring of 1798 appears to have been ungenial and severe, and Robert Aspland was again attacked by ague, the disease from which fen-born persons then rarely escaped. His enfeebled strength conspired with his strong family affection to turn his thoughts fondly to Wicken, the dirty lanes of which, he told several correspondents, had more charms for him than the gayest streets of London. Before his return home, a change of plan was determined on by the Ward Trustees. Influenced, probably, by the conviction that his house and varied occupations offered to the young man too many distractions of thought for continued study, Mr. Hughes advised Robert Aspland to spend the second year of his studies in England at Bristol. With some difficulty, Mr. Thompson's consent was obtained to this plan. The pupil, though sufficiently grateful for the advantages he had enjoyed at Battersea, felt his original regret revived that he had not been permitted at first to enter the Bristol Academy. Three changes of residence and teach-

---

* Leifchild's Memoir, p. 169.

ers, in the course of as many years, were not favourable to the pupil's steady progress. It may even be doubted whether the division of the time for study allowed by the Ward Trust, between England and Scotland, was the best possible arrangement. But all his feelings were absorbed in the idea of revisiting his family. His anticipations are thus expressed in a letter dated Battersea, April 16, 1798.

"I am extremely happy in the expectation of seeing my dear parents once more. With you, I feel the greatest pleasure. My *joys* are heightened by the pleasing idea that they heighten yours. My *sorrows* (I am not without them) are alleviated when I reflect that I suffer not alone, that a parent's bosom is opened to participate in every distress. * * * I dare say my dear mother will discern some difference in my person. That is great. But changes in sentiment and disposition exceed it. Oh! the revolutions which my mind has undergone since I left Wicken! Opinions have been formed; new evidence has appeared, and they have been thrown down, and others erected on their ruins. Thus we proceed through life. What a happy thing it is when we are making improvement!"

His final departure from Battersea was hastened by an engagement into which Mr. Hughes entered to supply the pulpit of Mr. Jay for six weeks, during the absence of the latter in Dublin.* And thus abruptly terminated his connection with Mr. Hughes. Beyond a call of civility and a letter written at a time when his mind was again in a state of doubt, to which Mr. H. returned an "imperious" answer, no further intercourse took place between them.

His return to Wicken was a joyful event to others besides his parents and himself. His worthy friend John Emons was constantly with him, seeking by his aid to solve a thousand doubts, and to gain what he valued above all things, religious knowledge. The diary at this time contains many entries of this kind:

"May 6th. Went to Soham with J. Emons, and heard Mr. B. Read as we went Lyttleton's Observations.—7th. Finished Lyttleton's Observations. To Soham with J. E. to prayer-meeting. I engaged.—10th. Read Clarendon and began 'Revelation Examined,' with J. Emons, in the orchard."

Nor was he less rejoiced to renew personal intercourse with his

---

* In those days Mr. Hughes was regarded as an imitator of Mr. Jay's pulpit style. If we may judge from his few literary remains, he soon outgrew this folly. It would certainly not recommend his temporary services to the members of Argyle chapel at Bath.

friend at Fordham, whose fine English character he particularly admired. His influence was immediately used to procure preaching at Wicken at the diminutive meeting-house built by his father. The diary has these entries:

"May 18. Helped to clear the meeting in the morning, which was filled with earthenware, &c.—Sunday, May 20. Rode to Soham on the mare. John spoke. Dine at Fordham. Heard Mr. Fyson. He preached at Wicken in the evening—great many people."

This was a memorable Sunday evening for the young student. His family and friends expressed their earnest wish that he should at once begin to preach. His doubts and fears, and his plea of youthfulness, (he was little more than sixteen,) were put aside by their encouraging assurances and their strong representations respecting the need which the village had of Christian instruction. He consented to make a trial on the following Sunday. The worthy blacksmith ever after prided himself as having been very instrumental in this decision. When during the week (which from Monday morning to Saturday evening was occupied with anxious preparation) the youth's spirits failed, John Emons' counsel and friendly wishes reassured him. The good man watched the progress of the sermon with almost a father's interest. When the work was nearly completed, and the intended preacher was "exercising," i. e. rehearsing the discourse, first in his father's garden, and afterwards in a corn-field at the back of the house, John Emons was a deeply-interested spectator, at first without the knowledge of his young friend. Nearly thirty years after, the old man was pleased to tell the story, on the very spot where he had stood an unknown listener, and where he had removed the tyro's fears by the confident prediction of his success. He finished the tale by the words, "Thus, Sir, I was your father's bushop."*

The day on which Robert Aspland for the first time spoke from a pulpit was May 27, 1798—Whit-sunday. The diary thus briefly records the event:

"Soham, with my mother—home to dinner. Soham in the afternoon—home to tea. Spoke at Wicken for the first time—a good congregation. Not *very* tired!"

The subject of the sermon was "Love to Christ;" the text, John xxi. 17 (in part), *Simon, son of Jonas, lovest thou me?* The sermon,

---

* The Cambridgeshire mode of pronouncing *bishop*.

as originally written, now lies before the writer, and occupies twenty small quarto pages. The doctrine, so far as it appears, is sufficiently "orthodox," comprehending original sin, Christ's deity, the Trinity and the atonement; but the general complexion of the discourse is practical, and four-fifths of it might, so far as its doctrine is concerned, have been preached by its author at any period of his ministerial life. It has the fault so frequently seen in young writers of sermons—indefiniteness, from the attempt to traverse too wide a field of doctrine and exhortation. In its style it is a remarkable production, considering the youth of the author. It is more simple than some of his subsequent juvenile productions. Like all his best sermons throughout his ministry, it is largely and happily illustrated by Scripture quotations. In this and some other good habits as a preacher, of which future mention will be made, he was probably fortified by observing the happy effect of illustrations from Scripture so frequently used by the preachers to whom he had listened during his residence in London. The following passage is perhaps the best which the sermon contains:

"We inquire not whether your relations or friends love Christ. No! Religion is a *personal* thing. If you would be religious, you must be religious for yourselves. The religion of others cannot profit you. There were many among the Jews who, ignorant of the nature of true godliness, wished to avail themselves of the name of Abraham, their renowned ancestor, and to shelter themselves under his religion. But they met with a severe reproof from John the Baptist (Matt. iii. 8, 9), *Bring forth, therefore, fruits meet for repentance; and think not to say within yourselves, We have Abraham to our father*, &c. Do not suppose that because you are Abraham's children according to the flesh, you are in the favour of God and free from his condemnation; for with God, the children of Abraham are such as imitate Abraham's faith and piety, and not merely the bodily offspring; for if this is to be spiritual, such spiritual children may be brought forth of all nations—yea, even of these stones. It is in vain, therefore, for you to expect any advantage from the goodness of others. When the angel swears by Him that liveth for ever and ever, that time shall be no more—when the Almighty comes to judge the world—when the books are opened and all mankind at his bar are waiting the decisive sentence, it will not then be asked whether such a relation was pious, or such a friend religious. No! We must then render an account of ourselves, and the consequences will be our own."

The following "Advice to Students of Divinity" respecting sermons was found in Robert Aspland's handwriting, and the MS. sufficiently resembles in appearance that of the first Wicken sermon, to justify the supposition that he possessed it and was guided by it in his early pulpit efforts. Whose the advice was, the paper does not state; but no one will suppose that it could have been originally penned by a youth not seventeen years of age.

"1. *Begin early to try to preach.* In all things, especially in speaking, a teneris assuescere multum est. St. Austin says, Ars concionandi in juventute discenda est. If you begin late, exercise the oftener.

"2. Take an analysis of a text or subject from any author and *discuss* it yourself, as well as you can. Explain it, illustrate it, prove it, adorn it, &c. Instead of purchasing a farrago of sermons composed by others, and to be repeated by you, learn yourself to compose.

"3. *Begin with easy subjects.* Take an easy piece of Scripture history, or a plain tale of a miracle, and observe times, places, circumstances, and so on. Nothing can be easier than to make a few pertinent remarks on each.

"4. Let your first essays be very short. A division into two parts will be sufficient. Examine these briefly, and with few or no ornaments.

"5. Exercise first in proper places. Not only pronounce your discourse in your room or in the field, but, the day before you preach, go alone into the place of worship where you are to preach, ascend the pulpit, familiarize yourself to the place, utter your discourse, &c. Preach in public first in a village among plain Christians.

"6. Take, if you can find such a person, a kind and judicious friend, and get him to attend your first sermons, to remark and correct your defects."*

Robert Aspland's first pulpit effort was, in the opinion of his friends and neighbours, eminently successful. He carried into the pulpit only a brief memorandum of the heads of his sermon, and spoke with perfect ease. His elocution was characterized by much of the animation of his best days, but wanted the relief of judicious pauses, and was injured by a slight nasal twang. This was subsequently pointed out to him by his Divinity Tutor at Bristol, and was entirely subdued.

His second public appearance was on the following Sunday in the pulpit of the Rev. Thomas Baron, the highly respectable Baptist minister of Cottenham, near Cambridge. It was recorded in the praise of Mr. Baron, that he was "an encourager of young men in religion, and of young preachers."† This worthy man is also entitled to honourable

---

* The substance of these Articles of Advice was given by Mr. Aspland, twenty years ago, to a young preacher, with the exception of No. 1 and the closing part of No. 2. He advised writers of sermons to be habitual readers of the best sermon-writers.

† Mr. Baron was by education an Independent, and a member of a society to

mention in this Memoir on another ground. He had not enjoyed the advantages of early education. The only training through which he had passed to fit him for the pulpit was preaching amongst Christian friends. His principal knowledge was of the Bible. He did not pretend to learning which he did not possess. He often lamented his want of education, and always recommended it to parents to teach their children all that they would learn and that could be taught. He was accustomed to say that he would submit to any bodily inconvenience to give his children education. In very early youth Robert Aspland listened to and caught the spirit of his strong and frequent remarks on this subject, and in consequence of them made the successful efforts to obtain a good education which have been previously detailed. This incident, which has already appeared in print* (though possibly without its full significancy being understood), is one illustration of the important results that may follow the utterance of our opinions in conversation, especially on the minds of the young.

Many of the inhabitants of the neighbouring villages now flocked to hear the "boy-preacher." His head might well have been turned by the popularity thus suddenly achieved; but he had, in addition to his own good sense, most judicious domestic advisers. In order that his services might not interfere with the regular duties of other preachers, he instituted at Wicken an early Sunday morning service, something after the plan of Robert Robinson's Morning Exercises. It began at seven o'clock, and lasted exactly an hour. This practice he commenced June 10th. He then attended twice at the Soham meeting-house, and

---

which the Rev. Joseph Maulden preached. "In this church Mr. Baron was observed by some of the members to have 'gifts for the ministry.' His gifts were tried in the usual manner, i. e. by his delivering an exercise before the members only of the church, the communicants, with closed doors. The result of this trial was, that Mr. B. was believed by the church to have gifts, and promising ones, but by his pastor to have none at all. There were not wanting those that imputed Mr. Maulden's decision to a mean jealousy of the young preacher, who certainly refuted practically his opinion; for, joining the neighbouring Independent church of Isleham, also in Cambridgeshire, under the charge of Mr. Lambert, where his 'gifts' were more properly appreciated, he came forth full of vigour and popularity. He came out about the same time as Mr. Andrew Fuller, of Kettering, with whom he was acquainted, and whose voice and manner he caught in no small degree, if he did not possess them naturally." (Obituary of Mr. Baron, by R. A., Monthly Repository, III. 164.) This incident in his early life probably made Mr. Baron eager beyond his brethren to welcome gifted candidates for pulpit usefulness.

* See Monthly Repository, III. 164.

in the evening preached again to the flock at Wicken, now increased to such an extent that the little chapel was incapable of containing them, and the service was conducted in the yard. He was induced to preach every Sunday during his stay in Cambridgeshire. The places not already mentioned at which he preached were Fordham, Isleham and Soham; but the principal scene of his preaching was Wicken. Here he carried on pastoral visiting and instruction as well as preaching, and a very strong feeling of affection sprung up in the minds of the simple villagers towards their boy-pastor. The evening previous to his departure from the village to resume his studies was one of sorrow to many. A prayer-meeting was held at the house of Mr. Fuller, and the brief record in the diary states that the "people were quite affected."

A few days before his departure, he wrote to his friend and pastor, Mr. Thomas, and thus apologizes for his abrupt assumption of the ministerial office of preaching:

"Wicken, July 12, 1798.

"You will be surprised to hear that I have spoken in public several times lately. It was by no means my intention when I left London, but I could not withstand the pressing importunity of friends whom I greatly respect, and whose esteem I highly value. And after I had consented to preach in one pulpit, to have declined it in another would have appeared like partiality, and would perhaps have given offence. I know not whether it is quite orderly; but, thus circumstanced, I am persuaded you and your friends at Devonshire Square will view it in a right light.

"Considering my youth, I am dubious whether I have acted with prudence, but I submitted to the judgment of others who in most respects appear to display caution and propriety of conduct.

"The motives which induced me to accept the invitations of my Christian friends were, if I may say any more on a subject which so nearly concerns myself, such as appear to me to be justified by the Word of God. I can truly say that I counted not the applause of men, nor aimed to obtain it. I wished to say something which might profit my fellow-creatures."

That he was at this time more eager to hear than to speak, was shewn by his making arrangements to spend the last Sunday of his vacation at Cambridge. He was accompanied by his father, and both were delighted hearers of Mr. Hall, who preached in the morning and afternoon. The following passage in his first letter home, after he reached London, exhibits Mr. Benjamin Flower, the noted political writer, as both a preacher and as the president of a society for religious conference. In estimating his criticism on their addresses, it must be remembered that the previous services of that day had offered for his contemplation the highest standard of pulpit eloquence.

"London, July 28, 1798.

"After I left you, I went to the meeting and heard Mr. Flower speak to about forty or fifty people. He got upon a favourite subject, *priests and sedition*. The text from Malachi iii. —. He is nothing of a speaker; I was quite disappointed; but he spoke excellently of *integrity of principle*, the necessity of maintaining it, the folly of deserting it. I was much pleased with that part of his subject; it exactly suited me; I trust it was useful. Several others attempted to speak. I do not much like the plan. It is making them all preachers, filling them with high notions of themselves, and blunting their appetite for instruction. It may have been useful in discovering talents which would otherwise have been concealed; but then every faithful minister ought to know his flock, to ascertain their worth, and to put their abilities into a proper channel for action. They several times pressed me to pray, and asked me to speak; but I did not; and I am not sorry that I did not."

In this letter there are many expressions of his affection towards the little Wicken flock, and of his earnest desire that Mr. Fyson and the ministers of the neighbourhood would keep up a religious service in the village.

CHAPTER IV.

DURING his brief stay in London, when on his way to Bristol, Robert Aspland renewed his visits to the house of Mr. Middleton. The friendship of this family was destined to exercise a large degree of influence over his future opinions, character and career. The mental activity, the interest in religion and the freedom of inquiry, which he here witnessed, were very attractive to him. In respect to theological sentiment, the ladies of the family were somewhat in advance of him, and had adopted opinions incompatible with the Calvinism in which they had been brought up, although perhaps they were at this time scarcely aware of the extent to which their *heresy* reached. With Sara, Mr. Middleton's elder daughter, Robert Aspland's friendship soon ripened into a warmer feeling, and the engagement which ensued gave occasion from this time for a correspondence, of which considerable use will be made in this Memoir, as it discloses in a very interesting manner his mental struggles and his theological progress.

It was about this time he became intimately acquainted with Mr. John Marsom, the author of the admirable essay " on the Impersonality of the Holy Ghost," who, besides carrying on business as a bookseller in Holborn, was a frequent preacher amongst the General Baptists.*
The General Baptist society meeting at Worship Street held at this time a Sunday-evening conference for the discussion of religious questions, at which Mr. Marsom's Scripture knowledge and familiarity with all the points of the Calvinistic controversy enabled him to take an important part. Robert Aspland often attended the conference. The diary has this entry, under the date Sunday, July 29, 1798:

---

* Mrs. Edney (Mr. Marsom's daughter) contributed to the 1st Series of the Christian Reformer (12mo, 1833, Vol. XIX. pp. 274, 364, 414, 465. 488) an obituary and a memoir of her excellent father.

"At Devonshire Square. Ezekiel xxxvii. 1. Dine at Mr. Overall's. Mr. T., Ps. cxviii. 22. To tea at Miss Middleton's. Went with them and M. P.* to the conference at Worship Street. Sup at Mr. M.'s (Marsom's); discourse on doctrine of the Trinity. My faith staggered. Referred me to Watts and Sir Isaac Newton."

His faith in the doctrine of the Trinity was, as will presently be shewn, for a short time re-established, chiefly through the influence of Dr. Ryland, his new theological tutor.†

He entered the Bristol Academy, July 31, 1798. Shortly before he quitted Mr. Hughes's, he was pained by the discovery that Dr. Ryland had conceived himself slighted‡ by his going to Battersea after the negociation was opened for his admission at Bristol. Mr. Andrew Fuller was solicited to act as a mediator, and was enabled to explain that the pupil's preference throughout was for Bristol, and that the decision in favour of Battersea rested entirely with the Ward Trustees. How Dr. Ryland received his pupil is described in a letter to his parents, of the date

"Bristol, August 3, 1798.

"After a journey of 120 miles and of twenty-one hours, Bristol appeared. The city stands low. It is surrounded by astonishing hills. When in the coach, we could see over it for miles. After breakfast, the gentleman who came with me led me to Dr. Ryland's. I was shewn into the parlour, and after waiting for a few minutes the Doctor appeared. As we always represent

---

* Miss Anna Maria Porter.

† Dr. Ryland was born A.D. 1753, Jan. 29, in the parsonage-house at Warwick, and was the son of the Rev. John Collet Ryland, Baptist minister, first at Warwick, and afterwards at Northampton. Of Dr. Ryland the extraordinary incident is told, that, such was his progress in the Hebrew language during childhood, he read a chapter of the Hebrew Bible to the celebrated Hervey before he was five years old. He began to preach in his seventeenth year, was united in 1781 in the pastoral office with his father at Northampton, and removed to Bristol in 1793, to undertake the joint offices of President of the Bristol Education Society and Pastor of Broadmead. He died in the year 1825, and his funeral sermon was preached at Broadmead meeting, June 5, by Robert Hall. From the discriminative and admirably drawn character of Dr. Ryland at the close of this fine discourse, one or two illustrative notes will be derived.

‡ Dr. Ryland possessed, according to Mr. Hall, extreme susceptibility of feeling, combined with gentleness and timidity. He was sometimes wounded where no unkindness was intended. "His sensitive mind was impressed with every variety of temper in those with whom he conversed; and if his peace was less frequently invaded from this quarter than might have been expected, it is to be ascribed to that reverence which his character so universally inspired. It seemed a sort of sacrilege to trespass upon so much innocence and piety."—Funeral Sermon, 3rd ed., p. 33.

to ourselves persons of whom we hear any thing, I had pictured to myself my tutor, but I had by no means done him justice. The openness of his countenance exceeded my expectations. He received me with the greatest affability. I had heard much in his praise, and my first interview with him confirmed all that I heard. The Academy is in a very pleasant part of the town,* not very crowded with houses, and just at the bottom of a hill, the top of which is the country. Here are a good parlour and an excellent library, books in most languages and of every description, besides a museum. Seven or eight students are come; most of them are very agreeable. * * * Wednesday morning was the anniversary of the institution.† We met at Broadmead meeting. 'Tis a capital place, large and at the same time elegant. It does not savour much of the *poor Baptists*. There were not many people. Job David,‡ of Frome, preached. He is a Socinian Baptist; consequently he was sure of not being liked. His sermon, however, was not very good. The latter part, in which he addressed himself to the friends of the institution and to the students, was good. * * * I am quite happy; so I hope my mother will be contented. We take Flower's paper, and I have seen the account of the

---

* The Academy was then in North Street, at the foot of the Kingsdown Hills. It is now in a still better situation in the same part of the city, in Stokescroft.

† The "Bristol Education Society," founded in 1770 by Dr. Caleb Evans. The first managers of it were, besides Dr. Caleb Evans, Rev. Hugh Evans, his father, Rev. James Newton, the Classical Tutor, Alderman Bull, Treasurer, and Thomas Mullett, Secretary. The library was increased by valuable legacies from Rev. Thomas Llewellyn, LL.D., and Rev. Andrew Gifford, D.D.—*Dyer's Life of Robert Robinson*, pp. 126, 127.

‡ Job David was born in Glamorganshire in 1746, where his father was a Baptist minister. In 1766, he proceeded to the Bristol Academy, where he remained till 1771. He settled first at Pennyfai, near Bridgend, with the church of which his father had been minister, but removed to Frome in 1773, where he was ordained, Oct. 7, by Rev. Daniel Turner, of Abingdon, and Dr. Caleb Evans. Here he continued thirty years. In 1787, Frome was visited by the late Dr. John Evans, then a student at the Bristol Academy, and "he witnessed with high gratification the harmony which subsisted between the pastor and his flock. No minister was more comfortably settled; the people were intelligent and kind, and the labours of the sabbath were crowned with success." Mr. John Foster succeeded Mr. David at Frome, and there are in the recently published Life and Correspondence some references to Mr. David and his opinions, in the usual "orthodox" strain. It is probable that the temper of the "orthodox" members of the society at Frome became less tolerant, and that this circumstance influenced Mr. D. to leave Frome in 1803, and remove to Taunton, where he succeeded Dr. Toulmin. In 1809, he removed for the sake of his health to Swansea, where he died, Oct. 11, 1812. (Mon. Repos., VII. 712—716.) During the past fifty years, the orthodox Dissenters have in some things gone back rather than advanced in liberality of spirit. This is in part, perhaps, the result of the distinct theological landmarks assumed by the different sects. What holy horror would be roused by a "Socinian" preacher now entering the pulpit at Broadmead!

execution of the Sheares, which affects me much. My blood boils—but farewell."

There were at the Bristol Academy in the session 1798-99, about twenty students, some of whom, however, were there for only a part of the session,—some leaving, and others coming to the Academy at Christmas. Their names and after-destination, so far as they can be ascertained, were as follows. 1. Francis Augustus Cox, born at Leighton Buzzard, March 7, 1783; settled first at Clipstone, in Northamptonshire, April 4, 1804, and removed to Hackney, Oct. 4, 1811, and has received the diploma of D. D. from Waterville, Maine, and of LL.D. from Glasgow. 2. Thomas Flint, succeeded his father-in-law, Rev. Benjamin Francis, at Shortword, 1800; resigned in 1803; and afterwards settled at Weymouth. 3. — Douglas, settled at Portsmouth, afterwards removed and kept a school in London. 4. Joseph Webb, said to have been a young man of fine taste. His health failed, and he died at Birmingham. 5. — Griffiths. 6. Thomas Roberts, settled with the Baptist congregation, King Street, Bristol. 7. Williams, died early of consumption, and never settled as a minister. 8. George Keeley, settled at Northampton, whence, after a residence of thirteen years, he emigrated to America. 9. Evan Jones, settled in Wales. 10. — Jenkin. 11. Benjamin Coxhead, settled at Winchester and at Wild Street, London; now resides at Newbury, but does not exercise the ministry. 12. Samuel Kilpin, is a highly-esteemed minister at Exeter. 13. William Thomas. 14. — Franklin, is settled at Coventry. 15. David Trotman, at Tewkesbury, but is now unsettled. 16. Joshua Marshman, afterwards D.D., was a missionary at Calcutta, in association with Dr. Carey and others; went to India in April 1799; died at Serampore, April 5, 1837. 17. Thomas Morgan, settled in Birmingham. 18. — Bicheno, son of a well-known writer on theological subjects. 19. Samuel Saunders, settled first at Frome and then at Liverpool.

His chief intimacy during his stay at the Academy, and the only one which survived his change of religious sentiments, was with Mr. Cox. Their academical studies began together, and for the last thirty-four years of Mr. Aspland's life they exercised their ministry in the same village.

Soon after the commencement of the session, Dr. Ryland placed in the hands of the new student the following question, to which he asked a written answer: "What is the character of a good minister of Jesus Christ? Do you aspire after this character, and hope you possess somewhat of its principal ingredients?" To this question, somewhat embarrassing to a very young and inexperienced man, he, after some thought and self-examination, gave in this answer:

"The good minister of Jesus Christ is one who loves God and bears an ardent attachment to Christ. He is one who, having partaken of the benefits of salvation, wishes and exerts himself that they may be extended to others. These are the primary qualifications of the preacher of the gospel; others, such as abilities, decidedness of character, &c., follow of course.

"It is often a question with me whether I possess the essential ingredients of the ministerial character, but hope generally preponderates, and this it is which induces me to aspire after it. Should Providence prepare the way, I feel a strong desire to be thus employed. And I think I may venture to say that it would give me the most heartfelt satisfaction to be in any measure subservient to the interests of virtue and truth."

The scholarship of the Bristol Academy, whatever it may be now, was not good half a century ago. Classical literature was probably carried to a greater height by Mr. Hall during his five years' tutorship than it had been by Mr. Newton, his predecessor, or than it was by his successors, Hughes and James. Many of the pupils from Wales came up to the Academy ill prepared in grammar knowledge, and, distracted as their attention immediately was by preparation for pulpit duties, in addition to a variety of studies altogether new to them, they had few opportunities of repairing past neglects. Robert Aspland and Mr. Cox found themselves at the beginning of the session somewhat in advance of their companions, and it is probable that their powers were not tasked in maintaining the lead in the class, of which the studies appear to have been in the Greek Testament, the Eclogues of Virgil, Selectæ e Profanis, Cicero's Orations and Horace. They found leisure for studies not included in the College course. Robert Aspland, notwithstanding the general acceptance of his pulpit services, avoided rather than courted public duty, and seldom preached except when there was no one else amongst the students to undertake the required service. He preached at Fishponds, near Bristol, at Chelwood twice, Downend twice, Thornbury twice, Bratton, in Wiltshire, George's chapel, and at Bridge Street, Bristol. But he was better pleased to be a hearer than a preacher, and records frequently the satisfaction with which he listened to Dr. Ryland's solid and well-prepared discourses. He occasionally attended at the Lewin's Mead chapel, and heard both Dr. Estlin and Mr. Rowe, but of the impression made no record appears. He once went to the French

Catholic church at the Hotwells and " heard M. —— preach an excellent sermon on miracles." His reading in theology and English literature was pursued during his residence at Bristol with great avidity; but in his miscellaneous reading he greatly needed the guidance of a cultivated and superior mind. The remarkable tenacity of his memory, by which he could recal, even in the closing years of life, the contents of books read in youth and never afterwards seen, enabled him to give classification and order to the knowledge and ideas which were the produce of this extensive but desultory reading. Still it may be doubted whether he ever entirely subdued the injurious mental effects of the neglect of system which characterized his studies during his college years. Although in after life no one could surpass him in the power, *whenever an emergency arose*, of bracing up his faculties and devoting his whole mind and will to a purpose,—and although, under such circumstances, the work he did was admirable alike for its completeness and despatch, yet in his ordinary literary pursuits, when there was no pressure from without, unity of purpose and persevering application were too often wanting. Had the studies of the English Dissenting academies at the close of the last century been elevated and regulated by affiliation with a higher institution, possessing the power of awarding literary and scientific degrees, like the present London University, it is more than probable that they would have produced a greater number of accomplished scholars and vigorous-minded men, and that the intellectual standard of English Nonconformity would now be (as it was at the close of the seventeenth century) greatly in advance of the age.

The letters which he wrote from Bristol will sufficiently describe his life there. The reader will find in them, at different times, very different feelings in respect to religious doctrine. Such differences are always found in a transition state of mind. There are ebbs and flows of faith. Many struggles have to be gone through before early convictions altogether lose their hold of the mind.

To his Parents.

"Bristol, August 31, 1798.

"I expected my father's letter several days before it came. I received it on the 23rd. It found me busy with Mr. James, our under tutor. I read it with eagerness. I can easily conceive that you felt yourselves dull the first sabbath after I left you. We had met so frequently together, that it began to be a thing of course. I assure you I felt myself equally, if not more dull.

I am happy to think preaching is not entirely forgotten at Wicken. When you see good Mr. Fyson, present my respects to him, and tell him that, after all, it is a great mercy that all preachers are not *farmers*. The week-day harvest would so engross their attention, that they would have no strength or inclination left to labour in the *harvest of souls.* * * *

"I went in the beginning of the month to see the French prison at Stapleton. The distance is about two and a half miles from Bristol. After a few minutes we were admitted, and a curious spectacle presented itself to us. A great number of men in a square yard fenced by low houses, mostly in rags, very dirty and variously engaged—many at cards, others at dominoes, some with books. A great number crowded towards us with little commodities which they had learnt to make in their leisure hours, each speaking or making some sign to attract our notice. Their goods were most curiously made, mostly of bone. What most struck me was the *guillotine*, of which they had a great number of various sizes. Their ingenuity is astonishing. In purchasing a few articles of them, I put a few questions to them in French. They were quite rejoiced to find I could speak to them in their own tongue, and began conversing immediately. They preserved their republican tone. They expressed great dissatisfaction with England, and the most ardent attachment to France. The love of liberty seemed written on their countenances. I was grieved on their account. To see a number of rational creatures crowded into a narrow space, deprived of air, separated from friends and surrounded by enemies, was to me no uninteresting scene. I left them with sorrow and with poignant indignation against the promoters of war."

To Miss Middleton.
"Bristol, Sept., 1798.

"Society I esteem one of the greatest privileges of life. Sameness of pursuits is indeed an inducement to acquaintance, but unless there be candour and openness of heart, my acquaintance with persons will be very distant. Out of seventeen or eighteen students, it would be strange if there were not some amiable dispositions; but most of them are, I fear, cramped by party-spirit. Unwilling or afraid to investigate, every thing novel is cried down as error; little acquainted with the human mind, they brand with ignorance or insincerity all who have independence enough to think for themselves. You know I love freedom of inquiry. It is hardly admissible here. If it is indulged, it will be at the expense of orthodoxy.

"Dr. Ryland is a very agreeable man. He is not one of the most liberal *Calvinists** (if I may use a term which I dislike), but his situation sufficiently

---

* This is Robert Hall's testimony to Dr. Ryland's theological spirit: "Though a Calvinist in the strictest sense of the word, and attached to its peculiarities in a higher degree than most of the advocates of that system, he extended his affection to all who bore the image of Christ, and was ingenious in discovering

excuses any dogmatism. He possesses great strength of mind, united with much simplicity of manners. He is plain, but very judicious. You hear from him few oratorical flourishes, few displays of eloquence, but neither will you hear those wanton flights and unkind insinuations with which they are too frequently connected. His sermons are calculated to instruct and to reform. He generally reads the greater part of his discourses. This is not the way to be popular. He has, however, a very large congregation, and, if riches create respectability, a respectable one. The meeting is a very spacious, handsome building, almost surrounded with vestries. Dissenters are a very numerous body at Bristol, and when I tell you they include the greater part of the Corporation, you will not be surprised to hear that they are very genteel Christians. They are too apt, I understand, to bring civil distinctions into the church; hence their frequent dissensions."*

To his Parents.

"Bristol, Sept. 28, 1798.

"I promised in my last letter an extract or two from Dyer's Life of Robinson. I dare say you are anxious to hear what is said of John Carlton; 'tis as follows: 'There was a person known by the name of poor John of Norwich (alias John Carlton), who was a kind of idiot, or at least passed for one, who had been acquainted with Robinson when a boy at Norwich. He had been *called*, i. e. had become religious under Robinson's ministry when a preacher in that city, and he could not be satisfied till he became a preacher. Whether the man was so sincere as Robinson apprehended, will not be inquired: Robinson at least thought him an honest man, though possessed of the understanding of an infant. He even encouraged him to preach, and actually signed a paper as a kind of testimonial, by virtue of which poor John strolled about the country and lisped nonsense, for he could not speak a word plainly: he frequently preached in Robinson's family: how many sinners he converted, or how many saints he comforted, is of little consequence. Robinson at least did not entirely lose his end; he endured this man's occasional visits, and

---

reasons for thinking well of many who widely dissented from his religious views. No man was more remarkable for combining a zealous attachment to his own principles with the utmost liberality of mind towards those who differed from him; an abhorrence of error, with the kindest feelings towards the erroneous. He detested the spirit of monopoly in religion, and opposed every tendency to circumscribe it by the limits of party."—Funeral Sermon, pp. 36, 37.

* The Broadmead society had been seriously divided a few years previously by a dispute between Dr. Caleb Evans and Mr. Hall. "After many months spent in this unseemly strife," says Mr. Hall's biographer, "a meeting between the belligerent parties was held in the presence of two friends of each, at the Mansion House, the Mayor of Bristol being one of the persons chosen by Dr. Evans." Dr. Gregory's Memoir of Robert Hall.

was the means of procuring him support.'* Thus much is said of dumb John, who was so popular at Isleham and elsewhere. Mr. Keeley, I think, told me that he is now in *Norwich workhouse*. There is something in good Mr. Fyson very much like Robert Robinson; he has at least the same cool, dry, witty method of speaking.

"I have had a short fit of illness, but have recovered. Bristol air agrees with me. I have preached but once since I wrote to you. It was at a place called Chelwood, in Somersetshire, nine miles from Bristol. 'Tis a Presbyterian interest, and they have service only in the morning. I rode back to Bristol, and was time enough for evening service. We rise every morning at six o'clock. On Lord's-day mornings, a few of us hold a prayer meeting. I frequently think of *you* then. How much the sabbath reminds me of you! Each of the students in turn delivers a sermon before the Doctor and students (one every week). It lately came to me, and I composed a short discourse from Daniel xii. 4, *Knowledge shall be increased*, in which I endeavoured to shew that a general increase of knowledge would precede and usher in *the latter-day glory*, and observed that the present state of things indicates that this *happy period is not far distant*. The Dr. and students expressed their approbation of the composition and ideas, but thought the sermon hardly *evangelical* enough. They would have wished me to introduce and insist upon the doctrine of Divine influences. Everlasting love, personal election, and a few other commonplace topics, can alone secure a man approbation. But I consider these topics of inferior moment, and seldom meddle with them."

To Miss Middleton.

"Bristol, Oct. 15, 1798.

"* * * I have sometimes considered the doctrine of *Divine influences*, and have generally felt the same difficulty as yourself. But will it not in some measure ease the subject, if we consider the agency of the Deity as operating on the hearts of men, not by force, but by *advice* carrying with it its own propriety? *Perhaps* this may in a degree reconcile the *freedom of the will* with *Divine interference*. That God does influence the human mind, is evident from the conversion of Paul—of——in short, of many Christians in the present day; and that all men are so involved in depravity and guilt as to incapacitate them for every spiritual exertion without Divine assistance, the present state of society appears to me to render equally evident. But how then to establish the *accountableness of man*, I know not. To recur to the sovereignty of God is unsatisfactory, because we generally suppose him to act with *design*. Should you meet with any thing tending to illustrate the matter, you will communicate it.

"The apparent contradictions and mysteriousness of Scripture have some-

---

* Dyer's Life of Robinson, pp. 136, 137.

times almost driven me to despair. Frequently have I sighed for non-existence! Frequently have I lamented that my lot was not cast in some remote part of the globe, where I might have lived at ease and indulged the native sentiments of my heart, free from those distractions which now sometimes agitate it. And more frequently have I been ready to accuse Providence for not permitting me to remain inattentive to religion and unapprehensive of futurity. And I assure you I have often been a prey to Deistical reflections; and though examination has tended to christianize my mind, you will readily believe that scepticism is not wholly excluded. I feel myself extremely happy under the tuition of Dr. R.; and if ever I attain that desirable enjoyment you mention, decidedness of sentiment, it must be imputed to him. The more I see of him, the more I admire him. He has not the art of shewing himself to advantage, but a little intimacy will reveal his worth. He is a good preacher. He gave us lately an excellent sermon in defence of Christianity, from John v. 39. The conclusion was so striking that I must give you it. 'Do you still wish the Bible were not true? You'd gain nothing by the change. You'd get leave to indulge your lusts, and you'd *obtain the prize of annihilation!*' Conceive the effect such a concluding address, from so respectable a man, must have had upon a crowded auditory. I dare say it made an indelible impression upon every reflecting person in the place. Perhaps I overrate it: what do you think of it? May we not pronounce it an excellent rhetorical stroke?

"I heartily wish you had heard him last sabbath evening; he gave us the best defence of the divinity of Christ that I ever heard, and what I must confess contributed in no small degree to settle my opinion on that controverted subject. As his ideas were new (at least to me), I shall make no apology for transcribing some of them from his notes, which I have just borrowed.

"Text, Matt. xxviii. 18, 'All power is given unto me in heaven and in earth.'

"'*All power in heaven and earth.* What can be comprehended in this expression? Does it include nothing more than a man like ourselves might receive and possess when distant many millions of miles, and incapable of knowing any thing about the present state of things upon earth, but by revelation or information of angels? Can it mean merely that the new dispensation of religion which he had set up should endure to the end of time? Then Moses might have said so 1490 years before him; and in what was Christ's power superior to that of Moses? Did he abolish various positive institutions, and appoint two new ones to continue to the end of time? Will this exhaust the force of his expression? Or does it only mean in addition that he had authority to command that the true God should be preached to the Gentiles, and that the future state and resurrection should be announced more expressly than by Moses? Is this enough? Does it include an assurance that the penitent should be forgiven on the mere ground of their repentance, though Christ had no particular influence in procuring their forgiveness, any more than any other good man,—only he in his ministry is supposed to have declared that God is so good as not to condemn those that ought to be acquitted? Is this all? Or does it include that the worshipers of the true God should be called by his name? Is this having all power, &c.? I can guess at no more that can be ascribed to Christ, if he was a mere man. While on this supposition,

"'We have to regret that his using such language and receiving such honours has occasioned a most awful mistake, and led thousands into idolatry for *sixteen hundred years* at least.

"'And Christ has been thus exalted *above measure* for so long time before his principal exaltation at the latter-day glory.

"'And the Jews have been so plagued for rejecting him, though their error *is nothing*, in not owning him for a prophet, *to ours*, in taking him for a *divine person*.

"'Never, surely, was any servant of God so *unfortunate*, and never was any so *incautious* as Christ, if he was merely a man and merely a teacher. In no instance can I see so little evidence of divine wisdom and prudence as in giving him so much honour. Never did such a deplorable event befal Moses or any of the prophets, except in the idolatry of the Church of Rome, *which had been foretold and condemned*, and even they never took *saints for deities*.'

"I should like to see a full attack of the Socinians on this score. There is ample scope for reasoning, and I think some arguments of this sort would be conclusive. What think you of this doctrine? I don't see how we can reasonably deny it. They who do, give Christianity a most unfavourable aspect: they represent it as little more than a republication of the law of Nature, and this ill accords with the many and expressive prophecies which foretold it, the claims of its first Founder and original propagators, or with the severe and awful punishments annexed to the rejection of it."

To his Parents.

"Bristol, November 23, 1798.

"I hope friend Fyson does not desert you. I have a most sincere affection for him. He is the best man around you. I long to see him. A few more days will introduce Christmas to us. I recollect John Emons telling me that till Christmas he should look back on the past summer; after Christmas he should begin to count on the next. It is probable I shall do the same. * * * My father has, I dare say, not forgotten our museum—the ancient Bibles; part of the Bible written by the Seventy Elders in the Greek language; the portrait of Oliver Cromwell, for which the late Empress of Russia offered £500. I could not then find the account of *Wicken*. I have since recollected the book, and will now transcribe some of it. 'At *Wicken*, near Soham, there was a house which the Lady Mary Bassingburn, in the fifteenth of Edward II., gave with several parcels of land to the convent of Spinney, on the condition that seven poor old men should be maintained in it, with an allowance to each of one farthing loaf, one herring, and one pennyworth of ale every day, and three ells of linen, one woollen garment, one pair of shoes and 200 dry turf every year.' Are there any traces of this donation at present? Is it included in what are called *the Poor's lands?*"

To Miss Middleton.

"Bristol, December 19, 1798.

" * * * I think I can easily account for the charge you exhibit against me. I will not plead an unsettled state of mind, nor will I urge an ardour of information; these perhaps would not satisfy you—I shall rest my defence on one single sentiment, detestation of slander. You cannot be ignorant that, as sceptical tenets have prevailed of late, malevolence has urged a certain class of Christians to charge the professors of them with enormities, which many of them would blush to repeat, and which arise, not from sentiment, but from character. This I account dishonest and unmanly, and whenever I have witnessed it have felt it my duty to oppose it and to expose its injustice. Thus, for instance, when I hear the Deists as a body charged with ignorance and repugnance to investigation, I cannot but repel the charge; and when I am told that their principles naturally generate selfishness and contract the heart, a review of the characters of some of their chief advocates gives the lie to the suspicion. And, again, who can forbear the most lively indignation when he reads from the pen of a Dr. Jon. Edwards that there never were above *twenty* or *thirty* moral characters among the Deists? (These are, I think, his very words.) Now I think you will side with me, and when you see that nothing but tacit assent to such notorious misstatements could have procured or preserved me the *esteem* of men, you must acknowledge that it was my duty to forfeit it. Are you satisfied? Can you give me any rule by which to conciliate the affections of others and maintain my own integrity and independence at the same time? However desirable, such a medium is, I fear, unattainable. But it is time to say something about our theological arrangements. I have given your plan another thought, and am more fully persuaded of its utility. I will suggest an idea or two. From what you have hitherto written on the subject, I conclude that your plan includes the Old Testament as well as the New. Now, will it not be more natural and more productive, to confine ourselves to the latter? I am aware that much stress is laid on Old-Testament Scriptures in Christian disputes, but surely with little propriety; for, however they may seem to confirm Gospel truths, they are most of them ambiguous at the best (being found in the prophecies), and many of them applicable to the Jewish dispensation alone. Afterwards, indeed, it would be useful to read the Old Testament with a critical attention to discover how far their economy extended, what were their morals, and what their views of futurity. Should this amendment (though perhaps I mistook your intention) meet with your approbation, we have nothing to do but to begin our Testaments, and read regularly through, entering under several commonplaces the passages we suppose favourable to them; and when we have done this, to reconcile, by the assistance of commentators and that best expositor, common sense, the texts which appear to clash. I shall begin immediately to pave the way for scriptural research, that I may lose no time after the receipt of your letter. But here I must request you not to be sanguine in your expectations from me, for the work with me must be very gradual. I will devote as much time to it as I possibly can, but I have no expectations of completing the scheme before Whitsuntide.

"Have you ever seen Gerrald's and Muir's trials for sedition? What sentiments of anger and detestation have they infused into my bosom! And when I think on the cruel fate of the former, I know not how to contain myself. Talents, worth, virtue, every thing that can render a man interesting, were concentrated in him. But he was a friend to liberty, and he has fallen a martyr in its cause. Yet he lives, and, as he boldly asserted on his trial, 'out of his ashes shall arise a flame to consume the tyrants of the earth.' His speech before the brutal justiciary of Scotland is a model of pure and energetic language."

To his Parents.

"Bristol, January 25, '99.

"I was not a little pleased with John Emons's letter. It reminded me of old scenes, and more than ever revived my *hankerings* after Cambridgeshire. After many affectionate observations and curious inquiries, he closes his letter, which is written in the most friendly style, thus. Did I not think him sincere, it would give me no pleasure; but as he is known to be right-down, I could not help being affected:—'I must conclude by only saying that the Christmas is over, and short days are past, and my hopes begin to revive at thoughts of spring's coming, when I hope the singing of birds will come, and you *as a turtle be heard in our land.*' * * * Oh! what pleasure and instruction I have derived from attending the lectures on Anatomy! Well might the Psalmist say, *I am fearfully and wonderfully made.* There seems not to be any thing deficient, nor any thing useless. Every part is formed with exquisite skill and nicety, and exactly answers the end for which it is designed. How infinitely inferior is every thing of human workmanship! I am more firmly than ever convinced of the existence of a Supreme Being. The dissection of a human eye furnishes stronger conviction on this subject than any speculative reasoning. We have had already nearly twenty lectures, and during the last week the lecturers have been dissecting before us. * * * My good wishes always accompany you in your meetings at Soham and Wicken, and not a sabbath passes without my thinking of you. Wednesday, I recollect, was my birth-day. I then began my 18th year. How fast time flies; and how mysterious as well as kind are the ways of Providence! Two or three years ago, I could hardly have believed that I should be where I am at present; and who knows what another such period may bring forth?"

To ———.*

"Bristol, Feb. 9, 1799.

"* * * Your character of Dr. Ryland raised my expectations and led me to conceive very highly of him. I am happy to inform you that I have by no means been disappointed. He is a most amiable man. So much good sense and general knowledge, connected with so much diffidence and modesty, cannot fail of endearing him to every one who is able to estimate character. His ideas of gospel truth are so reasonable and benevolent, that to receive them it is only necessary to become acquainted with them, and I hope his preaching and instruction have not been altogether lost upon me. Since I have been with the Dr., my religious sentiments have been much settled. Religious research only ends with life, but I hope I have been enabled to form some basis on which future opinions may safely rest."

To his Parents.

"Bristol, Feb. 19, 1799.

"* * * Your intention of building† gives me much pleasure. Go forward! Be not weary in well-doing, for in due time ye shall reap if ye faint not. I wish to hear of some real good done among you. I am more strongly than ever convinced that *to change the heart* is the sole prerogative of God; and this, instead of discouraging me or damping my hopes, gives me the greatest comfort, and renders the success of the word much more probable than if it rested with man. I used to question the truth of some of the commonly-received doctrines (election and reprobation for instance); but more diligent investigation has induced me to conclude that the plan of redemption is necessarily incomprehensible; and though some of the doctrines of grace may appear to clash with each other, 'tis my duty to receive them as revealed of God, and to rest satisfied in the belief that *what I know not now, I shall know hereafter.* * * * My kind love to Isaac; I shall expect a letter from him. He need not expect to be the tallest of the family. If I may believe persons here, I have much grown; and I can't call in question their statement, for I can look over the heads of most of the students."

To Miss Middleton.

"Bristol, March 14, 1799.

"* * * In a former letter you asked my view of the faith of the ancient

---

* Probably Rev. Timothy Thomas.   † A meeting-house at Wicken.

Jews. This is the first subject on which I may be said to have doubted, and my disbelief of this sentiment was the first step I took in the paths of heterodoxy. To suppose that persons living several ages before the Christian era, and who, we have no right to suppose, were favoured with more instruction on the subject than what is included in a few unconnected, enigmatical insinuations, had a proper conviction of sin, and depended on Christ's atonement for the forgiveness of it, appeared to me a palpable absurdity, which their *writings* totally disclaimed. And though my ideas are somewhat different now, I can't help thinking that the religious views of the O. T. saints were obscure and defective. I am hardly decided on the subject, but incline to the opinion that their hopes of salvation were founded on some *general* notions of satisfaction and of Divine benevolence, without any particular application to the Saviour. About the same time, without knowing that any one had openly avowed it, I warmly supported Warburton's hypothesis also, that the Jews did not believe in a future state. Many plausible arguments may be urged in defence of it; but when allowed its full scope, it does, I think, invariably lead to Deism. Reason revolts at the idea that God should fill a professed revelation of his will with *comparative trifles*, and leave his peculiar people uninformed of their high destination. This is not the only sentiment I have seen reason to change. My mind has of late undergone a complete revolution, and be not surprised to hear that *Calvinism* is at present in some measure triumphant. I am at least more reconciled to its leading doctrines. You are anxious to know the cause of this. 'Tis difficult to say whether it be the pure result of cool investigation—whether the influence which Dr. R. has gained over me—or whether it be the desire of escaping the censures and reproofs of the *faithful*. But as I by no means intend to exclude the first, I will give you the progress of my researches into the matter. As soon, then, as I had weighed the evidence of the Christian revelation, and had fully satisfied myself of its truth and authority, I resolved upon this principle, *That perfect consistency and simplicity in any scheme of religion is unattainable in the present imperfect state, and that 'tis our indispensable duty implicitly to receive whatever God has made known.* Thus prepared, I entered on the examination, and after many hesitations of mind concluded, that though the doctrines I have in part adopted are attended with great and invincible difficulties, they are less encumbered than their opposites. You will smile at my inconstancy. Well you may. I dare not ensure the continuance of my present belief a day. I aim at truth; if I miss it, it is involuntarily.

" You judge rightly of my attachment to Hall as a preacher. I have heard him with exquisite delight, and I think I do others no injustice when I state him to be the ablest man amongst the Dissenters. His talents render his conversation enviable. I hope to be delighted with it more than once in the summer. Your wishes will also be excited when you hear that Jay has been supplying at Bristol Tabernacle. I heard four of his discourses. The two first were excellent; I saw nothing extraordinary in the others."

In order to understand the letters of Robert Aspland that follow, some passages must be given from the replies of his correspondent. Independently of the important bearing they had on the after career of the subject of this biography, these letters present a very interesting picture of two minds engaged solely in the pursuit of religious truth, travelling in the same direction, but at different stages of the progress. In the reply to the last letter, the following passages seem to deserve attention.

"London, April 2, 1799.

"You tell me at present the leading doctrines of Calvinism claim your reception. This in your first letter from Bristol might have been welcome intelligence. You will perceive how different has been the result of our inquiries (though I trust pursued under the same impression of the necessity of receiving whatever God has been pleased to reveal), when I tell you that in your last it gave me surprise and concern. The former I soon repressed, recollecting that, however disposed to independence, the mind is formed for society, and, in connection with its advantages, is liable in some measure to receive its prejudices. I know likewise that 'tis probable my opinions may appear just as strange to you as yours did to me. My regret I cannot so easily overcome, because I see you likely to become the defender of a system which observation has taught me to consider as having a tendency to produce *rational* Deists, *wicked* professors and *intolerant* Christians, to furnish an unanswerable plea to the willing slave of sin, to discourage the *rational* though *sincere* believer, and to quiet the conscience of the indolent professor who once experienced strong emotions, perhaps conversion. I am happy to confess that a very great number of those who profess this doctrine are a credit to religion, but they are but half converts to their sentiments; they lay as much stress on the necessity of human exertions as those who maintain the freedom of the will; but surely this is not the Calvinism which you find the least encumbered with difficulties. If you are one at all, it must be a *high* Calvinist. But no! I recollect you have formed your decisions from Scripture, therefore I withdraw my last assertion. Till I can believe that *rendering* an account implies no *trust*, I must withhold my assent from moderate Calvinism. Till I can find some meaning very different to any I have ever yet been able to discover of such passages as Ezek. xviii. 32, xxxiii. 11; 1 Pet. i. 17; 2 Pet. iii. 9; Rom. ii. 4—6,—I cannot believe in personal reprobation. Those expressions which *seem* to favour this sentiment, upon close and candid examination will admit of another explanation. Their opposites are so obvious, that

I can't imagine how they can be made to speak any thing but their most direct language. Ah! my friend, can you dwell on this doctrine? When our minds become sublimated by the contemplation of Infinite Excellence and Perfection, the faint ray of intelligence in man fades on our sight, and we readily exclaim, 'Lord what is man, that thou art mindful of him! The nations are but as the dust of the balance.' But this is an elevation of mind which I can seldom long retain; and indeed that portion of self-love which God has so firmly rooted in every breast, in connection with the Scripture declaration of the value of the human soul, obliges us to consider its perdition as no trifling concern. Free-will has its perplexities, but to me they are of much less weight than those of the opposite opinion: the one contains difficulty, the other contradiction; a difficulty principally arising from our ignorance of what passes in the human mind. 'Who knoweth the things of a man, save the spirit of a man that is in him?' and for an explanation of this we must wait till that day when God shall judge the secrets of the heart. Mr. Fuller shews that it is not merely those who eventually receive the gospel to whom its invitations are addressed, by considering the character of Herod, Acts iv. 25, compared with Psalm ii. 10—12. On the preaching of John, we read of him, that he heard him gladly and did many things, though eventually he imprisoned and beheaded him. I think there can be no doubt but that he resisted the Holy Ghost. Peter tells the Jews that God sent his Son, that *every* one of them should be turned from his iniquities, Acts iii. 26; but that instead of a blessing, it would prove their destruction, v. 23, unless they repented and were converted in hearkening to the prophet which he sent, v. 19—'Ye *will* not come unto me that ye might have life.' 'Search the Scriptures,' &c. What an address to the understanding; what an assurance that the impediment to their believing resided only in their obstinacy and prejudice! To prove the duties of repentance and faith universal under the idea of man being prevented by a moral, not a natural inability, and then to assert that the latter is as total as the former, is indeed to make a distinction of sound, but not of sense. *Inability* is neither more nor less than *inability*, of whatever kind. The very essence of moderate Calvinism is to say, 'It is *your* duty to do that which God alone can effect.' For my own part, I cannot sanction the opinion of the slothful servant, Matt. xxv. 24. The conversion of St. Paul for a long time inclined me to Calvinism; but from considering all that he says of himself, it appears to me that he did not consider his conversion, although to him it must have been the greatest reality in the world, as necessarily implying his final salvation, nor the power of God as exercised towards him as superseding the freedom of his will. 1 Cor. ix. 27; Acts xxvi. 19; Gal. i. 15, 16.—I have been too much in the habit of expressing my sentiments freely, to suppose that you will require an apology for my having done so in the present instance. Perhaps, as you are only beginning to be right orthodox, you will be ready to say, Do leave the strong man in quiet possession of his new house. However, you still admit the use of reason in religion. If my arguments are weak, they will do you no harm; and if I am wrong, I would wish to have my error pointed out."

To Miss Middleton.

"Bristol, April 13, 1799.

" * * * If I felt seriously desirous of correcting your misapprehension of my principles of action, I could hardly forbear a smile at one part of your epistle, from which a reader, unacquainted with us both, would have gathered that I had deserted opinions once avowed, and had embraced the rigidly orthodox system, with all the virulence and malignancy of its *canonized founder*. You mistake, if you suppose me to be a *settled Calvinist*. (Were one of my brethren of the *sable order* peeping over my shoulder now, I might justly tremble for its consequences!) The strongest assertion I have made, or dare make, is, that I feel less repugnance to the popular belief than heretofore. My religious creed is yet to be formed, and will, I fear, remain as it is till this restless, fluttering something within (call it what you will), be released from its mortal shackles. One would judge from my undecidedness that I had adopted *Hume's* paradoxical aphorism, '*The perfection of human nature is to doubt;*' and I assure you I have sometimes thought it founded on truth. But amidst all my scepticism, I again repeat, I find much more satisfaction in moderate *Calvinism* (I don't like the frequent recurrence of this odious distinction) than in any other collection of tenets. I search for truth, and whenever I find it, whether in the Presbytery of Geneva, in the cloisters of Rome, or among the philosophers of the *great nation*, I am eager to make it my own. I inquire not whether the profession of it be reputable or advantageous—sufficient for me that it is truth; and neither the clamours of the multitude, nor the suggestions of the *more enlightened few*, shall induce me to relinquish it. Party names have long ago spent all their strength upon me; now their buzzing hardly molests me.—Having prefaced thus much, I proceed to tell you that I think your picture of the ill effects of my supposed sentiments is very much overcharged. We pretend not to secure them from perversion and abuse, but we think their moral impressions will suffer no disparagement by being contrasted with those of the opposite sect. Do they weaken human obligation, and cool the sacred warmth of disinterested love? Do they render men more deaf to the calls of mercy, less observant of social duty? You cannot for a moment suppose they do; and if, in any instance, they seem to cramp genius and benumb the mental faculty, more, I am persuaded, is to be attributed to the narrow and confined spirit of the day, than to them. As yet, they have not had a fair opportunity of expanding themselves. The leading-strings with which prejudice and weakness have fettered them, must be loosed before you can form a just idea of their influence on *mind*. So widely different, indeed, have been our views of this subject, that nothing has so much inclined me to the opinions of the party with which I am connected, as their *happy tendency*. This has, of late, appeared to me a prominent feature in their character, and, if I mistake not, is an excellency admitted by some of our opponents. The terms *we, our,* &c., you will say, little comport with the *unsettledness* I just spoke of. I only use them for brevity's sake.

"The Arminian controversy is very perplexing. You have, I will frankly own, the greatest *appearance* of reason and benevolence; but I can't help concluding that the real truth *inclines* the other way. The passages you have quoted, taken singly, weigh in your favour, but compared with and adjusted to others which you must bear upon your mind, do, I think, turn the balance against you. How to reconcile the doctrine of Divine influences with the 'freedom of the will,' I know not. But recollecting that 'now we see through a glass darkly,' I admit both on the testimony of Scripture. What else can I do? I give up all expectations of *simplifying* religion. Perfect satisfaction on every point I don't hope for. You charge the distinction of *moral and natural inability* with senselessness. Let me entreat you to re-consider it; it will well repay the most considerate attention; and while you blame Fuller's system as saying, 'it is *our* duty to do that which *God* alone can effect,' does not the censure rebound on yourself? You maintain that it is the incumbent duty of all men to believe the gospel; and yet you will not deny that '*faith is the gift of God.*' So of repentance, holiness and every other obligation. The Scriptures earnestly exhort men to the performance of them, and yet expressly say, that 'every good and perfect gift cometh from above.' But I have done. You dissent from me from principle and on mature investigation. I respect the difference which I could wish to remove. Whatever be the disagreement of our sentiments, let it not alienate our affections; rather let it lead us to court each other's information and correction. Let us shew that uniformity of opinion is not requisite to unison of heart."

His correspondent's rejoinder is dated "London, April 22, 1799."

" * * * Respecting your religious sentiments, if you can rest satisfied with moderate Calvinism, it will give me no great concern. Educational notions, lowered by feelings which from my childhood I recollect having experienced, long retained me in that class; but the beauty of holiness was ever that part of religion which engaged my affections. In Christians displaying moral excellence I discovered the excellent of the earth. As to the generality of those who denominate themselves exclusively the defenders of free grace and of unconditional salvation, the *malignity* of their tempers and the *consistency* of their principles startled me, and for a moment led me to doubt the divinity of revelation itself. Happily, I soon recovered from this mistake, though not without many ineffectual struggles to believe what I considered a true, though

F

awful system; at the same time attributing my want of conviction to the reasonings of the carnal mind and the withholden influences of the Spirit. My subsequent change you know. You mistake me if you suppose I deny the distinction between natural and moral inability; I only do so when held in connection with the doctrines of Calvinism. I believe that in the end moral inability becomes natural inability. This I think is exemplified in the Jews, who from inattention to their own Scriptures seemed really to want evidence of the Messiahship of Christ; and upon their turning to the Lord, it was declared that veil of unbelief should be taken from their heart. I acknowledge that every good and perfect gift cometh from above. I believe in the influences of the Spirit; but I believe them to be *rational* influences, and from Scripture it appears to me they are *universal;* for in any other sense I can't understand the meaning of St. Paul, 1 Cor. ii. 16, 17, warning them not to defile the temple of God—themselves being that temple—and yet liable to destruction. If the Spirit of God be irresistible, I am at a loss to comprehend such passages as speak of '*grieving* the Holy Spirit'—'*resisting* the Holy Ghost'—'*quenching* the Spirit'—'doing *despite* to the Spirit of grace.' This is the only mean I can find of reconciling Divine influences and free-will. Hard would be the task of that person who should undertake to work out his own salvation without a reliance on the God of all grace to work in him both to will and to do. Nor can I suppose that High and Lofty One that inhabiteth eternity can be induced to alter his resolves from any unforeseen event; for revelation assures us that his unspeakable gift preceded not only our transgressions, but our very being. But if Christ by the grace of God tasted death for *every* man, and yet those alone should have power given them to become the sons of God who believed in his name, I can reconcile that much more with Scripture, reason and benevolence, than the belief of *particular* redemption and its concomitant. But, as you say, 'I have done,' at least for the present. We are both of us too obstinate free-thinkers to be convinced by any thing less than an extensive view on the subject; and although in some points I may appear decided, yet in a variety of instances I must rank with the undecided. Mutual communication is desirable. Believe me, notwithstanding it is natural to me to express myself strongly on subjects which interest me, I am too firmly persuaded of the sacredness of private judgment, even in its *minutiæ*, to presume to be dictatorial."

Early in May, the College session at Bristol closed, and Robert Aspland bade adieu, not without regret, to his kind Tutors and to the companions of his studies. Of the latter, one, with whom he had been more closely associated than with any other student at the Academy, happily survives,—Dr. F. A. Cox, the distinguished Baptist minister, who has favoured the son of his old fellow-student with the following letter of academical reminiscences. It anticipates some of the after-events of this biography; but this is, on the whole, the proper place for inserting it.

"Hackney, March 18, 1846.

"My dear Sir,—In compliance with your request, I have been endeavouring to recal to mind some circumstances in the early history of my connection with your late distinguished father which might be fit to record; but I am afraid there are none worthy of your notice or that of the public. Many little occurrences, indeed, which, amidst the vivacity of youth, were full of interest and amusement to ourselves, are in vivid recollection; but they were only like sparkles on the stream of life, bright in the sunshine of the morning, and incapable of being retained or revived, so as to be impressed with any permanent character. I can only, therefore, deal in generalities, which you are at liberty to commit to the press or to the flames, as you may judge proper.

"I was less than sixteen years of age, and your father about seventeen, when we first met, by becoming students in the Baptist College at Bristol, then under the superintendence of Dr. Ryland. Both of us having received a degree of previous education by which we were a little in advance of many of the students, we constituted the entire class in some departments of literature; in consequence of which our acquaintance ripened into an intimate friendship.

"We took at the time the same relative stand in Latin, Greek and Hebrew. I often recur with great delight to our readings in Cicero together with the late Dr. Marshman, with whose eminence afterwards as a scholar and a missionary I always feel from this circumstance as if I had a sort of peculiar sympathetic participation. This, perhaps, belongs to the class of those foolish fancies, which, however, notwithstanding their nothingness, impart a kind of indescribable charm to the bygone days of existence.

"Your father and I commenced the study of Hebrew together. These were especially the times when, while engaged in this pursuit, the Psalter and the Lexicon or Bythner's Lyra Prophetica interchangeably in each other's hands, the one to look the root, the other to pronounce the word and work out the sentences, we intermingled our thoughts on every variety of topic that had occurred to us in general reading, as well as on the language immediately demanding attention. How often could we say on these occasions, 'Labor ipse voluptas!'

"Our kind President afforded us the use of the Museum, then a locked-up room, during a few hours of the week, when we hired a French master (that language not being included in the curriculum of the institution) to hear us read, for the purpose of perfecting our pronunciation, each having previously acquired the elements. This led us sometimes to go together to hear the French preacher in the city, whom we were able tolerably to understand. Here we had further opportunities of free conversation. Our intimacy was carried to the extent, that when either was appointed to preach at any place, the other would voluntarily accompany his friend and divide the services. This gave us a ride or a walk together, which tended still more to cement our juvenile attachment. It was also our fixed plan to visit each other at the residences of our respective relations during the academical vacations. It was on one of these occasions, when conversing in my father's orchard on the immortality of the soul, my friend first intimated his departure from orthodox opinions, by saying in reply to some remark, 'I *materially* differ from you.' Upon asking wherein, he answered emphatically, 'I tell you I *materially* differ —I am a *materialist*.' It is due, however, to his memory to say that this extreme of sentiment was afterwards utterly abandoned; but we continued to range on different sides of theological opinion. Once I spent nearly a week with him in the Isle of Wight, when we visited together its beautiful localities; and discussed the numerous points on which we took opposite views. Without conviction on either part, we allowed, by tacit consent, religious controversy ever after to cease.

"From the particulars to which I have referred, you will perceive, my dear Sir, that I had a pretty good opportunity of ascertaining the intellectual character of your estimable father at the outset of life; and for the purpose of stating, as you seemed to wish it, my views, I have been tempted so largely to introduce them. Having been often associated with him since, both in public and in private, I may state that my earliest impressions of him were corroborated by the subsequent intercourse of his whole life. The bud gave a certain indication of what the flower would be in its expanded maturity; and he was in the relative position and influence in which he appeared in the narrower circle of College association, what he afterwards became in the enlarged circumference of his public career.

"From the first to the last, he always seemed to me to possess great mental compass, energy and acuteness. If he did not know every subject, he was capable of knowing it, and never failed, I think, to succeed in the pursuit of any branch of language or literature that he attempted. He was gifted not only with an able, but an industrious mind. He was never satisfied with superficial glances at knowledge, and understood well the poetic admonition,

'Drink deep, or taste not the Pierian spring;'

though, by the way, he was no poet, and I question if he had any great taste for poetry; that is, for poetry as such, with its lighter graces and adornments. He had a clear judgment, but comparatively little imagination. He delighted far more to dwell in the land of reality, than in the regions of fiction or fancy. He had strong muscles and sturdy limbs for a lengthened walk through the fields of literature, but he had no wings to soar. He was severe as a student, close as a reasoner, dogmatical, perhaps, as a controversialist, vigorous as a writer, pleasing and impressive as a preacher, cheerful and instructive as a companion.

"But I must not proceed any further. You will doubtless think I have written enough—it may be, too much; for I am not his biographer; I am not required to be his eulogist; but, notwithstanding all differences, I shall never recal his memory in any other light than that of my valued friend. His departure is to me a fresh memento mori. The spring and the summer are gone; I feel that even the autumn is far advanced; and the falling friends around demonstrate that winter is near, with blight and barrenness and death. May you and I, my dear Sir, enjoy through the grace of Christ a well-founded hope of a glorious immortality!

"I remain faithfully yours,

"F. A. Cox.

"*To Rev. R. Brook Aspland.*"

CHAPTER V.

On leaving Bristol, Robert Aspland proceeded first to Newbury, where he paid a brief visit to Mr. Bicheno and preached at the Independent chapel. On reaching London, he became the guest of Mr. Thomas, who gave him a hearty welcome to his house and invited him to occupy the pulpit at Devonshire Square on the following Sunday. He was looking forward with some anxiety to his first appearance before a metropolitan congregation, when he received from the Ward Trustees a prohibition from preaching before the completion of his fourth year of study. The restriction was unusual, and does not appear to have been laid upon the other students on the foundation. This, coupled with the personal demeanour of the ruling Trustee, raised the suspicion that the soundness of his faith was distrusted. His perfect openness, both in behaviour and conversation, afforded to narrow minds abundant reasons for distrusting his strict orthodoxy. During his stay in London, he associated with persons of various opinions,—spent one day with Andrew Fuller, and attended the Missionary Society; and another with Mr. Marsom, Mr. John Evans, &c., and attended the annual meeting at Worship Street of the General Baptists.

At no time could the prohibition have been more painful. His letters to Wicken for months previous to his leaving Bristol shew how fondly he anticipated the renewal of his ministerial and pastoral labours in his native village. His interest in the work had been much increased by several confidential and affecting letters which came to him at Bristol from some of his Wicken hearers, expressing warm gratitude for religious benefits received through him. He had consulted his father and Mr. Emons as to the establishment of a Sunday-school to be carried on during the vacation. Anticipating numerous preaching engagements on his part, they did not encourage his proposal.

Ultimately, the Ward Trustees relaxed their prohibition so far as to allow his preaching at Wicken and similar places, and then his return to his father's house filled his own and some other hearts with joy. With what eagerness he returned to his ministerial duties appears from the fact, that in rather less than four months he preached forty times. The services at Wicken were, as in the previous year, timed so as not to interfere with the regular services at Soham. In addition to the Sunday services, there was another on each Tuesday evening. The congregation rapidly increased, and sometimes numbered not less than 300 persons. His father, deeply gratified by the popularity and apparent usefulness of his son, fitted up a barn as a meeting-house, and even this was sometimes inconveniently full. There is a tradition of their being obliged on one occasion to adjourn to the open green in front of his father's house, where the chesnut-trees afforded a grateful shelter from the heat of the sun. Besides preaching to them, he visited his flock, and the diary contains several entries of his visits to "poor neighbour Hills, of the Fenside," the wife of one of his hearers. She died before the close of his vacation, and the sermon which he preached on the following Sunday, from Amos iv. 12, was the first of the long series of funeral discourses which he was called upon to deliver.

The subjects of his village sermons were generally simple, and were in fact such as he loved to preach upon throughout his ministry. The Tuesday evening lecture was especially addressed to the young, and comprised the following subjects:—1. Supreme Importance of a Religious Life (Matt. vi. 33). 2. The Being of a God (1 Cor. viii. 6). 3. God is Love (1 John iv. 16). 4. Duty of studying the Scriptures (John v. 39), &c. His subjects on the Sundays were, Duties of the Sabbath-day (Exod. xx. 8). Sect of Christians every where spoken against (Acts xxviii. 22). Conduct of Felix (Acts xxiv. 25). Paul's Anathema (1 Cor. xvi. 22). Repentance (xvii. 30). Christ's Divine Mission (John vii. 46). Subjects and Employments of Heaven (Matt. v. 12). Glory of God (1 Cor. x. 31). Excuses for neglecting Religion (Luke xiv. 18), &c.

He was present at the Baptist Association, which met that summer at Olney; and in the same journey visited his friend Mr. Cox, and with him went to Weston to see some of the favourite haunts of the poet Cowper, and also to Woburn Abbey. He also made several short journeys in the counties of Essex and Suffolk, and was pleased with the opportunity of extending his acquaintance amongst the Baptist and Independent ministers of the places he visited. In one of his letters written at this time he describes a very interesting visit to Cambridge, the great attraction being the eloquence of Mr. Hall.

To Miss Middleton.

"August 26, 1799.

"* * * I wish I could number among my friends Maria Porter. I entertain for her a very high regard; and if I may draw a safe conclusion from her letter to me when at Bristol, she views me with esteem. Hitherto I have never felt myself at ease in her presence; consciousness of inferiority, I suppose, kept me at a distance; but should she favour my design I will endeavour to put on an air of equality. How is it that almost all the intelligent persons whose company I have enjoyed have left me with an apprehension that I lightly valued them? Is there any thing in reality forbidding in my countenance? Are my manners severe and overbearing? Tell me freely, that I may remove so great an obstacle to my happiness.

"The evening of the day you receive this (Wednesday), Robert Hall will, I think I am right, preach at Hammersmith. He is on his way to Bristol, and makes little stay in London. I spent the last sabbath but one at Cambridge.* You may judge how highly I was gratified. Hall certainly takes the lead of our preachers. Jay has merit, but is indisputably inferior to him. If I was enraptured with the preacher, I was carried into 'super-celestial raptures' with *the man*. I breakfasted and passed all the next morning with him. His conversation was one continued blaze of intellect. He has an inexhaustible store of information, and possesses a brilliancy of thought and a readiness and force of expression beyond almost any man I ever heard of. Oh! how truly humble, how abject did I feel in his presence! Never before did I view myself so insignificant, nor did ever dwarf despise himself so much by the side of the bulkiest giant, as I did in discourse with Mr. Hall. Wait for the rest till I see you."

In the autumn of 1799, he made preparations for his residence at Aberdeen. He quitted Wicken with the intention of continuing in Scotland until the close of the session 1800-1. He felt very deeply the separation for so long an absence from his family and friends. The prospect of it gave a tenderness and pathos to his closing services at

---

* The diary has this entry: "Aug. 18—Sunday. Fine morning. Preached from Matt. vii. 26, 27. Breakfasted—rode on mare by Upware to Cambridge—got there by 10. Went to meeting with Mr. W. Eaden, with whom I dined—heard Mr. Hall twice. Expounded in morning John xiii. 18, to the end. Funeral sermon in the afternoon, on 2 Cor. vi. 17, 18.

"Aug. 19—Monday. Breakfasted with Mr. Hall, with whom I spent the morning. What a prodigy! What strength and comprehensiveness of mind! How I felt my insignificance! Called at Pembroke College on Isaac Aspland," &c.

Wicken, and the preacher was in his turn deeply affected by the emotion of his hearers.

He did not carry with him to the University even that portion of orthodoxy which he had brought from Bristol. His constant perusal of the Scriptures, and his conversations with his amiable and sound-minded father, (in which their worthy neighbour, John Emons, often, and Mr. Fyson, of Fordham, sometimes, joined,) had renewed all his doubts about Calvinism, and given greater strength than before to his desire of a simpler and a more loveable system of Christian doctrine. He did not introduce into the pulpit any of the subjects which raised his doubts, and it was with no small satisfaction that he found he could succeed in imbuing the minds of his village congregation with deep religious convictions and Christian sympathies, without entangling them in the mazes of "orthodox" doctrine.

He spent a few weeks in London after leaving Cambridgeshire, and his intercourse there was chiefly with persons at least as far gone in heresy as himself. His own letters will best describe what occurred during his stay in London.

To his Parents.

"London, September 14, 1799.

"Mr. Thomas received me as usual. I spent the greatest part of the day with him. Yesterday I went with a party to Clapham, and dined with Mr. Thompson, one of the Trustees of Dr. Ward's institution. I have before mentioned to you the oddity of his character and the eccentricity of his conduct. Before I enjoyed the benefit of the exhibition, he opposed my entering; after some time he relaxed and behaved friendly; then, again, some how or other, he resumed his enmity, and even meditated my exclusion from the benefits of Scotland. His conversion from this hostile temper was effected by a letter I wrote to Mr. Smith. How long his goodness will continue I cannot tell. I pleased him, however, so well, that I am to go to see him again.

"Mr. Hughes is down at Bristol. Mr. T. wishes me to stay till his return, that I may gain from him every necessary information relative to Aberdeen. But I don't know that I shall, as Mr. Evans and others can sufficiently instruct me. I have been to Islington again to-day. Mr. T. presses me to stay some few days at his house. He says he would make me preach for him to-morrow, had I been *called out by the church;* but as I have not, he does not like to rifle the prejudices of some of his good people. He means, however, to give notice to-morrow of my preaching on Monday evening. I remonstrated against it, but to no effect. I called likewise to-day at Gillyatt's,* and brought home

---

* His first London schoolmaster.

Richard Warren. Would you suppose that G. behaved in a friendly manner? He asked me how I did as soon as he entered the parlour. I thanked him, and asked if he recollected me. 'Oh! certainly,' replied he, and then inquired about my situation, &c., and addressed me thus: 'You have talents—I know it—and will make a good classic. 'Tis a pity you could not procure admission into some of the large public schools at London'—and promised to get me an entrance, &c. I, however, excused myself on the ground of going to Scotland."

To the Same.

"London, September 21, 1799.

" * * * I forgot to mention to you that I had purchased a pair of boots of Citizen Thomas Hardy. I saw the good man, and I had half an hour's conversation with him on political subjects. He tells me that the societies are all dissolved, and that his friends despair of being able to effect any thing in England. He is a sensible but an illiterate person. I told him that I was no stranger to his name, and conveyed to him the congratulations of the Cambridgeshire patriots.

"On sabbath-day I was at Devonshire Square with brother William, both morning and afternoon, and at Surrey chapel in the evening to hear Mr. Jay. On Monday I went to Battersea, and spoke at Mr. Thomas's in the evening. My text was John vii. 46. I was by no means at my case,* and you will not wonder at it when I tell you my situation. At Battersea I fell in with Mr. John Foster, a minister of *heterodox* sentiments and a man of astonishing genius. He walked with me to Buckingham Gate, and, as you may suppose, we loitered in conversation on the road; so that before I got through the Park, 'twas half-past five, and they were to begin at six. I was startled, and with all my hurrying could not reach the meeting before half-past six. Without tea, in a great heat, deprived of study, how could I preach? But my hearers constituted a more serious difficulty still; for I had, on the one hand, to keep in with brothers and sisters of the church, who like nothing but folly and absurdity; and my character was at stake among some more sensible persons whom the report of my preaching had brought together. I like no place for speaking so well as Wicken."

He took his passage for Aberdeen in the smack the Hawk, Captain Campbell. It left the Thames on Saturday, October ——, he anticipating "fine weather" and "a pleasant voyage." The weather became bad and the wind grew contrary. After passing the Nore, his sufferings became intense, and brought on a complete prostration of physical strength and spirits. In the inner passage of the Yarmouth Roads (a

---

* This was not apparent to the auditors, who expressed their surprise at not only the talent, but the unembarrassed manner of so youthful a speaker.

channel of no small danger in rough weather), the captain was on the third day compelled to cast anchor. His inexperienced and suffering passenger took the opportunity of being put ashore at Corton, a village in Suffolk, between Lowestoft and Yarmouth, intending to proceed across the country to the great Northern road, and take the York or Edinburgh stage. The long-continued rains had, however, left the fens of Lincolnshire, through which he must pass to reach the North road, in a very unsafe state for travelling, and he found it necessary to return to London. Great was the astonishment of his friends there to see him so unexpectedly return, and he intimates that with some of them he might, had he chosen to act on their fears, have been regarded as the spectral apparition of him who they supposed was afloat on the German Ocean.

He immediately proceeded to Edinburgh, and thence to Aberdeen, by the mail.* Some of the incidents of his journey are detailed in his first letter from Scotland.

To his Parents.

"Aberdeen, Oct. 17, 1799.

" * * * I visited few of my friends.† So much explanation and detail would have been expected, that it would have been troublesome. The greater part of the day I spent with Mr. Marsom, bookseller, High Holborn, where I believe I have the most sincere and affectionate friends. Our acquaintance is not of long standing, but it is of the most unreserved kind. Mr. M. has the most perfect acquaintance with Scripture, and is the ablest Scripture critic I know. He is, however, *heterodox* in his notions; and though I may not approve of his explanations on the whole, I cannot fail to derive benefit from his instructions. He has written on several subjects,‡ and is, I believe, acknowledged to be an able writer. Our intimacy, however, is on the most equal

---

* As the recollection of the toilsomeness and expense of English travelling is daily becoming fainter, it may not be amiss to say that in 1799 the journey between London and Edinburgh occupied by mail 60 hours, by coach 80. The fare inside was seven guineas.

† On his unexpected return to London.

‡ In the year 1787, Mr. Marsom published the first edition of his treatise on "The Impersonality of the Holy Ghost." In 1788, he contributed to the Theological Repository, under the signature MARMOS, an able paper on 2 Cor. v. 1, vindicating the passage from the imputation of countenancing the idea of an intermediate state. (Theol. Rep. VI. 428—464.) About the same time he published "An Examination of the Rev. Mr. Elliott's Opinion respecting the Mode of Baptism." In 1798, he published "Animadversions on Mr. Paine's Letter to the Hon. Thomas Erskine," &c.

terms. He assumes nothing. Our conversation is free. When I please, I contradict, and can strenuously oppose without fear of offending. Mrs. Marsom is a woman of very great tenderness, and, what is more desirable still, to a fund of good sense adds fervent piety. Their daughter has the acuteness and judgment of the father, together with the religion of the mother. Such a family, you will readily believe, interested me much."

(Here follows a detailed account of his journey.)

"At Newark, the Trent had overflowed the lands for a considerable way. The roads were rough and bad almost all the way; so much so, that I never should have supposed, had I not been assured of it, that we were upon the great North road. Even in the inside of the coach we were extremely shaken. The harvest in the North of England is very late indeed. Much of the corn was standing,* and I think the greater part of it not gathered in. The reapers (whom they call shearers) are principally women. Indeed, I saw very few men. The harvest is much too late here; people apprehend that much of the corn must spoil.

"At Edinburgh I called on Mr. M'Lean, one of the Baptist ministers. I had no introduction to him. I had only seen his name prefixed to some of his publications. He seemed glad to see me. I learnt from him that the two students, who I supposed had left Aberdeen, were there still, which was no unwelcome intelligence. I also went to Dr. Erskine's, a minister in the Scotch Church. He expressed himself pleased to see me. Dr. Gordon, of St. Neot's, on whom I called on my way to Olney, had mentioned me to him, and he had for some time expected me. He is very old and infirm—a man of good talents, of some reputation as an author, and eminent for piety. Next morning I went and heard Mr. Fuller† at the *Circus* (a sort of playhouse). It is

---

* In his own more favoured and better tilled county, he had seen the beginning of the harvest in the month of August. The apprehension respecting the spoiling of the corn was sadly fulfilled. Wheat-flour rose to the enormous price of sixpence per lb., and was so bad in quality, that aged housewives residing in the Northern counties still tell of their trouble in the winter of 1799-1800 in making bread. The batch refused to rise, and the sodden mass would sometimes on the opening of the oven flow out in a continuous lava-like stream.

† The Rev. Andrew Fuller was now on a mission to Scotland (the first of a series of five visits) on behalf of the Baptist Missionary Society. His special object at this time was to make collections for the translation of the Scriptures into Bengalee. He spent for many years nearly a fourth of his time in journeys to collect for the support of the Baptist Missionary Society. Dr. Ryland tells us, in his Life of Fuller, that Mr. F. "kept a journal of this visit to Scotland," but parts of it are kept back, as Mr. Fuller's "opinions of some persons and things" were subsequently altered. He found the Scotch Baptists generally tinged with the sentiments of Glass and Sandeman. Dr. Ryland, in his valuable Memoir of his friend, specifies six points on which Fuller thought the Scotch

something extraordinary that on a week-day it is devoted to the purposes of amusement, and on the sabbath the Methodists use it. Mr. F. was civil, and by the invitation of Dr. Stuart, at whose house he was, I accompanied him to breakfast, where I saw Mr. Sutcliff. After breakfast we all went to the Scotch Baptist meeting. Their prejudices are great and their mode of worship singular. Hereafter I may give a more particular account of them. Mr. Fuller had no invitation to preach among them, and is not, I think, very candid towards them. To me, however, their modes of devotion were pleasing, as they savour so much of primitive simplicity. I am inclined to think that their church discipline is most scriptural. Mr. Sutcliff preached in the afternoon, and at night —— [the MS. is here defective] preached the collection sermon in the Circus to an astonishing congregation. Not only was the body of the place filled, but on the (curtain?) being drawn up, all the stage was crowded with hearers. The text from Gal. vi. 7,—the sermon very impressive. They gathered, I learn, above £80.

"I left Edinburgh the next morning, and as the weather was fine and the mail would be but one night on the road, I took an outside place. * * * We finished the journey by eight o'clock on Tuesday morning, and the high opinion of Scottish hospitality which the kind treatment I experienced at Edinburgh had given me, was confirmed by the conduct of a gentleman who rode a few miles with me in the morning. From some inquiries I made of him as a native of Aberdeen, he soon discovered that I was a stranger and learnt my intentions. At the close of our ride, he insisted upon my accompanying him home to breakfast. I consented, and was pleased to find that my companion was a respectable merchant, and moreover a very religious man. I was kindly treated, and after our meal and family worship he introduced me to Messrs. Coles* and Page,† the students from Bristol. They had no expectation of me this year, and were as surprised as they seemed glad to see me. We spent the day together. I met with the greatest kindness from them."

Arrived at Aberdeen, he had to choose between the two rival Col-

---

brethren were in error, in addition to a capital error respecting faith, in their definition of which, he complained, they entirely excluded the affections. The Calvinism of Scotland was and is too hard for the tastes of English brethren.

* The Rev. Thomas Coles had, like R. A., been a student at Bristol and under Mr. Hughes at Battersea. He settled, soon after leaving the University, at Bourton-on-the-Water, in Gloucestershire, where he remained, a very useful and respected minister, all his life. His name often occurs in John Foster's letters, who said of him, "I like Coles very much for his equal mixture of sense, piety, simplicity and kindness."

† Rev. Henry Page, who on leaving Aberdeen settled at Bristol as assistant tutor, and in 1802 as assistant minister at Broadmead. He afterwards removed to Worcester.

leges, King's, or the old College, and Marischal College. Many of his predecessors on the Ward foundation had entered King's College. There, in the years 1781-84, Robert Hall had studied under Professors Leslie, M'Leod and Ogilvie; and there also, 1787-90, Dr. John Evans and Mr. Hughes had studied; combining, however, with the Divinity lectures of King's those of Marischal College; the former read by Dr. Gerard, the latter by the still more celebrated Dr. George Campbell. Neither of these distinguished men was living in 1799, but Dr. Gilbert Gerard worthily occupied his father's Chair. The principal Chairs were thus filled in 1799:

	King's College.	Marischal College.
Principal	John Chalmers, D.D.	W. Lawrence Brown, D.D.
Greek	Hugh M'Pherson	Jo. Stuart, A.M.
Humanity	William Ogilvie, A.M.	—
Moral Philosophy	William Jack, M.D.	James Beattie and George Glennie, Assistant.
Natural Philosophy	Robert Eden Scott, A.M.	Patrick Copland.
Oriental Languages	James Bentley, A.M.	James Kidd, D.D.
Divinity	Gilbert Gerard, D.D.	Principal Brown.
Natural History	—	James Beattie, Jun.
Mathematics	—	Robert Hamilton.
Chemistry	—	Dr. George French.

Robert Aspland was probably guided by the advice and example of his new friends, Page and Coles, in entering himself a student of Marischal College. Mr. Stuart had the reputation of being an able and careful teacher of Greek, and to the study of the classics Robert Aspland determined to devote most of the time of his first session. By the advice of Mr. Stuart, who proved himself from the first a kind and most judicious friend, he engaged the assistance of Mr. Forbes, master of the Grammar-school, as a Latin tutor.

In accordance with the advice of the Ward Trustees and the strongly-expressed wishes of his Professors, he devoted himself entirely to his studies, neither preaching nor taking part in the school connected with the Independent chapel. To this some of the recent English students had given a large and, as their Professors thought, undue portion of their time. By the kindness of Mr. Evans and Mr. Hughes, he was introduced to Professors Ogilvie and Bentley, of King's College, and to Provost Crudens and Mr. Scott, at whose houses he found nearly all the social relaxation for which he had time and inclination. His health was at first injuriously affected by the severity of the climate and the change in the style of living; but before the close of the session he was again in the enjoyment of robust health.

Under the able instructions of Professor Stuart and Mr. Forbes, he for the first time felt a keen relish for the Greek and Latin classical authors. The lectures of Professor Kidd on the Hebrew Scriptures did not impress him with much regard for the learning or judgment of the Professor.

An employment to which he devoted a few hours in the week towards the close of the session, serves to shew the amiability of his character. The children of a poor relative of the person at whose house he lodged wanted instruction. He gave it to them, and found much pleasure in the task. In recording it in his diary, he says it made him happy, by reminding him of Mr. Wells and his own school-days at Hackney.

After reaching Aberdeen, the bent of his theological sentiments was all in one direction. Nearly all the preaching to which he listened, whether from the Aberdeen ministers or from the students at the Independent meeting, was hard and dry Calvinism, at which his taste and religious convictions now alike revolted. The Sundays were his least happy days, and with affectionate tenderness did his thoughts then turn to the little flock at Wicken. He earnestly encouraged his father to continue a regular Sunday evening service, and, when no neighbouring minister's help could be procured, besought him to undertake the preaching himself. Towards the close of the year, he drew up and sent to Wicken an address to his religious friends adapted to the last sabbath evening of the year. That his increasing heterodoxy was not unfavourable to the strength and purity of his devotional sentiments and his religious zeal, the extracts from his letters written from Aberdeen will serve to prove. They also shew his great anxiety to acquit himself well as a man of honour, and to be faithful to every implied trust in the new and embarrassing position in which he found himself from the progressive change of his religious opinions.

To his Parents.

"Aberdeen, Dec. 22, 1799.

" * * * Let me know in your next how you conduct the service, how many hearers, and how they receive the advice. I rejoice to hear of good being done. Nothing so much encourages me to qualify myself for teaching others, as to hear of blessings already attending my exertions; nor does any other circumstance so much confirm me in the propriety of the mode of preaching I have all along adopted. I am very badly situated for hearing. The Scotch preachers in general discourse in the same strain as the clergy in England, only they are much more dull. I have taken a seat at the Independent meeting here lately opened. They sing Dr. Watts's Hymns. The Scotch Psalms are worse, if possible, than those of Sternhold and Hopkins. Their singing is horrible. Everybody joins in it, and such discord I have seldom heard."

To Miss Middleton.

"Aberdeen, Dec. 30, 1799.

" * * * You must not suppose that I mean by extolling Nature to disparage Christianity. They do not jar. No! I have not lost any of my regard for the religion of Jesus. To it I am indebted for the chief solace of life, and from our mutual attachment to it I look for much of the happiness of our future union. There are situations in which I think I could fulfil the ministerial character to my satisfaction; but I must leave my present connections. How—when is this to be done? Give me your advice. I am no Calvinist, yet I am a member of an orthodox church. I am at present in an institution which I entered as agreeing with it (the church) in religious opinions. By my associating with the godly and soliciting their countenance, I have in a manner pledged myself to continue with them. At least, to renounce them will, I am sure, be looked upon as ungrateful and dishonourable. Oh! tell me what I am to do. I feel under deep obligation to good Mr. Thomas. To declare my heterodoxy will, I fear, much hurt, if not offend him. It will at once annihilate his expectations (which have, I fear, been sanguine) from my future character, and force him to think that all his kindness and services have been thrown away—nay, worse, that he has all this time been nourishing and giving reputation to an adversary. And I am by no means certain that a disclosure of my present sentiments, and the consequent expulsion from Devonshire Square which would immediately follow, would not deprive me of the benefits of Dr. Ward's legacy. The Trustees are not very partial to me. Mr. J. Smith has been my chief patron, and were he to withdraw his support (and in the case above mentioned he certainly would), I know of no one who would interest himself on my behalf. Yet, if such be the difficulties attending a declaration of my belief, those of concealing it are no less formidable. I am at present acting the part of a deceiver. While my views were unfixed, I was justified in adhering to the party whom I had joined; but now that the doctrine of the Trinity, of perseverance, and so on, makes no part of my creed, and is wholly excluded from my devotions, what is it but dishonesty to proceed as if I believed them all? Besides, the retreat will be more difficult hereafter than at present. Every year strengthens my obligations to my friends, renders their hopes more lively, and brings them nearer realization, and will at the same time diminish my character when my real sentiments are avowed. I have formed in my own mind the idea of a respectable character, and I shall only be contented as far as I resemble it. This prompts me to declare honestly and without reserve my opinions; teaches me that to regard *consequences* in such a matter is vicious; and encourages me by assuring me that the independence which can inspire so disinterested a step will more than support me under its event. I only wait, then, your advice. Give it freely. 'Tis an important matter, and be assured I will not proceed a step in this business without your advice."

To his Parents.

"Aberdeen, Jan. 28, 1800.

" I have a commission to deliver to my mother. Will she, some day, hear J. Emons's two daughters repeat, 'How precious is the book divine,' and give them from me a penny each? I put them, I recollect, upon learning it with the hope of the reward, and came away in their debt. You can't think what pleasure I take in singing the verses of that short hymn; it operates as a sort of charm upon me; drives away care, anxiety, uneasiness of every kind, and introduces me at once into religion and among my dear friends. If you should ask why this hymn in particular reminds me of home, I will tell you, and I do it with real pleasure, for I love to contemplate the circumstance. One sabbath, about four years ago, I was at Mr. Fyson's. In the course of the day, my friend and myself had a good deal of discourse about the Bible. At night, he, Nancy and I betook ourselves to singing, and, among others, fell into Market-Harborough tune and this hymn. I had never much noticed it before, and could not but deem it excellent, and our conversation in the fore-part of the day tended to make it the more impressive. But what made it most striking, while we were singing, * * *, the deist, entered. He seated himself. We continued our song; and the contrast between us made an impression upon my mind that will last for ever. We were speaking forth the praises of a book which he detested; our hearts were swelling with fervid gratitude to the Giver of every good for what he was execrating as the worst of curses; we were expressing our only comfort to be derived from a system which he had declared it was his chief happiness to reject. Such was the origin of my feelings on the subject. When you see Mr. F., you may remind him of the circumstance; it will at least bring to his recollection the pleasure of some of our gone-by interviews. Tell him I often think of him, and think of him with a sigh. I was always happy in his company. He was, I believe, one of the first friends my young mind cleaved to.

" The weather has been most dreadful here. We have had storms which you in England can have no conception of, and which the oldest people declare were never equalled. The sea for several days was most awfully agitated. The loss among the shipping is incalculable. There are five or six vessels now lying upon the shore within less than a mile from the town, and many have been totally destroyed. A day or two after the first storm, I went over to the Bay of Neg, just by Aberdeen, where several ships were reported to have been wrecked, and such an afflictive spectacle I never witnessed before! The shore of the Bay, at least a furlong long, was covered, entirely covered, with wrecks—masts, rigging, sides, ladings and bottoms of ships. Some of the relatives of the sailors and persons supposed to have perished were on the spot. There was the owner of one of the vessels, of which his own son had been captain, surveying the melancholy ruins, recognizing fragments of his former property, and gathering the sad certainty of the destruction of his son. I saw, too, a young woman, who had gone to the Bay fearing that her brother was among the lost, pick from amidst the ruins the jacket in which she knew him to have sailed from home. I could tell you more sad tales; indeed, every one's mouth has been full of them of late. Provisions of every sort are enormously dear. Great exertions are, however, making, and it is to be hoped charity will prevent much of the misery of the season. But Scotland is not like England. You are infinitely before the North Britons in every thing; the poor, especially, among you fare much better than the same class here. Here are no poor's-rates; no regular stated assessment; the supplies of many hundreds of wretches are entirely drawn from begging and from charity.

"I have of late, and particularly last Lord's-day, been reading the Life of David Brainerd, the missionary to the American Indians. It has much enlivened me in religion: such goodness of heart, such zeal, such humility, such constant and fervent devotion, has enraptured me. I see the necessity of living to God, and whatever may be my reasonings on religious topics, I do, after all, fall before Him a sinner, plead the merits of the Saviour, and only hope for forgiveness through his mercy. I thought of you on the 23rd.*

To Miss Middleton.

"Aberdeen, Feb. 7, 1800.

"* * * I often feel astonishment when I trace my present circumstances from their first beginnings. The kindness of Providence, as observable in this survey, excites within me the liveliest thankfulness. Seven or eight years ago I left home with scarce a friend beyond it. I entered situations with which our family was totally unconnected, and had, consequently, at so early an age, to act entirely for myself. Ambitious of distinction, I introduced myself to scene after scene, as my notions of honourable station advanced. And so propitious was Fortune, that, notwithstanding the disadvantage just referred to, and the more serious obstacles of temper, love of independence, firm adherence to private opinion, abhorrence of intrigue and intrusion, I soon saw myself surrounded by a pleasing circle of acquaintances and in the direct road to the attainment of the height of my wishes. Upon coming to Scotland, we were,

---

* His birth-day.

you know, apprehensive of a reverse. Our fears have been wholly contradicted. Without any exertion on my part, I have been introduced to many agreeable families, and in most of them am not, I believe, an unwelcome guest. In one instance or two, indeed, the appearance of Presbyterian suspicion and bitterness has warned me to retreat.

"I was gratified this morning by a call from my Professor.* He judged from my absence from the class that I was unwell; and, what is very uncommon with these gentlemen, wished to shew his concern in more than faint inquiry or distant condolence. I visited at his house since I wrote to Anna, and I must tell you how he dismissed me: 'Mr. A., you don't come often enough; I shall take it kind if you will look in whenever you have a leisure half-hour.'"†

Early in the year, he made the first direct disclosure to his friends in England of his departure from orthodoxy. He naturally selected his tried and always kind friend Mr. Thomas as the person first entitled to receive the necessary but painful disclosure. It is to be regretted that none of the answers to his letters to his former pastor and tutors are in existence. His letter begins with a reference to a communication made soon after his arrival at Aberdeen to Mr. Smith, the Ward Trustee. In it he had thus expressed himself: "I cheerfully embrace every opportunity of prosecuting religious inquiry, and wherever my researches may conduct me, I will honestly avow it; but I will give into no sentiments without the maturest and most impartial deliberation." After describing the plan of his studies and occupations at Aberdeen, his letter to Mr. Thomas thus proceeds. (The letter bears date Feb. 19, 1800.)

"In religion I am least happy. The Presbyterians are notoriously dull and formal, and the Seceders have in general little else to recommend them than their earnestness. Between them, good sense and devotion are banished from their assemblies. My chief, I must say only, religious enjoyment is derived from reading. Coles and Page are indeed agreeable; we are upon good terms, but something has prevented any close intimacy. Nature never

---

* Professor Stuart.

† He proceeds in this letter to make an apology for the egotism of such details, which he penned for the gratification of his correspondent, assured that she would interpret aright what he said of himself. The selections from the letters now given, especially those to his parents, are for the most part of that kind for which he felt it necessary to make this plea. The reader will not, however, draw the erroneous conclusion that egotism is the general character of his letters. The writer of this Memoir is desirous of making it, as far as possible, auto-biographical.

formed, I believe, our minds for association. Another cause of our distance is, perhaps, my declining to unite with them in their catechetical labours. I have kept myself disengaged, not because I am not desirous of communicating instruction, nor because I am averse to Sunday-schools, but from a principle of duty. I feel, Sir, particularly desirous that you should be satisfied of this; and as my conduct, without explanation, may appear censurable, I will take this occasion to disclose the motives to you. It will at once occur to you that I was restrained in a great measure by a desire of conformity to the will of the Trustees. You are acquainted with the prohibition they have laid upon me. You are not ignorant of the influence Mr. Thompson has upon the other members of the Trust; and you know as well as myself that his capricious temper would have taken offence at my teaching, and have imputed that in me to forwardness and self-will which has all along been allowed to Coles. This was one objection: another, equally strong, was the disapprobation the Principal of the College had expressed to Mr. Page of the schools. Would it have been justifiable in a young man just entering a seminary of learning, to have alienated from him, by unnecessary activity, its superintendents and teachers, and to have subjected himself to rebuke, perhaps to expulsion? Besides all this, I foresaw that to engage myself in this way would be to throw a great obstacle in the way of improvement. The occupation of the Sunday, and the connections into which it must have led me, would have usurped much of that attention which ought to be devoted to study. These considerations left no doubt what course I ought to take. They will, I flatter myself, be as satisfactory to you as they were operative upon me. Several causes have since concurred to make me pleased with my determination: one I am anxious not to conceal from you; it is, Sir, the unsettledness of my *religious sentiments*. I have seldom felt great confidence of opinion; of late, less than ever. Thus much a sense of the duty I owe to you has induced me to acknowledge, and I have done it the more freely because I am sure the confession will not be ill received or misapplied. The state it describes is not voluntary, much less is it desirable. My undecidedness would occasion me greater anxiety, did I not look forward to solidity of belief. I intend to pass the summer in Aberdeen, and to devote a great part of it to religious inquiry, that so I may either be confirmed in the tenets I have hitherto professed, or gather strong reasons for departing from them. Shall I, Sir, request your assistance and advice? They would, I assure you, be received with pleasure. The investigation is important. Should it betray me into error, it shall not be for want of impartiality or diligence."

To Miss Middleton.

"Aberdeen, Feb. 20, 1800.

" * * * My scepticism is momentary. However I speculate on systems, feeling and conviction both attach me to the substance of Christianity. Its simplicity, its morality, and its conformity to Nature, all plead powerfully to my reason on its behalf. And when I consider the awful grandeur of the Supreme Being, I rejoice in the new and living way discovered in the Gospel, by which mortals may approach him with confidence. When I consider the infinite purity of the great Creator, and my utter deficiency in that which can alone be pleasing to him, I feel the necessity of a Saviour, and throw myself upon his mercy for acceptance; and when I reflect upon the high powers of man, and their insignificancy and perversion in the present state of being, I am naturally led to receive with highest thankfulness the information of the New Testament, that this life is but as the moment of birth, the introduction to existence—that a future state will place man in a sphere suited to his dignity —and that his duration shall correspond to the greatness of his powers! This is the religion of the heart. It is my greatest solace.

"In accordance with your advice, I have at length written to Mr. Thomas, and as you without doubt feel interested in what I have said, I willingly transcribe a part of my letter to him. 'In religion I am least happy,' &c. (See the letter of the date Feb. 19.)

"I feel much happier now I have made the acknowledgment. A declaration of 'heterodoxy' would not now throw him into violent surprise, nor subject me to the imputation of dishonesty."

To his Parents.

"Aberdeen, March 9, 1800.

"* * * Your account of Mr. Sharpe* highly amuses me. But what if, after all, he should learn that his supposed convert has left the *old way* and turned a preacher of *error?* I perceive much goodness in his character, but, as Mr. Robinson said of old Mr. Berridge, I know how to estimate his good qualities without making myself a simpleton. True religion does not bluster; it is gentle and peaceable, and, like a quiet stream, is known rather by the fruits it nourishes than by any noise in its passage. You will remember me to all the ministers who visit you. I am eager to hear from Mr. Fyson. The sufferings of the poor at the present season are indeed distressing; you must see and hear a great deal of them. I can hardly guess what will be the consequence. Every where is heard the cry of scarcity. Enjoin upon the preachers at Wicken to discourse upon *charity*. We are so much occupied with preaching up a system, that the main part of godliness is neglected. Good works are, I will not say, the evidence of religion; they are religion itself; they alone can profit our fellow-creatures; they alone will pass the trial of Omniscience at the last day. Remember me to my friend J. E. Tell him to persevere; he need not be apprehensive of my deserting him; my conscience is not pliant enough to bend with interest. * * * I cannot forbear a smile

---

* Mr. Sharpe was an occasional preacher at Wicken.

at the idea of B.'s going to the Academy. Poor soul! much, much better will it be for him to keep to his *board*. He knows little of Bristol. He hears that he is going into a religious house, a house filled with preachers; but little does he calculate upon the giddiness of eighteen or twenty young men little acquainted with the world, or upon the ridicule and severity they would lavish upon a person so much older and, in general, so much inferior to themselves."

To his Parents.

"Aberdeen, April 13, 1800.

"Our session ended the first of April. I am perfectly free of College now—as much so as I was last summer—and shall continue so till November. 'Tis a very long time to view in prospect; and were I destitute of employment, would seem as long in the passing. But I foresee that it will be much too short for my purposes. I have many literary plans in agitation. That I shall follow up all is hardly to be expected; yet those in which I shall most certainly be busied, will allow of no vacancy in the time. You may wonder I have never informed you more concerning the College. The first character in it is the Rector, who is merely a nominal officer, and with whom we have nothing to do. The Principal is next. He must always reside in town. He is the proper Head of the College; he meets us once a week to exact fines, &c.; and, with the Professors, manages the internal concerns of the University. The present Principal is Dr. Brown, who is likewise Professor of Divinity and one of the preachers at the chief church in Aberdeen. He was Professor in a Dutch University, but at the Revolution in Holland was obliged to emigrate. The Principalship is in the gift of Government. Dr. B.'s hatred to anti-monarchical principles, and, I suppose, the recommendation of the Stadtholder, procured him this situation. You are now able to form some idea of his character; but you have not heard all. He is chaplain to the barracks here, and is just created one of his Majesty's Chaplains in Ordinary for Scotland. His character answers to his offices. His politics are venality itself; his religion is rancour and party-spirit. You may be sure I don't tremble before him. Besides him, there are eight Professors. It would be tedious to enumerate all the different Professorships. One or two of the places are almost sinecures. There are four principal classes, each of which a person must attend a session in order to be graduated; the rest are more left to the choice of the students.

"Since I wrote last, I have changed my residence. I have removed from one room in the back part of the house, to two, a pair of stairs lower, in the front. This I found absolutely necessary, not only for conveniency, but for health. My present rooms are every way agreeable; the sitting-room is tolerably large and decently furnished; the bed-room is very small; both are very airy; they look into the principal street, Broad Street, and directly front the College-gate. I dine, too, now in the same family of whom I hire my lodgings, which is very convenient. They are agreeable people; I receive much attention and enjoy every conveniency; indeed, I feel more at home at present than I recollect to have done in any situation since I first left Wicken. I find nothing objectionable, except it be a necessary addition of expense. Is it not singular that all the families which I have entered here have belonged to the Church of England? The present are very moderate; the other two were more stiff and high in their notions—not far, indeed, from Popery; but their opinions never for a moment distressed me; I was not sent here to make proselytes. We were always upon the best terms. I never once failed in my appetite because the mistress of the table thought it a duty to observe Lent, nor did I sleep the less sound because the good woman, my landlady, favoured praying for the dead. * * * My health is, as I predicted, perfectly established. I am surrounded with books; can converse with the greatest and best men of all ages; can take up one and lay down another, as I please; can read or sing, walk or sit still, without a soul to interrupt me; can stay at home or go out, as the humour prompts; can indulge thought free as the air, and have no dread of the racks of bigotry and religious ignorance; to crown the whole, can express all I feel and think, without the fear of interruption or abuse. All this is excellent; it is charming; it is the very essence of *liberty*.

"Your meetings of sabbath evenings must be very agreeable; the simplicity and want of form and pomp which, perhaps, rendered you unwilling at first to engage in them, do but make them the more engaging and more allied to primitive, apostolic Christianity. True religion is more likely to be advanced by your simple plan, than by ministerial show and consequence. Your meetings should not be tedious; the prayers should be very short; people seldom understand or join in them; and the Almighty needs not to be informed of every particular we want. Above all, the reading of the New Testament should be the chief employment of the hour. Some sermons, it is true, may be read to profit; but the greater part of them serve only to bewilder. If we want to know who of our fellow-creatures are under the displeasure of God, and whom, therefore, we ought to look upon with *pious indignation*, sermons will abundantly gratify our curiosity; but if we seek to know aright our Creator, his disposition towards his creatures, the duties he requires from us, the final state for which he has created us, we must recur to the simple revelation of Jesus Christ. While you are reading the Scriptures, do you not frequently feel the liveliest devotion excited? Does not here and there a passage warm your feelings? A plain, affectionate remark dropped at such a time, how would it interest! Coming from the heart, it would reach the heart; it would carry with it the impression of Nature; and you would instantly see the principle that prompted it diffusing itself through the hearts of your little assembly. But I only give the hint.

"I hope J. Emons will not drop all warmth in religion; but it is not for me, who am confirming every day in some of the sentiments he holds, to blame the freedom of his inquiries. The doctrine of the Trinity is the grand hinge on which the old system turns. It has, however, little support from Scripture. I will give you part of a letter which Mr. Robinson, not long before his death, sent my friend Marsom:—'As to personality in God, a Trinity of Persons, I think it the most absurd of all absurdities; and, in my opinion, a man who hath brought himself to believe the popular doctrine of the Trinity, hath done all his work; for, after that, there can be nothing hard, nothing inevident; the more unintelligible the more credible; and as this serves the purpose of producing implicit faith in pretended guides, priests will always try to keep it in credit. The Bible reads easy if we consider God *one*, Jesus the *Son of God*, and the Holy Ghost the *influence* of God; but this would spoil trade, the Scriptures would become plain and easy, and a learned priesthood would be unnecessary to make out and unfold that hard science, Christianity, to us poor blind creatures. Verily, my friend, priestcraft is at the bottom of all this burlesque upon religion; for such I account the grievance of one man's pretending to take care of another man's soul. The direct end of all their schemes is to cheat people into a disuse of their own understandings, and to pitch their eyes and place their affections upon a frail, and often a wicked, proxy.'

"I am going to-day to hear Page and Coles preach their farewell sermons. They leave Aberdeen by the first London vessel."

By the hands of the last-mentioned gentleman he sent letters to his late tutors, Dr. Ryland and Mr. Isaac James. To the former he expressed the liveliest gratitude for his instructions and constant kindness, described his studies, his intercourse with Page and Coles, and the change that had taken place in his religious opinions. He adds, "I will honestly avow that I am not satisfied of the scriptural authority of several Calvinistic doctrines." To Mr. James he wrote in the same strain, but broached his heterodoxy in the following playful passage:

"Some of my friends in England are apprehensive that this Northern atmosphere will prove injurious to my orthodoxy. Their fears are not entirely groundless. The air of winter is observed, I think, *to clear the ground of vermin*. But hush!"

In accordance with the wishes of the Ward Trustees, he sought from Professor Stuart, at the close of the session, a Testimonial, which was given in these terms:

"These certify that Robert Aspland, a native of Cambridgeshire, was a student in the Greek class of this University during the last session of College; that he was a diligent, attentive scholar; made a suitable proficiency in his studies; and behaved in all other respects very much to my satisfaction. It is therefore with great pleasure that I give this testimony to his merit. Given at Marischal College, Aberdeen, this ninth day of April, 1800, by

"Jo. Stuart, Lit. Gr. Pro."

One-and-twenty years after the date just given, the writer visited at Aberdeen the venerable Professor. He spoke with distinct and kind recollection of his pupil, and said he very soon after Robert Aspland's entrance in the class observed his heterodox tendency. The Professor was pleased to encourage his pupils to ask questions, and having interpreted a Greek passage to the class, Robert Aspland remarked, inquiringly, that a similar mode of interpreting a passage in the New Testament, which he quoted, would, so far as that text was concerned, be fatal to orthodox doctrine. Mr. Stuart said, with a smile, "Young man, I profess to teach, not theology, but Greek."

CHAPTER VI.

RELEASED from the College classes and separated from his class companions, Robert Aspland began his six months' vacation at Aberdeen well, dividing each day's studies between classics, theology and English literature. It is to be regretted that any thing interfered with his perseverance in so judicious a plan. With the advice and occasional assistance of Professor Stuart, invaluable would have been the course of study he had prescribed to himself. But soon there came letters from England, especially from the Trustees and some of his old religious friends, remonstrating with him for his indulgence in heterodox sentiments. It is unfortunate that none of these letters have been preserved. From the slight references to them found in his diary and some of his letters, it is probable that they were kind in spirit, though urgently dissuasive. They probably had on this account the greater power over him; for his first intellectual impressions were throughout life often moulded by his affections, though never by fear. He himself was aware of this tendency, and felt the necessity of jealously scrutinizing the opinions he felt disposed to adopt at the suggestion of friends. For a moment, the entreaties of his friends in England made him waver, and he struggled to return to *orthodoxy*, and to enjoy afresh the pleasures of his boyish faith. The process, however, was rather metaphysical than scriptural, as the following passage from a letter written at this time will shew. It is curious, as being, so far as is known, the last effort of his mind to adapt itself to the Calvinistic system.

To Miss Middleton.

"April 24, 1800.

"You will participate with me in the *pleasures of faith:* 'tis truly an exquisite enjoyment, but an enjoyment, alas! of which I had long deprived myself, to be able to say of any doctrine, 'This is truth; this I rely upon; this is the plain purport of Scripture.' A little attention to the sacred pages has fully convinced me of the universal superintendence of a particular Providence, and also of the necessity and importance of *prayer*; and from these I gather the doctrine of Divine Decrees (or, if you would rather, of Necessity), though the cold term appears to me—[here the MS. is defaced]; for there can be no other necessity than what arises from the will of the Supreme; likewise that of Divine Influences. Providence undoubtedly imports design; and Providence and prayer both seem to argue the necessity of intercourse between the Deity and the soul of man. My thoughts are yet hardly matured: what I have stated, however, appears to have force. Should these doctrines firmly establish themselves in my mind, they will force me to remodel my whole system: what other orthodox opinions they may introduce, I am not able to say; this only I can assert, that so far from degrading reason, I shall confer upon it the highest honour by bowing it to the will of the All-wise God."

His theological disquietude had broken in upon his plan of study. He felt increasingly the uncertainty of his future course and prospects in life, and he longed for the personal counsel and sympathy of his family and friends. Almost unknown to himself, these feelings had been growing in his mind, and they ripened very suddenly into action. This is the entry in his diary:

"Saturday, May 3. Spectator—Homer—Blair. After dinner, as I was looking over the Map of Holland, took the resolution to go into England. Dressed and went down to the pier to see for a ship. All agitation—wrote a letter to uncle William, informing him of my design."

Two days after, he embarked in a sloop, setting sail with a fair wind for Hull. He thus sportively alluded in a letter home to the possibility of the sloop falling into the hands of a French privateer:

"You will hardly hear from me again until you see me, which will be, perhaps, in a week, ten days or a fortnight. Should I be longer than that, you may conclude *I am gone to France*. I should like the opportunity of seeing the fooleries and vices of a degenerate people. But this is joke. There is not, I suppose, much danger. Should it happen, I should only lose some clothes and a few books. I have been expecting for some days your letter, but I shall have to go without it. I have not time now to explain all the reasons of my leaving Scotland, though I can give you the principal one in a few words—I want to see my English friends. I cannot express the pleasure I feel at the prospect of seeing so soon my dear mother and father, Isaac and our other friends. May the good Providence of our God bring us together again in safety, and may our meeting be blest to the best of purposes!"

Safely arrived at Hull, he hastened to London, where he passed a very happy week previous to his return to Wicken.

The summer and most of the autumn of 1800 were spent in Cambridgeshire. He devoted himself to preaching and teaching the young with greater ardour than ever. With his parents and friends he freely discussed all his theological difficulties, and the result of these discussions and his own scriptural investigations was the confirmation of his mind in the doctrines of the sole Deity of the Father of Jesus Christ, and of the Fatherly character of God.

His diary during this period has not been preserved; but several allusions are made in his letters to his labours in the villages around his father's house.

"Wicken, May 22, 1800.

"On Sunday I preach at home, at seven o'clock in the morning; and as my place here will be supplied at night, afternoon and evening I am to *speak* at Burwell, a large village at three miles distance. Thus you see I am full of occupation."

"June 5, 1800.

"I am engaged once on the Sunday and every night to meet the young people of the village."

"June 20.

"I preached a sort of funeral sermon last sabbath morning—the occasion suited my feelings. In the afternoon and evening I preached to a very crowded congregation at Isleham, my mother's native village, six miles distant. To-night I mean to dissect David's character—'Thou art the man.'"

"July 16, 1800.

"I am very busily employed. The service of the last sabbath evening added to my previous indisposition. I had to address an over-crowded congregation, and, what was worse, involved myself in a subject which took a discussion an hour and a half long."

"December 28, 1800.

"My little flock—how comfortable do I feel among them—welcomed as a neighbour, beloved as a friend, respected as an instructor! * * * We met on Friday night to tell our mutual *experience*. We were all happy: besides preaching again this afternoon, we meet for the same purpose in the evening."

What estimate those who knew him best at this time formed of his talents and aim as a preacher, is shewn in the following passage from a letter addressed to him by his nearest friend:

"June 30, 1800.

"—— paid us a visit last week; he thought he should have had a letter from you by this time. He said there was one thing which he thought to have mentioned to you, but which I could do for him—that was, to caution you against soaring above the comprehension of those whom you would instruct. I told him that, so far from aiming at sublimity, you rather studied simplicity;

and that the religion of all being derived from the same source, often rendered the eloquent plain and the plain eloquent. To this he in some measure assented, but said that your mind being so different to that of persons in general, there was some danger of your not being intelligible to every capacity; that Saurin, if he described Scripture ideas, would do it in language that would be above the common level. Take the compliment, or the caution, or both, as you think proper."

The friend whose advice is recorded above was probably the Rev. Timothy Thomas, to whom the following letter was written:

"Wicken, Sept. 21, 1800.

" * * * The mention of your two letters naturally leads me to repeat my sincere acknowledgments for them. I have read them with close and renewed attention; and whatever my opinion may be of the sentiments they disclose, or however desirous I may have been to examine some expressions which were fairly disputable, and to explain some passages of the letter which occasioned them, I shall ever consider the spirit that dictated them as that of the purest and most disinterested friendship.

"I have been too actively employed this summer to have had much time for speculation. Besides constant and frequent preaching and other necessary avocations, I have been engaged not unfrequently in the instruction of youth. The little attention I have been able to give to religious controversy has not attached me more firmly to *Calvinism*.

"Yet I am far from being indifferent to theological opinion. Concerning that body of sentiments, indeed, which is far removed from life, and which has been termed, not improperly, the *philosophy of religion*, I am little solicitous; and perhaps I shall not expose myself to much reasonable reprehension by suggesting, that whilst the great boundaries of truth are marked and fixed, within the channel they form, and ample enough it is, man is allowed to move and fluctuate, as inclination and a thousand other circumstances lead him. But over those truths which 'come home to men's business and bosoms,' which give 'the highest moment of impulse' to the springs of human action, I would exercise a wakeful, unremitting jealousy. I wish to form a system of belief that shall approve itself to the understanding, and I am equally concerned that my belief, whatever it be, shall afford full security for rectitude of heart and life.

"I forbear to say more, as I shall be ready to discuss these or any other topics with you when I return to London, which I expect will be about the 8th of October."

The approach of the Aberdeen session compelled him to form his plans for the future. Painful and distressing was the struggle through which he had to pass. With the Christian ministry were associated all his hopes and prospects. He had already made successful trial of his powers as a preacher and pastor; he was deeply interested in his studies, both general and theological; and an early settlement in life, involving as it did the happiness of one most dear to him, was an object to which he could not be indifferent. Yet the growth of his "heterodoxy" seemed to be closing against him every avenue through which he could hope to enter the Christian ministry. With the Arian and Unitarian ministers of England he had no acquaintance. From association with the latter it is probable he would have shrunk, as his views did not yet go beyond Arianism. His strong convictions respecting Baptism also would at this time preclude his thinking of a settlement with any but a Baptist church. With the General Baptists he had, through Mr. Evans and Mr. Marsom, some acquaintance, but it was too slight to warrant him in building upon it any expectations of a pastoral engagement with a church of that denomination.

It added not a little to the difficulties and anxieties of his position, that Mr. Middleton not unreasonably demurred to the prudence of entrusting his daughter's happiness to the care of one whose prospects were so uncertain and unpromising. These were the penalties which he had to pay for his religious freedom and sincerity. Great as were the sacrifices he had to make, he did not for a moment think of tampering with his conscience or concealing his opinions.

Carrying with him the affectionate sympathy of his parents, he proceeded to London about the end of October. Good Mr. Thomas, while he deplored his young friend's change of religious sentiment, was himself unchanged in kindness. To him, as the pastor of the church of which he was a baptized member, Robert Aspland felt the necessity of making a formal application respecting the propriety of continued communion at Devonshire Square.

To the Rev. Timothy Thomas.

"81, St. Martin's Lane, Oct. 29, 1800.

"Dear Sir,—I forgot to mention, when I saw you last, the difficulty I feel as to my connection with the people of Devonshire Square.

"I am of myself unable to determine whether the freeness of my religious belief ought to prompt a secession from a society more strict and rigorous in opinion; or whether, retaining my peculiar sentiments, but observing, as long as I am unmolested, a modest silence concerning them, I may be allowed to commemorate with you the sufferings of our common Lord.

"Were *my* feelings alone consulted, they would pronounce at once in favour of continuance with a pastor to whom I owe the highest esteem, and a company of Christians whom I regard with fervent affection. But if the laws of your church require the excision of a dissenter in opinion as an unsound and pestilent member,—if my stay among you would be any way the occasion of dissatisfaction, offence and dissension, I shall deem it a duty, however painful, to retire in quiet from your communion.

"As the next is the first sabbath in the month, I write that I may hear from you previous to the administration of the Supper. You will answer my question freely. Your decision will, I know, be the result of principle, and shall not therefore, whatever it may be, diminish aught from my respect."

The reply to this letter is not extant; but Mr. Thomas had no choice, according to the constitution of the church at Devonshire Square, in expressing his opinion that Robert Aspland could no longer be received by them as a communicant at the Lord's table.

The excision of the "heretical" member shortly after followed as a matter of course. The circumstance most painful to Robert Aspland connected with this affair was, that his conduct in relation to Mr. Thomas was by some unknown party misrepresented, and calumny for a moment alienated the kindly feelings of that worthy man. With the candour habitual to him, Mr. Thomas expressed his surprise and displeasure. The reply alone is preserved. It is without a date, but was probably written at Christmas-time, when the writer went down for a short visit to Wicken.

To the Rev. Timothy Thomas.

"Dear Sir,—Your letter equally surprises and grieves me. You have certainly been misinformed. One personal interview would, I am sure, correct the mistake; and, were not you engaged to-morrow, and myself obliged by appointment to leave London on Wednesday, I would not neglect for a day the clearing up of an affair which you view in so unpleasant a light.

"As your former letter was addressed to me as a member of the church of Devonshire Square; as its contents related to a part of religious conduct for which, in my social character, I am responsible; as it involved no private or delicate circumstances, but contained merely general advice founded upon open, steady principle, I cannot admit that to have introduced it in 'public' or even in *promiscuous* 'company,' would have been a violation of any of the rules of friendship. But this, Sir, although in my opinion perfectly allowable, I have not done. My memory does not furnish me with one instance in which a public company ever heard me so much as mention your letter. And I rely upon the consciousness of my own integrity, and of my respect for your character, that I never spoke to a third person of your expressions or conduct with unfairness and disrespect. Once, indeed, I recollect the subject of your note was talked over; but it was in a private, select circle of religious friends, and at the house of a fellow-member, one of your best friends. Otherwise than the general subject of discourse, I had forgot the observations which passed that evening, until a person who was present, and who remembers the conversation, reminded me, after hearing your last letter, that when in objection to your note it was asked, whether a minister did not arrogate to himself the rights of the people in forbidding a member from church-communion, I urged on your behalf that the letter in question was only an answer to a query, and was to be considered not so much prohibition as advice. This being the only time, in my recollection, that the matter has been discussed '*by myself and others,*' I am not at a loss for the source of the tale. Report, always unsure in its evidence, has in this instance greatly misrepresented. In a case like the present, you cannot object to give up names. When I know the authors of your information, I will refer in support of what I here advance to testimony which you will at once admit. Although I am little anxious lest my character should ultimately suffer, I cannot help feeling a little uneasiness that a momentary suspicion of its uprightness and consistency should cross the mind of one whom I highly regard, and whose good opinion I would therefore preserve to the last inviolate. And while I console myself with the assurance that further inquiry will end in my justification and your satisfaction, I trust to your generosity and goodness not to let vague, vulgar report deprive me of your esteem.

"I meant to have been at Devonshire Square yesterday, but my feelings overcame my fortitude. Avowed and argumentative opposition I can meet; but censure read only in hard and averted looks and in rough insinuations, or even silent pity, is a foe too formidable for me to encounter. It has no sensible, determinate shape. Fancy models it at will, and when her energy is lost in swelling its size and exaggerating its horrors, she sinks before the creature of her own formation."

Being no longer a recognized member of an "orthodox" church, he supposed himself not qualified to enjoy the benefits of the Ward Trust, which had been granted to him as a Calvinistic believer, and he hastened to replace in the hands of the Trustees the bursary which they had voted for his use.

"*To the Trustees of Dr. Ward's Exhibition.*

"Nov. 5, 1800.

"Gentlemen,—In my last letter of thanks, I solicited the continuance of your patronage; I now write to signify that I decline all further benefit of Dr. Ward's institution. An alteration of religious belief has produced this change of intention. With regret do I leave a situation from which I have derived pleasure and improvement; but as I am no longer a Calvinistic believer, I could not justify it to myself, to you, or to the religious world, to continue my dependence upon a Trust which has given me its support only under that character.

"I offer no excuse for myself. Free inquiry is a sacred, indispensable duty, and its result is the subject neither of praise nor blame. We are not allowed to prescribe to examination: we must follow as evidence leads. At the same time, to prevent any complaint of the abuse and perversion of your funds, I am anxious to have it understood that I intend to restore the sum, as soon as I find it convenient, which I have received from you for the purpose of education.

"I retire, gentlemen, thankful for your assistance, and happy in the consciousness that the step I now take is the impulse of honour and conscience."*

This was the greatest sacrifice of all, for by it he virtually excluded himself from the University and prematurely terminated his education. Had he possessed the knowledge which he afterwards gained of the liberal character of Dr. John Ward and his Trust, he might with perfect propriety have returned to Aberdeen and continued there two or even three more sessions.

His parents would without doubt have continued to furnish him with the funds necessary for his return to the University, had he thought it right to ask it at their hands; but so slight did the prospect appear to him of his ultimately being able to engage in the ministry, that he resolved no longer to burthen their generosity.

At this crisis in his history, Mr. Middleton proposed to him to turn his attention to trade, and offered him, should a trial of the experiment prove mutually satisfactory, a share in his own business. Not without hesitation and much mistrust of himself, his fitness for trade, and the suitableness of a London residence to his health, and, above all, not without pangs of mortification at the idea of giving up the profession of the ministry, he accepted Mr. Middleton's offer, and forthwith entered on his new duties at St. Martin's Lane.

---

* The late Mr. Ivimey, in his "History of the English Baptists" (Vol. IV. 499), described "Mr. Robert Aspland" as one "who had been educated at the Bristol Academy, at the expense of the Particular Baptists," and who "*relapsed into Socinianism.*" In the same passage allusion is made to "the deteriorating and destructive influence of that anti-scriptural system." Protestant Dissent has been unfortunate in some of its historians. Inaccuracy is not the worst fault of writers influenced by the petulant bigotry of Messrs. Bogue, Bennett and Ivimey.

CHAPTER VII.

The experiment of trade, to which Robert Aspland devoted the winter of 1800-1801, proved, to himself at least, unsatisfactory. His own hopefulness and the warmth of his affection, which was gratified by the society he enjoyed in Mr. Middleton's family, for a time made him believe that the experiment would be successful. But further experience dissipated the idea that he could with proper attention to business combine literary study. He tried, but in vain, to interest himself in the business. It offered no scope for his active energy, and it fell in with none of his tastes. For that portion of the business which related to *colours* he was almost disqualified by a physical peculiarity,* being to the close of life unable to distinguish their shades and combinations, and even some of the primary colours.

He did not enlarge his acquaintance amongst the Unitarians of the metropolis, nor did he preach more than twice during this winter in London. On both occasions it was for the Rev. John Evans at Worship Street.

The following letters describe his feelings at this time. The first is addressed to a gentleman of Aberdeen, with whom he had formed and kept up a pleasant intimacy during his stay in Scotland.

To Mr. Alexander Cooper.

" * * * You are wondering all this time where I am, what is my occupation, what are my plans. Your letter found me, as you expected, embosomed in village society, and sharing my time between literature and the heartfelt reveries of free, impassioned religion. In the autumn I left this pleasing

---

* The peculiarity is said to be not structural, but functional. It affected, but in a much greater degree, the late Dr. Dalton. From his case, it derived its modern name, *Daltonism*.

scene for London. Our love affairs, which had been some time ripening, had now reached their maturity. Consultation after consultation, grave as prudent, was held between fathers and uncles. The issue was a demand upon me, poor luckless, embarrassed wight, of a prompt, unwavering decision of my 'views and projects.' * * * It was proposed to me to relinquish my literary pursuits and accept a share in a genteel and lucrative trade. Your fancy will sketch the struggle I endured. I felt a secret contempt for the low traffic and drudgery of the world;—prejudices which I had before nourished, thus rising at this crisis in rebellion against me. I found it hard work to strip myself of those bold, high-aimed projects of eminence in which I used to invest myself, as I simply thought for amusement, or at most that I might pace my little sphere with somewhat more of confidence and self-importance, but which I had discovered were become part of my soul, and could not be separated without robbing it of its prime ornament and support. * * * In deciding in favour of business, I have, I confess, abandoned a fair, an enchanting path; but the one which I have now entered on is not without its charms. I enjoy the society and friendship of the best of women. The activity and bustle of the day makes me more sensible of the value of the retirement of the evening, and gives me a keener relish for conversation or books. My present situation promises a happy competency and a good portion of independence. Thus you see, Robert, dropping his literature, his public character and his wishes after fame, sits down for the remainder of life obscure, ignorant and happy."

To Mr. Isaac Aspland, Wicken.

"London, Nov. 19, 1800.

"Dear Isaac,—I need hardly say it gave me great pleasure to hear from you—to hear, especially, that Sally is at length out of danger, and that you are the father of a fine boy. Allow me to congratulate you and your wife on the occasion. I hope the young gentleman will live and prove a comfort to you and an honour to our family. I feel almost inclined to charge you to take care of him; for he has already raised such an interest in my heart, that I assure you I begin to anticipate the seeing of him. It would be full early to advise you to watch narrowly over his temper, but I can't help exhorting you to take care that he is not *killed with food*. We all of us, in reality, want little sustenance at a time; infants much less; yet the common custom is, as you know, to fill up their little stomachs to the brim; and whenever they cry, to stifle their voices with some sort of victuals. This, perhaps, is the chief reason why so many die in infancy. Now I am cautioning you, allow me to remind you of the promises you have given me to have nothing to do with the fooleries of churching and christening. Your good sense will teach you they are truly absurd: your sense of religion will inform you that they are ceremonies which God has not enjoined, and which consequently are of no obligation. Should you be desirous of some sort of religious dedication of the child, we can manage that amongst ourselves by prayer and a short address.

"You may suppose I feel strange and awkward in business—especially, too, in a business to which I was a total stranger. Our trade lies solely amongst the artists, and consists in colours and cloths for painting. My present situation is not without its disagreeables; but it has likewise many pleasantnesses, and after a year will, I expect, alter much for the better. I count much upon domestic enjoyments. It will give me inexpressible pleasure to see you and others of my friends under my own roof."

To Mr. Boyle, Aberdeen.

"London, Dec. 4, 1800.

"Dear Sir,—In beginning a letter to you, I must offer some excuse for not writing before: it was not because I had forgotten my promise, nor that I was insensible of the kindness of your request. I waited only that I might be able to pronounce with certainty upon my return to Aberdeen. I am at length forced of necessity upon a determination; and it gives me little pleasure to add, that by this determination I am debarred from seeing you again. When I left you, I intended, as you know, to return to Aberdeen to give something more of completeness to my education. An entire and unexpected change of private affairs has frustrated all my plans: of *scholarship* I have given up every idea, and my attentions are already engaged by business. With all my predilection in favour of my native country, I cannot think of having left Scotland but with deep and painful regret: the studies which so pleasingly employed me, and the kindnesses of friends whom I shall often recal with tenderness, have endeared it to me; and were I not made contented and happy, in spite of myself, by the affection and attentions of *dear and devoted friends*, recollection of the agreeable, improving situation I have deserted would frequently betray me into uneasiness and complaint. * * * I wrote to Professor Stuart some time since; but as I had not then made my final resolve as to Scotland, I will thank you to communicate to him the contents of this letter, together with my sincere respects. * * * The books left in your care, I will thank you to forward to London by one of the packets. Some of them are, I dare say, not worth the freightage; but as I have no inventory of them, and as several of them are odd volumes, I am unable to make any distinction. If there be room, you may send the scarlet gown, which I mean to keep as a memorial of past times."

The next letter, which is addressed to a Dissenting minister of Cambridgeshire, shews how quickly and fondly his thoughts turned to his family and the little flock at Wicken, and how reluctant he was to commit himself finally to a course of life which would shut him out from the ministry.

To the Rev. Thomas Nicklin.

"London, Dec. 6, 1800.

"I make no apology for writing to an old friend, nor shall I employ any art in introducing the design of this letter. You have often, and in terms which I am willing to believe proceeded from nothing but warm esteem, professed your regard for me: an opportunity in which your assistance will much oblige me now presents itself; I therefore avail myself cheerfully of your liberal and voluntary offers. You have perhaps heard that I have given up the ministry as a source of livelihood; not that I am weary of such an employment, nor indeed that I mean to discontinue it. My opinion is, that a minister who is independent on his people will be most likely to be happy in himself and useful to his charge. In pursuance of this plan, I have rested at London, instead of proceeding, as was expected, to Scotland. I am now in a business which promises to be both easy and profitable; but before I finally engage in it, I feel anxious to learn whether there are no situations in the country, to which I am ardently attached, and among my friends, whose company I cannot readily give up, which would be equally safe and agreeable." [Here follow a number of very minute inquiries respecting a business, that of a tanner, in the neighbourhood of Burwell, which he conceived might be purchased from its then possessor.] "I feel more interest in this matter, because the situation has always charmed me, and because it would allow me to continue my instructions at Wicken; and permit me to say that from our mutual society I should hope for much pleasure and profit. It will please me to hear that your health is well established. I suppose before this you have *been at the altar*. I shall therefore wish you and Mrs. N. every enjoyment of the hymeneal and connubial state. The benevolence of your disposition will, I trust, keep pace with the liberality of your fortune. I submit my requests to you with freedom, and rely upon your goodness for a cheerful compliance with them."

To Mr. William Aspland, Wicken.

"London, Dec. 20, 1800.

"* * * Had I not intimated to you my intention of engaging in trade, you would have been surprised upon the first information of my present employment. But although I have turned my attention to trade, I have not entirely deserted the ministry. I preach occasionally where opportunity and inclination lead. Thus I am free from restraint in my private inquiries and public addresses; and thus I am secure from a dependence, the most servile of all dependencies, upon the humours and caprices of the multitude.

"I am glad that the spirit of religion is in a measure alive amongst you. My joy on this occasion is founded upon a firm conviction that religion is necessary to full happiness in this life, as well as to 'life and immortality' in the world to come. Nothing less than a heartfelt interest in the gospel of

Christ is, I think, able to subdue the turbulency of passion, to withstand the torrent of worldly cares and anxieties, and to support under the pressure of mortal sorrows; as, certainly, nothing besides can lift the veil which parts time from eternity, and discover to us the last and high destiny of man. Religion, in her true, genuine appearance, is indeed lovely. Viewed in creeds, mass-books and formularies of worship, she is, I acknowledge, miserably changed: both gaudy and fantastic in dress, and severe and forbidding in demeanour and feature, she excites at the same time disgust and abhorrence. But her character, formed from the example and instructions of the Saviour, connected with the writings of his disciples, comprises every excellence which can fascinate and fix the heart. Were she more known, she would, as you have often heard me say, be better loved.

"You have heard, doubtless, that I intend to be at Wicken at Christmas. As there are but a few days before it will be here, I will thank you to communicate to my father the mode and plan of my intended journey, which will spare my writing to him expressly on the subject.

"My kind respects to my aunt. I hope William, my scholar, improves in reading, spelling and hymn-repeating."

To Mr. John Emons.

"London, March 18, 1801.

"Dear Friend,—As I promised to write to you, I feel uneasy at having neglected it so long; yet I must confess I am at a loss what to say. If I were to give way to my feelings, I should naturally touch on some melancholy strain, and thus, I fear, increase that despondency of temper to which you are of yourself too much inclined. And although I have no pressing necessity of sorrow, I have enough occasion for thoughtfulness.

"My situation affords me many pleasures, but I find business will not allow me so much leisure for books as I could wish, besides that it hinders me in a great measure from preaching; an employment in which, you know, notwithstanding the little success I have met with, I always took great pleasure. I am not finally fixed in trade, nor can I give up the idea of the ministry. I should hope to be able, because it may be necessary, to unite both. If, however, one must be sacrificed to the other, I shall not be long in deciding which shall become the victim. I pass now every where for a confirmed heretic.

"A vote of church exclusion is, I understand, issued out against me, for disbelieving the equal divinity of Jesus Christ, his atonement to Divine Justice for the sins of the elect, and for asserting (which I find was accounted the most crying and damnable error) that in the work of salvation man is expected to do his part. I do not blame these my former friends; they have executed, in their own opinion, an act—and to many of them, I believe, an unwilling act—of duty. And as I certainly entered among them as a Calvinist, which they maintain themselves inviolably to be, they might, perhaps, on a change of sentiment have right and power to expel me; yet one cannot help asking how it is that men with New Testaments in their hands could think of making the doctrines I have enumerated a test of orthodoxy—yea, of religion itself.

"In direct opposition to the first monstrous article, our Saviour renounces altogether every idea of supremacy. 'My Father is greater than I.' The second is founded on some few metaphors (and who will undertake to explain literally all the allusions and metaphors of the Scripture?), whilst it contradicts our first and simplest notions of Divine Perfection, by making him doom eternally the punishment of an innocent being, and take delight in his sufferings, and subverts all our ideas of justice by establishing that guilt and merit are transferable; that he who never sinned can be viewed and punished as a sinner, and that the sinner can be regarded as pure and innocent on account of the virtue of another; and, in short, opposes the whole tenor of revelation, which holds out redemption, not as a bargain between the Father and the Son, and something superior to either, dignified with the name of Justice; but represents it invariably as a free gift, proceeding from the love and pure grace of the Father. The last opinion, which makes men wholly passive in the salvation of their own souls, you as well as myself have long disowned. Were it not serious in its nature and consequences, one could hardly forbear laughing at its absurdity.

"I shall be extremely happy to pass again with you the hours we have spent pleasantly together at Wicken. That I can hardly expect. I may, however, see you before you expect; but if I should not be at Wicken within a month, I don't expect I shall be able to visit you for some time. The times are frightfully difficult. With your family, you must severely feel what I lament and dread at a distance; yet there is room for hope we may live to see better days.

"I hope you find pleasure in the religious meetings of our friends. Even should you not, you are at least secure from insult, from which you could not be at Soham. Remember me at home. Best wishes to yourself and family.

"P. S. Since I wrote this letter, something has transpired, about which I shall write to my father to-morrow. I will thank him to send to Soham for the letter."

In the promised letter he discloses to his parents a new and brighter prospect of life which had just opened upon him. His preaching at Worship Street, already alluded to, was the occasion of interesting in his behalf the Rev. John Evans, pastor of one of the three General Baptist societies which in 1801 assembled there. That kind and experienced man saw in the young preacher talents and dispositions that fitted him for usefulness and eminence in the pulpit, and he took the first opportunity of communicating his opinion to a General Baptist congregation in search of a minister.

To his Parents.

"London, March 19, 1801.

"Dear Parents,—I have frequently had occasion to consult you concerning the various situations I have occupied, and have often excited your surprise by new occurrences and resolutions. You may have guessed, both from the nature of the case and from some insinuations in my letters, that I did not feel myself altogether happy and contented in trade. Many things concurred to render this business interesting; the opportunity, in particular, it gave me of enjoying the society of friends whose worth and affection have for ever endeared them to me, seemed to invest it with the highest attractions. On this account I shall ever, I am sure, look back with pleasure and gratitude upon this last period of my life. But the enjoyments I have been favoured with have not always diverted my thoughts from the future; and, looking forward, I must confess my heart has often sunk at the prospect. I have been able to see scarcely any thing but a continuation of manual employments, of cares, of vexations, which I have at once despaired to surmount. At least, the labour of the ascent would, I judged, preclude all improvement and destroy all happiness. I have considered myself in the midst of a wilderness, where all was strange, rough and barren; and if I chanced to light upon a spot pleasant and familiar to me, fatigue from the past and apprehension from the future have incapacitated me for its enjoyment; and when I have left it, as I shortly have, it has served by its contrast to make succeeding scenes more savage and intolerable. My attachment to books and preaching you know. Taken from them, I seemed to be robbed of the food of life. I secretly pined and languished.

"These feelings often working, at length overflowed. I could no longer contain myself. I laid open my heart to friends whose views exactly met mine, and who very much assisted my resolutions. Through their zealous and diligent inquiries, to dwell no longer in detail, a pressing invitation has come to me from Newport, in the Isle of Wight, to go there for a few sabbaths as probationer. I have accepted the offer. I am to be there before the 12th April, and at Portsmouth, on the way thither, the sabbath preceding. My stay at Newport may not be long; but as I want a little rest and retirement before I go, and as I want also to take your advice on the subject, I mean to spend the intervening time, which will be about ten days, at Wicken. The letter of invitation reached me just after I had finished my letter to J. Emons. Something which I subjoined may perhaps have raised your curiosity. I have fixed upon Saturday, the 21st, for my journey. If you will order a horse (not my uncle's runaway) to meet me at Newmarket in the afternoon, you will see me at Wicken in the course of the evening.—We apprehended some opposition to our plan from Mr. M., who heard of it for the first time last night. He was unexpectedly mild and reasonable. He had doubtless perceived that the business was irksome to me, and could not therefore anticipate much success from my stay in it.

"The ladies are very cheerful. We all hope that Providence is directing us to some situation more happy and congenial to our feelings than this. I am sure we have your prayers that we may not be disappointed.

"The friends whom I have mentioned, and whose names it would be a crime to omit on this occasion, are Mr. Marsom and Mr. Evans. The latter I am going to visit this afternoon. He possesses a truly benevolent soul. The striking difference just occurs to me which there is between * * * and him, fellow-students. From the former I had a right to expect kindness and attention, but met with incivility and, what is infinitely worse, sly, insidious persecution. Mr. Evans, prompted only by goodness of heart, interested himself immediately and with warmth in my affairs, although almost a stranger to him. His letter to the Newport congregation was flattering and recommendatory. * * * You may order about Sunday as you please. I will preach, as you determine it, either in the morning and afternoon, or, omitting the afternoon, in the evening. Farewell."

The General Baptist congregation of Newport was, in 1801, a small but highly respectable society. Mr. Gabriel Watts, who had been pastor since 1794,* had a few months before resigned the pulpit through

---

* By the kindness of Rev. Edmund Kell, the present estimable minister of Newport, the writer is enabled to add some particulars respecting the previous history of the society.

"Of the origin of the General Baptist, now designated as the Unitarian, congregation in Newport, Isle of Wight, little is with certainty known. It is probable that Nonconformity is of very ancient date in this borough, as Robert Tutchin, of Newport, was among the ejected ministers of 1662, and 'was so well beloved by the inhabitants of this town,' says Calamy, 'that when he was turned out, they allowed him the same stipend as when he was their minister, so that they paid two ministers till the day of his death, and then interred him in their church. He had three sons,—John, Robert and Samuel,—that were all considerable men, and all silenced on the same day with him.' Vigorous seeds of Dissent were thus early sown, which appear soon to have produced a copious harvest; for the Dissenters of this town have always been among its most influential inhabitants, and considerably outnumber the members of the Establishment. Whether Mr. Tutchin himself formed a congregation is not recorded, though it may be conjectured that, like others of the ejected ministers, he would take advantage of such opportunities of preaching as were afforded him, till the Act of Uniformity enabled the Dissenters to profess their principles without molestation. The only certain knowledge we have is, that there was a Dissenting meeting-house, with a burial-ground attached to it, in Pyle Street, before the erection of the General Baptist chapel near the same spot, in 1728; and there

feeble health. The pulpit had been supplied for a short time by Rev. Thomas Rees, then a student from the Carmarthen Academy, and with so much acceptance to the congregation, that had his sentiments on baptism agreed with theirs, there is little doubt he would have been chosen as their minister.

The invitation to Robert Aspland to preach before the Newport congregation as a candidate for the pulpit, was communicated by Mr. Thomas Cooke. In his reply, he stated that his acceptance of their invitation was chiefly determined by " the persuasion he had, from the representation of friends, that the Baptists at Newport were equally pious and devotional in temper and conduct, and liberal in opinion." The trial or probation Sundays, times of great anxiety to all young

---

is reason to believe that that society was the parent stock from which also sprang the Presbyterian congregation, now called Independent, in St. James's Street. A funeral sermon preached by the Rev. Richard Clarke, the great-grandfather of the present Abraham Clarke, Esq., on the death of Mrs. Sarah Chick, in 1726, is among the oldest Dissenting documents extant in the town. From this sermon it is obvious that the writer had considerably diverged from the standard of orthodoxy. The Trust-deed of the chapel built in the year 1728, has annexed to it the signatures of several ancestors of the present members of the Unitarian congregation. It contains a clause, directing that if the worship conducted in it should ever be considered illegal, the Trustees should have the power to let the chapel, and distribute the proceeds among poor Christians, but should restore the chapel to its original use whenever it should be again lawful to worship there. No regularly-kept minutes of the proceedings of the congregation, before the year 1749, are preserved. The Rev. William Mott was then its pastor, but whether he was the immediate successor of Mr. Clarke is not ascertained. He was succeeded in Sept. 1751, by the Rev. John Sturch, son of a minister of the same name, who, from a published sermon in the possession of the writer, delivered Nov. 5, 1736, at Crediton, appears to have been an able and solid preacher. Mr. Sturch was ordained pastor of the church, June 21, 1753, on which occasion the charge delivered by the Rev. William Foot, of Bristol, was published. During his ministry in the year 1774, the chapel in Pyle Street, being inconveniently situated, was pulled down, and a new one erected in High Street. He was a man esteemed and beloved by persons of all sects and parties, and was the author of the first historical account of the Isle of Wight, and of a charge delivered on the ordination of the Rev. Thomas Twining in 1775. He hesitated not to avow Unitarian sentiments from the pulpit, and was himself what was called a Low Arian. This did not prevent an occasional interchange of ministerial services with the pastors of the Presbyterian (now Independent) chapel, one of whom, the Rev. John Potticary, married one of his daughters. His son, William Sturch, Esq., of London, was well known as a firm and liberal supporter of the cause of civil and religious liberty. For a short time previous to the close of his ministry, which continued for the long space of forty-three years, he was assisted by the Rev. Gabriel Watts, who succeeded him at his death in the year 1794. Mr. Watts continued pastor until the close of Oct. 1800."

preachers, were April 19th* and 26th and May 3rd. In addition to the Sunday services, the congregation met one evening in the middle of the week for prayer and exhortation. He found great diversity of religious sentiment in the congregation, but all appeared to him to be "liberal, candid and inquisitive." The chapel he described as "small, but neat, compact, and easy and pleasant to the speaker;" the town as clean and lively, and the surrounding country delightful. He found, till he went into a house of his own, a most comfortable home in that of a daughter of a former minister.

The congregation hastened to relieve the young candidate from his anxiety by a speedy decision. On entering the pulpit on the third Sunday, he found a note desiring him to convene a meeting of the members and subscribers at the close of the afternoon service. In the course of the evening, a deputation, consisting of six principal members of the congregation, waited upon him and reported that he had been by an unanimous vote chosen successor to Mr. Watts. Before giving his reply, he inquired whether they proposed any limitation to opinion? The answer which one and all gave was prompt and decisive—"You may go from the highest pitch of Arianism to the lowest pitch of Unitarianism, and give us no uneasiness!"

Without further hesitation, he at once, and with feelings of gratitude, accepted the office of pastor; and it was agreed between his friends and himself that he should on the following Sunday enter on his pastoral duties by administering the Lord's Supper. He hastened, in what he called "the happiest letter of his life," to communicate the pleasant tidings to her who shared in all his hopes. By the same post he reported the event to his friends at Wicken.

To Mr. Isaac Aspland.

"Newport, Monday, May 4, 1801.

"It will give you and my father and mother great pleasure to hear that I am now settled. I have no doubt that Providence has brought it about for

---

* He arrived at Newport on Friday, April 17. As the revolution in the mode of travelling which the present generation has witnessed is so great, it is well to notice the inconveniences to which our countrymen of the last generation were put in travelling. In 1801, the journey from London to Newport took two days; to Southampton, thirteen hours. From Southampton to Cowes, a voyage of fifteen miles, nine of which is river, the traveller was occupied from two to eight hours, according to the state of wind and tide. Robert Aspland was, in April 1801, the longer period. *Now*, the traveller could without difficulty get in eight hours from the fens of Cambridgeshire to the centre of the Isle of Wight!

my happiness and usefulness. The date of my services my hearers have handsomely agreed should commence at Lady-day last, so that now you are to consider me as their minister. We are above the superstition and impertinence of forms; in every thing we think and act for ourselves. Next sabbath afternoon I administer the Lord's Supper. Think of me at the time. Our service begins at three o'clock.

"A public ordination is agreed upon. When it will be, or who will officiate, is not yet decided. Here is a good opening for a school, which I am planning, and to the undertaking of which I have great encouragement.

"Poor Wicken! I have nearly done with it! At least I shall, I expect, see it henceforth only as a short visitor.

"Perhaps I may be in Cambridgeshire before Midsummer; if so, your prophecy will certainly be completed, for I shall not visit you *alone*.

"You must not leave Wicken on any account. My father and mother are inadequate to the business; it falls too heavy upon them now; if you go, it would, I fear, weigh them down.

"Take care of the garden. I have enjoyed many a happy hour in it, and am willing to hope I shall see it again with pleasure.

"My affectionate remembrance to my father and mother. I am very happy: it would be wrong in me to be otherwise. I hope the agreeableness of my prospects will make them happy too."

Before the month expired, Robert Aspland and Sara Middleton were united at the church of St. Martin-in-the-Fields. Miss Maria Porter was one of the few attendants at the simple ceremony. A visit to Wicken preceded the settlement at Newport, and never were parents happier in the happiness of their children than were his excellent and warm-hearted father and mother on this occasion.

A few days after his marriage, he received the long-delayed notice of his excommunication by the church at Devonshire Square. The temper of the document was as kindly as could have been expected.

To Mr. Aspland.

"No. 8, Haberdashers' Walk, Hoxton, June 3, 1801.

"Dear Sir—Agreeable to the desire of the church meeting near Devonshire Square, London, under the pastoral care of the Rev. Timothy Thomas, I transmit to you the minute of a past church-meeting which immediately refers to yourself.

"'The messengers appointed to inquire into the cause of Mr. Aspland's absence reported that, by their conversation with him, it appeared his belief in the doctrines of divine revelation was so different from what he professed it to be when he first became a member with us, and knowing that we considered such difference to be inconsistent with the nature and end of church-fellowship, he had on that account absented himself from uniting with us in public worship.

"'The messengers farther reported that he appeared to be confirmed in his rejection of the faith he formerly professed; on which account it was unanimously resolved, 'That he be no longer considered in church-fellowship with us, and that Mr. Sitch be desired to send him a copy of the above minute.'

"Sir, painful as the task has been, I have complied with the request of the church with whom I am connected, in sending you the above; but must beg to add one wish, that our changing opinions in religious matters may be for the *better*, and not tend to confirm us in *infidelity*. We cannot preserve too godly a jealousy of ourselves.

"May your ministerial engagements be abundantly blessed to all around you, and especially to that church over which you are planted!

"My best respects to your other part, not forgetting your dear self.—I remain, yours, "J. SITCH."

In what light the excommunicated member regarded this act of the church, will be seen in the following farewell letter addressed to his friend and former pastor.

To the Rev. Timothy Thomas.

"Newport, June 19, 1801.

"Dear Sir—Although I am widely separated from you by situation, and still more widely perhaps by religious belief, I cannot quietly consent that our intercourse should finally drop. I owe much to you; yet allow me to say that your personal services, much as they have benefited me, have not made upon me a more deep impression than the independence and generosity of your character. The late act of the church I impute not to you; or if I were to believe it had your support, I should applaud the resolution and piety of sacrificing feelings to religious truths.

"I am obliged to Mr. Sitch for the reluctance with which he announces the decision of his fellow-members, and for the good wishes with which he concludes his letter. Hereafter I may perhaps address him, and through him the church, upon my exclusion. As an act it cannot be revoked, but the nature, reasons and justice of it should be well understood.

"I am settled, happily settled, at Newport. Here is a congregation enlightened and affectionate. We all, I hope, feel the importance of Christian faith and practice, but we all feel equally a dread of invading each other's rights. Should a love of nature ever prompt you to visit the Isle of Wight, you would find in Mrs. Aspland and myself warm and sincere friends. It would be, I suppose, a mere compliment to invite you to my ordination; but if you could associate conscientiously in an act of religious worship with such men as Dr. Toulmin and Job David, your company would add to the pleasure of the occasion. The day is not yet fixed for the ceremony, but I could give you early information of it.

"I meant to have spared myself the necessity of this letter by calling upon you in passing through London. The shortness of our stay, however (we allowed ourselves but one day) prevented our leaving the town.

"Mrs. A. desires me to excuse her likewise for not accompanying Miss Thomas to the Exhibition. My sudden journey to town prevented the fulfilment of the engagement."

The first care of the young minister on his return to Newport was to make arrangements for his ordination, a ceremony to which he assented in deference to the wishes of the congregation. He would have refused this assent if he had regarded it as sanctioning the opinion that any man or body of men could rightfully interfere between the chosen minister and his people. He rejected the idea that any power could be conferred by any ceremony whatever; but he did not object to a religious service calculated to remind minister and people of their respective duties, and affording an occasion for united prayer for the Divine blessing.

The ceremony of ordination was, however, deferred a sufficient length of time to enable the young minister to go through the various duties of the pastor of a Baptist society.

On the Sunday previous to the ordination, he celebrated the public baptism at the chapel. Dr. Toulmin preached in the morning from Acts xviii. 8, "And many of the Corinthians, hearing, believed and were baptized." After the sermon, Mr. Aspland administered the ordinance to seven persons, two men and five women, and amongst the latter were his wife and her sister. He followed on this occasion the custom of Robert Robinson, immersing the subjects *forward*, thus giving the ceremony an appearance of worship and of voluntary service, as well as, in his opinion, conforming to the practice of the primitive Christians.

Some are still living who remember the service, and report that it was performed with equal ease and self-collectedness on the part both of the administrator and the candidates, and that the congregation was deeply attentive, and some present were affected to tears. In the afternoon, the minister addressed the newly-baptized persons, as also the church at large, from Heb. x. 22, 23, "Having our bodies washed with pure water, let us hold fast the profession of our faith without wavering." Dr. Toulmin preached again in the evening.

The ordination service took place on Tuesday, July 21st, in the presence of Revds. Dr. Toulmin; Russell Scott, of Portsmouth; John Mills, the aged minister of the General Baptist congregation, Portsmouth; John Fullagar; Mr. Stephen, of Ringwood; and a numerous congregation. Mr. Marsom and the Rev. John Evans were invited to attend and take part in the service, but were prevented by other engagements. Dr. Toulmin preached the sermon to the people from Matt. xvi. 18, "The gates of hell shall not prevail against it." He also subsequently gave an impressive and affectionate charge to the minister, from 2 Tim. iv. 5, " Endure afflictions." The afflictions on which he dwelt, as incident to the ministerial calling, were the bigotry or infidelity of the age, poverty, and the partial success of the ministry. The newly-ordained minister gave a brief address, expressive of his views respecting the service of ordination, and of his resolutions and wishes towards himself, his church and congregation. He declined to give, what neither the congregation nor his brethren had asked, a confession of faith, alleging that he was only on the threshold of inquiry, —that it would be presumptuous and rash in him to give a detail of articles of belief which he had adopted, as it were, but yesterday, and might see reason to reject to-morrow. He looked on a public avowal of particular tenets as an undesirable pledge for uniformity and obstinacy of faith. He dared not adopt a course by which he might hereafter find his religious inquiries stopped and blanked, just at the point where they promised to be successful, by a fear lest reference to ordination professions and promises should convict him of fickleness and inconsistency.

The other portions of the service were conducted by Mr. Scott (who read a very impressive selection of passages from the New Testament bearing on the connection of minister and people) and Mr. Mills.

An incident of a somewhat amusing character occurred, which is still remembered by the aged members of the Newport congregation, and is now told nearly in the words of a venerable friend who happily still lives to adorn his Christian profession.

Previous to the service, it had been agreed that there should be no laying on of hands—a ceremony which the minister to be ordained regarded as unwarranted in the present state of the Christian church, and tending to superstition.

" I have a distinct recollection of seeing Mr. Mills, when, in the ordination prayer, intercession was made for a blessing on the labours of the young minister, rise from his seat and place his hand on Mr. Aspland's curling locks; and I shall not forget how the colour mounted into his cheek, and by an indignant shake of the head he expressed his dissent from this unexpected addition to the ordination service. When Mr. Mills was afterwards asked how he came to violate the agreement entered into, he could only plead a sudden and irrepressible desire to make the day's work complete according to old General Baptist usage. He was a kind-hearted old man, and the matter was soon forgiven, if not forgotten."

The day of this service was rendered memorable by its being the birth-day of the Southern Unitarian Society "for the Promotion of Religious Knowledge and the Practice of Virtue on Unitarian Principles by the Distribution of Books." Dr. Toulmin* suggested the desirableness of establishing the Society, and assisted in drawing up the Constitution. Amongst its early patrons was the late William Smith, Esq., M. P., who being on a visit to the island at the time when the subscribers met to frame the Rules, assisted them by his presence, advice and a handsome subscription.

The following letter expresses the writer's happiness with his congregation:

To the Rev. John Evans.

"* * * I am very happy at Newport. My congregation possess among them, in a degree rarely seen, the ingredients which go to the composition of a minister's happiness — unanimity, liberality, confidence. I repeat my thanks to you, Sir, for your introduction and recommendation.

"The ordination service was filled up in the manner I delineated. We should have deemed the service more complete had we enjoyed your assist-

---

* The writer has before him the rough draft of the Rules, in Dr. Toulmin's MS., and appended to them are the autographs of the original members, viz.

William Cooke,	Abraham Clarke,
Rev. Thomas Dalton,	Lydia Sturch,
Rev. Russell Scott,	John Fullagar,
Rev. Robert Aspland,	William Dore,
John Brent,	William Lempriere,
Thomas Cooke,	John Kirkpatrick,
Samuel Price,	Robert Harris,
Joseph Brent,	William Mortimer,
Mrs. Sharpe,	
Mr. Jesse Middleton,	} not in autograph.

The Rev. Thomas Dalton, whose name stands second on the list, was Vicar of Carisbrooke. He was a decided Unitarian, and lived on very friendly terms with his General Baptist neighbours. He was an acquaintance of Dr. Priestley and Mr. Lindsey.

ance. Dr. Toulmin gave great pleasure by his sermons to all who heard him. I know not that he is eminent for originality or boldness of thought, but he certainly possesses in no scanty measure piety, goodness of heart, and gentleness and tenderness of manner.

"I have commenced, as you may have heard, pedagogue. My school is small, and probably will be so at present. What elementary book do you use in teaching geography? Bare names and definitions are hard and crabbed things in the mouths of boys, and generally, I have observed, give a distaste to the knowledge to which they profess to lead. I was taught geography *in verse*. The rhyme, as you will suppose, was doggrel, but it was easy; and though many years have passed since I last perused the book, broken passages still cling around my recollection. The materials, as far as I remember, were good, and the arrangement simple. The author was *Davidson*, I think an American.

" * * I have just received a fresh supply of Burke's eloquence. What a mighty genius! He knew well how to dispense magic with his wand. He leads his followers over nothing but enchanted ground, and, like other magicians, will not suffer them to think or inquire whither they are going. *Materiem superabat opus*.

"I have, Sir, re-opened our correspondence, and cannot but hope that it may not soon close. Letters conveyed to Marsom's will readily find their way to the island."

CHAPTER VIII.

PROSPEROUS and happy as the after-life of Robert Aspland was, it may be safely said that the early years of his pastoral life, passed at Newport, were the happiest of all. Most happily married, and soon surrounded by a young family, with a congregation harmonious, liberal and intelligent, his affections and tastes were gratified, and all the energies of his mind were called into healthy action. His time was divided between private study, including very careful and laborious preparation for the pulpit, the tuition of pupils, and pastoral duty. In the possession of high health and boundless spirits, and feeling the deepest interest in his theological researches and in the welfare of his flock, and, above all, exulting in the exercise of his mental and spiritual liberty, he was enabled successfully to encounter an enormous amount of physical and intellectual exertion. Notwithstanding his facility in *extempore* preaching, and his very limited stock of sermons, he made it a rule from the first to write his discourses; and although his occasional unwritten addresses were heard with much favour, he adhered to the rule to the close of life. Of thoughtless and careless pulpit exercises he entertained a feeling scarcely falling short of abhorrence. When reviewing his ministerial services at Newport, he thus forcibly expressed his opinion on this subject:

"A deep reverence of God and a proper respect for his audience will not allow a conscientious minister, who wishes to speak *as becometh the oracles of Heaven*, to discourse without mature deliberation and serious study. He will not offer the *blind for sacrifice, nor the lame, nor the sick*, nor address the Almighty in language with which he would be ashamed to approach an earthly *governor;* he cannot affront a Christian assembly with discourses which can never instruct or edify them, and may possibly expose them to derision. Following the apostolic advice, he will *give attendance to reading, exhortation and doctrine;* though, alas! he will often experience, with the Wise Man, that much study *is a weariness of the flesh; for in much wisdom is much grief; and he that increaseth knowledge increaseth sorrow.*"

It was a favourable circumstance that the congregation at Newport consisted of many persons who were, equally with their young minister, inquirers. They did not turn with weariness from the *theological* and purely doctrinal subjects which he at this time frequently discussed from the pulpit; but they welcomed them as aiding their own investigations and helping to build up their faith. In order to give somewhat of a systematic character to his pulpit instructions, he went through several of Paul's Epistles, taking each Sunday a longer or a shorter portion, according as it required explanation or afforded materials for thought. These discourses were not merely expository; he did not content himself with explaining, but illustrated many passages by reference, comparison and contrast; he removed objections and enforced exhortations. The advantages of his plan were, that he had always his subject ready; that, working upon a variety of matter, he could drop hints and observations, too insignificant of themselves to furnish the staple of a discourse, and yet such as would not readily unite with other topics; and that he had an opportunity of explaining fully, freely and regularly, the Christian doctrine as it was preached by the apostles and received by the first Christians.

In addition to the two regular services of the Sunday, there was a lecture every Thursday evening. On the first Sunday of the month, an evening lecture was substituted for the afternoon service, and in the afternoon the Lord's Supper was administered. Where an ample attendance can be secured, this arrangement offers some advantages. The communicants do not enter upon it wearied with a previous service; the minister is at liberty to discuss his subject at greater length; and members of the congregation, not habitual attendants at the Lord's Table, may be induced thereby to attend as spectators. One evening in the week (generally Tuesday) was devoted to a free conference on some religious subject, previously selected, at which the minister presided, opening the proceedings with an address explanatory of the subject to be discussed, and closing them with a summary judgment on the several opinions and arguments adduced. These meetings were usually held in his school-room, and were occasionally attended by others besides members of the congregation. With a view to the intellectual improvement and the social union of the latter, he encouraged the young people to meet together once a week for the purpose of reading aloud passages from the English classics, such as a paper from the *Spectator* or a scene from one of Shakspeare's Plays. On these occasions he always attended and gave his assistance. A president was chosen, whose duty it was to point out the faults of pronunciation and intonation in the reader. These meetings, besides being useful in other ways, brought him into close contact with all the members of his flock. They also served to develop talents and acquirements in some of the humbler members of the society, which might, but for them, have been unknown. A humble tradesman, a shoemaker, particularly distinguished himself, and established so warm an interest in the breast of his pastor and other friends, as to be subsequently aided to a situation more worthy of his talents.*

He also found time to take an active share in other societies of a more general character. He took his turn as lecturer to the "Philosophical Society;" and there exists an essay which he read on Caloric, the manuscript of which shews tokens of having been written in the midst of some chemical experiments. But he afterwards paid little attention to science, beyond occasionally reading a popular treatise or attending a course of lectures by Mr. Brande or his friend Mr. Phillips.

He also became a member of a political society previously existing in the island, which assembled annually to celebrate the Revolution of 1688. Elected to the office of president, it was his duty to open the meeting with an address suitable to the occasion. He did so in one of some length, which displays considerable historical inquiry and a just appreciation of both the virtues and the faults of William III. The peroration is vigorous and manly:

"Enjoying as we are at present the blessings of the Revolution, it would be ingratitude in us not to revere and celebrate its patriotic authors. Our ancestors, in achieving this great work, laboured less for themselves than for us. As Protestants, we owe the enjoyment of our religion—as Britons, our rights, to the Revolution of 1688. There is also a further and more important reason for keeping alive the memory of this great event, and that is the happy influence the constant remembrance of it will have upon our civil and political

---

* The ingenious person here referred to was the author of some very popular works for children. The title of one of them was, "The Yellow Shoestrings." He was gifted with a beautifully musical voice and exquisite taste in the expression of psalmody. For many years he led the psalmody at the New Gravel-Pit Meeting, Hackney. The writer will never forget the simple pathos with which he was accustomed to sing the single-versed hymn, beginning,

"Mercy, good Lord! mercy I ask."

condition. It stands in history, as La Fayette said of the American States, a monument to Liberty, upon which is written, 'Caution to the oppressor, courage to the oppressed.' It is not the least of the advantages of the Revolution that it prepared the way for the accession of the Hanover family to the throne. May they *remember*, to borrow an expression from Junius, *that, as the crown they wear was gained by one Revolution, it may be lost by another.* As it is from the Revolution that Parliaments derive their freedom, their power, their existence, let them remember that the freedom of the people is essential to their authority and being, and that whatever strikes at *that*, injures *these*. By the Revolution are we freemen; let us, therefore, ever hail the return of this day, which gave birth to its founder, with an association of festivity, patriotism and friendship. I conclude with giving, as a motto to this subject, this assembly, and, if you please, to this discourse, the words written upon the flag under which William was wafted to our native land, *The Liberties of England and the Protestant Religion.*"

Mr. Thomas Cooke, one of the few surviving members of the Newport congregation, has, amongst other things, recalled the following reminiscences of his former pastor:

"Mr. Aspland was very active; nor did he confine his activity to his own congregation. He re-modelled and made more effective a Book Society which had before existed. He was the means of establishing a Club for the friendly discussion of such subjects as might be proposed,* excluding only party politics and controversial theology. He invited his young friends to his house once a week to read selections from the best authors in verse and prose; and, indeed, was the life of every society into which he entered.

"He was a great admirer of country scenes, and usually came here *(Newclose)* on a Saturday to prepare his discourse for the following day. Having been accustomed to a flat country, he was not a very good judge of the distance of hills. Those in front of the room in which he wrote appeared to him so near, that he one day set off to reach them. He walked till he was tired, and then seemed but little nearer than when he set out, and the fatigue of his return altogether unfitted him for the duties of the following day."

In October,† 1801, the heart of the nation beat with joy at the announcement of the cessation of the disastrous war with France, which, since 1793, had been the occasion of a frightful expenditure of blood

---

* Before this society he read a very lively essay, still preserved, entitled, "Have the peculiar Habits and Manners of the Quakers contributed to the Support of their Moral Characters?" In this essay, his early prepossession in favour of the Quaker dress no longer appears.

† The Treaty of Amiens is dated March 25, 1802, but the preliminaries of a treaty of peace were signed on the first day of October preceding.

and treasure. In addition to the horror with which he viewed all war, Robert Aspland, in common with England's best patriots, looked upon the French war as unjustifiable on international grounds, and as undertaken by Mr. Pitt with a view to crush the rising popular spirit in England. He did not long delay to congratulate his parents on the return of the much-desired Peace.

"Newport, Isle of Wight, Oct. 23, 1801.

" Allow me to congratulate you upon an event welcome to us all, *Peace*. Your joy on the occasion as well as ours is, I am sure, heartfelt and warm. Did you make any rejoicings at Wicken? Our illuminations here were pretty brilliant. All our front windows, ten, were stuck full of candles, and consumed, I find, twelve or thirteen pounds. Hitherto we have not so much felt as anticipated the good effects of peace, but we must soon perceive a difference. It happens fortunately for us young housekeepers that the war is at an end. It has proved a vortex to this country, in which have been destroyed the lives, liberties and property of *Englishmen!* Viewing it as a politician, I think the peace highly dishonourable to Britain; but, as Fox said in his admirable speech to the electors of Westminster, 'If it is a bad peace, we must recollect it has been a bad war.' * * * People here dislike the peace. The Isle of Wight has been fed by the war, and can now no longer gorge upon the vitals of its mother country. Although we all illuminated, I believe most of the tradesmen would have lighted up with more pleasure if a bond had been entered into by the nations to make hostilities *eternal*. A friend of ours, Mr. Major, of Carisbrook, (whom we expect by and by to tea,) testified his joy by indubitable signs. Besides lighting up the tower of the church and several alms-houses, he illuminated every pane of glass upon his premises, in back and front. Upon a thorn hedge before his house, extending along the road, were 83 lights, emblematical of the French departments, and at a front window was the picture of *Buonaparte*, surrounded with a civic wreath. His house was open for the children and the poor.

" Your letter, my dear parents, is just arrived. It hath lowered the tone of my feelings. How, alas! are we constantly reminded of our mortality! What is life? Yes, father, it is vanity, and without the hopes of another world, it would be scarcely supportable. I hope that, as your old friends leave you one after the other, you will find a recompence in the characters and conduct of your children.

" I was ignorant of your birth-day, or it should not have passed among us without notice. And are you *fifty-five* years old? Well, I find consolation in the hope that we shall all meet hereafter, in that state where all the distinctions of weak and strong, young and old, shall be lost in immortality.

"I meant to have sent off my letter to-day, but the arrival of yours has disabled me; at every remembrance of you I am melted into tears. Adieu.

"I broke off yesterday suddenly. I return with pleasure to address you. Yesterday, for the first time, we had a dinner guest; in the evening we had several friends to tea. We have visited a great deal, and have received not a few tea visits. With all the people of our own meeting we are upon the most familiar terms, and several respectable people among the Independents have, by calling upon us, sought our acquaintance. We could not possibly have been placed in a situation more agreeable. As a minister I have nothing to complain of, nothing even to wish for; in point of society, Newport cannot be excelled, and our natural situation is pleasant and delightful to a proverb. I may have said as much before, but I am not tired of repeating it, since I know it will give you sincere pleasure.

"I am more than ever averse to Calvinism. * * It is my urgent request that you will buy and read a book written by Mr. Belsham against Wilberforce's work. It is entitled, 'A Review of Mr. W.'s Treatise.' In it you will find a plain and faithful statement of Unitarian tenets, with an exposure of the unscripturalness and folly of the vulgar creed. You will not find yourself overburthened with matter; the whole book is not large, and it is broken down into many short letters, addressed to a lady, the wife of W. Smith, M.P.

"Newport, Jan. 20, 1802.

" * * Last night the reading was omitted, from the length of the conference, occasioned by the presence of a Jew, who has sometimes looked in during the time of preaching, and who, I suppose, has some disposition towards inquiry, from his inclination to join the conference yesterday evening. He entertains some whimsical ideas about the lost tribes of his nation residing in an island surrounded by waves so violently tumultuous, that, except on their sabbath, no one can approach them. This is to account for their not being joined by the other Jews. He nevertheless spoke more reasonably in opposition to the commonly-received Christian system. What expectation can an orthodox believer entertain of converting a Jew or a rational Deist, while he maintains the paradoxical notion of a Triune God, as the object of worship, and of man, from whom worship is expected, as a moral and accountable, and yet as an incapable agent? The more we discover and admire the beauty and excellence of Christianity, the more thankful we feel in being released from the torturing shackles of such unreasonable opinions. We were much pleased with Cogan's reply to Wilberforce's 'Vital Christianity,' both with respect to matter and style. We are now reading his work on the Passions with very great satisfaction."

He hastened, on the birth of his eldest child, to make his fond parents the sharers of his happiness.

"Newport, March, 1802.

" * * In the dear mother and her innocent babe I find a perpetual source of happiness. To have a little tender creature committed to us to protect, to nourish, to instruct, to form for this world and the next, would be of itself a heavy charge, were it not lightened by our mutual endeavours, and the smiles and delights of infancy, and the fond feelings of parents. You sympathize with us, I doubt not, and I assure you we long for an opportunity of presenting to you this our little treasure, in which our hearts centre. She is plump, and, if we may judge from her present looks, will resemble more her mother than her father. But you must come and see her, and live with us, and help us to train her up."

The only drawback from his happiness was his separation from his beloved parents. Once and again he wrote offering them a home under his roof for the remainder of their lives. When his half-brother, Mr. Isaac Aspland, removed from Wicken and established himself in business in London, he urgently entreated his father to retire from the cares of trade, and to enjoy the calm and lovely retreat which the Isle of Wight offered. But the gratification of this wish was not conceded to his ardent filial affection. His father, perhaps wisely, thought the proposed change of residence and habits too great an experiment for persons approaching the grand climacteric of life. His mother he had the gratification of receiving as a guest more than once, but his father's intentions to visit him were never fulfilled.

To Mr. Jesse Middleton.

" Newport, 1802.

"I feel the kindness of your invitation and offer, which are powerfully seconded from Wicken in a letter we lately received; but I have no urgent call to leave the island at present, and a visit, however short, would interrupt my employ and duties, and I cannot help saying I have quite lost the taste for rambling; caused, doubtless, by the superior relish which there is in home; a home endeared by an *equal* wife, liberal friends, and now by a *smiling babe!* These attractions will be powerful enough, I hope, not only to confine my desires and presence, but also to draw you hither. We have room for you, and you will, I assure you, be welcomed as a friend and a brother.

" I have to discuss to-morrow a serious subject. I am brought in the course of my exposition to 2 Thess. i. 6, &c., which will oblige me, of course, to enter deeply into the nature of *future punishments*. The doctrine of eternal torments I cannot and will not believe; the doctrine of universal restoration is fascinating and brilliant, but seems to me to rest entirely upon the unsure and precarious foundation of philosophical reasoning and benevolent wishes; the middle or annihilating scheme is certainly more agreeable to Scripture, but little congenial with our feelings, or, to say the truth, with some of our firmest and most substantial opinions: for instance, no truth is more certain than that, in the punishment of the ungodly, some 'will be beaten with more, some with fewer stripes;' but for this equitable distribution, this proportion of suffering to guilt, the hypothesis in question makes no provision, unless, indeed, it call in to its aid the supposition that in the passage to 'destruction' there will be different ways, longer and shorter, and degrees of torture fiercer and less intense. That any of his rational creatures will be plunged by a wise and good God into everlasting oblivion is hard and horrible to believe; but that they shall be hurried into forgetfulness through pains and torments, through fire and brimstone, through scenes of progressive horror and anguish, who, venerating the character of the Almighty, and endued with the feelings and sympathies of human nature, can endure to think? This notion, like the vulgar one of eternal misery, strikes heavy upon my heart whenever I think of it. Of a future state I can hardly forbear sometimes saying, notwithstanding the lights thrown over it by Christianity, 'Clouds and darkness rest upon it.' I mentioned these difficulties some time ago to Marsom. I wish he would think of them and give me his ideas. I mentioned also the sermons of Bourn upon the subject, which I dare say are highly excellent. Mr. M. will notice this when he writes again. Remind him of the 8vo Life of King William. I can say no more."

To his Father.

"Newport, June 4, 1802.

"Dear Father,—We are surprised as well as pleased to find my mother with us. * * I hope that this visit is only the introduction to a permanent residence with us, an event which you know I much wish. * * We want to introduce you to our good friends here, and to shew you one of the most romantic and beautiful situations in England. I took my mother yesterday to the back of the island, among the rocks and cliffs which edge the sea. She will tell you what she thinks of the scenery. For my part, I feel, every time I survey it, new wonder and admiration. The day was tempestuous, but this added greatly to the grandeur of every object, and particularly of the water. * *

"I preached on the Thanksgiving Day,* contrary, as my mother will inform you, to my first intention and avowal. My text, I think, suited the occasion: Ezra ix. 13—15:—*And after all that is come upon us for our evil deeds, and for our great trespass, seeing that thou our God hast punished us less than our iniquities deserve, and hast given us such deliverance as this; should we again break thy commandments, and join in affinity with the people of these abominations, wouldest not thou be angry with us till thou hadst consumed us, so that there should be no remnant nor escaping? O Lord God of Israel, thou art righteous: for we remain yet escaped, as it is this day: behold, we are before thee in our trespasses: for we cannot stand before thee because of this.* I spoke freely, and considered the war both as an enormous sin and a heavy punish-

---

* Tuesday, June 1, 1802, was ordered to be kept as a Day of Thanksgiving for a General Peace.

ment. The Peace, I observed, was a blessing which should excite our thankfulness, and an interposition of Providence which we should improve. I viewed it as a call of God upon us to break off our sins by righteousness, and particularly those crying sins, the profanation of the sacred name of God by needless oaths, the persecuting men for conscience' sake, the oppression and cruelty practised in the East Indies, and, above every thing else, that horrible enormity, the Slave-Trade."

To his Parents.

"Newport, June 14, 1802.

"After being very much hurried, I left Town* in company with my two friends, Cooke and Harris. We were too experienced to trust to the chance of the outside of the coach, and therefore resolved to travel by night, it making little consequence to us the way we intended to return. Friday, however, was a very fine, tempting day, and we lost a pleasant journey. We took coach at Charing Cross, 5 o'clock Friday evening, and had the pleasure of being drawn quite through London, from Westminster to London Bridge, and thence through the whole length of the Borough. What surprised and amused us a little, was the turning of the coach up the Old Bailey, and its returning just before we reached Smithfield, and stopping at one of the doors of *Newgate*. We soon guessed the cause of this circumstance, and began to prepare for a set of curious companions; but the Londoners, who flocked around us in multitudes, seemed for a time uncertain whether to regard us as State criminals just arrived, or felons of importance about to be carried off towards Botany Bay. Eight poor wretches, chained and ironed and handcuffed by fours, were put upon the coach, and all night we had the clanking of their fetters to furnish us with materials of thinking. They had been brought, it appeared, from Lancaster, and were carrying down to Portsmouth, to be shipped for New Holland. They were unconcerned, and even hardened. A gibbet or two upon the road furnished them with not a little merriment.

"Tuesday, June 15.

"I am well pleased with my journey to London. I should like always to attend the annual Assembly. There is among my General Baptist brethren much good sense, liberality and piety, and not a small degree of zeal in some of them. 'Iron sharpeneth iron,' and the virtues of our fellow-christians raise and animate our own virtues. I have returned from London more disposed to religious activity and exertion. I have thought of and proposed to our friends something in the way of village preaching."

The first annual meeting of the Southern Unitarian Society was held July 15, 1802, at Portsmouth, on which occasion Robert Aspland had the pleasure of meeting Mr. Russell Scott and many other ministers

---

* After attending the General Baptist Assembly.

and friends. The preacher was Dr. Toulmin, who took for his subject, "The Doctrine of the Scriptures concerning the Unity of God and the Character of Jesus Christ." He vindicated the "perfect humanity" of Christ, denying that the Scriptures attributed to him a prior state of dignity. To this doctrine Mr. Aspland and several of his flock who were present were unable to assent, and to them, it is believed, Dr. Toulmin made reference in a note which appeared with the sermon when published.

"Some of the Society to which this discourse was addressed, it may be proper to remark, did not enter into the full force of the argument stated above, and embrace the doctrine of Christ's existence before his appearance in this world, in a state of dignity and glory. But *they* wish to be considered as decidedly of opinion that there is but one God and one Object of religious worship, and that this one God is the *Father only*, and not a Trinity consisting of Father, Son and Holy Spirit. On the other points, as friends of truth and free inquiry, they would preserve a candid temper."

What influence this discourse, and the conversation respecting the Scripture claims of Arianism which followed, had on the mind of Robert Aspland, there is no evidence to shew; but it is certain that not long after his mind was impressed as fervently as Dr. Toulmin's with the truth of the doctrine of the simple humanity of Christ. It was at this meeting that he was appointed Secretary to the Association.

In order that the next letter may be understood, it must be introduced by a portion of a letter from his excellent father.

Robert Aspland, Sen., to his Son.

"Wicken, July 24, 1802.

" * * * Our Calvin* was at Soham last sabbath-day. We met exactly at the meeting gate, and he shook hands with me very civilly. The meeting was very much crowded. We had a good Unitarian discourse, or, more properly, what an Unitarian might have delivered, with one or two exceptions: one was when, speaking of characters that make light of sin, he said, 'And they that make Christ a man, they make light of sin.' His text was Isaiah lv. 6—9. He dwelt much on the readiness of God to pardon and forgive sin on the sinner's returning to Him. After the evening preaching, John Emons had a little conversation with *the bishop* at his brother's. He thanked him for his *anathematic* letter, and told him 'he did not doubt that it was in kindness for him, but that he had missed the mark, and that he (J. E.) was not the character he supposed.' Mr. Fuller told him, 'he was full of fears for

---

* By this name Andrew Fuller was at this time designated.

him, and dared not stand in his place; and that he wondered and regretted that he was carried away by the opinions of a schoolboy.' J. Emons begged him not to repeat that remark, which was unfair. His sentiments, whatever they were, were the result of reading and thinking for himself. Scripture was quoted on both sides. John was resolute in vindicating his opinions. The *bishop* became very warm, and condemned him very bitterly. The dispute would have lasted longer, but they hurried him away, as he was going to R. Fuller's to investigate Mr. B——'s conduct. At parting, the *bishop* said, 'Well, friend Emons, I will shake hands with you as an acquaintance, but not as a brother.' John replied, 'Ah! Mr. Fuller, I doubt you have got too much the spirit of Calvin, and he caused one man to suffer death.' He walked off mumbling something to the contrary."

To his Parents.

"Newport, August 18, 1802.

"Your account of Fuller amuses me. I do not wonder he is enraged against me; against the cause of *Unitarianism* he must, from consistency, as Paul against Christianity, be '*exceedingly mad.*' It is almost strange that he did not preach against us. My best respects await my friend *John Emons* for his zeal and boldness. The story of *Servetus* was well put. They can never bear to hear of it. They affect to deny it; but Calvin's letters are yet extant, in which, after decoying Servetus into Geneva, he informed the magistracy of his abode, and *drove them* on to destroy him. Some of the Calvinists inherit *the temper*, as well as the doctrines, of their master. Nothing so much as their virulent, persecuting spirit confirms me they are distant from the truth. *Socinus* was a persecutor, but not to the extent of Calvin; and Unitarians do not attempt to excuse him (for his persecution was first published in English, I believe, by an Unitarian, Dr. Toulmin), nor will they suffer themselves to be called by his name, which would, they think, imply a recognition of his doctrines. They are called Socinians, but it is by their enemies, and by way of reproach.

"I forget whether I told you that Mr. Marsom was down at Portsmouth at our annual meeting. He came over to the island, and stayed a fortnight. The friends here were highly pleased with him. He possesses a very uncommon skill in Scripture interpretation. Indeed, his whole life has been nothing else than a study of the Scriptures. We spent a great part of the time he was with us in controversial discussion. We held three public conferences in the meeting, which were largely attended, on the Guidance of the Spirit, Future Punishment, the Resurrection, and, along with it, the Nature of the Soul. We maintained that the Spirit of the New Testament is not a person, but an influence; that the leading of the Spirit, strictly so called, was confined to the apostolic age; and that the influence of the Spirit now consists in the operation of the word of Truth. Concerning future punishment, we agreed in general that the notion of eternal torments is a libel on the character of the God of Love and Father of Mercies; that the restoration of all men, after a certain punishment, is a doctrine to be wished, but not made known in the Scriptures; that the doctrine of the destruction or utter extinction of the wicked, is more conformable to the general tenor, the particular expressions and most important images of Scripture, such as, 'not seeing life,' 'having the soul or life destroyed or killed,' being punished with destruction and perdition; and, among other things, particularly the parable of the Tares, and the representation of the lake of fire, which is the 'second death;' but that, however (at least, this was my language), it becomes us to say little about a doctrine which is so awful, and left so apparently undecided (at least, if we may judge from the variety of opinions which prevail concerning it), without using the very language of Scripture. And I am become more and more convinced, that would men once take to use only Scripture language, error, and that species of error which parades among us under the banners of Calvin, would gradually sink into ruin. But human creeds and human interpretations of Scripture have quite supplanted Scripture, and, astonishing as it may seem, a man, as soon as ever he stands up for the language of Scripture, and will use no other, is immediately looked upon as a proper object for church censure (whether among Established Churches or Dissenters) and church excommunication. Thank God! we are free to laugh at their absurdity and to despise their tyranny."

Another letter from Wicken must be given.

Robert Aspland, Sen., to his Son.

"Wicken, Sept. 7, 1802.

" * * * We go on as usual, and spend most of our time from Monday morning to Saturday night behind the counter. We have reason to bless God for the appointment of the sabbath-day. Were it not for *that*, our whole time would be devoted to the world. We continue to meet as usual, generally three times on the sabbath-day, which nearly fills up all my time. We read a section or two out of Doddridge once or twice in the day, and a sermon (sometimes two), either of Dr. Toulmin's or Lowell's. I want some animated practical sermons, if you can recommend some. We have not many hearers, and but few even of them appear to have any love for practical religion.

" I was at Cambridge about three weeks ago, and met Mr. Hall. He asked me where you were. I supposed he knew. He said he was sorry to hear you had gone off from orthodoxy: he asked me if I were not sorry too. What answer I made him, you may judge from his reply. He said, 'I thought you were too well grounded in religion thus to change your sentiments.' He went on to say, that our sentiments had a very bad tendency, as might be seen if they looked at Unitarian congregations. I told him I supposed quite the contrary from the little I knew of them; that there were many worthy persons amongst them striving with all their power to benefit their fellow-men. To this he said, 'No, no!'—and we parted."

To his Parents.

"Newport, Jan. 16, 1803.

"I am glad that you find pleasure in the Unitarian doctrine. It is increasingly dear to me. In the way of fair argument, it can never, I am persuaded, be in the least affected. It is unpopular and even odious, but this to me is rather a proof of its being the doctrine of *Jesus of Nazareth*, than otherwise.

"I preached a New-year's sermon to the Young, on Proverbs xxiii. 23. I have been also preaching several sermons on John xiv. 15, 16, 17, and shall preach several more. I have shewn that this language is a demonstrative proof that Christ was not God. Can God pray? Can one God pray to another God? Or can God pray to himself? I speak out boldly, and, doing so, I can never be followed by the multitude; but, thank God, I am following after Moses and the prophets, Jesus and his apostles.

"Cox has been in the island. I received and entertained him cordially.

"Young C——— has also been here and called upon me, and was very civil. He is clever, and, though a Calvinist, moderate. If he had known my political opinions in their extent, my hatred of priests, and particularly of Nonconformist priests, and my intimacy with Flower, he would have shrunk back from my door. He may, however, know this in part. I am glad, upon the whole, to observe that intolerance in its utmost rigours reigns chiefly among the old men and women who received the strait-laced education of the last century.

"Flower wrote me a very confidential letter not long since; and as he seems looking out for an habitation when he leaves Cambridge, I mean to invite him to the island.

"We are going to put up an organ in our meeting, which I hope will add greatly to the pleasure of our singing. I wish I could do any thing to enliven your little assembly. May you be happy, if you be not, in the common sense of the word, prosperous.

"Remember me to J. Emons. I suppose he battles it now and then with the old *Canaanites*. I should like to hear of his encounters."

At the beginning of the year 1803, he entered on a more capacious house, which he had been able to purchase soon after his settlement in the island. He soon added to his purchase a convenient garden, in which he took the greatest delight. The taste for a garden clung to him to the close of life. Here he loved to walk and talk, or still more silently to meditate and to collect his thoughts for the next sermon, and gather from the varying face of Nature illustrations of moral truth.

His new abode was soon darkened by sorrow—the loss of an infant, very shortly after its birth. It was a remarkable circumstance that, with a very large family, after this early bereavement death did not again enter his dwelling for more than forty years.

To his Parents.
"Newport, Jan. 25, 1803.

"My dear Parents,—You can sympathize with me in the occasion of this letter. Our dear little boy is taken from us by the hand of death! Seemingly well at first, he was soon attacked by the disease that carried off so many of your children, convulsions; and, after repeated and frightful shocks, died this morning, at nine o'clock.

"Poor lamb! This is an affliction we did not altogether anticipate; though, for myself, I must confess I had a secret dread of it. Our hopes, however, were ardent, and our grief is proportionably severe.

"We console ourselves with the assurance that he is not in pain. And religion cheers us with the enlivening hope, that we shall again meet our child in a world where he will be secure from death, and we from all painful bereavements like this. We bury the dear little body on Friday. Sara is in great distress, but, upon the whole, better than I expected. It does seem hard to have the tender child, for whom she suffered so much, torn from her breast. I hope she will fortify her mind with Christian considerations.

"Miss Middleton suffers deeply with us; almost too deeply, I fear, for her health.

"Time and the presence of our child whom Providence has blessed us with, will, I doubt not, moderate our sorrow. At present we cannot but feel that we have sustained a great, if not irreparable loss.

"It is so, but it is hard to say, on such melancholy events as this, when our hopes are all at once dashed to the ground—it is hard to say, 'It is well.'"

The Secretaryship to the Southern Unitarian Society was the means of first introducing him to the acquaintance of Mr. Belsham, which, notwithstanding many dissimilarities of temperament and taste, was afterwards cultivated on both sides in the most friendly spirit for more than a quarter of a century. What the "caution" alluded to in the following letter was, does not appear. It perhaps related to the Arian system of interpretation, for which Mr. Belsham had little respect.

The Rev. Thomas Belsham to the Rev. Robert Aspland.
"Hackney, May 9, 1803.

"Dear Sir,—I am very much obliged by your friendly letter, and am very sensible of the honour which has been done me by the Unitarian Society in asking me to preach their annual sermon. I cannot, however, but feel some regret that I so hastily accepted the office; and I sincerely wish, if it could be allowed without inconvenience, that I might be permitted to withdraw from the engagement. In the first place, I think the compliment ought to be first paid to the ministers in the neighbourhood; and it appears to me something too assuming to take a journey of a hundred miles to perform a service which every minister in the vicinage, who is a member of the Society, is at least equally well qualified to undertake. In the second place, I am equally unwilling either to be laid under restraint, or to give unnecessary offence; and from the caution you suggest, I cannot help apprehending that I may inadvertently wound the feelings and prejudices of some, and perhaps injure the cause I am expected to recommend; and this, I suppose, is what others apprehend likewise. Upon the whole, therefore, I think it would be better for me to defer preaching till the Society has acquired a greater degree of stability and vigour; and I shall be truly obliged to the Committee if they will release me from my promise, and will permit me for the present to postpone my official services upon the Society's anniversary.

"If, however, it should be really inconvenient to provide a substitute for me, I will endeavour, if Providence permit, to the best of my power, to perform the office; and the 13th of July will suit me as well as any day that could be named for the purpose.

"May I trouble you to present my best compliments to Mr. Kirkpatrick, with thanks for his very friendly letter, and for his kind invitation to Fairlee House, of which I propose to avail myself if I visit the island, and in the mean time shall take an opportunity of writing to him.

"It gives me great pleasure to find that my publications have had the good fortune to meet with your approbation. I must, as Dr. Priestley says of himself, expect that nine readers in ten will take part against me, and I must make the most of my tenth man. The esteem of the discerning few is ample compensation for the gross misapprehension or malignant misrepresentation of the many. Great is the Truth, and it will prevail; and though we may not see much good resulting from our personal exertions, it will not be forgotten that we have had it in our hearts to contribute to the sacred cause of pure religion and Christian virtue.

"If you ever come into this part of the world, I should be very glad to see you at Hackney—and am, dear Sir, very sincerely yours,

THOMAS BELSHAM."

Mr. Belsham's scruples were overcome, and on the 13th of July he delivered before the Southern Unitarian Society assembled at Newport an admirable discourse on the Study of the Scriptures.

The Rev. Thomas Belsham to the Rev. Robert Aspland.

"Hackney, Aug. 25, 1803.

"My dear Sir,—I have this day carried my sermon to Mr. Stower's to be printed, and he promises to let me have a proof on Saturday, so that I think it will be forthcoming by the middle or latter end of next week. I have desired that it may be printed of the same size and type as Dr. Toulmin's sermon, and that the paper may be a little better. As it seemed to be the wish of some of my friends, I have added the concluding prayer. Will you speak or write to our friend Scott to send up his excellent prayer before the sermon? * *

"And now, my dear Sir, I have to return my best thanks to you and to my other good friends in the island for the hospitable and friendly reception I met with amongst them, of which I shall ever entertain a grateful and pleasing recollection. My time was short, but, by the obliging contrivance of my friends, was well improved; and I do not know when I have passed three days more agreeably. The beauties and romantic scenery of the Undercliff have left an indelible impression upon my mind. The weather was uncommonly favourable, and we wanted nothing but to see a fleet steering up the Channel. I was very sorry that we were that day deprived of your company, which would have added greatly to the pleasure of the party. I am sorry that our friends from Chichester did not join us. I should have been glad to have met Mr. Youat, of whom I have heard very favourable accounts. I wish you may be allowed to hold the next meeting at Chichester,* but I am not quite so confident in the expectation of it as you appear to be. Persons who wish to stand well with the world do not like openly to join an obnoxious sect. Unitarianism, half a century ago, was the religion of the learned; it is now spreading among the lower classes of society, and is out of fashion in higher life; by and by it will become respectable from numbers, and then it will come into fashion again. But all this is the work of time, and, as honest Matthew Henry says, ' we must not *set our clock before God's dial.*'

"I shall be happy to hear from you, and still more glad to see you. In the mean time, with the warmest wishes for your increasing usefulness, I am, dear Sir, very sincerely yours, THOMAS BELSHAM."

To his Parents.

"Newport, Aug. 27, 1803.

"There is at Newport a Mr. Browne, who heard me on Sunday twice, and introduced himself. He is a Unitarian preacher at Warminster; but was three or four years ago in the living of Cherry-hinton, Cambridgeshire, and, some time previous to that, Fellow and Tutor of St. Peter's College. Conscience has made him what he now is. He gave us a lecture last night (Thursday), and will preach for me on Sunday, probably afternoon. He retains something of

---

* Although the next meeting was not held at Chichester, but at Portsmouth, a large accession of members from the former town took place, in 1804, when the sermons were preached by Mr. Marsom and Mr. Aspland, and the Secretaryship was committed to Mr. Fullagar, who some years afterwards became, and still continues, the zealous minister of the Unitarian society at Chichester.

clerical stiffness, but is intelligent and pleasant. He has just published a sort of Unitarian Liturgy, that is, Eight Forms of Worship, which he uses at his own meeting, and which I would use if I could. It is just the thing for you. I suppose you have no objection to a Form of Prayer. My objections to it have been removed a long time. It is, I think, the most decent and edifying way of conducting public service. The book in question is cheap and small. You can at least get it. Mr. Browne is about to publish a new Bible, of which I will tell you more when it comes out. With such a book in the hands of the congregation, you, who officiate, would be more at liberty; the congregation would feel a greater interest in the service; your numbers would, I think, increase; your devotions would be more respectable; and you would do away the necessity of waking the people every now and then with an explosion of *Methodist powder*. Their coming among you argues, as the doctors say, a *weak pulse*, a *low habit* of mind. There is with Mr. B. a Mr. Purn, who is, at the present time, a Fellow of Peterhouse, Cambridge, on a visit to the island, who has been to meeting and has visited me with Mr. B. He is also a Unitarian, and, I assure you, a very pleasant man."

To Mrs. Aspland (at Mr. Middleton's).

"September 7, 1803.

" * * * I mentioned in my last 'The Farmer's Boy.' It is certainly an interesting tale, but hastily written, and deformed with knotty, strange and mysterious incidents; but all modern romancers are guilty of violence to Nature. The characters are licked into a shape in the latter volume, but they are not master characters. The *ruffian* is not sufficiently humanized, though he is introduced in a striking manner, and acts a part which strikes the imagination; and his setter-on, a sycophant tutor, is made to act the villain without an adequate motive. The knight of the piece—so we may consider Lord Mount Talbot—is too sentimental, and there is too little delicacy in making Lady Lismore the pattern of every virtue—the willing wife of three husbands in succession. To the characters of Herbert and Rose, I have no exception to make, unless it be that there is not enough of them. However, the tale teaches two very good lessons,—the dangers of hasty and indiscreet attachments, and the misery consequent upon concealment between those who are to be together for life. Miss Gunning touches the generous chords of nature when she discourses on love. Take an example of delicate and happy description: 'The head computes by days and years; the heart's calendar is a calendar of moments—of moments so soft, so bright, they are the down on the wings of Time, and the grains of gold amongst the sand of his hour-glass.' Now take an example of bombastic allusion: 'A fresh supply of fuel was prepared to rekindle the dying embers; for fire, like friendship, expires by neglect.' I have said thus much of this work, because Anna knows, and you may probably see, the author, and to give you an opportunity of determining the correctness of my judgment by submitting these remarks to Anna Maria Porter and other novel-writers, who are better critics on this kind of writing than myself.

"Godwin is very amusing to me. To do him justice, he has some grand speculations. I think his characteristic quality—call it good or bad, which you will—is, pouring out his whole soul before you on every subject, and putting you in possession of all, whether treasure or lumber, that his mind possesses; and in this respect his mind resembles Lavater's Journal, and deserves a portion of the species of praise bestowed on it. This way of writing does of course give birth to absurdities and inconsistencies, but I do not know but it stands as fair a chance of truth as the mode of methodical deduction, which is obliged to explain every thing and make every thing bend to a system. At any rate, there is more honesty and simplicity in it. Bacon's Essays are read oftener than Locke's Human Understanding; and Godwin's 'Enquirer' will, if I mistake not, circulate more widely, if not last longer, than his 'Political Justice.'

"Yesterday evening, I heard B——, of R——, at the Upper-house. He has ingenuity, and a fluent elocution, and a sobriety of manner; but with him, and many other ingenious and sensible Calvinists, *orthodoxy is the rod which swallows up all talent.* Their wit, if they have it, has only one way of peeping into day, and that is by pushing out on its horns some new and fantastic ornament of the gothic and motley pile of notions within whose precincts they are imprisoned. When I hear these declaimers, I pity Christianity 'fallen amongst thieves,' and feel all the ardours of *Samaritan* charity and love. * * * I spent the evening, by express invitation, at Mr. Harris's (how very kind they are!), where we passed an unusually pleasant hour or two, talking chiefly on *Heraldry*,—a dry stock, you will say; but we took occasion from it to branch out upon a number of political and moral subjects. To cull flowers from what the vulgar term dry sticks, is the true and genuine science of life.

"I think of preaching to-night on Sleep. It will afford me occasion of making not a few moral and devout reflections. I made them to myself last night, from twelve to one o'clock, when I could not sink into obliviousness."

The Peace of Amiens was of short duration. In May, 1803, France and England were once more engaged in hostilities. Napoleon renewed the project of 1797, when large bodies of troops were assembled on the coasts of Normandy and Flanders for the invasion of England. In the autumn of 1803, it was all but universally believed that the First Consul meditated an attempt to plant the tri-coloured flag on the Tower of London. From its position between the coasts of England and France, the Isle of Wight was regarded, both by the inhabitants and the government, as exposed to peculiar danger of invasion. With the letter describing this state of affairs, the present Chapter must close.

To his Parents.

"Newport, Oct. 17, 1803.

"In the present state of trepidation and alarm, you must be anxious to hear from us, especially as we may be supposed from our situation to be more than others exposed to danger. We are, I assure you, in great apprehension; that is, the major part of us; for there are some here, as there are every where, who affect to despise the menaces of invasion, and to believe it wholly impracticable. Government, however, do certainly expect the French, and they have, I believe, given out that the Isle of Wight is likely to be one of the places of attack. We are well guarded, on the whole, with shipping— very poorly with troops, the whole island, volunteers and all, not containing more than 5000, though several thousands are daily expected, and many regiments are on the other side of the Channel, waiting the first signal to come over to our help. Our best defence and our chief trust is our *rocks*, which present a rough front and a fearless and threatening aspect to the enemy. Buonaparte will, I hope, find them *invincible*. The consequences of an invasion here would be dreadful, we should find it so difficult to get away. The ladies are beginning to migrate already. Boats are secured by order of government to carry away the women, old men and children, and portable and valuable property, on the first approach of the enemy's flotilla. The men must of course await the event, and I think it will be best for the women to await it also. Where can they go? What place will be safe? If Sara and the child should fly, they shall come into Cambridgeshire; certainly Wicken will be one of the securest situations in the world. You must not be surprised, therefore, to see the fugitives coming upon you without warning. London and all great towns would be a scene of dreadful riot if the enemy should be able to effect a landing. I would sooner be in the Isle of Wight than in them.—I am glad my profession excuses me from military service at this warlike period; yet, in case of extremities, I suppose I must do something, and indeed at such a time inactivity would be more intolerable than active danger. All classes of the inhabitants of Newport who are not enrolled in the volunteer corps have this day met, on a hill adjacent to the town, to arrange their services, and to receive directions how to act, should the alarm of invasion be given. They expect to receive pikes or some such weapon. Bills are stuck up by order of Lord Cavan, our military chief, informing us what signals will be given, both by day and night, should the French approach the coast. He has received orders not to sleep out of the island. All this looks very black; and I am told the farmers are ordered to burn their corn as soon as they see a French army; and the same directions have been given concerning the barracks, of which you know we have several.

"Still, I am not frightened, for I think that the chances are greatly against the success of an invasion. It is impossible for the Corsican to transport a large host into this country, without culpable remissness on the part of our

Ministers. Upon them, indeed, no reliance can be placed; they are babies warring with giant events. I hope as earnestly for their downfal as I do for that of Buonaparte. Ireland is, I think, the object of the invasion; though present times are so strange and eccentric, and the French are so wonderfully audacious, that I shall not be surprised at any thing; no, not should the capital of England become the seat of French usurpation and tyranny. I shall preach on Wednesday morning on the subject of our crimes and our danger, and the opening prospect of the large confused drama acting before us: text, Luke xxi. 25, 26. I shall write the sermon, for fear of being charged with sedition and removed to Winchester or St. James's."

CHAPTER IX.

The Proclamation enjoining the observance of a Fast Day on Oct. 19, 1803, declared that the people ought "to humble themselves before Almighty God, and in the most devout and solemn manner send up their prayers and supplications to the Divine Majesty, for obtaining pardon of their sins, and for averting those heavy judgments which their manifold provocations had most justly deserved." In strict accordance with this direction of the First Magistrate was the discourse prepared and preached by Robert Aspland at Newport. Passing by the popular and, from local circumstances, tempting subject of the threatened invasion, which not unnaturally was the staple of most of the sermons of the day, he chose the more difficult topic of "Divine Judgments on Guilty Nations." It required deep convictions in the preacher's mind, and a courageous application of his principles to the political and moral state of the country, to rescue such a topic from the merest commonplace. Robert Hall, in preparing his discourse for the same occasion, at first meditated an "enumeration of our national sins," but confessed* that "he was diverted from it by observing that these themes, from the press at least, seem to make no kind of impression, and that whatever the most skilful preacher can advance is fastidiously repelled as stale and professional declamation." "The people in general," he added, "are settled into an indifference so profound, with respect to all such subjects, that the preacher who arraigns their vices in the most vehement manner, has no reason to be afraid of exciting their displeasure; but it is well if, long before he has finished his reproofs, he has not lulled them to sleep." There was no drowsiness in the chapel at Newport; the congregation, largely increased on

---

* See the Preface to the second edition of his Sermon, entitled "The Sentiments proper to the present Crisis."

this occasion by the presence of persons usually attending Methodist and Calvinistic places of worship, listened with interest that never once flagged to a discourse which far exceeded the ordinary length of sermons. In a prefatory address, the preacher disclaimed fasting as part of the Christian discipline, and while he denied the magistrate's right to interfere with the religion of the people, vindicated his obedience to the Royal Proclamation as a simple act of patriotism. After explaining his text and shewing how applicable some portions of the prophecy fulfilled at the destruction of Jerusalem were to the circumstances by which they were surrounded, he selected, as national sins calculated to draw down the Divine judgments, eagerness for war, the oppressions practised by earthly rulers, the alliance of the Christian religion with the civil power, the wrongs of Ireland, the subjugation of the East Indies, the countenance given to Slavery and the Slave-trade, the multiplication of oaths, and the severity of the Penal laws. In the latter part of the discourse, he held up the events then acting on the theatre of the world as the prelude to some mighty display of God's providence. With an ardour which the wisdom of after years taught him to regard as unduly sanguine and enthusiastic, he ventured to anticipate the speedy fulfilment of prophecy in the destruction of the Papal power and of all allied ecclesiastical establishments, and in the national restoration of the Jews. The sermon closed with an "eloquent peroration,"* descriptive of the illustrious era designed to close the long series of God's providential arrangements.

The improved taste of Mr. Aspland in later periods of his life enabled him to perceive, and he was free to acknowledge, some gaudiness in the style and some exaggeration in the sentiments of his Fast Sermon in 1803. But he reflected to the last with satisfaction on his having thus early published his protest against the cruelties of the Penal Code of England. To appreciate the value of his contribution to right views on this subject, it should be remembered that it preceded by several years the humane, yet slowly successful, efforts of Romilly to wipe the stain of bloodguiltiness from the Statute-book of his country. As the

---

* Of this glowing passage (as the readers of the Christian Reformer have been already informed by him whose able and friendly pen traced in our last volume the "Tribute to the Memory" of Mr. Aspland,—a paper of which frequent use will hereafter be made by the writer of this biography) a beneficed clergyman, the late Rector of Old Swinford, in Worcestershire, "availed himself—perhaps without being aware of the source whence he filled his urn—certainly without acknowledging the obligation."—C. R., N. S., II. 103.

sermon is now somewhat rare, the passage reprobating the severity of the Penal Laws of England is here extracted. Other passages might be quoted of greater verbal power, but not one more pure in style or more wise in sentiment.

"The only legitimate object of punishment in a State is the public good, including, when it is not in irremoveable opposition to the welfare of the community, the good of the offender himself. The life of a delinquent can never be justly taken away, unless its continuance be necessarily incompatible with the order, that is with the existence of society, and unless his character be such, which can rarely happen, as to exclude all possibility of reformation. What a waste of human blood, then, is every year made on our scaffolds; whilst almost every succeeding year sees also a deeper dye added to the too sanguinary hue of our penal statutes. This severity defeats its own end: the number of crimes having multiplied in England, as has been frequently shewn by moral writers, in exact proportion to the increase of its capital punishments. The frequency and publicity of spectacles of death in a State, deprave the hearts of the common people by familiarizing them to an awful act of justice, which, in obedience to humanity and that it may be a salutary restraint upon crimes, ought never to be contemplated or witnessed without terror. Another unhappy consequence of the extreme rigour of our penal laws is, that all the discriminations which morality establishes between different acts of delinquency are confounded by it. *Death* is the utmost severity that the law can inflict on the most atrocious criminal; yet this severest and last of human punishments is denounced in our Statute-book, and actually inflicted in the course of our criminal jurisprudence, upon numberless offences. If we inure the people to scenes of blood, under the forms and sanctions of justice, can we wonder that in periods of riot and convulsion, they should practise in return all the unsparing ferocity which the juridical institutions and practice of their country have taught them? Our legislative errors thus punish themselves: and if there be a Creator of man, and if he have not altogether forgotten the child of his own image, the wanton barbarity with which we immolate so many human lives on the altars of custom and commercial policy, in spite of the remonstrances of experience, humanity, philosophy and religion, must excite against us the Divine anger, and expose us to its rebukes and corrections. The Supreme Being is addressing us with the thunder of his power, with the voice of his judgments—*'What have ye done? the voice of your brethren's blood crieth unto me from the ground.'*"

The preacher was urgently pressed by many of his hearers to print the sermon, but at first declined from an unwillingness to expose himself too early to the ordeal of public criticism. Subsequently, when he became acquainted with the prevalent tone of the Fast Sermons published by Dissenting ministers,* in which the warmth of their patriotism had, in his opinion, seduced them into a more warlike tone than became the ministers of a religion of peace, and in some cases into the expression of undeserved and fulsome praise towards the King's Ministers, he so far complied with the request previously made to him as to place the manuscript in the hands of his friend, Mr. Benjamin Flower, of Cambridge, with permission, if he saw fit, to print it, with any additions he might choose to make.

Mr. Flower instantly perceived that the discourse of his young friend was characterized by great power, and believing that it would prove a timely antidote to the more courtly effusions of other Dissenters, immediately announced it for publication. The following letter reports progress.

Mr. Flower to Rev. Robert Aspland.

"Cambridge, Jan. 29, 1804.

"Dear Sir,—In the first place, let me congratulate you on the safety of Mrs. Aspland and on the addition to your family.† Mrs. Flower unites with me in best wishes, hoping that the little one may be spared, and prove a grain of *salt* to be added to the little handful remaining in this corrupt world, which may preserve it from putrefaction.

"In the next place, I must entreat your patience for a few days delay in the publication of your sermon. The fact is, no time has been lost in printing; but when I took my pen in hand, I found my work increasing. The sermons of Hall and Fuller, the more I read them, the more mischievous I thought their tendency. I have one long note on the injustice of the war, which I

---

* Some excellent sermons, quite free from the faults mentioned above, were printed on this occasion by Mr. Belsham, Mr. Wellbeloved, Mr. Rowe and Mr. Richard Wright. On the other hand, Mr. Hall's discourse, magnificent as a specimen of heroic eloquence, was open to the charge of befitting the mouth rather of a general leading his troops to battle than of a Christian minister, and of strengthening the hands of those who were disposed to abridge rather than extend constitutional freedom. Dr. Rippon delivered on the same day a sermon at the Drum-head in the fort, Margate, which he afterwards repeated before the East Kent Association of Protestant Dissenters, and before his own congregation at Carter Lane, in which he indulged in encomiums upon Mr. Pitt, equally infelicitous and unbecoming the pulpit. According to Dr. Rippon, the Right Hon. William Pitt "made *half* a globe tremble," and was himself "an ornament and long-continued blessing to the *whole* globe." But even this bad taste and want of truth was exceeded when the Dr. came to speak of George III., whom he described as "the friend of the universe," and as one in whose person God "had beatified the British empire with the best of earthly monarchs."

† The child here referred to lived but a few days. Its death was recorded in a letter inserted in the last Chapter. The date of that letter (the error is in the original MS.) should have been not 1803, but 1804.

have written to remove the wretched ignorance which prevails in the religious world on the subject. I think I shall make *Hall* appear *little* in a way that neither his friends nor foes can expect, and shall put a *bit* in the mouth of this fiery steed which will make him champ and snort and foam a little, but which will not be found out till they come to the concluding note.* I have given *Evans* a gentle trimming.† The Preface will contain about 24 pages, principally of remarks on Hall's abominable sentiments respecting national sins, the respect due to rulers, &c., and vindicating the right of discussion and of resistance, &c. * * * I really am not sorry that we set up this joint protest against the servility and corruption of the times. Rippon's sermon is come to a third edition.

"In a letter I received this morning, I am informed George Clayton has accepted an invitation to settle at Lock's-fields (Walworth) meeting. My wife was, upon the whole, pleased with his company when she was at Southampton. I shall be too late for the post if I add any thing more than that, with Mrs. F.'s kind respects, I remain, dear Sir, yours sincerely,

B. FLOWER."

That Robert Aspland's sermon obtained an immediate and a wider circulation by the aid of Mr. Flower's well-known name, is probable; but that the good fame of the publication was aided by the remarks of

---

* Mr. Flower very rashly hinted a charge of plagiarism against Mr. Hall, alleging that some of the thoughts and expressions in "The Sentiments proper to the present Crisis," were borrowed from a pamphlet, recently published, entitled, "What have we to Fight for? An Address to the Freeholders of Middlesex, &c., on their Duty as Britons at the present Crisis." A candid critic would find no justification for a charge of plagiarism. The coincidences are such as may easily be accounted for by the obviousness of the sentiment. But even if Mr. Hall did borrow, such is the transmuting power of genius, what he received in iron he paid back in silver. Mr. Hall met the charge, in a letter addressed to the Monthly Reviewers, with the declaration, " that he had never heard of the pamphlet on which he was supposed to have committed a plagiarism till he read the extracts in Mr. Flower's notes, and that he had never seen the pamphlet itself to that day."

† Mr. Evans, in his Fast Sermon at Worship Street, published " with an Account of the Destruction of the Spanish Armada," had noticed with satisfaction that the Prayer drawn up for the use of the Established Church on the Fast Day had a clause indicative of good wishes for *Dissenters*. Mr. Flower objected that the Prayer was hypocritical, inasmuch as the Bishops supported the Penal laws against the Dissenters which disgraced the Statute-book.

This portion of the Prayer is worth preserving as an ecclesiastical curiosity: "And give us all grace to put from us all religious dissensions, that they who agree in the essentials of our most holy faith and look for pardon through the merits and intercession of the Saviour, may, notwithstanding their differences upon points of doubtful opinion and in the forms of external worship, still be united in the bonds of Christian charity, and fulfil thy blessed Son's commandment of loving one another as he has loved them."

the honest and fearless printer, can scarcely be maintained. There is in both Preface and Notes a tone of personal acrimony which the present writer will not justify; and he will not conceal his regret that Mr. Hall and Mr. Fuller, both of whom had been friends of Robert Aspland in the days of his orthodoxy, should have been the objects of Mr. Flower's attack in this publication.

The "Divine Judgments on Guilty Nations" excited considerable attention. In Mr. Vidler's Magazine,* the sermon was welcomed " as one born out of due time, and as, among Fast Sermons, what the apostle of the Gentiles was among his brethren, *greater than them all.*" In more orthodox circles, especially amongst the Baptists, it met with a different reception. The wounds of some who resented the author's secession from the ranks of orthodoxy, if not still festering, were green. The attack by his associate on two of the greatest of their leaders was naturally resented, and a portion of their anger fell on him. One of the principal Dissenting publishers in London was Mr. William Button, who united with the business of bookselling in Paternoster Row, the pastorship† of a Baptist church in Dean Street. He had been Mr. Flower's agent heretofore, and his name appeared on the title-page as one of the publishers of the sermon. But it was placed in the *Index Expurgatorius* of the Baptist Inquisition. The resentment of the divine proved stronger than the acquisitiveness of the bookseller, and not a copy of the obnoxious pamphlet would the reverend trader sell. Nevertheless, a large impression was sold off in a few weeks. As the work cannot be smothered, its author and his ally must be crushed. This work is undertaken, but anonymously, by Mr. Fuller,‡ in the *Theological and Biblical Magazine* for April. The review opens thus:

"Mr. Aspland is a young man of some talents. We suppose this may be his first essay as an author. He promises to be a proficient in the Socinian school, having learnt with ease to explain away a Christian duty which does not suit him, and to shew how little the Scriptures may be made to mean. His performance is a clever thing of the kind; some may think, however, that it would have been quite as much to the honour of so young a man to have

---

* "The Universal Theological Magazine and Impartial Review," Vol. I. 164.

† He was ordained in 1755, and presided over the church at Dean Street more than forty years. He resigned the pulpit in 1813, and died in 1821. In the opinion of the historian of the English Baptists, his example did not recommend the union of a secular and a sacred calling.

‡ See Mr. Flower's Preface to the second edition of the Fast Sermon, p. vi.

introduced himself to the world under some other character than that of a national censor."

Mr. Fuller probably remembered that this "young man" had as a youth of not sixteen years withstood him in the field of politics in Mr. Thomas's parlour,* and before he was twenty had taught some of the Cambridgeshire Baptists to stray from the orthodox fold. In now publicly rebuking an opponent for the equal crimes of youthfulness and judging for himself, Mr. Fuller indulged both his resentment and a constitutional arrogance of temper. But his treatment of the youthful "heretic" was mild when compared with his assault on Mr. Flower, than which nothing more coarse or venomous ever disgraced the periodical religious press.†

The Fast Sermon has been dwelt upon at some length, both because its publication was a critical event in the life of Robert Aspland, and because the little controversies which it led to throw some light on the spirit of the age.

It was about this time that he began to contribute to the periodical literature of the Dissenters. It may be convenient here to enumerate the articles which are known to be his, published previously to his assuming the Editorial functions. To the IXth volume of the Universal Theological Magazine he contributed first an excellent letter,‡ signed *A Nazarene*, reprobating the demand of a confession of faith at a minister's ordination. The remonstrance was occasioned by the report§ of an ordination at Portsea of Mr. John Kingsford. The Rev. Daniel Taylor gave the introductory discourse, and afterwards called upon the minister "for the confession of his faith." The same number of the Magazine also contained a brief report of the meeting of the Southern Unitarian Society. The following passage is deserving of notice:

"The Society took into consideration the propriety of adding to their Rules some more explicit declaration of their sentiments and design; and resolved unanimously to signify to the public, that by calling themselves Unitarians,

---

* See Memoir, Chap. iii.

† Both Mr. Aspland and Mr. Flower were defended, and the reviewer in the Theological and Biblical Magazine rebuked, by a contemporary but anonymous writer in the Universal Theological Magazine, I. 313—317. The letter is signed *Justus*.

‡ P. 66.

§ Vol. VIII. p. 166.

they mean only to avow their belief in and desire of promoting the doctrine of the simple Unity of God; the Unity as opposed to the Trinity; and the advocates of which are Unitarians in contradistinction from Trinitarians."

This ground, probably taken at this time, in part at least, from a lingering attachment to Arian principles, was subsequently and through life maintained from considerations of a more catholic nature. Though he soon discarded the doctrine of the pre-existence, he was unwilling to make any distinctions between the worshipers of the Father of Jesus Christ, and asserted the equal title of him that received and him that rejected the doctrine of Christ's pre-existence to the Unitarian name. Mr. Belsham, following Dr. Lardner, was disposed to limit the title Unitarian to a stricter use, and hinted his disapprobation of the Magazine report in the following letter:

Rev. Thomas Belsham to Rev. Robert Aspland.
"Hackney, September 13, 1803.

"Dear Sir,—I see a very *cautious* account of our meeting in Mr. Vidler's Magazine. I am much mistaken if such caution will answer the purpose of those who use it.

"I had the pleasure of hearing Mr. Vidler last Sunday se'nnight, and was much pleased with his plain and energetic manner of treating his subject, and with the numbers, the seriousness and the attention of the audience."

His second contribution to the Magazine* was an essay, with the signature *Sibboleth*, on Cant Religious Terms. This was his definition of his subject:

"All those terms which are used without any clear, determinate ideas attached to them, or to which are affixed ideas that do not belong to them, according to the usage of the best writers, or which are limited to the expression of a part only of their genuine meaning,—as also all those that are adopted as the watchword of a party, which are intended, like another freemason's sign, to distinguish and certify that party at all times and in all places, and which are repeated as often as the common forms of salutation, may, without hypercriticism or captiousness, be called CANT TERMS."

The terms selected in the essay for illustrating the subject are, "Orthodoxy," "Evangelical," "Grace" and "Gracious;" and, to relieve the essay from the charge of partiality, the author censures the incorrect use of the term "Virtue," as including piety as well as morality; the narrowness of the term "Brother," given by the General Baptists to their teachers; and the bigoted assumption of exclusive

---
* Vol. IX. pp. 188—195.

reasonableness in the title "Rational Dissenters." He was also the author of Remarks on J. M.'s (Marsom's) Observations on John xii. 40, 41, by *A Nazarene*,* controverting the application of the passage to Jesus Christ. Mr. Marsom replied,† and not without justice complained of the harshness of some of the expressions of " A Nazarene." Robert Aspland's rejoinder appeared in the Ist volume of the New Series of the Magazine, p. 24, and occasion was taken not merely to retract the expressions which had pained Mr. Marsom, but to pay a well-deserved compliment to him for his admirable tract entitled, " The Impersonality of the Holy Ghost," which was commended for " the ingenuity of the criticisms, the fairness of the reasoning, and the simplicity of the style." His other contributions to Magazine literature previous to 1806, so far as they are known, were unimportant.

We now return to his private correspondence, and find the letters to Wicken written at the beginning of 1804 still dwelling on the threatened invasion.

To his Parents.

"Newport, Jan. 2, 1804.

" I have waited some time in expectation of the articles you were so good as to send us before I wrote; they, however, are not arrived; nor are we certain that they are not giving the fishes in the Channel a Christmas treat, for about the time that they ought to have been here a vessel from Portsmouth to Cowes was lost. Indeed, the weather for the last fortnight has been unusually boisterous and the sea tremendously rough. This, more than any thing else, I believe, has kept Master Buona from paying us a visit; as all accounts state that he has embarked, and only waits a clear course and a favourable wind. If, as is also reported, Suffolk and Norfolk are the intended points of attack, you are not much more secure from danger in your obscure corner than we are in the Isle of Wight; the only danger in all places is, that of being pillaged by a lawless soldiery, French or English; and everybody living in the vicinity of the military operations and the invasion, must expect to suffer from these ruffians. The alarm has greatly subsided here. We can talk of invasion with as much indifference and pleasantry as they do in the Highlands of Scotland.

" You have heard, I suppose, that Mrs. Flower has been at the Isle of Wight. Every thing seemed to promise us the addition of them to our circle of friends, but I believe they will not settle in the island. House-rent is generally high, and the distance from London, Mr. F. thinks, would be injurious to his business, that of general and book printing."

---

* Vol. IX. p. 266. † P. 307.

"Newport, Jan. 10, 1804.

"This day week (Tuesday, the 3rd inst.) we were in great confusion, the town having been alarmed early in the morning with a report that the French were at the back of the island. The volunteers were under arms all day, expecting every minute to hear the drum beat to arms, and to march against the enemy. It was not till towards evening that the alarm completely subsided. The regulars had been marched out of Newport in dead of night, and were just prevented, by the arrival of the commander-in-chief, from frightening us out of our wits with their drums.

"I now begin to think that the invasion of this country is altogether impracticable. At least, it must be attempted soon or never. Buonaparte has, I guess, well nigh run the length of his tether. He begins to find that there are some things impossible even to him; and I hope he will soon find, also, that there are degrees of tyranny which it is not in human nature to bear."

"May 25, 1804.

"* * * What think you of the new Administration? We were all *tired* to death with Mr. Addington; Mr. Pitt, I believe, will *worry* us to death. It is a wretched Ministry, and cannot possibly stand long; at least my wishes lead me to expect as much.

"I might have forgotten my dislike to the general tenor of the British Government, had not my feelings been renewed by the odious and oppressive Income Tax—a tax which indicates that we are greatly fallen from the proud spirit of our forefathers, and that the last barrier to the liberties of the people, that of public opinion, is broken down.

"We are both well. I was confined with an ulcerous sore-throat a few weeks back, and was unable to preach two Sundays. Mr. Potticary preached once each day for me, and Mr. Fullagar (our friend who writes in the Magazine) the other times. He is a pleasant and acceptable speaker, and will be very useful."

The next letters open the prospect of a change of residence.

The Rev. Thomas Belsham to the Rev. Robert Aspland.

"Hackney, May 23, 1804.

"My dear Sir,—I trouble you with these lines at the joint request of Mr. Shore, of Meersbrook, and his son, Mr. Samuel Shore, of Norton Hall, near Sheffield; who are desirous to know whether you are disposed to listen to an application from them to settle with a small congregation at Norton, of which they are the principal supporters. The place is lately built, and about the size of your own. The congregation used formerly to assemble in Mr. Shore's hall. It consists of seventy to a hundred hearers, but I believe there are few subscribers besides themselves, *i. e.* the family of Shores, who are indeed most truly respectable and liberal. * * * They have hitherto had Pædo-baptist ministers, but I do not imagine that a difference of opinion upon that subject would be attended with any inconvenience or regarded as an objection.

"When Mr. W. Smith was visiting at Mr. Shore's two months ago, he undertook to write to you upon the subject; but as they have heard nothing about it from him or you, they presume that he has been too busy in settling the *ministry* of the nation, to think of settling the *ministry* at Norton. As, however, the time is short—for their present minister, Mr. Williams, leaves them at Midsummer—they wish to know whether you are disposed to listen to an application from them, and to take the matter into consideration. Otherwise, it will be necessary for them to be looking out elsewhere.

"When you have made up your mind upon the subject, I request the favour of a line from you, and in the meantime, with compliments to Mrs. Aspland, I am, dear Sir, very sincerely yours, THOMAS BELSHAM.

"Your eloquent and manly discourse upon the late Fast has deservedly attracted much attention and applause."

In his reply, Robert Aspland expressed his regard for the Newport congregation, yet admitted the desirableness of a change, if it would free him from the drudgery of a school, or enable him in any way to devote a larger portion of his time to study and the ministry. The letter also reveals considerable theological progress. The passages which describe this are too important to be omitted.

To Rev. Thomas Belsham.

"Newport, May 28, 1804.

"* * * I should like to officiate among a congregation *purely Unitarian*. I came to Newport an Arian in sentimemt, and found the greater part of the people such. I have gone on to Mr. Wilberforce's 'half-way house,' and have unfortunately left them behind me. This circumstance lessens in some degree the cordiality which I think ought to subsist between a minister and his congregation,* and opposes a kind of barrier to my inquiries and pulpit discussions, not very agreeable to my views of Christian independence and honesty.

"My laxness with regard to baptism is an objection to my serving a church in whose constitution the rite is accounted fundamental. I am not (far from it!) a Pædo-baptist, but I consider that both parties have lamentably exaggerated the importance of an unimportant ceremony."

In accordance with a suggestion made by Mr. Belsham, Robert Aspland, as soon as his holidays set him at liberty, paid a visit to Norton. With the character of Mr. Shore, of Meersbrook, and of his son

---

* Some member of the congregation remarked to him about this time the change observable in his preaching, in a tone that fell on his ear like a reproach, and he felt compelled to plead the charter of perfect liberty that had been granted him when he undertook the pastoral office.

residing at Norton Hall, he was greatly delighted; and they were increasingly desirous of securing his services both as a minister and as a tutor to the young people at Norton Hall. His decision was, however, necesssarily postponed. He visited Wicken, Cambridge and London, before he returned to the island,—at the latter place preaching at Worship Street, Parliament Court, and at the Gravel-Pit, Hackney.

He was greeted by his flock on his return to Newport with unusual affection, mingled with an anxious apprehension of receiving a confirmation of the rumour which had preceded him, of his intention to quit them. The difficulties of coming to a decision were greatly increased by the tokens which daily greeted him of their sincere attachment. He found that he had unconsciously formed an exaggerated estimate of their dislike of his bolder theology, and he was much touched by their generous offer to increase their subscriptions by nearly a third, in order to retain his services and to release him from the burthen of a school. His decision was at length made to remove to Norton.

The Rev. Thomas Belsham to the Rev. Robert Aspland.

"Hackney, Sept. 30, 1804.

"My dear Sir,—I thank you for your letter announcing to me your acceptance of the invitation from Norton; and as I doubt not that you have acted upon the best principles and to the best of your judgment in the case, I firmly believe that it will prove ultimately beneficial both to yourself and to the public; though I acknowledge that I feel deep regret that talents like yours should be buried in so obscure a retreat. But you must often come to town to edify and instruct us here. We need it much, for there are few in these times who can endure *sound* doctrine.

"I know nothing of the conduct of Mr. Vidler's Magazine; but I should have a much better opinion of it if it were under your direction. Many thanks to you for your kind present of your second edition. What an infamous, lying libel is that of Andrew Fuller upon B. Flower! Such, forsooth, is the superior excellence of the Calvinistic above the Socinian scheme! But I suppose the elect may do what they please. God sees no sin in his people.

"The death of my brother Kenrick was a very awful and affecting visitation of Divine Providence. It is severely felt in the circle of his family and near connections, and in the present state of things it appears to be an irreparable loss to the cause of rational Christianity, which had very few warmer friends or abler advocates. If I did not believe pure Christianity to be the cause of God, and, consequently, that its ultimate success is certain, I should almost despair of its progress, when I see the lights of the world, one after another, withdrawn, and so few rising up to supply their places. But we may safely trust Infinite Wisdom with the direction of its own concerns; and we are sure that if the cause of truth and goodness is not accelerated in that way and by those instruments which human sagacity prescribes, it will be carried on in a better way and by more efficacious means. We know in whom we have believed.—The Queen's book is come out, with an Introduction by the Bishop of London, and *stereotyped* by Lord Stanhope. I have just dipped into it. I presume it is the Catechism which she learned when she was a child, and which she still faithfully adheres to. I have just glanced over it as it lies in Johnson's shop. It is a mass of absurdity. Even the Wilberforces and Thorntons will be ashamed of it.

"It teaches us that Christ's descent into hell is the first degree of his *exaltation*, and that after his resurrection he went there, body and soul, to shew himself to the devils and damned spirits, in order to frighten them.

"This doctrine is, I dare say, as new to you as it was to me; and as, though it may be palatable food to a German taste, it requires some time for an English stomach to digest it, I shall leave you for the present to ruminate upon it; and, with compliments to Mrs. Aspland, I remain, dear Sir, your affectionate friend and faithful servant, THOMAS BELSHAM."

To his Parents.

"Newport, Sept. 25, 1804.

"Dear Parents,—In my last I left you, as I myself then was, in suspense about the invitation I had received from Norton. It may be interesting to hear the history of my proceedings in the business, as well as to know my final determination." [Then follows a statement, the substance of which has been anticipated in the previous narrative.] "Thus you see my mind is made up. My friends here fully justify me, and are, I believe, convinced that I have behaved handsomely to them. I have received another invitation from a congregation at Warminster, about to be vacated by Mr. Browne, whom I mentioned to you last year. Of course I have declined this, and stand engaged to go to Norton next Lady-day. We are all well. Mr. Marsom is now with me in the *trinity* capacity of friend, usher and curate."

The healthful air of Derbyshire, and the prospect of having at Norton a spacious house, revived in his mind the desire which he had so strongly felt and urged when he settled at Newport, that his parents should spend the closing years of their lives under his roof. His excellent father, who felt his strength declining, was now not unwilling to entertain the idea. But in the designs of God's providence it was otherwise arranged. In October, Robert Aspland was hastily summoned to Wicken on account of his father's serious illness. He arrived not only in time to receive his blessing, but had the satisfaction to see him revive, and left him not without the hope of his going on to convalescence. Robert Aspland's letters during the remainder of that month were frequent and most affectionate, full of considerate suggestions for the comfort of the invalid, and all written in the largest and boldest character of his always good manuscript, to suit the failing sight of his sick parent. On the first of November, his fears were again aroused by the report of a relapse. He again hastened to Wicken, and the sequel is best told in his own sorrow-charged letters.

To Mrs. Aspland, Newport.

"Wicken, Nov. 5, 1804.

"My dear Sara,—Our worst fears are realized. Isaac met me at Newmarket this morning, and informed me—of what, I must confess, I expected yet dreaded to hear—my poor father left the world on Saturday morning.

"We are all here again; William alone was in time to behold his father alive. My arrival earlier, there is reason to believe, would have given great satisfaction to the dear patient, who had something which he wished to communicate, but could not make himself understood, on account of the failure of his speech. He seems to have suffered much;—the pains of dying were protracted from Wednesday night—the time when the letter was written by my uncle to me—to the period of his departure. My uncle and aunt have been extremely assiduous in alleviating my mother's affliction; they are much affected by this melancholy occurrence.

"You may conceive that ours is now a house of mourning. My feelings are too confused for me to describe. I can scarcely bring myself to believe that I have lost for ever a revered and beloved parent. As yet I have not ventured to look at the overthrow of life and sense in so dear and venerable an object.

"Wednesday afternoon is fixed upon for the funeral,—a melancholy and dreadful ceremony. There is something in the pomp of death, as exhibited in a country burial, more awful to me than all his pangs. Before you receive this I shall, I suppose, have passed through this afflictive office.

"*Here* I am obliged to *assume* a fortitude which really I have not. Inwardly I am a prey to a thousand gnawing remembrances, but it is necessary that I should put on an appearance of serenity, and exemplify the lessons I inculcate. Not that I am destitute of motives to equanimity and resignation. Something I have learnt from Philosophy, much from Christianity, to mitigate the terrors of the grave. In my father's case, two considerations are of great avail to strengthen and support me: first, his good and useful life; secondly, his title to the resurrection of the just. In some moments I consider him as asleep, rejoice that I shall soon lie down with him, and exult in the firm hope that we shall both awake together and be re-united to our dear friends and relatives in indissoluble connection. The hopes that it inspires into mourners I consider as the primary and most essential part of our religion.

"Remember me kindly to Mr. Marsom. His spouse, daughter and grandson drank tea at St. Martin's Lane with me on Sunday. Mrs. M. is perfectly willing that Mr. M. should stay with us *as long as he can be useful;* but I would recommend him, if he would recover (or, if he please, preserve) her affections, to write a very loving and dutiful epistle.

"Love to our girl. Kiss her from papa, and tell her that poor grandfather talked of her to the last."

To Mrs. Aspland, Newport.

"Wicken, Nov. 8, 1804.

"To-day (Thursday), my dear Sara, you will receive the mournful intelligence of my poor father's death. I know it will deeply affect you, but I hope you will not suffer it to affect you *too* deeply. He was, truly, a good man and a tender parent. Poor Isaac and I often say to one another, 'We shall not look upon his like again.' My mother, after the first gush of sorrow on my arrival, was tolerably composed until yesterday, when we had to pass through the awful ceremony of interment. While we retained the corpse in our possession, our loss seemed to be but partial—we could testify our respect by visiting and watching around it, and vent our sorrow by dropping our heart-wrung tears upon it—but the taking it away seemed to be such an affecting remembrance of our loss, and the house seemed such a perfect void! About 3 o'clock, nearly all the respectable parishioners assembled at the house, to the number, I dare say, of fifty. It was most trying for us to see all the funereal preparations carrying on around us; my mother could scarcely support it. Never shall I forget the overpowering moment when the venerable remains were carried out into the street through the parlour, that room where you and I and the poor deceased have passed so many pleasant hours. My mother, who was up stairs, flew to the window to see the melancholy train, and was well nigh distracted. What between leaving her in that state, and going up to the church to deposit my poor father in the grave, you may suppose what were our feelings. I cannot describe them.

"The corpse was carried by eight respectable farmers, and was accompanied to the church, the distance of a mile, by hundreds. Oh! it was an exquisite gratification to share the sympathy of the whole village; though this very circumstance, by its reaction, by exciting our sympathy for them, sharpened the edge of our grief. Their tears and sighs attested their heartfelt concern, and they reminded us that we were not the only mourners; that the poor had lost their best friend—such a friend as they could not expect to see again.

"According to universal custom here, the Church service was read over my poor father. I did not like singly to oppose it, though I am persuaded, could we have consulted him, he would have forbidden it. I never heard it before, however, in a disposition so little captious and implacable; it is in a manner consecrated for ever in my eye by this day's use of it. We sang in church— I say *we* when I mean a few of the congregation, for it was not every one that *could* sing—that fine, truly fine hymn of Dr. Watts's, 'Why do we mourn departing friends.' Often before have I admired it; I never *felt* it till now. This sad event has done me good. You can't conceive with what delight I have read the xith chap. of John and the xvth of 1st Cor., or what beauty I perceive in the Christian doctrine of the resurrection. Without such a stay, how could I support the loss of *such a father?* He was no common man. I should have mourned over him as an acquaintance; I should have lamented him for life as a friend. As a parent, his death will form a new epoch in my life, a new source, I trust, of Christian sympathies, and a new and powerful motive to piety. The scene at the grave was doleful: the mourning crowd, the dreadful grating of the ropes as they were drawn from under the coffin, and the first clods of earth rattling with a frightful reverberation upon it, and the idea that nothing now remained of a father so tender and beloved but a— name! We *once had* a father.

"On our return, we found my mother much better than we expected, as she was, indeed, all the evening, and is this morning. Mrs. Cross has been very kind, and was, poor girl, much affected; so was Isaac, as you would expect from the natural tenderness of his heart.

"Miss Fyson has been here several days, and has proved a source of comfort to us all. Mr. Fyson was at the funeral, and will preach a funeral sermon here on Sunday afternoon (to begin at 2 o'clock), a service which will be very distressing. You will, I know, sympathize strongly with us. This is the last service of a public kind we can render to my father's memory, and one in which we must feel a strong interest from the consideration of his being much attached to religion—sincerely desirous of seeing it prosper at Wicken—and a sort of minister in his own little place.

"Of a nature with this letter is a piece of melancholy news I have to communicate concerning Robert Hall. Would you believe it? His 'mind is overthrown'—he is a lunatic! I don't wonder much, but I *do* grieve. Farewell, my love. R. ASPLAND."

The funeral sermon was preached, according to appointment, on the following Sunday, by Mr. Robert Fyson. His text was Numbers xx. 29. Adopting the style of his favourite master, Robert Robinson, he gave a nervous and feeling portrait of the virtues of his departed friend, and then pathetically added, "The fathers, where are they? The prophets, do they live?" After a moment's pause, occasioned by his own and others' emotion, he turned towards the surviving Robert Aspland and added—"Yes! I see the image of my much-respected friend before me. The son inherits the character of the father. Long may he sustain it—an honour to himself and a blessing to the world!"

With one more letter written from the house of mourning, this Chapter must close.

To Mrs. Aspland.

"Wicken, Nov. 12, 1804.

" * * * What an age does it seem since I left you! Such a train of events have been crowded into the narrow space of ten days, that they appear upon retrospection like so many months. Indeed, the loss of so excellent a father has quite shocked and deranged my ideas. But for you, the dear Sara and a few more, I could adopt the sentiment which I have so often admired in Thomas, of keeping a beloved friend company even in death. 'Let us also go, that we may die with him.' We can scarcely bring ourselves to believe that my dear father is gone for ever. My poor mother often starts from the dream that he is only on a journey. He is on a journey, but, alas! one in which there is no circuit or return. We shall go to him, but he will not come to us.

" This house, and indeed the whole country, is to me a solitude, bereft as they are of their best inhabitant. It is not that such a particular form is vanished—that so much life is extinguished; but that an uncommon portion of sense, a rare sum of virtue, and an enviable degree of usefulness, are all annihilated at a stroke. The poor have lost a patron, the parish a man of real respectability and unsullied amiableness, my mother an invariably kind and tender partner, and we, my Sara, a parent who loved us both with a warmth which even I, who loved him so much, knew him so well, and praised him, as you know, so highly, was, I confess, ignorant of. His life and comfort, as my mother loves to tell, hung upon ours, and all his future prospects (oh! how illusory!) were connected with our prosperity. Can we forbear mourning over such a ruin? Must we not rejoice in a religion which promises to repair it?

" I must give you the conversation of a poor man with my mother, which I have just overheard. 'How do you do, Mrs. ?' 'I don't know how I do; I can't settle to anything.' 'Aye! I don't wonder at it. Yours *is* a loss; but it is not yours only. Everybody here has lost a true friend. If half the farmers of Wicken had been taken off, the loss would have been less. Well! make yourself as easy as you can. We did not all come into the world together, and we can't go out together.' "

CHAPTER X.

The illness and death of his father prevented his fulfilling an engagement to deliver at Newport, on the evening of November 4th, a discourse on "The Revolution of 1688, considered in a Religious View." The discourse was delivered on his return to the Isle of Wight, and had he been swayed only by the wishes of his hearers, it would have been committed to the press. This was, however, prevented by the disinterested and certainly judicious advice of Mr. Benjamin Flower. Independently of the disadvantage to a minister's fame and usefulness of his being regarded as a political preacher, Mr. Flower probably thought that the sermon on the Revolution submitted to his judgment would not add to Robert Aspland's literary reputation. The topic was, however, a favourite one with him through life. He loved to welcome, both in conversation and from the pulpit, the anniversary of a day signalized by the abdication of despotic power, by the annihilation of religious intolerance, and by surrounding the British Throne with the fence of law. With such examples before him as Tillotson and Hoadly and Watts and Foster, he entertained no doubt of the propriety of the subject to any Protestant pulpit. The following passages will sufficiently indicate the character of the discourse.

The Revolution of 1688 unstained by Blood.

"The manner in which the Revolution was accomplished, is another indication of the interposition of Him who 'hath the hearts of all men in his hand, and turneth them whithersoever he will;' 'who changeth the times and the seasons; who removeth kings, and setteth up kings.' No tumult, no massacres attended it; no imprisonments, no confiscations, no legal murders. Other revolutions have rushed upon the world like 'burning comets,' awful in their approach,—and from their horrid hair

'Shaking pestilence and war.'*

---

* Par. Lost, B. ii. l. 710.

This ascended the horizon, like the orb of day, in silent, serene and cloudless majesty,—scarcely perceived by mankind until they felt and exulted in its gladdening influence. Of such transcendent value is a wise and equitable constitution of government, that no labours or sufferings ought to be spared in order to establish it on lasting foundations;—in the present instance we see this grand object obtained without suffering, almost without labour, as if ' not by might nor by power,' (as was said by the prophet of a similar event in sacred history,) ' but by the spirit of the Lord of Hosts.'

"The complete success and lasting benefits of the Revolution should lead us to ascribe it to God : ' He is wonderful in counsel, and excellent in working.' The design of this great and national event was bold and comprehensive,— no less, in short, than the utter overthrow of tyranny, temporal and spiritual. Had it succeeded but partially, occasion would not have been wanting for our admiration and gratitude; that its end has been so fully answered, we ought to acknowledge with devout astonishment and pious joy. Since this illustrious era, Britain has enjoyed, without interruption, the blessing of a free government and the light of the Protestant religion,—the happy consequence of the temperate change and judicious establishment that were then effected. The principal agents in the Revolution were men of enlightened minds and of religious principles, men whose reverence of the Deity, whose knowledge of human nature, whose sound morality and warm patriotism, qualified them to be, as they have been, the legislators of ages. Oh! how unlike the rash, furious, nefarious actors in the late commotions of an adjacent kingdom!—who, sordid in their manners, brutal in their maxims, detestably selfish in their projects, and flagitious to a proverb in the exercise of their blood-stained power, fattened upon the miseries of their country, and in their desperate struggle for supremacy cared not if they had crushed the world! The epoch of their crimes differs as widely from the era we are contemplating, as the red, angry, terrific corruscations of a volcano do from the benign and cheerful light of day. In the results of the two Revolutions we see, in the one case, independence and freedom circulating throughout all the classes of a populous empire, and inspiring sentiments of contentment and personal dignity unknown but in the perfection of the human character; in the other, a subtle and searching despotism overspreading a considerable portion of the civilized world, poisoning the springs of human felicity, and vitiating and destroying the elements of moral and intellectual improvement. Their equally signal but infinitely different effects betoken the one event to have been administered by a wise and righteous Providence as a scourge; the other, which we are calling on you to contemplate with pious gratitude, as a blessing."

Civil Rights secured through desire of Religious Liberty.

"The Revolution of 1688 comes naturally to be considered under a moral view, on account of its intimate connection with the Protestant religion, which first gave it birth, and afterwards owed its protection to it. Men's religious fears prompted their desire of political change. Had the infatuated James aimed at arbitrary power only and unconnected with Popery, he would to a certainty have accomplished his purpose; our ancestors were not excited to resistance by the horrid aspect of tyranny, till it was rendered more horrible by the baleful colouring of superstition. Their piety happily aroused their patriotism: the freedom of their consciences and the glory of their God impelled them to assert their civil and domestic rights. In the reasons which moved them to renovate the form of their government, were blended the noblest motives which can actuate the human breast; but a zealous regard to the purity of the Christian faith was their most predominant and conspicuous sentiment. I consider the leaders in the Revolution as taking up anew the characters and principles of the Reformers, and carrying on the improvements which they had begun; but which, owing to the circumstances of their times, they had been constrained to leave imperfect."

The following glowing passage follows an argument to shew the necessity of the Revolution to carry on the work begun at the Reformation:

"True honour is paid to the characters of the Reformers—not by him who remains fixed to the spot which they had reached centuries ago, and who, from this borrowed eminence, assails with reproach all who are looking forward to farther progress—but by him who reveres them as admirable patterns, but dares not give himself up to them as infallible guides—who is animated by their spirit and invigorated with their principles—who is a follower of them as far as he conceives them to have been followers of Christ. To the bigot, who calls himself their champion, while he is in fact reversing their maxims and calumniating their characters, the shades of these holy men would say, could we call them up from their quiet abodes—'With your mind and temper, you would have been the first to oppose, to slander and to persecute us, had you lived in our day of peril and rebuke; in the time of the first publication of the gospel in these lands, you would have stood up for the established impieties and idolatry of heathenism, and have hurried the founders of our faith to prison and to death:—at Athens you would have poisoned Socrates; at Jerusalem would have crucified Jesus. 'Ye be witnesses unto yourselves that ye are the children of them which killed the reformers and the prophets. Fill ye up, then, the measure of your fathers.''

"Considered in any other light than as the precedent and beginning of a series of improvements of the same kind, the Reformation loses all its significancy, propriety and value, and can be esteemed nothing better than a lawless rebellion or pernicious schism. It involves an absurdity to suppose that it exploded one arbitrary system of faith, only to establish another; and implicates the Reformers in presumption and folly, to imagine that they determined that no one hereafter should imitate their own example, and that the narrow step which they had taken out of the region of error was the goal of perfection, and should be the boundary of the human mind. Sufficient was it for them to explore the path of truth; to their posterity it belongs to pursue it. Glorious was their design of emerging from Popish darkness—heroic their determination to follow the light of truth; and the highest encomium that we can render to their memories consists in following up their principles and completing their plans. But let us not, at the same time, mistake their merit and misapply our praise. It is the boldness of their design, rather than the completeness of its execution, which demands our admiration and applause; and they must be regarded as our benefactors, less on account of the actual acquisitions, than the example of industry and patience which they have bequeathed us."

The study of the Constitution of England, and especially of its renovation in 1688, had a salutary and corrective influence on his political opinions, which, when mellowed by further reading and observation, settled down into a firm and hearty attachment to that great political party of which Mr. Fox, Earl Grey and Lord Holland, were the representatives.

A portion of his correspondence during the interval between his father's death and his own removal from Newport is worth preserving.

*To the Gentlemen of the Philosophical Society, Newport, Isle of Wight,— addressed to Rev. John Potticary.**

"Newport, Nov. 23, 1804.

"Dear Sir,—It is with some reluctance I now write to request that you will signify to my friends of the Philosophical Society, that, owing to the multiplicity of new engagements brought upon me by the rapid approach of

---

* The Rev. John Potticary was originally an Independent minister, and had settled with the Independent congregation at Newport. He was born 1763, was educated at St. Paul's School, and studied for the ministry at the Independent College, Homerton. He married at Newport a daughter of the Rev. John Sturch. He retired from the ministry to devote himself to a boarding-school. In 1806, he removed his establishment to Blackheath, in Kent, where it enjoyed considerable celebrity. Amongst his pupils there were Mr. Benjamin D'Israeli (who at that time observed the rites of the Jewish faith), the present Lord Congleton, Mr. T. M. Gibson, now M.P. for Manchester, and others whose names are not unknown to the public. His adoption of Unitarian sentiments and occasional preaching in Unitarian pulpits did not interfere with the success of his school. He habitually worshiped, during his residence at Blackheath, at the General Baptist chapel at Deptford, of which the Rev. William Moon was then minister. Mr. Aspland's intimacy with Mr. Potticary continued till the death of the latter, which took place at Bath, March 3, 1820.

the time of my removal from Newport, and the late calamity which my family has sustained, I shall be unable to attend their meetings any longer. I would not withdraw my name till the last moment of my stay in the island, could I reconcile myself to the idea of being an inefficient and useless member, for this I am sure I should be constrained to be. It being about my turn to lecture, I feel a little indelicacy in making this request at the present moment; but I do it from the certain conviction I entertain of being in my present situation incapable of doing justice to any chemical subject which might fall to my lot, joined to my fixed opinion that a careless, unstudied lecture would do harm rather than good to the interests of the Society.

"Assure the gentlemen of my esteem and good wishes. I shall ever look back with pleasure on our little but unanimous and profitable exertions, and in whatever part of the world Providence shall hereafter place me, shall heartily rejoice if I be so fortunate as to find such scientific friends as I have found at Newport.

"Might I presume to leave any advice with the Society, it should be solely that they adhere with firmness to their laws, and aim rather to increase their knowledge than to enlarge their numbers.

"I should fear the charge of presumption in addressing this admonition to gentlemen who are so well qualified to judge and act for themselves, did I not know that you and they are bent on the improvement of the Society, and will therefore receive with pleasure the opinion of any individual who wishes it well.

"Believe, my dear Sir, that I am yours and theirs, with the warmest esteem,
ROBERT ASPLAND."

The Rev. Thomas Belsham to the Rev. Robert Aspland.
"Hackney, Feb. 13, 1805.

"My dear Sir,—I heard of, and sincerely sympathize with you in, the melancholy event which summoned you into Cambridgeshire; nor was I surprised, and much less was I offended, that it was not convenient to you to make Hackney in your way either going or returning. You oblige me highly and will gratify my friends exceedingly by your kind offer of assistance either on the first or the last Sunday in March; and as both those days are equally convenient to me, I beg that you will suit your own convenience.

"I rejoice to hear that you are so well satisfied with the choice that you have made. I sincerely hope that your retirement at Norton may answer your views and expectations, and be the means of qualifying you for more extensive usefulness; for I cannot bear the thought of your being buried for life among the glens and mountains of Derbyshire.

"I am glad that my animadversions upon Smith's[*] plausible and imposing

---

[*] Subsequently to the publication by Mr. Belsham of his Funeral Sermon for Dr. Priestley, Dr. Smith (then the Rev. John Pye Smith) addressed to that

letters meet with your approbation. Those letters display so much pompous ignorance and self-conceit, that at first I did not intend to take notice of them. But my friends hearing how much they were cried up by the Calvinists as a most learned and unanswerable work, urged me to take some notice of it, and have at last prevailed upon me to promise that my reply shall appear in a separate publication, when I have finished the series of Letters in Vidler's Magazine, which will be by the first of April. I have no expectation of either opening the minds or stopping the mouths of determined Calvinists; but it will be doing something to excite attention to the subject; for truth must gain in the end by examination and inquiry.

"Your friend Mr. Potticary misapprehended my meaning in the sermon to which you allude. After stating that some interpreters denied that there was any reference to Christ in the prophecy in question, and that others understood it in a double sense, my words are—'But though I am not satisfied entirely to reject the symbolical, or, as it is improperly called, the double sense of prophecy, I see no reason to admit it in this instance; as I think that if this prophecy be considered as a direct prediction of Christ, it will sufficiently explain the whole context,' &c.

"I am glad to hear so good an account of Mrs. Aspland, and I sincerely wish that every addition to your family may be an addition to your comfort. My sister begs her compliments to you and Mrs. Aspland, and unites with me in hoping that she will favour us with her company at Hackney with you. We have a bed at your service, and we hope that you will both stay with us as long as you can.

"I am, dear Sir, very sincerely yours,

T. BELSHAM."

The last Sunday of Robert Aspland's pastorship at Newport was February 24th, 1805. His farewell address was spoken on the evening of the following Wednesday. The discourses of the Sunday were occupied with a review of his preaching during his ministry at Newport. His text was 1 Cor. iv. 1: "Let a man so account of us as of the ministers of Christ and stewards of the mysteries of God." Thus did he explain his doctrine respecting the person of Christ:

"Following the course of my inquiries and convictions on this subject, I

---

gentleman a series of letters, animadverting on several of the statements in the Sermon. Mr. Belsham not considering it a fit occasion for a separate pamphlet, replied in a series of letters in the Universal Theological Magazine, Vol. II. pp. 250, 306; Vol. III. pp. 39, 88, 142. Mr. Belsham was afterwards induced to collect and publish these letters, under the title of "A Vindication of certain Passages in a Discourse on occasion of the Death of Dr. Priestley, in Reply to the Animadversions of Rev. John Pye Smith. 1805."

have sometimes thought it my duty in my public ministry to express myself in terms which a few years ago would have appeared strange to myself, and which may have been as little familiar to some of you as it would then have been to me. But I have never dared to consult what would be popular, but what was scriptural, and the Scriptures appear to me to teach most clearly that Jesus of Nazareth was a man—a true and proper man. So the evangelists, so the epistolary writers speak of him, and so he speaks of himself. It is only, I conceive, by applying figurative expressions in a literal sense, a sense contrary to that intended by the writers of Scripture, that a different idea has been entertained of his person.

"The notion of Jesus being God Almighty is utterly irreconcileable with the whole tenor of the Bible, and contradictory to the uniform representations of himself and his apostles. He was certainly a person, and a separate person from the Being whom he speaks of under the titles of God and the Father, the Being in whose name he spoke, to whom he prayed, by whose authority he conducted his heavenly mission, and whom he invariably takes care to distinguish from and to represent as greater than himself. If he himself were perfect God, then there is not one God, there are at least two Gods, and Christianity is a refined system of polytheism and idolatry. I see not, besides, on this plan, how we can clear our Lord from the charge of deceiving the people; for his language and conduct are at variance with his real meaning,—*this* setting up himself as God, and *those* declaring that 'there is but one God, the Father—his Father and our Father, his God and our God.'

* * * * * *

"The doctrine of Christ being a pre-existent spirit, I consider equally unscriptural, though as harmless in its tendency as an error can well be. You will remember that I am now speaking for myself alone, and without the most distant idea of depreciating the impartiality, good sense, learning and piety of the advocates of the opinion in question; to many of whom I look up as my superiors in every great and estimable quality, and to some of whom I confess myself indebted, under Providence, for whatever correct knowledge of the Scriptures I possess. But in religion, 'one is our Master, even Christ,' and from this authority I think myself entitled to reject the notion of his existence prior to his birth of Mary.

"This opinion is supported only by a few obscure passages of Scripture, while it is opposed by its uniform and constantly-recurring language. In itself it would be the greatest miracle on record; and taking it in that light, it is singular enough that it never should be appealed to, as all other miracles are, in proof of our Lord's mission. It seems likewise to refine away the real and proper humanity of Christ, and is scarcely reconcileable with any of those scriptures which speak of him as the Son of Man and the lineal heir of David, and which represent him as 'made in all things like unto his brethren.' And it is not, I think, a slight argument against it that (a concession allowed by some of its ablest defenders) it is of little or no practical utility, and, whether true or false, makes not scarcely a visible difference in the nature of the Christian religion.

"These arguments are, I am aware, rendered nugatory in the minds of many excellent Christians by a pious fear of degrading the character of the Saviour of the world. But can it be any degradation of him to think and speak of him as he describes himself, as his apostles thought of him, and as the New Testament represents him? Would not the same sentiment befriend any doctrine, however corrupt, which professed to magnify the person and authority of Christ—the reversal, for instance, of the language of Paul in the xvth chapter of this Epistle, and the prediction of a period when God the Father shall deliver up the kingdom to the Son and become subject to him, that the Son might be all in all? And amidst all our fears of dishonouring Jesus, is there no occasion for a fear of infringing upon the honour of God, who acknowledges no equal, and will not 'give his glory to another'?"

On the subject of Baptism—on which his mind had, as has already appeared, undergone some change—he thus expressed himself:

"Baptism I have represented as an act of personal and voluntary obedience —a badge of individual and practical Christianity—a vow of virtue and devotion. The Lord's Supper I have defined to be, on the one hand, a symbol and token of Christian fellowship and a pledge of fraternal love, and, on the other, a memorial of the death and resurrection of Christ, and a memento of his second coming.

"These rites I have importuned no one to perform, because they lose their nature when they are not voluntary, and are useless when they are not observed from principle. On all subjects, but on these particularly, I have ever said, 'Let every man be fully persuaded in his own mind.' The voice of bigotry may condemn this latitude of conduct; but I am acquitted by my own conscience, and am emboldened to hope for the approbation of the Supreme Being, who declared even under the Jewish dispensation, a dispensation of forms and shadows, that he desired mercy rather than sacrifice—virtue than bodily service."

In these solemn words did he close his review of his teaching from the Newport pulpit:

"Such is the outline of the doctrine which you have heard me at various times deliver. I submit it to you and to Almighty God under a deep sense of imperfection, and with a humble prayer that it may not have been wholly unprofitable to you, or unworthy of the Divine blessing. Wherever it has been defective or erroneous, may your enlightened judgments enable you to distinguish it! As far as it has been scriptural, may it be accepted of Jesus, the Mediator of the new covenant and the head of every man, and especially of every Christian teacher! I implore your candour and indulgence, your kind remembrance, and your prayers at the throne of Divine Grace."

If the services on this day tried both his own feelings and those of his much-attached flock, much more so did the farewell service on the following Wednesday evening. The burial of a member of the congregation preceded the service, and thus additional mournfulness was given to the occasion. A contemporary diary describes the whole service as painfully affecting, equally to the preacher and his hearers. A large congregation attended, including many of the Independents of Newport. The Rev. Robert Winter,* with rare courtesy, gave up his own customary Wednesday-evening service in order to pay a farewell token of respect to a neighbour of another faith.

Before this time, Mr. Aspland had assisted the congregation at Newport in their efforts to secure the services of a suitable successor.† It will somewhat surprise those whose knowledge is derived solely from the recent Memoir published by Mr. J. E. Ryland, to learn that they looked, in the first instance, to Mr. John Foster, who soon after became celebrated by the publication of his Essays. He had been settled about a year at Frome, where he succeeded Mr. Job David. This circumstance appears, from the following letter, not to have been known at Newport, although the rumour of his having left Downend had travelled thither.

---

* This very respectable minister was grandson to the noted Rev. Thomas Bradbury, and was born in London, 1762. He studied at Homerton. In 1783, he settled with a congregation at Hammersmith. He was afterwards successively minister at Salters' Hall and Hanover Street; and in 1803, he settled in the Isle of Wight. In 1806, he returned to London, at the call of the Independent congregation at New Court. In 1809, he received from New Jersey the diploma of Doctor in Divinity.

† The successor to the pulpit at Newport was Rev. John Tingcombe, who removed thither from Plymouth in April, 1806. He had been a pupil of Mr. Belsham at Daventry. In 1815, Mr. Tingcombe removed to Bridgwater; and the pulpit was, during a portion of 1816 and 1817, occupied by the Rev. Benjamin Goodier, whose name will recur in a future portion of this Memoir. When he was compelled, by ill health, to seek a still milder climate, the congregation was supplied by Rev. William Hughes, who had been previously minister at Sidmouth and Leather Lane, in London. In July, 1818, Rev. William Stevens, now of Maidstone, became the minister, and remained so until April, 1823. He was succeeded by Rev. Edmund Kell (son of the late Rev. Robert Kell, of Birmingham), who was educated at Glasgow and York. The congregation still enjoys his efficient services. In 1826, the chapel was enlarged, and additional Sunday-schools were built. In 1830, an endowment of the yearly value of £30 was added. Connected with the chapel is a Library containing 1000 volumes, and a Sunday-school that numbers more than 100 scholars.

Rev. Robert Aspland to Dr. Cox, Fishponds, near Bristol.

"Newport, Isle of Wight, Dec. 11, 1804.

"Dear Sir,—I avail myself of the slight acquaintance with which you were pleased to honour me whilst I was at Bristol, to solicit information concerning a gentleman who is known to no one whom I have the pleasure of knowing so well as to yourself. A rumour has reached me that Mr. Foster has removed from Downend; will you be so obliging as to inform me whether the report be true, and, if so, whether Mr. Foster be yet settled satisfactorily and immoveably? Being myself about to leave my present congregation, whom I sincerely respect, I feel naturally anxious to be able to resign them into the hands of some gentleman of talent and respectability. On looking round, I perceive no one who is disengaged so likely to win their approbation as Foster; and I must confess I should feel not a little flattered in having such a successor. My application, however, presupposes that he has left, or is leaving, your neighbourhood; for it would be most invidious and cruel to seek officiously to rob you of a man, who knows so well how to make conversation intellectual and society alluring. In the obvious and universal dearth of men of original, enlightened and active powers of mind, you have found him, I doubt not, an invaluable companion, and his loss must every where be felt, I should imagine, to be irreparable. For the same reason, it is desirable that, if he be looking out for a new situation, he should choose a society which will be competent to appreciate his talents and profit by his instructions; such, I conceive, is the General Baptist congregation of this place, who, few in number, are select, intelligent and liberal. Among them Foster would take his proper rank, and preserve his much-loved independence. I leave a circle in which I have received much pleasure, and attained, I hope, some improvement, only at the instance of an invitation to a situation still more promising— promising with respect to facilities of study and literary attainments. The rumour which has occasioned you, Sir, the trouble of this letter, implies at least that Foster has relinquished the profession of Calvinism,—a system which I must confess I always thought uncongenial to the feelings of his heart, and ill adapted to the natural elasticity of his mind.

"The less a man is bound up in the rigours of party, the better, I conceive, he would suit my friends of the Isle of Wight.

"It gives me pleasure to learn that you are about to communicate to the public some portion of that light which has so long and so successfully guided your practice in the treatment of the most awful malady with which Providence afflicts our nature. May your science meet with the honour it deserves, and your benevolence with the usefulness it desires! You know, I presume, that Miss ——, of the Isle of Wight, is married to Mr. ——, a manufacturer of ————. She enjoys sound health. I am now reminded of her, as I have often heard her speak with apparent delight of the kindness of yourself and Mrs. Cox. Please to present my respectful compliments to your lady."

It is to be regretted that Dr. Cox's reply to these inquiries respecting Mr. Foster has not been preserved. It may be presumed that he did not discourage the proposed application to his friend; and, with much confidence, that he did not allege Mr. Foster's relapse into Calvinism as an obstacle (and it would have been an insuperable one) to his forming an engagement with a society of more than *heretical bias.*

Whatever was Dr. Cox's reply, it led to a direct application to Mr. Foster, on behalf of the Newport congregation, by Mr. Cooke. Mr. Foster appears to have declined the invitation, not on the ground of theological differences, but on the score of his failing health. Two or three years previously, a morbid state of the thyroid gland had begun to trouble him.* The disease was aggravated by the exertion of public speaking, and he was apprehensive, at the time when Mr. Cooke applied to him, that the suspension, if not the entire cessation, of pulpit duty was inevitable,—an apprehension which was realized in the course of the following year.† Mr. Aspland hastened, on learning Mr. Foster's illness, to express his friendly sympathy.

Rev. Robert Aspland to Rev. John Foster, Frome.

"Newport, Feb. 8, 1805.

"Dear Sir,—I should not now trouble you with a letter, were I not desirous of expressing my sincere concern on account of your very alarming disease. As a Dissenting minister, I could not forbear condoling with you, though a perfect stranger; my knowledge of your character and our former acquaintance, however slight, excite within me a lively sympathy in your affliction.

"Mr. Cooke's letter was written at my recommendation, and I had flattered myself with the possibility of your succeeding me here. My disappointment was doubly painful from the cause of your declining the invitation being so calamitous. What effect has the last remedy to which you allude produced?— and what are your prospects, should you be ultimately obliged to renounce your present profession? These inquiries are prompted solely by a desire to serve you, and a wish that you would make use of my house in Derbyshire during some part of the ensuing summer. If change of air be at all serviceable to you, you might expect much from the salubrious breezes of the High Peak, and your company would be truly gratifying to both Mrs. Aspland and myself. We leave this place at the end of the present month, and hope to be settled in our new residence about the middle of May, after which we

---

* See Ryland's Life of John Foster, I. 280.

† "Mr. Foster resigned his ministerial charge at Midsummer, 1806." Life I. 284.

shall be extremely happy to receive you at any time as a visitor. Norton, to which we are going, is a village in the county of Derby, six miles from Chesterfield, four from Sheffield, and is sufficiently known in the neighbourhood as the seat of my friend and patron, Samuel Shore, Esq. There are direct conveyances to it from Oxford and Birmingham, as well as London.

"Your friends in the neighbourhood of Bristol seem not to know of the complaint under which you labour, as I judge from Dr. Cox's silence about it in a letter which I lately received from him, in answer to one I sent with inquiries concerning you. You should not deprive them of an opportunity of testifying their sympathy and indulging their kindness. Your talents and virtues entitle you to more consideration than you claim.

"I am, dear Sir, yours sincerely and affectionately,
ROBERT ASPLAND."

On leaving Newport, Robert Aspland had arranged to spend a few weeks at Wicken, in order to settle the affairs of his late father, before he established himself at Norton. He devoted a few days to a visit to his wife's relatives at St. Martin's Lane; and on the Sunday following his departure from the Isle of Wight, he fulfilled a promise to preach at the Gravel-Pit, Hackney, for Mr. Belsham. It was a singular coincidence that Mr. Belsham had only a few days previously (Feb. 27th) received from the trustees of Essex-Street chapel an urgent invitation to succeed Dr. Disney in the Essex-Street pulpit, which the latter gentleman intended to vacate on the ensuing Lady-day. Of these circumstances Mr. Aspland was wholly ignorant, until Mr. Belsham, on the Sunday in question, confidentially intimated to him that he meditated the acceptance of the invitation to remove to London. Under these circumstances, it was natural that some of his friends, amongst them Mr. Belsham, should suggest to him the probability and the desirableness of his succeeding to the Hackney pulpit. He stayed, however, in London at this time only a few days. His diary records his paying a visit to "the venerable Mr. Lindsey," by whom and Mrs. Lindsey he was received with marked kindness. At Wicken, the duties of consoling his surviving parent and settling her affairs, so as to enable her to be free from the cares and responsibilities of trade, occupied his attention. The agitation of mind which the suggestions of his friends had excited soon subsided, as the following extracts from letters written at this time will shew.

To Mrs. Aspland.

"Wicken, March 11, 1805.

"My mother counts on being near us, but she wishes we were going to settle *nearer London*. On this subject I feel little anxiety. In truth, I expect the matter will blow over. I am not strong enough in reputation for *London*. * * * I am not fit for a successor to *Price* and *Priestley*, and too sudden a rise might be as prejudicial as too protracted an obscurity. Besides, I wish not to encounter, while our children are young, the fogs and foul vapours of the metropolis, nor to introduce them into a style of living which they will be unable to keep up. Glad am I that the determination of this affair can never be in my own hands; most cheerfully do I leave it to *Providence*."

To Miss Middleton.

"Wicken, March 12, 1805.

"You know my predilection for worm-eaten, rusty-covered books. Not unfrequently has this taste procured me rich and exquisite entertainment. It led me this morning to look over a collection of mouldy volumes, and to select from among them a tattered book of poems by FRA. QUARLES. This author I had always looked upon as a mere gospel oddity, and his poetry no better than the unmeasured doggrel of John Bunyan; but I have found him, to my surprise, a true poetical genius! His humour is sterling—his versification sometimes equal to Dryden, if not to Pope—his descriptions the true symbols of nature—and his morality sound, impressive and touching. I have found that both Milton and Young have gone before me in reading and admiring and copying him. With such an author before him, I less wonder, though I can never cease to wonder, at MILTON's force and sublimity. The *Paradise Lost* was not a fairy and magic fabric; it was compiled of materials borrowed no less from Du Bartas and Quarles, than from Lucan, Virgil and Homer. I shall give you some extracts from an historical poem of Quarles's, entitled 'The Historie of Samson.' The following is part of the speech of the Angel to his mother, proscribing the 'law-forbidden meats' that she was to forbear to taste during the time of her pregnancy:

'The hunch-back camel shall be no repast
For her; her palate shall forbeare to taste
The burrow-haunting coney, and decline
The swift-foot hare, and mire-delighting swine;
The griping goshauke, and the tow'ring eagle;
The particolored pye must not inveigle
Her lips to move; the brood-devouring kite;
The croaking raven; the owle that hates the light;
The steele-digesting bird; the lazy snaile;
The cuckow, ever telling of one tale;
The fish-consuming osprey, and the want,*
That undermines; the greedy cormorant;
The indulgent pelican; the predictious crow;
The chatt'ring stork, and the ravenous vultur too;

---

* *Want*, the old English name of a *mole*; still used in the Isle of Wight.

>   The thorne-backt hedgehog, and the prating jay;
>   The lapwing, flying still the other way;
>   The lofty-flying falcon, and the mouse,
>   That finds no pleasure in a poore man's house;
>   The suck-egge weasell, and the winding swallow,
>   From these she shall abstaine————.'

"I admire in this description, and I think you will, the individuality and fine painting of the epithets; and this is one of the most certain marks of genuine poetry.

"The following is the picture of Delila when first seen by the 'brawny-thighed' hero, and of a fond and transported lover:

> 'Not farre from Azza, in a fruitful valley,
> Close by a brooke whose silver streams did dalley
> With the smooth bosom of the wanton sands,
> Whose winding current parts the neighb'ring lands,
> And often washes the beloved sides
> Of her delightful bankes with gentle tides,
> There dwelt a BEAUTY, in whose sun-bright eye
> Love sate enthron'd; and, full of majestie,
> Sent forth such glorious eye-surprising rayes,
> That she was thought the wonder of her dayes:
> Her name was called Delila the faire;
> Thither did amorous Samson oft repaire;
> And with the piercing flame of her bright eye,
> He toil'd so long, that, like a wanton flie,
> He burnt his lustful wings, and so became
> The slavish pris'ner to that conquering flame:
> She askt and had: there's nothing was too high
> For her to beg, or Samson to deny:
> Who now but Delila? What name can raise
> And crowne his drooping thoughts, but Delila's?
> All time's mispent, each houre is cast away,
> That's not employed upon his Delila:
> Gifts must be given to Delila: no cost,
> If sweetest Delila but smile, is lost:
> No joy can please, no happinesse can crowne
> His best desires, if Delila but frowne.
> No good can blesse his amorous heart, but this,
> He's Delila's, and Delila is his!'

"More I cannot transcribe. Our folks are tired with waiting for me to read. 'Tis well if I don't open the Bible upon simple Samson and lascivious Delila! Good night. God bless you all!

"Wednesday morning.—King's Arms, Leadenhall Street: send there early on Saturday morning for a box or package, which will contain, among other things, a pair of very fine wild ducks, and a leash of smaller fowl, consisting of a couple of teil and a widgeon. Present them to your father, with my compliments, and request him to send either the leash or the pair, as he thinks proper, to Mrs. Belgrave, with my sincere respects. The apples, I suppose, Miss Sa. will look on as her own property; make her to understand they come from papa and grandmother. I would not advise the birds to be kept longer than is necessary, though the fen fowler who brought them to me tells me *it is grand to have such grand birds high.* Thus you see I am quite a provident and prudent son, nephew, brother, husband and father. In the former part of the letter I regaled your wits; now I am catering for the less intellectual part of you.

"Thursday morning.—Did you observe the moon last night? It was encompassed with the most 'beauteous halo' I ever saw,—the mystic ring of glory which seems hung out as the emblem of peace and friendship. I fancied you were looking on it with me, and this thought shed a refreshing pleasure upon me. My friend Emons, with whom I had gossiped away all the evening, first observed it on going out of doors, and challenged me to explain the cause of it. I conjectured, but was more disposed to spiritualize, as you will guess, than to expound.

"I have just determined to ride over to Ely again to-day to meet my friend the lawyer, to give him directions concerning taking up my little estate there, and proving my father's will. I shall get upon the London road, and shall no doubt feel myself the better for it."

He rejoined his family in London before the close of the month, on the last Sunday of which (March 31) he had in the morning the high gratification of hearing Mr. Belsham preach his initiatory sermon at Essex-Street chapel, from Matt. xvi. 13, "Who do men say that I, the Son of Man, am?" In the afternoon and evening of that day, he himself preached the annual charity sermons at Worship Street. At the latter service, he had as hearers several members of the Hackney congregation. At its close they waited upon him as a deputation, and informed him that, by an all but unanimous vote,* the Committee of the Gravel-Pit congregation had resolved to invite him to preach as a candidate on probation for two Sundays. They assured him, such were the feelings of the congregation towards him, that the probation would be a mere matter of form. He subsequently received a written application to the same effect, and his last act previously to leaving London for Norton was to address the following letter to the Treasurer of the Gravel-Pit congregation:

---

* The Committee was a large one, consisting of 24 principal members of the congregation. The Rev. John Edwards, previously of Birmingham, was put in nomination at the same time. For him, 3 members recorded their votes, and 19 for Mr. Aspland.

To Francis Ronalds, Esq.

"London, April 2, 1805.

"Dear Sir,—I beg you will transmit to the Unitarian congregation at Hackney the warm sense which I entertain of the honour they have done me in the invitation which you have so obligingly communicated. Their good opinion of me both flatters and humbles me: it is flattering that my zeal has earned me the approbation of a society of Christians so enlightened and respectable; it is humbling that I am constrained to feel my incompetency for a situation eminent beyond example for the great powers of its ministers for a series of years, and for the high cultivation of its people. The deference, however, which, as a public teacher, I owe to the voice of so large a body of Christians, would have led me to comply at once with their request, had I been entirely free to follow my inclinations.

"It is not unknown to many of the subscribers to the Gravel-Pit, I believe, that I have long pledged myself to accept of the pastoral office in the Unitarian chapel at Norton, Derbyshire, and that I am also obliged by the tenor of my engagement to be there by the ensuing Sunday. I am thus, of course, prevented from acceding to their immediate wish of preaching at Hackney the two next Sundays; and I have so high an idea of the sacredness of the pastoral contract, that my sense of Christian honour will not allow me either to seem to regard it as insignificant, or to attempt personally to dissolve it. At the same time, I will frankly confess—and I assure myself, from the known liberality and candour of the Gravel-Pit congregation, that the confession will not be prematurely divulged or misconstrued—that were it possible to remove all impediments consistently with my honour and the satisfaction of my highly respectable friend and patron, Samuel Shore, Esq., I should be truly happy to devote myself to the service of a society—were this their unanimous will—whose well-known character insures the respectability, the improvement, the usefulness and the comfort of their pastor.

"I am, dear Sir, with every sentiment of respect and esteem for yourself individually, and for the congregation at large, your obliged, humble servant,
ROBERT ASPLAND."

For his journey into Derbyshire he had provided himself with a horse in Cambridgeshire. This is his account of his journey:

To his Mother.

"Norton, April 8, 1805.

"Dear Mother,—I arrived here only on Saturday evening. The journey did not in the least fatigue me. Mr. Shore's family expected me with some anxiety, and welcomed me with very great kindness.

"I left London comfortable, under the assurance that you were getting better. I set off on Tuesday, at noon. Mr. Jesse accompanied me on a hired nag the first day, and the first stage of the second day. We slept the first night at St. Alban's, and breakfasted at Market-street, in the neighbourhood of Dunstable. Here Mr. Jesse left me; but on the road to Newport-Pagnell, where I dined, I picked up a tolerably pleasant companion, who accompanied me as far as Derby; that is, I suppose, about eighty miles. He was an old traveller, and was therefore of great use to me.

"The second day, I ended my travels at Northampton. On the Thursday morning it was wet, and, lifting up the window of the inn room to look at the weather, whom do you think I met? My old friend Cox, who was overjoyed at seeing me, and by such an accident too. He lives at Clipstone, and had come to Northampton on business. We rode together to Market-Harborough, which is within four miles of his village; there, as I could get no further on account of the wetness of the day, we dined and spent the day at a very comfortable inn. He left me in the evening, but not without making me promise to visit him, and also to preach for him, on my return.

"From Market-Harborough, I rode on Friday morning to Leicester to breakfast—from thence to Loughborough to dine—and to Derby to sleep. At Leicester I called on Mr. Deacon, the General Baptist minister, who was glad to see me, and made me also promise to give him a sermon when I next pass through the town. After a wet morning on Friday, we had a pretty comfortable evening, and had not an unpleasant ride into Derby. That day I travelled about forty-five miles. Saturday was my last day. I left Derby after breakfast, and got here to tea, the distance about thirty miles. My horse stood the journey very well, and looks as fresh as ever. He shines in the stables, even among coach-horses.

"Before I left town, I had an application from the congregation at Hackney. How it will terminate I know not. I am more pleased with Norton the more I see of it."

He commenced his duties at Norton on Sunday, April 7th, by a sermon on social worship, from Gen. iv. 26; and on the following day began his instructions to the young people of the family at Norton. So agreeable did he find the occupation and the society of the families at Norton and Meersbrook, that he began to think he could be more than content if Mr. Shore did not see fit to release him from his engagement.

CHAPTER XI.

His uncertainty as to his destination continued for several weeks after his arrival at Norton. A few extracts from a familiar diary, penned for the eye of his dearest friend, will indicate some of his employments and feelings:

"Norton,* April 8.—'Woke at half-past six. Read Bubb Doddington's Diary about an hour. Took a walk over *our* house and garden till nine.† Talked over a little Latin with my pupil. Rode to Sheffield with Mrs. and Miss Shore. Called on Mr. Nayler, the Unitarian minister, who is going into business at Manchester. Returned to Meersbrook at five to dine, where we met General Roberts and his aide-du-camp, Captain Gossip, who have been reviewing to-day some volunteers in the neighbourhood, and are to inspect to-morrow Mr. Shore's corps in the Park.‡ Thanked God I was not a soldier. Could not talk and would not talk. Listened with impatience for the step that should announce tea. Became interested in the intelligent talk of my female scholar.§ Rode home about ten by the light of a most silvery moon, talking over Mars, Sirius, Perseus and Andromeda.

---

* Norton Hall, in its ancient state, was one of the picturesque old houses of our country gentry. Some portions of it were of high antiquity; others appeared to be built about the first of the Stuart reigns; and some of the best apartments had been added by the Offleys. There was a fine old entrance-hall, with a gallery, and in this room the Nonconformists of Norton and the neighbourhood had been long accustomed to assemble for public worship. Mr. Newton, the neighbour and friend of Mr. Shore, on his death left a sum of money for the building of a chapel at Norton. This was done in 1790, and the Hall was no longer needed as a place of worship. Norton Hall was rebuilt by Mr. Samuel Shore in 1812—1814.

† The minister's house at Norton, a spacious and commodious building, was originally built by Mr. Joseph Offley for the residence of the Rev. Mr. Lowe, who had a very flourishing school there about the middle of the last century.

‡ "When the country armed in its defence in the year 1803, Mr. Shore appeared in the novel character of a military officer, and raised a company of volunteers, chiefly from amongst his own tenantry and dependents, whose services were accepted by the Crown."—Mon. Repos., N. S., III. 70.

§ Miss Elizabeth Maria Shore grew up an accomplished and benevolent lady.

"April 9.—An idle, though a very pleasant day. Met Dr. Bagshawe, the neighbouring squire and present high-sheriff of Derbyshire,* in the Park at the review; was prevailed upon to accompany him to Sheffield. My concern at the uncertainty of my destination is daily augmented by the kindnesses of both the families of the Shores,† who are amongst the excellent of the earth.

She was acquainted with the original languages of the Scriptures, devoted much time to the poor, superintended a village school, and formed a village library for the improvement of her poor neighbours. She sank to rest, after a few hours' illness, Jan. 11, 1834, aged forty.—See Christian Reformer, 1834, p. 87.

* The Oakes, the seat of the Bagshawe family, is about a quarter of a mile from the village of Norton.

† They belonged, as Mr. Aspland remarked some years after, to "one of the few families of our hereditary gentry who have from generation to generation professed and consistently maintained Dissenting principles." Samuel Shore, Esq., of Meersbrook, the head of the house in 1805, was born Feb. 5, 1737-8, and was baptized by Mr. John Wadsworth, the Presbyterian minister of Sheffield. He resorted for seven years to the school of the Rev. Daniel Lowe, the Presbyterian minister of Norton. In 1759, he married the elder of two daughters of Joseph Offley, Esq. Of the peculiar circumstances attending the alienation and recovery of the Offley estate, Mr. Hunter has published a singularly interesting narrative. Norton Hall, the park, demesne and manor, were assigned to Mrs. Shore. During her life, Norton Hall was their constant residence. She died there in 1781. On the marriage of his son, he removed to Meersbrook, which had been the abode of his father. In 1761, he served the office of high-sheriff for the county of Derby. In early life, Mr. Shore acted as a magistrate of the West-Riding of the county of York; but when Parliament refused to listen to the application for a repeal of the Test Laws (a movement in which he had actively assisted), he felt it to be his duty to discontinue his magisterial services, and thus offered a dignified protest during the remainder of his days against the impolicy and injustice of the law excluding Protestant Dissenters from offices of trust and honour. He just lived to see the Test Act abolished, and his name (together with that of his son) appears in the list of Stewards of the Dinner to commemorate that great event which was held at the Freemasons' Hall, June 18, 1828, and presided over by the Duke of Sussex.

To Mr. Shore's varied services to the cause of liberal Dissent, this brief note will only allow a passing reference. He was the active and generous friend and patron of Mr. Lindsey and Dr. Priestley; the latter of whom dedicated to Mr. Shore his History of the Christian Church, as to one "whose conduct had long proved him to be a steady friend of Christianity, and whose object it had been to preserve it as unmixed as possible with every thing that has a tendency to corrupt and debase it."—The Mrs. Shore to whom Mr. Aspland refers in his diary was of course the second wife; she was the only daughter of Freeman Flower, Esq., of Clapham, in Surrey. The writer had the pleasure of visiting this venerable couple in the year 1825. They spoke with kindly interest and much freshness of recollection of Mr. Aspland's brief residence at Norton. Mr. Shore, notwithstanding his great age, retained not only polished manners, but intellectual vigour. As he stood for a moment beneath his own bust, sculptured by Chantrey (a native of Norton), with his silvery hair and finely moulded head, almost as white as the marble, the writer thought he saw the finest specimen he ever beheld of extreme age, and the happiest resemblance in marble of the

I am not inclined to make angels of them; you know I ever avoided transporting myself into raptures of friendship for them; but they do gradually steal upon my affection, and all that I hear from everybody nourishes the growing sentiment.

"April 10.—After attending in the morning to my little pupil, I rode through a succession of close, rugged, grotesque and almost impassable lanes to my friend Mower's, of the Woodseats.* The house stands on the edge of the Derbyshire moors, secluded from every strange eye, and the inmates seemed wild and fearful. With some difficulty I obtained admission, and was sorry to find my political friend confined to his room. He received me with a kind of enthusiasm. His physiognomy denotes both eccentricity and benevolence. I regretted not seeing his lady, who is very accomplished. He married her out of Dundas's, now Lord Melville's, family. Dined and slept at Meersbrook. Mr. Shore, Sen., is a truly respectable and pleasant gentleman. He has a large stock of knowledge, and, what is more, good principles. He is very candid, but at the same time ardent. Mrs. S. is perhaps my favourite, if I may use that term in relation to a family where there is not one whom I do not highly esteem. They are all considerately attentive. The house is being now thoroughly cleaned; the garden had been previously attended to. As to settling here, I feel little anxiety. Upon the whole, I incline to wish it; though I make no doubt of being able, if the Hackney people choose me, to accept an offer from them with honour.

"April 11.—Dined at Dr. Bagshawe's, with Mr. Ward, of Sheffield, and Mr. Calton. Home to Meersbrook about nine. Glorious decision in the House of Commons in the case of Lord Melville!

"April 24.—Letter to-day from Mr. Rutt.† The Hackney business proceeds."

---

human countenance. Mr. Shore died at Meersbrook, Nov. 16, 1828, in the 91st year of his age.—See M. Repos., 1829, and Rhodes's Peak Scenery, 8vo, p. 268.

Samuel Shore, Esq., of Norton Hall, was the second son of Samuel Shore, Esq., of Meersbrook (the eldest son died in his eighth year), and was born 1762. He was a pupil first of Mr. Lowe and then of Mr. Holland at Bolton. In 1778, he entered the Warrington Academy. He subsequently studied at Geneva. Returning to England in 1782, he entered himself a member of Lincoln's Inn and kept the necessary terms. He married, 1788, Miss Foye, of Castle Hill, in the county of Dorset. He served the office of high-sheriff for Derbyshire in 1832, and died Nov. 1, 1836, in the 75th year of his age.—See Christ. Ref., 1836, p. 909.

* This gentleman had sought his correspondence and friendship, previous to all personal acquaintance, simply from political sympathy, excited by accidentally meeting with his Newport Fast Sermon.

† The writer cannot pass by the name of this good man without offering a humble tribute of reverence for his memory. He was foremost amongst the members of the congregation who desired Mr. Aspland's settlement at Hackney,

The purport of this letter was to inform him that the Gravel-Pit congregation had all but unanimously decided, on the previous Sunday, to invite him to preach for two Sundays on probation, assuring him, at the same time, that this was a mere form, and on his compliance with which he would certainly be elected; and stating that Mr. Belsham strongly hoped he would comply with the invitation.

A few days after, being at Meersbrook, his kind friend Mr. Shore, "looking benevolence itself," entered the room where he was, and said, "Here are two letters which I feel it my duty to lay before you. The one from Mr. Belsham I should have shewn you before; but I waited in expectation of the other, which, however, did not arrive till this morning. My son and I have nothing more to say than that we wish you to consider yourself at perfect liberty to act as you think proper." The second letter was from Mr. Ronalds, the Treasurer of the Gravel-Pit congregation.

---

and for five-and-thirty years he continued to render him unfailing service. Mr. Rutt had lived through evil times, and had an enthusiastic and high-toned love of liberty, civil and religious, the ardour of which men of the present age can scarcely understand. The personal friend of Price and Priestley and Wakefield, even if he had no other claims upon us, would be an object of our respect. But as the biographer of Wakefield (in conjunction with Mr. Arnold Wainewright) and the editor of Dr. Priestley's Works, Mr. Rutt has achieved a permanent place for himself in the annals of religious literature. He edited and enriched with his annotations the long-neglected Life of Calamy. A similar service he rendered to Burton's Cromwellian Diary, and he also edited the "Correspondence of Samuel Pepys." Of his contributions to the periodical literature of the Unitarians, occasion will hereafter arise in this Memoir of speaking. His conversational powers were great; his utterance rapid, emphatic and distinct. His memory was retentive and accurate; and he poured forth even in ordinary conversation, with admirable profusion, the varied stores of his well-furnished mind. In addition to all this, he had a good Christian heart, which warmed to every kind and virtuous sympathy. Early in life he promoted with great zeal "the Jennerian discovery of vaccine inoculation." In age, he gave his aid and blessing to the Domestic Mission established in Spicer Street, Spitalfields. Those who enjoyed familiar intercourse with Mr. Rutt, either at Bromley or Clapton, could not but be pleasantly impressed with the patriarchal simplicity and affectionateness with which he presided over a large and very interesting family. It is certainly to be regretted that no extended memoir of Mr. Rutt has been given to the public. "Memorials" of him have indeed been printed, but they have been strictly limited to "private circulation." It is beautifully remarked in the Preface, that though "too much divorced from learning by fortune, he still loved it; his ardent desires for the advancement of his species in knowledge or freedom, did not interfere with his fond love of all the vestiges of the past; and his humanity, though embracing all varieties of sect, colour and climate, had its deep-rooted centre in his own home."

Rev. Thomas Belsham to Samuel Shore, Esq.

"* * * The probation sermons are little more than matter of form, and will, to a moral certainty, be followed with an almost, if not altogether, unanimous invitation to him to become the morning preacher. It is not, my dear Sir, for me to prescribe to you or to Mr. S. Shore what part you should take in these circumstances. If it appear to you both that by removing to Hackney, Mr. Aspland's usefulness may be greatly increased, and that his distinguished talents, activity and zeal, may be rendered greatly instrumental in promoting Christian truth, piety and virtue, I have no doubt that with this (prospect?) both yourself and Mr. S. Shore would be ready to make a sacrifice of your own views and wishes (however painful or unexpected) to the public good. Of the probability of this result you are fully competent to judge."

Rev. Robert Aspland to Mrs. Aspland.

"Meersbrook, April 27, 1805.

"* * * What, you will ask, are my views and feelings? To be frank, they are not discordant with those of our friends in Town. The zealous attachment of the Gravel-Pit society affects me with like sentiments. The advantages of Hackney are in themselves great, and the situation becomes doubly desirable on account of its being so gratifying to our friends in St. Martin's Lane, and so likely to administer to the comfort of my mother." (After describing the interview with Mr. Shore, the letter proceeds)—"I could say nothing; but I endeavoured to *look* gratitude. * * * The upshot of the business, I can now say, will be my settling at Hackney. Thus, my dear love, is our lot about to be fixed. What do we not owe to that indulgent Being who is favouring your husband and friend so far beyond his deserts! God grant that his mercies may never fail to impress us with the liveliest gratitude!"

The diary has this entry under May 1:

"To receive the Kirkpatricks" (pupils who it was at one time proposed should follow him from Newport to Norton). "So it *was* to be; but true is it, we know not what a day may bring forth. Now, it seems, I shall scarcely settle here myself. By another May-day what greater changes may not occur. Last year at this time, let me remember, my dear father was living, and we were expecting with all the impatience of affection to meet in the ensuing month!"

He stayed at Norton and Meersbrook till the middle of May, accompanying Mr. Shore and his son in a visit to Wakefield, where they went to attend a meeting of the Trustees of Lady Hewley's charities.*

---

* They spent two evenings, in going to and returning from Wakefield, at Mr. Edmund's, of Worsborough, near Barnsley. Mr. Edmunds had married the younger Miss Offley, and took the Brampton estate. Mrs. Edmunds died a little before this.

Upon this occasion he had the pleasure of making the acquaintance of the Rev. William Wood, of Leeds, and the Rev. Thomas Johnston, of Wakefield. He left his generous friends at Norton and Meersbrook with feelings of regret, and often in after periods of life spoke of them with affectionate respect, and dwelt on the pleasures of his brief residence in Derbyshire.

The " probation" Sundays at Hackney were May 26 and June 2. If they had their anxieties, they were not without their pleasures; for of the former day portions were spent in the society of Rev. John Kentish, Mr. Marsom and Mr. Rutt; and of the latter, in that of Mr. Belsham and of Mr. William Smith. At the conclusion of his second service, the Committee met and resolved, by an unanimous vote, to recommend him to the choice of the congregation; and on the following Sunday, the election was confirmed by an equally unanimous vote on the part of the congregation.

John Towill Rutt, Esq. to Rev. Robert Aspland.

"London, June 14, 1805.

"Dear Sir,—I was sorry to understand to-day that Mr. Ronalds had not written to you, from his not having taken your direction. I am the more vexed at this, because I am a little implicated in some neglect as to furnishing him with it. As I have not seen Mr. R. to-day, lest he should not write officially to-night, I trouble you with this letter to say that the business was finished on Sunday last as I expected, and I think as satisfactorily as you would desire. Mr. Johnston and Mr. Travers, at their own suggestion, moved and seconded the resolution to agree with the Committee in the choice of you as pastor and morning preacher. I was authorized to state the full concurrence of Dr. Pett, who was absent on a journey, and of Mr. Christie, who was detained from attendance by the indisposition of his family. It is wished that you would commence as early as possible.

"Should you not immediately find a house to suit you at Hackney, I wish you would inform me before you engage any temporary residence. * * * We design to spend the months of August and September at a house of Mrs. R.'s father's by the sea. We shall take all the family except one servant, who with our house would be at your, Mrs. A.'s and your family's service, should you not be more agreeably provided. We might possibly leave Hackney the last week in July.

"I remain, dear Sir, yours sincerely,

J. T. RUTT."

Of those members of the Gravel-Pit congregation that joined in this election of a pastor, a few venerable friends survive. One of them,

Mr. John Christie, has favoured the writer with his reminiscences on the subject, which shew that there were not wanting some out of the congregation who thought the election a hazardous experiment.

"I have thought it right to give you these few facts, as many judicious and respectable individuals, at the time your worthy father became our minister, wondered at our congregation, an old Presbyterian society, choosing a minister so very young, preaching to a Baptist connection, and immediately following such venerable and distinguished men as Belsham, Priestley and Price. The truth is, the congregation was inquiring and intelligent, and they reckoned that in having Mr. Aspland as their minister, they would have a man of great talent and extensive usefulness, or, as he would have phrased it, 'serviceableness' (for that was his favourite word in such a connection). And the congregation was neither mistaken nor disappointed in their choice, as the experience of forty years demonstrated."

In compliance with the earnest wish of the Committee, he entered with little delay on the duties of his office. His initiatory service at the Gravel-Pit took place on Sunday, July 7, 1805. The devotional and sacramental services were (as was then his custom) *extempore*. He selected as the subject of his first sermon, the Liberal Spirit of the Apostles and the Benevolent Design of the Christian Ministry, taking for his text 2 Cor. i. 24: *Not for that we have dominion over your faith, but are helpers of your joy.* In a contemporary letter, written by a hearer of this sermon, it is observed, " The composition and delivery were quite satisfactory: at the pathetic parts, Mr. Aspland's voice was just altered enough to indicate his sensibility without endangering his self-possession."

How deeply his mind was impressed with the weight of responsibility resting on him, as the successor of the distinguished men who had preceded him in the Hackney pulpit, several passages in the sermon express. He describes them as " men of irreproachable virtue, enlightened and steady devotion, laborious inquiry, fearless attachment to truth, deep and extensive knowledge, philosophic liberality and unbounded benevolence."

"I still hear their instructions reverberating within these walls; I see the images of their minds in the surviving attendants on their instructions; I am encompassed with a thousand recollections which tell me that *the place whereon I stand is holy ground:* I consider myself as occupying, alas! how unequally, the place to which these *messengers of God ascended*, to improve you with their wisdom, and to delight you with their eloquence; and from which they *descended* to dignify private life by their virtues, to bless the domestic circle by their kind affections, and to ameliorate society by their useful inquiries: with *Jacob* at *Bethel, I am afraid, and say, how dreadful is this place! this is none other but the house of God, and this is the gate of heaven.*"

Towards Mr. Belsham he thus expressed his feelings of respect and gratitude:

"To my immediate predecessor, I am prompted, no less by my unbiassed esteem of his character, than by private friendship, (if he will pardon my speaking thus publicly of the favours which he has conferred upon me,) to offer the tribute of my feeble praise. Cheerfully do I join with you, brethren, in admiration of the profundity of his theological researches, of the clearness and solidity of his reasonings, of the manliness and perspicuity of his writings, of his apostolic zeal for the unsophisticated truths of the gospel, of his equable temper, and affable manners. Long may he continue to display, in another place, the same talents and excellencies, which for a series of years edified and charmed this congregation!—may his abilities and virtues be as properly estimated *there*, as they were *here!*—and may a good Providence crown his labours with its blessing, and make him, in the midst of a dark and erroneous age, a *burning and a shining light!*"

In this fervid strain did he apostrophize his two most distinguished predecessors, Price and Priestley:

"Standing in a situation where I am so forcibly reminded of their characters, may I be indulged likewise, in expressing my high veneration of the two philosophical friends, the equal champions of rational religion, who in succession, and within the memory of most of you, asserted from this place the claims of religion, and the rights of human kind! Noble and generous spirits! accept our reverence and gratitude! *Though dead, ye yet speak!* Your memory lives among us; your virtues constrain our homage; your sufferings awaken our sympathy; your instructions, immortal as your names, enlarge the sphere of our knowledge, amplify and elevate our conceptions, exalt and invigorate our virtuous ambition, liberalize our faith, extend the boundaries of our charity, and evangelize and quicken our hope. *Dying in Jesus, your slumbers are blessed, and your works follow you.* Oh! that a portion, however small, of your spirit might descend upon one of the least in the train of your successors, who now invokes your remembrance; and that all who witnessed your example, and enjoyed your labours, may partake of your dignities in the *resurrection of the just*, and prove your *hope, your joy, your crown of rejoicing, in the presence of our Lord Jesus Christ at his coming!*"

In complying with the request of the congregation that he would print his sermon, he was enabled to acknowledge in the Preface his obligations to the Unitarian congregation at Newport, and also to the two Messrs. Shore, by whose liberality he had been able to accept with honour his present station.

His settlement in the neighbourhood of London at this time opened to him many social and intellectual pleasures, of which he partook with very keen relish. Hackney itself was the residence of several persons of high cultivation,—Rev. Thomas Belsham, Dr. Pett, Rev. John Pickbourn, Mr. Rutt, and occasionally Rev. — Dewhurst. In neighbouring villages, within the reach of an easy walk, were Mr. and Mrs. Barbauld, of Newington, and her brother, Dr. Aikin; Rev. Jeremiah Joyce, of Highgate; Rev. John Evans, of Islington; Rev. Dr. James Lindsay, of Bow; and the learned and amiable Rev. El. Cogan, of Walthamstow, the only survivor of the group. In London, in addition to his old friends, he now enjoyed the society of Dr. Abraham Rees; and at Essex House, the residence of Mr. and Mrs. Lindsey, in occasional morning visits, he not only saw the venerable confessor of Unitarianism, but many other distinguished friends of liberal Christianity. He renewed and improved into intimacy his acquaintance with the biographer of Robert Robinson, the upright, learned, amiable, but very eccentric George Dyer.*

To the House of Commons he sometimes went, when there was the prospect of a debate, and was upon several occasions rewarded by hearing Charles Fox, Lord Henry Petty and Mr. Grattan. He was at this time an occasional (though rare) visitor to Covent Garden Theatre, attracted by the noble acting of John Kemble and Mrs. Siddons.

He entered on his duties at Hackney simply as morning preacher. For a time the congregation indulged the hope that Mr. Belsham would be at liberty, and not be indisposed, to accept the afternoon preachership at the Gravel-Pit. When it became evident that Mr. Belsham's services were secured by his friends at Essex Street, other candidates were heard for the afternoon preachership at Hackney. That change

---

* Well did Charles Lamb say of his friend Dyer, that "for integrity and single-heartedness he ranked among the best patterns of his species." He was the kindest and gentlest of men, with a soul full of admiration for all that is truly great. His eccentricity was greatly increased by his defective eye-sight, and by his extraordinary absence of mind. His whole life was one of learned poverty and self-denial, borne with uncomplaining cheerfulness. For eleven years he was almost incessantly engaged on Valpy's Edition of the Classics, in 141 vols. His eye-sight entirely failed him shortly after the completion of this work. He died in his chambers at Clifford's Inn, March 2, 1841, aged 85, within a few days of the death of two octogenarian friends, Mr. Rutt and Mr. William Frend.

in the hours and domestic habits of the Dissenters about London had not taken place (although there were even then some symptoms of its approach) which prevents a large portion of our congregations from attending an afternoon service. Being disengaged in the afternoon, he was applied to to undertake the afternoon duty at Worship Street, and subsequently was invited by the congregation of Newington Green to become their afternoon preacher. In making this application, they reminded him that his great predecessor, Dr. Price, had sustained the proposed relation to them whilst minister of the Gravel-Pit.

He saw fit to decline both applications, knowing that it was the anxious wish of many of his friends at Hackney that he should be their sole pastor, and not thinking himself at liberty to defeat their wishes by making any other engagement for the afternoon. Before the close of the year, the matter was satisfactorily settled by his being elected the afternoon preacher. That the election was not unanimous (44 to 17 upon the ballot), only shewed that there were some in the congregation still anxious for the services of two ministers, to which they had been so many years accustomed.

During his early years in the ministry at Hackney, Mr. Aspland was not without his difficulties and anxieties. The taste of some of the aged members of the society had been formed on a model of preaching very different from his. Mr. Belsham's calm, well-argued and condensed appeals to the intellect of his hearers, and his lucid expositions of Scripture, had indisposed them to appeals to feeling, and the episodical introduction of topics not necessarily connected with the subject in hand, which sometimes characterized his successor's *early* sermons.

Those who felt any of their spiritual wants or tastes ungratified at the Gravel-Pit, could with little difficulty place themselves anew under their former pastor at Essex Street. There were also a few timid persons who were alarmed at the prospect of changes in the hour of the second service, and other lesser points proposed by their young and ardent pastor. From these and from other (as the result shewed, mere accidental) causes, there was within the first twelvemonth of his ministry a diminution in the number of families in the Hackney congregation. There is no reason why these things should not be disclosed. The statement, taken in connection with Mr. Aspland's subsequent success, may be the means of guiding and consoling others pressed by a similar anxiety. In what spirit he bore this trial, a large extract from a letter to the Treasurer of the congregation will shew. The first portion of it relates to an inadvertent irregularity on the part of that officer, which had been made the occasion of secession by a dissatisfied member.

Rev. R. Aspland to John Towill Rutt, Esq.

"Hackney Terrace, May 2, 1806.

"Dear Sir,—I thank you for a sight of Mr. ——'s letter. It does not surprise me.

"You ought not for a moment to take to yourself an iota of blame for his secession. The notice was, it is true, irregular, but no man of common sense or common feeling would make that irregularity a subject of censure after the notice was *revoked*, and an *apology* made for its being irregularly issued. If all the congregation had withdrawn their subscriptions on this occasion, you might have lamented their folly, but you ought not in justice to have reproached yourself. If an inadvertence is to be reckoned in all cases a *misdemeanour*, it is high time for us to quit society and to commence *anchorites*.

"I think the business should be got rid of on Sunday, not on Mr. ——'s account, but on account of some remaining subscribers who are 'perplexed with fear of change;' though having paid rather dearly for our object, it is vexatious to fall short of it.

"I consider, my dear Sir, the latter part of your letter a new proof of your friendship, which, I assure you, I regard and have ever regarded as one of the greatest privileges of my present situation.

"The state of our congregation is, I confess, truly lamentable. Were we called upon to make any great exertion, we should, I fear, find our weakness. This, however, grieves me, I assure you, less with regard to myself than to our cause. I should, indeed, be mortified, if I found that my inability for a situation which I had presumptuously accepted should prejudice the interests of truth and afflict my friends; but I shall never allow myself to repine at any desertion as a preacher, because it is the tenure of my profession, and I have made up my mind to it. Perhaps the more I am driven back by such desertion upon other exertions, the better it may be for my moral and intellectual improvement.

"I beg, my dear Sir, you will consider that I am fully aware that the withdrawment of so many families from the Gravel-Pit must materially injure our finances, and consequently that the minister's salary must undergo a proportionate reduction. I entreat, therefore, that your delicacy may not be permitted to throw upon you a greater burden than you ought, relatively to the rest of the congregation, to bear. I thought it my duty to touch on this topic, considering you for a moment in your official capacity as Treasurer of the meeting.

Be assured, my dear Sir, that I feel nothing of despondence; it is not, happily, in my nature so to feel. Providence may, after a little temporary adversity, give us, as a congregation, a season of prosperity. If not, we have meant well and endeavoured earnestly, and have therefore no reason on any side to be dissatisfied. I sometimes, however, ask myself, not in reproach, but simply in curiosity, whether I may not have mistaken the situation for which nature intended me. She, I sometimes think, has fitted me for a more obscure and quiet life than I now occupy, and may mean to punish my ambition in aspiring to the Gravel-Pit pulpit, by forcing me to see from thence empty pews. Since this little tumult has arisen, I have compared myself to the country mouse, on a visit to the town mouse, whom the racket of London so disturbed, that she parted, notwithstanding her rich living and luxuriant abode, for her hollow tree and the fare of the open fields."

The public and political events of the years 1805 and 1806, made a very deep impression on his mind. He was particularly struck with the removal by death of not less than four chiefs and leaders, " two eminent in counsel and two in arms." The latter were Lords Cornwallis and Nelson; the former, Mr. Pitt and Mr. Fox. Towards the latter he was habituated to indulge feelings approaching in their warmth to personal attachment. He was fascinated by the venerable simplicity of Mr. Fox's character—" the vast comprehension of his mind—his natural, heartfelt, convincing and commanding eloquence—his political wisdom, amounting almost to prophetic sagacity." On Mr. Pitt's death, it was with satisfaction and hope that he saw Mr. Fox called to administer the embarrassed affairs of the nation, distress having at length forced the Sovereign to set that value upon his talents which he had been so reluctant to acknowledge. When, in a few months' time, Mr. Fox's valuable life was closed by death in September, 1806, Mr. Aspland was deeply impressed and even affected by the nation's loss. Knowing the feelings of his flock on this subject to be in unison with his own, he took the occasion to address them on " The Fall of Eminent Men in Critical Periods," and dwelt on the bright features of Mr. Fox's character as a friend to popular liberty, as guided by moderation, as the advocate of justice and humanity, and the steady promoter of peace. The remarks that follow on the two latter topics were favourably received by the public.

"Never, during the whole of his long Parliamentary life, was his voice lifted up to justify oppression or persecution: never did the injured or oppressed appeal to the British senate that he did not exert his noble eloquence on their behalf. He made the cause of all that were wronged his own; and, even where he failed, through the perverseness of the times, of procuring justice for them, he in a measure compensated their sufferings by lending his great talents to their cause, and by drawing towards it the sympathy of mankind. In him, the most discordant sects and the most distant provinces found an ever-ready defender and a generous patron: he pleaded (and with what strength of argument, what rich variety of illustration, what dignity of sentiment, what majesty of diction!) for the equitable privileges of the Roman Catholic and the Protestant Dissenter; and he contended, with an eloquence alternately indignant and pathetic, for the rights of the harassed Irish, the oppressed Hindoos, and the suffering Africans. He brought into office the same just and benevolent principles which he had maintained while out of power. One of the first acts of his late administration, (too short, alas! for his own glory and our happiness!) was a measure for the restriction of the Slave-Trade, and by his means, a solemn resolution was voted by the Senate and laid before the Sovereign, on the justice and policy, the duty and necessity of 'the total abolition (to use his own strong expression) of the abominable traffic.' In discussing the former of these measures, he declared on behalf of himself and such of his colleagues as had voted with him on the subject when out of office, in a fervour of philanthropy, which quickly communicated itself to the breast of the country, and rekindled our warmest hopes, that 'they still felt the total abolition of the Slave-Trade as a step involving the dearest interests of humanity, and as one which, however unfortunate this administration might be in other respects, should they be successful in effecting it, would entail more true glory upon their administration, and more honour upon their country, than any other transaction in which they could be engaged.' Could party-spirit so far blind this nation as to render it insensible to his merits, the grateful African would commemorate his name, and plead with the Parent of the Universe, in language which is not disregarded in Heaven, for a blessing on it.

"He was on all occasions the STEADY PROMOTER OF PEACE, and, as a peacemaker also, our religion enjoins us to bless his memory. He reprobated the wickedness, he deplored the calamities of war, begun unjustly or protracted unnecessarily. He opposed, with all the vigour of his great mind, that unnatural and violent struggle between America and England, which terminated in the disruption of the Colonies from the mother country; he unmasked the false pretences, demonstrated the utter injustice, and foretold the ruinous consequences of the late war—a war which impoverished this nation, desolated a great part of Europe, filled the world with misery, and sowed every where the seeds of future hostilities; and he deprecated with all his profound wisdom, all his manly eloquence, the contest in which we are now unhappily involved, beginning with a violation of the national faith, and likely to end in the aggrandizement of that overgrown and menacing power which it was designed to check and reduce. On every favourable opportunity he interposed his pacific counsels. He was the advocate of human nature; he spoke its wishes and sustained its cause; and mankind looked up to him as their patron. When, at length, the necessity and distress of his country, which, let it be remembered, he predicted, imperiously demanded the aid of his great powers, and he took the helm of affairs, he began, in the true spirit of his character, negociations for peace; and Providence, in its inscrutable justice, has removed him from us, while the event of those negociations is yet uncertain. He expired, breathing those wishes for peace which it had been the purpose of his life to carry into effect; and peace, whenever we obtain it, will be considered by a grateful country as the legacy which he has bequeathed to us: his memory will be associated with the blessing, and will be for ever honoured in the association.

"We feel and cannot but feel—we lament and must deeply lament his loss—but we do not feel or lament alone; ALL EUROPE sympathizes with us!—for there is not a civilized nation that did not confide in his integrity and revere his wisdom."

The sermon was printed and published, " in testimony of the admiration felt by the Gravel-Pit congregation for Mr. Fox's character as a statesman." In the Preface, the author expressed a hope " that this token of the warm sympathy of a considerable society of Protestant Dissenters might afford a ray of comfort to the disconsolate minds of Mr. Fox's personal friends, and especially to that illustrious Nobleman who was not more nearly related to Mr. Fox by consanguinity than by congeniality of talent and principle."

Lord Holland acknowledged the sermon in the following letter, which was the beginning of a correspondence continued at intervals, with frankness and kindness, to the closing years of his life.

Lord Holland to Rev. Robert Aspland.
"Holland House, Oct. 9, 1806.

" Sir,—I have to thank you, which I do most sincerely, for your feeling and eloquent sermon. You are kind enough to say that one of your motives in publishing was to soothe my uncle's immediate and personal friends, and I hope, therefore, you will not consider it vanity in me, on whom you have bestowed such flattering and undeserved expressions, saying that you have had the gratification of fully attaining your object as far as I am concerned. For of the various productions the late melancholy event has given rise to, none have afforded me such real pleasure as this warm and affecting testimony paid to his public character; and the topics you have selected from his public life are those which were nearest to his heart, and which I hope those who were attached to him will never forget or abandon. His public exertions in the cause of humanity and toleration are well known, and most justly described in your work, but none but those who knew him intimately and privately can judge or even believe how anxious he was to promote them, and how secondary to them every other political object was in his mind during the whole of his life up to the very close of it.

"I am, Sir, with great truth, your very obliged, humble, servant,
HOLLAND."

CHAPTER XII.

The pressure on the intellectual powers of a young preacher during the early years of his ministry, especially if his congregation is numerous and intelligent, is great, and sometimes felt to be severe, leaving little energy for other pursuits. The mental activity of Mr. Aspland, however, was such, that within a very few months of his settlement at Hackney he voluntarily undertook literary and public duties of a very arduous nature. With that intuitive judgment which characterized all his public labours, he was enabled, notwithstanding the disadvantages of youth, inexperience, and a very slight acquaintance with the Unitarian public and their ministers, at once to chalk out for himself a line of duty and usefulness by which his whole after-life was directed.

He saw that the great want of the Unitarians of England was union and organization. A slight review of what had been previously done in London in the way of general organization and in promoting Unitarian literature, periodical and otherwise, may not be out of place or unacceptable. Several causes had conspired to increase the isolation both of individuals and congregations amongst Unitarians, which is in some degree the result of their habitual recognition of the rights of private judgment. During a large part of the 18th century, the old Presbyterian congregations of England were undergoing a gradual transition from a nominal "orthodoxy" to avowed "heterodoxy." The progress of the different congregations was in the same direction, yet not always equal in degree. The theological differences amongst the hearers in many cases influenced the preachers to practise a cautious reserve, which they justified to themselves by considerations of respect for the consciences of their people. When Mr. Lindsey, at the call of conscience, nobly forsook his benefice and opened in London a place for Unitarian worship, and Dr. Priestley and others fearlessly attacked the orthodox system from the pulpit and through the press, a new spirit began to arise amongst the liberal Dissenters of England. Of this the most visible fruits were, 1st, a "Society for promoting the Knowledge of the Scriptures," established in 1783, which published two volumes of theological disquisitions of considerable value, under the title of "Commentaries and Essays;" and, 2ndly, the "Unitarian Society for promoting Christian Knowledge and the Practice of Virtue by the Distribution of Books," established in 1791. Each of these Societies rendered good service to liberal theology. The first made its appeal simply to the very limited circle of Biblical students, and confined its labours to the illustration of Scripture. It was virtually superseded by the "Theological Repository," resumed by Dr. Priestley in the year 1784,* which was composed on a more comprehensive plan, and by seeking to promote religious knowledge in general, and courting rather than avoiding religious controversy, attracted a much larger share of public attention.

Of the Unitarian Society, the birth was untimely. The absorbing interest of the French Revolution, then in its early glory, gave to the first public meeting of the Society, held in London, April, 1791, a very political tone.† The toasts and speeches were made the subject, more than once, of Parliamentary comment, and were fastened in the public mind, to the prejudice of the Society, by the angry eloquence and bitter sarcasms of Mr. Burke. The horrible outrages at Birmingham soon after occurred; and it was not unnatural that the conductors of the Unitarian Society should avoid attracting unnecessary publicity to their

---

* The "Theological Repository" was begun in 1769 by Dr. Priestley, with the concurrence of Dr. Price and Rev. John Aikin, and with promises of support from Mr. Cappe, Mr. Samuel Clark, of Birmingham (who died, however, at the close of the year, before his promise had been fulfilled), Mr. Merivale, of Exeter, Mr. Scott, of Ipswich, and Mr. Turner, of Wakefield. Volumes were published in each of the two succeeding years; and in 1784, 1786 and 1788. In addition to the contributors named above, there were articles by Mr. Cardale, of Evesham; Mr. Mottershead, of Manchester; Thomas Amory, Esq., of Wakefield; Mr. Brekell, of Liverpool; Mr. Waters, of Ashburton; Mr. Lindsey; Mr. Hazlitt, of Maidstone; Mr. Badcock, of Barnstable; Mr. Willetts, of Newcastle; Mr. Palmer, of Macclesfield; Mr. Mackay, of Belfast; Dr. Toulmin; Dr. John Wright; Dr. Williams, of Sydenham; Mr. Gill, of Gainsborough; Rev. William Lillie, of Bingley; Dr. Calder; Mr. George Walker; Mr. Job David, of Frome; Mr. Marsom; Mr. Benjamin Carpenter; Mr. Wakefield; Mr. Wiche, of Maidstone; Mr. Bretland; Mr. Foljambe; Mr. T. F. Palmer; Mr. Garnham, of Cambridge; Mr. Evanson; and Mr. Henry Toulmin. See Mon. Rev. LIV. 134; Mon. Repos. XII. 526, 601, 602.

† See Belsham's Life of Lindsey, Chap. x.

proceedings, and confine them to a quiet annual meeting, with an occasional sermon,* and the publication of Unitarian books. There was another circumstance, not of an accidental kind, which perhaps diminished the usefulness, by narrowing the circle, of the Unitarian Society. This cannot be better stated than in the words of Mr. Belsham, who suggested the plan of the Society, and who was the author of the Preamble to the Rules:

"As the object of the Society was by no means to collect a great number of subscribers, but chiefly to form an Association of those who thought it right to lay aside all ambiguity of language, and to make a solemn public profession of their belief in the proper Unity of God, and of the simple Humanity of Jesus Christ, in opposition both to the Trinitarian doctrine of Three Persons in the Deity, and to the Arian hypothesis of a created Maker, Preserver and Governor of the world, it was judged expedient to express this article in the preamble in the most explicit manner. This was objected to by some, as narrowing too much the ground of the Society, which, as they thought, ought to be made as extensive as possible. But the objection was easily overruled, it being the main intention and design of the Society to make a solemn, public and explicit avowal of what, in the estimation of its members, was Christian truth; to enter a protest against the errors of the day; to unite those who held the same principles, and who were scattered up and down in different parts of the country, in one common bond of union; and to encourage them to hold fast their profession, and to stand by and support one another."—*Belsham's Life of Lindsey*, pp. 297, 298.

It is by no means certain that a more comprehensive policy on the part of the Unitarian leaders in 1791, and an attempt to combine in joint and friendly action all the worshipers of the Father of Jesus Christ, without regard to their opinions on the subject of Christ's pre-existence, would have been at once successful. But the course actually pursued tended to put the Arian and Unitarian bodies into a position of mutual hostility. Arianism at this time numbered some very earnest champions amongst the Presbyterian ministers of England, and their opinions were shared by some individuals in most congregations, and in some instances by whole congregations. In the metropolis, in 1791, the Arian party was composed of Dr. Abraham Rees, the popular minister of the chapel in the Old Jewry; Dr. James Lindsay, of Monkwell Street; Mr. Thos. Tayler and Mr. George Lewis, of Carter Lane; Mr. Butcher, of Leather Lane; Mr. (afterwards Dr.) John Evans, of Worship Street; and Mr.

---

* Even this was not attempted till 1806.

Hugh Worthington, of Salters' Hall. It is a singular fact that not one of the pulpits in these chapels is now occupied by an Arian minister, a result perhaps hastened by the decided stand taken by Mr. Lindsey, Dr. Priestley and Mr. Belsham.

The Unitarian Society expended in the first fourteen years of its existence (from Feb., 1791, to Dec., 1804), chiefly in printing and purchasing books, £2555. To it, within this period, we are indebted for the thirteen duodecimo volumes known by the general title of "Unitarian Tracts," containing works by Price, Priestley, Lindsey, Belsham, Disney, Frend, the Toulmins, Lardner, Hopton Haynes, Dr. Hartley, Rogers and Mason. The result was satisfactory; and, considering the inability from age of Mr. Lindsey to take any great share in public meetings, and Mr. Belsham's almost constitutional distaste to popular movements, the success of the Society was surprising. Still it can hardly be alleged that a subscription list, not including quite 150 names, and raising less than £200 per annum, was all that the Unitarian body could effect in 1805. Little had been done to bring the Unitarians of different parts of the kingdom into personal communication, and the publications of the Society did not include any periodical work.

The rise and progress of religious periodical literature is a subject of some interest. How large a share the Presbyterians took in the periodical literature of the 18th century, is not generally known. At the close of the previous century (1691—1696), Dunton led the way in his "Athenian Gazette." In 1704, Defoe began his "Review," which, it is admitted, "pointed the way to the Tatlers, Spectators and Guardians." In 1716, and two following years, appeared the "Occasional Papers," by Drs. Grosvenor, Avery, Wright, Evans, Lardner, Lowman, Earle and Simon Browne. In 1739, was published weekly, the "Old Whig," conducted by Dr. Avery, which ranked amongst its contributors, Dr. Caleb Fleming, Dr. James Foster, Dr. George Benson and Mr. Towgood. In 1761, Dr. Joseph Jeffries published "The Library," in which he was assisted by Lardner, Kippis, Radcliff and Alexander. In 1794, and five following years, appeared the "Protestant Dissenters' Magazine," amongst the numerous contributors to which were Dr. Toulmin and Mr. John Evans. Two years before this, in 1792, Mr. B. Kingsbury commenced "The Christian Miscellany, a Religious and Moral Magazine." He was assisted by Dr. and Henry Toulmin, Rev. J. Holland, Rev. W. Turner and others; but the Magazine expired on the completion of its eighth number. Of Dr. Priestley's "Theological Repository," in six vols., mention has been already made; and to the Magazine originated by Mr. Vidler, reference will be presently made.

In devising plans for combining in joint action all the elements of strength of which he found the Unitarian body in possession, Mr. Aspland was probably very much guided by the experience he had gained in the "orthodox" camp. At Mr. Eyre's school, and under his father's roof, he had learnt the charm to religious people of a monthly Magazine, detailing the progress of the plans in which they are interested, and sometimes assisted his master by writing out Missionary reports for the Evangelical Magazine, of which he was one of the originators and early editors. Amongst the Baptists, he had seen the beneficial effects of periodical assemblages of the members of different churches. This experience had been confirmed by his subsequent observation of the practice of his friends the General Baptists, in holding in London an annual assembly, for the transaction of business, for religious exercises and social union.

His first labour was to establish a periodical, in whose pages all the friends of liberal Nonconformity might record their thoughts and detail their plans of usefulness. In carrying out his purpose, his sense of justice and his regard for a very worthy man interposed a serious difficulty. The friend alluded to was Rev. William Vidler, minister to the Universalist congregation assembling at Parliament Court, Bishopsgate Street. Born of humble parents at Battle, in Sussex, and brought up to his father's trade of a stonemason, Mr. Vidler had, by the strength of his religious convictions and the clearness and power of his intellect, risen above the difficulties of his humble place in society and deficient education, and come to be the head of the Universalist body. He left the Established Church, and became first an Independent Calvinist, then a Particular Baptist. He early became a preacher, and continued his ministry, in spite of the remonstrances of his parents and the persecution of other members of the family. In 1792, he embraced the doctrine of universal restoration. This brought him to the knowledge of Mr. Winchester; and, on that gentleman's departure for America in 1794, he was invited to succeed Mr. W. as pastor of the congregation he had established at Parliament Court. In 1797, Mr. Vidler, in conjunction with Mr. Teulon, began to publish in monthly numbers, "The Universalists' Miscellany, or Philanthropists' Museum: intended chiefly as an Antidote against the Antichristian Doctrine of Endless Misery." One of the early and most valued contributors to the Miscellany was the Rev.

Richard Wright.* This led to personal intercourse and a warm friendship between the two. Mr. Wright was further advanced than his friend in "heterodoxy," and exercised for several years a very beneficial influence over him. In 1802, Mr. Vidler became, like his friend, an Unitarian. In that year, his Magazine changed its title to "The Universal Theological Magazine: intended for the Free Discussion of Religious Subjects, to which Persons of every Denomination are invited."

---

* Of Mr. Vidler, Mr. Wright left the following record in his unpublished MS. Autobiography, kindly lent to the writer by the Rev. John Wright, B. A., of Macclesfield:

"My acquaintance with Mr. Vidler commenced at a time when we were both in peculiar circumstances, having lost almost all our former religious connections and acquaintances through the change which had taken place in our opinions, and having formed scarcely any new ones. Each of us was glad to find a new friend, and to have a person with whom we could freely communicate on all theological subjects. We met each other at first with caution, and attempted, in as delicate a way as possible, to feel out each other's views. At that time he had not departed so far from the reputed 'orthodox' system as I had done, and had evidently some fears of Arianism, and much more of what he called 'Socinianism.' Our acquaintance soon became intimate, our correspondence frequent, our minds quite open to each other, and our friendship firm, and it continued to the time of his death, when, I hope, it was only interrupted to be renewed beyond the grave. When together, at different times, we discussed many points in theology with entire freedom, and I believe mutually assisted each other in the understanding of the Scriptures, and in attaining to a clear knowledge of divine truth. * * *

"Mr. Vidler was a man of an open and generous heart. He possessed a great deal of firmness and decision of character. He was a champion for religious liberty and free inquiry. His piety was rational and highly-toned; it supported him through many great troubles, and produced calm resignation to the will of God. In conversation he was ready, deliberate, free, and sometimes jocular; but always preserved a becoming degree of gravity. He was one of the best *extempore* preachers I ever knew; but whether it was that he had not the same confidence in his powers in London as in the country, I know not, he always appeared to me to preach much better in the latter than in the former. Wherever he went in the country, he had generally large audiences, and almost always commanded deep attention. He did not publish much; indeed, writing was to him a laborious work, especially in the latter part of his life, owing to his hand shaking very much. In controversy he displayed considerable talent when it occurred in conversation or at conferences. He had read much, and formed a strong inclination for reading and study. Considering the disadvantages under which he laboured in early life, the difficulties through which he had to make his way, and the unfavourable circumstances which attended him, he did much for the improvement of himself, the cultivation of his talents, and the promotion of the cause of pure and genuine Christianity. I owed much to him for the encouragement he gave me to undertake and proceed in various labours, and for introducing me to many of my new connections. Probably our acquaintance was a link in the chain of both our lives on which much depended."

In 1804, the title underwent another change, "The Universal Theological Magazine and Impartial Review." The work was continued until the close of the year 1805. Mr. Vidler's change of opinions had diminished year by year the number of its original supporters. His own want of literature prevented his Magazine from obtaining, in the latter years of its existence, any considerable circulation amongst Unitarians, and his very limited acquaintance with Unitarians had not enabled him to enlist a sufficient number of new and competent contributors. When Mr. Aspland removed to the neighbourhood of London, he found Mr. Vidler under considerable anxiety respecting the Magazine, which was struggling for existence, and burthened with a growing weight of debt. He immediately gave literary help to a considerable extent. To the list of papers contributed by Mr. Aspland to the Theological Magazine, mentioned in Chap. IX., must be added, the series of articles on Archdeacon Blackburne's Life and Works, those on Foster's Essays, a brief Life of Paley, and several smaller articles of Review.

Having tried his wings in these lesser flights, before the close of the year Mr. Aspland undertook to relieve Mr. Vidler of his responsibility as an editor, and also made a pecuniary arrangement with him, in consequence of which the whole property was transferred, with its liabilities, to the new editor.

It was a matter of prudence to give to the new series of the Magazine, which aspired to a different and wider circulation than the old, a new and general title. The title first thought of was one now so familiar to the Unitarian public, THE INQUIRER; but that ultimately chosen was doubtless in great measure suggested by Dr. Priestley's excellent periodical, The Monthly Repository of Theology and General Literature. A prospectus of the intended work was widely distributed, which stated that it was the editor's purpose to endeavour to blend literature with theology, and to make theology rational and literature popular; to be the advocate of scriptural Christianity; to guard the Protestant privilege of liberty of conscience; and, acting on the principle that a bold and manly habit of religious investigation is favourable to truth and virtue, to open the pages of the Monthly Repository to all writers of ability and candour, whatever were their peculiar opinions; so that there might be at least one periodical work in which the rational Christian, of whatever sect, might clear himself from misrepresentation, and expose persecution to the hatred of the world. He aimed to diffuse a spirit of inquiry, to enlarge the circle of knowledge, and to give a new impulse to the sentiments of peace and charity. The work was to consist of two parts, a Magazine and a Review. The former to contain Biographical Sketches, Moral and Theological Disquisitions, Political Criticism, Select Poetry and miscellaneous Original Communications; the latter to consist of a brief analysis of works on Morals and Theology, with an impartial examination of their merits. To these two parts were added an Obituary, a Monthly Catalogue of New Books, and copious Intelligence, religious, politico-religious and literary. The editor also stated his purpose to annex to each volume an annual Retrospect of Theology; a purpose which it is to be regretted he did not fulfil, the Intelligence, as he stated, surpassing in copiousness his expectations, and supplying his readers with ample materials for the Retrospect. However copious the materials may be, it requires a practised eye to select those that are important, and sound judgment to assign to them their relative places. From any writer possessing these requisites, a periodical Retrospect of Theology would be of great value. The new editor received from the several friends to whom he applied for literary assistance, the most gratifying assurances and promises, and his desk shortly after groaned under the pile of his correspondents' favours. A large part of the month of January was allowed to glide away before the selection of articles was made for the opening number. So little time was left for the printing of the last sheet or two, that the unpractised editor was compelled to spend the whole of the night but one before the day of publication in the dreary reading-room of a printer's office in Paternoster Row, to correct the proofs the moment they were ready for his eye. With the aid of this forced march, all was ready in time for the "Row" on the last day of the month, and there were fewer typographical errors* than, under the circumstances, might have been anticipated. The writers in the first No. of the Monthly Repository, so far as they were known to the editor and marked in his copy, were, *Mr. J. Spurrel*, of Hackney—Memoir of Rev. Edward Evanson; *Mrs. Cappe*, on the Indiscretion of Preachers; *Rev. S. Palmer*, of Hackney; *Rev. Rochemont Barbauld*—Dialogue on a Reflection of Dr. Jortin's; *Rev. William Turner*, of Newcastle—Dissenting Congregations in Northumberland and Durham; the late *Rev. Newcome Cappe*—Explanation of 2 Cor. v. 21; *Rev. John Holland*, of Bolton—Review of Cappe's Dis-

---

* One blunder had the effect of conferring a diploma on a humble village preacher named in the Intelligence. Instead of D[aniel], he was printed Dr., and the title stuck to him.

courses; *Mr. J. Evans*—Review of Parker's Lectures and Obituary of Mr. Pine; *Rev. H. H. Piper*—Obituary of Rev. Joseph Denney; *H. C. Robinson, Esq.*—Translations from Herder and Goethe. Most of the other articles were from the pen of the editor.*

---

* It is to be regretted that the Editor did not mark, in the subsequent volumes of his copy, the names of the authors. It may not merely gratify curiosity, but furnish materials to biography, to give the names of the principal writers throughout the first volume, where they are not distinctly stated. It is with great interest that the writer contemplates the names of the survivors in this list, and is enabled to state that several of them are amongst the most valued contributors to the *Christian Reformer*. It is perhaps an unparalleled circumstance that, after the lapse of forty-two years, six writers are found continuing voluntary literary assistance to the same or a similar periodical work.

Rev. W. Richards, Lynn—The Cambro-British Biographical Sketches, pp. 63, 120, 172, 229; obituary of Rev. D. Thomas, p. 271; Guilym Emlyn, p. 585.

John Towill Rutt, Esq., wrote under various signatures—as, T. O., p. 75; J. O., p. 76; Verax, p. 80; Laicus, p. 178; L. L., p. 180; A Friend to Civil and Religious Liberty, p. 182; A Gleaner, p. 283; Socius, p. 340; N. L. T., p. 568; Selector, p. 569; Whistonius, p. 594; J. T. R., p. 670.

Mr. David Eaton—Anti-magog, p. 79; Objections to the Unitarian Fund considered, p. 188.

Edward Taylor, Esq.—No Bigot, p. 650.

Mr. Benjamin Flower—Amicus, p. 81; Remarks on Life of Evanson, p. 247; A Plain Christian, pp. 583, 654; review of Bourdaloue's Sermons, p. 606.

J. E. Gambier, Esq.—S. D. R., p. 575.

Mr. Marsom—on John xiv. 16, 17; Ephes. i. 14.

Rev. Samuel Palmer, of Hackney—Censure of the Evangelical Magazine's Misrepresentations of Priestley's last Moments; Moderator, p. 289; Memoirs of Rev. Samuel Clark.

Rev. John Kentish—Review of Kenrick's Sermons.

Mr. John Christie—Review of Memoirs of Priestley.

Rev. Dr. Toulmin—Integritas, p. 626; Life of Rev. W. Robertson, D.D., pp. 109, 180, 226.

Rev. John Evans—Obituary of Rev. M. Naile.

Rev. L. Holden—An Observer, p. 528; Life of L. Holden, p. 561.

H. C. Robinson, Esq.—Parable from Lessing; Lessing's Education of the Human Race, p. 412.

Rev. John Kenrick—Translation from Paulus, p. 197.

Rev. W. Turner—Vigilius Posthumus, p. 544.

Miss Middleton—Cuvier's Eulogy of Dr. Priestley.

Mrs. Aspland—Plea for Candour, p. 241; Charlotte Richardson's Poems reviewed, p. 380.

Rev. H. H. Piper—Review of Montgomery's Poems.

Mr. J. Spurrel—Spence's Recantation, p. 246; Vindication of Memoirs of Evanson, p. 366; on the Eclectic Review, p. 475.

W. H. Reid, Esq.—W. H. R., pp. 254, 347, 481.

Rev. L. Carpenter—On 1 John v. 7; on Mental Pursuits; on an Improved Version of the New Testament.

Rev. Josiah Townsend—Thoughts on Baptism, pp. 300, 661.

Rev. W. Severn, of Hull—Sabrina, p. 463.

The editorship of the Monthly Repository brought Mr. Aspland into correspondence with the friends of liberal theology both at home and abroad. Amongst the earliest and ablest supporters of the work, two names deserve especial mention—Mr. J. T. Rutt and the Rev. John Kentish. There is not a volume of the Monthly Repository for the long series of twenty-one years, that was not enriched by their wisdom and learning or adorned by their taste. It is just to add, that the Rev. William Turner and the late Dr. Toulmin contributed many valuable articles, the former to the whole series, the latter to nine volumes and a half,—all that were published before his decease in 1815.

For a time, the Magazine was a heavy pecuniary burthen; but with that hopefulness and disregard to mere pecuniary interests which distinguished him through life, Mr. Aspland persevered, until it acquired, first, a circulation that paid its expenses, and ultimately one that was slightly remunerative.

In the first No. of the Monthly Repository it was announced that a plan was in agitation for establishing a Society for promoting Unitarian preaching among the poor, and the editor invited the communications of all persons favourable to the object. To the origin of this plan our attention must now be turned.

Amongst the General Baptist friends in London with whom Mr. Aspland had become acquainted, was Mr. David Eaton, a theological bookseller and occasional preacher. He was born in Scotland, of very humble parentage, and received little or no education. Abandoned in childhood by a profligate father, a common soldier, and living with his mother, who was in a state of abject poverty, his desire to learn a trade was long frustrated. On the death of his mother, when he was fifteen years of age, he was induced by a message from his father to remove to York. After some vicissitudes, he learnt the trade of shoemaking. To redeem himself from poverty, he worked during two years eighteen or nineteen out of the twenty-four hours. The consequences were, as might be expected, a serious illness which brought him near to death. Soon after this, he happily became acquainted with a fellow-craftsman

---

Rev. Jer. Joyce—A. B., p. 337; A. L., p. 372.
Rev. Job David—Theophilus Senex, p. 534.
Rev. S. Parker—p. 337.
Rev. R. Allchin, Maidstone—A. N., p. 601.
Rev. Daniel Jones—Calvin and Servetus.
Rev. Thomas Madge—Want of Zeal in Unitarians.
Rev. C. Wellbeloved—Vindication of Mr. Cappe's Discourses.

in the same city, Francis Mason. Through his influence he was led to join a society of Baptists, consisting of persons in the humble rank, but gifted with intelligent and inquiring minds. They " had just made the amazing discovery that the doctrines of the Trinity and of the Atonement are not to be found in the New Testament! They did not know that there was an Unitarian in the world besides themselves, and were perpetually occupied in devising means how most effectually to declare this great discovery to others."*

David Eaton soon became a teacher amongst his new friends. His natural sagacity and strength and soundness of intellect, qualified him to be a leader amongst the York Baptists. He had the good fortune to attract the notice of the Rev. Charles Wellbeloved, and by him was introduced to the venerable Newcome Cappe. The interest excited in their minds by Mr. Eaton's description of the struggles and unassisted progress of the little band of inquirers, induced him to compose a brief history of their proceedings. Their favourable judgment of the little work being confirmed by that of Mr. and Mrs. Lindsey, who shortly after paid their last visit to York, it was (by Mr. Lindsey's assistance) printed and published in 1800, under the title of " Scripture the only Guide to Religious Truth: a Narrative of the Proceedings of the Society of Baptists in York, on relinquishing the Popular Systems of Religion from the Study of the Scriptures."

Acting on the principle adopted by the York Baptists, to search the Scriptures and form his own religious opinions, Mr. Eaton soon outstripped his colleagues in theological liberality. Finding that his views of church discipline were, from their comprehensiveness, displeasing to his associates, and dreading the consequences of a conflict of opinions, he resolved to leave York. By the aid of Mr. Rutt, he was introduced to a small Unitarian congregation at Billericay, in Essex, of which he became for a few months the minister. He soon, however, removed to London and established himself in the book trade. Before leaving York, Mr. Eaton, rejoicing in his newly-acquired views of truth, and believing that there were every where persons who would equally rejoice to possess them, if plainly stated and earnestly enforced, revolved in his mind some plan of attacking the strongholds of orthodoxy by means of popular Unitarian preaching. He communicated

---

* See Mrs. Cappe's deeply interesting letter to Mrs. Lindsey, inserted in the Christian Reformer, Vol. XV. (12mo series), pp. 345—349. In the same vol. is a biographical sketch of Mr. Eaton, from the pen of Mr. Aspland.

his ideas and wishes to Mr. Wellbeloved, who was always ready to give kind and indulgent attention to the views of his humble neighbour. Mr. Wellbeloved thought the times were scarcely ripe for so great an undertaking.* He conversed with Mr. and Mrs. Cappe on his favourite subject. They trusted that truth was silently making its way, but deemed open and decided hostility to established doctrines imprudent and untimely. He continued, however, with honest zeal to urge his views, until Mrs. Cappe asked him to detail them in writing. He did so, and she was sufficiently interested in the plan to advise him to send it to Mr. Lindsey. That venerable confessor expressed his warm approbation of the plan, and that he should rejoice to see it carried into effect, and would assist those who would undertake it; but added, that he was prevented by age and infirmities from taking any active part in it. On his removal to London, Mr. Eaton communicated his plan to Mr. Rutt, and nothing will better convey to our minds a sense of the discouraging state of things in the beginning of the century, than the fact that this clear-sighted and courageous man, though deeply interested in the scheme and approving highly of the object, yet was appalled by the difficulties that seemed to lie in the way, and thought the Unitarians of England were not ready for a general association. For a time Mr. Eaton's plan slumbered. On Mr. Aspland's settlement at Hackney, Mr. Eaton and he often met, both at the house of Mr. Rutt and in London.† There were many reasons for their mutual sympathy. Both were strong-minded men; both were the architects of their own success in life; both, after difficulties and struggles, had reached the same theological conclusions. The strong individuality of Mr. Eaton's mind and manners was probably attractive to his companion, who always found a charm in the society of self-raised men, and greatly preferred their ruggedness to the polished feebleness of commonplace persons.

Mr. Aspland listened with deep interest to the suggestions of Mr.

---

* See Mr. Eaton's interesting account in the Mon. Repos., XX. 337, 479.

† The long sittings of the two friends, previous to the birth of the Unitarian Fund, in which their deliberative powers were commonly stimulated by the fumes of their favourite weed, gave rise to a ridiculous report respecting Mr. A.'s employment of his time. The foolish story, with many exaggerations, reached the ears of Mrs. Lindsey, who had little tolerance for the old Presbyterian usage of the pipe, and expressed herself in the decided way habitual to her. Her comments came back to the person principally concerned, and an explanation ensued which was satisfactory to all parties.

Eaton, which fell in with his own convictions and wishes. His energetic mind and sanguine temperament enabled him to overlook all immediate obstacles, and to see beyond them a course of useful and successful exertion. In short, Mr. Eaton found what he had been seeking for eight years—a leader able and willing to introduce his plan to public notice and successfully to work it out.*

The first council that was called together upon the subject consisted, in addition, of Rev. W. Vidler, Rev. John Simpson† and Mr. Marsom. Mr. Aspland, with the concurrence of the friends present, proposed the printing of Mr. Eaton's plan. It appeared accordingly in the "Universal Theological Magazine" for Sept. 1805, Vol. IV. p. 127, under the title of "An Address to Unitarian Congregations."

In his Address, the author laments that the Unitarians have adopted so few of those active measures which the experience of other Christian denominations recommended. The efficacy of popular preaching is dwelt upon, and the authority of Dr. Priestley, " that great friend of truth and patron of religious inquiry," is adduced in favour of popular plans for disseminating Unitarianism. The argument is somewhat embarrassed by the doubtful position, that " the poor can best instruct the poor." The writer proceeds to say that many friends and advocates of pure Christianity were rising up whose labours needed pecuniary support. " Whatever is done for those who have been regularly educated for the ministry, and who by change of sentiments become Unitarians, it is not recommended that they who now follow any

---

* It is to be regretted that Mr. Aspland's repugnance to seeing his own name and conduct unnecessarily dwelt upon in the pages of his Magazine, induced him to strike out of Mr. Eaton's narrative (Mon. Repos., XX. 480) that portion which related to his own share in originating the Unitarian Fund. But the writer more than once received from Mr. Eaton's lips an account of the matter. He always spoke with gratitude of the generous support his plans received from the young minister of the Gravel-Pit chapel.

† Mr. Simpson was a very worthy minister among the General Baptists. He was a native of Yarmouth, and became an associate and intimate friend of John Wesley. After a successful ministry of some years among the Methodists at Yarmouth and Lowestoft, his mind became unsettled on the subject of the influences of the Spirit. On communicating his difficulties to Mr. Wesley, that penetrating chief pithily said, "*Samson*, the Philistines are upon thee—escape for thy life!" His opinions were finally Unitarian. He was afternoon preacher at Worship Street for about fourteen years. He published, in 1802, "Plain Thoughts on the New-Testament Doctrine of Atonement." He lived many years at Hackney. His life was protracted till his 92nd year, when he died, Oct. 14, 1824, leaving many descendants. One of them is the present zealous minister of Chatham, the Rev. J. C. Means.

manual labour should be taken from that sphere of usefulness. Nothing more is intended than that such assistance should be given as would indemnify them for unavoidable loss of time, enable them to fit up a place of meeting and support its expenses, and give encouragement to all prudent exertions."

The "Address" succeeded in exciting considerable attention. In the following No. of the Magazine, a writer signing himself H. D. W. (pp. 200—202, understood to be Mr. D. W. Harvey), professed his intention, with a view of forwarding the plan, to move certain resolutions at the next quarterly meeting of the Unitarian Society. Another writer (*Festina Lente*, pp. 258—260) requested H. D. W. to reconsider his purpose, alleging that the Unitarian Book Society was usefully pursuing its own objects, that the scheme for encouraging popular preaching had already received promises of support, " and the further promotion of it was in the hands of a friend to the cause, whose zeal and ability would not suffer it to languish."

The preliminary discussion in Mr. Vidler's Magazine was not productive of unmixed good. The premature and very unnecessary introduction of the subject of the employment of lay and uneducated preachers, was not unnaturally distasteful to some of the older Unitarian ministers, and shook their confidence in the judgment of the promoters of the scheme. But sufficient support was offered to justify immediate action. The first actual meeting of the Society was held Feb. 11, 1806, at the house of Mr. Ebenezer Johnston, Bishopsgate Street. The chair was taken by Mr. John Christie, who for so many years discharged the office of Treasurer to the great advantage of the Society. The members of this preliminary meeting were few in number, consisting, in addition to the Chairman, of Mr. Ebenezer Johnston, Mr. Joseph Holden, Mr. John Sowerby, Mr. D. W. Harvey, Rev. W. Vidler, Rev. James Pickbourn,* Mr. Eaton and Mr. Aspland.

The principal resolutions passed were,—

" I. That it is desirable to establish a Fund for the promotion of Unitarianism by encouraging popular preaching.

---

* Rev. James Pickbourn for many years conducted an academy for young gentlemen at Hackney. He pursued his studies for the ministry under Dr. Jennings. He officiated one year at Harlestone and four years at Brentwood. He was subsequently appointed Librarian by Dr. Williams's Trustees. In 1777, he opened his school, which he continued till 1804. He published a " Dissertation on the English Verb," and another on " Metrical Pauses." He left at his death (which took place, May 25, 1814, in his 79th year) £1000 to the Presbyterian Fund. See Mon. Repos., Vol. IX.

"II. That by Unitarianism we intend the system of doctrines which is included in the belief and worship of One only God, the Creator and Governor of the world, in contradistinction to doctrines generally termed 'orthodox.'

"III. That the uses to which the Fund shall be applied shall be, 1, To enable poor Unitarian congregations to carry on religious worship; 2, To reimburse the travelling and other expenses of teachers, who may contribute their labours to the preaching of the Gospel on Unitarian principles; 3, To relieve such Dissenting ministers as, by embracing Unitarianism, subject themselves to poverty."

A Committee was appointed to prepare the Constitution of the Society, and to Mr. Aspland was assigned the office of Secretary, the duties of which he continued to discharge for many successive years.

Mr. Belsham was named as a member of the Committee. He declined to serve. The motives by which he was actuated appear in the following passage, written by him several years after, marked by the habitual candour of his mind:

"But the Society which at present holds the foremost rank, and engages the most general and warmest support of the Unitarian body, is that which is called the Unitarian Fund Society; the professed object of which is to encourage popular preaching, and to engage missionaries to visit different parts of the country, and, wherever there is an opening, to preach pure and uncorrupted Christianity in opposition to popular and prevailing errors. Some of the ministers employed in these missions, though not possessing the advantage of regular education, are men of very popular talents and very extensive information; and by the great success with which their labours have been attended, they have abundantly proved that simple, unsophisticated truth has charms to captivate even the most ordinary minds, when it is exhibited to them in a clear and affecting light, and demonstrated the fallacy of the commonly-received opinion, that Unitarianism is not a religion for the common people. This being a new experiment, in which unlearned ministers were chiefly employed, many of the more learned and regular members of the body stood aloof, and declined to give countenance to a proceeding of the prudence and propriety of which they stood in doubt. Some do not yet (1812) approve it, and others who wish well to the design do not regard it as within the field of their personal exertions. But after the success which has attended the efforts of this Society, no person who is a real friend to the cause can consistently be hostile to its principle."

At the first half-yearly meeting of the Unitarian Fund, held May 29, 1806, the Secretary read a report of the proceedings and prospects of the Society. From this report, which was never printed, the writer is, by the kindness of the Committee of the Unitarian Association in entrusting to his care the early Minutes, able to make the following extract, which, while it serves to shew the obstacles which the Unitarian Fund at first met with, indicates the spirit by which they were in the end happily overcome:

"It is to be regretted that the Society is regarded by some of our Unitarian brethren with a dubious sort of feeling, bordering upon suspicion and dislike. They think we shall degrade the Unitarian cause, and put ourselves on a level with the Methodists. Their fears originate in their love of Truth, and ought to be respected; but let us ask in what particulars we are likely to become what is feared? The Methodists are praiseworthy for their zeal—their zeal as displayed in the fervour of their devotions, and their activity in popular preaching. * * *

"This question resolves itself into two or three principal inquiries, the bare statement of which is, one would think, sufficient for our purpose. In the first place, Is the Unitarian doctrine the doctrine of the gospel? Is the gospel intended for the poor, or can it be understood by them? Is it the duty of Christians to propagate the gospel; and, if it is, is it not right to propagate it by the methods taken by our Lord and his apostles, and which have always succeeded? The Unitarian that shall negative these questions will excite my wonder, as will the Unitarian in an equal degree who, granting them, shall yet deny merit to the Unitarian Fund. * * * We shall, I trust, convince our elder brethren, who like the brother in the parable will not come in, that our claims are not arrogant, our conduct not unworthy of our cause. Whether we succeed or not in satisfying their minds, it will still be meet (to accommodate to our purpose the words of the father in the parable alluded to) that we should make merry and be glad, for popular Unitarianism was dead and is alive again, and was lost and is found."

Of the proceedings of the Unitarian Fund, occasions will hereafter arise of speaking. It need now only be added, that it rapidly rose in favour with the Unitarian public, and numbered before the close of the year nearly 200 subscribers. There were not wanting the names of several "elder brethren" among the subscribers and donors, including Mr. Lindsey, Mr. Belsham, Mr. Barbauld, Mrs. Cappe, Mr. Kentish, Mr. Holland, Mr. Corrie, Mr. Rowe, Dr. Toulmin, Mr. Turner and Mr. Yates.

CHAPTER XIII.

In the year 1807, Mr. Aspland introduced at the Gravel-Pit a series of weekly Conferences on religious subjects. The meetings were held each Wednesday evening during the winter season, beginning at a quarter to seven o'clock. They were opened and concluded with singing and prayer. The subjects of discussion were arranged and published at the beginning of each season, and comprehended a great variety of topics in theology,* interpretation of Scripture, moral philo-

---

* A list of the subjects of Conference for one season may be added with advantage. Of the following season the subjects will be found appended to the *Plea for Unitarians*, pp. 137—139.

1812.
Dec. 9. The probable Consequences of an universal Circulation of the Bible, "without Note or Comment."
16. The Grounds of the Reformation from Popery, in the 16th Century.
23. Whether the Reformation left any of the prevailing Corruptions of Christianity unreformed?
30. Characters of the "Man of Sin," 2 Thess. ii. 3, &c.

1813.
Jan. 6. Whether any part of Christian Doctrine be proposed to the Belief of Mankind as a *Mystery*?
13. The Calvinistic Doctrines of Election and Reprobation.
20. Whether the Declaration, Mark xvi. 16 (*He that believeth and is baptized, shall be saved; he that believeth not, shall be damned*), be applicable to Men of the present Day?
27. The Innocency of Mental Error.
Feb. 3. The Apostles' Creed.
10. The Athanasian Creed.
17. Moral Effects of War.
24. Scriptural Authority for Infant Baptism.
March 3. Peculiarities in the Doctrine and Discipline of the People called Quakers.
10. The idea of Christianity as a Reformation, Heb. ix. 10.
17. Whether Infallibility be claimed by the Prophets, Apostles, or Evangelists?

sophy and ecclesiastical history. The meetings were open to all comers, of every variety of faith. The minister presided; and on him devolved the important task of summing up each evening's discussion, supplying deficiencies, explaining difficulties, and striking the balance between the conflicting arguments adduced by the speakers. These meetings were continued for a long series of years. To the young and to religious inquirers they proved interesting and eminently serviceable. From the first they were remarkably successful, attracting within their sphere persons of every variety of belief and unbelief. To all, a fair hearing was granted. For the conduct of meetings of this kind, Mr. Aspland possessed remarkable qualifications. His personal bearing, without any thing of priestly assumption, was sufficiently dignified to maintain order and decorum, and sufficiently familiar to encourage perfect freedom of discussion. His patience and firmness were sometimes tried by personal attacks, but assailants using weapons of this kind generally retired with the mortifying consciousness that they had only lowered themselves. Generally speaking, the discussions, though animated, were sober and improving. The summing up was often a masterly performance, and exhibited copious knowledge, vigorous logic, and skill in assigning to the several arguments their respective place and weight. He had many able assistants, both amongst the members of his own congregation and ministers and laymen of other societies. Messrs. Rutt, Christie, Parkes, Young, Hart, Fearon, Talfourd, W. H. Reid and Marsom, may be named amongst the laymen who took part in the Conferences. Mr. Vidler, Mr. Barbauld, Mr. Simpson and Mr. Gilchrist, were amongst the divines who gave their help. It is believed that many persons were made Unitarians by means of these discussions. A clergyman* ministering in the parish of Hackney made public through the press his

---

    24. Whether the Old Testament reveal the Doctrine of a Future State of Existence?

    31. Agreement between the Church of Rome and the Established Protestant Churches.

April   7. Doctrines common to all Christians.

    14. Love to Christ on Unitarian Principles.

    21. Whether any Scheme of Church Discipline can be devised which shall sufficiently discountenance Immorality, without infringing upon Christian Liberty?

    28. Whether the Character of God, as revealed in the Scriptures, warrants the expectation of the Final Happiness of all Mankind?

* Rev. H. H. Norris, in 1813. See his "Practical Exposition of the Tendency and Proceedings of the British and Foreign Bible Society," p. 207.

complaint of this "debating assembly, at which the mysteries of the Christian faith are all in their turn brought under discussion, with that freedom of inquiry which admits every one to deliver his opinion." To this clerical critic this appeared an "outrage upon Christianity." He deplored the fact that these Conferences were "so attractive to the young and inconsiderate" that they frequently "attended them in great numbers."

The spirit in which Mr. Aspland and the members of his flock engaged in these Conferences was thus described by himself:

"Not being under any other restraints than those of Scripture and Reason, we judge that we cannot act more wisely than to communicate to each other our doubts and difficulties, our discoveries and persuasions. We dare to *search the Scriptures*, because we dare to avow the doctrines which in our judgments the Scriptures teach."*

The Curate of St. John's had asserted that at the Gravel-Pit Conferences "every one might deliver his opinion in any language which an unchastised imagination might suggest." In setting right his censor as to a matter of fact, Mr. Aspland rebuked his want of charity:

"No, Sir, there are bounds within which the 'Moderator of the Assembly,' as you very properly style the minister who presides upon the occasion, confines all the discussions; what they are, I may, perhaps, best explain by saying that he would not permit any speaker to use such language, with regard to the members of your Church, as you have used, in your book, with regard to Unitarians."

The Hackney Conferences, indirectly as well as directly, made heavy demands upon the minister's time. They who were preparing to join in the discussion, often came to him for advice and the loan of books. In his hospitality, his house was the home of those that came from a distance to join in the Conference. Earnest theological discussions often sprung up at his supper-table, surrounded by Conference guests, which were carried on beyond midnight, and sometimes adjourned till the next day. The diary has sometimes entries of this kind the day after the Conference:

"1807, Jan. 22.—Messrs. Vidler and Marsom stayed dinner. Talk all the morning of baptism and first chapter of John. I read to them Cappe's Dissertation on Baptism."

A little before this time Mr. Aspland had given up the doctrine of

---

* "Plea for Unitarian Dissenters," pp. 122, 123, *note*.

the perpetuity of baptism, but to the end of his life he abstained from the practice of infant baptism, using in its stead a simple service of dedication. Mr. Cappe's theory in the Dissertation referred to is, that it was on the part of the baptizer only a form of reception to instruction, and on the part of the baptized an acknowledgment of the truth of the pretensions of the person who baptized; and he further held that the term *baptism* might be used wherever there was a reception of a proselyte to information and instruction, even where the rite was not literally used. Mr. Aspland often, at this period of his life, had to defend his new convictions on the subject of baptism against Messrs. Wright, Vidler, Toulmin and others.

Other additions to his public services, undertaken by him shortly after the establishment of the Conferences, were the catechising of the children in the Sunday afternoon, and the delivery to the young people of the congregation of a lecture on some scriptural, theological or historical subject, immediately after the close of the morning service. The addresses were short (occupying in delivery about twenty minutes) and popular, and generally consecutive in subject. One course was on Prophecy; another, a series of Sketches of Ecclesiastical History; another, on the Primitive Church; another, on the three Creeds of the Apostles, the Nicene and the Athanasian; another, on the English Deistical Writers, &c. The substance of many of these lectures may be found in the early volumes of the *Christian Reformer* (duodecimo series). The numerous, intelligent and deeply interested assemblages of young persons in the lecture-room at the Gravel-Pit, were abundant reward to their pastor for his exertions. Sometimes, in addition to his regular and laborious Sunday duty, he undertook a third service in the evening in London, and occasionally took his turn in a week-evening lecture established by Mr. Vidler in the neighbourhood of Stratford.

His duties at home were not unfrequently interrupted by calls abroad to distant places, to preach charity sermons and to plead in behalf of the Unitarian Fund. In the year 1807, he had the gratification of re-visiting his friends at Meersbrook and Norton; and his diary records the pleasure which he derived from the interesting and able conversation of many of the guests assembled to meet him, amongst whom were Chantrey and Montgomery. At the same time he visited Nottingham, to preach the school sermon, and passed several very happy days in the society of Rev. James Tayler and Rev. John Grundy, and of the principal members of the High-Pavement congregation, amongst whom were many persons of cultivation and refinement. It happened that the election of a Member of Parliament was going on in the town. The Liberal candidate was Dr. Crompton. At the invitation of one of the sheriffs (an Unitarian), Mr. Aspland went more than once on the hustings, and was present when the poll was closed. This accidental circumstance subsequently occasioned him the annoyance of receiving the Speaker's warrant to attend and give evidence on the subject of the election before the Committee, Dr. Crompton being beaten, and having petitioned against the return. It was natural enough that Dr. Crompton's party availed themselves of the evidence of one residing near the metropolis, of respectable station and unbiassed by local feuds. But Mr. Aspland's memory was too definite and unyielding to give that help to the case of Dr. Crompton which his leading counsel, Serjeant Heywood, knew was wanted, and the Doctor's petition was voted "frivolous and vexatious."*

---

* As an illustration of the manner in which, forty years ago, and till the Reform Act, elections were carried on, and as a document of some local interest, insertion may be given to a paper in Mr. Aspland's handwriting, entitled, "Evidence, as far as I can recollect it, concerning the Nottingham Election, May, 1807."

"I was present at the Nottingham election on Saturday, the 16th of May, 1807, about three hours in the forenoon, when I heard proclamation frequently made for closing the poll. Between the proclamations there were considerable intervals. I heard Mr. Smith demand of the returning officers the close of the poll, and heard Mr. Balguy declare that he would close it the first moment he could legally. Mr. Smith, I remember, declared the conduct of the sheriffs to be 'shameful,' and seemed to intimate that he would bring them to account. Immediately afterwards, Mr. Smith hastily and angrily left the poll-booth.

"I was on the hustings likewise on the afternoon of Monday, the 18th. I entered about four o'clock, and remained till the close of the poll, about an hour. Soon after my entering the booth, a conversation took place between Dr. Crompton and Mr. Balguy, which lasted some time, concerning the close of the poll. Mr. Balguy wished Dr. Crompton to consent to it. Dr. Crompton said that he could not and would not do so, as he believed he had considerable chance of gaining the election, and at any rate wished to be respectable on the poll. Dr. Crompton also said that if Mr. Balguy had determined to close the poll before the *fifteenth* day, he ought to fix on a time, say Wednesday at twelve o'clock, and give the electors notice of it. From this period proclamations were frequently made for closing the poll, against which Dr. C. still protested. At the close of one of the proclamations, several persons came up and voted. Immediately afterwards, proclamation was made; but before the crier had proclaimed the first proclamation the third time, I saw a voter present himself, who, I heard some one declare to Mr. Balguy, had taken the necessary oaths in the ante-room, and demand to poll. Upon this immediately Mr. Balguy declared the poll to be closed, and that this voter had been purposely kept back, with a view to protract the election.

Mr. Aspland was about this time (July 4, 1807) a guest of Serjeant Heywood's, to meet an interesting party. Instead of the brief record in the diary, the fuller narrative of Mr. Belsham will be used.*

"The zeal of the Dissenters, and particularly of the Dissenting ministers in Yorkshire (in behalf of Lord Milton), in favour of the late Administration, and the disdain with which they generally treated the cry of 'No Popery,' has given the leaders of that party a more favourable opinion of Dissenters, and induced some of them to desire an interview with a few of the Dissenting ministers in London. Accordingly, we were invited to dine at Mr. Serjeant Heywood's about a fortnight ago. The party consisted of Lord Holland, Lord Lauderdale, Lord Howick (the late Earl Grey), Lord Stanley, Mr. Whitbread and Mr. W. Smith, on the one hand; and per contra, Dr. Rees, Mr. Jervis, Mr. Aspland, Dr. Lindsay and myself. I expected it to have been an insipid party, but it proved otherwise. Dr. Lindsay (late Mr. Lindsay, of Monkwell Street), who, you know, is a bold and intelligent man, told Lord Howick that when he was in power he did not go far enough. 'You will do no good, my Lord,' said he, 'until you do something for the people. If you were to come in again to-morrow, you would be turned out the next day if you brought forward any measure that was offensive to the Court. *If you would bring forward your own plan of Parliamentary Reform, you might do some good, but till then you can do nothing.*'† Lord Howick, who is a very

---

"Before my giving my evidence, Serjeant Heywood (principal counsel for Dr. Crompton) wanted to persuade me that I remembered many things which I did not: and on my examination, for refusing to seem acquainted with some matters that were brought up, I was complimented by the counsel against the Dr. with having a *very bad memory*. My examination was short, and upon the whole respectful, on the part of my examiners: no questions were put to me by the Members of the House of Commons.

"After me, they examined Carrington (I think his name was), whose vote was refused. It appeared that he had taken the oaths several days previous to the close of the poll. He was questioned why he did not present himself to vote before, and whether he had not been kept back by Dr. C. or his agents. To the latter part of the question he answered in the negative; but to the former he would not for a time give any other answer than that he did not choose to vote before: the adverse counsel insisted upon the reason of his *not choosing;* he stopped the examination by answering at last, 'I thought, as I was a free man and had a free vote, I might have free time.' ROBERT ASPLAND.

"N. B. Till I entered the hustings on the 16th, I had never seen any of the candidates. I gained admission by one of sheriff Oldknow's tickets.

* In a letter to Rev. Mr. Broadbent, of Warrington. See Williams's Memoirs of Mr. Belsham, pp. 574, 575.

† The italics are not Mr. Belsham's. Dr. Lindsay's words were prophetic, although the fulfilment of the prophecy was necessarily delayed by Earl Grey four-and-twenty years.

proud, reserved man, gazed with great attention and amazement on our friend Lindsay, not having been used to be addressed with so much freedom and so little ceremony, but he did not appear to be at all offended; and with the greatest politeness and good humour replied, 'He was now as much a friend to Parliamentary Reform as ever, but he was fully persuaded that if he should bring forward a measure of this kind into the House, at present, he should be left in a very small and a very unpopular minority;' and Lord Holland added, 'That the people stood in great need of being enlightened, for he was fully persuaded that if we had at this time a House of Commons which spoke the sense of the great mass of the people, we should be in a much worse situation than we are at present.' I thought all this very good sense, but my friend Lindsay was not convinced. The conversation, however, was kept up with great spirit and good humour till half-past ten o'clock, when we parted. The clerical guests liked the party very much, and I hope that the political guests were not displeased. We all agreed that Lord Holland was a most amiable and agreeable man, and that he had much of the appearance and style of his late admired and regretted relation."

Towards the end of 1808 (Nov. 3), the venerable Theophilus Lindsey, whose life had been protracted to his eighty-sixth year, gently breathed his last, after a week's illness. For five-and-thirty years he had been an Unitarian confessor, having resigned his living in the month of November, 1773. Mr. Lindsey's infirmities had prevented frequent intercourse with the minister of the Gravel-Pit, but Mr. Aspland's occasional morning visits to Essex House had confirmed the feeling of reverence which familiarity with Mr. Lindsey's history and writings had previously excited. When the news of his death reached him, he felt, with Mr. Belsham, that the world had lost "one of the most upright, consistent and eminently virtuous characters which ever adorned human nature." He was permitted the privilege, extended only to a few, of beholding the remains of the confessor at Essex House, and on a subsequent day (Nov. 11), of following them to their last earthly resting-place in Bunhill Fields, where Mr. Belsham performed the funeral service.

On the Sunday following Mr. Lindsey's death, Essex-Street chapel was closed, as a suitable token of grief for the silence of that voice which had there first, and for so many years, preached the words of truth and righteousness. In reply to a request to Mr. Belsham that he would preach at Hackney on that day, Mr. Aspland received the following expressive note:

"Saturday afternoon.*

"My dear Sir,—You should not have had the trouble to ask twice, had it been for your own convenience only, had it been in my power to have assisted you to-morrow. But, under the present oppression upon my mind, I feel myself utterly incapable of officiating in public. I could wish for the next week that I had wings like a dove, that I might fly into the wilderness.—I am, dear Sir, very sincerely yours, "T. BELSHAM.†

"I rejoice to hear of your good success in your missionary tour."‡

Although Mr. Lindsey had never been personally connected in any way with the congregation at Hackney, it was felt by both minister and people that his death was an occasion that demanded an expression of their estimate of "his many and great virtues, and of his services in the cause of Truth." Some members of the congregation had long enjoyed his personal friendship, many had received light and conviction from his writings, and all had admired his example and revered his character. On the Sunday following that set apart for the proper funeral sermon at Essex Street, Mr. Aspland gave expression to the feeling that pervaded his flock, by preaching a sermon suitable to the occasion. He appropriately selected the character of Abraham as resembling in one material quality that of the deceased confessor, and hence described "the duty and reward of sacrificing temporal interests on the altar of Truth." This sermon, which was afterwards printed, was enriched by a "Tribute of Gratitude, Affection and Respect, to the Memory" of Mr. Lindsey, which was from the pen (the statement is now, by permission, made public for the first time) of the Rev. John Kentish. This able memoir, which displays "intimate acquaintance with the subject, and great felicity of expression," was at first intended for the *Monthly Repository*, after having been delivered to the numerous and respectable congregation of the New Meeting, Birmingham. The pulpit draped with black cloth, and the mourning garments of a very

---

* Nov. 5, 1808.

† The funeral services had been long foreseen by Mr. Belsham with great anxiety, and were executed with much pain, under the fear that he might not do justice to the subject and occasion. See Mr. Belsham's diary, Memoir, p. 582.

‡ Mr. Aspland had just returned from an interesting missionary tour in Kent, where he visited the churches at Tenterden, Cranbrook, Rolvenden, Maidstone and Chatham. He was accompanied during a portion of the tour by Mr. Richard Wright. The consequences of this tour were very beneficial to the Unitarian Fund. For Mr. Laurence Holden, the minister of Tenterden, Mr. Aspland entertained high respect.

crowded audience, as well as the preacher's sermon, shewed the feelings of the Hackney congregation to the memory of Mr. Lindsey.

It was probably to mark her sense of this tribute to the memory of her deceased husband, that Mrs. Lindsey presented to Mr. Aspland the Greek Bible which had been his. On the first leaf there is inscribed, in the firm and well-proportioned manuscript, so indicative of her character*—THIS BOOK BELONGED TO THE LATE THEOPHILUS LINDSEY, AND IS NOW PRESENTED TO THE REV. ROBERT ASPLAND AS A MEMORIAL OF HIM, AND AS A TESTIMONY OF THE RESPECT HE BORE HIM FOR THE ZEAL AND SERVICES MANIFESTED IN PROMOTING TRUTH, BY SPREADING THE KNOWLEDGE OF THE DIVINE UNITY, BY HIS FRAIL REPRESENTATIVE,

MARCH 30TH.   H. LINDSEY.
ESSEX HOUSE, 1809.

Mr. Aspland had, in the previous year, named his third-born son "Theophilus Lindsey."

Our narrative must now return to Cambridgeshire. In Soham events had been for some time going on, the progress of which he watched with deep interest.

In 1803, Mr. John Gisburne, who had been a Wesleyan preacher, joined the Baptists, and became assistant to Rev. Andrew Fuller, at Kettering, in whose family he resided nearly six months. The Baptist church at Soham wanting a minister, Mr. Fuller recommended Mr. Gisburne. After preaching a few months, he was invited to become the pastor. He objected to their covenant of church-fellowship and articles of faith (which had been drawn up by Mr. Fuller during his ministry at Soham), subscription to which was demanded from every member. He expressed a strong aversion to the shackles of subscription to a creed, and advised the people to adopt the Scriptures in the place of the covenant and articles. They did so, and Mr. Gisburne became their minister. His services were acceptable, and the church increased. Mr. Fuller heard of their proceedings with displeasure, and attempted to effect Mr. Gisburne's removal from Soham, but unsuccessfully.

From time to time Mr. Aspland heard from his relations in Cam-

---

* Mr. Belsham truly said of this excellent and vigorous-minded woman, "She entered into all his (Mr. Lindsey's) views, she applauded the generous purpose of his heart, she encouraged, comforted, animated him, and, if possible, even went before him in the career of Christian glory."—Funeral Sermon for Mrs. Lindsey, p. 23.

bridgeshire, some of whom were connected with the Soham Baptists, reports of Mr. Gisburne's preaching and course of reading which excited his curiosity. He became acquainted with him, and found him to be an inquirer after Christian truth. In 1808, Mr. Gisburne avowed his adoption of Unitarianism. The congregation became agitated and divided, but the majority continued to support him. The minority seceded. Things were in this state in August 1808, when Mr. Aspland visited Cambridgeshire. He was requested by Mr. Gisburne to preach for him at Soham, and, having ascertained that the majority of the congregation concurred in the request, he consented to preach on the following Sunday afternoon. On approaching the town on that occasion, he was met by a mob of Mr. Gisburne's opponents, who endeavoured by their clamours to frighten him and prevent his undertaking the service. He rebuked them, and warned them of the consequences of disturbing public worship. They were intimidated by his presence, and the service proceeded without interruption, his sermon (on 2 Tim. i. 7) being listened to with great attention by a large and respectable congregation. The subsequent proceedings of the Soham Calvinists were detailed in the Fifth Report of the Unitarian Fund, whence the most important facts are selected. After their secession, the congregation flourished and appeared heartily united. The seceders perceiving this, and fearing that by leaving the society they had contributed to give it a decidedly Unitarian character, resolved to return in a body and to cast out Mr. Gisburne. They now attended the public worship, and, for the sake of preserving a right to vote in the affairs of the society, attended the Lord's Supper—the test of church-membership. At various meetings they endeavoured to accomplish their purpose of ejecting the minister, by questions put to the vote, but were always left in a small and constantly lessening minority. Thus defeated, they became outrageous, and proceeded to the length of interrupting the public worship. On several Sundays they raised a tumult in the meeting-house. One method of annoyance pursued was to bring books of controversy to the meeting-house, and read them out during the religious service. On a Sunday in October, the interruptions were so coarse and violent that Mr. Gisburne was unable to proceed with the service, and felt himself compelled to appeal to the civil power for protection. But the officer called on, properly enough, declined to act without a warrant. The disturbers were emboldened by this refusal of the officer to do his duty, and, with a trustee at their head, ventured, after the morning service, to lock up the doors. Mr. Gisburne was for waiting for legal redress, but one of his friends, who was also a trustee, resolved that the place should be open as usual in the afternoon, and accordingly opened a window in it by force, through which Mr. Gisburne entered, and from within turned back the lock of the door. Upon this, the constable who in the morning had refused to act, took Mr. Gisburne into custody. He was detained in custody five hours, and then brought before two clerical magistrates, who bound over the Calvinists to prosecute him at the next Cambridge assizes.

For any minister placed in circumstances like those of Mr. Gisburne, Mr. Aspland would have felt compassion; but the locality, his knowledge of the character of the persecutors, and his sympathy with Mr. Gisburne's religious opinions, greatly increased this feeling, and there was mingled with it a deep sense of the outrage that had been committed on religious liberty. He immediately stood forward to protect this persecuted man; and his representation of the circumstances enlisted the sympathy of many friends, including all the members of the Committee of the Unitarian Fund. The latter were precluded by the constitution of their Society from having any thing to do with law proceedings, but individually they gave Mr. Aspland authority to do whatever was necessary for the protection of Mr. Gisburne. He secured the services, as attorney for the defence, of Mr. John Wilks, afterwards so well known as the Secretary of the Society for the Protection of Religious Liberty. The opinion of Mr. Gurney (afterwards Baron Gurney) was taken, and by his advice cross-indictments were prepared against the persons who had disturbed the worship on the morning previous to the locking-up of the doors.

On the approach of the assizes in March, Mr. Aspland felt it to be his duty to go down to Cambridge and watch the progress of these extraordinary prosecutions. Thither, too, went Mr. Andrew Fuller, who, naturally enough, was requested by the Calvinists from Soham to do what he could in their behalf. Mr. Fuller and Mr. Aspland were looked to as the respective guides of the two parties. Both were acquainted with the leading Dissenters of Cambridge, who felt a painful interest in the prosecution, believing that, if carried on, it would entail great disgrace on the cause of Nonconformity. They offered to mediate, but their first efforts were frustrated by Mr. Fuller's influence. In a conference between Mr. Fuller and the mediators, the indictment was read. It immediately struck the Cambridge friends that it was founded on the *penal* laws against Antitrinitarians. They the more earnestly pressed for a compromise. The offer to withdraw the indictment against Mr. Gisburne if he would retire from the meeting-house, was by Mr. Aspland's advice rejected, who urged Mr. Gisburne "to stand the event of a trial, however disastrous the issue, rather than thus bargain away his reputation." Subsequently, Mr. Fuller consented to refer the matters in dispute to arbitration, each party to withdraw the indictments and to pay its own expenses. In a personal conference between Mr. Fuller and Mr. Aspland and the rest of the two parties, it was agreed to choose two referees from amongst the Dissenters of Cambridge. Notwithstanding the reference, the indictments were carried before the Grand Jury. It was proved by the Calvinist witnesses themselves that their leader, Thomas Emons, had in the midst of the service challenged Mr. Gisburne to substitute Mr. Fuller's book against the Socinians for the Bible. A juror unacquainted with matters and names of religious controversy, asked the witness, "What book was mentioned?" Upon this the foreman, Sir Charles Cotton, interposed with the remark, "*It does not signify whose book it was; no book can be put in competition with God's word.*" So clear were the merits of the case, that the Grand Jury threw out the bill presented against Mr. Gisburne, but found the bills against his persecutors. This unexpected result struck terror into the Soham Calvinists. They were now at the mercy of the friends of him whom they had designed to crush. With scrupulous honour, Mr. Aspland used, and with success, his influence in carrying the proposed arbitration into effect; and the result was that the arbitrators, two orthodox Dissenters of Cambridge, awarded Mr. Gisburne a sum of money as compensation for the chapel, which he agreed peaceably to resign into the hands of the Calvinist minority. For the time, Mr. Fuller seemed moved by the honour and generosity of his Unitarian opponent, and in the freedom of social intercourse admitted that some of his censures, in former days, of his heretical brother were not deserved.

The money awarded to Mr. Gisburne was the first contribution to a fund for raising an Unitarian chapel at Soham. Mr. Aspland gave all his assistance in promoting the fund, and with this and money derived from other sources, in the course of a few months after the close of the Cambridge prosecutions, a neat chapel was erected. It was opened April 3rd and 4th, 1810, by Mr. Aspland, Mr. Wright, Mr. Madge, and many other Unitarian friends from London and other parts of the kingdom.

The good humour with which the Calvinist chief had parted at Cambridge with his opponent was soon disturbed. He made a claim of the payment of the costs contracted by his party in getting the indictments withdrawn, affecting to regard them as the proper costs of Mr. Gisburne's friends, and therefore to be paid by them. The claim was of course not conceded.

Comments were freely made on the conduct of Mr. Fuller in abetting legal proceedings against a fellow-christian based on the penal statute against the impugners of the Trinity. Eighteen months after the transactions at Cambridge, Mr. Fuller put forth a short pamphlet, which he entitled, "A Narrative of Facts relative to a late Occurrence in the County of Cambridge, in answer to a Statement contained in a Unitarian Publication called the Monthly Repository." The statement referred to was in the Monthly Repository for August, 1809, and was, in fact, the Fifth Report of the Unitarian Fund. One portion of the pamphlet is an impeachment of his opponent's honour for not allowing the costs of withdrawing the indictments to be paid out of the money awarded by arbitration to Mr. Gisburne. The other and more important part was a defence of himself against the charge of having endeavoured, in the spirit of persecution, to enforce the penal laws against Antitrinitarians. This is his defence:

"Advising with a few of our Cambridge friends, we first heard the indictment read. It struck them that it was founded on the *penal laws* in force against Antitrinitarians, on which account they pressed a compromise. At that time I had not sufficiently thought upon the subject. I knew my object was not to prosecute Mr. Gisburne as an Antitrinitarian, but merely to prevent the place of worship being wrested from its rightful owners. * * * On Wednesday morning, about half-past eight or nine o'clock, having had further conversation with one or two of my friends at Cambridge, I waited on our counsel, *Mr. Best*, to whom I stated this among other difficulties, as nearly as I can remember, in the following words:—*It is the opinion, Sir, of some of our friends, that our indictment rests upon the ground of the penal laws against Antitrinitarians, and that if we go into Court, it must be to enforce them. If so, Sir, we cannot go; for, whatever we may think of Antitrinitarian principles, we disapprove of all penal laws on account of religious opinions.* Mr. Best did not deny that the indictment rested upon that ground. I then asked him, seeing we could not in conscience go into Court on such a principle, whether he would not recommend a compromise? He answered, he would. From him I immediately proceeded, with an attorney, to Mr. Aspland and his friends, who I had been given to understand had expressed a willingness to settle the affair by arbitration. We found them so disposed, and acceded to that mode of adjustment."

To Mr. Fuller's "Narrative" Mr. Aspland replied in a series of Letters to John Christie, Esq., Treasurer of the Unitarian Fund, entitled, " Bigotry and Intolerance Defeated ; or, an Account of the late Prosecution of Mr. John Gisburne, Unitarian Minister of Soham, Cambridgeshire: with an Exposure and Correction of the Defects and Mistakes of Mr. Andrew Fuller's Narrative of that Affair."

Mr. Fuller is asked to explain (*note*, p. 59) why the indictments were pressed to a decision. Had he and his party at once, on the agreement to arbitration being entered into, withdrawn their witnesses, the witnesses on the other side would have retired of course, and much trouble and expense would have been spared. The continuance of the proceedings after Mr. Fuller's recognition of the fact that they were based on a persecuting statute, is fatal to his reputation as a friend to religious liberty. Thus powerfully was the well-deserved rebuke administered :

" Mr. Fuller first heard the indictment read in company with some of his *Cambridge friends*. It struck them, but not him, that it was founded on the penal laws against Antitrinitarians. Mark the effect of habit! The well-read, liberal, private gentlemen of Cambridge, though Calvinists, were quick to discern and prompt to expose intolerance. They had been the hearers (occasionally or regularly), and some the companions, of ROBERT ROBINSON, that brilliant genius who kindled up the flame of religious liberty in the bosoms of all that knew him, and from the lightning of whose wit and eloquence the malignant spirit of persecution instinctively shrunk away. * * When the indictment was read, the Cambridge friends were struck; there was persecution in the formulary of law; they felt the blow, and they protested against the iniquity. There spake the mind of Robinson! * * Much as they were struck, the mind of Mr. Fuller was unaffected. He does not pass for a man of dull and slow apprehension, but his sensibilities were not awakened by the stirring up of penal laws against Antitrinitarians. He is quick of discernment as to heresy; he can see an Arminian under the mask of Calvinism, and in the detected Arminian can discover the future Socinian; but he could hear an indictment read in which, word after word, and line after line, were the direct characters of persecution, and yet not perceive the *malus animus*, the detestable meaning. * * Mr. Fuller 'had not sufficiently thought upon the subject.' Thirty years' reflection and discourse as a Dissenting minister, had not prepared him to feel instantly and act decidedly in a case of persecution! For the greater part of that time he had been at warfare with the Socinians, but he had not catechized his heart so as to know that there were some hostile weapons, and amongst them indictments, which his honour would not allow him to use. * * A whole night did Mr. Fuller sleep upon this indictment!—a thorny pillow, surely, for a Christian head! He was pushing a proceeding which his friends warned him would issue in persecution. * * He could not at once resolve to desist. I solemnly declare that I would rather bear the utmost severity of all the penal laws against me as an Unitarian, in their combined force and most rigorous administration, than I would have passed such a night as Mr. Fuller went through, if he felt as he ought."—Pp. 38—41.

To this exposure Mr. Fuller published no reply; in truth, none could be made. This was felt by his two biographers, one of whom, Dr. Ryland,* has passed over the matter with perfect silence, not even giving a place in his enumeration of Mr. Fuller's publications to the "Narrative of Facts;" and the other, the Rev. J. W. Morris,† has more candidly pronounced a deliberate verdict of disapprobation of Mr. Fuller's conduct. The whole passage deserves attention.

"The mental and moral energy of Mr. Fuller's character was evidently allied to something like misanthropy, or at least a disposition to indulge the most unbounded suspicions of human nature, which in too many instances produced rashness and dogmatism in the opinion he formed of others. Some may be disposed to attribute this to his superior discernment and acquaintance with mankind. It is true he studied this subject; but he studied it till he could see nothing to commend, where he found any thing to censure. 'To think ill of man and well of men,' was with him an established axiom; but it would be a rare thing to arrive at the latter sentiment through the medium of the former, or to feel benevolently towards the individual of a species which we have previously agreed to vilify and condemn. Mr. Fuller's ideas on the abstract doctrine of human depravity might be perfectly correct and scriptural; but it does not follow that the position they occupied in his thoughts, or the effect they actually produced on his feelings, must needs be equally unexceptionable; and when the mind becomes accessible to every suspicion, this is not likely to be the case. The constitutional tinge given to his moral and religious system,

---

* "The Work of Faith, the Labour of Love, and the Patience of Hope, illustrated in the Life and Death of the Rev. Andrew Fuller, &c. Second Edition, with Corrections and Additions: chiefly extracted from his own Papers. By John Ryland, D. D." London, 1818.

† "Memoirs of the Life and Writings of the Rev. Andrew Fuller. By J. W. Morris." London, 1816.—For its honest and faithful delineation of the character of Mr. Fuller, this work received emphatic praise from Robert Hall.

infused into his preaching and conversation a style of malediction neither the most favourable to usefulness nor adapted to form an amiable trait in the Christian character. * * *

"With his zeal for whatever he believed to be true, his want of forbearance towards moral and heretical offenders, and the paramount importance he attached to an inflexible integrity, he would have been in danger in darker times of employing other arguments than those which sober reason would approve. * * *

"It is extremely painful to advert to particular instances of this kind of severity; and if truth, justice, honour and impartiality, did not imperiously demand it, we would not advert to the unhappy transactions in which he was concerned at Soham, in the year 1809, in a dispute between his former friends and a party of Socinians who claimed a right to their place of worship, and to the incorrect and unsatisfactory statement he was induced to make of those transactions nearly eighteen months afterwards, in defence of his own conduct. Under no pretence whatever can we attempt to justify those transactions, nor the part which Mr. Fuller took in them, nor the means which he afterwards employed to exculpate himself from the charge of wishing, indirectly at least, to avail himself of those disgraceful statutes since repealed by the legislature, to secure what he considered the rights of the injured party; much less can we agree to consider him as having been influenced by any sinister or dishonourable motive, of which he was utterly incapable. The whole was a downright and palpable mistake, founded indeed, as in many other cases, on a large quantity of misinformation, and a wilful design of accomplishing the supposed ends of public justice. There is no need of any farther comment. His 'Narrative of Facts' relative to these occurrences, which we have consigned to oblivion, instead of classing it with his other publications, admits but of one apology. It was written long after the facts had taken place, and must be attributed, as his eloquent and judicious friend observed, to 'a most unhappy lapse of memory,' though unfortunately there are some other 'facts' which demand a similar apology."—P. 488.

In the year 1819, Mr. J. G. Fuller, a highly respectable printer of Bristol, put forth in the Baptist Magazine for June a vindication of his father's memory from the charge of persecution. From his statement it appears that Mr. Fuller composed a reply to Mr. Aspland's Letters, which, however, was never published. The only material statement is the following:

"It was a conviction of the injustice of Mr. Gisburne's proceedings towards the people whom he professed to serve, and not antipathy to his religious tenets (of which, however, I have the same opinions that I always have had), that made me feel as I did towards him. That which Mr. Aspland has all along attributed to a persecuting spirit, was no other than indignation against what I considered as disingenuous conduct."

He adds, that the subject on which he had not sufficiently thought was, " not the unlawfulness of persecution, but the nature and bearings of the indictment."

It will be seen hereafter that the proceedings at Soham and Cambridge were observed by others besides Unitarians and Calvinists, and proved to the satisfaction of some men in power the necessity of extending to Unitarians, as well as other Dissenters, the protection of the law. For this reason, as well as on account of the curious picture which the affair exhibits of the spirit of a portion of the religious world in England in the beginning of the nineteenth century, these details have been given.

CHAPTER XIV.

During the early years of his ministry, it was Mr. Aspland's practice to record in a journal the subjects of his sermons, the places where he preached, the religious and other public meetings which he attended, and all incidents of importance arising out of or connected with his ministerial and public life. Of the early portions of this journal the substance has been embodied in the previous Chapters of the Memoir. These will not be repeated (except in one or two instances, for the sake of some connected fact or remark), but other portions of the journal are worth preserving. The contemporary notes, however brief, of an acute observer of events are always valuable, and furnish both indications of character and materials for biography. The gleanings now proposed, and which it is deemed desirable to throw together, with only a few occasional notes, extend back to the autumn of 1805.

"1805. Sept. 15.—Mr. Belsham preached for me this morning. Excellent sermon on Christian Faith, John xx. 29. After an early dinner, I accompanied Mr. Simpson to Worship Street, where I preached in some sort, as at Newington Green, as a candidate.

"Dec. 1.—Victory off Trafalgar. Buonaparte at Vienna. What shall I do on the approaching *lugubrious* Thanksgiving-day? Lie I will not; rejoice I cannot.

"Dec. 5.—Thanksgiving-day for the naval victory off Trafalgar, Oct. 21. Service at the Gravel-Pit this morning. Congregation not large, and composed in a great measure of strangers.

"1806. Jan. 26.—Gravel-Pit. Morning, *Reflections on the Fugitive Nature of Man*, written particularly in allusion to Mr. Pitt, who died on Thursday, 23rd instant, and to Lord Nelson, killed in the battle of Trafalgar.

"Feb. 23.—After service, a poor Somersetshire man applied for a book on the grounds of our belief; brought him home, and gave him Priestley's three tracts and Disney's six ditto.

"June 8.—Birmingham, New Meeting, Sunday morning—charity sermon—Job's Character. Noble congregation. Collected £102.—Sunday afternoon, Old Meeting. Excellent congregation—£58.

"June 11.—Melbourne, Derbyshire. Preached this evening (Wednesday) at the General Baptist meeting-house—minister, Mr. Whitaker—from Acts viii. 8, extempore. Small congregation.

"June 15.—Birmingham, Sunday morning, Old Meeting, for Mr. Kell. Sunday afternoon, New Meeting, for Mr. Kentish and Dr. Toulmin. Very good congregation. The numbers, respectability and zeal of the Unitarians in this place at once surprised and delighted me.

"July 13.—Mr. Cogan, of Walthamstow, and I this day exchanged. The congregation at Walthamstow exceedingly small.

"Sept. 14.—News reached me before service of Mr. Fox's death, which so affected me that in reading Ps. ciii. verses 15, 16, to the end, I knew not how to go on.

"Sept. 28.—Went this morning to re-open the old meeting in Southwood Lane, Highgate, at the instance of Mr. Treacher (Paternoster Row) and under the auspices of the Unitarian Fund, which means to keep the place still open.

"1807. Wednesday evening, Jan. 7.—This evening a meeting for Prayer and Religious Conference was opened at the Gravel-Pit. We met at first in the vestry, supposing that not more than twelve or eighteen persons would attend; but the vestry being soon filled, we were constrained to adjourn to the lecture-room. I opened the meeting with prayer, and stated at some length the use and design of a conference. Mr. Simpson followed, and stated his experience of such meetings and his opinion of the best plan. Mr. Rutt expressed generally his approbation of the meeting and his conviction of its usefulness. Mr. Christie and Mr. Spurrel severally declared their cordial approbation of the conference, and delivered their opinion as to the mode of carrying it on. Mr. Simpson concluded with prayer. Question for next evening (proposed by Mr. Christie) is, 'The Evidence from the Scriptures in favour of a Future Universal Restoration.'

"Who would have anticipated such a beginning of such a meeting at the Gravel-Pit? 'O God! prosper thou the work of our hands; the work of our hands prosper thou it.'

"Jan. 11.—After morning service, I proceeded to deliver my first

Lecture to the Young in the lecture-room, and found it, to my astonishment, crowded, so that it was with difficulty I got in. Thus, through a good Providence, this plan also seems to succeed.

"Wednesday evening, Jan. 14.—Gravel-Pit conference. I introduced the service with a prayer. The question, 'The Evidence from the Scriptures in favour of a Future Universal Restoration.'

"1. Mr. Parkes* began with reading an examination of the passages relating to future punishment, adopting occasionally the two schemes of Destruction and Restoration to repel the third, of Eternal Torments.

"2. Mr. Simpson spoke, expressing the congeniality of the doctrine of the Restoration with his feelings and wishes, but his incapacity of finding it in the Scriptures, some passages of which supposed to teach the doctrine, he examined.

"3. Mr. Barbauld, who had come without its being known to the conference, declared strongly for Restoration. He admitted it was not to be found in particular passages, but might be inferred from the tenor and was included in the genius of Christianity. He attempted to shew particularly the indefensibleness of the scheme of Destruction.

"4. Mr. Christie spoke in favour of Restoration.

"5. Mr. Marsom spoke in behalf of Destruction, taking notice of some passages of Scripture brought forward by Mr. Barbauld. But the time being up, he was constrained to conclude abruptly. The subject being hardly entered upon and the speakers by no means exhausted, it was agreed to adjourn the discussion to next Wednesday evening, altering a little the question, and making it, 'The Evidence from the Scriptures as to the Future Condition of all Mankind.'†

---

* Mr. Samuel Parkes, the well-known writer on Chemistry.

† So interesting was this discussion, that it was adjourned four successive weeks. At the second meeting the journal records, "Larger company than we yet have had—a considerable number of ladies and some *poor persons*, whom I was particularly glad to see with us. Mr. Rutt concluded in prayer—short, but comprehensive—animated and correct."—At the close of the fifth discussion Mr. Aspland summed up, stating some arguments for eternal misery, and concluded with expressing the persuasion that the wicked would be punished, that the righteous would be rewarded, and that all would in the end be well. The excitement of this protracted discussion led to some inconvenient violations of the rules of the conference, and is supposed to have acted very injuriously on the health of Mr. Barbauld, whose ardent zeal in behalf of the doctrine of Restoration made it no easy task for the Chairman to keep him within the limits prescribed for the speakers.

Mr. Barbauld died Nov. 11, 1808, the day of Mr. Lindsey's burial. He was found drowned in the New River. Miss Aikin, in her biography of Mrs. Bar-

"Feb. 8.—Wednesday evening. After prayer, I stated that the irregularity which had crept into the conference had obliged us to think of new measures. Accordingly, two Moderators were chosen as subsidiary Chairmen. * * * Question, 'The Efficacy of a Death-bed Repentance.' Conversation not brilliant, but Christian. The only peculiarity of the evening was a speech from a Jew, who if he had not been flurried would have spoken well.

"March 18.—Wednesday evening. Conference. Quest., Rom. viii. 14, 'For as many as are led by the spirit of God, they are the sons of God.'

"1. Mr. Simpson reviewed the connection of the passage—the spirit, the gospel.

"2. Mr. Marsom. The passage an argument. The spirit, the spirit speaking by prophets and apostles.

"3. Mr. Christie. Spirit opposed to flesh, heavenly-mindedness to sensuality.

"4. Mr. Eaton. Spirit, miraculous powers.

"I concluded with stating that the apostle probably comprehended in the word Spirit the several ideas that had been advanced, and indeed the whole system of means by which God under the gospel influences the human mind.—Mr. Rutt prayed.

"April 29.—Seventeenth and last conference for the season. Question, 'The Influence of the Mosaic Institutions upon Domestic Happiness.' After praying, I opened the question very much at large with a view to draw forth discussion, it being generally thought the subject was scanty. Mr. Simpson followed, objecting to the rigour of the

---

bauld, alludes to this distressing circumstance when she speaks of "the pressure of anxieties and apprehensions of a peculiar and most distressing nature, which had been increasing in urgency during a long course of time." Mrs. Barbauld recorded some of her feelings by those striking lines entitled "A Dirge," beginning,

"Pure Spirit! O where art thou now!"

She communicated to the Monthly Repository a short but admirable Memoir of Mr. Barbauld (III. 706). Particular mention is made in the following passage of his earnest zeal for the doctrine of universal restoration: "Of the moral perfections of the Deity he had the purest and most exalted ideas; on these was chiefly founded his system of religion; and this, together with his own benevolent nature, led him to embrace so warmly his favourite doctrine of the final salvation of all the human race, and indeed the gradual rise and perfectibility of all created existence. He preached many sermons on this doctrine, which he defended, both in the pulpit and conversation, with a zeal and enthusiasm which his congregation and his friends cannot but well remember."

Jewish law; to whom Mr. Rutt replied, pointing out some provisions of the law favourable to domestic happiness. Mr. Christie took up Mr. Rutt's argument and pointed out other instances of the excellence of the law. Mr. Bone mentioned some things in the Mosaic economy favourable to freedom and independence.

"May 17, 1807. — Nottingham, High-Pavement; annual charity sermon for the school; large congregation; collection £35; accounted good. The Unitarians at Nottingham flourishing. Messrs. James Tayler and Grundy, ministers. Schools in excellent order. Large and handsome meeting-house.

"Oct. 4, Sunday.—Interwove with prayer, a prayer against national crimes, war in particular, and for the oppressed and afflicted Danes.* This prayer, I now learn (Oct. 27), gave infinite offence.

"1808. Jan. 24.—Sermon on Sleep† (written on the Saturday), made at the request of Anna, out of a few notes of a week-evening lecture at Newport. Heard by Mr. Joyce, who requests me to draw up the art. *Sleep* for Nicholson's Cyclopædia now preparing for the press.

"March 16.—Conference. Question, 'The Calvinistic Doctrine of the Imputed Righteousness of Christ examined by the Light of Scripture.' After prayer and opening, Mr. Vidler undertook to state the orthodox opinion fairly and favourably. *Acting*, however, does not become him!

"March 27.—Committee meeting in vestry to consider of taking a lease of the meeting-house.‡ The lessors ask seventy guineas.

"April 6.—Gravel-Pit conference. Question, 'The probable Condition and Employment of Mankind in another World.' I suggested that a future state would be a state of probation—possibly a mutable

---

* The history of war scarcely furnishes an instance of a more indefensible and unrighteous attack on a brave and neutral power than the seizing of the Danish fleet, consisting of eighteen ships of the line and fifteen frigates, by the English fleet. The defence offered by the Government was, that the Danish fleet would have fallen into the hands of France, and that it was expected the Danes would quietly surrender. This anticipation, if really entertained, was disappointed. The Danes resisted, though vainly, at the cost of two thousand lives of their citizens and the conflagration of a portion of their capital. By a national outrage like this, well might the spirit of a Christian minister be stirred within him, and the outpouring of his heart be listened to without "offence."

† See Vol. of Sermons, 1847. Sermon X.

‡ The Gravel-Pit meeting-house had been built on a lease granted by St. Thomas's Hospital, which was now expiring. On this subject many and some anxious meetings were held during this year.

state—so that, though heaven be eternal, man's abode in it may be temporal. This idea was once started by Mr. Rutt in a conference on the destruction of the wicked.

"April 17, Sunday.—Sermon on the Discriminating Influence of Christianity on Moral Character, John vii. 46. Very large congregation. Several Jews were present, brought by Mr. E. Johnston, who expressed themselves gratified; also a Mameluke (a Mahometan), brought by Mr. Wood (a late convert at the Gravel-Pit), who attended the lecture likewise, and was introduced to me by Mr. W.

"Aug. 8 (at Harlow).—This morning, after breakfast, Mrs. Flower set me to work. She had before importuned me to write for B. F.'s Political Register, and I had offered to give her a paper if she would furnish me with a subject; upon which she took me to the counting-house, gave me a pipe of tobacco, and told me to write on the *Impudence of Counsel at the Bar;* a subject suggested by her husband's late proceedings against ——.* I was obedient, and penned the letter which appeared on the subject in the next No. of the Political Register.

"Aug 14, Sunday (Wicken).—I had engaged to preach for Mr. Gisburne at Soham, and after an early dinner walked thither with Isaac and John Emons. Gisburne met us half-way. When we arrived at Horse Fen Droveway, within a mile of the town, we came suddenly upon a number of men waiting apparently to receive us, whom we instantly recognized as the Calvinistic party. I shook hands with the ringleader, Thomas Emons, accosted the rest, and pushed through them. They followed. The spokesman inquired if I were going to preach. I answered, Yes. He told me they wished me not to preach, and had come out to prevent me. I asked, By what authority?—made

---

* A lamentable quarrel had arisen between Mr. Flower and a brother-in-law, consequent on the settlement of the father's affairs. Serious imputations were thrown on Mr. Flower's character by a son of his brother-in-law, many years after the transactions referred to took place. Mr. Flower proceeded against his nephew for defamation. The trial took place before Sir James Mansfield and a special jury, in the Court of Common Pleas, London, July 25, 1808. The damages were laid at £2000, but the jury gave only such damages as would carry the costs of the action, influenced in part by Serjeant Lens's unscrupulous speech in defence, and in part by a strong and not unnatural distaste to family quarrels. Mr. Flower published a "Statement of Facts" as a Preface to a Report of the Trial. Those who are curious in studying such documents will find it highly seasoned. If the nephew were guilty of defamation, the uncle was not innocent of railing.

him confess that the majority of the church and congregation were with Mr. Gisburne, and silenced his arguments. Thus we walked into the town, I at the head of about thirty people, friends and foes. When we reached the town, the people flocked to see what was going forward; but I advised the Calvinists, for their own sakes, to be quiet. They took my advice, the greater part dispersing; a few came to hear me. Independently of this party, I found assembled within doors a large and respectable congregation. The circumstance of being beset in the way did not flurry me; the subject I had chosen was appropriate, viz. *Christianity the Spirit of Fortitude, of Love, and of a Sound Mind.* Under the pulpit sat my father's friend and the friend of my youth, Robert Fyson, of Fordham, who in his blunt way and loud voice thanked me before all the congregation for my sermon, and, on my relating what had passed on the road, vented a philippic against the bigots of the place which struck a few Calvinists present with surprise. In conclusion, he pressed me to go to Fordham to preach in the evening; but finding I was engaged at Wicken, agreed to go thither, as did his daughters and other Fordham friends, as well as many from Soham. On coming out of the meeting, I found a crowd of people around the gate of the meeting-yard, and John Emons and brother Isaac encountering some of the Calvinists. Not wishing to engage in a controversy with mere ignorance and prejudice and brutal passion, I passed through the multitude and walked on to Wicken with friend Fyson and others.

"Evening.—A large congregation assembled early at our little chapel. At the time of beginning I found it difficult to get in. There were many about the door and the yard. I preached on 'Unitarians being a sect every where spoken against,' a long discourse. The people were attentive, though it can hardly be hoped they went fully into the subject. The remark at the conclusion of the service was, 'Old times were reviving, and that I was now regarded as ten years ago in the Calvinistic fervour of youth.' To me the reflection was a melancholy one, as it struck me with a feeling of pensive regret that he, my ever-to-be-lamented father, who took such delight in my usefulness, was no longer capable of encouraging or assisting my services. But he rests from his labours and is blessed!

"Sept. 18, Sunday.—Gravel-Pit. It happened well that the latter part of the sermon this morning was on the duty of Christian liberality, for Mr. Johnston assembled the Committee after service to propose *building a new place*, the bargain for the old one being broken off, and we being warned out by Lady-day. Everybody came into the plan.

"Oct. 2.—Gravel-Pit. Mr. and Mrs. Potticary from Blackheath, with Mr. Conybeare, grandson of Bishop Conybeare and Master of Christ Church, Oxford, present. A fortunate sermon (on the Lord's Supper) for an Oxonian to hear!

"Oct. 9.—The Committee again met and resolved to build a meeting-house on freehold ground, with room for a burial-place. Only nine gentlemen of the Committee were present, and they put down their names for £800.

"Christmas-day.—The Committee came to a resolution to purchase a piece of freehold ground, adjoining that taken for the meeting, for a parsonage-house.*

"1809. January 4.—Conference. Question, 'The Reasons for continuing the Rite of Baptism in the Christian Church.' Prayer as usual. In opening the conference, I requested the discussion to be confined to the positive side of the question. Let such as hold the perpetuity give their reasons, and let others, if they choose, examine them.— Mr. Simpson argued for the perpetuity on two grounds,—the nature of baptism an act of personal religion, and the commission to baptize all nations. Mr. Marsom confined himself to the apostolic commission, which he contended could not be proved to militate against the perpetuity. Mr. Christie and Mr. Mears made some observations; and I took up the apostolic commission and shewed that it limits itself; that it was addressed to Jews, and intended only for Jews; and the only commission given to a Gentile apostle for the Gentiles (Paul's) said nothing of baptism, nay excluded it, for he was not sent to baptize. Mr. Christie concluded in prayer.

"Jan. 25.—Conference. This morning we began to feel at Hackney the effects of the thaw after the immense quantity of snow. At noon I was going to the children at the Gravel-Pit by way of New Cut, but found the road overflowed with water, which ran into the houses. I succeeded by way of the Church Well, but found the water rising fast there also. In consequence I sent the children home.* * * In the

---

* This good resolution was never carried into effect. Spiritedly as the collection began, the sum expended on the chapel greatly exceeded both the estimate and the amount raised, and a debt hung on the building for a sufficient number of years to efface the resolution from the recollection of its promoters.

afternoon Mr. Marsom came, and after reading together for an hour or two, we attempted to get to the Gravel-Pit. The New Cut was completely flooded still; at Church Well the water was lower, but even there it was over the tops of Mr. Marsom's boots. He went to reconnoitre at the Gravel-Pit, to determine whether the conference could go on or be deferred. He presently returned and told me there were about a dozen persons, upon which I went round by Church Street, and got put across the water in a ferry cart. We had nearly twenty persons, but only three speakers, viz. Mr. Marsom, Mr. Mears and myself. Subject, *State of the Dead*. We were all of one mind, viz., *that the dead are dead*, and not alive in whole or in part.

"Jan. 29.—Mr. Stower* here, who brought proof-sheets of *Monthly Repository*, and took copy for the new edition of Lardner's Works which I have engaged to edit.†

"Feb. 1.—Conference. 'Introduction to Gospel of John.' Speakers, Mr. Simpson, Mr. Marsom, Mr. Ellis and Mr. Parkes. I maintained the *Word* to be Christ, but objected to and endeavoured to expose the rendering of the *Improved Version*, John i. 1, *a God;* as if Christ were a created or demi-god.

"March 8.—Conference. Question, 'Whether the Constitution of

---

* The well-known (to Unitarians at least) printer, and the author of the "Printers' Price Book."

† This scheme was nipped in the bud by the interference of some booksellers, with whose interests the proposed edition would clash. From the Prospectus, which was widely distributed, the following short passages are taken:

"Dr. LARDNER has justly obtained the appellation of THE PRINCE OF MODERN DIVINES. With his name is associated the praise of deep erudition, accurate research, sound and impartial judgment and unblemished candour. The publication of his great works constituted a new era in the annals of Christianity; for, by collecting together a mass of scattered evidences in favour of the authenticity of the evangelical history, he established a bulwark on the side of truth which infidelity has never presumed to attack. His 'Credibility' and his 'Collection of Jewish and Heathen Testimonies,' may be said to have given the Deistical controversy a new turn, and to have driven the assailants of the gospel from the field of Christian antiquity, in which they esteemed themselves securely entrenched, into the by-paths of sarcasm and irony.

"In applause of Dr. Lardner, all parties of Christians are united; regarding him as the champion of their common and holy faith. Archbishop Secker, Bishops Porteus and Watson, and Doctors Jortin and Paley, of our National Church; and Doctors Doddridge, Kippis and Priestley, amongst the Dissenters, have done public homage to his learning, his fairness and his great merits as a Christian apologist. The candid of the literati of the Roman Catholic communion have extolled his labours. And even Morgan and Gibbon, professed unbelievers, have awarded to him the meed of faithfulness and impartiality."

the Apostolic Churches be a suitable Model for Christian Churches of the present Day?' Many speakers. This is the last conference but one this season, and the last I shall attend, as to-morrow morning I set off for Cambridge with Wilks, the attorney, in consequence of John Gisburne, the Unitarian minister at Soham, Cambridgeshire, being under prosecution for a *riot* in opening the doors of his meeting-house, which the Calvinists had shut up.

"JOURNEY TO CAMBRIDGE, MARCH 13, TO THE ASSIZES (having long neglected to record this very interesting journey, I must now content myself, Jan. 9, 1810), with a brief account of it as far as an imperfect memory and the press of business will allow.

"Monday, March 13.—Mrs. Wilks, wife of J. Wilks, the attorney, called at Homerton Row in a post-chaise, about nine o'clock in the morning, and took up S. and myself. Wilks had gone forward by stage-coach. We all met to dinner at Harlow, Mr. Benjamin Flower's. Here we left Mrs. A., and we three proceeded in the evening by chaises to Cambridge. 'None ride so fast as those whom a *lawyer* drives.' Wilks has the knack of bribing the post-boys into a gallop. We reached Cambridge about nine o'clock in the evening, and drove to our lodgings on the Market Hill, which I had by letter got Mr. Staples to take for us, and of which Mr. S. informed us by a letter. Wilks and I presently called on Mr. Staples, and inquired after Mr. Gisburne, whom, however, we could not find.

"Tuesday, 14.—To-day I met ―――― at a book-stall, and presently introduced him to Wilks, who was shocked at his appearance. ―――― was dressed as follows: a white beaver hat, blue coat, white waistcoat, corduroy breeches and white stockings. Wilks suggested that we must change his dress or lose our cause, he being our chief witness before the Grand Jury, who it was feared would be prejudiced against such a comically-dressed parson. It was agreed that he should go and look for a clerical suit. He did, and presently came back with a good black hat, covering a powdered head, a black coat and black silk waistcoat. All these he had found ready for him, and as suitable as if made on purpose, at a brother Unitarian's, alias a *Jew's*. The cost was twenty-eight shillings! We congratulated him on his happy metamorphosis, but he remarked that there might be one inconvenience attending his change of appearance—if confronted with his own witnesses in Court, they would not know him.

"I spent the morning in perambulating the Colleges and recalling the associations of my boyish days. In the evening, my brother Isaac and the rest of our witnesses assembled, and were invited to the great room at the Black Bear, which we engaged for the assizes. We informed them that the adversary had indicted three persons, namely, Gisburne, Isaac Aspland and John Emons. We gave them but little comfort.

"Whilst here this evening, Mr. Staples and Mr. Wm. Hollick called upon me to express their fear of the trial, if proceeded in, disgracing the Dissenters, and their wish for an accommodation. I found they were misinformed as to the state of the case, and of course prejudiced. *Mr. Andrew Fuller* was come as the head of the Calvinist prosecutors, and had tutored these gentlemen. After narrating matters to them, I stated of course that, as *defendants*, we had nothing to offer or to do; we were only prepared to meet a prosecution.

"Wednesday, 15.—This morning early, we met our witnesses, and prepared them for their examination. I was called away from them by Messrs. Hollick, Nutter and Audley, who came to talk of some scheme of saving the Dissenters from disgrace. I could only refer them to Andrew Fuller. 'If,' I said, 'they would agree to an arbitration to settle all the points in dispute, we were willing to agree to any feasible plan, though we were not to be frightened into any unseemly concessions.' They regretted that *Andrew* would listen to no accommodating measure—'he was sure of a triumph.' I told them at last they must not reckon too fast, as we had drawn up indictments against the Calvinists.

"So we parted. I found our witnesses had all flown. Wilks had taken them to wait at the Grand Jury room-door, for he had put his indictments into the hands of the Clerk of Assize the moment he got to Cambridge, on the Tuesday, and obtained a promise that they should be presented first if his witnesses were ready to attend and follow them up.

"On going to the Shire Hall, I was met by Mr. Hollick, who told me that an arbitration was acceded to by Andrew Fuller's party; but the witnesses on both sides were now in attendance, and so the matter went on.

"[The general Case and the Result are described in the Abstract of the Report of the Unitarian Fund, drawn up by myself, and published in Monthly Repository for August, 1809.]

"On the Market Hill I saw Andrew Fuller, whom I had not seen since I met him in Edinburgh, in the year (I think) 1800. I accosted him. He began to be high, but by firmness I brought him down. We had much conversation about the proposed arbitration. He had the effrontery to take credit to himself and party for not prosecuting Gisburne for blasphemy! Mr. Nutter invited me to dine with Andrew at his house, to which I consented. I plied him with theological conversation, and obtained some curious concessions from him as to his written charges against the Unitarians and his verbal charges against myself. All in tolerable temper. Whilst with him, Wilks brought me notice of the glorious termination of the affair, which chagrined Andrew beyond expression.

"The rest of the day was taken up in the development and exposure of the prevarications of the party.

"We met Gisburne and his friends at the great room in the evening, who were of course overjoyed. They drank 'Wilks and Liberty;' and John Emons recollected a line of an old song about Marquis Granby, which he applied to the victorious attorney, who, like the hero, chanced to want hair, viz.,

'We'll crown his bald head like a Cæsar.'

"16.—This morning met Andrew again and again; walked with him, his arm locked in mine, about the town; and after the termination of the affair, about noon, we parted on good terms.

"Saturday, 18 (Wicken).—I spent the afternoon at the Hall, Squire Rayner's, where I accidentally met John Aspland (of Soham), schoolmaster, with whom I had a long desultory religious chat. The old gentleman stood up zealously for the religion established by law.

"Sunday, March 19.—Morning, Wicken, to a good congregation; afternoon, Soham, in Gisburne's temporary place. A great crowd. A hundred persons, at least, from Wicken. Andrew Fuller at the old place at the same time.

"Evening, Wicken, *Right to the Tree of Life*. A crowded congregation, some from Fordham, and even from Isleham.

"April 23.—To-day, laid up again with the Cambridgeshire ague.

"April 30.—After service, the congregation chose thirteen trustees for the new place of worship.

"May 14.—To-day, the Gravel-Pit charity sermons were preached by Mr. Houghton (late of Norwich), now come to Prince's Street, Westminster. I preached for him. Congregation very thin. It must spoil a preacher to have to do with such a handful of hearers. I think, if I were with such a people, I should revive them, or they would kill me. There is but one service at Prince's Street; the afternoon discontinued since Mr. Jervis left (for Leeds). This is also the case at Dr. Lindsay's, Monkwell Street, and Mr. Coates's, St. Thomas's, Borough. The palsy has taken *one side* of us; may be the left; but the right cannot be considered secure.

"May 28.—I deferred giving the concluding lecture to young persons on account of a meeting of the congregation to consult on the Trust-deeds of the new meeting-house. Immediately on coming home, I was seized with an ague fit and obliged to go to bed. Mr. Platts, of Boston, was at Mr. Christie's, but he had no sermon with him. I therefore gave him a MS. of the late Mr. Turner's, of Wakefield, sent to Monthly Repository, and he read a discourse on Jonah iv. 1—'Admonition to be drawn from good men's failings.' It was singular enough, this was Mr. Houghton's text and subject a fortnight before.

"June 11.—Dudley. Charity sermon. The collection above £50. The singing fine.

"June 13.—Warwick Tract Society. I attended the service at the New Meeting, Birmingham. Mr. Corrie preached a very good but somewhat metaphysical sermon. The Society afterwards dined together. I gave a detailed account of the prosecution of Gisburne. The story brought in several subscriptions.

"June 15.—By coach to Nottingham, and spent the evening with Mr. Tayler.

"June 16.—By coach to Lincoln. Fell in, on the road to Newark, with a young Calvinist Baptist parson, just hot from Bristol, who abused and vilified Mr. Belsham, but whom I brought to confession. I forced him to give me his name, which was J———.

"June 18 (Horncastle). This morning I went to the parish church and heard a sermon preparatory to Confirmation: the Vicar, Mr. Madeley, afterwards expressed his sorrow that he should have been so unfortunate in his subject. In the evening I went to the Methodist meeting. My preaching at Horncastle was talked of, but prejudice had been there before me, and even Mrs. W. gave out that her nephew denied the *foundation*, i. e. I suppose, the *atonement*.

"19, Monday.—George Weir took me a long ride, both of us on horseback, to Tower on Moor, Tattershall and Coningsby, where I called upon my old fellow-student, William Thomas.

"22, Boston.—Association-day. (Vide M. Repos. Vol. IV. p. 406.)

"July 9, 1809.—Gravel-Pit.—Well pleased to be at home again. *One's own people* the best people to preach to.

"August 7, Monday.—Dined to-day by invitation with Mr. Vidler's congregation of Parliament Court, at Canonbury House, Islington. About sixty persons present. The meeting, upon the whole, pleasant. I proposed ' Mr. Vidler and the Congregation of Parliament Court,' and also read a part of Mr. Wright's letter from Scotland of the date July 26th, with remarks; gave likewise ' To the Ashes of Michael Servetus,' and expatiated on the character of the deified murderer, John Calvin, and told the story of Symkiss, the shoemaker here, who was refused by a magistrate of Worship Street a parish apprentice because of his Unitarianism.

"August 8, Tuesday.—This evening I attended a lecture of the celebrated Joseph Lancaster's, on Popular Education, at a large room formerly belonging to the Paul's Head in Cateaton Street. Began at six o'clock and lasted till near nine.

"Lancaster is a philosopher without learning, or what is called knowledge. He has anatomized the human heart, and can find something in every youth's affections of which to lay hold. He has no pretensions to eloquence, but he has a great body of interesting facts, which are much better. His system is a blessing to the country, and will prove such, it is to be hoped, to the world.

"Forty of his poor scholars were in the room, and went through a part of the Lancaster exercise. The appearance of one of them, a monitor, of the name of Norris, interested the whole company, a lad of a fine countenance, of great firmness and assurance of manner, and a warm friend apparently of Lancaster's. The room, which will hold 300 persons, was nearly filled.

"August 20.—Met the Building Committee in the vestry upon the plan of new meeting. Mr. Edmund Aikin* has been chosen architect.

---

* Mr. Edmund Aikin was the youngest son of Dr. John Aikin. He gave his services gratuitously. His intended liberality, however, proved, as it generally does in such cases, very costly to the society. To exercise a watchful and stringent economy in respect to an architect who gives his plans and labour, is ungracious and impracticable. The result is commonly unsatisfactory to both parties. Neat and comfortable as the interior of the New Gravel-Pit chapel is,

The plan exhibited to-day is for a building to seat 500 persons, an oblong square, with an octagonal roof; the galleries to be in that shape, and to go round the meeting, or to occupy five out of the eight sections.

"August 29.—At eight o'clock in the evening I met a party of the poor of the Gravel-Pit congregation, who are desirous of establishing a Benefit Society, at Mr. Bainbridge's. We discussed the plan of the Society, and also about the New-meeting singing, &c., and sang several hymns. These humble persons were very cheerful, and apparently pleased at my meeting them. I have great hopes of a new era at Gravel-Pit from this circumstance.*

"September 2.—Anna brought home the charity sermon which I had drawn up at the request of David Eaton. It appears that the clergyman who had ordered the discourse for a brother clergyman in the country, after having looked at it (though he took it home), returned it, saying, 'He wanted a sermon for an hospital, and this was all about Job.'†

"Sept. 17.—In the afternoon had as a hearer Mr. Houghton, of Prince's Street, who came with Mr. Spurrel's family. I engaged myself to sup, with Mr. H., at Mr. Spurrel's. When we arrived at Shore Place, it occurred to us that we might hear a slice at least of an orthodox sermon, so we went to the Baptist meeting-house, and heard an *experimental* discourse from John ii. 4; the preacher, as we afterwards learned, ———. He ran on with text after text, interlarded with a little savoury exclamation and interrogation. We had a pleasant evening at Mr. Spurrel's. Mr. Houghton's infantine simplicity makes him a truly interesting companion. It is eccentricity without wit, without any thing dazzling or brilliant, but it is amiable eccentricity. You give him credit for much talent, and I believe he possesses it.

"Sept. 24.—There was a call of the whole congregation after service.

---

it is both externally and internally deficient in proper ecclesiastical style. At no period was ecclesiastical architecture in England at a lower ebb than at the beginning of the present century.

* This sentiment often appears in the diary and journal. Thus, "I should rejoice to see more of the poor among us, hearing what we consider the *gospel preached*." "Many poor present—felt animated by this circumstance."

† The subject of the sermon was, *Job a Father to the Poor*. Mr. Eaton, at a subsequent period to this, became a well-known agent for supplying clergymen, wanting the ability or the industry to compose, with manuscript or pseudo-manuscript sermons. He lithographed a series of sermons, chiefly his own, which had as much merit as sermons destined for the general use of the clergy could *safely* possess. They are discreetly and decorously dull.

At the request of several, I attended. The plan of Mr. Aikin was submitted to the auditory and approved, and it was resolved to begin to build immediately. The unanimity was disturbed only by ———, who protested against the proceedings of the congregation, because they would not agree to declare the place ANTI-TRINITARIAN* in the Trust-deeds.

"Thursday, Sept. 28.—This morning I was present at the laying out of the ground for our New Gravel-Pit meeting, along with Mr. Munn, the auctioneer, Mr. Aikin, the architect, Mr. Seabrook, the contractor, and Mr. Ashpitel, the surveyor of the estate. My hopes from the burial-ground increase as the building advances, and I must strive to prevail upon the Building Committee to increase it by the purchase of another lot or two of land in addition to the three already secured. This was the first day workmen were employed upon the ground.

"Monday, Oct. 16.—Laying the foundation-stone of New Gravel-Pit meeting, Hackney. We had a fine mild day for our purpose. About four o'clock the Committee and others met at the vestry of the Old meeting, whence we proceeded to the site of the new one. A large company was there assembled. In the back of the place in the centre of the eastern side, the stone was raised up by a temporary pulley. I first ordered it to be let down that the inscription might be read. It being sufficiently perused, the stone was again raised. I now took the trowel and spread the mortar on the foundation of brick; then we lowered the stone and I squared it, which being done, from the platform, on a spot near to which the pulpit is to stand and facing the east, I deli-

---

* The Gravel-Pit congregation acted on this occasion in strict accordance with the principles and usage of their Presbyterian ancestors. Thirty-four years afterwards, when the Dissenters' Chapels Bill was before the House of Lords, the congregation pleaded this fact as a strong reason for the passing of the Bill, alleging that the society had ever continued faithful to the English Presbyterian principle of liberty of conscience; that the whole cost of the chapel and burial-ground was raised by themselves, without a single known contribution from any person holding what are called orthodox opinions; that, adhering to the principle of non-subscription to human articles of faith, in preparing their Trust-deed they resolved to insert no creed as binding their posterity, but left the meeting-house and its appurtenances to the operation of the English Presbyterian principle of the right of private judgment, both to individuals and congregations. The petition, which received much attention, was presented to the House of Lords, Thursday, May 2, by the Marquis of Lansdowne.

vered an Oration.* A good many of our 'orthodox' neighbours were present, and had an opportunity of hearing Unitarianism stated without

---

* This Oration was subsequently published. It contains the inscription on the foundation-stone:

"SACRED TO THE ONE GOD, THE FATHER.
This Stone is laid as the Foundation of a Building for the Use of the Congregation of Unitarian Christians assembling in the Gravel-Pit Meeting-house in this Vicinity, Monday, October 16, Anno Domini 1809.
ROBERT ASPLAND, *Minister.*
EBENEZER JOHNSTON, *Treasurer.*
EDMUND AIKIN, *Architect.*

The *Oration* was a brief statement of and apology for the principles and opinions of the Gravel-Pit congregation. It was well calculated to excite the curiosity of strangers to their faith, as the two passages now quoted may serve to shew:

"Your religious principles, my brethren, in furtherance of which you associate as a church and design to rear an edifice on this ground, are at once distinguished by their simplicity and their agreement with the Scriptures. Your belief is, with very few exceptions, and those comparatively unimportant, expressed in that unquestionably ancient, but certainly not apostolic, symbol of faith, called the Apostles' Creed, the simplest and best composition of the kind, next to the confession of the Messiahship of Jesus in the New Testament, which was ever framed. You hold, professedly and as a body, no articles of faith which are not, and have not been always, held by the universal church; the difference between you and other denominations of Christians being, that whilst you confine yourselves to the few plain truths which the gospel makes essential to salvation, they have, under pretence of tradition or of deduction and explanation, added to them a mass of propositions, historical and metaphysical, at which, according to a Prelate of the English National Church, 'reason stands aghast, and faith itself is half confounded.' In matters of revelation, you esteem it a duty to adhere strictly to the law and the testimony; and it is the peculiar privilege and distinction of your system of opinions that it may be wholly and fully set forth in the words of sacred writ;—a circumstance which ought, methinks, to bespeak the patience and candour of such as deem us most erroneous, if not to excite a suspicion that there must be something human in a creed which is not expressly and literally derived from the Word of God."—Pp. 9, 10.

"I cannot conceal that we have as a congregation something wherein to boast. It is not that we are considerable in number; it is not that we are respectable according to the standard by which society measures respectability; it is not that heretofore our pastoral chair has been filled by men of unrivalled eminence; it is not that we are of long standing in the Christian world; but it is this glorious peculiarity, which I pray to God we may never forfeit, that we allow unbridled liberty of conscience! History tells us of a Grecian robber who, having taken travellers, measured them by his bed, and if too long cut them shorter, and if too short stretched them longer;—a fit type for the invaders of Christ's jurisdiction, the violators of Christian liberty, the framers and imposers of human creeds and articles of faith, engines to rack and torture the free-born mind. *O my soul*, is the exclamation of us all, *come not thou into their secret; and unto their assembly, mine honour be not thou united.* Delivered from the house of bondage

being misrepresented. Mr. Palmer* was in the field, and was very busy in quieting some boys, who at a little distance were noisy. Some of the Homerton students† were also present. We afterwards dined together at the Mermaid, to the number of 120, Mr. Rutt in the chair, and had a most agreeable day. Mr. Remington brought his £100 subscription to the dinner. An account of the dinner, &c., appeared in the *Morning Chronicle*.

"Sunday, Oct. 22.—This morning we had a very crowded auditory, the most numerous, it is said, that has been in the Gravel-Pit since Dr. Priestley's Farewell Discourse, though I think there were as many on the occasion of Mr. Lindsey's funeral sermon. I preached on *Christ's Kingdom not of this World*. The sermon contained some striking extracts, as appears to me, from the defenders of conscience in the Church of England.

"Dec. 21.—Dined at Mr. David Eaton's, with Mr. Middleton and Mr. P——, the Swedenborgian. He is a complete mystic, of slender

---

ourselves, we abhor the thought of enslaving others. We hold no creed but the New Testament, every man's interpretation of which is to himself the true standard of orthodoxy. Our communion is open to all that are sound in character. We think that virtue is of more importance than speculative belief, and that the worst heresy is a wicked life."—Pp. 15, 16.

* This was the venerable Rev. Samuel Palmer, the successor to the pulpit of Hunt and Barker and Matthew Henry and Bates at Hackney, and the Editor of *The Nonconformists' Memorial*. He was upwards of fifty years pastor of the Independent congregation at Hackney, from 1762 to 1813. His "orthodoxy" did not narrow his sympathies. His social intercourse and his literary alliances were not limited to his own religious party. Of the *Monthly Repository* he was a friend from its commencement, and to its pages he was a frequent contributor. He honoured the Editor with his friendship.—Amongst the boyish but fondly-cherished recollections of the writer of this note, is his seeing in his father's library, about the year 1812 or 1813, three divines of most venerable and attractive appearance in the clerical costume of the last century, one of whom was Mr. Palmer, who in a manner combining dignity, kindness and pleasantry, gave him his blessing, and wished him to be like his father in every thing, *except his heresy!*

† The learned and most estimable Dr. J. Pye Smith, the head of the Academy, was present on the occasion of the delivery of this Oration, with several of his pupils. From the lips of one of them, since distinguished in public life, the writer heard it stated that on their return to the Academy a discussion ensued respecting the statement of Unitarian principles given in the Oration. The Professor questioned, while the Pupil (already, though unconsciously, beginning to diverge from the strict line of "orthodoxy") defended, the justness of the exposition of Unitarianism contained in the Oration. This was the beginning of a change that not long after led to that pupil's abandonment of Calvinism and retirement from the Homerton Academy.

parts and confined knowledge—dogmatical, yet he seems to be naturally benevolent, and his peculiarities make his conversation for once interesting. He speaks highly of the kindness of Dr. Priestley and his congregation to him at Birmingham.

"Dec. 29.—I was introduced at Mr. Foster's,* Bromley Hall, to my new hearer, Mr. David Ricardo,† and his lady. He is sensible and she is pleasant.

"REVIEW OF THE YEAR 1809.—I preached this year 102 sermons and composed 42. Much of my attention has been directed to the *Monthly Repository*. We have printed of this 1250, and probably sold, including back Nos., 1000. The work gains publicity. The affairs of the Gravel-Pit have this year worn both an important and a pleasing aspect. The number of hearers has not decreased, and if a few subscribers have been lost, others have been gained. * * * The lectures to young persons continue to be well attended and practically useful. The conferences are, I think, better attended than ever, and in proportion as they become known, will probably be the means of enlightening many of the inhabitants of Hackney, who would otherwise have no opportunity of hearing the truth. But the great object which has

---

* This was Mr. Thomas Foster, for more than fifty years a respected member of the Society of Friends, in which he was born and educated. He was led early in life, by reading William's Penn's works, to embrace Unitarianism. Through the medium of Mr. William Rathbone, also a member of the Society of Friends, he became a subscriber to the London Unitarian Book Society. In the autumn of 1810, he printed in the *Monthly Repository* some remarks on the Yearly Meeting Epistle which were afterwards distributed amongst the Friends. This circumstance led to proceedings being taken against him by the Society, and eventually he was disowned. He defended himself in "A Narrative of the Proceedings of the Society called Quakers, within the Quarterly Meeting of London and Middlesex, against Thomas Foster, for openly professing their Primitive Doctrines concerning the Unity of God. 1813." He was a man possessed with a simple and earnest love of truth, with a sound head and a truly warm heart. Mr. Aspland had the greatest esteem for him. He continued till 1818 to reside at Bromley Hall, where his friends were ever welcome, and where the most agreeable society, both in and out of the circle of the Friends, was constantly found. He then removed to Evesham, where he resided about ten years. He died at Rushwick, near Worcester, July 9, 1834, in the 75th year of his age.

† Mr. Aspland had the happiness to interest more than one Jewish family in the truths of Christianity. His sermon on the death of Mr. Lindsey had a considerable circulation amongst intelligent members of the Hebrew faith. One of them pronounced it "a noble funeral sermon for Abraham himself." Mr. Ricardo continued to attend at the Gravel-Pit until his removal to the western side of London.

occupied our attention has been the new meeting, which was begun about Michaelmas and is to be ready for use at Midsummer, which I suppose will be Michaelmas again. However, it is now (Jan. 1810) in great forwardness. The roof is nearly on. It was thought unwise to begin building at such a season of the year, but there were reasons which led to its commencement at this precise period; one was the necessity of losing no time, on account of the precarious tenure by which we hold the old place. * * * A favourable contract has been obtained. The builder has engaged to erect the meeting-house for £1800; the whole expense is calculated at £2700; but it will certainly not be less than £3000, if it do not reach £3500. The sum at present subscribed is, I believe, £2200.

" Hitherto Providence has remarkably smiled upon us, for the weather has been milder than was almost ever known. The workmen have not been hindered one whole day. As was said of the last Jewish temple, there has been scarcely a serious shower in the day-time since the building was commenced. There has been a great deal of rain, but it has fallen entirely in the night.

" Of late, a question has been started with regard to the new building which has provoked much debating, and, it is to be feared, some ill-blood. The idea was suggested by Mr. Frend on the day of laying the stone, viz., that of having vaults under the meeting. The foundations are laid very deep, and there will be a great excavation. It was thought that therefore this underground space might be turned to account, and that the arch-work of the vaults would both strengthen the house and keep it dry and warm. But much opposition immediately arose.* .... I was rather zealous for the vaults, believing that the plan (drawn up with great care on a new principle, adopted in the new church at Wakefield, and improved by our architect, Mr. Edmund Aikin) was perfectly safe, that all objections would presently subside, and that much permanent benefit would result from the work. My sentiments and speeches were, however, somewhat misrepresented in reporting; and from the whole affair I have learnt a lesson or two—as, that the peace of a church may be broken by trifles, where there is a previous want of congeniality or union, or inattention in bringing a plan forward to people's feelings and prejudices; and that a minister

---

* This scheme was on many accounts properly withdrawn and unanimity restored.

cannot be too delicate in his interference in the secular affairs of a congregation. I have now finished this journal of the year. * *

"Every year increases the arduousness of my situation. May every year also increase my usefulness! May Providence strengthen, guide and bless me in my public character!"

CHAPTER XV.

Before resuming the extracts from Mr. Aspland's diaries, a few passages from the letters of his correspondents at this period deserve a place.

From Rev. Joshua Toulmin, D. D.

"Birmingham, May 4, 1809.

"I lose no time to forward to you Mr. Robinson's 'Historical Account of the Congregations in Cambridgeshire,'* as received, about thirty-four years since, from the late Mr. Josiah Thompson, of Clapham.

"The pressure, noise and uproar at the Crown and Anchor,† I could scarcely have borne. But the object of the meeting is perfectly congenial to my principles and feelings. May it be pursued with vigour, extent and success!

"As to the conduct of this town, or its silence on the late very interesting proceedings in the House of Commons, I am ashamed of the town, and ashamed for it, as I say here. Our Dissenters and Whigs are timid. They fear the influence of the clergy. The men who take the lead are Tories of the old school or of the Evangelical class. It is supposed that any attempt, especially if made by Dissenters, to carry a vote of thanks to Mr. Wardle, would be violently opposed and overpowered by great numbers. A private letter has been sent by post to many gentlemen, calling upon them to come forward, but without effect. I could wish that some of the London papers, with a keen pen of satire and censure, would animadvert on the conduct of this town—more censurable as here is no corporation and borough influence to pervert and bribe us."

"Birmingham, July 17, 1809.

"I shall deliver to-morrow to my young friends some arguments in favour

---

* This very interesting account was printed in the Monthly Repository (Supplement), Vol. V. 621—632.

† One of the numerous popular meetings held at this time to express an opinion respecting the charges against the Duke of York of corrupt distribution of his patronage as Commander-in-chief.

of the perpetuity of the Christian rites, especially baptism. I have half a mind to transcribe them for your Repository. I am about eight or ten days hence to baptize publicly a worthy, thinking, serious young man, who has read on the subject *pro* and *con.* You will perceive I am still the Baptist. Human nature, it appears to me, requires ritual services. The promulgation of religious truth requires it; the preserving the memory and awakening attention to important facts require it. I enclose a list of my publications. The publisher of the Universal Magazine has obliged me with an impression of twenty copies of my Memoir of Mr. Lindsey. One asks your acceptance to accompany my other pieces which you have collected."

"Birmingham, Aug. 13, 1809.

"I have perused most of the Repository, and am particularly pleased with Mr. Belsham's spirited and masterly defence of the Improved Version,* and with the reviews of Bishop Warburton's Letters and of Jones's Illustrations. The latter has raised my desire of seeing the work itself.

"Mr. Charles Lloyd, above a week since, wrote to me about Coventry. I almost immediately recommended him to the attention of the congregation there, and proposed, if they turned their views to him, that they should write to him, as the most direct way of coming to a conclusion on the point.

"The apostle says, 'I was not sent to baptize, but to preach.' Our Lord's repeated declaration is, when speaking of the Mosaical sacrificial institutions, 'I will have mercy, and not sacrifice,'—an Hebrew idiom to denote preference. Permit me to do, as Archbishop Newcome has done, to refer to Bishop Pearce's commentary in loc.

"It was well judged, methinks, to advertise Mr. Belsham's answer to the Quarterly Review, otherwise the writer and patrons of that publication would not, perhaps, have known of it, or would have been able to plead ignorance. The merit and excellence of the strictures, likewise, recommended the notification of them."

"Paradise Street, August 26, 1809.

"I return with sincere thanks my good friend's ingenious, interesting sermon on Sleep. To be capable of saying so much, and so much to the purpose, on a sleepy subject, shews how much your thoughts were *awake* when you composed it. Indeed, I am truly obliged by your indulgence, and I have faithfully adhered to the restrictions you laid me under. I have only to regret one effect arising from the perusal—that when I am in the very act of slumbering, I am roused by an untimely recollection of what you say respecting the attack of sleep commencing in the forehead; attempting to oppose my opinion to yours, by asserting it is in the eye, I lose the power of closing

---

* In reply to the Quarterly Review, which, in its second No., assailed the Improved Version with true clerical rancour and contumely.

it, for any sleepy purpose, for some time.—I am greatly obliged by the tender of your love, and beg you and your dear Mrs. Aspland will accept a return in kind and degree, assuring you that your conversation exceedingly entertains, and your well-regulated zeal truly animates, your very faithful friend."

"Birmingham, Dec. 19, 1809.

"It is not to be supposed that you compare the critiques in the Review with articles themselves, otherwise I should think the meagre, left-handed praise given of my neighbour Mr. Fry's sermon,* you would not have thought equal to its merit, which in my idea rises much above the run of discourses from the pulpit. To me it appeared peculiar in point of sentiment and composition. Wonder not that I feel concerned for my friend's reputation under present circumstances, when I am on the eve of giving a volume to the public and to your critic. Well! the Rubicon is or soon will be passed."

"Birmingham, Feb. 1, 1810.

"I owe, and I beg you to accept, my cordial thanks for the present of your Oration. I admire it for the appropriate sentiments, the conciliatory address, the judicious collection and application of scripture, the devotional spirit, and the concluding paragraph. A lady who, though she is afflicted with bodily blindness, has a mind in a high degree enlightened, wishes that a copy of it, guarded from injury in a box, had been or could now be, for the instruction of some distant times, lodged near the foundation-stone.

"Some of your remarks on the Jubilee meet my approbation, but the reference to the New Meeting I did wish had not appeared.† It appeared to me

---

* The reference is to a funeral sermon, preached at Coseley, Dec. 11, 1808, by Rev. Richard Fry. Mr. Fry was a Dissenting minister, settled successively at Warminster, Billericay, Cirencester, Coseley, Nottingham and Kidderminster. He was brought up, and exercised his early ministry, amongst the Independents; but while at Billericay embraced Unitarian sentiments. The last twenty-nine years of his blameless and useful life were passed at Kidderminster, during the greater part of which he officiated at the Old meeting in that town. The infirmities of age induced him to resign the pastoral office in 1835, and he died March 12, 1842, in the 83rd year of his age. See an interesting tribute to his memory in C. R. 1842, p. 317.

† See Monthly Repository, IV. 695—697. With the celebration of the fiftieth anniversary of the Accession of George III. to the throne, on Oct. 25, 1809, called the Jubilee, Mr. Aspland did not warmly sympathize. He regarded it as a mere political measure, designed to serve the interests of a party, in whose proceedings he did not concur. He thought that it was devised with a view to divert the public mind from the consideration of the nature of the Administration and the state of the country. It was the professed object of the celebration to express thanksgivings to God for the length of the reign of George III. He could not regard that reign as, upon the whole, prosperous and happy. It was pre-eminently a warlike reign; and, recollecting the rivers of human blood that had been spilt during the half century preceding 1809, he could not, with his abhorrence of war, in Christian sincerity make it the subject of religious thanksgiving.

too jesting for the occasion and for the dignity of your work. A friend was much disturbed by it. In general, I believe it has not made much impression; several were pleased with it. Is not much caution proper when politics are introduced into a work of a religious nature, as they do not exactly fall in with its leading design, and may tend to bring an odium on it and the tenets defended in it?

"Have you seen how I am trimmed in the Eclectic Review for November?"

From Mr. Benjamin Flower.

"Harlow, Feb. 12, 1809.

"I suspected, by a paragraph in some of the papers, that there was some jarring about a new edition of Dr. Lardner's Works, and the Prospectus of Hamilton's confirmed that suspicion. Your letter explains matters. I thank both you and Mr. Stower for thinking of me; but I must at once explicitly decline undertaking the matter; not that I am afraid of London booksellers, the body of whom I have long had a contemptible opinion of, but it would be impossible for me to print ten or even five sheets a month of the work, without adding considerably to my establishment, which I have no wish to do. My Reviews nearly employ half our time; and although we are sometimes slack of work, yet there are few months in the year in which we could accomplish more than two or three sheets of any work.

"William Clayton's Ordination service is to be published; and I hope, as it will with propriety come under your cognizance in your Review, that you will notice the folly of attributing an expression in a parlour, used by Mr. Hall (about spirits being liquid death, &c.) in one of his jocular strains, to an ordination service. The expression was used to Mr. Smith, of Foulmire, in conversation. Mr. Smith was very fond of smoking, and would sip over a glass of brandy and water, but was never known to be intemperate.

"What shocking scenes of profligacy in high life, and in the different departments of Government, are now exhibiting before the House of Commons! That House may be resolved to clear the Duke of York, but can never clear him in the opinion of the public."

The Editorship of the Monthly Repository was the occasion, from a very early period, of Mr. Aspland's engaging in familiar correspondence with many Unitarians resident in America. Portions of their correspondence were from time to time published in the Magazine; other

---

The situation of the country in 1809, was, in his opinion, sufficient condemnation of the Jubilee. Large armies were wasting away by disease in the marshes of Spain and Holland; at home there was distress and bankruptcy, and a general distrust of the capacity and virtue of public men. The power most hostile to England was at its height, and apparently bent on destroying the independence, if not the existence, of England. Well might a Christian and a Patriot think this was not a fitting time for a Jubilee!

portions, containing personal and other details of considerable interest, were properly withheld. Time has, however, removed the objections that then existed to their publication. One of his earliest Transatlantic correspondents was Mr. William Christie, the correspondent and friend of Dr. Priestley.*

---

* This vigorous-minded and courageous man deserves a fuller biography than has yet been awarded him. The outlines of his story are given by himself in the Preface to his "Dissertations." He was a merchant of Montrose, in Scotland, of active mind and possessed of some learning. He collected a valuable theological library, and devoted his leisure to the study of the Greek Testament, with the aid of commentators, fathers and critics. Early in life he had read with deep interest the writings of Dr. Samuel Clark, and had imbibed many of his opinions. The result of his studies was the rapid progress of his mind from Arianism to proper Unitarianism. Previous, however, to this, the final state of his mind, he avowed his heresy to his townsmen of Montrose with an intrepidity which none can estimate who have not resided in Scotland, where the yoke of Calvinism is insufferably heavy on the public mind. As early as July, 1781, we find Mr. Christie corresponding with Dr. Priestley, and informing him that so great was his own unpopularity amongst his countrymen, that he did not suppose any Scottish clergyman would, if requested, baptize his children. By Dr. Priestley's mediation, the Rev. Caleb Rotherham, of Kendal, in August of that same year, visited Montrose, at Mr. Christie's expense, and baptized the children. He collected around him a congregation at Montrose, to whom he preached, and this little band constituted the first Unitarian society in Scotland. In 1783, he became personally acquainted with Mr. Lindsey, who was much pleased with him, and astonished with the variety of his learning and the extent of his reading. He remarked, too, on his mental quickness and agreeable elocution. In 1784, he printed a work on the Divine Unity, consisting of a series of discourses which he had delivered at Montrose. A little before this, Mr. Christie was delighted by receiving from Mr. Thomas Fyshe Palmer, then a member of the University and a fellow of Queen's College, Cambridge, a letter expressive of his opinion that the Liturgy of the Church was antichristian, and her Articles an injurious violation of Christian liberty, and declaring his determination to decline all preferment, and devote himself to the study of the Bible and to preaching the Divine Unity. Mr. Christie joyfully welcomed Mr. Palmer to Montrose, and was assisted by him in the pulpit until he removed to Dundee in 1785. When the disgraceful riots took place at Birmingham, Mr. Christie was led to publish his opinion on the subject of ecclesiastical establishments, in an essay designed to shew their hurtful tendency. In November, 1792, he took his farewell of his flock at Montrose in a discourse which was afterwards published. In 1794, he removed to Glasgow, and preached to the little congregation of Unitarians there, of which Dr. Benjamin Spencer had been hitherto the minister. Here Mr. Christie composed and delivered his "Dissertations on the Divine Unity," which he afterwards printed in America. It was at this period, being in the maturity of his life and mental powers, that he made up his mind on the subject of the person of Christ, and deliberately rejected the doctrine of his pre-existence. While in Glasgow, he issued proposals for publishing a series of Lectures on the Revelation of St. John, but did not receive the necessary encouragement. In 1795, he was induced, by the threatening aspect of public affairs and other con-

"Philadelphia, 3rd February, 1809.

"Rev. Sir,—I only received your letter of the 21st March last, on the 29th of July; and I was then so closely engaged in correcting and preparing my *Dissertations* for the press, as well as superintending several other literary works, that I could not spare sufficient time to write you in the manner I wished. Your enclosures were very acceptable, particularly the Third Report of the Committee of the Unitarian Fund. I rejoice in the progress of Unitarianism, and particularly admire and applaud Mr. Wright for his laborious and useful exertions in propagating Unitarianism among the people at large. Such a man may be called an apostolical character.

"I never saw more of your *Repository* but the Prospectus, till very lately, when a friend procured me a sight of the numbers for January and May last. I find by the first of these, that the two pamphlets I sent Mr. Lindsey in 1807, had reached him; and by the last, that the Church-Alley Constitution had been sent you by some other person. In your remarks on these pieces, you point out some of the defects of that Constitution; but I think the gross usurpation of legislative authority in the church of Christ (the dire spring of so many public evils in the religious world) made by those persons of this

---

siderations of a more personal nature, to emigrate to America. Before he reached New York, he was prostrated by a nervous fever, and soon after landing several of his family were attacked by yellow fever. His first settlement was at Philadelphia; but in 1796, he removed to Winchester, in Virginia, carrying with him an earnest zeal for the diffusion of scripture truth. In 1800, Dr. Priestley described him, in a letter to Mr. Lindsey, as exerting himself zealously, though with little success, at Winchester, where he had delivered his "Dissertations," and published a tract on the Unity of God and the Humanity of Christ. His undisguised avowal of his opinions proved, according to Dr. Priestley's testimony, very injurious to his interests. He held an office in the College at Winchester, but found it necessary to resign it; his school was from a similar cause unsuccessful. In 1801, he removed to Northumberland, much to the satisfaction of Dr. Priestley, who did every thing in his power to uphold him there. He had the melancholy duty, in 1804, of speaking over the grave of his distinguished friend, and the address was afterwards published. He also added to the Memoirs of Dr. Priestley, published by his son and Mr. Cooper, "A Review of Dr. Priestley's Theological Works." After spending a year at Pottsgrove, where he conducted an academy, Mr. Christie removed, early in 1807, to Philadelphia. He was invited to become their preacher by the surviving members of the congregation, then scattered, to which Dr. Priestley began to preach in 1796. Differences of opinion arose, to which there are allusions in the letters given above from Mr. Christie and Mr. Taylor, who were at that time a little alienated, but were both pure-minded and good men, and both distinguished by their love of truth. A division into two congregations was the result. Mr. Christie's life was protracted till his 74th year. He died in New Jersey, Nov. 21, 1823. A tribute to his memory was communicated to the Monthly Repository (Vol. XIX. 363) by Rev. James Taylor, who, whatever differences of opinion he had had with his departed friend, was prompt in expressing his reverence for his inflexible integrity, his deep-seated piety and his benevolent feelings.

city, should have been more fully animadverted upon, and set in a stronger light than what you have done. You are acquainted, undoubtedly, with the Bangorian Controversy, that afterwards occasioned by the Confessional, and the decision of the celebrated Dissenting synod about ninety years ago, when all subscriptions to human formulas were declared against, and the sufficiency of the Scriptures were affirmed, by a majority of four votes. If such a daring infringement on Christian liberty had been made by any overbearing individuals in any liberal congregation in England, it would certainly have been much censured; and it should be remembered, that such an attempt is as little justifiable in America as it would have been in England, and that it is no extenuation, but an aggravation, of the matter that the offence was committed by Unitarians, who are supposed to possess more light and information than others. Though this constitution has the appearance of being formed upon democratic principles, yet in its exercise and management it is perfectly aristocratical; and matters have been under the control of three persons, who, from their situations, connections and influence, have been always able to secure a majority in their favour. I am sorry to add, that some of these leaders not only acted imperiously and unwarrantably in framing and carrying through their constitution, but since that time endeavoured, by undermining and insidious arts, to thwart the progress of our late little independent society, and foment divisions in it; and were but too successful with some of the members, though the majority stood firm. You will find a brief account, in the Preface to the *Dissertations*, of the causes of the suspension of this society, Note, pages xxx, xxxi.

" After all I have said, however, I make no doubt but that in your account of the proceedings here you intended well, and thought it best to treat the subject mildly.

" I read with some surprise your account of Dr. Priestley's Memoirs. Surely, if any person in England inclines to write the Life of Dr. Priestley over again, he has a right to do it. Several accounts have been given of the lives of Dr. Watts, Dr. Johnson, and others, and so there may be of the life of Dr. Priestley. But what has been done in this country ought not to be depreciated, more especially as it came from a person so nearly related to Dr. Priestley, and so well acquainted with all circumstances.

" With respect to my labours on the subject, I was actuated by honourable and upright motives,—a desire of doing justice to Dr. Priestley's theological productions, and making the world better acquainted with their worth and useful tendency; and I derive no emolument whatever from the sale of the publication.

" For the politics of this country, I refer you in general to the American newspapers which are sent over to England, and I suppose you may have an opportunity of seeing. The laying on of the embargo and its continuance has been approved by the generality of the people of the United States, as is evident from the late elections, which have been carried by great majorities in favour of the present administration. Some opposition has been made in New England; but it is even thought there that a majority of the people will discover the propriety and necessity of the measure.

"The same religious denominations exist here as in Great Britain. These all in general adhere to the tenets of their respective sects; nor is it an easy matter for any opinion, new to them, however true and ancient in itself, to make an impression upon them; guarded as they are by Articles, Liturgies, Confessions, or by prejudices of long standing. A benevolent and generous mind, however, must contemplate with pleasure that Religion labours under no restraint in this country, that all sects with respect to civil rights are on an equal footing, and that the most numerous and wealthy have no prerogative over the smallest and least opulent.

"My *Dissertations* were published and advertised near three months ago in four different papers in this city. Including subscribers and purchasers, there are about seventy copies in circulation. I have reason to believe that they have made some favourable impressions on individuals; and their effect, I apprehend, will be greater hereafter, and when their author is removed from this world.

"The Unitarians in Church Alley, I understand, keep up their meetings regularly, and they have had (I am informed) this winter, as well as the last, evening lectures, in which they assert and defend the principles of Unitarianism.

"For my part, though I can never give up my Christian liberty and yield to their *usurpation*, and must ever continue to disapprove of what I think to be wrong, when I am led to speak upon the subject; yet, as preachers and propagators of divine truth, I wish them every degree of success. Men may have acted extremely wrong in some respects, and yet be highly useful and beneficial to their fellow-creatures in other important particulars.

"Wishing you and all our friends in England the most eminent and lasting success in your pious and useful undertakings, I remain, Rev. Sir, yours in the faith of the Gospel, WILLIAM CHRISTIE."

*From Mr. James Taylor.**

"Philadelphia, May 8, 1809.

"Dear Sir,—On the 3rd of January, I replied to your much-esteemed favour of 27th May, and have the satisfaction to learn from my friends, to whose care I addressed my letter, that it arrived safe.

---

* Mr. James Taylor was by birth a Scotchman. He emigrated to America about 1791. He was to the close of his life a frequent correspondent of Mr. Aspland's. To the Monthly Repository he contributed, amongst many other things, a series of articles, exhibiting varied talent and a very amiable spirit,

"At that time, opportunities for Great Britain were exclusively confined to the sailing of the British packets, which rendered it difficult to send any parcels or packets across the Atlantic. Happily, a great change in our political relations has taken place, as you will learn from the daily prints. In consequence of this, the commercial intercourse is again restored; and we have at present the additional satisfaction of hoping that an amicable arrangement will also be made with France. To all who love peace and abhor violence, this must be good news.

"Mr. Wood, son of the late Rev. Mr. Wood, of Leeds, who sails for England to-morrow, will convey this to you. At the same time, you will receive a discourse by my good friend Mr. Eddowes* on the early treatment of children, of which I beg your acceptance. Mr. E. is a layman, like the writer of this scrawl; he is related by marriage to Mr. Belsham. I hope he will soon find it convenient to furnish you with an account of our little society. It continues to flourish, and gradually to increase. We have no wish to attract the gaze of the crowd. It is our aim to engage the attention of those who are willing to think for themselves, and to induce those who perceive the truth, openly to avow it, and, by their example, to illustrate its excellence."

"Philadelphia, Nov. 21, 1809.

"* * * It is greatly to be lamented that too many Unitarians do not lay sufficient stress on instrumental duties. While many of the reputed orthodox

---

entitled, Critical Synopsis of the Monthly Repository, by an American, commencing with Vol. XIX. He undertook to assist Mr. Eddowes in the latter years of his ministry, and after Mr. Eddowes' withdrawment from the pulpit he continued his ministry. He died at Philadelphia, where he had resided upwards of fifty-two years, April 30, 1844. He was described by the United States Gazette as a clergyman who *had preached as he believed, and practised as he preached.*

* Mr. Ralph Eddowes became the minister of the first Unitarian society in Philadelphia, after Mr. Christie's retirement from the office. He was a native of the city of Chester. He was educated at Warrington. He took a very distinguished part in the public proceedings of that city. He asserted successfully, by an appeal to the House of Lords, the rights of his fellow-citizens, in a long struggle respecting the validity of the Charter of the Corporation. In 1793, to the lively regret of the people of Chester, he emigrated to America and settled at Philadelphia. He continued to be the minister of the little congregation at Philadelphia (for some time jointly with Mr. James Taylor, the writer of the letter given above) till the autumn of 1820. In then tendering to them his resignation of the ministerial office, he desired them to record in the archives of their church that he was thankful to God that he had been "led to a more diligent inquiry into the grounds of the Christian revelation, his firm and deliberate conviction of its general truth, and more particularly of those views of it to which the great and fundamental doctrine of the DIVINE UNITY either directly or collaterally leads." Mr. Eddowes published a volume of Sermons, which were characterized by vigour of thought.

appear to regard them as substitutes for virtue, if not as really superior to the fruits of righteousness, not a few of those who wish to be accounted rational, act as if they imagined that in religion the end may be attained without the use of means, and as if the injunctions of our Lord to confess him before men, and similar precepts, were a dead letter as regards those who lived after the days of the apostles. I am not sorry that some of the old nominal Unitarians are going off the stage: however exemplary their private characters may have been, their public services were worse than useless, while the warmth of their political principles was but a miserable substitute for the frigidity of their religious zeal. Mr. Lindsey was a noble example to the contrary, therefore his memory will live in the hearts of generations yet unborn. You were peculiarly happy in your choice of a subject for so interesting an occasion, as well as in the introduction of the direct address which is found in the body of your discourse, the perusal of which at once refreshed and delighted both Mr. E. and the writer of this—nor will its circulation stop here; for I mean to put it into the hands of a number of my friends.

"I have now the Repository for August, and look with no small degree of anxiety for the account of Mr. Wright's missionary labours in Scotland. Mr. W. is a man beyond all price; and in Scotland he will probably do more good than in any other place. Here, the people have neither the same degree of curiosity, nor the same spirit of religious investigation as with you. The American character is cold, and the perfection of our religious liberty produces indifference to religious subjects. The episcopal clergy are sensible and judicious, moderately orthodox, complete Arminians, but cold and frigid; while, among the Presbyterians, Baptists and Methodists, you meet with all the Puritanism of the 17th century, both as to quaintness of language and illiberality of sentiment; and these sects are the great and overpowering majority.

"I do not believe that any Unitarian preacher could make his living here by keeping a school. A Roman Catholic is not objected to, but an Unitarian is a monstrous being. However, as our services are gratuitous, we cannot be starved into silence. I am the more particular in stating this, because it is a circumstance that ought to be known on your side of the Atlantic. Some of my brethren would wish much that we had a large church and a popular preacher; and they are sanguine in their expectations that a gentleman of popular talents might form a numerous society. I wish this were practicable at present, but I do not believe it, and therefore I would not be guilty of holding out prospects which I do not believe would be realized. To draw a great number of people together, the preacher must have a strong voice and an impassioned manner; he must speak without book, *and be sure to repeat the cant phrases:* without these qualifications, whatever might be his learning, his talents, his eloquence, or his respectability of character, he would meet with obstacles which would require an independent fortune to enable him to surmount. In illustration of these remarks, I might advert to the case of Mr. John Sherman, a gentleman (as I am credibly informed) of pleasing manners and exemplary character; and, as I know from actual correspondence and the perusal of some of his discourses, of superior talents as an investigator of truth and a teacher of Christian morals. Yet this worthy man is at this moment a preacher to two congregations in a sequestered part of the State of New York, and with means of support so scanty, that his own manual labour is necessary to enable him to provide for his family. He informs me that the sale of the Improved Version, which was re-published at Boston, has excited much alarm among the 'Evangelical believers.'

"As Mr. Mellis has undertaken to procure some particulars respecting Thomas Paine, who died some time ago at New York, I will only remark, that he had long ceased to be respected by those of sober habits and correct deportment.—I will endeavour to get Mr. Eddowes to commit his thoughts to paper now and then for the Repository; but you will see from our tracts, a set of which, so far as we have gone, you will receive with this, that we have taken many articles from you, not, however, without acknowledging the obligation.

"Mr. Christie, as I understand, continues to read proof-sheets. His family attend us regularly. His secession from us was fortunate in one respect; for he was so unpopular, that no stranger went more than once or twice to hear him, and we were reduced to a very small number. Since he discontinued his services, we have gone on harmoniously and have gained ground.

"Last Sunday evening Mr. Christie attended us for the first time since his secession. The text was 2 Kings v. 18, 19; the subject, the duty of exercising candour and forbearance towards those who frankly lay before us their convictions, although we may be unable to prevail on them to go so far as we might wish or deem necessary, concluding with an address to Unitarians, urging on them consistency of religious conduct. I mention this occurrence, because this was the precise point on which Mr. Christie and I split. He was for denouncing Trinitarians as idolaters, whereas I deny that we have any right thus to brand them. It is enough that we try, in the spirit of meekness, to convince them that they are in error. Their consciences ought to be respected. It is our business to judge *ourselves*, to beware of sinful conformity, and to avoid every approach to that illiberality in our own language and conduct which appears to us so absurd and reprehensible when we perceive it in others."

"Philadelphia, Oct. 27, 1810.

"In my last, I mentioned that the re-publication of the Improved Version in this country had excited much alarm among the 'makers of silver shrines.' One of them in particular, filled with wrath, and armed, or at least supposing that he is armed, with the thunderbolts of Heaven, has not only sent us to hell, but attributed to us the most diabolical of motives. I send you now the article alluded to (the author of which is Rev. J. M. Mason, D.D., of New York), with some remarks thereon by my friend Mr. Eddowes; also the 9th and 10th Nos. of our tracts. The volume was completed by the re-publication of the 1st part of Mr. Wright's excellent work, entitled the 'Anti-satisfactionist,' which is doubtless in your possession.

"Having been in habits of intimacy with Dr. Mason, I first tried to convince him that, even supposing the sentiments of Unitarian Christians to be erroneous, unless he could first substantiate either his own claim to infallibility and to a knowledge of the hearts of others, or could convict them of immoral conduct so as to fix on them the charge of duplicity and treachery, he was not justified in making such strictures. To this he replied, not by a reference to the Improved Version, but by giving his verdict on Socinianism. I then asked him to point out the chapters and verses in which there had been either the suppressions or the mutilations which he had spoken of, and called on him to produce evidence in support of his assertion that 'the editors and circulators of the Improved Version were an Iscariot band,' &c., quoting the words of the paragraph and note. In about a fortnight he wrote, saying, that the whole system of Socinianism was a complete subversion of the gospel, except as to the doctrine of the resurrection; that his remarks applied to the whole volume, including the notes as well as the text; and that he had said nothing about any man's motives or conscientiousness in circulating the Improved Version, nor 'is there a syllable in the paragraphs of the Magazine alluded to which requires such a construction.' He then, forgetting Judas, talks of Paul before his conversion, and says 'we need be no worse than him in his *sincerity* before his conversion to perish eternally.'

"On mature reflection, as Dr. M. is a man of very high standing in what is called in Scotland the Burgher Church, and as he had so egregiously committed himself,—and, besides, as he would neither retract what he had asserted, nor come forward to defend it, for you see how he flies from the ground,—it was deemed advisable to print 1000 copies of this little tract, not for sale, but for dispersion, in the hope that some service might thereby be done to the cause of truth, by exhibiting the true spirit and genius of Calvinism.

"I am aware that such details as these can be no farther interesting to those on your side of the Atlantic than as they may serve to exhibit the temper of the Evangelical, or rather extra or super-evangelical, folks in this land of *boasted* religious liberty. I say boasted; for so far as the power of the clergy reaches, and so far as their influence can avail, many of them rule with an iron rod. I ought, however, to add that there are some honourable exceptions. Even among the Presbyterian clergy, the paragraph alluded to has been found fault with, and by some of them been pointedly reprobated.

"The excellent Bishop of Pennsylvania (Dr. White), true as he is to his own church, is a model of Christian humility, meekness and candour: he was one of those who uniformly treated the never-to-be-forgotten Dr. Priestley with attention and kindness. Towards the latter part of the Dr.'s life, his hearing was much impaired. When in Philadelphia in 1801, as no Unitarian place of worship was open, he generally attended that episcopal church in which the Bishop preached (for this good man preaches twice every Lord's-day). Knowing the Dr. to be dull of hearing, Bishop White always spoke much louder than usual when Dr. P. was present; and one afternoon I actually saw the Bishop acting as pewopener to the Dr., the sexton not being immediately at hand. These are little matters, but they are unequivocal tokens of real benevolence, and I relate them with pleasure."

Before resuming the extracts from the diaries, it is necessary to mention a humble but very useful Society which Mr. Aspland had the satisfaction of assisting to establish. In noticing in the Monthly Repository (III. 625) the proceedings of the Religious Tract Society (founded in 1799), he expressed his earnest wish that means could be found for the publication and distribution of moral and religious tracts, which, without being controversial, should yet accord with Unitarian principles. He invited the co-operation of those who concurred in the desire. The Rev. Lant Carpenter came forward to second the suggestion, and recommended the formation of a London Committee to carry it into execution. Mrs. Mary Hughes, of Hanwood, in Shropshire, a lady of cultivated mind and warm benevolence, whose name will hereafter recur in this Memoir, offered in furtherance of the scheme not only a handsome donation in money, but the more valuable contribution of a tract suited for circulation amongst the poor. This was her "William's Return, or Good News for Cottagers," a delightful story, which has had, and still deservedly continues to enjoy, a wide circulation. This well-timed offering was the best practical argument for the proposed Society, which was established without delay. Mr. James Esdaile was appointed the Treasurer,* and Mr. Aspland undertook the Secretaryship, the duties of which he continued to perform during the two first years of the Society's existence, and then was succeeded by Rev. Thomas Rees. The second tract was from the pen of Rev. Richard Wright, and the third from that of Mrs. Cappe. The

---

* The original Committee of the Christian Tract Society included also Messrs. Joshua Brookes, Christie, James Esdaile, Jun., Thomas Foster, William Frend, Thomas Gibson, Ebenezer Johnston, Samuel Parkes, J. T. Rutt, R. Wainewright and Dr. Samuel Pett.

other writers of the early publications of the Society were Mrs. Price (a niece of Mrs. Mary Hughes) and a few others. Before he quitted office as Secretary, Mr. Aspland was enabled to report that the Society had printed 52,000 tracts, of which more than half had been put into circulation.

The usefulness of this Society has been tested by an experience of more than forty years, and there are few Unitarians accustomed to visit the dwellings of their poor neighbours who cannot call to mind some instance of pleasure and moral benefit rendered by its publications. At the time when it was established, there were comparatively few publications for the poor that were not disfigured by a sectarian spirit, or by other objectionable qualities. This, happily, is no longer the case; yet it is to be hoped that the sterling excellences of the Christian Tracts, and the increasing demand for such works, will ensure to the Society a succession of supporters as liberal and successful as were its founders. To our excellent Domestic Missionaries, the interesting tales and addresses bearing the names of the authors already mentioned, of Henry Ware, J. Johns, and of living writers of ability and piety, cannot but prove useful auxiliaries.

CHAPTER XVI.

"1810. Jan. 4.—Walked to Mile-end Road to dine, for the first time, with my new hearer, Mr. David Ricardo. Dr. Lindsay and Mr. T. Foster of the party. After tea, we had a long debate on the natural evidences of a future state.

"Jan. 21.—To-day received from Mrs. Barbauld a little collection of Hymns* for the commencement of worship, used at Norwich, among which are three of hers which I have not before seen.

"Jan. 23.—At the House of Commons on the opening of the session. Got in after two hours' hard squeezing. The debate was good and lasted till five in the morning,† when the House divided.

"Jan. 28.—Morning sermon on the *Justice of God*. The large Committee (of 24) met to-day to consider the propriety of having any inscription on the front of the new meeting. When I left the lecture-room, I was requested to go to them in the vestry to deliver my opinion; but this I declined. Young Mr. Harris, of Maidstone, dined with us.

"Feb. 4.—Morning sermon, *Peace in the Church*,—an useful topic, meditated for some time, but begun yesterday and finished this morning.—This morning Mr. E. Johnston brought to the Gravel-Pit Mr.

---

* Mr. Aspland was now compiling his Selection of Hymns for Public Worship.

† Of this debate he recorded his impressions in Mon. Rep. V. 42. It turned upon the disgraceful Walcheren expedition, and the recent duel of Mr. Canning and Lord Castlereagh. Mr. Peel seconded the address. The opposition speakers were Lord Gower, Mr. Ward, Mr. Ponsonby and Mr. Whitbread. The other speakers were Lord Bernard, Mr. Peel, Lord Kensington, Mr. B. Bathurst, Lord Castlereagh, Mr. Canning and Mr. Perceval. For the address, 263 voted; for the amendment, 167.

Wyvill's* Petition to the House of Commons, and instructed Street to give out that a Petition for the Repeal of the Test Act lay for signatures in the vestry. This Petition I declined to sign, because I considered it inexpedient and ill drawn up. The original design of Mr. Wyvill was good, to present a Petition, signed by Churchmen only, for the abolition of all penal statutes. Why the design has been abandoned, I know not. As it is, the Petition will have but little effect; few Dissenters will take it up, and it may hamper the Catholics in their application to Parliament. If they gain their object, our relief will follow.

"Feb. 18.—Last week a paper was drawn up, at the request of some parishioners, by Wilks, the lawyer, and circulated in the parish, calling a general meeting to oppose parish aristocracy. I find it is imputed to me, for two reasons: first, that it contains some hard words; and, secondly, that it is violent. This determines me to have nothing to do with parish politics.—We read to-day Eachard's 'Causes of the Contempt of the Clergy.'

"Feb. 25.—Anna read to us Mrs. Hughes's too affecting story of the 'Twin Brothers.'

"Sunday, April 22, I spent at my friend Benjamin Flower's at Harlow, on occasion of the melancholy event of the death of Mrs. Flower.†

---

* The Rev. C. Wyvill, of Burton Hall, in the county of York, a zealous friend of civil and religious liberty, the author, in 1792, of a "Defence of Dr. Price and the Reformers of England." He early in life declined clerical duty and ecclesiastical preferment, but did not openly secede from the communion of the Established Church. He took much interest in Mr. Lindsey's Reformed Liturgy. He died March 8, 1822, in the 83rd year of his age. The petition referred to in the diary was presented to the House of Commons on Friday, June 8, 1810. It is inserted in the Mon. Rep. V. 311.

† Of this interesting lady, Mr. Aspland inserted a brief memoir in the Monthly Repository, V. 203—206. With considerable intellectual accomplishments, she united a remarkable degree of enthusiasm and fortitude. It is a romantic circumstance that Mr. Flower's imprisonment in the year 1799, by the House of Lords, for a breach of privilege in commenting on the political character of the Bishop of Llandaff, gained him this lady's hand. She had been an admiring reader of his political publications, and had suffered some persecution for her independence and spirit. When Mr. Flower was thrown into Newgate, she felt irresistibly called upon to visit him in his prison. The prisoner was naturally and deeply touched by this expression of personal sympathy growing out of congenial political sentiments, and had the happiness, on regaining his liberty, to make the lady his wife. She left at her death two daughters. One of them survives, and is the accomplished authoress of "Vivia Perpetua," and of various musical compositions.

I walked down on Good Friday; the next day was the funeral. On Sunday morning, Mr. F. assembled a few friends in his parlour, and I spoke to them on the *resurrection*. In the afternoon we heard Mr. Severn preach the funeral discourse. Evening, I spoke again to about fifty persons, chiefly orthodox, in Mr. F.'s parlour, a continuance of the morning subject. The good Calvinists heard me with the greatest liberality, and several of them thanked me.

" Wednesday, June 13.—Anniversary of Unitarian Fund. Dr. Carpenter preached. Great and good day! Mr. Rutt read the greater part of the Report for me.* But after dinner I spoke on the beneficial tendency of Unitarianism as a reason for promoting it, and on the penal statutes against us.†

" Sunday, June 17.—Charity sermon this morning at Gravel-Pit, by Dr. Carpenter, on ' That the soul be without knowledge is not good.'

---

* Mr. Aspland had only just recovered from a severe attack of quinsey, a complaint by which he was repeatedly attacked.

† On the back of a letter still in existence are preserved some hints of this address. " Why propagate Unitarianism? Because it is Christianity and we are Christians. Happy effects—benevolence contemplates them with joy. Case of a family mistaking the character and designs of a common parent, and on that account disunited and miserable. One fancies that as soon as he was born he was inoculated with disease; another, that spies and tempters have been placed around him; another, that he has no place in his father's testament, but is cut off for beggary. On the other side, one fancies that his father selected him as a favourite, and poured his heart's blood into his veins, giving him a kindly and a kindred nature; another, that fondest and most partial regards are fixed upon him, that he cannot alienate parental benevolence by disobedience, or increase it by obedience; another, that his name is in his father's will, and that for him a large and unequal portion of goods is destined. Thus the family is divided. One party looks on the other with a jealous eye—one abject, the other supercilious—and they cannot speak peaceably to each other. Now would it not be kindness to go to these children to rectify their errors, and set the unhappy part of them at ease with regard to their father's designs, and all at one with each other? This is the condition of the Unitarian amidst believers in the partiality, the injustice and the cruelty of the Heavenly Father."—Of the proceedings at this anniversary Mr. A. penned an interesting account in the Monthly Repository. Mr. Frend, the eminent Algebraist and Actuary of the Rock Insurance Office, informed the company that he had been consulted by some of the leading Catholics to solve a curious problem, viz., How long, calculating from the divisions in the House of Parliament for several years past, it would be before the Catholic question would be carried? In working the problem, he found the increase of toleration was $2\frac{1}{2}$ per cent. per annum, and that in twelve years the friends of toleration would be a majority. It did credit to Mr. Frend's acuteness that, in 1821, a Bill for the relief of the Roman Catholics was carried through the House of Commons by a majority of 19. Eight years' further agitation was necessary to complete the actual solution of the great problem.

The congregation large and the sermon much approved. Collection upwards of £35. I preached for Mr. Houghton, Princes Street, Westminster. In the evening, heard Mr. Grundy, of Nottingham, at Parliament Court, who preached a bold sermon against the Plenary Inspiration of the Scriptures, and delivered it well.

" June 21.—The procession on Sir Francis Burdett's coming out of the Tower! A tiresome and mortifying day.*

" Oct. 28.—*Last Sunday at the Old Meeting.* Preached from Joshua iv. 19—22, 'The Association of Ideas with Places morally considered.'" From this sermon, which, though hastily written, bears the impress of considerable previous meditation, it may be well to extract the closing paragraphs:

"It has been a custom in all ages to place together the Temple and the Tomb—a custom growing out of a natural and useful association of ideas. The House of Prayer is not rendered melancholy by being surrounded with the remains of those that once came up to it to take sweet counsel and to unite their thanksgivings; on the contrary, it is hereby endeared to the feelings as well of piety as of friendship: while the house appointed for all living is in such a position divested of some of its terrors and enlivened as by the light of the sanctuary. When the angel sought to banish fear from the hearts of the faithful women that came early to our Lord's sepulchre, and to excite their best affections, he said, *Come see the place where the Lord lay.*

" I have been led to the subject of the association of moral ideas with places by the circumstance of our now worshiping for nearly the last time as a people in a building which has been for a long time eminently distinguished by the virtues and talents of a succession of its former ministers, and by the number, the light and the zeal of the multitude that have come up hither in company. How many ideas, some pleasant and some painful, must we ever connect with this humble edifice! Painful it is to reflect upon the friends, the fathers and the prophets who have finished their religious course—though the pain may almost be converted into pleasure when we again consider that they finished their course well, that they fought the good fight and kept the faith, and that

---

* Sir F. Burdett had been sent to the Tower on a vote of the House of Commons that he had been guilty of a breach of privilege in writing and publishing, in Cobbett's Weekly Register, a libellous Letter to his Constituents. At the expiration of the session he was released, and instead of proceeding by Tower Hill, and placing himself in the procession of friends anxious to celebrate his release, he took a boat at the Tower stairs, went a little way down the river, and then, mounting his horse, rode to his country house.—Interested as Mr. Aspland at this time was in Sir F. Burdett, he saw reason, long before his secession from the popular ranks, to distrust the soundness and comprehensiveness of the principles of this once popular idol.

henceforth there is laid up for them a crown of righteousness. Pleasant it is, on the other hand, to look back upon the wise and salutary instructions, the reasonable and purifying devotions with which these walls have in some distant seasons at least resounded; and to contemplate the influence which this place may have had upon the faith and practice of the neighbourhood and of a still more extended circle. In the review, it must give high satisfaction to the older members of our society that they have long contributed to maintain a station where there has been a wise and holy and benevolent contending for the faith once delivered to the saints.

"But, endeared as this place is to many of you, I must congratulate you, my brethren, on the occasion of our removal from it. We do not, thanks to a good Providence, relinquish it because the sacred interests of Truth and Righteousness have failed in our hands; we do not depart divided and broken by dissensions and dispirited; we do not flee to avoid the rage of persecution. The God whom you serve has put it into your hearts to raise a more spacious and commodious edifice for his worship; and we are about to enter upon it under the most pleasing auspices. May we consecrate our new House of Prayer by carrying into it the spirit of love and a sound mind; may that place be equally distinguished with this (I do not say for the talents and virtues of its ministers, for that we cannot expect, but) for the zeal, the charity and the unanimity of its attendants; may we experience the fulfilment of the promise that in all places where God records his name, he will come into them and bless those that tread their floors; and may all that have assembled here, and all that shall assemble there, be raised up together in the resurrection of the just, to enter upon an inheritance which is incorruptible and undefiled, and that fadeth not away."

"Sunday, Nov. 4.—*Opening of the New Gravel-Pit Meeting.* My Selection of Hymns used for the first time to-day; though, as the congregation were not all supplied with books, the hymns were printed off in a little pamphlet. I read out of the new Bible which, before the service, Mr. Knight, our Treasurer, had very gallantly laid upon the cushion, in face of the congregation, but which, alas! I found prostrate on the floor on my entrance into the pulpit—a sad omen, as the 'orthodox' would say. The cushion and Bible were a present from the ladies. The sermon was a vindication of the worship of One God, from Rom. xv. 5, 6.* The day was very unfavourable, dull and rainy—roads bad;

---

* This spirited and very striking sermon was printed at the request of the Gravel-Pit congregation, and has been long out of print. Its object was to shew the true purpose of a Christian society, to explain the apostolic view of pure worship, and to vindicate the practice of Unitarians as worshipers of one God in one person. Towards the close of the discourse, the preacher very skilfully

but the place was quite full. Persons of all denominations. The singing had been long practised beforehand, and was quite delightful. The place turns out quite favourable for the voice.

"Tuesday, Nov. 6.—This day was held the congregational dinner of Gravel-Pit, to celebrate the opening of the New Meeting. One hundred and one or two dined at the London Tavern; Mr. Christie was chairman. Mr. ——— entered his protest against the principle of the New Meeting deeds, but declared he should oppose no longer; and as a proof of reconcilement, gave twenty guineas more towards the new building— a good ending. Mr. Belsham's health was given and received with great ardour. He made a very good speech in reply. The greatest unanimity prevailed.

"Friday, Nov. 9.—Mrs. ——— sent for me to a servant of hers, who is in a dreadfully low way, and has been more than once on the point of destroying herself. I saw that she laboured under the

---

availed himself of the circumstance of their meeting on the anniversary of the Revolution of 1688, to allude to the singular legal position then occupied by the Unitarians:

"On this day 122 years back, appeared off the British shores the deliverer of our fathers from Popery and arbitrary power. One of his first acts on the Throne to which he was called by the suffrages of the people, was the grant of Toleration to Protestant Dissenters. But it must not be suppressed, that from the benefit of the Toleration Act such as oppose the doctrine of the Trinity are expressly excepted, and left to feel the weight of all the precedent heavy statutes against Nonconformity. We only, of all who separate from the Established Church, are unprotected by the law. But, blessed be God! he has not left us defenceless, but has shielded us by the large and growing liberal sentiments of the times, and by the tolerant disposition of the successive Monarchs of the Hanover family. If I may speak without indelicacy of the present Sovereign, whose domestic calamities almost forbid an allusion to him at the present moment, I would remark, and with gratitude and respect, that during his long and eventful reign he has uniformly acted upon the resolution, said to have been taken up and avowed by him in early life, that he would suffer no persecution for conscience' sake. I am not, as you well know, accustomed to practise adulation towards the great; my praise of the Prince on the Throne is drawn out by my subject; it has certainly the merit of being sincere; and in addition to it I will state my firm belief, that whatever sentence history may pass upon the character of the present reign, there will be at least this one feature of it which posterity will contemplate in the most pleasing colours; they will look with warm approbation on the page where it shall be recorded that every subject of the present government was protected in his religious profession, even though put by the letter of the law without the pale of Toleration." The preacher added his anticipation (happily soon to be fulfilled) of the repeal of the statutes against Unitarians, "which the legislature would shudder to re-enact, and which no magistrate would consent to put in force."

weight of guilt, and brought her to confess that she had been seduced and debauched by a young man, and had taken abortive medicines. She could not believe that she could live, or that God would forgive her. I stayed with her two hours, read the Scriptures to her, and prayed by her; I left her somewhat relieved and comforted.

"What an illustration is this poor creature's case of the scriptural truth, that 'she that liveth in pleasure is dead whilst she liveth!'

"Sunday, Nov. 11.—Sacrament to-day, on account of the opening being the first Sunday. A good many of the poor, whom I hope to see frequently. The unhappy young woman was twice at meeting. I lamented that there was little in the morning sermon that could reach her case, though I rejoiced that in the afternoon there might be something in the sermon for her, the subject being 'The Comforts of Religion.' In the evening, I went to Parliament Court to hear my friend Benjamin Flower on the *Day of Judgment*. A good plain sermon and a good audience.

"Dec. 11.—The Londoners are becoming bankrupt.* The ice is broken, and flaws and cracks are spreading on every side, and the greater part of the mercantile men will, I fear, be under the water. This is the effect of war, the sin of which Providence is visiting upon the heads of its chief promoters."

The calamitous nature of the times told unfavourably upon the pecuniary condition of the Gravel-Pit congregation, which found itself embarrassed with a debt of £1500 above the estimated cost of their undertaking. But before the close of the year, the congregational prospects a little brightened, nearly one-half of the deficiency having been raised. Nor had Mr. Aspland been quite free from other anxieties, growing out of the opening of the New Meeting. In anticipation of this event, he had, with a large amount of labour, been preparing during the greater part of the year his Selection of Hymns. There were but few collections then in being that were not more or less orthodox in their complexion. He desired to form a volume of devotional poetry that should be strictly Unitarian in its spirit, yet should not be deficient in the warmth and fervency which are the proper attributes of sacred song. In order to enrich it with hymns not previously known or in use, he looked carefully through the English Poets, and sought in various quarters original contributions. One principle was adopted by him, the

---

* The Gazette of Nov. 9 contained the names of 54 bankrupts.

neglect of which in other collections sometimes offends: he did not think himself at liberty to alter what he used further than by omission and transposition. He observed that "he did not feel himself competent to improve the poetry which he had selected, and he could not allow himself to debase it."

When the volume was completed, the author was somewhat disheartened by the scruples of some of the members of the congregation about its use, possibly on account of his admission of " some hymns which glow with very fervent feeling towards the Saviour, and which, to an unpoetic mind, might seem to approach too near the character of worship." The introduction of these hymns he thus vindicated in the Preface:

"In the hymns on the divine mission, the spotless character and the high exaltation of Jesus, will be found some glowing expressions, of the correctness of which there may be a doubt. They have not been adopted, however, from inadvertence, but after mature deliberation. Gratitude and honour are eminently due to the author and finisher of our faith; and *to bow the knee* to him, to celebrate his excellencies, to acknowledge his authority, and to anticipate his second coming and his society in heaven, is, according to scriptural language and apostolic usage, *to glorify God the Father*. Some of the strongest expressions on the subject of Christ's honours which will be here met with, are derived from the New Testament; and that they may be appropriated to the use of Christians of the present day, was evidently the opinion of the greatest advocate of Unitarianism in modern times, Dr. Priestley, from whose Collection hymn 359, on *Looking to Jesus*, has been taken, in which there is an adoption of one of the boldest figures in the book of the Revelation. 'We are too scrupulous in our public exercises,' says an elegant writer, with some of whose compositions the present volume is enriched,* 'and too studious of accuracy. From an over-anxious fear of admitting any expression that is not strictly proper, we are apt to reject warm and pathetic imagery, and, in short, every thing that strikes upon the heart and the senses. In our creeds let us be guarded; let us there weigh every syllable; but in compositions addressed to the heart, let us give freer scope to the language of the affections and the overflowing of a warm and generous disposition.'"

Great as his disappointment would have been, had the volume not been adopted by those for whose use it had been prepared, and acutely as, with his ardent temperament, he felt these crosses, he put aside personal considerations in an absorbing anxiety for the peace and welfare

---

* Mrs. Barbauld. *Thoughts on the Devotional Taste. Miscellaneous Pieces*, pp. 233, 235.

of his flock, and addressed the Committee in these considerate and conciliatory terms:

To Richard Knight, Esq., Treasurer of the Gravel-Pit Congregation.

"My dear Sir,—I apprehend that there is a division in the opinions of the congregation with regard to the merits of the Selection; and if you and the Committee think the same, I should wish the book to be at once quietly withdrawn. Unanimity is particularly desirable at the present juncture; and I should have much to answer for to myself, if I were to divide the society upon any question relating to any thing of mine.

"I certainly did think that I had contributed by the Selection to the improvement of Unitarian worship, and in this notion have been supported by many much-respected friends and some congregations;* but it is unquestionably for the Gravel-Pit society to determine whether the adoption of the work would be an improvement in their particular case; and if, as I suspect, their decision, or that of any considerable number of them, is against my opinion, I shall bow respectfully to their will; consoling myself with the reflection, common to disappointed projectors, that I have meant well.

"Having failed in obtaining the best *possible*, I shall sit down contented with the best *practicable*, assured, however, that in all your determinations you have the interests of our common society as much at heart as myself, and that you are altogether better judges than I can pretend to be of the fittest means to accomplish our ends."

The result of this exercise of forbearance was the all but unanimous adoption of the Hymn-book by the congregation.

The year 1811 is memorable in the history of English Nonconformity, from the attempted alteration of the 1st of William and Mary, c. 18, commonly called the "Toleration Act," and from the united and successful opposition to the attempt made by all classes of Dissenters. Mr. Aspland took a very active share in the proceedings instituted by them to uphold their religious liberty, and a narrative of the circumstances hence becomes a necessary part of this Memoir.

The Prime Minister was Mr. Perceval. The attempt to alter the Toleration Act did not, however, proceed from any member of the Government, but from Viscount Sidmouth, who was at that time out

---

* In acknowledging a presentation-copy of the Hymn-book, Mr. Belsham writes, Sept. 10, "I return you many thanks for the kind present of your Selection of Hymns, the principle of which I highly approve, and which I have no doubt will be, in my estimation, the best Collection extant. I hope you will have no board of soi-disant critics to sit in judgment upon them, and to prevent their being adopted by your congregation."

of office. Two years previously, his attention had been drawn to the subject of the licences of Dissenting ministers. Throughout the kingdom, a new class of preachers had arisen, men without education, but influenced by great zeal, who succeeded in carrying away with them large bodies of men as ignorant as themselves. Instead of seeking to remedy this undesirable state of things by the only effectual remedy, the introduction of a general system of education, and by stimulating the educated ministers of religion to greater zeal and the adoption of a more popular method of teaching, he rather directed his thoughts to the best mode of excluding illiterate men from the ministerial office. He consulted the Bishop of Gloucester, who, while he prudently advised him rather to consult in the first instance the principal men among the Dissenters, expressed his wish to see some restriction put on the licensing of Dissenting teachers,*—such as, that they should be of age, that they should be of known and approved character, and that the licences should be for a specific place; and that a minister going to a new congregation should obtain a new licence. Lord Sidmouth, to prepare the way for legislation, moved in the House of Lords, June 2, 1809, for a return of licences granted to Dissenting ministers in the several dioceses of England and Wales since 1780. The return was ordered from 1760. The returns illustrated strikingly enough the illiteracy of many who had taken out licences.† Lord Sidmouth received from the clergy great encouragement to remedy the abuse by legislation. By some of them it was urged that the abuse of toleration led to other evils beside the dissemination of doctrinal errors; that contempt was instilled into the popular mind, by some who had the protection of the licences, for the religious and civil institutions of the country; that the labours of the regular clergy were defeated by them; that the common people were taught to despise and reject the Church Catechism and Book of Common Prayer.‡ These statements, recently for the first time made public by a panegyrical biographer, are important, as shewing some of the influences under which Lord Sidmouth prepared his celebrated Bill. He contented himself, in 1810, with announcing his pur-

---

* See the Life and Correspondence of Lord Sidmouth, recently published, by the Dean of Norwich, Vol. III. p. 39.

† In the county of Middlesex, out of 285 licences taken out at the sessions of the peace, the words, "Dissenting, Minister, Teacher, Preacher, Gospel," were misspelt by the applicants who signed the rolls not less than eighteen different ways.

‡ Life of Lord Sidmouth, III. 44, 45.

pose to introduce a Bill, and by professing his intention to do nothing hostile to the Dissenters. "He considered the Toleration Act as the palladium of religious liberty, and had not the slightest intention of proposing any infringement of it." In the following year he put himself into communication with Dr. Coke, the Wesleyan minister, and believed he had gained not merely his assent, but his "zealous approbation" of the intended measure.* On May 5, Lord Sidmouth laid a Bill before the House of Lords, the principal enactments of which were, 1, to limit the benefit of 19th Geo. III. to the ministers of separate and registered congregations; 2, to prescribe, as a preliminary for obtaining a minister's licence, the signing of a certificate of appointment by certain "substantial and reputable householders belonging to the congregation;" 3, to extend the benefits of the Act to persons not ministers of separate congregations, provided they exhibit at the quarter sessions a certificate, signed by reputable and substantial householders, to the effect that they are ministers of their sect or persuasion, that they have been known to them a certain time, and that they are persons of sober life and conversation, and of sufficient ability and fitness to preach and teach; 4, to extend the privileges of the Act to such probationers of the ministry as shall exhibit at the quarter sessions certificates of character, &c., of a certain number of Dissenting ministers; 5, to require the magistrates to administer the necessary oaths and declarations, and to record the certificates.

This Bill was calculated to awaken the suspicions, if not to rouse the actual fears, of the Dissenters. The speech with which it was introduced, though moderate in its tone, did not quite conceal the influence of a selfish Church-of-Englandism, alarmed at the prospect of having "an Established Church, but a sectarian people." †

---

* The Dean of Norwich has published extracts from a very singular letter of Dr. Coke's, in which he states the fear of the Wesleyans that academies for the instruction of their ministers would expose them to the inroads of Unitarianism. After stating that the Wesleyans had no academies, he adds, "As we believe that the Unitarian sentiments and doctrines were introduced among the Dissenters by their means, and as we have no regular confession of faith (the Thirty-nine Articles of the Church of England excepted), we should be in greater danger of fatal errors than the Dissenters, if we had academies like them."—III. 47.

† The Bishop of Chichester, in a Charge delivered about this time at Lewes, expressed his fears that, owing to the rapid growth of Dissenters and Sectaries, the religion of the Church of England would cease to be the religion of the majority of the people.

To Unitarians, whose ministers are generally settled with a particular congregation, and are persons of education, Lord Sidmouth's Bill would have been practically innocuous. Its inconveniences and penalties would have fallen chiefly on the Methodist body. But this consideration had no influence in diminishing their opposition to a Bill which involved a principle inconsistent with religious liberty. Mr. Aspland felt that the Methodist stood upon the same ground of conscience with himself, and that if the follower of Whitfield or Wesley were sacrificed to the bigot one day, the Baptist, the Independent and the Presbyterian, might be demanded to be given up the next.*

No existing organization of Dissenters included the numerous bodies of Methodists who had risen up subsequent to the recognition of the "Three Denominations." It was therefore deemed prudent to summon a general meeting, to include all Protestant Dissenters and other friends to religious liberty, in order to bring into one unbroken line the whole body of the opponents of Lord Sidmouth's Bill. The meeting was held in London on the 15th of May. The resolutions stated that there were at least two millions of Protestant Dissenters in England and Wales, inferior to none in patriotism and loyalty; that though they considered the right to worship God according to individual judgment, as an inalienable right, yet they had lived satisfied under the Act of Toleration, which they perceived with extreme regret was now attempted to be violated; that the foundation of Lord Sidmouth's Bill was incorrect, and the introduction of it not justified by any necessity, but would be highly injurious to the country if passed into a law; that, disregarding all doctrinal and ritual distinctions, they would co-operate in every legitimate effort to prevent the Bill from passing into a law, and oppose the smallest diminution of the Act of Toleration; and, encouraged by the declaration of the Prince Regent that he would deliver the constitution unaltered to his Father, they trusted that the proposed innovation would never obtain the sanction of his authority.

At this meeting Mr. Aspland took an active part. He was placed on the Committee to whom the opposition to the Bill was entrusted.

---

* See Reflections on Lord Sidmouth's Bill in Mon. Repos. VI. 501. When, more than thirty years after, the Wesleyan Methodists, under an ignorant delusion, imagined that the Dissenters' Chapels Bill was designed exclusively to benefit the Unitarians, and therefore with much clamour opposed it, Mr. Aspland reminded a friend of the ungrateful return of this body to the Unitarians, than whom none were more earnest in procuring the rejection of Lord Sidmouth's Bill.

With such successful vigour did this Committee act, so "energetic and unparalleled"* were its exertions, that the floor of the House of Lords was inundated with a flood of hostile petitions. Religious and political organization had not on any previous occasion produced this now not uncommon effect, and both the House and the public were astonished. When the Bill came on for a second reading, Lord Liverpool, on behalf of the Government, declined to support it, remarking that the Toleration laws were matters which the Legislature should not touch, unless under a paramount necessity; and that the great disquietude which the Bill had occasioned rendered it desirable that it should be dropped. Lord Sidmouth made a show of persevering; but after an interesting debate, in which the Archbishop of Canterbury, the Lord Chancellor, Lord Holland, Earl Stanhope, Earl Grey and others took part, on a motion of Lord Erskine, the Bill was without a division defeated.

The biographer of Lord Sidmouth pleads that he was deceived throughout the transaction by the impression he had derived from his earlier communications with leading members amongst the Dissenters, believing, on the strength of their representations, that the measure was more palatable to them than was proved by the result to be the case. In a note, the name of Mr. William Smith, M.P., is given; and Dr. Pellew quotes a written memorandum of Lord Sidmouth's as follows: "Mr. Smith repeatedly told me that the Bill was so reasonable in its principle, and so just and moderate in its provisions, that he could not oppose it. *The clause relating to probationers was introduced at his suggestion.*"—Vol. III. p. 65, note.

That this imputation upon Mr. Smith's honour was not justified by the facts of the case, will be believed by those who knew him well. Prudent and unduly cautious he was sometimes thought to be, but no man doubted his inflexible integrity. That Lord Sidmouth deceived himself as to the extent of Mr. Smith's approbation of the professed objects of the Bill, the statement of some indisputable facts will shew to be more than probable. Mr. Smith occupied the responsible situation of Chairman of the Deputies appointed to protect the Civil Rights of Dissenters. To the Deputies in general, and no doubt to his intimate friend Mr. Smith in particular, Mr. Belsham alluded in the following passage of his Letter to Lord Sidmouth: "I observe in the resolutions of

---

* Mr. Belsham's Letter to Lord Sidmouth, &c., p. 35, note.

some of the Committee upon this occasion, that an oblique censure has been passed upon certain individuals who communicated with your Lordship upon the subject, and who are supposed to have led your Lordship to conclude that the great body of moderate and respectable Dissenters of all denominations were favourable to your Lordship's Bill; and their mission and authority is disavowed. To whom in particular these resolutions point, I am not informed. It is, however, maintained that your Lordship, in your eloquent speech upon introducing the Bill, did express a conviction that the measure you were about to propose would be approved by the body of Dissenters at large. Your Lordship, no doubt, communicated with those from whom it appeared probable that you would derive authentic information. Who the individuals were, I know not. But it has happened to come to my knowledge that, among others, were some of the highest respectability, who I dare say did not represent themselves as delegates of a *body which did not then exist*,* but who were in fact the proper representatives and delegates of the only body which the Dissenters acknowledge as appointed to watch over their civil concerns, and who consist of Deputies from a large number of the most respectable congregations in London; nor have I yet heard that these delegates have been disavowed by their proper constituents. With these gentlemen I have heard that your Lordship held repeated and confidential communications; and it is probably owing to some mutual misapprehensions that your Lordship was led to conclude that the Dissenters would be favourable to the measure. *Indeed, it is peculiarly unfortunate that an abstract of the Bill was not shewn to those gentlemen previously to its being introduced into the House, which was, as I understand, your Lordship's intention, as it would then have had the benefit of many calm and judicious observations. For in the shape in which it appeared, it could not but create universal alarm.*"—Pp. 34—36.

From this statement, it is clear that the Chairman of the Deputies had not seen even an abstract of the Bill before its introduction into the House of Lords. The proceedings of the Deputies were printed and published in 1813, in a volume entitled "A Sketch of the History and Proceedings of the Deputies." The proceedings connected with Lord Sidmouth's Bill occupy pp. 83 to 122. They include the account of

---

* In a note, Mr. Belsham explains his reference to the general meeting of Dissenters which has been described.

an interview with Lord Sidmouth as early as May 11th, 1810, when a Sub-committee, appointed for the purpose, detailed to Lord Sidmouth the serious objections entertained by them against the measure as explained by him. When the Bill was actually introduced, in the following year, " the Chairman immediately summoned a meeting of the Committee."—P. 95. Active measures were taken to oppose the Bill, and when the opposition proved successful, the Deputies recorded their sense of the vigilance and ability of Mr. Smith's proceedings in the following resolution :

" That William Smith, Esq., M.P., the Chairman of this Deputation, is desired to accept our warmest thanks *for his vigilant attention to the subject of the late measure ever since it was first announced in Parliament; for his ready and obliging communications with the Committee, in their attempts to dissuade the noble author from actually bringing the same forward; and for his able and active assistance in obtaining its rejection.* And that this Deputation entertains a strong and grateful sense of his constant and zealous support of civil and religious liberty, and of the rights of Protestant Dissenters on all occasions."—P. 116.

These documents prove Mr. Wm. Smith to have been in active opposition to the Bill from its first announcement. It is morally impossible he could have given Lord Sidmouth those private assurances of support now for the first time asserted in print by Dean Pellew.

The only circumstance that gave Mr. Aspland anxiety in opposing Lord Sidmouth's Bill was, that his course was not sanctioned by the judgment of Mr. Belsham, who, much as he disapproved of some things in the Bill, believed it capable of amendment, and thought it contained some things worthy of being preserved. The following letters passed between them subsequently to Mr. Belsham's publication of his Letter to Lord Sidmouth.

Rev. Robert Aspland to Rev. Thomas Belsham.

" Hackney, June 25, 1811.

" Dear Sir,—I have great pleasure in conveying to you a letter from our young people, in acknowledgment of your kindness in presenting them with a copy of the ' Calm Inquiry.' It is, I need not add, wholly their own ; and it will, I am sure, gratify you at least, as a declaration of their attachment to the great principles of your excellent volume.

" I have to thank you for the *Letter to Lord Sidmouth*, though I am persuaded I shall not give you offence by saying, that I am not prepared to think either so favourably of his Lordship's intentions,* or so unfavourably of the exertions of the Dissenters,† as you appear to think. I judge of Lord Sidmouth's views from his various motions and prefatory speeches, and particularly from his opening speech on bringing forward the business this session, in which, as was remarked to us by the Marquis of Lansdowne, when we waited upon him, he openly declared hostility to the Dissenters.

"I cannot see that we owe his Lordship either apology or reparation. His Bill, as far as it was declaratory of the intent of the Toleration Act, was erroneous, and some of its provisions were vexatious and intolerable. And from his Bill only could we judge of his design; though I doubt not that, after the expression of public opinion, it would have been modified in a Committee. But what can we think of a Bill, amending the Toleration Act at the present day, which repealed no one penal statute?

---

* Mr. Belsham states (p. 3) Lord Sidmouth's intentions to have been, "to exclude from the Christian ministry the ignorant and the vicious; to extend the benefits of legal toleration to many respectable persons who are now protected only by connivance; to render the law intelligible and uniform; and to make it imperative upon the magistrate in the cases to which the statute was intended to apply." At p. 39, he avows his conviction that Lord Sidmouth's "objects were reasonable and important, and that his intentions were upright, honourable and liberal."

† Mr. Belsham's Letter opens with a satirical description of some of the extravagances of the opponents of the Bill, of which the following is a specimen: "Some among us, of more than ordinary penetration, clearly foresaw that your Lordship would never rest satisfied till you had obtained a revival of the famous Writ de Hæretico Comburendo; and were persuaded that, like Bishop Gardiner, of *pious* and *merciful* memory, your Lordship's appetite would be whetted by the odour of a roasted heretic."—Pp. 1, 2.

The celebrated Sydney Smith did not share Mr. Belsham's respect for Lord Sidmouth, or his ridicule of Nonconformist fears. In one of his masterly articles in the "Edinburgh Review," his opinion is thus stated: "If a prudent man sees a child playing with a porcelain cup of great value, he takes the vessel out of his hand, pats him on the head, tells him his mamma will be sorry if it is broken, and gently cheats him into the use of some less precious substitute. Why will Lord Sidmouth meddle with the Toleration Act, when there are so many other subjects in which his abilities might be so eminently useful; when enclosure bills are drawn up with such scandalous negligence; turnpike roads so shamefully neglected; and public conveyances illegitimately loaded in the face of day, and in defiance of the wisest legislative provisions. We confess our trepidation at seeing the Toleration Act in the hands of Lord Sidmouth, and should be very glad if it were fairly back in the Statute-book, and the sedulity of this well-meaning nobleman diverted into another channel. The alarm and suspicion of the Dissenters upon these measures is wise and rational. They are right to consider the Toleration Act as their palladium."—Works of Sydney Smith, Vol. I. p. 233.

"I fear the way in which you speak of the uneducated* amongst our teachers will pain the feelings of these individuals, who, to say the least, are doing good where learned men could not find their way. To hurt their minds was not, I know, your design, and being fully assured of this, I venture to make the above remark.

"No apology, I trust, is necessary for what I have written; but if any be required, your candour will suggest one for me in the interest which I have taken in this affair, and in the concern I entertain for the reputation of those with whom I have particularly acted.

"I am, dear Sir, yours very respectfully,

ROBERT ASPLAND.

"P.S. I have been for some time meditating a publication on the Sidmouth affair. Should I proceed and give my thoughts to the public, I may possibly refer to your Letter; but in doing so, I shall not forget the respect which is due to you from the friends of freedom, or lose the diffidence with which I in particular should dissent from your opinions."

Rev. Thomas Belsham to Rev. Robert Aspland.

"Hackney, June 25, 1811.

"My dear Sir,—I am much obliged to the young persons of your congregation for their kind and respectful letter. I am glad that the Summary of Lectures originally drawn up for their use was acceptable to them. And it will give me unspeakable satisfaction if, in concurrence with your active exertions, it should be the means of promoting truth and virtue among the rising generation in your flourishing society.

"I do not wonder, nor am I at all offended, at your disapprobation of many things in my Letter to Lord Sidmouth. I wrote with extreme reluctance, knowing the offence it would give to many; but I wrote from a sense of duty, to obviate as far as lay in my power the foul and, as I think, unjust aspersions which were cast upon Lord Sidmouth's character. And upon this subject I regarded myself as more competent to judge than many others, because I was acquainted with facts which could not be known to them.

"I heard Lord Sidmouth's opening speech, and I will take upon me to say, in opposition to Lord Lansdowne, that it was not a declaration of hostility to the Dissenters. On the contrary, he evidently expected that his Bill would have been acceptable to the general body of Dissenters, with very few exceptions, and was astonished to find how unpopular it was. It is true, it *does not*

---

* At p. 19, Mr. Belsham writes, "After having *tried his gifts* till he is tired, honest John will return in peace to his bodkin or his awl, perhaps convinced that he has mistaken his vocation, or more probably denouncing the vengeance of Heaven upon the ungodly crew who refuse to listen to the admonitions of so divine a teacher."

repeal penal laws, nor does the Toleration Act itself. The Act of W. and M. exempts persons who comply with its conditions from certain penalties. The Act of 19 of Geo. III. comprehends many who could not be benefited by the Act of Wm. and Mary; but Lord Sidmouth's Bill extends the provisions of the 19th of Geo. III. It protects many who are at present unprotected, and it makes the Act imperative upon the magistrate, which many now consider as discretional. These are, unquestionably, great advantages; but they are countervailed by the exclusion from toleration of those who could not obtain certificates, and by the absurdity and vexatious nature of the certificates themselves.

"You very naturally observe that 'from his Bill only we could judge of his design, though, *after the expression of public opinion,* it would have been modified in the Committee.' I happen to know that, antecedently to any the least suspicion of the opposition which would be made to the Bill, he was ready to have introduced many material changes; viz., to have thrown out all the clauses relating to probationers, and to have altered the wording of the certificates, so as to have made them as unexceptionable as possible. There was scarcely an alteration which could be suggested to which he was unwilling to accede, so desirous was he of making his Bill acceptable to the Dissenters, and all this before he dreamed of the opposition he met with. But this, though known to me, could not be known to the public, which, therefore, must judge by appearances, and that judgment must of course be harsh. It appeared to me, therefore, that justice to Lord Sidmouth required that I, who knew his sentiments, should attempt his vindication.

"He is excessively hurt at being charged with a *design* to abridge the Toleration Act. He certainly did not design it. His views of it were too contracted; but his design was to extend it *upon the whole.*

"He was ignorant, but appeared to me desirous to be informed, and to listen to reason. He needs instruction rather than rebuke.

"Certificates are so customary in the Establishment, that he had no suspicion that they could give offence to the Dissenters. It is plain that he is an entire stranger to the habits, feelings and prejudices of the Dissenters; he wants, and is willing, to be set right.

"I acknowledge that my expressions against illiterate preachers are strong, but my argument required it. I wished to state and prove that even the miserable fanatics who could obtain no testimonials to their character and talents ought not to be exposed to the penal laws. I am obliged to state the worst supposable case.

"I wished the opposition to the Bill to have been conducted by the Committee of Deputies and by the general body, which I have no doubt would have been ultimately successful. I dread lest the energies of your Committees should be retaliated upon us another day by the clamour of—The Church is in danger!—I have often wished that I had not gone to the opening speech; but having heard it, and having by my subsequent communication with Lord Sidmouth acquired, as I think, a distinct knowledge of his views and principles, I could not in justice withhold my testimony to his character, though I was sensible it would give much offence. You, my dear Sir, have the same right to publish your ideas on the subject, which I doubt not you will do with your usual candour.

"I am, very sincerely yours,
THOMAS BELSHAM."

CHAPTER XVII.

Lord Sidmouth's ill-advised attempt to give new stringency to the Toleration Act, led in the following year to a partial revisal of the laws affecting Protestant Dissenters. In the long series of years that had intervened since the passing of the Toleration Act, only one law had been passed, for extending the relief granted by the Toleration Act to Protestant Dissenting ministers and schoolmasters. Until 1779, the benefits of the Toleration were limited to those who subscribed the doctrinal Articles of the Church of England. By the Act of that date, subscription to the Articles was remitted, and in lieu of it a declaration was substituted of being a Christian and a Protestant. The Statute-book was, however, encumbered with several unrepealed persecuting laws, such as the Conventicle and Five-mile Acts. It would have been a poor defence of these relics of perhaps the worst and most disgraceful period of English history, that they were practically inoperative; but they wanted even this defence. In remote parts of the country, where the Dissenters were few and weak, magistrates were still found not ashamed to make occasional use of these generally discarded weapons of persecution. As one of the Committee of the *Protestant Society for the Protection of Religious Liberty*, Mr. Aspland took an active part in consultations to devise the best mode for obtaining the repeal of the obnoxious laws. Mr. Belsham thus addressed him with his advice and encouragement:

Rev. Thomas Belsham to Rev. Robert Aspland.

"Tuesday, Dec. 17th.

"My dear Sir,—Most cordially do I wish success to your proposed application to Parliament,—an application most seasonable and judicious, and which will, I trust, in its main object be successful. Indeed, it must be so.

The voice of the delegates of 800 congregations of Protestant Dissenters must be heard. They will grant your request from a sense of justice, from fear, from policy—and, though last, not least, out of *spite to the Whigs*.

"Will you excuse my suggesting the hope that you will not clog your main object by connecting it too strongly with things of minor importance?

"The main and primary object, which ought never to be lost sight of for a moment, and to which every thing else should be sacrificed, is the *repeal of the penal laws*, particularly those mentioned in the 7th section of the Toleration Act. This they cannot refuse to grant, because these persecuting Acts have been lately enforced. And this is all which, as Dissenters, we can claim as a *right*. For no person could then be called to account for preaching or administering the sacraments.

"If we go further and ask for privileges and exemptions, the magistrate has then a right to demand a test, or, in other words, a description of the persons to whom those exemptions should be granted. The Act of the 19th of Geo. III. sets this matter nearly upon its proper basis. It grants exemptions to ministers of congregations who make a declaration to which no Christian can object. But it wants to be made *imperative* upon the magistrate; he should be *required*, instead of *empowered*, to administer the oaths. And if, in order to obtain this important object, you should consent that every applicant should bring a testimonial to his character and to the competency of his qualifications for the ministry, signed either by two *qualified* ministers or four respectable householders of his congregation, they will, I think, be pleased with the concession, and you will gain a great benefit without the sacrifice of any principle.

"I deprecate the entangling this important object with the trifling question of exemption from parish rates, of which the adversaries of religious liberty would lay hold as a handle to overturn the whole. At any rate, such a clause as that should only be proposed when the Bill is in the Committee, and by no means constitute a substantive part of the Bill. The same may be said of a clause for the repeal of the Antitrinitarian laws.

"I hope you will excuse the liberty I take of suggesting these hints. I most sincerely wish well to the cause, and I think that there never were better hopes of succeeding than at present.

"I hope Mr. Wyvill's Petition will be withdrawn: it can excite no interest and will do no good.

"Wishing you all possible success in your active exertions to promote the best of causes, I am, dear Sir, most sincerely yours,

T. BELSHAM.

"P. S. When you have determined upon your Reading Library,* please to

---

* Active exertions were at this time made, under Mr. Aspland's direction, to establish an Unitarian congregation at Reading, in Berkshire. Mr. Vidler, of

accept from me a copy of the Calm Inquiry, the Improved Version, and the Summary of Evidences, as a contribution to it. Vidler's conduct seems to have been most admirable."

Before the close of the year 1811, he, together with Mr. John Wilks and others, had an interview with the Prime Minister on the subject,* who listened favourably to their case. Early in the spring of the following year, the negociations were renewed with the Government, the Methodist "Committee of Privileges" taking the lead, seconded by the Protestant Society and the Committee of Deputies. The subject was one of the last which occupied the attention of Mr. Perceval. On Monday, May 11, Mr. Aspland, in company with Mr. Wilks and Mr. Mills, had a satisfactory interview with him at three o'clock in the afternoon, and two hours after, as he was entering the House of Commons, he was shot by a deranged assassin.†

Parliament Court, rendered great aid. See Report of Unitarian Fund, 1812, and Mon. Repos., VII. 768.

* In a familiar letter to his mother, dated December 21, 1811, he thus wrote: "This day week I waited, with four other gentlemen, on Mr. Perceval, the Prime Minister. He received us very graciously. We are to go up to him again; and we have every reason to believe that we shall get some of the persecuting laws repealed."

† The facts, as described by Mr. Aspland at the time, were these. "The assassination grew out of commercial transactions in the Russian empire. A merchant there, by name *Bellingham*, had a dispute relative to his business, which being referred to arbitration was given against him, and it ended in his being thrown into prison. He conceived that the English ambassador and consul were not sufficiently attentive to his complaints, and he came to England with this idea strong in his mind, impressed deeply by the indignities he had suffered, and heightened by a derangement to which he appears to have been subject. Here he laid his complaints before Ministers, Members of Parliament, and the Bow-street officers, but nowhere obtained that attention to which he thought himself entitled. Hence he formed the idea of sacrificing a public man to his resentment, with a confused notion of teaching them their duty; and it fell to the lot of the first Minister to receive the fatal blow. He was coming into the lobby of the House of Commons, when he received a pistol-shot, the ball piercing his heart; and, advancing only a step or two, he fell, and expired in a few minutes.

"Having perpetrated the act, Bellingham retired to a seat behind, where he was seized soon after, with a very unnecessary degree of violence, for he did not betray the slightest wish to escape, nor did he make any resistance. After an examination, in which he confessed the fact, and corrected with great coolness the evidence of some of the witnesses, he was committed to Newgate, and four days after was brought to his trial. In prison, and at the bar, he manifested the same firmness of mind, rejecting the plea, that had been set up for him, of insanity, complaining of the injuries he had sustained in Russia, and of the neglect of government towards him, both at home and abroad, and justifying

Lord Liverpool succeeded to the Premiership, and shewed, at least equally with his predecessor, a willingness to redress Dissenting grievances. Before the close of the session, a Bill was introduced into and passed both Houses without opposition, repealing the Conventicle and Five-mile Acts, and, while it imposed the necessity of obtaining licences both for preachers and places of worship, gave to all persons, not exceeding twenty in number, the right to meet in an unlicensed place. On the third reading of the Bill in the House of Commons, Mr. Wm. Smith "congratulated the House and the country on the singular progress of the Bill through the House, to that, its last, stage, without having provoked the expression of one sentiment of hostility against it. This he could not help looking upon as a most auspicious sign of the rapid advance of liberal and enlightened opinion." In the House of Lords, Lord Sidmouth, without offering opposition to the Bill, expressed his regret that no qualification was demanded from persons professing to teach and preach. Lord Liverpool, after a careful explanation of the provisions of the Bill, observed, " that an enlarged and liberal toleration was the best security to the Established Church,—a Church not founded in the exclusion of religious discussion, but, in its homilies, its canons, and all the principles upon which it rested, courting the investigation of the Scriptures, upon which it founded its doctrines." The Bill received the warm support of Lords Holland, Stanhope and Erskine; and, having obtained the Royal assent, was designated in the Statute-book as 52 Geo. III. c. 155.

---

his act, in which he maintained that there was no peculiar malice against the unhappy object, who fell a victim to the neglect of government in doing justice. The sentence of death he received with the utmost composure, which he retained during the trying interval to the time of execution, which was employed in pious conversation and acts of devotion, for he was a very serious member of the Establishment, and in writing. His fortitude did not forsake him to the last; for previous to his execution, on the third day after his condemnation, just before he stepped on the scaffold, he was examined by the Lord Mayor and Sheriffs, in the presence of a number of persons, before whom he justified the act, and denied the concurrence of any accomplice. He looked upon death as a haven from his troubles, and was launched into eternity, without betraying a symptom of remorse, or losing at any time his fortitude." (Mon. Repos., VII. 342.)

There was something revolting both to our sense of justice and humanity in the frightful speed with which Bellingham was doomed and executed. His crime was committed on Monday, May 11th. On Friday, May 15th, he was convicted; and on the morning of Monday, May 18th, his lifeless corpse was in the hands of the surgeons for dissection. He was subject to hereditary insanity.

It was wisdom in the Unitarians not to endanger the new Toleration Act, by pressing the consideration of their peculiar grievances, at a time when the temper of the legislature was matter of uncertainty. But it would have been strange if they had not desired to benefit by the liberality manifested by the Prince Regent's Government.

Mr. Aspland was the first to act in this important matter.* On July 8, 1812, he called together the Committee of the Unitarian Fund,† and laid before them a paper on the subject of the legal condition of Unitarians. The result was, a resolution that it was expedient that the Unitarians should put themselves into communication with the Government on the subject of the penal laws which aggrieved them. A sub-committee, consisting of Mr. Aspland, Mr. Christie and Mr. Vidler, was appointed to confer with Mr. Belsham.

Rev. Thomas Belsham to Rev. Robert Aspland.

"Essex Street, July 10.

"My dear Sir,—I am just returned out of the country and have received your two notes, and I shall be very happy to meet you and the other gentlemen whose names you mention, to confer upon the most proper and effectual means of obtaining what I think cannot be refused, the repeal of those penal laws which press upon the Unitarians. Will Monday at twelve o'clock be a convenient time for you and them?"

The conference ended in a written request, signed by Mr. Belsham and the members of the sub-committee, to Mr. William Smith, M. P., to endeavour to procure the insertion of a clause in the pending Toleration Bill protecting Unitarians. Mr. Smith, however, seems to have prepared a distinct Bill, and the immediate result of his labours is detailed in the following letter:

Rev. Thomas Belsham to Rev. Robert Aspland.

"Essex Street, July 15, 1812.

"My dear Sir,—Mr. W. Smith's exertions in our favour have been most

---

* It appears by the Report of the Unitarian Fund, 1813, that Mr. Aspland had previously corresponded with Unitarians in different parts of the kingdom, and ascertained that they were ready to support by petitions any application that might be made to Parliament for the repeal of the penal laws affecting them.

† Of the gentlemen who composed that Committee, three members survive, Mr. Christie and Mr. Samuel Hart, of Hackney, and Mr. William Hall, now of Liverpool. To each of these gentlemen, but especially the first-named, the Unitarian cause in England is indebted for many valuable services.

meritorious and unwearied. At two o'clock this morning he was obliged to defer his motion till to-day. I called upon him this morning; he shewed me his Bill, which is short but complete. He has conversed with Lord Castlereagh, Lord Liverpool and the Archbishop; they, *individually*, are all with us; they acknowledge the reasonableness of the thing, and I believe would have had no objection to its being included in the Toleration Act, had it been in time. But the Archbishop must consult his brethren and act with them; and the Bishops are all gone out of town, in reliance that no *more good* should be done than what they have already consented to. It is the universal wish that the measure may not at present be pressed. And our end, I think, is sufficiently answered by having our case brought forward into notice, and particularly to the notice of the Cabinet and the Archbishop. Mr. Smith also said that all the Lords were going out of town, so that there would be nobody to introduce the Bill into the other House. Upon the whole, I took the liberty to say to Mr. Smith that I was confident the Unitarians would regard themselves as under great obligations to him for the pains which he had taken; that our great object was to shew that we are alive to our situation; and that we desire and think ourselves entitled to the same privileges which other Protestant Dissenters possess; and it cannot be doubted that in due time they will be granted. But at present I have taken the liberty to answer for my brethren that we shall all be perfectly satisfied with that way of disposing of the measure which Mr. Smith himself may judge to be most expedient, leaving it to him to persist in it or to withdraw it as he may think proper. I think it cannot be doubted that it would be carried another session; but Mr. S. says they talk of revising the whole penal code, and that this Act will probably be repealed with the rest. I thought it proper to tell Mr. Smith that, if he thought it advisable, we could in a few days procure hundreds of signatures to a petition, that it might appear that he did not bring forward the measure without authority from the Unitarians. But this at present he declined. And I imagine that the names of those who signed the request to him are pretty well known.

"Next to Mr. Smith, our best friend is that eminent saint, Mr. Andrew Fuller; his attempt to revivify the dormant statute in the case of Mr. Gisburne has been of infinite service to us; had he renewed his Christian attack, or had any of his disciples imitated his holy zeal, our triumph would have been complete and immediate. Lord Liverpool, upon hearing it, said it altered the case very much indeed. And if any debate should come on, your friend Andrew will be very handsomely worked about it. I told Mr. Smith that the case was very correctly stated in your Letters to that gentleman, and, at his desire, I ordered Hunter to send him a copy, which I took the liberty to direct him to send as *from the author*. If the *author* does not approve of this, I will be answerable for the price.

"I am glad you are going down to Brighton* to open the chapel there. I received a letter from Mr. Bennet upon the subject. I have got five pounds towards the expense from Mr. Selby, and I mean to give as much myself, and I hope among my friends to collect a little more.

"With compliments to Mrs. Aspland, I am, my dear Sir, very sincerely yours,
T. BELSHAM."

In the following year Mr. William Smith carried through the House of Commons, without any difficulty or opposition,† a Bill for repealing so much of the 9th and 10th of William and Mary, *and of all or any other Act or Acts of the English, Scotch, British, Irish, or United Parliaments, as imposed penalties on those who interpreted the Holy Scriptures inconsistently with the Holy Trinity as laid down in the Thirty-nine Articles of the United Church of England and Ireland, except so far as they related to ministers of the said United Church.*

When the Bill was carried to the House of Lords, an objection was taken to the informality of the clause which is printed above in italics, it not being regular to repeal any Act of Parliament without its being distinctly specified. It was not known that any other English statute existed making it penal to deny the doctrine of the Trinity. Nor did any one anticipate the danger which subsequently arose to Unitarians enjoying endowments and foundations created anterior to the admission of Unitarianism to strictly legal toleration. Had this singular result of the Hewley suit been foreseen, there can be no reason to doubt that the mischief would have been cured by an additional clause in the Trinity Bill of 1813, establishing the Unitarians in the enjoyment of the religious foundations they had inherited from their fathers. A new Bill was immediately introduced which repealed the clauses in the 19th Geo. III., and in the *Toleration* and *Blasphemy* Acts of William and Mary, which related to the denial of the Trinity. It also repealed

---

* The chapel was opened July 22, 1812. Two sermons were preached on the occasion by Mr. Aspland; that in the morning, on the Existence of God; that in the evening, on Christian Liberty. See Mon. Repos., VII. 525.

† His success exceeded the expectations of the Committee of the Unitarian Fund, who, presenting their Report immediately after Mr. Smith had obtained leave to introduce his Bill, observed, "That it will at once pass both Houses is too much to be expected; but if it excite discussion it will do good; and though unsuccessful at present, the way may be preparing for its future complete success." In nearly similar terms did Dr. Priestley write to Dr. Estlin in 1792, just before Mr. Fox's motion for the repeal of the penal laws against Unitarians. See Rutt's Life of Priestley, II. 182.

the Blasphemy Acts of the Parliament of Scotland passed in the reigns of Charles II. and William III. This Bill passed very quickly through all its stages in both Houses of Parliament. In the House of Lords, on the question of the third reading, the Archbishop of Canterbury (Dr. Sutton)* took occasion to remark upon the well-merited character of the Established Church of England for its due attention to the principles of genuine toleration; and added, "that the Church was always remarkable for its tender regard with respect to the religious scruples of individuals," and that "on those principles he had no objection to the passing of the Bill." The Bishop of Chester (Dr. Law) said that "the Bill was not brought forward in consequence of penalties actually imposed on Unitarians, who already enjoyed perfect toleration;" but added, "he was pleased such a Bill was introduced, as affording an additional proof that intolerance was no part of the character of the Church of England." The Bill received the Royal Assent, July 21, 1813. It is marked in the Statute-book as 53 Geo. III., c. 160, and is entitled, *An Act to relieve Persons who impugn the Doctrine of the Holy Trinity from certain Penalties.*

Twenty years previously, a similar Bill was brought forward by Mr. Fox, in consequence of a petition signed by Christians of different denominations, and, though supported with all his eloquence, "was instantly and indignantly opposed and crushed by all the power of government, and by the fascinating eloquence of celebrated politicians,† who too frequently succeeded in making the worse appear the better

---

* Except in his opposition to the Roman Catholic claims, Dr. Sutton was the unvarying friend of religious liberty. This was shewn by his conduct on Lord Sidmouth's Bill, by his support of the Unitarian Marriage Bill, and by his conduct on the repeal of the Sacramental Test. In his Letter of Expostulation to the Rev. H. H. Norris, Mr. Aspland held up the Archbishop of Canterbury as an example of the "more excellent way" of Christian charity. "I had the high satisfaction of hearing him, in the House of Lords, in the last debate (Tuesday, May 21, 1811) on Lord Sidmouth's abortive Bill, declare himself broadly against all intolerance, and assert for all Christians the inalienable rights of conscience. He said, and with a fervour which bespoke sincerity, that 'however he might lament what he conceived to be the errors of Protestant Dissenters, it was to be recollected that the Bible was the foundation of their religious belief, as well as of that of the Established Church, and was, or might be, in the hands of every member of the empire; and it was to be recollected also, *that the best of* INTERPRETATIONS *were but the interpretations of* MEN, *and that the best of men were liable to error.*'"—P. 93.

† Pitt and Burke. The Bill was moved May 11, 1792, and rejected by a majority of 79.

part." Well might Mr. Belsham, surveying the contrast which 1813 presented to 1792, say,* "I can scarcely persuade myself to believe that it is real. The whole has the appearance of a wonderful and delightful vision." The passing of the Trinity Bill was celebrated by resolutions adopted by various Unitarian societies in London and the provinces, and by the preaching of thanksgiving sermons. No one rejoiced on this occasion more than Mr. Aspland. He gave utterance to his feelings on an early Sunday,—the first on which he met his flock after the passing of the Act,—in a discourse on Micah iv. 3—5. The concluding portions of this sermon (which was not printed) will not be read with diminished interest from the fact that one or two passages were used by him in that part of his "Plea for Unitarian Dissenters" in which he commented on Mr. Norris's lament over the liberality of the times.

"The last Sunday that I met you within these walls, there existed laws which declared against us a sentence of outlawry if we mutually professed the opinions which bind us together, which we have learned of our only Master in religion, Jesus Christ, and which, under a solemn constraint of conscience, we could not and cannot but believe and avow. *Those laws are no more;* they have expired without a struggle, and are now only remembered as the ghastly apparel of a spirit of persecution, which is laid for ever. Unitarians are henceforward a legal sect in England, on a level, in point of toleration, with those Dissenters that approach nearest in doctrine to the Established Church. Under these circumstances I could not meet you to-day, after a short absence, without strong emotions of gratitude to the God of Peace and Freedom, nor could I have justified myself in passing by so favourable an opportunity of exhorting you to pious gratitude, to Christian patriotism, and to persevering and increasing labours in the cause of Truth and Virtue.

"Vanity does not, that I am aware, betray me into an over-estimate of the importance of the legislative measure to which I refer:—it is a measure of relief to the consciences of many thousands of our fellow-countrymen, as well as to our own; it is a blessing to our children, our children's children. And by it there is abolished not only an instrument of oppression to no inconsiderable body of Christians, but also an instrument of disgrace to our country; for unjust and cruel laws are a stain upon a country's honour, and her best chil-

---

* See his admirable discourse preached at Essex Street, July 25, 1813, pp. 4, 5, entitled, "The Sufferings of Unitarians in former Times urged as a Ground of Thankfulness for their recovered Liberties." Another Thanksgiving Sermon, equally worthy of the occasion, preached at the New Meeting-house in Birmingham, by Rev. John Kentish, was published.

dren will rejoice most when they are wiped away. The repeal of a persecuting statute is a virtual assertion of the rights of conscience, and therefore, though the statute may be of little consequence, the repeal is of the greatest: it is a boon to other sects as well as that immediately contemplated by it, inasmuch as it is a declaration that religion is not amenable to man's tribunal. We cannot contemplate this as a single unconnected measure; persecution was once a strong and massy building; the first stone that was removed from it prepared the next to fall; stone after stone, buttress after buttress, was thrown down; we have just seen a main pillar tumbled to the ground; the little that remains of the ruinous fabric shakes with every gust of public opinion; and presently not one stone shall be left upon another.

"We are not selfish in our joy. Our gain is no man's loss; it is a gain also to all the wise and good amongst our countrymen. We have sacrificed none of our fellow-christians or fellow-men to save ourselves; we have made no surrender, no compromise, no stipulation. We have not sunk, or agreed to postpone, any claim which as Christians we think that we can justly or may prudently prefer. And it would be strange indeed if we should be less disposed, because we are more able, to help any of our fellow-christians who may yet be held in the inner wards of the house of bondage.

"It may be said in diminution of the good of the measure under consideration, that the statute which has been repealed had become obsolete. This was a good reason for its repeal, but none for our contentment under it. That a bad law sleeps, is no earnest that it will never be awakened; and though it be not in exercise, it may breathe a noxious spirit and pollute and afflict a community with bigotry. The arrows of reproach that have been so frequently cast upon Unitarians were dipped in the poison of persecuting laws that were reputed to be dead: now that this source of acrimony and virulence is dried up, it may be hoped that our antagonists will meet us with more honourable weapons, remembering the apostolic maxim, that *though a man strive, yet is he not crowned, except he strive lawfully*.

"For these reasons you do, I persuade myself, join with me in thanksgivings to Almighty God, our Help and our Shield, with whom alone is the guidance of the public mind and the control of the powers of this world, and who for benevolent purposes speaks peace to the nations, and commands the kings and judges of the earth to be wise and to be still, remembering that He is God. In wisdom, doubtless, he permitted our fathers to see the rod of persecution suspended over their heads, that thereby they might be excited to greater watchfulness, to a closer examination of the grounds of their faith and the motives of their profession, and to the cultivation of a habit of dependance solely on the Divine arm; but in great goodness has he removed the scourge, as if seeing that we have borne temptation well, and are prepared to enjoy liberty without the danger of licentiousness. * * *

"Amongst the strong reasons for our thankfulness to Almighty God, we cannot overlook our condition as members of a free and enlightened country,—a country fertile in the richest productions of the heart, in manly sentiment, in liberality, in generosity, in charity, in candour. Under the influence of these endowments of the public mind, we were safe even with positive laws against us. We thank our countrymen, next under God, for their fair and liberal interpretation of our profession and conduct: and we shall not love them the less, nor will they, I trust, entertain the less respect for us, because we henceforward enjoy as a right what was before a charity. The recovery of the right we owe to them, and we feel it a bounden duty to use it for general good. Our loyalty, our reverence of the genuine constitution of our country, was not, we presume to think, questionable, whilst we were in the letter of the law deprived of some of its essential benefits; it shall not, I may venture to promise, be doubtful, although there are a few great civil privileges still denied to us; but loyalty will, we hope, be ever with us a sincere desire of the improvement of our country in whatever is laudable and great, and tending to our own happiness and that of the rest of the world—a reverence of public authority for the sake of virtue, peace and freedom. Such is the only loyalty which a wise government will accept, or which enlightened citizens can proffer. We say from the heart, May our country prosper! May its power be perpetual! But we should esteem it treason against human nature not to add, May its prosperity spring from its virtue! May its power never be parted from Justice and Mercy!

"On this day of congratulation and joy and triumph, it is scarcely possible not to look back with the mingled sentiments of painful sympathy and thankful admiration to our forefathers, who, by their labours and sufferings, upheld and adorned and sanctified our cause,—the cause, as we believe, of truth and righteousness. They sowed in tears, that we might reap with joy. They wrote and preached and prayed for a long series of years with little apparent success, and were sometimes in danger of their liberty and life, always assailed with reproach and calumny. Till within a short time, the Unitarian doctrine was confined to the books of the learned and the closets of the curious. We have lived to see the pure doctrine of the New Testament spread amongst a large mass of our countrymen: we have seen the poor opening their understandings to receive the religion of the fishermen of Galilee: we have seen unbelievers embracing the truth as it is in Jesus, and rejoicing in the words of truth and soberness: we have seen houses of prayer dedicated in every part of the empire to the Only True God, the Holy One of Israel, the God and Father of our Lord Jesus Christ: and we have, lastly, seen the Legislature of our country almost voluntarily stepping forward to acknowledge us as Christians, and to hold out to us, for the precarious shelter of public opinion, the substantial and durable protection of law. And seeing and feeling this, can we withhold the just tribute of admiration and applause to those great and good men, now no more, to whose characters and exertions we owe the prevalence of our opinions, and the estimation in which we are held by our country! Let us shew our esteem of the departed advocates of truth by imitating their example; let us do, in the security of law, what they did in the face of danger; and as evil report did not terrify them from the duty of avowing an unpopular faith, let not good report seduce us from the fulfilment of our obligation to make known the truth, which requires only to be made known in order to gain general acceptance."

The passing of the Trinity Bill was, we have seen, materially assisted by the Unitarian Fund Society.* The remainder of this Chapter will be devoted to a review of the proceedings of the Society, to which Mr. Aspland for a long series of years devoted much time and all the energies of his mind. From the foundation of the Society in 1806, to 1818, he was uninterruptedly the Secretary; and the careful minutes and the annual reports written by his hand, and preserved in the archives of the *Unitarian Association*, shew how assiduously he laboured in carrying out the objects of the Society. The ministers and laymen who assisted were amongst his warmest friends, and the executive of the Society was for many years chiefly supplied from the members of the Hackney congregation. It would be an act of injustice not to specify the very zealous services of Mr. John Christie, then an eminent London merchant, who was for a long period the Treasurer of the Fund.

In reviewing the success and the failures of the Society, it must be borne in mind that it entered upon a path wholly untrodden, and nearly all its first steps were in a great measure so many experiments. Hitherto there had been no general organization amongst the Unitarians of England, and no systematic Unitarian missions. The Unitarian Book Society had sent forth its silent missionaries; but its publications had not found their way to the homes of the poor, but were for the most part confined to the middle classes. An unwillingness to interfere with this excellent Society prevented the promoters of the Unitarian Fund from making the publication of books and tracts a part of

---

* The Rev. John Kentish, in his sermon preached on the anniversary of the Society, June 1, 1814, alluding to the cruel enactments against persons denying the Trinity, described "the repeal of them, since their previous anniversary meeting, as the honour of the age and reign," and congratulated the members that it "had been effected in part through the instrumentality of their Society." See Sermon, p. 29.

their original plan. Their objects were stated in the PREAMBLE, which was agreed to at a meeting of the Committee held at Mr. Rutt's, March 23, 1806:

"It has long been a subject of complaint among Unitarians, and a topic of reproach to their adversaries, that so few active measures have been taken to diffuse among the lower classes of the people the doctrines of Rational Religion. A knowledge of this, together with a conviction of the necessary connection between Truth and Righteousness, has prevailed upon a number of individuals, zealously concerned for the spread of Scriptural Christianity and the promotion of the happiness and improvement of the Poor, to institute a Society for the encouragement of Popular Preaching on Unitarian principles. The Society is not insensible of the laudable efforts that have been made to instruct the public mind in the knowledge of pure Christianity by the distribution of books. Those efforts its members have witnessed with pleasure, and have as individuals assisted. They are persuaded, however, that addresses from the pulpit are more suited to the habits of the Poor than addresses, equally excellent, from the press, and that the encouragement of Unitarian worship is one of the best means, as it is the natural consequence, of disseminating the Unitarian doctrine."

The first object to which the Committee directed their efforts, was to secure the co-operation of well-known Unitarians, in various parts of the country, as corresponding members. Honourable mention is made in the first Report of the services, in behalf of the Society, of Rev. John Holland, of Bolton, and Rev. Lant Carpenter, of Exeter. The information supplied by correspondents enabled the Committee to direct their labours to the promotion of Unitarianism in various parts of England, Scotland and Wales. Chapels long closed were re-opened, ministers in straitened circumstances were encouraged and enabled to continue their labours amongst the poor, new congregations were assisted, and, above all, itinerating missionaries were sent forth nearly to every part of the kingdom. The annual meetings of the Society were long objects of great and increasing attraction, and, by moulding and giving expression to public opinion amongst the Unitarians, by rousing sympathy and emulation, by diffusing information respecting the progress of Unitarianism throughout the world, were of great practical use.

In arranging and assisting in the conduct of the anniversary meetings, Mr. Aspland was singularly successful. The report — often a wearisome part of a public meeting — in his hands was always attractive and interesting. His natural and animated elocution, and the hopeful expression of his countenance, commanded the attention of his audience through statements often exceeding an hour in duration. In the discussions which not unfrequently ensued he generally took an active part, keeping or drawing back the attention of the meeting to whatever was important in the argument, conciliating by his temper and judgment friends whom the argument had a little warmed, and often, by a happy suggestion, guiding an apparently divided meeting to an unanimous decision. The least agreeable part of a public meeting is, that it gives weak, ignorant and conceited persons, especially if they are gifted with a happy insensibility to signs of the impatience and distress of those around them, the opportunity of being very troublesome. To this inconvenience, meetings of Unitarians are particularly exposed by their habitual freedom and latitude of opinion and expression. When required, Mr. Aspland did not shrink from the painful duty of silencing an unqualified, a mischievous or a disorderly speaker, by a timely appeal, or, if necessary, by a pithy rebuke. In encounters of this kind he was aided by habitual presence of mind, self-command and a natural dignity of manner, against which little but self-important opponents found it vain to struggle. In private intercourse he was sometimes dogmatical, and in rebuking what he regarded as intentional impertinence, stern; but in public meetings there was little or nothing of this, and whatever little there was, was for the protection, and carried the concurrence, of the meeting at large. To himself, the anniversaries of the Unitarian Fund Society were most gratifying. They were, in fact, gatherings of his most intimate friends and fellow-workers from all parts of the kingdom; the sentiments uttered on those occasions were generally those which he most fondly cherished. His house and the houses of neighbouring friends were usually at Whitsuntide filled with country brethren and other guests. He had the high gratification of beholding the steady progress of the Society, and of welcoming, in successive years, as friends and allies several who in the outset stood aloof. The following is a list of the preachers before the Society, together with the numbers attending the annual dinner, and the name of the chairman.

			Preacher.	Chairman.	No. of Guests.
1	1806	Nov. 26	Rev. J. Toulmin, D. D., Birmingham	J. T. Rutt, Esq.	70
2	1807	Oct. 21	Rev. R. Aspland	E. Johnston, Esq.	100
3	1808	June 8	Rev. J. Lyons, Hull	W. Frend, Esq.	150
4	1809	May 24	Rev. T. Rees, Newington Green	W. Sturch, Esq.	190

	Year	Date	Preacher.	Chairman.	No. of Guests.
5	1810	June 13	Rev. L. Carpenter, LL.D., Exeter	J. Young, Esq.	200
6	1811	June 11	Rev. J. Grundy, Manchester	J. Christie, Esq.	240
7	1812	May 20	Rev. W. Severn, Hull	J. T. Rutt, Esq.	270
8	1813	June 9	Rev. E. Butcher, Sidmouth	W. Frend, Esq.	300
9	1814	June 1	Rev. J. Kentish, Birmingham	E. Johnston, Esq.	300
10	1815	May 17	Rev. T. Madge, Norwich	J. Young, Esq.	280
11	1816	June 5	Rev. W. Broadbent, Warrington	W. Frend, Esq.	260
12	1817	May 28	Rev. W. J. Fox, London	J. T. Rutt, Esq.	308
13	1818	May 13	Rev. N. Philipps, D.D., Sheffield	J. Christie, Esq.	250
14	1819	June 2	Rev. J. Yates, Birmingham	W. Frend, Esq.	300
15	1820	May 25	Rev. R. Scott, Portsmouth	Rev. R. Aspland	300
16	1821	June 13	Rev. W. Hincks, Exeter	W. Smith, Esq., M.P.	330
17	1822	May 19	Rev. J. Morell, LL.D., Brighton	W. Hammond, Esq.	—
18	1823	May 21	Rev. H. Acton, Walthamstow	J. T. Rutt, Esq.	280
19	1824	June 9	Rev. J. G. Robberds, Manchester	E. Taylor, Esq.	250
20	1825	May 25	Rev. C. Berry, Leicester*	W. Smith, Esq., M.P.	300

In speaking of the results of the Unitarian Fund, the chief place must be assigned to the laborious and successful missions conducted by Richard Wright. Before the Society was organized, this excellent man, prompted by his earnest zeal to promote Christian truth, entered upon, though on a very small scale, the work of an Unitarian missionary. In early life he had embraced strict Calvinism. Following out his system, he felt for a short time all the painful influences of a religion of gloom and fear. He did not cease to be an inquirer, and soon saw reasons to modify his creed. Passing through the important stages of Arminianism and Sabellianism, he became, after years of thought and study of the Scriptures, a believer in the simple humanity of Christ and the paternal mercy of the Father. As soon as he was fully convinced that Unitarianism was the doctrine of the Gospel, he felt an ardent desire to communicate his views to others. He resented the assertion that Unitarianism neither was nor could be the religion of the common people, and resolved to make the experiment of preaching it to them on as large a scale as he possibly could, in a plain and popular style.† With these views he became, without patronage or help,

---

* All these sermons were printed and published, except those of Mr. Aspland, Mr. Rees, Mr. Grundy and Mr. Severn. When, at the annual meeting of 1807, a resolution was unanimously passed that Mr. Aspland should be requested to print his sermon, he declined on two grounds—1, the annual publication of the Report made the printing of Sermons unnecessary; 2, it was necessary to prevent the publishing of the sermons from growing into precedent, and no opportunity would be so favourable for doing this as the present.

† See "A Review of the Missionary Life and Labours of Richard Wright," Chap. i.

an Unitarian missionary, visiting parts of Norfolk, Cambridgeshire, Lincolnshire, Sussex and Yorkshire. For these services he was, immediately after its establishment, elected an honorary member of the Unitarian Fund Society. His subsequent engagement as its missionary is thus described by himself in his (MS.) autobiography:

"On the formation of the Unitarian Fund Society, I was invited to engage as one of its missionaries, which I did, and have acted in connection with it from its commencement. This opened to me new and extensive scenes of usefulness, and brought me into connection with the general body of Unitarians throughout Great Britain. For several years I acted only as an occasional missionary, devoting at first about one-third, and afterwards nearly half my time to the objects of the Fund, and at the same time continued in my office as pastor of the church at Wisbeach; at length, finding it inconvenient to act both as a missionary and the pastor of a particular congregation, and being applied to by the Committee to act as a perpetual missionary, I resigned my office and income in Wisbeach, and have since that time been employed in missionary labours eight or nine months in the year, and three or four of the winter months I devote to study and writing, performing during that time, now and then a short journey, and preaching occasionally in the town where I reside."

Mr. Wright was admirably qualified for his work as an Unitarian missionary. He had a very clear mind and a strong understanding. Without any pretensions to grace or ornament, his style was simple and his elocution earnest. His knowledge of the Scriptures, and of the doctrines of the different religious sects, was extensive and accurate. To this he added knowledge of human nature, the result of his own close observation of men of all ranks of society. Few men surpassed him in the power of wielding a close but unartificial logic. He devoted a large portion of his leisure to writing down his thoughts—a habit which no doubt assisted him in correctness of reasoning and the power of compressing his style. Though small in stature, he possessed great muscular strength, and could without difficulty walk thirty or forty miles a day. He would frequently preach in the evening, after walking twenty or even thirty miles. He was habitually self-denying and economical, and he was rewarded for his temperance by equal and cheerful spirits. His only luxury was tobacco. The use of this he often turned to good account, seating himself quietly in the parlour of a way-side inn, or, if permission was given him, by the kitchen fire of the farmer, or in the one room of the cottager; and, listening to the conversation of those around him, he embraced any opportunity that arose of turning the conversation into a religious channel. His various information and obliging manners, especially his habit of being pleased with whatever was offered him in a kindly spirit, however humble it might be, made him a welcome guest wherever he went. He was systematic in all his arrangements, and punctual in the fulfilment of an engagement. Above all, he was deeply interested in his work as a missionary. He fulfilled it faithfully, never allowing the gratification of curiosity or offered pleasure to turn him aside from his prescribed path. Though his judgment was calm and well-balanced, his temperament was sufficiently sanguine to make him always hopeful as to the result of his labours. This was the right spirit; for though it might occasionally beguile him and others into anticipations which the result did not confirm, there is no doubt that it often enabled him to achieve success which a man of phlegmatic temperament would never have aimed at. His greatest obstacle was the ignorance of the masses of the people.* Notwithstanding this prevailed to a great extent, his success was sufficient to reward himself and his supporters.

Between Mr. Wright and Mr. Aspland there was the freest and happiest intercourse for nearly thirty years. There were many congenial qualities in their characters. The similarity of their religious experience, and the strength with which each held their new faith, were strong ties. He recognized at once the fine qualities and serviceableness of Mr. Wright. In the very first Report of the Unitarian Fund, we find him expressing "gratitude to a good Providence for having raised up so fit an instrument of the designs of the Society." To Mr. Aspland's ear, Mr. Wright's north-eastern provincialisms were not unmusical, although his own speech was remarkably correct; nor could he be displeased with his friend's assiduous use of the pipe, although it even surpassed his own.

One of the early and most gratifying proofs of Mr. Wright's skill as a religious teacher, was seen in his conversion of a Baptist minister at

---

* This obstacle is happily in the course of being removed. Our own day has accordingly witnessed amongst the intelligent masses in the Midland and Northern counties a gratifying aptitude for receiving instruction in liberal theology. How invaluable would the labours of such a man as Richard Wright now prove! But not of every day's growth is his ardour of feeling, combined with sobriety of judgment; his controversial skill, combined with piety; his freedom of speech and thought, combined with moderation and wisdom.

Hull to Unitarianism. Of this gentleman some account is due in this Memoir, as he became one of Mr. Aspland's intimate friends, and was on several occasions his chosen companion in his summer tours.

James Lyons was born, 1767, at Seaford, in the N. of Ireland, his father being superintendent of a timber-yard at that place. He received only a plain education, but even in early youth shewed signs of precocious talent and quick sensibility. The zeal of the Wesleyan Methodists, and their exciting strain of preaching, caught his boyish fancy, and, much to the annoyance of his father, who was a Presbyterian, he joined the new sect, and became first a local, and then a circuit, preacher amongst them. His first pulpit efforts were made when he was only sixteen years of age. At nineteen, he was enrolled as one of their regular ministers. It was probably on account of his abilities and success that, at twenty-one, he was called to England, receiving first an appointment in Wales, and next in Devonshire. His opportunities of acquiring theological knowledge had hitherto been few, but he was earnest in the pursuit of truth. Falling in with some persons of the Baptist persuasion, he found himself unable to resist the arguments which they adduced from Scripture in favour of their peculiar tenet. He did not hesitate to quit the Methodist communion, and was publicly baptized. He was immediately engaged as assistant minister to a Baptist congregation at Devonport (then Plymouth Dock), under the pastoral care of Mr. Birt. He was called to London to supply the Baptist church meeting at East Lane, Walworth, in the interval between the pastorship of Mr. Joseph Swain, who died April 14, 1796, and Dr. Joseph Jenkins, who succeeded him in April, 1798. Before this time, however, Mr. Lyons had removed to Hull, as co-pastor with the Rev. John Beatson, who had then been settled nearly twenty-seven years as pastor of the Baptist church in George Street in that town. Mr. Beatson was a correspondent of Robert Robinson, which is a presumption that he was without bigotry. He was regarded by his contemporaries as "a close thinker," and was the author of some theological works. In 1798, Mr. Lyons married the daughter of his co-pastor, and the union was the source of much happiness, her " character being distinguished by simplicity, truth, affectionateness and undissembled piety."* On the death of his father-in-law, Mr. Lyons became sole pastor of the church. He had been from the commencement of his

---

* See Monthly Repository, V. 90.

ministry at Hull not altogether free from theological difficulties, especially relating to the Trinity, yet was on the whole an "orthodox" believer. The unscripturalness and apparent contradiction involved in the usual phraseology of *three persons in one God*, was not without difficulty to his mind. He consulted Mr. Beatson on this point prior to his ordination, who informed him that he disapproved of the term *person* in relation to the Trinity. By his advice Mr. Lyons adopted in his confession of faith the statement, that there were three *distinctions* in the Divine essence, called *Father, Son and Holy Spirit*. The doubts which occasionally arose in his mind he stifled by the reflection, that the Trinity was a profound mystery, to be believed, but not to be understood. He read chiefly on the orthodox side of the question, yet was not able to overcome his doubts on the equality of Christ with the Father. About the year 1805, the publications of Mr. Wright, through the agency of Mr. Severn, the Unitarian minister, began to be widely circulated in Hull. Finding that some of the younger members of his congregation were shaken by Mr. Wright's arguments, Mr. Lyons procured some of his books, especially his "Essay on the Unity and Supremacy of the One God and Father," and his "Anti-satisfactionist." The perusal of these works satisfied him of the necessity of calmly reviewing his whole religious system, and ascertaining by a thorough scrutiny the Scripture evidence for it. He applied himself to this important task, and, while not declining the help of controversial writers on both sides, he chiefly studied the New Testament. He read it through several times, dispassionately estimating, as he proceeded, the arguments for and against the "orthodox" faith. Towards the close of the year 1807, he reached the clear conviction that the doctrines which he had hitherto professed were not supported by Scripture, but were corruptions of Christianity.

With characteristic honesty, he hastened to communicate to the deacons of his church his change of opinions, stating that he was prepared to submit the reasons that had led to the change to his flock, if they desired it; but if not, he offered to continue with them for two months, or till they could procure another minister, on the understanding that he should preach on practical topics, and avoid in the pulpit matters of controversy. On Saturday, December 5, he was informed that it was the wish of the deacons and other principal members of the congregation, that he should at once resign the pastoral office and take his farewell of them on the afternoon of the following day. He addressed them, from John v. 39, on *The Right and Duty of a Faithful and Fearless Examination of the Scriptures.* He avowed his new conviction that he had hitherto preached to them doctrines opposed to truth and injurious to the best interests of human nature, and expressed a hope that his public renunciation of his errors would induce them carefully and dispassionately to study the Scriptures, and ascertain the certainty of the doctrines which they professed. His sermon was subsequently published, and had a large circulation.

Thus terminated, with feelings of regret on both sides, a pastoral relation which had subsisted for nearly eleven years. Mr. Aspland and Mr. Wright hastened to offer a brotherly welcome to one who had, in thus separating himself from all his religious associates, given such unquestionable proof of his love of truth and his moral courage. His services as a missionary were immediately secured by the Unitarian Fund Society, and he proceeded under their patronage to Scotland. In Glasgow he had the happiness of assisting some religious inquirers, less advanced than himself, and helped to form the rudiments of an Unitarian congregation in that city. He afterwards undertook other missionary engagements under the direction of the Unitarian Fund. Possessing considerable pulpit talent, his services were sought by several congregations. He accepted, in 1808, an invitation from the Presbyterian congregation assembling in Crook's-Street chapel, Chester, to succeed Mr. Thomas, who had been compelled by bad health to withdraw from the ministry.

In 1808, he preached the annual sermon before the Unitarian Fund, and gratified his respect and regard for the excellent man who had been one of the chief instruments of leading him to a liberal theology, by drawing a portrait of the Unitarian missionary:

"Missionary work requires a peculiar constitution, the habit of extemporaneous speaking, a considerable acquaintance with doctrinal subjects, and a readiness in producing Scripture arguments in a striking form. To instruct the lower orders of the people, a minister must be able to enter into all their views and feelings, to simplify every subject which he brings before them, and to bear with much patience their misconceptions of what he conceives to be most plain and obvious. He must be prepared for many disappointments, and be possessed of that deep and habitual piety, ardent zeal and firmness of mind, which will cause him, in the midst of opposition and in the most discouraging circumstances, to be steadfast and unmoveable. He must love the truth more than ease or reputation; he must be a man of cool and comprehensive prudence, of mild and conciliatory manners, and of enlarged candour and liberality."*

The year after he settled in Chester he lost his wife, who died Nov. 11, 1809. She retained the moderate Calvinism in which she had been educated; but her personal goodness appears to have extracted from her theological system the sting of intolerance. Forgetting her creed, she indulged the belief that good men of the most opposite sentiments would finally meet in perfect harmony in the presence of their Heavenly Father in a better world. This made her easy in her husband's change of sentiment. Three children survived their mother, who did not, as they grew up, adopt their father's religious views, and this discordance of sentiment was the occasion of much mutual distress. Mr. Lyons, in 1813, dissolved his pastoral relation with the Chester congregation, and although he occasionally supplied temporary pulpit vacancies (at Parliament Court, Newport, Reading, &c.), he did not after this enter into any permanent ministerial engagement.

The social circle was that in which Mr. Lyons especially shone. Warmth of feeling, a rich and copious style of narrative, irresistible pathos, humour, both refined and broad,† were the instruments by which he delighted his friends, winning from them at will either smiles or tears. He had moral courage to rebuke with stern contempt whatever was mean and base, while his heart seemed to swell with generous sympathy whenever any thing noble was placed before him. He formed a second matrimonial alliance with a widow lady of Chester, who survives him. He continued to reside in that city and its immediate neighbourhood during the remainder of his life. He was induced, probably by his sympathy with the liberal politics then professed by the head of the house of Eaton, to take great interest in the election struggles of Chester. Differing as he did from many of his closest friends, and forgetting sometimes the dictates of self-denial, he yet retained to the last his Chester friendships. He died at the Iron-bridge cottage, near Chester, Sept. 13, 1824, aged 57 years.

Mr. Aspland (whom, in conjunction with Mr. Joseph Swanwick, he

---

* "The Dissemination of Unitarian Principles recommended and enforced, in a Sermon," &c., p. 27.

† His *Irish* stories were characterized by great power and beautiful delineation of the best parts of the national character. He had at his command all the variations of dialect and brogue that mark the different provinces of Ireland.

had appointed an executor of his will) thus described his character in a brief obituary memoir:

"His early and best habit of preaching was extempore; he was fluent and animated, and his manner was free and manly. His elocution was agreeable. He had a mind of considerable powers, and with early cultivation would have been distinguished in any profession. He was a cheerful companion, and his conversation abounded in humour and pleasantry. His affections were warm; his disposition generous. From feeling and principle he was a lover of his species, and a declared enemy of all intolerance and oppression. With the excellencies of this cast of character, even friendship cannot claim for him an entire exemption from its defects; but this may be said with perfect truth, that they who knew him best were his most steady friends, and now cherish his memory with the most tender regard."*

The other missionaries employed by the Unitarian Fund were Mr. Phillips, of St. Clear's; Mr. Bennett, of Ditchling; the students of the new Hackney Academy, of whom the next Chapter will furnish some particulars; and Mr. Henry Winder.† Of the last-named gentleman the following interesting account appears in Mr. Wright's autobiography (MS.):

"This was an extraordinary person. He was brought up without ever being taught to read. For many years he was a common soldier; and while in the army taught himself to read, became a preacher, and acquired a considerable degree of religious knowledge by attention to the Scriptures. He became an Unitarian, to use his own words, 'without reading any other Unitarian book but the Bible.' Soon after he left the army, being a Baptist, he was invited to become the minister of the General Baptist church in Norwich. He accepted this invitation; but in the outset would make the engagement for but one year. His opinions soon alarmed his congregation; but he conducted himself with so much prudence, and defended the doctrines he believed so ably, that in the course of a few months he brought his hearers to assent to the truth of them; and in less than twelve months from the time he began his ministry in Norwich, he was unanimously chosen as their pastor and ordained among them. In a short time he acted occasionally as an Unitarian missionary. In the summer of the year 1815, he removed to Wisbeach, where he continued to the time of his death, which took place about two years after. Mr. Winder certainly possessed great natural talents. His understanding was acute and penetrating, his judgment discriminating and comprehensive,

---

* Monthly Repository, Vol. XIX. p. 629.

† Mr. Winder died July 31, 1817, aged 45 years. Further particulars respecting him will be found in the Monthly Repository, Vol. XII., in part from the able pen of Mr. Edward Taylor.

and he was capable of expressing his conceptions with much conciseness, in a clear manner, and of giving point to what he said. I have heard him deliver truly excellent and masterly discourses, and have wondered, considering how little he had read and the great disadvantages under which he laboured, how he had acquired such clear and enlarged views of things. He followed the suggestions of a superior natural understanding, thought with entire freedom, spoke as freely as he thought, and was cramped by no rules. Considering that he knew nothing of grammar, his language was much more correct than might have been expected. In company he shewed a good deal of modesty and diffidence. At public meetings he would deliver speeches which surprised and gratified the most respectable companies. Yet in the outset of a speech he would sometimes tremble, but even then he did not discover confusion of thought. He was a grand production of nature, superior to the artificial productions of the schools."

CHAPTER XVIII.

In the spring of 1812, Mr. Aspland was invited by the managers of the *Society for the Relief of the Necessitous Widows and Fatherless Children of Protestant Dissenting Ministers*, to preach the annual sermon in behalf of their charity. He felt happy in complying with their request, both on account of his cordial approbation of the Society, and because as a Protestant Dissenting Minister he felt a natural pride in having his name added to the long and honourable list of ministers who had in successive years advocated its interests. The Widows' Fund was established in 1733, chiefly by the zealous exertions of Dr. Samuel Chandler, who used his not small influence with the opulent Dissenters of his day in obtaining a capital fund and annual subscriptions sufficient to establish the Society on a safe and permanent footing. It was, like most of the institutions originated by the English Presbyterians, catholic in its spirit, extending its benefits to the families of such ministers of the Presbyterian, Independent and Baptist denominations as at their death stood accepted and approved as such by the body of ministers of the denomination to which they respectively belonged, and who died so poor as not to leave their widows and children a sufficient subsistence. Its management was entrusted to twenty-seven laymen. The annual sermon is preached alternately in a chapel belonging to each of the Three Denominations. At the institution of the charity, the annual allowance to the widows of English ministers was five pounds, but the managers were enabled in the years 1765, 1767, 1776, 1785, 1800, 1805, 1809 and 1811, to make a series of additions to the allowance till it amounted to fifteen pounds.* To the widows of Welsh

---

* It is much to be regretted that, since 1817, the allowance has been diminished, in consequence of the declining state of the funds. For many years the

ministers the allowances were on a smaller scale. The Widows' Fund is one of the very few remaining institutions amongst the Protestant Dissenters in which the Three Denominations continue to act with unbroken harmony. The list of the preachers is a curious historical document, and is here inserted, beginning with Dr. Chandler, the founder of the Society.

			Minister of the
1735.	Dr. Samuel Chandler†	Presbyterian	Old Jewry.
1736.	Dr. Samuel Wright†	Presbyterian	Carter Lane.
1737.	Dr. Henry Miles	Presbyterian	Tooting.
1738.	Rev. Samuel Wilson†	Baptist	Prescott Street.
1739.	Rev. John Barker	Presbyterian	Hackney.
1740.	Rev. John Denham	Presbyterian	Gravel Lane.
1741.	Dr. John Guyse†	Independent	New Broad Street.
1742.	Rev. Jos. Burroughs†	General Baptist	Paul's Alley.
1743.	Rev. Edward Godwin	Presbyterian	Little St. Helen's.
1744.	Rev. Henry Read	Presbyterian	St. Thomas's.
1745.	Rev. Samuel Price	Independent	Bury Street.
1746.	Dr. Jos. Stennett	Baptist	Little Wild Street.
1747.	Rev. Michael Pope	Presbyterian	Leather Lane.
1748.	Dr. Samuel Chandler†	Presbyterian	Old Jewry.
1749.	Rev. John Richardson	Independent	Lime Street.
1750.	Rev. Robert Cornthwaite	General Baptist	Mill Yard.
1752.	Rev. Thomas Newman	Presbyterian	Carter Lane.
1753.	Rev. Francis Spilsbury	Presbyterian	Salters' Hall.
1754.	Rev. John Halford	Independent	Horsleydown.
1755.	Rev. Charles Bulkley	General Baptist	Paul's Alley.
1756.	Rev. W. Bush.		
1757.	Dr. George Benson	Presbyterian	Poor Jewry Lane.
1758.	Dr. David Jennings	Independent	Gravel Lane.
1759.	Rev. John Brine	Baptist	Curriers' Hall.
1760.	Dr. John Hodge	Presbyterian	Crosby Square.
1761.	Dr. William Prior	Presbyterian	Goodman's Fields.
1762.	Rev. Thomas Towle	Independent	Aldermanbury.
1763.	Rev. Samuel Fry	General Baptist	Fair Street.
1764.	Dr. William Langford	Independent	Weigh-house.
1765.	Rev. Edward Pickard	Presbyterian	Carter Lane.
1766.	Dr. Thomas Gibbons	Independent	Haberdashers' Hall.

annuities were reduced to ten pounds; since 1841, they have advanced to twelve pounds. The present Treasurer of the Society is Stephen Olding, Esq., Clement's Lane, Lombard Street.

† This mark is put to indicate that the sermon was printed.

1767. Dr. Josiah Thompson ....Baptist ....Unicorn Yard.
1768. Dr. James Fordyce ......Presbyterian......Monkwell Street.
1769. Dr. Andrew Kippis ......Presbyterian.....Princes Street.
1770. Rev. Samuel Brewer ....Independent......Stepney.
1771. Dr. Samuel Stennett ....Baptist ....Wild Street.
1772. Dr. Richard Price........Presbyterian......Hackney.
1773. Dr. Thomas Amory ......Presbyterian ....Old Jewry.
1774. Rev. Joseph Barber .....Independent......Founders' Hall.
1775. Rev. Benjamin Wallin....Baptist ....Maze Pond.
1776. Rev. Thomas Tayler ......Presbyterian .....Carter Lane.
1777. Dr. Abraham Rees ......Presbyterian.....Old Jewry.
1778. Rev. William Ford ......Independent .....Miles' Lane.
1779. Rev. A. Booth ....Baptist ....Prescott Street.
1780. Rev. Thomas Urwick ....Presbyterian......Clapham.
1781. Rev. Hugh Worthington..Presbyterian......Salters' Hall.
1782. Rev. Thomas Morgan ....Presbyterian.....Goodman's Fields.
1783. Dr. Daniel Fisher.. ......Independent......Plasterers' Hall.
1784. Rev. John Martin........Baptist ....Grafton Street.
1785. Rev. Joseph Fawcett ....Presbyterian......Walthamstow.
1786. Rev. Robert Jacomb ....Presbyterian......Salters' Hall.
1787. Rev. — Palmer.
1788. Rev. James Dore .. ..Baptist ....Maze Pond.
1789. Rev. Thomas Jervis ......Presbyterian.. ...Princes Street.
1790. Dr. Joseph Towers ... .Presbyterian......Newington Green.
1791. Dr. Benjamin Davies ....Independent......Fetter Lane.
1792. Dr. John Rippon ....Baptist ....Tooley Street.
1793. Rev. George Lewis ......Presbyterian .....Carter Lane.
1794. Dr. Robert Winter ......Independent.....Carey Street.
1795. Rev. John Fell ....Independent.
1796. Rev. John Evans ....General Baptist .Worship Street.
1797. Rev. Thomas Belsham ...Presbyterian......Hackney.
1798. Rev. Benjamin Carpenter .Presbyterian.....Stourbridge.
1799. Rev. John Clayton ......Independent......Weigh-house.
1800. Rev. Andrew Fuller......Baptist ....Kettering.
1801. Dr. John Humphreys ....Independent.
1802. Dr. James Lindsay ......Presbyterian.....Monkwell Street.
1803. Rev. James Knight ......Independent ....Colliers' Rents.
1804. Rev. Robert Hall ....Baptist ....Cambridge.
1805. Dr. Thomas Barnes .. ..Presbyterian .....Manchester.
1806. Rev. T. N. Toller .. ..Independent......Kittering.
1807. Rev. William Jay........Independent .....Bath.
1808. Rev. James Hinton ......Baptist ....Oxford.
1809. Rev. James Manning ....Presbyterian .....Exeter.

1810. Rev. J. Winter ....Independent......Newbury.
1811. Dr. John Ryland .. ..Baptist ....Bristol.
1812. Rev. Robert Aspland †....Presbyterian......Hackney.

Mr. Aspland chose for his subject, "The Beneficial Influence of Christianity on the Character and Condition of the Female Sex." The sermon contains a comprehensive survey of the condition of women under the several forms of Heathenism, under the laws of Moses, and under the influence of Christianity, and deduces from the survey an argument for the immeasurable superiority and consequent truth of the religion of Christ. It is one of the most elaborate and successful of his occasional sermons. The following passage is one of many that might be advantageously quoted from it:

"It may seem wonderful that in the dark ages, when every vestige of the truth as it is in Jesus, and almost of civilization, was swept away, the esteem in which Christianity holds females should have been retained. But agreeably to the mysterious and adorable plan of Providence, which brings good out of evil, this was one of the accidental benefits of some of those abuses and corruptions of religion which were otherwise so pregnant with mischief. The extravagant value set upon *celibacy* led to a reverence of female chastity; and the idolatrous respect paid to the *Virgin Mary* reflected back honour upon her sex. Even the *crusades*, those wild sallies of religious enthusiasm and martial ardour, contributed to soften the temper and to refine the manners of the European nations. The heroes who had acquired fame under the banner of the Cross, emulous at home of their renown abroad, entered into bonds of *chivalry*, an eccentric but lofty institution, in which the genius of Christianity was unsuitably enshrined in 'the pomp and circumstance of war;' every member of the order solemnly engaging, on taking up the profession of arms, to be *the husband of widows, the father of orphans, the protector of the poor, and the prop of those who had no other support.*

"In these instances, the errors of the human heart were overruled by Christianity for the good of society. The salutary precepts of our religion mingled with human weakness and folly, and corrected their baneful tendency, and even in some measure changed their nature. In its decline and fall, Truth preserved its majesty. When its authority was most feeble, it still gave law to superstition, idolatry and war, curbed their licentiousness and fierceness, and controlled them, in violation of their natural tendency, to render service to chastity, courtesy and mercy."—Pp. 23—25.

In connection with this sermon, the following letter is introduced,— the only one found in Mr. Aspland's papers,—from the highly popular and celebrated minister of Salters' Hall.

Rev. Hugh Worthington to Rev. Robert Aspland.

"Northampton Square, April 22, 1812.

"My dear Sir,—I have been repeatedly deceived in my hopes, or should have sent a much earlier reply to your very kind letter. Through the whole of last week I strongly hoped to be able to get over to Hackney and personally wait upon you. Then (having been disappointed by a cold severity of wind, which my weak lungs cannot bear) I thought it probable we might have ten minutes' conversation at the Library: there business was so protracted, that my intention was frustrated. Accept these honest apologies.—Now to business.

"I *feel* the honour done me by you and your friends in the request so handsomely conveyed by your pen, and if it were only to shew that difference of opinions does not weigh with me in cases of charity, I should wish to come on the morning of the 24th or 31st of May, as you and the managers may settle— but there are two difficulties which hang as a dead weight on the wheels of action: one is, my poor state of health, so liable to interruption; the other, of which, perhaps, you are not aware, that I advocated the cause of your schools several years ago, and no man should receive the honour or be called to the service *twice*. Consider these things; look out for vigour and novelty, and, according to the rule of Virgil, 'let the aged horse be unharnessed.'

"But, my dear friend (for such I must call you), I have a petition to present to you, which I *entreat* you to consider and grant. Your sermon for the Widows' Fund opened an argument so strong, so little and seldom examined, so clearly stated, so cautiously and yet so eloquently enforced, in favour of the Christian religion, that you *must publish it*. I have spoken of it from the pulpit—I must have it in the parlour—I must send it to my relations. Put me down for a dozen copies, or more if necessary. The entire composition is ready without further revisal, 'paratus ad unguem.'

"Earnestly hoping you will attend to a request in which multitudes secretly concur, I remain, Reverend and dear Sir, your much obliged and affectionate brother, HUGH WORTHINGTON."

Amongst the small congregations who received aid from the Unitarian Fund was a General Baptist society at Wedmore, in Somersetshire. On the death of its pastor, Mr. Moses Naile, in 1806, they found themselves unable to raise a salary of £20 per annum, and had no one in the society able to conduct their public worship. By the mediation of Rev. Daniel Jones, of Trowbridge, a worthy but unlearned man, named Webley, belonging to the Baptist church at the latter place, undertook to preach at Wedmore. The Committee of the Unitarian Fund from time to time voted small sums, both to increase his very scanty salary, and to enable him to devote himself for a few months to study, under the direction of his friend and former pastor, Rev. D. Jones.* Mr. Webley continued to discharge his duties, much to the satisfaction of the Committee, until the latter end of 1811, when Mr. Aspland received from him a communication to the effect that he could no longer receive assistance from or continue his relations to the Unitarian Fund, in consequence of an entire change of opinion respecting the person of Christ. He stated that a careful perusal of the Scriptures, undertaken with a view to settle some doubts which had arisen in his mind, had convinced him that the miraculous conception of Christ, his pre-existence and atonement for sin, were Scripture doctrines, and had also satisfied him that Christ, as to his divine nature, was co-equal and co-eternal with the Father. He had not gone on to Calvinism, but still firmly believed in the universality of Divine love. His letter expressed warm gratitude to the members of the Committee in general, and to Mr. Aspland in particular, for past kindness, and regret at the dissolution of the acquaintance; and concluded with the prayer that they might all meet in heaven, "where they should all see as with one eye." In conformity with Mr. Webley's request, Mr. Aspland immediately wrote an answer to his letter, which, for the strength of its arguments and the gentleness of its spirit, appears entitled to a place in this Memoir:

To the Rev. S. Webley.

"Hackney, Nov. 20, 1811.

"Dear Sir,—Your letter to the Committee of the Unitarian Fund, dated the 15th instant, I have read with very mixed emotions of mind; though, I assure

---

* In the Report of the Unitarian Fund read to the general meeting, reference was made to Mr. Webley's case. The passage is interesting as shewing some of the influences under which the Unitarian Academy afterwards arose. "It will be recollected that Mr. Webley, now filling an useful station at Wedmore, Somersetshire, received his preparatory instruction for the ministry under the sanction of the Society. The success of the plan in this instance has made it appear desirable to the Committee that it should be again acted upon, on favourable occasions. This is likewise known to be the opinion and wish of many persons of eminence and weight in the Unitarian body. But at the same time the Committee have considered, in viewing particular cases which have been brought before them, that the education of young men for the ministry is not one of the first and most direct objects of the Society, and that in no instance would it be allowable to apply their funds to the purpose of a complete learned education. The utmost, they conceive, that your Committee would be warranted in doing, would be the placing of promising persons, already acceptable preachers, under some popular and zealous minister, for the sake of being inducted into English literature and put in the way of studying to profit, and this only when it can be accomplished with little expense."

you, with no angry or unfriendly sentiments towards yourself. Before I submit the letter to the Committee, I think it right to address a few thoughts to you on the subject of your change of opinions, which, I am persuaded, you will take in good part and consider with serious attention.

"So far, my dear Sir, from blaming you for your manly avowal of your dissent from the principles of the Unitarian Fund, I applaud your integrity and courage. While our Society is intended for the promotion of what we consider the most glorious, but long-lost, truths of the gospel, we are not so inconsistent as to attempt to remove the fetters of reputed orthodoxy from men's minds, solely to put on our own chains in their stead. Our object is in part accomplished, if we set the human mind upon inquiry, whether inquiry lead *to us* or *from us*; and you, I conceive, will ever thank us, even if you retain your new and, as I must think, unscriptural and erroneous notions, for having incited you to think for yourself, and supplied you with the means of forming a rational judgment upon the gospel.

"We shall regret your departure from us, if, indeed, your conscience shall ultimately compel you to depart, because we entirely approve of your character and conduct, and, from your evident and increasing improvement, entertained great hopes of your usefulness in the cause of pure religion; but we shall assuredly never disesteem you for using the liberty, which we are so forward to claim for ourselves, of free inquiry and independent judgment, nor regret the aid which we may have furnished towards your acceptableness and respectability as a religious teacher.

"With regard to ourselves, therefore, you may set your mind at rest; but there are higher obligations which you are under to *Truth*, and you are, I am persuaded, solicitous that you may not be negligent of these. As a Christian minister, the New Testament is your sole authority for your faith; but how you reconcile to that sacred volume the opinions to which you declare your conversion, I am utterly at a loss to conceive. I have no expectation that a short letter (such only as I have time to write) will produce any great effect upon your mind; yet, let me ask of you, where in the Christian Scriptures you find the *divine nature* of Christ, and, above all, his *co-equality* and *co-eternity with the Father?* You surely know that these terms are not scriptural, that they are merely of human invention, relics of popery; and not only are they not in Scripture, but (which challenges your solemn inquiry) nowhere in Scripture can terms be found which are equivalent to them, or which can signify the ideas which they convey. Now when language cannot be found in the Bible to express opinions, the presumption surely is, that the opinions intended by such language are human and not divine.

"For my part, I cannot open the Scriptures without perceiving the strongest assertions of the humanity of Christ and the unity of God; and how these primary doctrines of revelation can consist with those which you have adopted, it behoves you seriously to consider: the consistency between them, I will venture boldly to say, cannot be made out but with the help of idle fictions of men, which will serve the hypothesis of Transubstantiation as well as that of the Trinity.

"With your new sentiments, you have, I take for granted, adopted new objects of worship; and can you feel in the worship of 'Gods many and Lords many' perfect satisfaction in your own mind that you obey the requirement of the 'man Christ Jesus,' which demands the absolute and unequivocal worship of *the Father, the God and Father of our Lord Jesus Christ?* The questions of the miraculous conception and pre-existence of Christ have, I conjecture, first and principally puzzled you; but you ought to know, that however these are answered no way affects the principles of the Unitarian Fund, which are simply the Unity, sole Worship and unpurchased Love of the Universal Father.

"You say you are still a believer in the universality of Divine love, and yet you avow the strange and unscriptural notion of Christ's being literally 'a propitiatory sacrifice for sin,' by which you mean, I conclude, that God would not forgive sins without a satisfaction (where, then, is *forgiveness?*), and that he would not have been propitious or kind but for Jesus Christ (what, then, becomes of his eternal love?). The scheme of the atonement is utterly at war with the gospel declarations of *grace* being *free*—of mercy being a *gift*, not a *debt*—the spontaneous bounty of heaven, not the result of a contract or bargain. Where, my good Sir, does Jesus Christ represent his death as necessary to enable the Father to pardon his own children? In what other light does he ever place it than that of a testimony to truth and righteousness, an instance of obedience to the will of God and a preparation for a resurrection, the grand example of the merciful design of heaven to raise all mortal men to a state of life and immortality?

"I grant the word *sacrifice* is used of the death of Christ, as it is of the almsgivings of the churches, but, in the one case as well as the other, is, I am persuaded, after a careful examination, merely figurative. A *vicarious* or *substitutive* sacrifice the death of Christ could not be without being wholly dissimilar to the sacrifices of the law, not one of which was of that description; besides that it is in itself absurd and impossible, as well as repugnant to the express declarations of Scripture, that one being should *morally* represent another, and that the innocent should be punished for the guilty.

"You believe, I presume, that Christ was God, and that the real Christ died to satisfy divine justice; but let me seriously ask, *Did God die?* If he did, welcome Paganism! and let Wedmore, which is memorable in history as the scene of the baptism under the great Alfred of an army of Danes, be again signalized by a return to the heathen mythology. If he did not, then either Christ did not die or Christ who died is not God. You may distinguish between the *natures* of Christ, but where do you learn from Scripture that he has more natures than one? You will probably, agreeably to the fashion of the times, allot him *two* natures; but you might just as well, as far as Scripture is concerned, ascribe to him two hundred or two hundred thousand. This is an awkward device to get rid of the clear, decisive testimony of the New Testament concerning the *Son of Man*.

"Your new theory amounts to nothing at all, if God did not die; if it were a mere man that died, a man is then wholly competent to the work of salvation, and the divinity of Christ is useless. 'But the union of the divine nature with the human stamped an infinite value upon Christ's suffering.' *There was no union, if the divine nature suffered not when the human was torn in pieces.*

"Ah! my friend, there is surely in this system, which you seem inclined to adopt, a forgetfulness, if not a distrust, of the Father of all, of Christ as well as us. Why should not his appointment and approbation of Christ be accounted all-sufficient both for the honour of Jesus and for the efficacy of his mission? It is not enough, then, according to the apostolic doctrine, that 'God anointed Jesus of Nazareth with the Holy Ghost and with power, and was always with him as he went about doing good!'—You may not, indeed, go all lengths with the believers in the divinity of Christ; but you cannot, in my view, *consistently* stop short of the horrid nonsense of God Almighty dying, in order to make God Almighty good and kind.

"Believe me, good Sir, I do not state these things thus strongly in order to harass your mind, but merely to warn you of the tendency and consequences of your new faith, of which I would fain persuade myself you are not fully aware. If, indeed, you see all these consequences, and can look at them and the Scriptures at the same time with an undaunted face, I shall admire your courage, whatever I may think of your creed.

"You seem to intimate a belief that you have been led in your inquiries by the Holy Spirit. That you have not been guided by an evil spirit I am fully prepared to admit; but I must demur to your statement of divine influences when I see you adopting sentiments so offensive (as I cannot but deem them) to the clearly revealed will of God. Divine teachings, you know, are claimed by men of almost all sentiments, and claimed most eagerly by the greatest fanatics, by the followers of Joanna Southcott more than by Calvinists, and by them more than by you;—this assumption, therefore, goes no way in a controversy; the only proper question is, what is the doctrine of Jesus? *His word is spirit;* he teaches me that God is One; that he himself is not God, but man; and that God is a Father, and always acts a fatherly part towards all his children: and if an angel from heaven were, in spite of these divine teachings, to preach to me the Trinity, the deity of Christ, and the incapacity or unwillingness of the Almighty to pardon sin without full satisfaction, I should, as I valued my soul, hold his doctrine accursed.

"That the exercises of your mind have been very painful I am well persuaded; the operation of putting out an eye cannot take place without extreme anguish; and will you pardon me for saying that I consider you as having been employed of late in extinguishing the light of your mind. You, no doubt, think you have been, on the contrary, brought out of darkness. Be it so:—let the Scriptures, then, determine between us; but, as we differ about their judgment on the points in controversy, let us refer our cause to the Judge of all the earth, who will do right and make truth manifest; in the mean time, not judging one another, nor claiming any dominion over faith, but helping each other's joy.—You will not, I trust, consider my remarks as angrily made or harshly enforced; you request to hear from me, and I give you, as a Christian friend and brother, my free thoughts. If they are good, treasure them up; if bad, reject them; but, at any rate, consider them before you determine upon their value.

"When you have thought over my letter, give me your answer; in which I shall be obliged to you to state whether the congregation at Wedmore have changed with you, or whether your new opinions will affect the connection between you? If you have declared your Trinitarian principles to the church, it would, perhaps, be candid to let them hear this letter.

"As to the future, you need not be under anxiety; for, besides the protection of a good Providence, which you have, in common with all the children of men, your new creed will make you more popular than you could have been with your old one, and, if not at Wedmore, yet elsewhere, will procure you warm friends and zealous patrons.

"My recommendation would scarcely be of service to you with Trinitarians, but if in any thing I can serve you, I shall be happy to testify that, notwithstanding your desertion of the faith which I glory in, I am your well-wisher and Christian friend and brother,

 (Signed)   "ROBERT ASPLAND.

"N.B. I intended to write a short letter, but have been insensibly drawn on to this length by the interest which I take in your welfare. Perhaps you will frankly tell me by what steps and with what progress you have arrived at your Trinitarian conclusions."

Mr. Webley sent a rejoinder,* and assured Mr. Aspland that he took his letter in good part, and regarded it as a new proof of his friendship. The Committee, in reporting to their constituents Mr. Webley's change of faith, said of him, "Whatever be thought of his opinions, he cannot be too much esteemed for his integrity and openness and gratitude."

The increased demand for ministers fitted for missionary labours, and

---

* The correspondence is printed in the Monthly Repository, VII. 722.

disposed to undertake the charge of the less important congregations amongst the Unitarians, led Mr. Aspland and many of his friends about this time to take active measures for founding an Unitarian Academy for the training up of popular rather than learned ministers.

The subject was first discussed at a meeting of the Unitarian Fund Committee, held May 16, 1811, at which Messrs. Eaton, Richard Taylor, Rutt, Christie, Burford, Hall, Freeman and the Secretary, were present. At a subsequent meeting of the same persons, their deliberations were assisted by Mr. William Frend, who took a warm interest in the subject. On the 30th of May, a meeting of "friends of the Unitarian cause" took place, at which resolutions were passed declaring it to be highly expedient that an Academical Institution should be established to educate a succession of useful and acceptable preachers; that it should be denominated THE UNITARIAN ACADEMY; and that its objects should be to teach the students theology and the branches of study immediately connected with it, and to exercise them in and habituate them to the best methods of communicating religious instruction. The plan was speedily agreed upon, and adopted by a general meeting held June 6. It prescribed that the students should be under the care of a Principal Tutor who should board and lodge them; that the young men eligible as students should (except in special cases) be between the ages of eighteen and twenty-five; and that the period of study to each pupil should be limited to two years.

The founders of the Academy believed that it might be so conducted as to provide a succession of teachers qualified for communicating scriptural instruction to the common people; that, with the means and within the time allowed, the students might acquire a fair portion of general knowledge, and might learn to read the Scriptures in their original tongues. They proposed to make the instruction purely theological. In this respect and in the limited period of instruction, it differed entirely from the higher and more important institution at York, then and for so many subsequent years presided over with such eminent success by the Rev. Charles Wellbeloved.

The name UNITARIAN was given to the Academy, not for the purpose of pledging either its students or supporters to any particular system of faith, but because it expressed the leading opinion of those who interested themselves in its formation, and their expectation of its results. They used the term *Unitarian* in its broadest sense, including under it all Christians that agreed in the sole worship of one God, the Father, whatever might be their views on minor topics, or their practice in less important matters. They desired that the freest inquiry should be encouraged in the students, feeling assured that investigation properly conducted would end in the perception and acknowledgment of truth. The friends who united in founding the Academy were well aware that its success must in a very great measure depend on the abilities and energy of the Principal and Theological Tutor. From the first they looked to Mr. Aspland to undertake this laborious and responsible post. He might well have pleaded that his ministerial duties, the education of his large and rapidly-increasing family, his editorship of the Monthly Repository, and the conduct of the Unitarian Fund, involving him, as it in reality did, in a kind of general agency for the Unitarian body, were work enough for one man. But he was now in the prime of life, in his thirtieth year, his vigorous frame unbowed by sickness, and his mind eagerly intent upon promoting truth and religious knowledge, and without hesitation or fear he consented at once to enter upon the new and laborious path which duty opened before him. His friends, Mr. Christie and Mr. Richard Taylor, undertook respectively the offices of Treasurer and Secretary, and with them were associated Mr. Frend, Mr. Rutt and Mr. Dewhurst, as members of the Committee of Management. Of the last-named gentleman mention will presently be renewed in connection with a more important office in the Academy.

Immediate and active measures were taken for conciliating to the new institution the required pecuniary support. In many quarters objections were felt, and in some were expressed. The preliminary proceedings were objected to as hasty, and confined to too small a body of persons. It might have been expedient to have enlisted a larger number of persons in both town and country as founders of the institution; but practically it is well known that any plan, to be successful, must be in the first instance devised by a few thoughtful minds, and afterwards carried into execution by a few intelligent and resolute persons. To some, the term *Unitarian* was objectionable. They wished a place of theological study to be free from a sectarian brand, which they regarded as unfavourable to the impartial search after truth. To a small number, the broad definition of the term *Unitarian* was unacceptable; the latitude which included Arians, high and low, and which might include some Trinitarians, seemed to them inconsistent with a proper regard for Scripture truth. Some of the more zealous friends of the College at York feared that the new institution might be the means of diverting some portion of the support given, or likely to be given, to their favourite institution. Others objected to the limited period of instruction as utterly inadequate to the communication of a sufficient basis either of general or scriptural knowledge. This last objection was felt very strongly by Mr. Belsham. He had never, since the breaking up of the former College at Hackney, abandoned the idea of the re-establishment of a liberal academical institution in or near the Metropolis.* He watched with anxious interest the preliminary proceedings of the founders of the Unitarian Academy, prepared with considerable care the scheme of an institution which might combine the support of all that were favourable to a Metropolitan Academy; and when his hopes were disappointed by the adoption of a period of education limited to two years, he thus expressed his feelings:

Rev. Thomas Belsham to Rev. Robert Aspland.

"Friday Evening.

"My dear Sir,—I thank you for your obliging note. I am grieved at the resolutions of yesterday, which will, I fear, paralyze my exertions.

"My object is the same with that of the gentlemen who then met. I wish for ministers eloquent, able, popular, zealous and well-informed, willing to adapt themselves to the capacities of the inferior classes of society; and this I consider as amply provided for upon my plan. My wish was to combine all parties and all objects, which appears to me very feasible. Let the plan of education be complete, and provision made for four, five, or even six years' employment of the student; but let it be left to the discretion of the Divinity Tutor, in connection with the Committee, to reduce the time in particular cases, and to direct the particular course that every student should pursue. My plan comprehends the whole of theirs, but theirs does not and cannot comprehend mine; and mine has the advantage of including a description of persons who will not support the other.

"If the two-year plan is adopted, I cannot wish you to be the Tutor; the country is better than the town; and Mr. Wright would conduct such an institution to great advantage. But to my plan your co-operation would be essential. You would do what I wish to see done; you would direct the attention of the pupils to theology; you would make them practical, popular,

---

* Perhaps the finest passage ever written by Mr. Belsham was this pathetic lament over the fate of the Hackney College: "The spirit of the times was against it. It fell—and the birds of night, ignorance and envy, bigotry and rancour, screamed their ungenerous triumph over the ruins of this stately edifice; while virtue, truth and learning mourned in secret over the disappointment of their fond hopes and of their too highly elevated expectations."

active *divines,* in which our London institutions hitherto have been wofully deficient.

"I should regret to see you at the head of a two-year institution, when the orthodox around us have abandoned that system, and have flourishing Academies for a complete education.

"I wish to see you take the lead in an institution supported by the great body of liberal Dissenters in the Metropolis and elsewhere,—a situation that should be respectable, useful and lucrative; for, with a rising family, you ought not to be expected to give your labours gratuitously. In these circumstances I should be happy to give you all the assistance I could; and I should rejoice to have a Committee chosen which possessed your entire confidence, and with which you might act in perfect harmony.

"However, if the other plan be adopted, I shall comfort myself with the conviction that it must terminate in my plan at last, though probably not till it is too late for me to give it any aid. The impracticability of communicating all the knowledge which is requisite, in so short a period, will make it necessary to add another year and then another, till the course is complete. And perhaps this may be the better way. I have seen so many of these half-education schemes either come to nothing or terminate in a regular institution and a complete course, that I can have no doubt of the ultimate issue of this. At all events, I sincerely wish that your usefulness and comfort may continually increase—and am, dear Sir, most sincerely yours,

T. BELSHAM.

"I sincerely wish well to all the able, active exertions of such ministers as Mr. Wright, &c., to promote the great cause of truth and virtue; but you know my disinclination to public dinners.

"I am obliged to your friend Mr. Evans for his good hints, to which I shall attend as I am able.

"Can you send me the names of half-a-dozen worthy ministers to whom my 'Calm Inquiry' would be of use?"

Notwithstanding his disapprobation of the term of study adopted at the new Academy, Mr. Belsham gave to its conductors much seasonable aid, freely and kindly counselling them in the choice of Tutors, and after a time assisting them with pecuniary grants over which he had control. His letters and notes to Mr. Aspland contain repeated reference, always in a friendly strain, to the Academy. From a large number of them, the following is selected as very honourable to him:

Rev. Thomas Belsham to Rev. Robert Aspland.

"Essex Street, Nov. 17, 1813.

"My dear Sir,—I have this day paid into Mr. Christie's hands £110 for the Unitarian Academy. As I have no other way of communicating to the generous but unknown donor the information of the method in which I have disposed of his liberal benefaction but through the medium of the Monthly Repository, I request the favour of you to insert it in the following manner:

"For the Unitarian Academy, a benefaction from an unknown
  friend, through the hands of Rev. T. Belsham £100 0 0
"Two years' interest upon the same 10 0 0
                       £110 0 0

"In this way our unknown friend will see that, though I have kept his money for two years, I have not been making any advantage of it for myself, which may perhaps induce him to repeat his liberality.

"The reason of my keeping it so long was, the hope that by this time the managers of your institution might have raised the term of education from two years to four or five, in which case I had hoped that we might have very considerably enlarged the amount, and even added the income of the remaining funds of the College. This I have no doubt will be the case ultimately, though I may not live to see it. In the mean time, I heartily wish you and them the best success in promoting the cause of learning, truth and virtue, though it be not exactly in the method which in my estimation would appear most eligible—and am, dear Sir, very sincerely yours,

                 T. BELSHAM."

However urgent the want of an Academy might appear to its founders, their appeal to the Unitarian public was responded to neither promptly nor liberally. A list of subscriptions and benefactions endorsed 1812, i.e. the year after the plan had been made public, shews that at that time the life subscriptions and donations amounted only to £453. 10s., and the annual subscriptions to £130. These amounts were afterwards considerably increased, but the funds were never such as gave promise of stability to the institution. Pecuniary considerations had little weight in any part of his life with Mr. Aspland, and he proceeded to carry into execution the plans agreed upon with undiminished zeal. The state of the funds probably occasioned a modification not originally contemplated, viz., the admission into the Academy of a few lay students. This arrangement, while it largely increased his own personal labour, protected him from pecuniary loss. He removed, at Michaelmas, 1812, from Homerton to a more spacious dwelling, with suitable gardens, called Durham House, situated in the Hackney Road.*

---

 * It had been previously occupied by his friend Mr. Samuel Parkes, the author of several works on Chemistry.

With himself the Committee had associated the Rev. John Bickerton Dewhurst as Classical Tutor, an arrangement most congenial to his wishes, and full of promise to the Academy.

Mr. Dewhurst, the eldest son of the Rev. Edward Dewhurst, a Presbyterian minister, was born at Cottingham, near Hull, Oct. 1, 1770. His school studies were conducted under the able and vigilant direction of the Rev. Joseph Milner, the learned master of the Grammar-school at Hull. He was distinguished as a pupil by precocious tastes, and the diversity and accuracy of his knowledge. He far surpassed his companions, even of riper years, though many of them were not defective in talent, and some afterwards rose to distinction. If the persuasions of his master, who was a zealous Churchman and a very popular preacher of Calvinistic theology, could have prevailed with young Dewhurst, he would, like his friend William Dealtry, have proceeded from the Grammar-school at Hull to the University, and his conformity would doubtless have been rewarded by emoluments and honours not inferior to those of his companion and friend. Finding his persuasions ineffectual, Mr. Milner took his pupil by the hand and said, "My young friend, above all things avoid the errors of the Socinians."* He resolved to qualify himself for the Christian ministry amongst the Protestant Dissenters, and with this view entered, in 1792, the Academy at Northampton, conducted by Mr. Horsey. His tutors found him, on his entrance into their classes, better instructed than many were on leaving the Academy. His classical, which were his favourite, studies were continued under Mr. Forsaith. He continued at Northampton the usual period of five years, and impartially devoted himself to each branch of study provided in the academic curriculum. Mr. Horsey detected and deplored one defect in his character, a want of self-reliance and a disposition to think too meanly of himself. "What all others saw and admired, he could scarcely be induced to believe existed." This peculiarity developed itself on his quitting the Academy in a great and growing distaste to all kinds of public speaking. After fulfilling a temporary and brief engagement with the congregation at Halifax, and acting as an occasional supply to some of the congregations in the Midland counties, he came to the unfortunate conclusion that he was not qualified for usefulness in the pulpit, and resolved to devote himself to private tuition and the pursuits of literature.

---

* See the memoir of Mr. Dewhurst, by Mr. Rutt, in Monthly Repository, VII. 729, whence the facts related above are derived.

In the same year that he quitted Northampton, he entered the family of Mr. E. L. Mackmurdo as tutor, by whom he was greatly valued, and treated with that consideration to which his virtues and his learning so fully entitled him. His contributions adorned several of the best periodicals of that time. To the *Annual Review* he contributed the articles belonging to the department of Classical Literature and Biography. To the *Athenæum* he contributed a series of "Classical Disquisitions." To the *Monthly Repository* he contributed only two articles in the third volume. When the Unitarian Academy was planned, he was still in Mr. Mackmurdo's family, and with them was a regular attendant on Mr. Aspland's services. He frankly acceded to the proposal to become the Classical Tutor in the Academy, much to the satisfaction of all concerned. "He was," says Mr. Rutt, "eminently apt to teach, and knowing beyond most scholars of his time what could be discovered by literary research, he was well fitted to guide the inexperienced to the more prompt acquisition of their limited but important object." The time for the commencement of his new duties had nearly arrived, his colleague was closely occupied in superintending the domestic arrangements for the comfort of the students, when he learnt that Mr. Dewhurst was seriously ill. He had long been otherwise than well, but had neglected seeking medical advice, and with enfeebled powers, sadly needing rest and change, had pursued with iron resolution his accustomed studies. The result was fatal; for when the exhausted frame would no longer sustain the unremitted toil and he fell, his medical advisers found that the vital energy was spent, that diseased action of the head had set in, which baffled all their skill. After a few days' struggle, the most distressing characteristic of which was his apprehension of the loss of intellect, he died in the evening of Oct. 5, 1812.

Deeply as the premature departure of this accomplished and excellent man was deplored by a large circle of admiring friends, by no one was his loss more deeply and for a longer period felt than by Mr. Aspland, on whom the undivided burthen of the Academy now fell. He gave utterance to his sorrow both at the grave of his colleague in Bunhill Fields, and in an address to the congregation of which Mr. Dewhurst had so recently been a member. From the former we derive the tribute to Mr. Dewhurst's memory which follows:

"He was no common character. His modesty, indeed, concealed his great worth and his extraordinary acquirements from casual observers, and his premature death has cut off the hopes which his friends and the friends of literature and religious truth had fondly entertained, that his great talents and rare acquisitions would be employed for the lasting benefit of the public. He was possessed of an eager thirst after knowledge; in pursuit of it was a pattern of regular industry, and was distinguished by a retentive, capacious, well-ordered and serviceable memory. His learning was deep and solid. His knowledge was more wonderful than his learning, for there were few subjects on which he was not thoroughly informed: yet no man was more free from pedantry and all kind of ostentation. His contributions to various literary works are marked by accuracy, judgment, simplicity and perspicuity of style; qualities which might eventually, if such had been the will of Providence, have elevated him to the rank of the best and best-known writers of his age and country. To his honour be it mentioned, that, though employed occasionally in anonymous criticism, he never took advantage of that tempting opportunity of indulging in personal reflections, nor made a single remark under cover of secrecy which he was not ready to own and able to defend.

"The same traits that characterized him as an author distinguished him as a man—sound judgment, simplicity, candour. His manners were so amiable that there were few that knew him that were not his friends. Enemies, I believe, he had none, nor was it possible that he should have had any. Unobtrusive, quiet and retired in his habits, he might appear sometimes reserved; but his real affability made him easy of access, and no one, but through his own fault, could long enjoy his conversation without both pleasure and profit.

"From his strong understanding, his extensive learning, his habit of patient research, and his freedom from all professional bias, he was well qualified to judge of the evidences in behalf of revealed religion; and his decision was such as every well-informed inquirer would expect, and every Christian would wish; and his belief in Christianity seemed to be of growing importance to him. But he distinguished between the Christianity of the New Testament and the Christianity of popular profession, and held a system of truth which he had drawn for himself from the original sources of divine knowledge.

"With enlightened zeal he united great candour. He could not admire and approve indiscriminately, but he was a gentle censor; in this and all points conforming himself to the standard of whatsoever things are just and true and pure, lovely and of good report. He was prudent in his affairs, temperate in his enjoyments, of uniform goodness and habitual piety. In a word, he was *a disciple whom Jesus loved*.

"On his death-bed he reaped the fruits of his virtues: gratitude for his instructions, esteem of his character, friendship and anxiety for the interests of learning and religion, surrounded him with willing, eager and faithful attendants. All that professional skill, and all that the generous kindness of friends, and the tender assiduities of relatives, could do to arrest disease or to alleviate its pressure, was done; and now there mingle in his grave as sincere tears as ever bedewed a corpse."

Rev. Robert Aspland to Mr. Isaac Aspland, Wicken.

"Durham House, Oct. 24, 1812.

"Dear Brother,—We hoped before this to have seen my mother, but suppose now we shall see you first. We are recovering a little from our bustle, and are in expectation of some of the students coming in.

"But, alas! how vain are all human plans! The learned and excellent young man with whom I was to have been joined in the conduct of the Academy, and without whom I should not probably have undertaken it, is no more. At the time I was getting into my house, he was sickening for his last illness, and died on the 5th instant. I buried him in Bunhill Fields on the 12th, and last Sunday preached his funeral sermon. This is to me a great and afflicting loss; but all is shadow rather than substance on this side the grave: 'every man walketh in a vain show.'

"In the last No. of the Repository you will have seen Mr. Dewhurst advertised as one of the Tutors of the Academy, and in the next you will read his obituary.

"There is another death which, in connection with the Repository, is somewhat affecting, that of the Rev. Job David, who wrote the account of Mr. Howell, lately deceased, in the last No., and whose own obituary will be in the No. following.

"These are lessons, Isaac, which come home to our hearts."

CHAPTER XIX.

Notwithstanding discouragements sufficient to dishearten many men, Mr. Aspland entered on the conduct of the Unitarian Academy with energy, and presided over it during its brief existence in a manner to give perfect satisfaction to its supporters. During the first year, he undertook the entire instruction (excepting Hebrew) of the young men. In the years 1814 and 1815, the Mathematical department was undertaken by the Rev. Jeremiah Joyce. The engagement of Mr. Joyce as his colleague gave him much satisfaction. He was pleased to be united with a man whom in his youth he had looked up to with pity and veneration as a possible martyr to English liberty, and whom in after years he admired for his various attainments and loved for his social worth. The events of Mr. Joyce's life and his various publications are recorded in a Memoir of him which Mr. Aspland published in the Monthly Repository (Vol. XII. 697—704). He closes it by expressing the satisfaction which its publication gave him, as connecting his name with that of Mr. Joyce. Thus did he draw the character of his "ever-lamented friend:"—"His character may be summed up in a few words—probity, industry, simplicity, fortitude, benevolence and rational piety. A remarkable plainness of appearance and straightforwardness and perhaps bluntness of manner, which characterized Mr. Joyce, sometimes led superficial and distant observers to form an erroneous notion of his temper. On a nearer acquaintance they discovered that, under a somewhat rough exterior, there lay all the amiable and virtuous dispositions which qualify a man for friendship and social and domestic happiness. In company Mr. Joyce was unobtrusive and even retiring, yet not so as to abstract himself from his companions, much less to appear to watch their discourse: his countenance shewed that he took an interest in whatever was the subject of discourse, and he was not backward to take his share in conversation when he could communicate pertinent information, or bear testimony to what he considered to be truth. The ordinary state of Mr. Joyce's mind was calm and equable, but he was sometimes excited to considerable warmth of feeling and to a correspondent strength of expression. He displayed this earnestness chiefly when exposing the misrepresentations of sophists and the calumnies of bigots. He was tolerant and indulgent to all but baseness and hypocrisy."

Mr. Joyce's connection with the Unitarian Academy was terminated by his accepting an invitation to superintend the education of the younger branches of a noble family. His performance of his duties as Mathematical Tutor, though brief in duration, had gained for him the esteem and gratitude of his pupils and the friends of the Academy.

A Classical Tutor was for a short time found in the person of the Rev. Thomas Biggin Broadbent. This excellent young man, the son of the Rev. William Broadbent, of Warrington, was born March 17, 1793. After passing through a course of elementary instruction, first under his father and then under a clergyman of Manchester, he entered in 1809 the University of Glasgow. His academic course was distinguished by industry and success; he gained prizes in all his classes in which they were given; in the Greek class he carried off the first. He took his Master's degree, April, 1813. He spent some time after leaving the University, still pursuing his studies, under his father's roof. Between Mr. Broadbent, Sen., and Mr. Belsham a strong friendship existed, and knowing well the classical attainments of his friend's son, it was natural that he should exert his influence to obtain the benefit of them for the Unitarian Academy, in the prosperity of which he felt a growing interest. His mediation was ultimately successful, although, as his letters shew, there were many difficulties to overcome. Mr. Broadbent's residence in London during two years was made serviceable to religion and sacred learning by his undertaking, in addition to his Tutorship, the supply of the pulpit at Princes Street, by his assisting in the preparation for the press of an edition of the Improved Version, and by his transcribing for his venerable friend at Essex Street a portion of his Translation and Exposition of the Epistles of Paul.

Rev. Thomas Belsham to Rev. Robert Aspland.

"Essex Street, May 19.

"My dear Sir,—I have this morning heard from Mr. Broadbent, and I regret to say that he and his son finally decline our proposals. Shall I venture to ask him again to make trial, if it is but for a year? I know not where else we can look for help. And I dread the thoughts of the London interest falling into the hands of unknown adventurers.

"Have you seen Wright's Letters to me? They are written with temper, but they require little reply. It affords, however, a tempting opportunity of giving a rapid view of the argument from early testimony, which my friend Wright's Letters help to confirm. But I fear I should occupy too many of your pages and too much of your readers' patience.

"Mr. Turner's account of Warrington is interesting, but he ought not to go off scot free for his attack upon the theological discussions of Daventry. Warrington cold morality and theological ignorance and indifference have ruined almost all the Presbyterian congregations in Lancashire.

"Adieu, my dear Sir. May the good work long prosper in your hands, and may you find able coadjutors.—Yours most sincerely,

T. BELSHAM."

"Essex Street, May 25, 1814.

"My dear Sir,—I enclose two pounds from my worthy friend, Percival North, Esq., as a donation to the Unitarian Fund.

"I cannot help flattering myself that if you succeed in engaging Mr. Broadbent for the next session as your Classical Tutor, it may pave the way to a permanent connection, which appears to me an event devoutly to be wished.

"I know his father means to come to town next summer to take his son back to Warrington. Would there be any impropriety in asking Mr. Madge to change turns with him? It is hardly probable he will be in London two years in succession, and I dare say he would like to preach your sermon.

"I think you should ask £100 for a lay-student; it is no more than fifty pounds thirty years ago; and you can hardly afford to take them for less, unless your numbers very much increase, which I sincerely wish they may.

"It is not at all necessary to depart from the original plan of your institution; but I think the public should be fully apprized that provision is made for giving a complete education to those who are desirous of it, whether intended for the ministry or for other professions.

"Wishing you all possible success in your active exertions to promote the interests of truth and virtue, I am, dear Sir, most sincerely yours,

T. BELSHAM.

"I hear that our friend Pickbourn has paid the debt of nature. Life in his circumstances was no longer desirable."

"Manchester, Sept. 20, 1814.

"My dear Sir,—I must take to myself the blame of all the eccentricities of my friend T. Broadbent; but I will answer for it that when he once begins to move in his regular orbit, he will pursue his course as steadily as old Saturn himself.

"By the desire of my friends at St. Alban's, I have been prevailed upon to stay over the Sunday, and I have *peremptorily* fixed to return to Essex Street on Monday morning. I have requested my sister to provide a piece of roast beef for our dinner at four o'clock; and I now request you to favour us with your company to meet us at that time, and to allow me to introduce my young friend to you. I have, for the present, recommended it to him to take lodgings in Arundel Street, as being nearly equidistant from his two charges at Westminster and Durham House. If this should be found inconvenient, it will be easy to form a new arrangement. And though I shall be far from opposing any plan which may be conducive to his comfort and usefulness, I shall regret if he removes his quarters to an inaccessible distance from me.

"I cannot help flattering myself that this proposed winter visit of my friend Broadbent to London may issue in his permanent connection with the metropolis; and I cannot but congratulate myself upon having been instrumental to so auspicious an event. I am sure that you will find him a most able and amiable colleague; and I have no doubt that his services will be highly acceptable at Princes Street.

"He desires me to give his best respects to you and thanks for your kind letter: he is greatly obliged to Mr. Christie for his kind invitation, which he hopes to be able to accept another time, though circumstances prevent him from waiting upon him next Sunday.

"If you cannot meet me on Monday, I will accompany Mr. B. to your house on Tuesday morning; and with my best compliments to Mrs. Aspland and all friends who may do me the honour to inquire after me, I remain, dear Sir, your affectionate friend and obedient servant, T. BELSHAM."

The manner in which Mr. Broadbent discharged his duties as Classical Tutor during the years 1814—1816, was described to be such as secured "not only the improvement, but the affection and gratitude of his pupils,* together with the high approbation of his learned colleagues and the managers and supporters of the institution."†

He resigned his office at the close of the session 1815-16, but did not long survive. By his very sudden death, under circumstances peculiarly striking and affecting, Nov. 9th, 1817, prospects of no common usefulness and happiness were in a moment destroyed.

A successor to both the Mathematical and Classical department of the Academy was found in Rev. John Morell, LL.D. He was descended from Huguenot ancestors, and was born at Maldon, in Essex,

---

* Mr. Goodier said, "Mr. Broadbent is a most agreeable teacher, and were I in health I should have almost every advantage for mental improvement."

† Mr. Belsham's Memoir of Rev. T. B. Broadbent, M.A., Mon. Rep. XIII. 2.

May 16, 1776.* His parents were attached to the principles of the Independents, and destined him for the ministry amongst the "orthodox" Dissenters. He received his academical education at Homerton, and subsequently settled with congregations at Foulmire, Blandford, Daventry and Enfield. The latter charge he was induced to resign in 1802, partly from a failure of his voice and partly from a change in his religious views. He devoted his talents, subsequently to this, to the education of the young. For this employment, according to the testimony of one of the most gifted of his pupils,† he was eminently fitted both by the constitution of his mind and the compass of his attainments. On the breaking up of the Academy at Hackney, he settled at Brighton, where he officiated at the Unitarian chapel as minister, conducted a flourishing school, and educated or assisted to prepare several young men for the ministry. The closing years of his life were spent on the continent and in the city of Bath, where he died April 11, 1840, in the sixty-fifth year of his age.

With the aid of such colleagues,‡ Mr. Aspland had the happiness of beholding the Academy realize during its short career many of the hopes of its founders; and had not his own health broken down under his heavy and complicated labours, and the funds proved quite inadequate to the required expenditure, it might probably have been continued with advantage for many years longer.

The plan of the Academy, as has already appeared in Mr. Belsham's letter (of the date May 25), soon outgrew the narrow limits at first assigned to the period of study. At first, two years was the term appointed for the course of study of each student; but power was given to the Committee to extend it. Experience soon taught the managers of the institution that two years were not sufficient for the objects at which they aimed. The uncertainty as to the length of the course prevented the Tutors and students from making from the first the best arrangement of it. The addition of a third year to the course of instruction had not, therefore, removed all the inconveniences of their original plan. In 1816, the Committee recommended to the Governors of the Academy to extend the curriculum to four years in the case of those whose studies included the classics, and to limit it strictly to two with

---

* See Rev. J. Reynell Wreford's interesting Memoir, appended to the Funeral Sermon preached by Rev. Henry Acton.

† Rev. Henry Acton.

‡ The Hebrew teachers were Mr. Bright and Mr. Bolaffey.

those whose studies were confined to English literature and general theology. But, alas for human plans! in four years the Academy had ceased to exist.

From the first, the students were practised in whatever would assist to make them useful and effective preachers. Exercises in elocution, particularly the reading of Scripture, and extempore prayer in the family, were much encouraged by their Theological Tutor. He also wished them to take part in the weekly religious conferences held at the Gravel-Pit lecture-room. Between the managers of the Academy and the Committee of the Unitarian Fund there was cordial co-operation. The pulpits of several chapels kept open by the help of the Fund were often supplied by the students of the Academy. Their vacations were spent chiefly in missionary excursions, in which, under the judicious guidance of Mr. Wright or some other experienced friend, they gained knowledge of human nature and acquired facility in popular addresses, while they improved their health and acquired strength and spirits for the severer duties of their studies. By two of the Hackney students the writer has been favoured with their recollections of their studies at the Academy.

The Rev. John Smethurst says, "With respect to our studies, the order of the different pursuits was often changed; but the general rule, I believe, was, that we were three days of the week with Mr. Aspland, who gave us instruction in History (ecclesiastical and general), Rhetoric and the Belles Lettres, Composition, particularly that of a sermon and its delivery. I have his lectures on the latter subject in shorthand, which I copied from his manuscript. We had also, and I think previously to the last-mentioned course, some lectures on Prayer. In addition to this, your father gave us more general directions in our theological studies by pointing out the authors he wished us to read, mentioning the difficulties we might expect to meet in making up our minds on this or that subject, and helping us to get over them, &c.

"The rest of the week was devoted to Classics and Mathematics,— two days to the former and one to the latter. Mr. Broadbent was our Classical Tutor, I think, for two sessions, but I am not quite certain whether it was one or two; and Mr. Joyce took the Mathematical part. Dr. Morell, however, during my last year, was both Classical and Mathematical Tutor. In Mathematics, Horsfield and myself, who formed a class, got through Bonnycastle's Algebra and Euclid, and during our last year did a little in Trigonometry.

"In Classics, we read together Virgil and Horace, Quintus Curtius, Livy, some of the minor Greek Classics, and a little of Homer.

"To fill up odd hours—of which, by the way, your good father seemed to think we had far more than was really the case—he had us with him to read Grotius, which, being considered extra work, made his crabbed Latinity any thing but a favourite with us; and I have to this day something like my old feelings on this subject whenever I consult his 'Annotationes.'"

The Rev. William Stevens says, "The Tutors, during the first year of my term, were Mr. Broadbent for the Classics, Dr. Morell the Mathematics. In the second, Dr. Morell was both Classical and Mathematical Tutor, the students attending at his own house at Homerton. On the Dr. removing to Brighton, Mr. Fox was appointed to the Classical Tutorship. Much the largest portion of the labour devolved upon Mr. Aspland,—Divinity, History, Mental and Moral Philosophy, the Pastoral Office, Composition and Elocution; in which last, if I might particularize one above the rest, he certainly took very great pains, evidently aware that it matters but little what talents, attainments or character, a minister may have, if he has a bad elocution he will never be a popular preacher. Admirable and pure as his own elocution was, this care could not but be of very great advantage to the students, some of whom came with dialects that pretty strongly marked whence they came. I believe we were all deeply sensible of the advantage we thus received. The teaching of languages formed no part of Mr. Aspland's province as Tutor, but nevertheless we read Grotius de Veritate with him; and in addition to the subject matter, it was an exercise in Latin construing which, from the extremely minute and careful analysis to which it was subjected by him, I shall ever regard as one of the most profitable lessons of that kind I enjoyed during my stay at Hackney. If my memory serves me, your father's lectures were three days in the week, from eleven till about two, and this through the whole of my term, with the exception of two or three months at the close, when he had a long and very serious illness. As domestic Tutor he likewise frequently gave up considerable portions of his time to the students, in such manner as prolonging the breakfast hour much beyond what would have been necessary, by exercising them in reading, and reading with them, papers from the Spectator, Rambler, Poetry, &c. I believe there was not one among them who was not deeply sensible of and grateful for the kindness and fidelity with which

Mr. A. laboured to fit them for the office they were intended to fill."

It was the custom at the Academy for each student in turn to perform the duties of monitor, one of which was to keep a general diary of the proceedings and studies of the pupils. An extract or two from one of the volumes of the diary, which has alone escaped destruction, will shew something of the discipline.

"1813. Oct. 4.—Began at $6\frac{1}{2}$. Studied Latin till breakfast. Cooper prayed and Goodier read Psalm viii. Studied our various lessons—Testament, Delectus, Grammar, Vocabulary, and Selectæ e Profanis, till Mr. Aspland came in. Then we first read to him, and afterwards he read to us, Dr. Taylor's Charge to his Pupils; then went over our lessons, and read the Parable of the Prodigal Son. Afterwards we studied Hebrew, and read Vidler's last letter to Mr. A. Goodier studied Logic. After dark, Goodier read Matthew viii. in R. T. and Improved Version, and a part of chap. vii. in Latin Testament, and together we read Watts on the Improvement of the Mind, and the 1st chapter of Job and the 1st of Matthew; prayed and went to bed. At supper, Mr. A. read the two first books of Pope's Essay on Man.

"Oct. 5.—$6\frac{1}{2}$. Wrote a little, studied our Latin lessons. At breakfast, Mr. A. read Psalm li. and Acts i., also Bingley's Animal Biography. We then studied again till Tutor came in; then he read to us the Prodigal Son, in the words of Mr. Bourn, of Norwich, who by turning it into modern language, and considerably enlarging it, has entirely destroyed its beautiful simplicity. We then went over all our lessons. In the afternoon I went to London. Goodier read Latin and Logic, and worked one hour in the garden. Spent the evening in the parlour. Read Monthly Repository to Mrs. A. After supper, G. read the Messiah, by Pope, to Mr. A. Mr. A. read Book iii. of the Essay, and we then each read the Fable of the 'Farmer's Wife and the Raven,' and after conversing some time retired to the study. Read John iii. and Matt. iii., prayed and went to bed.

"Oct. 15.—$6\frac{1}{2}$. Wrote diaries. Composed a little of our themes. I read and Cooper prayed. Wrote a little more; then studied Latin lessons; read our themes to Mr. A. when he came in, and he corrected them; then a part of our lessons. We studied Latin till after dinner. Cooper wrote. Went to see Mr. J——, &c. Read Watts an hour. We then wrote for some time; then I studied Logic till $10\frac{1}{4}$; then supped. I read a chapter in Mason's Pastor. We afterwards conversed some time with Mr. A., chiefly on *Grotius*. In the study we read two chapters, prayed, and went to bed about 12."

The system of instruction pursued by Mr. Aspland with the young men preparing for the ministry, was rather to turn their attention to the best authors on the several subjects of study, than to deliver set lectures. The class was always small, and instruction was best communicated in the most familiar manner. Two or three series of lectures were, however, prepared and read to them on Ecclesiastical History, including a description of religious sects and denominations; Athanasius and his Creed; English Deistical Writers; and Sketches of the Protestant Reformation. These lectures were necessarily popular in their character. They were used in the Lectures to Young Persons at the Gravel-Pit; and some of them were afterwards printed in the early volumes of the Christian Reformer (First Series, in 12mo). Other lectures were read by him to the students, particularly five on the Composition and Delivery of a Sermon, and ten on Prayer. These lectures, although never printed, have had during the last thirty years a considerable circulation through MS. copies amongst students of theology. They abound in judicious observations, in references, the fruit of an extensive perusal of English divines and critics, and in illustrations of excellencies and defects in sermon-writing, taken from the works of writers of eminence. The introductory remarks may serve as a specimen:

"In preaching, as in praying, there is an *art*, the knowledge and practice of which will greatly assist a preacher, making his duty more easy to himself and more profitable to his hearers.*

"The first inquiry for a candidate for the pulpit is, What is the end of preaching and the final object of his profession? The end and object is the promotion of truth and virtue, and this is to be attained by instruction and persuasion.

"'There are two abilities requisite (says Bishop Wilkins†) in every one that will teach and instruct another,—a *right understanding* of sound doctrine, and an *ability* to *propound, confirm* and *apply it* unto the edification of others. And the first may be without the other: as a man may be a good *lawyer* and not a good *pleader*, so he may be a good *divine* and yet not a good *preacher*.'

"Every man who pretends to instruct others owes it to his own character, and to the respect to which every other man is entitled, to fit himself for the work which he undertakes. And as there are many ways of doing the same thing, it behoves him to seek out the best and to observe it diligently.

"Much more is this the duty of a preacher, who is to be an example no less than a teacher of excellence, who is under a more peculiar responsibility to God Almighty, and whose employment is of such great importance, having reference to the souls of men and the solemn realities of eternity.

"No man ever excelled in a profession who did not estimate it highly and

---

* "Wilkins' Ecclesiastes, p. 1. 8vo, 1704. † "Ut sup., p. 2.
‡ "The divine alluded to is *Gaspar Streso*. See South's Sermons, I. 158.

entertain a love of it. The best preachers have been also the most pious men, and the most shining examples of theological learning. Perhaps, too, it will be found that they who have written the best sermons were habitual readers of the sermons of others, and zealous admirers of the greatest masters in this department of letters.

"In a preacher, success will depend much upon his mind and character. What a learned foreign divine said of the English preaching may be said of all, *Plus est in artifice quam in arte;* so much of moment is there in the professors of any thing to depress or raise the profession.

"The knowledge of theology is the first qualification of a preacher, but every species of knowledge will be found serviceable to him. History will supply him with examples of moral truths, and attestations to the truths of religion; science will furnish him with proofs and illustrations of the Being and Providence of God; and even works of fancy will enkindle his genius, and enable him to enlighten and enliven the subjects of which he treats, and to clothe the plainest ideas with the beauties of imagination. Livy has a striking passage of the utility of all sorts of knowledge to a Greek warrior, Philopæmen;* and a fine writer of our own remarks that Plutarch made use of all other authors, and mixed them up in his own style, which has thus a peculiar excellence,—like the Corinthian brass, which had in it various metals, and yet was a species by itself.† In like manner, the divine may amass and amalgamate in his mind all sorts of knowledge, and appropriate and hallow every thought by consecrating it to the service of the sanctuary.

"There is a connection between knowledge in general and virtue; the connection is more close and obvious with regard to moral and theological knowledge. The motto of a learned and eminently pious and eloquent divine, Dr. Henry More, should be the motto of every preacher and student, *Amor Dei, Lux Animæ.*

"It is a remark of Lord Bacon's, that the sermons of our English divines contain a complete body of moral truth and practical wisdom. We may add, that they exhibit also a history of our language and even of our manners, and that they abound in examples of every kind of beauty of style. The study of them is of the first importance to a preacher, for let his original talents be what they may, it is only by setting before himself the best models that he can expect to avoid faults and to attain to excellence."

---

* "Erat autem Philopæmen, &c. Liv., l. 35, § 28.

† "Dryden, in Life of Plutarch prefixed to Plutarch's Lives, 8vo, I. 46. Sir Joshua Reynolds (who read amongst his earliest books this work of Dryden's; see Malone's Life of him, prefixed to his Works, 8vo, I. 7) uses very happily this same simile of the Corinthian brass to illustrate the necessity of an artist's studying and incorporating all the styles of painting. Six Discourses on Painting, Works. I. 173. For the real history of the Corinthian brass, consult Dr. Jennings's little tract, entitled, An Introduction to the Study of Medals, p. 21.

The following is a list of the young men who entered the Unitarian Academy, as students in theology, during its continuance under Mr. Aspland's roof:

When entered.		Afterwards settled, &c.
1812. Oct. 29.	John Hancock (Evesham)	did not pursue his studies more than one session.
	Thos. Cooper (Framlingham)	Moreton Hampstead, Jamaica, Hanley, Dorchester.
1813. April 21.	Benjamin Goodier (Failsworth)	died, at Montauban, July 23, 1818, aged 25.
Oct. 16.	Francis Knowles	left the Academy November 11. Nantwich, Park Lane.
1814.	John Smethurst (Failsworth)	Moreton Hampstead.
	Thomas Walker Horsfield (Sheffield)	Lewes, Taunton, Chowbent; died August 26, 1837, aged 45.
	G. Fletcher	} did not pursue their studies long.
	Joseph Webb (Framlingham)	
1815.	Joseph C. Meeke	Colchester, Reading, Stockton, Northampton, Lewes.
Sept. 6.	William Stevens	Newport, Isle of Wight, Maidstone.
1817.	Frederick Horsfield (Sheffield)	continued his studies under Dr. Morell. Cirencester.
	Neil Walker (Dundee)	Wisbeach.

Of these gentlemen, several are now performing their ministerial duties, and some are engaged in the education of the young, and the position occupied by most of them is honourable to themselves and to their Alma Mater. Of two of Mr. Aspland's pupils at the Academy, more especial mention may be indulged in, their death having done away in their case with that necessity for reserve which delicacy and sincerity impose on the biographer when alluding to the living.

Benjamin Goodier was the son of John Goodier and Sarah Taylor, his wife, who followed the occupation of weavers at Hollinwood, between Manchester and Oldham. He was the second of four children, and was born April 25, 1793. His father was a man of good sense and some literary cultivation.* For a time John Goodier conducted a

---

* Of this the writer has before him most satisfactory evidence in a memoir (MS.) drawn up by him of his gifted and amiable son.

day-school, but was compelled to give it up in consequence of the delicate health of his wife, who was unable to bear the noise of the children. At a very early period, Benjamin developed a sweet and gentle disposition, together with great talents for the acquisition of knowledge. His parents were members of the ancient Presbyterian chapel at Dob Lane, connected with which was a library, containing many books suitable for the young, which had been established in 1790 by Mr. Darbishire. Of this library young Benjamin Goodier made use before he was six years old; and so decided was his taste for literature, and so early matured his character, that he was in his twelfth year appointed librarian. He followed his father's trade of weaving, and notwithstanding scanty resources, often made still more scanty by sickness in the family, he found means to buy books, and to exercise habitual charity to the poor around him. Just as he was entering on manhood, an unfortunate accident, by which he was precipitated overhead in a mill-pond and narrowly escaped with life, brought on a severe attack of rheumatic fever, and probably gave a shock to his health from which his constitution never entirely recovered. Feeble as his frame was, his mind was zealous and strong in devising plans of usefulness and improvement. He established the Sunday-school at Dob Lane, and instituted in the same place a meeting for the improvement of the young, similar to that which he afterwards recommended for general adoption in the Christian Reformer, Vol. I. p. 307. His father thus describes the circumstances which led to his joining the Academy at Hackney:

"In 1812, he was very successfully engaged in conference meetings in the Woodhouses with the Methodists on doctrinal subjects, and afterwards with the preachers belonging to the New Jerusalem church at the same place; but in August the same year he was invited by them to their meeting in Manchester, at which he acquitted himself so much to the satisfaction of the Unitarian gentlemen who attended that meeting, that a subscription was entered into to send him to the Academy at Hackney."

During the months that intervened before this plan was carried into execution, he was enabled, by the kind assistance of the Rev. D. Jones, minister of Dob Lane, to conquer the elements of the Latin language.

His residence at Hackney is remembered by the members of Mr. Aspland's family with deep and affectionate interest. The worth and loveliness of his character was instantly felt by his new associates. His progress in his studies was both rapid and sure. One who had at this time frequent opportunities not only of observing, but also of assisting his progress, has thus described him:

"He was a rare example of great rapidity of mind united to indefatigable industry. Such was his progress in every study he entered upon, that all his tutors derived the highest gratification from instructing him. Whilst devoting his hours to the acquirement of science and of languages, the moral ends of these studies were never absent from his mind; nor did he content himself with gaining stores of knowledge, but already began to perform the duties of a Christian minister; he occasionally filled the pulpit, in various places, in a very acceptable manner, and many of our readers must recollect with pleasure the good sense, piety and acquaintance with the Holy Scriptures, apparent in the speeches he made at the religious conferences carried on in the lecture-room of the Gravel-Pit meeting. His conversation in private society was not less interesting and instructive; he seemed to think every moment lost that was not employed on some useful subject; yet he had none of the harshness or pedantry which sometimes belongs to the hard student; he was constantly amusing as well as intellectual. He was equally admirable as a learner or a teacher: in company with persons whose judgment he revered, he would easily and unobtrusively lead to topics on which he hoped to gain information: when conversing with young children, of whom he was particularly fond, and who eagerly sought his society, he divested instruction of dulness; and even when listening to the silly arguments of a weak-minded disputant, he failed not to treat him with the patience and consideration due to every fellow-creature; for if the ludicrous absurdity of some remark forced a smile into his countenance, that smile was so full of candour and benignity, that it could scarcely hurt the feelings of him who had caused it. With all this gentleness and modesty, he possessed that manly independence of thought essential to the pursuit of truth: the writer of this article does not remember, on any other occasion, to have seen him look so indignant as in repeating a conversation in which it had been taken for granted, from the attachment he had expressed for his theological tutor, that he had adopted some religious opinion because it was believed by that gentleman."*

One or two extracts from his familiar letters will help, better than any formal description, to portray his life at Durham House. Writing soon after his arrival (May 8, 1813), he says,

"From what I have said, you may be sure that I find my situation as comfortable as I could expect. I have indeed a goodly heritage, but not so comfortable as home: politeness and civility reign in this family, but these are not so sweet to me as the openness and unceremonious friendship I have

* Mon. Repos., XIV. 70.

enjoyed at home. The chapel is a new and elegant building, with seats for about 700 persons. Last Sunday I received the Lord's Supper there: about a hundred persons stayed, which I am told is fewer than usual."

In June 1813, he thus writes:

"Before I came here, I sometimes heard the Academy called 'a hot-bed.' As a proof that this name is very applicable, I need only tell you, that on Sunday, 30th of May, I preached '*for the great man*' (as he styles himself), Mr. Vidler, who was at that time making the greatest efforts to disseminate Unitarianism at Chatham. His chapel is in Parliament Court, Bishopsgate Street; the same in which the annual meetings of the Fund are held: it is a neat building, with galleries on three sides, capable of holding five hundred persons. On the opposite side to the pulpit is a small organ. The congregation was raised by Elhanan Winchester, the great Universalist preacher. Think what were my sensations when I stood up in that pulpit! For a raw, inexperienced country lad, who had scarcely been six weeks from home, to enter a London pulpit and address a congregation in which some powdered heads were assembled, was rather a bold undertaking. To stand in a pulpit which is regularly *filled* by such a man as Mr. Vidler, and which has been filled by such men as Aspland, Grundy, Wright, Winchester, &c., was an arduous undertaking; it made me tremble. My text was, 'What must I do to be saved?' Mr. A. sent my fellow-students with me to criticise a little, or rather, I should say, to see how I acquitted myself, and report to him accordingly. Their report was very favourable to me; I was not, however, contented with it; I wished to know what faults I had committed, or what blunders I had made, and was urgent with Mr. Cooper to tell me," &c.*

His first vacation he spent in missionary labours in the villages of Cambridgeshire, in supplying at Wisbeach for Mr. Wright, and in a missionary journey in company with that excellent man.

In the early part of the summer of 1814, there appeared some alarming symptoms of pectoral disease. By the earnest advice of Dr. Pett, he felt constrained to relax in his studies, and shortly after to leave the Academy. He found consolation in this distressing trial by devoting himself to the promotion of Unitarian worship at Oldham. He visited a number of towns and solicited subscriptions with such success, that a chapel was built at the cost of about £600, and was opened for public worship Jan. 4, 1816.

Indulging in the hope that his health would improve, he consented to accept the office of minister to this little congregation, so dear to him. He resided for some time in the family of a kind relative at Dukinfield,

---

* See Mrs. Hornblower's interesting Memoir of Rev. B. Goodier, pp. 20, 21.

whose family he instructed. In the summer of 1816, he visited the Isle of Wight, intending to pass only a few months there, preaching to the congregation at Newport, and benefitting his health by the mildness of the climate. But he suffered a severe relapse, and was henceforth entirely disabled from public services. He spent portions of the following year with friends in Shropshire, Liverpool and Chester, who watched his declining strength with affectionate solicitude. From the house of Mr. Freme, of Liverpool, one of the kindest of his friends, he thus wrote, in the autumn of 1817, to Mrs. Mary Hughes:

"My good doctor (well he deserves the name) was too sanguine. I continue at present in much the same state as when Mr. Aspland was here, which was better than he seemed to expect to find me; had he stayed, I almost believe I should have been better still, for, as you say, his conversation is exhilarating in a very high degree. I could not but regret his very short stay with us,— much too short, I think, for the importance of the place, where he is very little known, and where he needs only to be known to be admired and loved. After his departure, I was more and more disposed to lament the shortness of his visit, and to envy you the pleasure of his company. I had hoped to have some religious conversation with him; and, like another Boswell, had formed a plan of registering his almost every word, thinking that it might prove the last interview I should ever have with him. He talks so delightfully, and at the same time so rationally, on the character of God, the proofs of his essential and universal goodness, and on the Christian's hope in death, that his conversation on these subjects is valuable to all, but especially valuable to me, struggling very likely myself with a disease that generally proves fatal. To be deprived of so good an opportunity for improvement in heavenly-mindedness was indeed a serious disappointment; however, I hope that my loss was a gain to him, and that his excursion in North Wales tended to establish him in that health which was so necessary for the discharge of his important duties."

The deep-seated disease which had deprived him of his strength was still making fatal progress. Before the close of 1817, he was ordered by his medical advisers to proceed to the South of France. He found a temporary home at Bordeaux, and thence proceeded to Montauban. Here he lived long enough to create in the minds of many persons who had the privilege of his acquaintance, a deep interest; but died, after enduring sufferings of the severest kind with the sweetest patience, on July 23, 1818. Such was the respect and affection which his gentle virtues and Christian piety had created, that his remains were followed to the grave, not only by all the resident English of the place, but by all the Professors of the College, by the students, and by the Protestant ministers of Montauban. In piety and practical religion, Mr. Goodier greatly resembled Henry Ware; and, taking into view the manner in which the former of these two equally faithful servants of God broke through all the difficulties of poverty and imperfect early education, we may well believe that, had his life been protracted, his career would not have been less distinguished nor less abundant in the fruits of religion and righteousness than that of Mr. Ware.

In connection with Mr. Goodier's history, room must be found for two letters.

Rev. William Johns to Rev. Robert Aspland.

"Manchester, Aug. 8, 1818.

"Dear Sir,—On Wednesday last, Mr. Goodier, of Hollinwood, near this town, received a letter, written the 25th of July, communicating the intelligence of the death of his son, which took place on the 23rd of the same month. He died at Montauban, where he had resided a few months. Mr. Goodier, the father, has desired me to write to you and suggest the propriety of your drawing up a memoir, to be inserted in the Repository. I certainly know no person so proper for the task as yourself, if you will undertake it. What you may know concerning the last year or two of his life I am ignorant; but Mr. Freme and myself will cheerfully communicate what we know, if you desire it. Mr. Freme has received several letters from him from France, and I have seen several to his father. In all these there is a complete unity and consistency of character to the end. The last letter to his father (written July 12) is admirable. He wrote to Mr. Freme on the 15th; but that letter I have not seen. Of these interesting letters we can furnish you with copies, if you think that it will facilitate the undertaking. They can be easily sent. The liberality of Mr. Freme and Mr. James Freme has been very great. His friends in this neighbourhood, upon being informed of the contents of his last letter to his father, immediately subscribed above £20, and more would have been done in a few days, if the report of his death had not arrived. We shall have no difficulty, in concert with Mr. Freme, in making proper arrangements in regard to his concerns. One thing, however, the voice of humanity and a correct national feeling loudly calls for—the liberal remuneration of those strangers whose conduct towards our deceased friend during a most trying and painful affliction, requiring the most unremitted, patient and even servile attention, has in a very exemplary degree been kind, humane and affectionate.

"I hope your own health is restored, and that Mrs. Aspland and every branch of your family is well. I shall be glad to hear from you as soon as convenient on the subject of this letter. I have been *very* much engaged, or else I should have written immediately upon hearing of poor Goodier's death, and likewise more fully.

"I am, dear Sir, yours most truly,
WILLIAM JOHNS."

Rev. Robert Aspland to Rev. William Johns.

"Hackney Road, Sept. 3, 1818.

"Dear Sir,—I am but just returned from a journey into the West of England, or your kind favour of the 8th ultimo would not have remained so long unanswered.

"The death of our excellent young friend was announced to me on the road; and though I heard of the event without surprise, I could not fail of being deeply affected by it. He was upon the whole the best young man I ever knew. Had his life been spared, with restored health, he would have been of great importance to our connection: and until very lately I often pleased myself with reckoning upon the services which he seemed raised up to render to the cause of truth and righteousness. It has, however, pleased the Infinite Wisdom to close his probationary account, and we must console ourselves with reflecting that few mortals have ever been called to the eternal world at once so young in years and so ripe in virtues.

"I cannot decline any labour that would perpetuate our departed friend's memory or do honour to his name, but I do not think that I am the fittest person to draw up his memoir. Of his short history previous to his coming to the Academy, I have little or no knowledge, and I have few, if any, documents to illustrate his character in reference to the period between his removal from my house and his death. There must be many of his Lancashire friends who in point of information are much better qualified than myself to undertake his biography, and none of them, I presume, who cannot command more leisure for the purpose. My long illness, from which I can be only said to be recovering, has thrown upon me a weight of neglected business which every addition renders truly formidable.

"You will quite understand, therefore, that my wish is that you or some other friend of Goodier's in the neighbourhood of his native place should draw up the account for the *Mon. Repos.*, but that at the same time I will not refuse the work, if it be declined by those that are more conveniently circumstanced. Should it be imposed upon me, I must be supplied with all the documents that are judged necessary or useful by his family and friends.

"You can perhaps inform me whether the funds in the hands of his friends be sufficient to liquidate all the claims upon him, and to remunerate his kind attendants in France. If further help be wanting, I will cheerfully endeavour to raise something in this neighbourhood.

"Believe me, dear Sir, yours very truly,
ROBERT ASPLAND."

In consequence of Mr. Aspland's severe and protracted indisposition, the memoir in the Monthly Repository was written by Mrs. Middleton, the authoress of *The Widow* and other Christian Tracts.*

Thomas Walker Horsfield was the other pupil at the Academy whose useful but too short career claims a brief record in this Memoir. He was born at Sheffield, November 6, 1792. Of his early years it is only recorded that he was connected in business with Mr. James Montgomery, the poet, who entertained great regard for him, though he deplored his Unitarianism and his devoting himself to its ministry. He entered the Academy in 1814, where, according to the testimony of a friend who knew him well,† he " availed himself in the most creditable manner of the great advantages which he enjoyed at this time, especially of the highly valuable instructions of his Tutor, Mr. Aspland, in divinity and pulpit eloquence, of whom and of whose family he always spoke in terms of the warmest gratitude." At the conclusion of his academical course, he settled, in 1817, as minister of the Presbyterian congregation of Lewes. His services were continued here with ability and acceptance upwards of ten years. His Sunday-evening lectures, delivered in several successive winters, were remarkably attractive and useful. He found leisure for many public and some literary pursuits. Of the former kind may be mentioned the Mechanics' Institution,—said to be one of the best conducted in the kingdom,‡—which he established and assisted by delivering scientific lectures. His contributions to topographical literature *(The History and Antiquities of Lewes*, 2 vols. 4to, 1824; and *History and Antiquities of the County of Sussex*, 2 vols. 4to, 1835) procured for him a Fellowship from the Antiquarian Society. He had married soon after his settlement at Lewes, and to maintain an increasing family he added a boarding-school to his other labours.

He removed, in 1827, to Taunton, and again, in 1835, to Chowbent. Here his prospects of usefulness and comfort were such as to promise a satisfactory field for the exercise of all his matured powers; but in the summer of 1837, he was attacked by dangerous sickness, which in little more than a fortnight terminated his life. He expired August 26, in the forty-sixth year of his age. As a preacher he was vigorous

---

* In the year 1825, a much fuller Memoir was published by Miss Roscoe.

† The late Rev. Henry Acton. See Christian Reformer (8vo), V. 66.

‡ See Rev. W. James's Memoir of Rev. H. Acton, p. xvii, where it is stated that the Institution grew out of a small literary society, of which Mr. Acton was an early and zealous upholder.

and effective. The style of his compositions and his method of delivery sometimes reminded a hearer of those of his former Tutor in theology. During the latter years of his life, he devoted a portion of his leisure to landscape painting. He was possessed of considerable versatility of talent, but it was as a preacher and a writer that he chiefly excelled, and his early death was a serious loss to the Unitarian body.

CHAPTER XX.

In the last Chapter, with a view of bringing together the circumstances connected with the Unitarian Academy, some of the events of a series of years (1812—1818) have been alluded to; but it is necessary to return now to the earlier period, in order to notice some things worthy of recollection, both in Mr. Aspland's correspondence and publications.

In the year 1812, he preached, on a Sunday morning in November, a discourse on the Proofs of God's Providence in the State of Infancy and the slow Growth of the Human Being. Taking as his text Psalm viii. 2, he adopted the remark of Dr. Geddes, that the whole of the Psalm is "a strong and natural argument against the Atheist." Confining himself to the argument suggested by the text, he shewed that it is not an unmeaning truism that the infant state is the first state of all the human race; for hereon rests an irrefragable argument for the Supreme Providence. No difference can be greater than between the human being in infancy and the same being in maturity; yet every man was an infant, and every infant not arrested in its progress by death will grow up to manhood, there being folded up in the babe all the powers and faculties which in their full display and active exercise constitute the perfection of life. One instance of growth from infancy to maturity would be an object of ceaseless wonder, an inexhaustible study; but every adult human being has exhibited such an instance, and has been from his cradle upwards a witness, whether conscious or unconscious, willing or unwilling, of his Creator's matchless perfections.—Again, the *growth* of the human creature is a continued act of Providence. It implies that with the preservation of life, and happy life, there is a perpetual advancement and improvement of the powers both of body and mind,—an advancement and improvement which is at the same time gradual and imperceptible, universal and harmonious. A retarded or quickened, an irregular or disproportioned growth, occasions deformity and disease. When, therefore, we consider, on the one hand, of how many various parts, some of the most exquisite make and delicate operation, the human frame is composed, and, on the other, the comparatively small number of cases of habitual or permanent defect or irregularity or disorder in the body or mind of man, how can we possibly avoid the conclusion, that there is an unseen, all-wise Power which watches, guards, leads and perfects our nature?

On the discourse, of which this is a summary, remarks were made by some of the hearers, which came to the pastor's ear, to the effect that the argument was superfluous and untimely. Self-complacent critics of this kind, wiser than their teachers,* are to be found in most congregations. A few days after, Mr. Aspland received from an unknown correspondent the following gratifying letter:

To the Rev. Robert Aspland.

"London, November 24, 1812.

"Sir,—It is with pleasure I take the liberty of informing you, that the sermon you preached last Sunday morning has effectually removed every atheistical opinion which I have for years entertained, and which has harassed and perplexed my mind with feelings I am at a loss to describe. To you alone, dear Sir, am I indebted for this happy change of sentiment, and shall ever regard you as an honoured instrument under Divine Providence in having effected a revolution in my religious notions, and caused me to place a firm reliance upon the existence of a Deity, and a confident hope of participating in his mercy hereafter. Might I hope that you will one day commit your discourse *to the press*, in the sincere hope that it may have the same good effect upon others that I myself have derived from it?

"I am, dear Sir, most gratefully yours,

A. B."

He never learnt who his correspondent was; but at a later period of his ministry he had the satisfaction of rendering a similar service to an accidental hearer, who made himself personally known, and who continued for many years to express gratitude to him for having released him from the bondage of infidelity.

---

* Dr. Robert Robinson, in his Directions to Young Ministers, warns them that they will find some of their hearers " will not be content with judging for themselves only, but will take upon them to teach their ministers what they would have them to teach."—Appendix, p. 130.

Mrs. Cappe* to Rev. Robert Aspland.

"York, June 16, 1813.

"Dear Sir,—I have just received your letter, which could not fail of being extremely gratifying to me. It has assuredly been one of the first wishes of my heart† that Mr. Cappe's views of Christianity should excite attention,—in part, perhaps, because they were his, yet still more, if I do not deceive myself, because I believe them to be just, and consequently the only ones that can furnish an effectual answer to the objections of unbelievers, and produce entire conviction of the great truths of the gospel, on calm, enlightened and philosophic minds. You will see that Unitarianism, properly so called, forms but a part of these—an essential part, however, and of great importance to be established; yet I am convinced that many conscientious members of the Establishment (and among these are some of the most excellent persons I have ever known) do in reality worship one God alone, however confused may be their language, and absurd and contradictory their creeds. I thank you for sending the Dissertations to Dr. Cogan,‡ which I really consider as an

---

* Of this excellent woman it is scarcely necessary to say, that she was the daughter of the Rev. Jeremiah Harrison; that she was born at Long Preston, in Craven, June 3, 1744; that she married, in 1788, the Rev. Newcome Cappe, of York, whom she survived more than twenty-one years; and that she closed a most useful life at York, July 29, 1821, leaving behind her an interesting autobiography, which was published in 1822, under the title of "Memoirs of the Life of the late Mrs. Catherine Cappe."

† In the obituary of Mrs. Cappe in the Monthly Repository (XVI. 495), Mr. Kenrick, after speaking of her marriage to Mr. Cappe, says, "Her greatest delight in this new relation was to assist in preserving from oblivion a record of the knowledge and talents of her husband. To her the Christian world owes it that the eloquence of Mr. Cappe is not already become a faint echo in the ears of his few surviving auditors, and that the labours of his life in the investigation of the Scriptures do not remain locked up in an unintelligible short-hand. But the history of this portion of her life may be best learnt in the Memoir of Mr. Cappe prefixed to his Critical Dissertations, and since separately printed,—a beautiful specimen of truly Christian biography, to which we trust that few of our readers are strangers. With the same zeal and affection with which she had soothed and supported his decline, she endeavoured to do honour to his memory and promote the diffusion of his works. His fame was far dearer to her than her own: one of the highest gratifications she could receive was to know that his eloquent and powerful defence of the doctrine of Providence had enabled some mourner to exchange the spirit of heaviness for the garment of praise; that some heart, perhaps in a distant land, had been warmed with the love of religion by his animated praise of virtue and devotion; or that some seeker after Christian truth had found in his critical principles the solution of difficulties in the language of Scripture by which he had been long perplexed."

‡ This eminent philosophical writer was, during his residence at Clapton, an attendant at the Gravel-Pit. The writer well remembers a visit which, in company with his father, he paid to him at Clapton. His benevolent and noble

obligation, and with whose writings Mr. Cappe would have been delighted. I wish also that he should see the notes I have subjoined to my 'Life of Christ;' and as I have not the honour of being known to him, will you do me the favour to send him the copy which accompanies this letter, and of which I beg his acceptance?

"I am glad you approved the paper* I sent some weeks ago for the Monthly Repository; the sequel you will receive in this parcel. I feel very anxious to see the review of Mr. Belsham's Memoir of my late most excellent and invaluable friend—one of the first of human characters. Great as is its merit, invaluable the information it contains, and excellent as the temper with which in general it is written, there are a few expressions that pained me exceedingly, particularly what is said in page 201 of the 'peccability and moral imperfection' of our great Exemplar—a mode of expression not authorized, in my opinion, by any thing published either by Mr. Lindsey or even by Dr. Priestley. This I should not have noticed if it were not too common among Unitarians, in their zeal against Orthodoxy, to institute inquiries and make use of phraseology in itself extremely objectionable, unfavourable to the progress of truth, and of a tendency to lower the high veneration and affectionate attachment so justly due from Unitarians, as well as others, to the character of him who, to use his own highly figurative but emphatic language, was 'the Way, the Truth and the Life,' and whose relation to us is perfectly unique.

"I communicated your letter to Mr. Wellbeloved, who desires his compliments and gives you free liberty to put down his name, in addition to those of Mr. Turner, Dr. Carpenter, &c. You will rejoice to hear that the young men† who are to leave our institution this year are characters of the greatest promise in every respect, and indeed that the whole state of the College gives reason to hope that the indefatigable labours for many years of the excellent Theological Tutor, aided as he now is by such able coadjutors as Mr. W. Turner and Mr. Kenrick, will eventually prove a blessing to society at large. We lament the loss of Mr. Dewhurst, and shall rejoice to hear that you have the prospect of supplying his place, although it can hardly be hoped that it should be done completely. When you see Mr. Eaton, remember me kindly to him—to Mrs. Aspland also; and I am, dear Sir, your obliged friend,

CATH. CAPPE."

---

countenance and dignified manners were most impressive. He died at the house of his brother, the Rev. E. Cogan, of Walthamstow, Jan. 24, 1818, in the 82nd year of his age. The funeral address and sermon were delivered by Mr. Aspland, and from his pen was the Memoir of Dr. Cogan inserted in Vol. XIV. of the Monthly Repository.

* On Mr. Cappe's opinion respecting the miraculous birth of Christ, Mon. Repos., VIII. 37, 183.

† The students who left the College in 1813 were Messrs. Manley, Joseph Hutton, Henry Turner and George Kenrick.

At the close of the first session of the Unitarian Academy, in the summer of 1813, he made a series of visits into Lincolnshire, Norfolk, Worcestershire, Lancashire, Cheshire and Shropshire, preaching in each of these counties, and inviting the support of the congregations whom he addressed to the Unitarian Fund and Academy. It was in this journey that he first visited Mrs. Mary Hughes, whom he had long known as a writer and admired as a correspondent, and whose friendship he and the other members of his family assiduously cultivated during the remainder of her life.*

Mary Hughes, the youngest daughter of the Rev. Edward Hughes, Rector of Norbury, in the county of Stafford, was born in 1756. She had the misfortune to lose her father in infancy. Her mother, to whom she was most devotedly attached, was a woman of great Christian worth, imbued with warm devotional feelings and a strong sense of practical religion. From her excellent parent she early learnt to practise rigid self-denial, in order to extend the circle of her personal charities. During a considerable period of her life, her pecuniary means were limited; but she set apart one-fourth of her income to be expended in charity. When her income increased, she gave half of it in the same way, and afterwards a still larger proportion.† The family resided at Hanwood, a country village about four miles from Shrewsbury. With the aid of her second sister, she established, and for many years carried on with great success, a Sunday-school, to which the villagers' children of the neighbourhood of Hanwood resorted. The history of this benevolent undertaking is pleasantly told in her interesting story of "The Sunday Scholar."‡ Mary Hughes and her sisters were brought up as members of the Established Church, of which their father had been an exemplary minister. At Hanwood they enjoyed the society and friendship of the clergyman of the parish, the Rev. Edward Harries, who resided on his paternal estate at Ascott, about a mile from Hanwood. This gentleman's opinions and history exercised a very important influence on the religious opinions of Mrs.

---

* In token of this friendship, he named his youngest daughter, born 1814, after this excellent woman, *Mary Hughes*.

† See the interesting but too brief memoir by her neice, Mrs. Price, in Mon. Repos., XX. 114.

‡ The "Sunday Scholar" was a Mr. Edward Morris, who afterwards settled in Glasgow, where he filled a commercial situation and was much respected. In religion he was a Wesleyan Methodist, and occasionally did duty as a local preacher.

Hughes and her daughters. He had been brought up in the Highchurch principles of his family, and studied first at the Grammar-school at Shrewsbury, and afterwards at Magdalen College, Cambridge. Before he left the University, a great change was made in his political views by the perusal of Mr. Locke's "Letters on Government" and the "Independent Whig." On leaving Cambridge, he took orders, and was inducted into the livings of Cleobury Mortimer as well as Hanwood, both in Shropshire. The secession of Theophilus Lindsey, in 1773, from the Church, and his resignation of the vicarage of Catterick in consequence of his adoption of Unitarian opinions, made a deep impression on the mind of Mr. Harries, and induced him to review the grounds of his religious system. The result was his conviction that the doctrine of the Trinity was not contained in the Bible. He did not at once withdraw from the Established Church, but satisfied his conscience by omitting in his use of the Book of Common Prayer all that now appeared objectionable to him. His parishioners were not disposed to find fault with the liberties he took with the Liturgy, and as he did not openly teach Unitarianism, many of them were probably unaware of the great change which had taken place in the opinions of their pastor. The church was never better attended than during the services of this heterodox minister. The Hugheses were induced to examine the new religious opinions of their friendly pastor with great care, and the consequence was that they were led to adopt them with a full conviction of their truth. Mary Hughes, then about eighteen years of age, was absent from home during the whole time that this important change was going on. On her return, she was not only surprised, but grieved and shocked, at the new and strange opinions adopted by her mother and sisters. Like them, she too entered on a course of inquiry into the scriptural evidence of the doctrines which she had hitherto undoubtingly held as "orthodox," and with a similar result. She embraced the doctrine of the Divine Unity with ardour, and during a not short life made it her untiring aim to promote it amongst others.

Fortunately for his peace of mind and religious consistency, Mr. Harries was soon rescued, by a letter of remonstrance from his Bishop, from a situation so perilous to religious integrity as the clerical office in a Trinitarian Church must ever be to a Unitarian. He had previously resigned the living at Cleobury; he now parted with the advowson of Hanwood. Previously to his retirement from the Church, he explained to his parishioners what his new opinions were. He afterwards kept up a religious service on Unitarian principles at his own house, which was attended by several of his neighbours, and amongst them by the family of Mrs. Hughes. Preaching in the High-Street chapel, Shrewsbury, a few months before his death, he said, "There have been many excellent books written by great and good men, with the best design, to reduce Christianity to the belief and worship of the One True God; but the plainest book on this subject is the New Testament." He bore to the last a consistent religious profession, and during his last illness he exhibited the consolatory and elevating tendency of his religious views. He died February 1, 1812, and the virtues of his exemplary life were recorded in a brief but faithful Memoir by Mary Hughes, than whom no one had been more deeply and beneficially influenced by his opinion and example.

The formation of the Christian Tract Society was the occasion both of her becoming an authoress and of her forming an acquaintance with its Secretary, so soon to ripen into friendship. Mrs. Hughes was upwards of fifty years of age when she composed "William's Return," the first of the long series of tracts with which she enriched the early volumes of the Society's publications.* Its instant success chiefly delighted her because it opened to her an untrodden walk of useful benevolence. From that time, composition was one of her greatest pleasures, and beguiled many hours of weariness and suffering. The judgment which Mr. Aspland formed of her tracts has been confirmed by that of thousands of readers, in both England and America. They are "as profitable to the instructor of the poor as to the poor themselves; they display an intimate acquaintance with the human heart, and a peculiar knowledge of the wants and feelings of persons in humble life."

The following letter is valuable from the biographical particulars which it contains, and is a fair specimen of the writer's head and heart.

---

* Their titles are, 1. "William's Return, or Good News for Cottagers." 2. "The Twin Brothers, or Good Luck and Good Conduct." 3. "Henry Goodwin, or the Contented Man." 4. "An Affectionate Address to the Poor." 5. "Friendly Advice to the Unlearned." 6. "The Sick Man's Friend." 7—12. "Village Dialogues," Parts I.—VI. 13. "Advice to Female Servants." 14. "A True Friend, or the Two Nurse-maids." 15. "Sick-Room Dialogues." 16. "The Sunday Scholar." 17. "The Good Grandmother." 18, 19. "Family Dialogues, or the Sunday Well-spent," Parts I. and II. 20. "Address to Sunday-school Teachers."

Mrs. Mary Hughes to Rev. Robert Aspland.

"Hanwood, January 23, 1812.

"Dear Sir,—I know not how sufficiently to thank you for the many kind and flattering expressions of regard contained in your last letter. Your approbation of what I have done to advance the benevolent views of the Society has continually incited me to proceed; and if the simple productions of my pen, which have multiplied under your fostering hand, have improved or instructed any, it is to you the obligation should be acknowledged. Had I been fortunate enough to possess such a friend earlier in life, I might have hoped to attain a higher degree of usefulness; but I am most thankful to be able to contribute something towards the furtherance of the best and noblest of all causes.

"My father and only brother were ministers of the Established Church; but my mother, who had the most sensible and candid of all minds, together with my two elder sisters and myself, were convinced how absurd and unscriptural her doctrines were, by 'Lindsey's Apology' and a few other books which were put into our hands by our much-esteemed friend and neighbour, Mr. Harries, of whose secession from the Church, many years ago, you have probably heard. From that time we have attended him on Sundays at his own house, or that of another of our neighbours who held the same opinions; but our little congregation never increased. Mr. Harries studiously avoiding all doctrinal subjects, the few who occasionally dropped in, had no chance of having their prejudices in any degree shaken. Thus I have lived the greater part of my life without having any opportunities of conversing with zealous and well-informed persons who thought as I did. Indeed, I never had the least knowledge of one of that description, except Mr. Rowe, the present minister of the chapel in Lewin's Mead, Bristol, whom during his residence in Shrewsbury I saw now and then, but in such circles as prevented my gaining any thing from him. It is, however, to him that I owe the pleasure I now feel in addressing you; for nearly five years ago, when he made a short visit in this neighbourhood, he mentioned the Monthly Repository, which we had before never heard of; and that most interesting work opened the Unitarian world to my view, and has ever since been such a source of pleasure and instruction to me, that I have only pictured my own feelings in describing those of Henry Goodwin with respect to it.

"You see, dear Sir, how much I presume upon your friendship, by my venturing to say so much of myself. I need not say how much I rejoice to be assured of your recovered health, or how much I thank you for your kind wishes respecting my own. I have long been an invalid, and had last year a long fit of illness, but am at present better than I had been for many months previous to its commencement, except that it has left a weakness and a degree of inflammation in my eyes, which I regret chiefly as a check upon my favourite avocations of reading and writing, making the little I could otherwise do still less.

"I lament, with you, the coldness and worldly-mindedness of many rational believers, a stronger proof of which could not be given than a diminution in the sale of the Repository. To view our Maker as he is, all goodness and benevolence, does not seem to excite a degree of love and gratitude sufficient to animate them to exertion; the base principle of fear appears to have a more powerful influence on the generality of people than the brightest and most glorious hopes and expectations. 'This,' Hannah More would triumphantly say, 'clearly proves the deep corruption of our nature.' But we shall not be forward to join her in throwing our crimes and follies on our first frail progenitor, or rather in believing that an infinitely *just God* formed a weak, fallible creature, and to punish his transgression caused all his successors of the human race to be born with hearts 'desperately wicked' and inclined to evil continually. You will guess that I have been reading 'Practical Piety,' a work which, though much that is good is taught in the course of it, as far as I have gone, leaves a gloomy, disagreeable impression upon my mind, unfavourable to a *love* of our Creator, or a *cheerful* performance of the duties he requires from us.

"I received a letter a few weeks ago from an entire stranger, dated Cradley, near Stourbridge, who, after expressing much approbation of my small publications, tells me that she lives in a very populous neighbourhood, that the people are both depraved and ignorant in an uncommon degree, and that in her frequent visits to their sick rooms she feels herself much in want of a proper book, as they often request her to read to them. This deficiency she thinks I can supply; and though I have little hope of succeeding, I have promised to make the attempt. Such a work, well executed, would certainly be very useful, but I do not feel at all equal to the undertaking. I fear I cannot write with sufficient force and plainness to reach the hearts of such a description of people. When I have made a trial, I shall turn with pleasure to the subject you propose, which may perhaps be introduced in a work on the proper observance of the Lord's-day, which is a matter of high importance to all, but little considered with respect to themselves by the higher classes. With this, Mr. Rees will receive another short essay, which I have been encouraged to write by the favourable reception of the first. It is like the first, but I fear hardly so good. The kind partiality which you express for what I write, gives me an additional motive for wishing them more worthy of your approbation: but have the goodness to remember that I shall feel highly obliged by your pointing out any faults.

"I think you have already published a small work similar to the one which you now mention having in hand, and I hope to have the pleasure of reading it soon after you receive this. Nothing can be more desirable than publications of that kind; for the best hope we can entertain for the reformation of mankind must arise from a more careful and enlightened attention to their early impressions.

"I am very particularly gratified by Mrs. Aspland's kind notice and approbation; be pleased to present my best thanks and affectionate regards to her. My sisters and Mrs. Price beg to unite in the same to you, with, dear Sir, your much obliged friend, M. HUGHES.

"I enclose a five-pound note,—one guinea as an annual subscription from Mrs. Warten, of Cruch Mede, near Shrewsbury, and three guineas as the commencement of an annual subscription from my eldest sister, Mrs. Hughes, both for the Unitarian Fund. You will have the goodness to acknowledge both in the Repository; and the remaining sixteen shillings will remain with you till I send something for the new Academy, for the commencement of which I look with some impatience.

"You will be so good as to add my sister's name to the list as an annual subscriber of two guineas, and mine for a donation of ten; and both will be ready when called for.

"I will take an early opportunity of sending the packet to Mr. Case. He is a most worthy and amiable man, but has not always exerted his talents as he might have done. He thinks nothing less than a *miracle* could animate his congregation, or fill the empty seats in his chapel."

It was with no common pleasure that Mr. Aspland, in the year following the date of this letter, visited his amiable correspondent. All his expectations were fulfilled.* Though she was feeble in health, her conversation evinced a vigorous mind and zeal in behalf of pure Christianity, not less ardent than his own. He was deeply struck with her disinterested benevolence. Although gifted with talents that rendered her society attractive to the most intelligent, she appeared to think she was never so worthily employed as when, by the efforts of her pen or by familiar conversation, she was imparting knowledge to children, or to those who had arrived at mature years without the blessings of education.

Some extracts from two letters written shortly after his first visit to Hanwood, will best shew the exhilarating effect on his mind of the society of the amiable circle.

Rev. R. Aspland to Mrs. Aspland.

"Chester, Sept. 13, 1813.

"My dearest Sara,—To-day you are to write to me; and though I should

---

* See Christian Reformer (First Series), Vol. XI. p. 36.

like to have your letter before I give you one, yet I cannot any longer delay the delightful task of assuring you that I am well, and as happy as I can be away from you and the dear little ones. I am with friend Lyons.

"My journey to Evesham was as pleasant as such a journey could be, and left me so little fatigued that I kept up and awake all the Tuesday, walked about the town, dined and supped in parties, preached with sufficient animation to a large congregation, and did not go to bed till near midnight. I was entertained very hospitably at the house of Mr. New.

"Next morning, Wednesday, I was up by half-past three, and off at four in a chaise for Worcester, where I arrived in time for the Shrewsbury coach. I rode to Kidderminster outside, but was there driven inside by the rain. My companions were a clergyman, his wife and niece; the husband a meek, religious, benevolent man,—the wife, travelled, accomplished, spirited, shrewd, and generally very reasonable,—the niece, mild, good and communicative. From my conversation, they concluded me to be a young priest of their own sect, and treated me with marked kindness, which subdued me so, that I did not open myself upon them when they praised the present ministry and lifted up their hands at the *horrid Socinians*. The coach reached Salop so late, that I judged it best not to go on to Hanwood that night; and so took up my rest, in the company of my pleasing coach party, at a comfortable inn.

"I walked on Thursday morning, before breakfast, to the village of our *correspondents;* the distance four miles, the walk most interesting, the Welsh mountains directly in front. Is it one of my peculiarities that I took heavy and reluctant steps to Hanwood? I was really embarrassed in prospect of the interview, fearing that on both sides there might not be the personal liking that both must desire. However, on I went, and passed along a very small rural village, to a neat laurel-encircled house, beside a little church with a rustic appearance, and a churchyard crowded with ancient yew-trees. The face of the servant who opened the door, and her quick step after I had been put into a parlour opening upon a garden, with a pretty wood rising behind it, sufficiently indicated that I was not an unexpected or an unwelcome visitor. Presently came in a lady who, with a face suffused with a deep blush, told me she was my correspondent; with her was a little one, Mary Ann, whose instantly apparent fondness broke the awkwardness of the interview. After a short interval, Mrs. Isabel Hughes, the eldest sister and mistress of the house, appeared; after another, Mrs. Price; and lastly, her mother, the grandmother. Breakfast was prepared for me, theirs being over; and a quiet, cool, respectfully tender conversation commenced. I was not, or fancied I was not, quite well. I could not talk with spirit. A walk to two beautiful spots close by roused me a little, and brought us nearer together. Our familiarity increased at a neat, orderly, frugal, but hospitable and cheerful dinner-table; but I sunk completely in the tea-parlour, and the fear of being dull made me stupid. Supper, however, and a *pipe* brought me about, and now we began to know each other, and the time passed away delightfully unheeded till one o'clock in the morning, when we separated after a short prayer, or rather thanksgiving, to our Almighty Friend who had brought us together. I slept, as I told my happy knot of friends, *in the lap of peace.* Conversation was renewed with our meeting at the breakfast-table, and was running on pleasantly, till, alas! I was snatched away by a letter from Mr. Lyons, whom I was to meet by appointment in a few hours at a distance of thirty miles! I must resume this subject in two or three days, for I am summoned to dinner, and at Chester dinner is a serious thing.

"I met Mr. Lyons in Wales on Friday night, and arrived at Chester on Saturday morning. I preached twice yesterday, when a collection was made for the Fund. To-morrow we start again for Wales. My return will be gladdened by the expectation of your letter.

"Farewell, my very dear wife; make my love to Sara and Brook and the rest, and assure Anna of my warm affection. I am, Sara, your

ROBERT."

"Friday, Sept. 17, 1813.

"My dear Sara,—I am just returned from our Welsh excursion, and have been refreshed by your welcome letter. Thanks to a good Providence that you are all well, and that all is comfortable at Hackney! My letter met yours on the road, and I am pleased to reflect that for once I have been better than I promised, and have given you an agreeable surprise. I have you now a little in my debt, and I am so happy under the new character of your creditor in an epistolary account, that I am using my pen on a large sheet with a view to the post to-morrow: to-day it is not open.

"You want portraits of the Hanwood group. Alas! you know I am no painter: I cannot distinguish colours, nor have I a recollection of faces: but I will describe the happy circle as well as I can.

"*Mary Hughes* is rather a small woman, not handsome nor elegant, but of a soft and expressive physiognomy: *I think* of a fair complexion and light hair. Her eye I call to mind with pleasure: the tones of her voice are plaintive. She may be about the size of my mother: as I guess, she is about forty-eight years of age. Her conversation is exactly in the style of her writing—even, sensible, pleasant and benevolent.

"*Mrs. Hughes (Isabel)* is a large woman, with a strong-featured face, once I suppose handsome, a gentlewoman in her manners, but plain, *bordering on* bluntness, frank, and evidently kind-hearted, and giving indications of very strong sense. She is the mistress of the house—feels herself such—and is so treated by the family; though there is no appearance on her part of conscious superiority in conversation, but the contrary. She and the others take pleasure in Mary's reputation.

"*Mrs. A. Hughes* (the mother and grandmother) reminded me of Mrs. Wakefield, in her person (though somewhat larger) and manners. She is a widow. I should think she has more spirit than either of her sisters: at first reserved, she soon grows animated in conversation, and she fully keeps up the character of the family for sense.

"They fully intend, i. e. Mrs. H. and Mrs. Mary, to visit us in the spring, and they are most positive that you shall spend some of the next summer at Hanwood, with Sara or another or others of your children.

"I found the family quite eager about our A——, and I wish she would write, and that you would adopt a plan of regular correspondence.

"When I arrived here, I was so filled with the remembrance of Hanwood, and so grieved at having been hurried away from them, that I wrote a sort of *love* letter to Mrs. Mary, inviting a letter to me on my journey, and intimating a wish and almost a hope that I might be able to take Shrewsbury on my way home. This, however, I cannot do without being out a fourth Sunday, which I dare not contemplate. I should have great pleasure in repeating my visit to the *Holy Family*, and might do some good; but the good and the pleasure might be bought too dear. What think you?

"Near Hanwood is Ascott, where lives in genteel style Mrs. Harries, the widow of the late Unitarian seceding clergyman, whom I met, and who gives us a pressing invitation to the neighbourhood.

"The three last pages are written this morning (Saturday), just before my departure for Liverpool. Love to the children and Anna, from your ever affectionate, ROBERT."

At Liverpool he was the guest of Mr. and Mrs. Freme, and under their ever hospitable roof he was prostrated by a severe inflammatory attack, which for a few hours endangered his life; but through prompt and skilful medical treatment, seconded by the kindest and tenderest nursing on the part of his hostess, he was restored in a few days sufficiently to travel home, but was compelled to forego some public engagements in Manchester and its neighbourhood.

Rev. Robert Aspland to Mr. Isaac Aspland.
"Hackney Road, Oct. 30, 1813.

"Dear Isaac,—I have the pleasure to state that my health is improved and improving. I had a very sharp attack at Liverpool. With two physicians and a surgeon about me at one time, and that time one o'clock in the morning, I thought myself in some danger. My complaint was an obstruction in the bowels; however, by the blessing of God, I got speedy relief, and, though bleeding and a course of medicine and low living much reduced me, I have, I trust, been mending ever since my return.

"My engagements are rather more numerous than they should be for my health and comfort; but my friend Mr. Joyce has kindly stepped in to my assistance in the Academy, in which I have now four pupils, three for the ministry.

"This day nine years, Isaac, we saw our dear father a corpse. How swiftly have the seasons run round! In nine years more, which will pass as quickly as the last, we may be as he is. It is certain that we shall go to him, though he will not return to us. Happy are we, if we can persuade ourselves of a resurrection to life, and of a re-union with our dear father, and with all wise and good men, in a purer and better world. Were I at Wicken at this time, I should visit the revered grave, and renew my love of his character and my hope of partaking of that reward which I am confident he will receive from our Heavenly Father.

"Make my love to my mother. This is a dark season of the year for her; but you will, I doubt not, by your kindness, make her feel as little as possible the loss of him whom we are not again to see in the flesh.

"I had a faint expectation of seeing your son here; I would have done my duty to him, and have endeavoured to make him happy if you had entrusted him to my care.

"I am able to write letters to-day (Saturday), having the promise of assistance to-morrow from my good friend Madge, of Norwich, who is now on a visit to me. Goodier, the only one of the students whom you know, is this morning gone down to Reading, where I am to be, opening the new chapel, on the 24th of next month. Tell my mother, Cooper, the other student, whom she knows, is going on admirably. I believe I told her that Hancock stays at home through illness. Yours truly,

ROBERT ASPLAND."

The establishment in Hackney of an Auxiliary Bible Society in the year 1812, and the angry controversy to which it led between certain members of the Established Church, were the occasion in the following year of calling Mr. Aspland into conflict with one of the clergymen of the parish.

The design of incorporating the parish in an auxiliary district of the Bible Society was promulgated by some lay members of the Church, but at once opposed by the Vicar, Dr. Watson, and by the Curate of St. John's Chapel, the Rev. H. H. Norris, M.A., on the grounds usually taken by clergymen of High-church principles, viz., that the object of the Bible Society is better provided for by the Society for Promoting Christian Knowledge, which with the Bible distributes the Book of Common Prayer, and that union with Dissenters is inexpedient, and calculated to " produce strife, animosity and dismemberment of the

Church."* At a meeting of the vestry, held Nov. 26, 1812, the course taken by the clergy was approved, and the meeting unanimously agreed to this, amongst other resolutions—"*That an indiscriminate distribution of the Bible has a tendency to lessen the reverence due to that Sacred Volume.*" This singular resolution, and the un-protestant spirit in which the resistance to the Bible Society was carried on, gave occasion to an ingenious *pasquinade*, professing to be "The Address of Patrick O'Flanagan to the Clergy, Gentlemen of the Vestry, and other Opposers (if other there be) of the Hackney Auxiliary Bible Society." The writer† in this amusing satire assumes the style of a Catholic priest, and hails the clergy and vestry of St. John's, Hackney, as coadjutors. The Address was eagerly sought and read by all classes of persons in the parish; and when Mr. Norris collected and published all the documents of this parish controversy, this was included as one of several "Socinian contributions to the cause of the Bible Society." It was preceded by about forty pages of preliminary observations, in which Mr. Norris indulges in a series of bitter remarks on the Im-

---

* Mr. Norris's first letter to Mr. Freshfield, "Practical Exposition," &c., p. 4.

† The authorship of the "Address" was by general consent given to Mr. Aspland, but was not acknowledged by him. One or two brief extracts from it will enable the judicious reader to judge whether the style indicates the author:— "Your position is as much common sense as it is piety. * * * Diminish the circulation of the Bible, and you will increase its value in public estimation. Lodge the treasure in the hands of the priest, who, more properly than the magistrate, is the *custos utriusque tabulæ*, which, by a free translation, I render, *the preserver* (and a preserver is not a *distributor*) *of the sacred records*. Or, at most, imitate your forefathers, and allow only a *parish Bible*, to be chained to the altar and consulted on holidays alone, and then in the presence of the curates or keepers of souls, who shall see that the common people carry away nothing that would be pernicious. Ogh! that the Bible should ever become (as the proposers of the new institution would make it) *cheap*. * * * Perhaps, however, very dear brethren, it may not be possible to prevent at once the circulation of the book *so hard to be understood* and so easily *wrested* to mischief; in that case take counsel of your own resolution (2nd of Set II.); let none have it but such as 'upon due inquiry shall be found likely to make a right use of such a gift.' By this means, you will keep it out of the hands of Anabaptists, and all the sects of the New Light; regular church-goers alone will obtain it, and from them no abuse of it is to be apprehended, 1st, because it is the fundamental article of their faith to believe only what the Church believes; and 2ndly, because there cannot be much abuse where there is little use. One charge you must lay upon such as you select for the reception of Bibles, and that is, never to put them into the hands of their children till they have got by heart and understood the Catechism and the Three Creeds. *Understand* all these they never will, and thus, my dear brethren, you are safe." Patrick O'Flanagan dates his address from *Bonner's Hall*.

proved Version,—the religious conferences at the Gravel-Pit,—the eccentric Unitarian advertisements of the late Mr. Clarke, of Swakely House,—the Rev. William Turner's Secretaryship of the Newcastle Bible Society,—on the conciliatory demeanour towards Socinians fostered by the Bible Society,—on the sympathy of Socinians with Mahometans, and the resemblance of the Koran and the Improved Version. Mr. Norris entitled his volume, "A Practical Exposition of the Tendency and Proceedings of the British and Foreign Bible Society; begun in a Correspondence between the Rev. H. H. Norris and J. W. Freshfield, Esq., relative to the Formation of an Auxiliary Bible Society at Hackney, and completed in an Appendix containing an entire Series of the Public Documents and Private Papers which that Measure occasioned, illustrated with Notes and Observations. Edited by the Rev. H. H. Norris, M.A., Curate of St. John's Chapel, Hackney, and Chaplain to the Earl of Shaftesbury." London, Rivington. Pp. 440. It was dedicated to Dr. Howley, the Bishop (elect) of London.

There was but little in this volume that required reply. It was characterized throughout by abundant railings and deficient reasonings, by a loose style, by the want of a definite object,* and by the absence of all perceptible arrangement. Only a small portion of its censures of the Unitarians was original. The more biting invectives were borrowed from Leslie, Whitaker and Nares. The mere confutation of such an opponent promised little glory. But there were, on the other hand, reasons sufficiently strong which induced Mr. Aspland to enter the field against the assailant of his religious denomination. The private character of Mr. Norris was held throughout the parish in deserved honour, and gave some weight to his opinions. The controversy had attracted great attention both from Dissenters and Churchmen, and the occasion was a favourable one for dissipating some prevalent misconceptions respecting Unitarianism, and for exposing the deformity of bigotry. He accordingly prepared a reply,† which was published under the title of "A Plea for Unitarian Dissenters, in a Letter of

---

* Justly enough did Mr. Freshfield complain to his reverend opponent: "When I consider the matter of your Letter, I find it like an ignis fatuus, constantly leading in directions not tending to the object; and if I stop where it most usually rests, I shall find myself engaged about forms and shadows, and neglecting the substance."—Letter VI.

† The "Plea" was composed and printed in less than a month, notwithstanding the author's distracting cares of the Academy, the pulpit, the Monthly Repository, and general public business.

Expostulation to the Rev. H. H. Norris, M. A., on that Part of his late Work against the Hackney Auxiliary Bible Society which relates to Unitarians." 8vo. Pp. 139.

To estimate the whole merits of this work, the reader must make himself acquainted with that to which it is a reply. A straggling, confused and desultory assault may be harmless to those attacked; but every one accustomed to literary exercises knows that to reply to such an attack effectively, and to make the defence interesting to others than those whom the local controversy concerns, is a very difficult task. That Mr. Aspland succeeded in overcoming the difficulty, is proved by the fact, that two large editions of his " Letter of Expostulation" were called for by the public, and that three different portions of it were subsequently reprinted as popular Unitarian tracts.* The tone of the Letter is, considering the provocation, sufficiently courteous; justice is done to Mr. Norris's character, and the sincerity and disinterestedness of his conduct in the controversy respecting the Bible Society fully admitted; at the same time, his " unhappy spirit" is exposed, his numerous mistakes are corrected, and the folly of some of his charges against Unitarians is proved. But the charm and lasting value of the " Plea" consist in its numerous illustrations drawn from English ecclesiastical history and literature, and the admirably selected passages from the writings of some of the best authors and preachers of the Church of England. Mr. Aspland confined his expostulation to Mr. Norris's remarks on Unitarians, leaving the defence of the Bible Society to other writers. He thought it undesirable to take the subject out of the hands of " orthodox" Protestants, able and willing to rebuke the Popish tendency of some of their own ecclesiastics; and in the infancy of the Bible Society he held it to be inexpedient, knowing the strength of religious prejudice, that Unitarians should needlessly put themselves in the front rank of the supporters of the Society.

One or two short extracts will sufficiently illustrate the spirit of the " Plea." The first is a passage of rebuke:

" You, however, reckon it amongst the sins of the Bible Society, that it promotes a ' conciliating demeanour towards Socinians'! Whither, Sir, would you carry us back? What age of darkness and bigotry would you recal? I

---

* 1. On the terms Unitarian and Socinian (pp. 64—73). 2. Reasons for Distrusting the Genuineness of the Socinian Epistle to Ameth Ben Ameth, Ambassador from the Emperor of Morocco to Charles II. (pp. 97—103). 3. The Unitarian's Creed (pp. 124—131).

seem, in reading your book, to be transported to the times of Parker and South and Laud: I almost suspect that the *principle* of persecution is not so abhorrent to your mind as the practice of persecution would be to your heart: I say, involuntarily, 'This writer is one born out of due time;'—he and his age do not agree; his language is adapted to other ears, his maxims to other times than ours. With what books can he have conversed? Our Milton, our Chillingworth, our Locke, our Jeremy Taylors, our Hales', our Tillotsons, our Jortins, our Paleys,—have they all lived in vain for him? Can an individual remain stationary, while the world is moving on to improvement? Can the sacred flame of Christian charity beam full upon his face from a thousand works, splendid both in argument and eloquence, and strike no warmth to his soul? Is he, is one man in the kingdom, not aware, by happy consciousness, that the age of uncharitableness is over? Would not he, who, at a time like this, when every man is making a tender of his charity to his neighbour, hangs upon the memory of penal statutes with a sort of fond regret, have been in danger of *smiting with the fist of wickedness*, if the legislature had not mercifully, to him as well as his neighbours, tied up his hands?

"These reflections, Sir, you have forced upon me, though I do again willingly acquit you of an injurious design; for it is the character of such as are *calling down fire from heaven, to consume,* but not to cheer, *not to know what manner of spirit they are of."*—Pp. 37—42.

The other extract is the closing passage of the "Plea:"

"A controversy on the points of faith in which we differ, conducted with good temper, and in a becoming manner, might be useful to us both; for we have each of us, I dare to say, some persuasions to lay down, and others to take up, before we become 'perfect men in Christ Jesus.' In such a controversy, however, you would have an obvious advantage over me: should you make me a convert to your Church, I should lose my present right and title, and should be very unlikely, at my age, to acquire a right and title of any other description, to the Christian ministry;—but should I happily convince you of the truth of the Unitarian doctrine and of the duty of Unitarian worship, you will have only to step from one church into another; the congregation at the Gravel-Pit will welcome you into their communion, glad to shew you that they are not irreligious, immoral, violent, or very different from their fellow-christians; and your honest conviction and ingenuous profession will give you Holy Orders in all the Unitarian churches in the empire."—P. 133.

Mr. Norris made no reply to the "Letter of Expostulation." From many friends, amongst them Dr. Parr, did Mr. Aspland receive letters expressing approbation of his work. By none was he more gratified than by the letter which follows, from one who in experience and skill then surpassed all writers on the Unitarian controversy.

Rev. Thomas Belsham to Rev. Robert Aspland.

"Essex Street, Nov. 28, 1813.

"My dear Sir,—I thank you for the copy of your Letter to Norris: you have handled him as he deserves; and, without departing from the character of a gentleman, you have given him some severe thrusts. If it is possible, he will be ashamed of himself: at any rate, his party will be ashamed of him. The passages which you cite from Tillotson, Watson, &c., will teach him, or at least others, to qualify the bitterness of their language when speaking of the Unitarians. You have admirably and unanswerably exposed Leslie's character, and have completely put down the foolish story of Ameth Ben Ameth.

"I think you have borne a little hard upon Dr. Enfield, Dr. Priestley, and others of that standing, who, labouring under all manner of abuse from their orthodox opponents, took to themselves the name of rational Christians, or rational Dissenters,* as a counterbalance to that of Orthodox, Evangelical, &c., assumed by their opponents. Indeed, I never quarrel with any party for giving themselves a good name, as they are sure to be sufficiently plied by their adversaries with epithets of evil repute. Have you a sufficient voucher for the Prince of Orange refusing an Oxford degree from a principle of conscience?† Dr. Powell, who is an Oxford man, told me he would not sign the Articles at matriculation. If he is to be the husband to our future Queen, we may well say *Orange boven*.

"I am sorry to hear you were so ill as not to be able to preach to-day. I

---

* The passage objected to by Mr. Belsham is at p. 94 of the "Plea," note: "At present, the Unitarians are, as they have long been, the *heterodox*; but they have sometimes appeared to wish to recommend themselves as *orthodox*, under the designation of *rational Christians*, as assuming and invidious a phrase as ever a party decked itself withal. When and where it was fabricated I know not; it is of more consequence to state that it is nearly fallen into disuse. In its behalf it has been pleaded that it is meant only to distinguish such as allow from such as deny the use of *reason* in religion. But this is not its proper import, nor would it ever be taken generally in this sense: besides that the interpretation assumes a false position, no Christians are wholly against the use of reason in religion, they are simply for defining the boundaries of reason; at least, they do not reduce their supposed principle to practice, for, with an amusing inconsistency, they reason against reason, and argue against argument. Whether a sect be *rational*, is the same question as whether it be *orthodox*, or *right*, or *sound*; and, for my part, I have never heard the phrase *rational Christians* used, without thinking of the concluding line of Milton's sonnet, 'On the new Forcers of Conscience under the Long Parliament,' from which I take my motto,

'New Presbyter is but Old Priest writ large.'"

† "The Prince" (of Orange, a suitor, favoured by the Prince Regent, for the hand of the Princess Charlotte) "is said to have refused to subscribe the Thirty-nine Articles for the Doctor's degree, leaving the University in possession of its honour, and content with carrying away his conscience inviolate."—Plea, p. 132, note.

fear you do not take sufficient care of yourself. I was happy to learn from Mr. Vines that every thing passed off so well at Reading, notwithstanding Mr. Vidler's indisposition. I hope that interest will be permanent and prosperous.

"I am much shocked to hear of the death of my old friend Palmer:* we were fellow-townsmen, and have been intimate for more than half a century. When I saw him last he was remarkably well. He had his failings; but in morals and consistency of character I look upon him as far superior to one whose praises have lately been so much blazoned abroad, and who, had he died ten years sooner, would perhaps have deserved all that his most partial friends are now inclined to bestow. I cannot expect to continue long after the friend of my youth; and I rejoice to see that the good cause is going on with increasing speed, and that a succession of able advocates are rising up for the defence of Christian Truth, and to fill up the places of those who will in a short time be dismissed from their labours. That you, my dear Sir, may long be spared as a burning and a shining light to the Unitarian churches, is the earnest wish and prayer of your affectionate friend and servant,

T. BELSHAM.

"My best compliments attend Mrs. Aspland."

---

* The Rev. Samuel Palmer, the venerable pastor of the Independent congregation at Hackney, and the editor of the Nonconformists' Memorial, died on the morning of the day on which this letter is dated. Mr. Palmer was born at Bedford; but was Mr. Belsham's senior by nine years. On the Sunday previous to his death, he had celebrated the fiftieth anniversary of his ministry at Hackney.

CHAPTER XXI.

Soon after the publication of the "Plea for Unitarian Dissenters," Mr. Aspland committed to the press "Three Sermons," two of which he had recently preached before several public societies. The subjects of these discourses were—I. The Unitarian Christian's Appeal to his Fellow-christians on the Christian Name. II. The Apostles' Creed concerning the One God and the Man Christ Jesus. III. The inseparable Connection between the Unity and the Benevolence of God. It would be wrong to conclude, from the controversial strain of a large portion of his occasional sermons, that he was indifferent to "the common faith of Christendom." The application of Christianity to the practical purposes of life formed the staple of his pulpit addresses. On suitable occasions, such as public lectures and the meetings of religious societies, he felt it to be a solemn duty to vindicate Christianity from corruption and abuse, believing as he did that while error existed in the world, controversy was the only means left of preserving or reviving truth. In the language of Dr. Disney,* he reminded those well-meaning and candid persons who, having themselves attained to pure Christianity, dislike and discountenance controversy, that their aversion "is no other than their declaring their earnest desire to establish the *end*, while at the same time they inconsistently and peremptorily protest against the only *means* which can effect it."

Like the "Plea," the Sermons are illustrated by notes containing choice passages from some of the best English divines. The little volume found acceptance with the public, and when a second edition was called for, the author prefixed a reprint of a Sermon on Religious

---

* See Memoirs of Dr. Sykes, p. 364.

Liberty, which had been originally preached by him before the Western Unitarian Society in 1812.

When the Sermon on the Christian Name was first addressed to his own congregation, the appeal with which it concludes, urging Unitarian Christians to honour their profession by activity and zeal, was illustrated by the following narrative, which is valuable as a proof that the goodness of God, earnestly preached, will sometimes melt to repentance hearts that would be proof against the terrors of the Lord.

"I was yesterday called to attend the death-bed of an utter stranger, who wished to make a confession before he quitted the world, and I should leave off assured that this discourse had answered its end if I could convey to you the impression which the scene has made upon my own mind. The dying penitent had to confess no great crime, no habitual vice (God grant that in this respect your death-beds may be as easy as his!) but he wished to unburthen his mind of a painful sense of *religious negligence*. For years, he said, he had known the truth, but had lived as if he had never known it; serving Mammon more than God, and doing nothing for the promotion of that great cause for which Jesus laid down his life. He wished me to make use of his experience to warn the thoughtless, inactive professors of *pure and undefiled religion*, that there is no peace at the last but in the consciousness of having *kept the faith, fought the good fight and finished a good course*. Yet he acknowledged the unspeakable goodness of his heavenly Father, that he should now find comfort in those views of truth which he had so long slighted. The last time he mixed with his fellow-christians was in this place, a few Sundays ago, when he heard a sermon, designed to shew that all divine punishment in this world and the next is corrective and purifying; the subject touched his heart: he could have left the world unconcerned, if the goodness of God had not been set before him: but before this he melted into repentance, gratitude and love. He expressed to me his pleasure in the prospect of *the rest which remaineth* for him in the grave; he had served the world, he added, and the world had ill-requited him; he had neglected God, but God was mindful of him in the decay of his nature, and was *laying underneath him his everlasting arms, and making all his bed in his sickness*. Having in a moment of pain dropped a word which might seem to indicate impatience, he immediately added, 'But shall I not quietly wait for my heavenly Father, who has so long waited for me? I have been,' he concluded, 'an undutiful child; I have been scourged for my benefit; I hope my sufferings have been sufficient; if not, I am in the hands of God for eternity, and he will not afflict me above measure and without end. Tell,' said the failing voice, the speaker taking me by the hand, 'Tell your friends what I say, what I feel; it may do good to the living.'

"I have fulfilled my promise, and I have only to add my prayer to God that this death-bed attestation to the value of truth may not have been made in vain."

Mr. Aspland's next publication was, "A Selection of Sermons, in Chronological Order, from the Works of the most eminent Divines of Great Britain, during the Seventeenth and Eighteenth Centuries; with Biographical and Critical Notices." The general title was given to the work of "British Pulpit Eloquence." For such a work he was well qualified by his familiarity with the lives and writings of English theologians. He had no sympathy whatever with those who in modern days affect to despise the pulpit eloquence of England, but thought, with Dr. Johnson, that subsequently to the Reformation the English language had "been chiefly dignified and adorned by the works of our divines." The first preacher selected is Richard Hooker. In strictness, he belongs entirely to the sixteenth century, in the last year of which he died; but his sermons were not published till after his death. They are only seven in number: that selected is certainly in every respect the best; it is entitled, "A learned Sermon of the Nature of Pride." It is to be regretted that no specimen is given of Bishop Andrews' preaching. Fuller, in his Worthies of England, styles him a "peerless prelate," and "an inimitable preacher in his way." His style was indeed peculiar and very artificial, but one of his sermons would have well filled up the gap between Hooker and Chillingworth. The specimens of the pulpit eloquence of the seventeenth century are taken from Chillingworth, Jeremy Taylor, Henry More, Richard Allestree, Benjamin Calamy, Barrow, Wilkins and Whichcot. It will be observed that all are Church-of-England divines. In the Preface, the editor declared that he made it a point of conscience "not to prefer authors on account of their theological creed." Although the work was published anonymously, and through a bookselling firm not identified with heretical books, it was regarded with suspicion by that not small class of theological readers and book-buyers who refuse confidence to every volume that comes to them unstamped by a sectarian *imprimatur*. The sale of the numbers was so small, that the work terminated on the completion of the first volume. Had its editor been encouraged to proceed, not merely South and Tillotson (both his special favourites), but several of the more eminent Nonconformists, such as Baxter, Howe, Manton and Bates, would doubtless have been enrolled in his list of eloquent divines of the seventeenth century.

The biographical sketches which precede each sermon, though necessarily brief, are full of important matter, and indicate the writer's familiarity with the theological literature of the period, and his possession of an accurate judgment. If for no other reason, the non-completion of the selection is to be regretted, because it broke off this series of useful biographical sketches. What became of the impression of "British Pulpit Eloquence," is now not remembered. Probably it became the prey of some of those Adjutants* of unsuccessful literature who seize divines and poets with equal avidity, and, with catholic impartiality, relish orthodox and heterodox reams alike. As the volume is now of rare occurrence, two or three extracts from the Memoirs may be acceptable.

HOOKER.

"Hooker has left behind him a rare character for simplicity of mind, strength of understanding, purity of heart, benevolence of life, and warm and unaffected piety. His main work, the Ecclesiastical Polity, though a fragment, sprung up at once into public favour, and has maintained its place amongst standard English books. It is controversial, but not uncharitable, and abounds in deep thoughts and manly eloquence. Pope Clement VIII. pronounced of it, that 'it would get reverence by age, and that there are in it the seeds of eternity.' Three successive English sovereigns, Elizabeth, the first James and the first Charles, were professed admirers of Hooker; the last unhappy prince recommended him to the study of his son, Chas. II. And his name is scarcely ever used by our best writers but with certain epithets which denote the highest respect, as Learned, or Judicious, or Venerable, or Immortal. Of his style, Bishop Lowth says, in the Preface to his Introduction to English Grammar, 'that in correctness, propriety and purity, he hath hardly ever been surpassed, or even equalled, by any of his successors;' and Bishop Warburton, in his book on the Alliance between Church and State, often quotes from him, and calls him 'the excellent, the admirable, the best good man of our order.'"—Pp. 3, 4.

CHILLINGWORTH.

"Chillingworth is distinguished as an author by closeness and cogency of reasoning, and by clearness and strength of style; on account of which qualities, Mr. Locke recommends him to be 'read over and over again.'

"Besides the celebrated persons already mentioned, Chillingworth numbered amongst his friends the ever-memorable Mr. John Hales, of Eton, and Lord Falkland: this enlightened and accomplished nobleman was joined with Chillingworth in a common saying at Oxford in their day, namely, 'that if

---

* For the useful functions of the gigantic crane so called, see the Cyclopædias, &c.

the great Turke were to be converted by naturall reason, these two were the persons to convert him.'

"We have not the means of judging accurately of Chillingworth as a preacher; none of his sermons were published by himself; and there is reason to apprehend that, with the exception of one, they were not printed from his manuscripts. There is in them a frequent hardness of phraseology which the author would have worn down in going over his composition with a view to the press; and there are sentiments occasionally which the reader will not know how to receive from the author of 'The Religion of Protestants.' Still, as Des Maizeaux remarks, a judicious reader may soon perceive that they come from a masterly hand: he will find in them a noble simplicity, attended with sublime and exalted thoughts, and a constant unfeigned zeal for the glory of God and the good of men's souls.

"The Roman Catholic writers have succeeded in making a general impression amongst biographers that Chillingworth did not acknowledge some of the fundamental doctrines of his church; and Hobbes, of Malmesbury, who knew him, pronounced 'that he was like a lusty fighting fellow that did drive his enemies before him, but would often give his own party terrible smart back blows;' but it is justly said by Granger, in summing up the character of our author, that Chillingworth, Tillotson and other great men who have employed the force of reason in religion, though under a proper restraint, have been branded with Socinianism."—Pp. 29, 30.

Jeremy Taylor.

"Bishop Jeremy Taylor was one of the completest characters of his day. His person was uncommonly beautiful, his voice musical, his conversation pleasant, his address engaging. To sum up all in a few words,—'this great prelate had the good-humour of a gentleman, the eloquence of an orator, the fancy of a poet, the acuteness of a schoolman, the profoundness of a philosopher, the wisdom of a counsellor, the sagacity of a prophet, the reason of an angel, and the piety of a saint.'[*]

"The British pulpit is indebted to Jeremy Taylor, more than to any other divine, for its reformation. He was not without some of the faults of his age; but he set an example of excellencies, in the presence of which all blemishes disappear. He was 'the Barrow of an earlier date,'[†] but superior to Barrow in the force of his expressions, and above all in the splendour of his imagery. In some points there is a great resemblance between these two eminent orators, and one remark made by a very competent judge (Dr. Parr) upon them both is strikingly just: 'Without any attempt to preserve the peculiar forms of philosophical investigation, without any habit of employing the *technical* lan-

---

[*] Rust, Fun. Serm., pp. 20, 21.
[†] Birch's Life of Tillotson, 2nd ed., 1753, p. 22.

guage of it, without any immediate consciousness of intention to exhibit their opinions in what is called a *philosophical point* of view, their incidental representations of man in all the varieties of his moral powers and his social relations, have so much depth, so much precision and so much comprehension, as would have procured them the name of philosophers, if they had not borne the different and not less honourable name of Christian teachers.'"—Pp. 76, 77.

During the year 1814, Mr. Aspland found time to edit an edition of Hopton Haynes's "Scriptural Account of the Attributes and Worship of God," and prefixed a brief biographical sketch of the author.

It was at this time also that he planned and made preparations for publishing a second Unitarian Magazine. He saw that there was room for a periodical which should diffuse religious knowledge and promote scriptural inquiries amongst a humbler class of readers than those for whom the Monthly Repository was adapted. He also wished the Unitarians to have a periodical less controversial, and marked by a more decided practical bent. Had he consulted his pecuniary interests, he would scarcely have embarked on this experiment. The Repository, now in its ninth year, had only recently begun to yield more than its actual cost. During its early years, it was a source only of loss. Some of his friends foresaw that the second would eventually endanger the prosperity of the first Magazine. His hopeful temper, however, combined with his earnest desire of usefulness, made him disregard these prudential considerations. There was, five-and-thirty years ago, but little literature, especially of a religious kind, suited to intelligent artizans. The early race of scholars, as they left the Lancasterian and the Sunday school, and rose to manhood, found little that met their wants in either the standard literature or the periodical publications of the day. There were no precedents, therefore, to justify great expectations of success for a religious Magazine adapted to humble readers. It was found difficult to adopt a title which should be significant without being sectarian and arrogant. That eventually adopted was, "The Christian Reformer, or New Evangelical Miscellany." The new Magazine was warmly supported by many of the habitual contributors to the Monthly Repository, especially Mrs. Mary Hughes, Mr. Wright and Mr. Marsom. The first No. made its appearance on the first day of the year 1815, and, notwithstanding many hindrances and difficulties, it continued to enjoy the editorial superintendence of its founder for thirty years, during nineteen of which it preserved its original duodecimo form; during the last eleven, it was increased in size and price, and became a kind of successor to the Monthly Repository, which had then passed into other hands, and had ceased to supply the religious wants of the Unitarian body. The early volumes of the Christian Reformer were largely indebted to the ready pen of its editor. If any one is surprised how he could, with the numerous avocations of his pulpit, the Academy, the press, the weekly conference, and general business, both private and public, find leisure for the conduct of a second Magazine, the only solution of the difficulty that can be offered is, that it accords with experience that it is the busy, not the disengaged members of society who do all the new work that is perpetually arising and demanding attention. The spare minutes of the energetic man are often more productive of practical results than the days and weeks of the loiterer or the bustling trifler. This is one of the numerous exemplifications of the Divine promise, *Whosoever hath, unto him shall be given, and he shall have more abundance.*

The year 1814 is memorable in European history, through the downfal of Napoleon, and his consequent retirement to Elba, and the conclusion of the war with France, which had for so long a period agitated all Europe. No one more cordially welcomed the return of Peace than Mr. Aspland. On the 7th of July, which was set apart by Royal Proclamation as a day of Thanksgiving, he poured forth in fervent strain his abhorrence of war and his joy at the restoration of peace. Taking for his text Ps. xlvi. 8—10, after a brief explanation of its words, he thus addressed the members of the Gravel-Pit congregation:

"When on various occasions during the late dreadful war the supreme authority of the nation invited the people to fast and pray for success to our fleets and armies, we found ourselves unable to comply with the request; for we worship not the God of Britain merely, but the God of the whole earth; and we should have feared the Divine rebuke by the mouth of the holy prophets, and especially of the Prince of Peace, the Lord of Life, if we had dared to implore from heaven the destruction of our fellow-creatures.* On these days we chose rather that the shutting up of the doors of this House of Prayer should expose us to hard surmises, than that we should seem to approve and countenance war, the greatest of all evils under the sun, and the most subversive of the design of our religion. Here the command of God and the command of man seemed to us to be at variance, and we thought it right, acting

---

* In a familiar letter to his mother, dated Jan. 13, 1814, he wrote—"This is the Thanksgiving day" (for the defeat of Bonaparte at Leipsic, &c., and the triumph of the confederate armies); "but I feel no gratitude, and can express none, for the shedding of blood and the making of widows and orphans."

under the responsibility of our Christian character, to obey God rather than man. At the same time, it may be observed that in this country Proclamations for the religious observance of special days are not of the nature of laws; the disregard of them is no breach of the peace, nor liable to any punishment; they are, as they have been just termed, requests and invitations, and have no further authority than that which is given them by every individual or every independent assembly of Christians; they do not even bind the ministers of the Court religion: and therefore, judging them not agreeable to the spirit of the gospel, we should have acted the part neither of good citizens nor of faithful Christians, if we had not dissented from the common practice for conscience' sake.

"But on this happy day our judgment and our feelings, our patriotism and our piety, concur to urge us to listen to the call of our rulers, and to join the multitude, and to come up to the House of God in company."

After powerfully depicting the physical horrors of war, he proceeded thus earnestly to describe its evil influences on manners and morals:

"The young of one sex are tempted by the high valuation of martial prowess to despise the common and cheap virtues of domestic life; and the young of the other sex imbibe a taste for outward glare and glitter, for the show of festivity and for personal decoration, and an admiration of the spirit of pride and boasting and defiance. Revenge becomes a national passion: our children lisp in threats, and the lips of that part of society to whom gentleness and kindness are thought peculiarly to belong, grow too familiar with the language of malediction. We acquire insensibly a love of war; our houses are ornamented with its ensigns; venal writers accommodate themselves to the prevailing inclination, and the Gospel of Peace is forgotten, or is perverted to the public wish, and the few that dare to assert it are just tolerated, or more probably vilified and held out to scorn."

From this sermon, which was never printed, one still longer extract is offered, on account of the calm wisdom with which it surveys the war and appreciates the terms of the peace.

"The long war which is just brought to an end was begun on principles and pretences which can never be enough condemned; but its character was changed in its progress, and though originally unjust, it might in the end and for a time be necessary. It raised in France a fierce military despotism, infuriated by a wild ambition, which allowed of no repose and seemed to tolerate no show of independence in Europe. The Continent had fallen, or was falling, under one master, who knew no law but his will, and pursued no object besides military greatness. Nothing was heard from one extremity of the civilized world to the other but the clang of arms. Hosts such as were never before marshalled to battle, were rolled hither and thither at the nod of one despot. Little was wanting to the peace of all nations; but how different a peace from that which we this day celebrate—the peace of a desert, the silence of the grave! In this juncture, Divine Providence interposed; the elements fought against the troubler of kingdoms; that political strength which was considered to be as iron and brass, melted away; and after falls and changes more wonderful than any which history has on record, almost all Europe is in a state of external quiet, if not of internal repose.

"These extraordinary scenes have been so arranged by the hand of Almighty God as to keep down and rebuke human pride. So far from any individual person or power having brought about what we witness, no one calculated upon such a strange result. Events followed one another with a rapidity that outstripped imagination. All that the leagued powers of Europe had to do, was to follow the openings of Providence. They did follow them—let it be here acknowledged—with moderation and even with humility. There seemed to be the stillness occasioned by awe of the present Deity. Magnanimity and mercy presided in the breasts of princes, at their councils and over their armies. The voice of the people was practically acknowledged to be the voice of God, and thus the great vital principle of legislation and government which it was the earliest object of the war to extinguish, was in its issue acknowledged and confirmed. If the principle shall be hereafter generally recognized and revered, we may say, in adoration of the mysteries of Divine Providence, that the revolutions and calamities of a quarter of a century will not have been in vain.

"In the terms of pacification there is something to deplore, though much to admire. The unexpected, unaccountable provision for the revival of the Slave-trade has already excited in the public a sentiment of disgust and indignation which clears our national character from reproach; but perhaps we are not sufficiently alive to the injustice and cruelty of dooming one virtuous and happy people as a sacrifice to the peace of Europe. On behalf of the high contracting Powers it must be admitted that the resistance of Norway was not to have been expected; but surely it would have been more consistent with their general equity and magnanimity to have adopted new and conciliatory measures on discovering the spirit, the noble spirit, of that patriotic country: it may not be yet too late,—the unintended, unforeseen injustice to Norway may be compensated at the approaching general Congress; and in prospect of such a desirable event, it is only to be wished that the people of this free and enlightened country had, in the constitutional mode of expressing their sentiments, united the wrongs of the Norwegians with those of the Africans.

"With these abatements, the Treaty of Peace is entitled to our unqualified praise: it was framed in the spirit of peace. The parties to it appear neither as conquerors nor as conquered. There is no assumption on the one side, nor submission on the other: there is no triumph, no degradation. Admirable provisions have been made for preserving the balance of power and the independence of the several European states; and, with the blessing of Providence, we may look forward to peace and happiness for ourselves, and our children and our children's children."

Mr. Aspland cheerfully united with the Dissenting Ministers of the Three Denominations in preparing and presenting an Address of congratulation to the Prince Regent on the restoration of Peace. The Address was read by Dr. Rippon. It contained a strong expression of regret at the renewal of the Slave-trade on the part of France. The reception of the ministers on the occasion was described as gracious and cordial; but neither in his diary nor in any of his letters does there appear any particular allusion to this, which was probably his first visit to the Court of the Sovereign. He was not singular in feeling little respect at any time for the personal character of George IV. The letter that follows is dated on the day preceding that of the presentation of the Address.

Rev. Thomas Belsham to Rev. Robert Aspland.

"Essex Street, July 27, 1814.

"My dear Sir,—I have no holidays this year but what Mr. Joyce allows me while I take a journey in the months of August and September. I should be happy to assist you on the day you mention, but it is our Communion-day, and the last day of my preaching in Essex Street before I enter upon my journey.

"I can do nothing for Brighton but raise a little money.* In this way I can engage for a guinea a day for twenty mornings during the season; but where to look for supplies I am utterly at a loss; and being so soon about to set off upon my journey, I can take no active part.

"Happy you that are about to figure in the splendour of the Regent's Court! On some accounts, I should not much dislike to be one of the party. But I absented myself because I thought I should be out of town when the Address was carried up. Had it been an *open Committee*, which it might have been, I might perhaps still have joined you. I admire the Address much, and I doubt not you will be most graciously received.†

"I give you joy on the late addition to your family, and the safety both of the mother and the child. May your comfort increase as your family enlarges!

"I am happy if my Thanksgiving Sermon met with your approbation.‡ When

---

* The reference is to the new Unitarian chapel at Brighton.

† The Address and the Prince Regent's Answer will be found in the Monthly Repository, IX. 516, 517.

‡ The Sermon was entitled, "The Prospect of Perpetual and Universal Peace." In a review of it, Mr. Aspland commended the argument as weighty and the sentiment as delightful.

shall we see yours? Some of my friends who heard it were highly gratified. You warn me to expect censure. But I flattered myself that everybody would concur with me in the expectation of the *latter-day glory* of the Church.

"The silly Bishop of St. David's has been making another violent attack upon me in the Gentleman's Magazine, and I have been busy the last two or three days in answering a fool according to his folly; but I doubt whether Mr. Urban will receive it.*

"My sister unites in affectionate respects and congratulations to yourself and Mrs. Aspland, with, dear Sir, yours very sincerely, T. BELSHAM."

Shortly after this, Mr. Aspland underwent great anxiety respecting his excellent mother, whose age and declining health warned him that her departure could not be very distant. Instances have already been given of the depth and tenderness of his filial affection. It had been his strongly-expressed and repeated wish that his surviving parent should find a shelter in her widowhood under his own roof. But, with characteristic good sense and self-denial, she declined his filial offer, on the ground that her simple and independent habits, suitable enough for a retired country village, would not harmonize with those of a large household in the vicinity of the metropolis. Disappointed in his wish of personally ministering to her comforts, he soothed her declining years by frequent visits, and by letters (written in large characters, suitable to her failing sight) much more frequent, in which, with patient kindness, he detailed all those little family incidents, the relation of which is inexpressibly interesting to an affectionate relative. Here and there are references to passing events of a more public character, a few of which are subjoined.

"April 13, 1814.—All other news is swallowed up in that from France, which overwhelms us with astonishment. Who could have believed that the great Emperor would have ended his career as a fugitive and captive! Peace, thanks to Providence! is the joyful result, and I hope it will be found that the cause of Liberty has not suffered by twenty years of bloodshed.

"The children are at home for the Easter holidays. Last night they had a treat in seeing the illuminations, which I suppose are to be repeated this evening, if not to-morrow. I put up a few candles to save my windows; but I reserve myself for the signing of the definitive treaty, when I promise the young folks a bonfire. I never lighted up for a victory, but I can do it honestly on such an occasion as this."

---

* The reply to Bishop Burgess was admitted by the Editor of the Gentleman's Magazine. Both the attack and the reply were reprinted in the Monthly Repository, IX. 602—610.

"June 28.—My friend Ben. Flower is leaving Harlow. Brook and I paid him a parting visit last week. Thus Providence brings friends together for a little while and then separates them. Happy country beyond the grave, where there is no parting!"

"August 13.—My friend Madge, of Norwich, is coming up to town next week, which will enable me to go down for the following Sunday to Brighton. The Sunday after, should my supplies hold out, I shall probably be at Reading. After that, the Academy commences, and I must consider myself a close prisoner till Midsummer, unless the frost should enable me to give you a few days, which I much wish, at Christmas. But I am writing about distant times, whereas we know not what shall be on the morrow. Let us then commend ourselves to the care and keeping of Heaven, and rejoice only that our times are in the hands of God.

"My newspaper this morning hints at something alarming in the state of the Continent, on account of which Parliament is to meet unusually soon. Napoleon is reported to have left his island. Some scheme may be planning which will require his military skill. The home news is, that the Princess of Wales has left England; everybody wonders why? I suspect that, whatever may be the cause of her departure, the Prince meditates a divorce and is dreaming of a new wife."

"Nov. 14.—At this period of the year,* dear Mother, it is natural that you should feel oppressed with heavy thoughts; but at the same time we are Christians, and cannot sorrow without hope. Every year, as it passes, shortens the distance between us and departed friends. After some few more revolutions of years, all that have lived will live again, and live together, and live for ever. * * * We had yesterday an annual collection for discharging the debt on our building. We have just agreed to purchase a piece of ground on the north side of the meeting, for the sake of enlarging the burial-ground. This will cost us £250. One of the reasons for the purchase is, that by it we shall make it possible to enlarge the meeting-house, of which the want of accommodation for an increasing congregation makes us think."

"April 17, 1815.—You saw probably by the Repository that I was to preach for the Unitarian Society for distributing Books, at Essex Street, on Thursday last. We had a good congregation. I preached a long sermon, the greater part of it in the midst of a thunder-storm. The sermon is, much against my will, to be printed."†

"May 29.—We have now got through the bustle of Whitsuntide. Our meeting was numerous and pleasant. Mr. Madge gave us an admirable ser-

---

* It was the month in which, ten years previously, his father died.

† The sermon was entitled, "The Power of Truth." It contains some fine passages, but is as a whole less complete than his printed sermons usually are.

mon, which is to be printed. * * * War is, I fear, certain. The end must be left to Providence; but whatever it be, this country must suffer.

"Poor Andrew Fuller is, it seems, gone. It will, I doubt not, fare better with him than he was disposed to allow or to wish with regard to some others. An infirm temper and a narrow education kept him the dictator of a mere party, though his talents were adapted for more extensive usefulness. However, it is pleasant to think he will rise, or soon become a different man, at the resurrection of the just."*

"October 20.—Next month we begin the Unitarian winter campaign. I have to superintend our Wednesday-evening conferences, to deliver a lecture to the young at the close of the morning's service, and to take part in three courses of lectures, namely, at Parliament Court and St. Thomas's on Sunday evening, and at Worship Street on Thursday evening. This, in addition to other duties, will be no light work, but, with health and the blessing of God, I hope to reach the spring in comfort."

"Nov. 14.—I rejoice that the last accounts of you were so favourable, though I have been much disappointed in Saturday's box not being yet arrived, for by that I expected a letter in your own hand. * * * I thought of you much last night, for in consequence of our being infested with thieves, I was obliged to scour and load and fire off your pistols. We shall probably give the rogues the same warning often during the winter, which threatens to be one of many crimes. But do not be alarmed for us. We have a house full of folks, and some of us are strong-boned and stout-hearted, and nearly six feet high."

Early in the following year, he was summoned to Wicken by the tidings of his mother's increasing illness. He stayed with her to the close of her life. It is not without much hesitation that the two letters which follow, written from the house of mourning, are inserted in this Memoir. While it has been felt that some portions of them express feelings too sacred for the eye of strangers, yet, as a whole, they give so clear an insight into one portion of the writer's character, that biographical fidelity requires their insertion.

Rev. Robert Aspland to Mrs. Aspland.

"Wicken, Sunday Morning, February 4, 1816.

"My very dear Sara,—I have a melancholy satisfaction in telling you that the conflict is over, and that my dear mother has entered upon her long sabbath. She breathed her last ten minutes before nine o'clock last night. Her faculties were bright to the very moment of dissolution, and to her probably,

---

* Mr. Fuller died May 7, 1815, aged 61.

to me certainly, it was a consolation that I received her parting breath, and that her hand was locked in mine in the final struggle.

"O, *that* moment! I felt the power of death. Never will the image be erased from my mind or heart. God of our fathers! what is man? what the condition of our nature? Alas! 'the *bliss* of *dying*' is the impertinence of a song. It is, as my dear mother told me again and again, *hard work*. Her sufferings for the last week were beyond description: she longed and prayed for death, and the King of Terrors really approached as her deliverer. Since Sunday she had not been in bed: on Wednesday she took to an easy chair in the parlour, where she expired. Besides her principal complaint, her weariness and watchfulness and the soreness of her limbs were sufficient to have put an end to her life. It appeared that she had a presentiment upon her mind of a lingering and painful death. Her sighs and groans, and her articulate prayers, were for as easy a dismission as was consistent with the will of Providence. Yet, do not fear, my love, that she was in religious trouble of mind. No: her views of the other world were commonly clear, and her feelings frequently broke out in comforting passages of holy Scripture: the last words that she uttered, and this in the article of death, were, *Pray, Father;* and these were repeated. She had some time before (a few minutes only) repeated with unwonted strength, *Come unto me, all ye that labour and are heavy laden*—here her breath failed, and I took up the remainder of the delightful words—*And I will give you rest*—and her looks, directed towards me, expressed *hope* and *satisfaction*.

"Thank merciful Heaven, the corpse is most lovely! I gaze upon it with more of pleasure than pain. *No more sorrow*, as the dear sufferer frequently said; no more care and anxious and sad expectation. I still see the smile that allured my infant feelings, and I can hardly believe, as I stand beside the bed, that the form is not about to awake refreshed out of sleep. But this sleep will last through the night, and I shall not see her again conscious and intelligent until the last morning.

"In this trial, how have I wanted your sympathy and counsel! yet it would have been too much for you—but oh! my dear Sara, must one of us in all probability be to the other what I have been and shall long be to my mother, a sad, helpless spectator, a bowed-down mourner! The Father of mercies spare us in the failing of heart and flesh! * * *

"Be so good as write on Tuesday without fail, and let the direction be in a large and legible hand: your letter will then come to comfort me after the melancholy duties of Wednesday.

"In all respects, this is a dreary sabbath. We shall endeavour to lighten it by a religious service with a few friends here in the evening; amongst them, and chief, my uncle William's family, who have been most affectionate in their attentions.

"Farewell, my very dear wife; give my love to the dear children and Anna, and believe me yours, R. A."

"Wicken, Thursday.

"My dear Sara,—Your kind letter came into my hands last night, and was soothing to my spirits, after the melancholy preparations and agitating duties of the day. Long may we be spared (if such be the will of the Supreme Disposer) to support and comfort each other!

"The funeral took place yesterday. It had been made easier to me by my dear mother's having, as you know, given precise directions concerning it. These were of course punctually fulfilled, and in their fulfilment we saw with sad satisfaction new proofs of that practical wisdom for which, in her own station, my mother was eminently distinguished.

"The coffin was of oak, with little ornament, and nothing black except the face of the inscription-plate. The body was dressed in the clothes worn by the dear deceased, all white, and the head rested upon a pillow. The lining of the coffin was flannel. How much simpler and better than the customary trappings of undertakers! To the last, the corpse was a pleasing object— pleasing at least to me. I closed the lid with my own hands, taking a reluctant leave for ever of a form interesting to me through a thousand recollections.

"By her own desire, none but my uncle's family were invited to the funeral. The clergyman attended at the house—not the curate, but the incumbent —this we took as a mark of respect. The body was borne by eight poor men, chiefly such as were under pecuniary obligations to my mother; they returned to the house to have a plain meal and a dollar each. Though so few were invited, the procession was not small; the greater part of the inhabitants of the village attended us to church. In the midst of the service there was sung a hymn from my Selection, *Why do we mourn departing friends*, &c. The body was finally placed upon my dear father's—a cold bed, but one of which the expectation gave pleasure to at least the former of these sufferers. Having performed the obsequies, we returned to a house which, in the absence of even the corpse, appeared to me empty.

"We had a bitter day, but the frost and snow made the roads more passable. I took it as a peculiar mark of respect that the surveyors of the parish had the path swept by the parish labourers all the way up to the church.*

"Write on Saturday; I shall want comfort on the Sunday. I have the funeral sermon to deliver in the afternoon; the service begins soon after two; the text allotted me is 1 Pet. i. 4. I long to be with you, though my mind will linger about this spot. Your own ROBERT."

---

* The letter goes on to detail his intentions with respect to his mother's property, his purpose to double the legacies left by her to relations, and to present a "memorial of gratitude" to one relative who had been very kind to her in her sickness.

CHAPTER XXII.

THE year 1816 was also darkened to Mr. Aspland by the loss of several valued friends, amongst whom were Rev. Jeremiah Joyce and Rev. William Vidler. By the death of the former gentleman he lost not only a friend, but a zealous and punctual coadjutor in the administration of Dissenting trusts and charities, and an able correspondent of the Monthly Repository. Mr. Joyce was engaged on the composition of a series of articles on Natural Theology, thirteen of which he lived to complete, and they appeared in Vols. X. and XI. of the Magazine. On March 29th, Mr. Aspland, accompanied by the students of the Academy, had listened with no small pleasure to Mr. Joyce's admirable sermon before the Unitarian Society, on "the Subserviency of Free Inquiry and Religious Knowledge among the Lower Classes of Society to the Prosperity and Permanence of a State." The interest of the service was painfully heightened by the circumstance, that within a few doors of the chapel (in Essex Street) lay the corpse of the preacher's elder brother, Mr. Joshua Joyce, who had died very suddenly early that morning. To his brother Joshua* Mr. Joyce was very tenderly attached; but such was his sense of the importance of fulfilling his engagement to the Society of which he was the Secretary, that he sub-

---

* Two circumstances entitle this good man to our respect. By his forbearing, with equal generosity and justice, to exercise all his rights as his father's heir, his younger brother Jeremiah was enabled, on coming of age, to quit a mechanical employment, and to gratify his natural bent and serve mankind, by devoting himself to literature and the Christian ministry. When, in 1794, his brother's life was endangered by the charge of high treason, to the untiring exertions of Mr. Joshua Joyce did the accused, in part at least, owe their successful defence. The prisoners were served with the names of 421 persons as the panel from which the jury would be selected. In the short space of ten days, he succeeded, with the assistance of friends who equally appreciated the importance of the crisis, in

dued his personal grief so far as to deliver his discourse with considerable fervour. The exordium was uttered with a faltering tongue, but the agitation of his spirit afterwards gave depth and animation to his delivery, and he was rewarded by the sympathy and close attention of his hearers. In less than three months Mr. Joyce himself died. On the 21st of June, Mr. Aspland received from him a letter, written in his usual cheerful and friendly style, in which he promised to prepare an article (one of the series alluded to) for the following month. On the evening of that day Mr. Joyce suddenly expired. Brief tributes to his worth were paid by Dr. Shepherd, Mr. Rutt and Rev. Thos. Jervis, but the memoir was entrusted to Mr. Aspland, and appeared in the Monthly Repository, XII. 697—704.

On Friday, August 23rd, died Rev. William Vidler, in the 59th year of his age. In him popular Unitarianism lost a disinterested and very able advocate. Mr. Aspland had during more than eleven years found in him a zealous associate in many public labours, and a fast personal friend. Masculine sense, an ardent love of religious truth, an accurate knowledge of the peculiarities of the different Dissenting sects of England, a strong dislike to bigotry, and great fearlessness, were some of the qualities that were common to both of them. Independently of their frequently being associated together in the performance of public duties, the conversation and character of each was attractive to the other. In early life, Mr. Vidler was of a lean, feeble, and it was feared consumptive habit; but during his latter years he had become excessively corpulent,* and neither severe bodily exercise nor habitual abstinence could keep in check his constitutional tendency. Latterly, asthma had disabled him from public speaking, and occasioned him much distress. During his long confinement, Mr. Aspland frequently saw him, first at West Ham, and afterwards at the residence of his son-in-law in London. Throughout his sufferings, of which he

---

ascertaining the character and political bias of all these jurymen. Horne Tooke gratefully acknowledged that himself and friends were more indebted to the exertions of Mr. Joshua Joyce than to those of any other man, in defeating the prosecutions. The creatures of the Government were detected, and a tyrannical Minister was baffled.

* In one of their journeys together to visit the churches in Kent, as they were ascending Shooter's Hill, the hind wheel, on Mr. A.'s side of the carriage, having lost its linch-pin, became disengaged, and rolled backwards down the hill, but Mr. Vidler's weight prevented an overturn and kept the carriage *in æquilibrio*.

early foresaw the issue, he was self-possessed and often cheerful. His death-bed was serene and hopeful. On the 21st of August, Mr. Aspland saw him for the last time; he expressed perfect satisfaction with the religious views he had adopted, his conscience bearing him testimony that in every change of his views he had been actuated solely by the fear of God and the love of Christ, and an earnest desire to do good to mankind. He gave with much calmness instructions respecting his funeral. When his friend, much affected by the scene, rose to take his leave, Mr. Vidler clasped his hand with warm affection, and said with great solemnity, *Before the face of the Master, the Friend, the Brother—before the face of Jesus Christ, I expect to meet you again. Farewell!* Two days after, he breathed his last. Such a death-bed as this, and that which he had recently with still deeper emotions stood by at Wicken, entitled Mr. Aspland to say, that "the Unitarian doctrine had nothing to fear, if examined by the characters which it had created and modelled," many of whom had shewn " proofs of the power of their religion to give support under the pressure of affliction, and to yield consolation and good hope in the decline of nature and the immediate prospect of dissolution."

Mr. Vidler was buried by his friend in the ground of the New Gravel-Pit meeting-house, and, at the earnest request of many members of the Parliament-Court congregation, the funeral oration was printed in the Christian Reformer (1st Series, Vol. II. p. 425). On the following Sunday evening, Mr. Aspland preached the funeral sermon to a densely crowded audience. He had written for the occasion a sermon on the subject of *Reproach for the Sake of Truth the Christian's Glory;* but when he entered the pulpit so long occupied by his departed friend, he became dissatisfied with his written discourse, and, giving free way to the emotions which filled his heart, while the congregation were singing the hymn, he sketched out the plan of an entirely new address from 2 Tim. iv. 6—8. If the writer may trust his youthful recollections, assisted as they are by the judgment of older friends, this purely extempore sermon was appropriate and deeply impressive.* The biogra-

---

* At this period of his life he retained all his powers of extempore address. They were shortly after again tested in the pulpit at Parliament Court. After the commencement of the service on the evening of November 17, 1816, he discovered that he had left his sermon-case at home. He had previously preached twice at Hackney that day, once extempore, but he immediately gave, without the slightest embarrassment, a sermon on a third subject without the aid of a note.

phical sketch of Mr. Vidler's life and character with which it concluded was subsequently expanded into a full memoir, and published in three parts in the Monthly Repository (Vol. XII.). Mr. Vidler's writings will have given the present generation but an inadequate idea of the man, whose person and manners were thus described by his friend:

"Notwithstanding the imperfectness of his education, his knowledge was very extensive. He had read most of the standard books, in the English language, in the various departments of literature; and his clearness of conception and retentiveness of memory often enabled him to surprise his more intimate friends by the exhibition of his acquirements. He was quick in his perceptions, but at the same time patient in his inquiries and cool in his judgment. His conversation was formed after the model of the style which prevailed a century ago, and was occasionally quaint, frequently proverbial and generally sententious, but always intelligent and commonly tinctured with good-humour. Instances have been already given of his presence of mind in sudden altercations, and his smartness in repartee. Under offence, he assumed great severity of countenance, and administered rebuke in a tone and manner which compelled it to be felt; but he was habitually willing to be pleased, and into whatever family he entered, his presence commonly diffused cheerfulness throughout the whole circle. He was fond of children, and on entering a room where they were, immediately attracted them to his knee. His heart was soon affected by any tale of distress, and in an early period of his residence in London he was much imposed on by persons affecting an equal degree of distress and of religion; in such cases he sometimes gave away all the money that he possessed; yet if he suspected fraud, no one expressed quicker or stronger indignation. His bodily make, tall and upright; his step, regular and firm; and his countenance, open and unvarying, indicated great courage. Mr. Teulon says of him, that 'he was a man to whom fear seemed unknown.' In short, his was the old English character mellowed and refined by the gospel.

"As a preacher he excelled chiefly in strength of reasoning, simplicity and perspicuity of style, and an open, manly elocution. His voice was clear and strong, his look penetrating, his attitude erect and self-possessed, and his person dignified. He would sometimes indulge in the pulpit an ironical turn of expression, which produced a striking effect. In prayer he was less happy than in preaching, and he was accustomed to acknowledge the difficulty which he found in discharging this part of his public duty to his own satisfaction. His devotional exercises as well as his sermons were framed in a great measure in the language of Scripture, and this often gave them an interesting appearance of solemnity. Of the merits of his pulpit services we must judge by their effects; and in this point of view a high rank must be allotted to him amongst popular divines, for there have been few preachers who have been able to make upon the minds of an auditory so deep an impression, not of feeling merely, but of knowledge and truth."

The condition of the Protestants in the South of France excited amongst the friends of liberty in England, in the years 1815 and 1816, much alarm and sympathy. In the month of July in the previous year, a massacre had taken place, in which hundreds perished, in the city of Nismes, and a still larger number fell victims in the neighbourhood. The restored Government of Louis XVIII. shewed little disposition either to punish the offenders or to take the necessary steps for protecting the oppressed. During several subsequent months in that and the following year, the whole Protestant population of the South of France continued to live in a state of terror, their places of worship closed, their persons often insulted, and their houses frequently disfigured by their enemies during the night time by emblems of destruction. The Government of this country were appealed to by the Dissenting ministers of the Three Denominations and other public bodies to use their all-powerful influence in behalf of religious liberty, but with little effect. It was supposed that the French Protestant party in the Southern provinces looked with no favour on the restoration of the Bourbons, and therefore they were denied the sympathy of the English Government and their Tory adherents. An attempt was made by the ministerial journals first to discredit the existence of the persecution, and then to conceal its severity. Odium was heaped on those who stepped forward as the advocates of the persecuted.* The difficulties of the case were greatly increased by the time-serving duplicity of some of the leading Protestants of France. It was Mr. Aspland's painful duty to expose one notable instance of this. Mons. Marron, President of the Protestant Consistory, wrote (probably at the instigation of the French Government) an official letter to the Dissenting ministers of London, disclaiming and rebuking their interposition as unnecessary and mischievous. Little did he know the character of his correspondent when he enclosed this false and heartless letter in a private communication to Mr. Aspland, dated Dec. 11, 1815, in which he stated that the proceedings of the London ministers had created in France a strong sensation, that the French Protestants were consoled and gratified by them, and that the result was likely to be highly bene-

---

* In one ministerial journal the ministers of the Three Denominations were stigmatized as "treble-faced rogues."

ficial.* It was deemed necessary, therefore, to rouse the public mind of England by public meetings, resolutions and speeches, and by a subscription in behalf of those of the Protestants of France who had suffered loss. In the labour and responsibility of these measures, Mr. Aspland took his share, and was rewarded by being brought into personal communication with Lord Holland, a nobleman whose sympathies were throughout life on the side of the oppressed, and with whom attachment to religious freedom was a first principle. In the English House of Commons, the cause of the French Protestants was pleaded with all the ardour of benevolence by Sir Samuel Romilly; and although Lord Castlereagh, relying on an obsequious majority ever ready to uphold any ministerial measure, derided his plea and maligned his motives in introducing the subject, his object was answered, and public opinion coerced the lethargic Cabinets of England and France to do what was necessary for the protection of the Protestants of the latter country. To this subject reference is made in the following letter.

Mrs. Cappe to Rev. Robert Aspland.

"York, Jan. 4th, 1816.

"Dear Sir,—I am very glad to find, from a notice in the last number of the Repository, that the Sermons, of which I have so lately been the editor, will be reviewed in the number for the present month. It is not that I wish them to be praised beyond their merit, of which different persons may probably think very differently, and which no one can appreciate so highly as the editor; but, as I think them eminently qualified to stimulate the reader to high degrees of moral excellence, and to raise the tone of religious sentiment, I certainly do wish that they should not fall lifeless to the ground, of which there may be some danger, from the want of patronage on the one hand, and the operation of prejudice on the other. Had they been recommended by a certain portion of orthodoxy, how great would have been their celebrity!

"I have now decided to venture upon a second edition of the former volume on devotional subjects, it having been long out of print and frequently inquired for, and shall put it into the hands of the printer as soon as the paper, already ordered, shall arrive. The great discouragement is the immediate expense and the long-protracted accounts with booksellers, so harassing to persons unaccustomed to business, and especially if from age the memory becomes

---

* In the Morning Chronicle of Feb. 3, 1816, it is stated that M. Marron "acknowledges that he wrote to the Rev. R. A., and with a profligacy of expression unworthy of a minister of religion, and especially when connected with the calamities of his brethren, he says, '*he might have gilded the pill*' and '*have softened the crudity of his refusal*' *(disclaimer)*."

incorrect. I avail myself of an opportunity, by the reports, of sending you another paper, a sort of sequel to the former, which you will be so good as to insert as soon as is convenient. I rejoice in the increasing respectability of the Repository, and, as I hope, in its increasing circulation and celebrity also. What a singular fact it is that such a torpor should prevail in our *establishment* respecting the persecutions of the Protestants in France! Mr. Welby has done his utmost in our small congregation (small, being overshadowed by a magnificent cathedral, &c. &c.), and the contributions have been as ample as could be expected; but I do not yet hear of any other effort. I wish the Methodists would come forward. I ought, indeed, to have excepted the Quakers, many of whom here are liberal and enlightened, as well as most actively benevolent.

"Dear Sir, your sincere friend,

CATH. CAPPE."

Rev. Thomas Belsham to Rev. Robert Aspland.

"Essex Street, July 22, 1816.

"Dear Sir,—The enclosed letter from Mr. Vanderkemp was given to me this morning by Miss Joyce, as appertaining to the Unitarian Society; but I see it contains something intended for the Monthly Repository, and therefore I transmit it to you. I rather suspect that the paper signed Crito, a copy of which, if printed, is desired to be sent to the American ambassador for his father, was drawn up by the old President himself. But I only judge so from that circumstance: and I think that I recollect having heard, many years ago, that his sentiments were similar to those of the enclosed paper, which, however, cannot be called Christian.

"I also enclose a little pamphlet by Sylvanus Gibbs, of Plymouth Dock, which he sent to me for you: and with every good wish for your health, comfort and success, I am, dear Sir, very sincerely yours,

T. BELSHAM."

The remarkable paper to which Mr. Belsham alludes was published in the Monthly Repository (XI. 574—576), under the title of "Syllabus of an Estimate of the Doctrines of Jesus compared with those of others." There can be no doubt of the correctness of the conjecture of Mr. Belsham, that it was the production of John Adams, the seconder in Congress of the Declaration of Independence, and the successor, in 1797, of Washington in the Presidency of America. The son of this distinguished man, John Quincy Adams, was at this period residing in England as the representative of his republic, and occasionally honoured Mr. Aspland with an exchange of visits.

The letter that follows is inserted as the only memorial found in Mr. Aspland's papers of one for whom he entertained great respect, and of whom he wrote (1817) in the following terms: "This intrepid man was Secretary to the Corresponding Society. He was the first whose life was sought on pretence of high treason by Mr. Pitt. An honest jury delivered him from the fangs of his persecutors; and he is still living, an example of enlightened patriotism, unimpeachable virtue, and the unostentatious profession of religion."

Thomas Hardy to Rev. Robert Aspland.

"30, Queen's Row, Pimlico, Nov. 15, 1816.

"Dear Sir,—With this I send you a letter of mine to a few friends who meet annually to commemorate the Fifth of November, but not merely for the acquittal of Thomas Hardy on that day, but for the acquittal virtually of thousands. * * *

"The Corresponding Society (which has been so basely calumniated) began in the latter end of 1791, in consequence of a conversation I had with a friend respecting the unequal representation of the people in Parliament. That conversation suggested the propriety of instituting a Society with the view of ascertaining the opinion of the people on that question by corresponding with other societies that might be formed, having the same object in view, as well as with public-spirited individuals. * * *

"The first meeting of the London Corresponding Society was held on the 25th of January, 1792, consisting of eight persons. * * * How strange and how very amusing it was for me to see a plan exactly similar recommended to the adoption of the British and Foreign School Society, by a Royal Duke, five-and-twenty years afterwards,—a plan which is now also in full practice by Missionary and Bible Societies! The same means that were used to promote the success of Parliamentary Reform in 1794, were charged as a crime against the London Corresponding Society.

"The first address and resolutions which the Society printed, and which were published very extensively, were dated April 2, 1792. From that time the Society became known to the public. Societies were then formed in different parts of England, Scotland and Ireland, in quick succession, for the same laudable object. A constant correspondence was afterwards kept up with each of these societies. The London Corresponding Society was considered the Parent Society. This was the reason why Burke, in one of his mad rants in the House of Commons, designated it as 'the mother of all mischief.' At this period the numbers increased rapidly, and political knowledge was diffused generally throughout the nation by means of small tracts, which were well adapted for giving information to persons of every capacity, and also by political discussions and conversations in the various meetings. The members increased in about two years to an amount far exceeding all the electors by whose suffrages the House of Commons is at present chosen. The popular societies becoming so numerous, and petitioning for Reform also becoming so general, began now to attract the notice of Government, and created an apparent alarm, which was fed and increased by the lying and interested misrepresentations of the agents of the Ministry. * * * After many efforts to suppress the rising spirit of the country for a Reform of Parliament, the prosecution, imprisonment and banishment of individuals for what they termed sedition, proving ineffectual, the Ministry at last had recourse to a still more iniquitous measure, that of charging us with HIGH TREASON. * * * Twelve men, among the many thousands in the nation who were equally engaged in the same benevolent and patriotic cause, were now singled out as the *first* victims. The State Trials, as they are called, began on October 25, 1794, with the trial of myself (who was supposed to be the most helpless of the band), which lasted nine days, and on another memorable 5th of November I was honourably acquitted. The then Attorney-General, Sir John Scott, now Lord Eldon, took nine hours to deliver his opening speech on that trial. The trial of John Horne Tooke was next in order, which lasted five days; and on the 21st of November he was also honourably acquitted. The trial of John Thelwall next succeeded, which lasted three days, and he was also honourably acquitted on the 5th of December. The other prisoners whose names were included in the same indictment, were two days afterwards brought to the bar and honourably discharged. Thus ended the momentous trials of 1794. I cannot help mentioning here the names of our excellent advocates on that trying occasion, Erskine and Gibbs, now the Right Hon. Thomas Lord Erskine and Sir Vicary Gibbs.

"Perhaps you may desire to know how many of those twelve men who were destined in the councils of erring mortals to die on a certain day still survive. I shall only mention the names of those who have already paid the debt of nature. The first of them who died was Thomas Holcroft; the next, John Augustus Bonney, Stewart Kyd, John Horne Tooke, Thomas Wardle, and lately, Jeremiah Joyce. If the recapitulation of the above circumstances shall have communicated any interesting information or recalled any pleasing or useful recollections, it will add to the happiness of, dear Sir, yours with great respect, THOMAS HARDY."

The year 1817 opened gloomily. The war was at an end, but its enormous cost bowed the nation down, and there was a general stagnation of trade. Social distress engendered political discontent, and led to an angry cry for Reform. The Government and their party, unused to popular control, endeavoured by harsh prosecutions and other threatening proceedings to keep down the expression of discontent. In one or two instances, political antipathy fomented religious animosity, and led to results which seemed for a time to endanger toleration. At Liverpool, some proceedings of a very extraordinary character took place, the mention of which will serve to shew how great has been the progress of liberal feeling in the last thirty years.

Mr. John Wright (a brother of Rev. Richard Wright) had opened a room for preaching and religious lectures in Marble Street, in that town. An advertisement on the subject of these lectures, inserted in the *Liverpool Mercury*, March 28th, 1817, attracted the jealous attention of the Mayor (whose name also was John Wright), and he sent an informer to watch the services at Marble Street. In the following month, proceedings were taken against Mr. Wright, in the first instance on a charge of holding meetings for worship in a place not duly licensed, and subsequently on the more serious charge of blasphemy. The alleged blasphemy was the delivery of a lecture, in which the doctrines of the Trinity and Atonement were discussed and denied, and also the doctrines of an intermediate and of any future state.* The magistrates, under the guidance of Mr. Statham, the Town Clerk, notwithstanding the production of secondary evidence proving that the room in Marble Street had been licensed in the Bishop's Court at Chester twenty years previously, on behalf of the congregation then assembling in it, convicted Mr. Wright on the minor charge, and committed him for trial at the ensuing assizes at Lancaster on the more serious charge of blasphemy. In reply to the prisoner's demand to know under what law he was charged, the Town Clerk informed him that it was "under the common law."

These proceedings awakened immediate and anxious attention. Mr. Aspland brought them without delay under the notice of the Committee of the Unitarian Fund,† and it was resolved that the solicitor of the Society should at once put himself into communication with Mr. Wright and his friends, and make an early report of his opinion on the case. It was matter of regret and animadversion that the Committee, at a subsequent meeting (May 12), in the absence through illness of their Secretary, received and resolved to act on the advice of their solicitor, not to interfere by supporting Mr. Wright, in the state of the question for which he was under prosecution.

---

* For the latter part of the charge there was no evidence. The informer, little acquainted with theological discussions, probably confounded the denial of a separate or intermediate state with the denial of man's immortality. The lecture which led to this charge was, in fact, a printed one, and formed No. 14 of the volume of "Evangelical Discourses" published by Rev. R. Wright in 1811.

† Minutes of Unitarian Fund Committee's proceedings, April 22, 1817.

Mr. Belsham, greatly to his honour,* remonstrated against the decision of the Committee, in the latter part of the following letter.

Rev. Thomas Belsham to Rev. Robert Aspland.

"Essex Street, May 26, 1817.

"My dear Sir,—I am much obliged by your communication, and am glad to hear that the good cause is going on so prosperously on the other side the Atlantic.

"I dare say that Mr. Taylor's anecdote of Bishop Seabury may be correct.† But it does not at all militate against mine, which relates a private communi-

---

* Mr. Belsham reiterated his views still more urgently on Mr. Rutt in the following letter. The incidental mention of the absence of both the Secretary and Treasurer at this critical moment, may explain, though it does not justify, the inaction of the Unitarian Fund Committee.

"Tuesday, June 10, 1817.

"Dear Sir,—I take so little part in the administration of the Unitarian Fund, that it may seem officious in me to obtrude any advice. But I cannot help fearing that, by neglecting as a body to take up the cause of Mr. Wright, they are not consulting their reputation or their interest. To profess, as one main object of the institution, to protect Unitarian missionaries, and to shrink back in the very first instance from supporting a respectable teacher against a malicious prosecution, appears to me and to many others inexplicable. I wonder not at the conduct of the Protestant Society; but I am a little surprised that the Deputies have not taken up the cause. This, however, gives a very glorious opportunity for the Unitarian Fund to come forward, to take up the cause, to offer to defend Mr. Wright to the utmost extent of their means, to open a correspondence with the Committee at Liverpool, and to request the assistance of the friends of Christian truth and of religious liberty. I have no doubt that these resolutions, if properly circulated, as they should be, and the sooner the better, would immediately raise a sum of money much larger than would be necessary, and would leave a large balance in the hands and for the purposes of a Fund so liberally and judiciously applied. Whereas, if the Fund as a body deserts the cause of Mr. Wright, I have no doubt that many will take great offence, and the consequences will be injurious both to the character and the revenue of the Fund.

"I have given Mr. Aspland my sentiments upon the subject; but I hear he is out of town, and Mr. Christie is also absent. I write to you upon the supposition that you are an active member of the Committee; and the case admits of no delay, this being the proper time for the Unitarian Fund to take it up, as the Deputies have declined. And if the Fund still continues to decline interfering, some other method must be thought of to support Mr. Wright's cause, as money is wanted immediately.

"Though not of the Committee of the Unitarian Fund, yet, as an old subscriber, I have presumed to give an opinion, which you, my dear Sir, and the managers, will adopt or reject as you and they may see to be expedient.

"I am, very sincerely yours,

T. BELSHAM."

† In a letter dated Philadelphia, Jan. 24, 1817, Mr. James Taylor had thus written to Mr. Aspland:—"In Mr. Belsham's Memoirs of Mr. Lindsey (Chap. ix.), there are two anecdotes of the late Bishop Seabury, one of which is incor-

cation between Bishop Seabury and Dr. Styles, communicated in a private letter from Dr. Styles to Dr. Price, and by Dr. Price to Mr. Lindsey or Dr. Priestley, and upon their authority inserted in Mr. Lindsey's Memoirs from a letter now in my possession. This occurred previously to the public meeting, and is not at all inconsistent with what Mr. Taylor relates as having occurred at the meeting, and in which, to do Bishop Seabury justice, it does not appear that he took any part, the application being probably made by some officious friend.

"I am very much concerned to find that your health is still in so precarious a state as to prevent your attending the Fund meeting on Wednesday. I should rejoice to hear that you had determined to lay aside all business and all care for the present, and to take a journey into the country on horseback for a month. This, I should hope, would set you up completely. But if you do not mend soon, and that very materially, I beg you would have *other*, if not *better* advice; and do not trifle with any complaint which threatens to affect the lungs.

"I will take care that Mr. W. S. shall see your review of Southey. At present he is at Norwich, condoling with Pratt and Co.

"I am surprised to hear from Edgar Taylor that the Unitarian Fund, *by the advice of Mr. Wilks*, have determined not to support Wright. I do not wonder that the Protestant Society will not take up his cause, nor should I be surprised if the Deputies rejected it; but as to the Unitarian Fund, it seems to me to be completely a *casus fœderis*, the defence of a man who is prosecuted for being a Unitarian teacher. I think Mr. Wilks's advice should be received with caution. I have been told that he is solicitor to a confederacy of Calvinists who threaten to eject all the Unitarian ministers in Staffordshire from their chapels and their glebes, under pretence that they were given or bequeathed by Calvinists. They have begun with Wolverhampton.

---

rect; the facts, as lately received from a respectable friend, are as follow: At a commencement, after the gentlemen had assembled and taken their seats, it was announced to Dr. Styles, the President of Yale College, that Bishop Seabury was in the meeting-house, or place where the commencement was held, and a request was made that the President would invite him to take a seat on the stage, which had been appropriated for the accommodation of the Trustees and Governors of the College and other distinguished characters. Dr. Styles replied that there were already one hundred Bishops in the house who had not been invited to take seats on the stage.—My authority is Dr. Freeman, of Boston. I was induced to make the inquiry which led to Dr. Freeman's communication, in consequence of a conversation with Bishop White, the Episcopal Bishop of Pennsylvania, a most excellent man, who complained that injustice had been done to Bishop Seabury, and related the circumstances referred to. The other fact, relative to Dr. Seabury's breathing on a candidate for ordination, I believe to be correctly stated by Mr. Belsham. It is of more importance than the other. The late Rev. Dr. Lathrop, of Boston, was present and saw the Bishop act thus."

"With my best compliments to Mrs. Aspland, and with the most earnest wishes and prayers for the speedy restoration of your health, and for the long continuance and increase of your comfort and usefulness, I remain, dear Sir, very sincerely yours, T. BELSHAM."

Lord Holland made the prosecution of Mr. Wright the subject of conversation in the House of Lords, and attributed it to a very reprehensible circular which had been a short time before issued by Lord Sidmouth from the Home Office. Finding that public attention was aroused by their proceedings, the Magistrates and Town Clerk of Liverpool adopted the prudent course of dropping the prosecution.

But the doctrine laid down by the Town Clerk of Liverpool, that the denial of the Trinity was still an offence at common law, singular as it appeared to be, when viewed in connection with the Act recently passed by the legislature " to relieve persons who impugn the doctrine of the Holy Trinity from certain penalties," was shortly afterwards revived in another court, with an appearance of authority which naturally alarmed every true friend of religious liberty.

In the month of July, 1817, the case of the Wolverhampton Chapel was argued in the Court of Chancery. This chapel had been erected about the year 1701, in John Street, Wolverhampton, by a congregation of English Presbyterians. The trust-deed declared that the building was intended as a " meeting-house for the worship and service of God." The founders probably held orthodox opinions. About the year 1770, the minister, Mr. Cole, was an Arian. He was succeeded by Mr. Griffiths, an Unitarian. A secession of some members of the congregation holding Calvinistic opinions then took place. Some pecuniary benefactions were made to the chapel by certain worshipers therein between the years 1770 and 1800, the donors holding Arian or Unitarian opinions. In 1813, a Mr. Steward, then professing Unitarian opinions, was appointed minister for a term of three years. In 1816, he renounced the profession of Unitarianism and avowed himself to be a Trinitarian. The congregation were unwilling to renew the engagement of Mr. Steward, but gave him three months' residence to afford him time to find another situation. At the end of that time he refused to quit. Mr. Benjamin Mander, one of the seceders in 1780, now re-appeared to support Mr. Steward against the trustees. A "Case" was drawn up and circulated amongst the Independents as one " of great importance to orthodox Dissenters," inviting pecuniary aid on behalf of Mr. Steward. This Case was sanctioned by the names of nine Independent ministers.* Thus supported, Messrs. Mander and Steward filed an information in the name of the Attorney-General to restrain the trustees and the congregation from ejecting Mr. Steward. Amongst the grounds on which the judgment of the Court of Chancery was solicited against the trustees, were—1, That Unitarianism was *now* illegal, and therefore that an Unitarian congregation could not lawfully hold any property; 2, That, Unitarianism not being tolerated at the time of the erection of the meeting-house and the date of the endowments, Unitarians could not be the lawful possessors of the property.

The case of the relators was argued by Sir Samuel Romilly, Mr. Hart and Mr. Shadwell. What was the opinion of Sir Samuel Romilly will presently be stated in his own words.† Mr. Shadwell denied the legality of impugning the Trinity. He referred to the case of Mr. Wright at Liverpool, reminding the Court that a prosecution was at that time pending against an individual for impugning the doctrine of the Trinity. He further declared that Unitarian doctrines were blasphemous and wicked, and the professors of them ought not to be protected by the Court. Lord Chancellor Eldon, while he declined to state, sitting as he did in a Court of Equity, what would be the effect on the common law of the passing of the Acts for relieving Unitarians, confidently affirmed that in the House of Lords, at least, it was never intended by them to alter or affect the common law.

---

* The names of these nine gentlemen who thus violated the first principle of Protestant Dissent were, J. A. James (Birmingham); Thomas Scales (Wolverhampton); John Steward, John Hudson and James Cooper (West Bromwich); James Dawson (Dudley); John Berry and John Hammond (Handsworth); and John Richards (Stourbridge). Having mentioned their names, it is right to add that one Independent minister, Mr. James Robertson, of Stretton-under-Fosse, came publicly forward and rebuked these nine patrons of the Case, characterizing their proceedings as " an attempt to revive the laws of persecution against the abettors of religious opinions different from their own." "This," he added, "is the *real* but *disgraceful character* which belongs to them." Mr. Robertson's pamphlets were entitled, " Religious Liberty applied to the Case of the Old Meeting-house, John Street, Wolverhampton," and " Infringements on Religious Liberty Exposed," &c.

† It is due to the memory of this distinguished man to add, that in the course of the argument in the Court of Chancery, he clearly indicated what he thought of the spirit which had put the law in motion against persons holding Unitarian sentiments. " *God forbid that any persons, whether Unitarians or Jews, or holding any description of religious opinions, should be prosecuted on that account! There can be no person so illiberal as to cherish such an idea, and in my opinion it would be most illiberal to attempt any legal interference on such subjects;* but, at the same time, I apprehend that a Court would be bound to say that it would not carry any trust for such purposes into effect."

It is not necessary for the purpose of this Memoir to enter at present any further into the history of this tedious and harassing suit, which, after two long periods of inactivity, was only recently finally decided, and the enormous costs of which swallowed up the entire value of the property.* It was, however, necessary to give a brief outline of the suit, which led to very important results, and made a very material change in the position of the English Presbyterians relatively to the two other denominations. In anxious councils how best to meet and ward off the disastrous consequences of religious litigation, Mr. Aspland took a full share with the friends of religious liberty in both England and Ireland till very near the close of his life.

His first step was to call the attention of the Committee of the Unitarian Fund to the doctrines laid down in the Court of Chancery with regard to Unitarians.† A resolution was immediately passed recommending the ministers who were members of the Committee to confer with the other Antitrinitarian ministers in London and the neighbourhood upon the propriety of convening a meeting of Unitarians to deliberate upon the measures necessary to be taken in the present juncture for the protection of their civil rights. Of the result of the deliberations thus recommended mention will hereafter be made.

The subject of Blasphemy, and the propriety of regarding it as a civil offence, engaged his earnest attention. Finding no work in which the subject was fully discussed and in a liberal spirit, he prepared first for his congregation, and afterwards for the public through the press, a series of discourses on it. From a careful collation of those scriptures which relate to the sin of blasphemy, he shewed that, according to its etymology, it meant no more than evil-speaking, against whomsoever directed; that, in a religious sense, the Hebrew word was restricted by the earlier Israelites to evil-speaking against God; that in this sense, and this sense only, blasphemy was a capital crime by the Jewish law; that in this its most rigid meaning, the word is rarely, if ever, applied by our Lord and the apostles; that it is never applied by them to thoughts or opinions or simple error; that they have not given any sanction to its being considered as a civil offence and avenged by tem-

---

* The hapless lot of the relators should be a warning to those who are tempted to go into Chancery for the gratification of their bigotry. The costs of the Trustees were ordered to be first paid, and the residue of the estate was far from being sufficient to cover the costs of the promoters of the suit!

† Minutes of Unitarian Fund Committee, Aug. 1, 1817.

poral punishment; that *constructive blasphemy* (or the holding of opinions from which an opponent may draw a conclusion that he thinks dishonourable to God) was an artifice of the Pharisees in order to ensnare and destroy our Lord and the first disciples; and that the history of the doctrine is a narrative of the progress of uncharitableness, the charge of constructive blasphemy having been often brought against the holiest men, and advanced with the most zeal by men the most depraved and wicked. With regard to real blasphemy, he stated that, though he held it in utter abhorrence, he would leave it on earth to the punishment of the prompt, bold and stern indignation of all virtuous minds. He proved it to be the effect of the doctrine of constructive blasphemy to convert every church and every court of justice into an Inquisition.

To these discourses, when published, Mr. Aspland added an Appendix on the state of the Unitarians with regard to legal protection. He thus confutes the dogma that the Trinity Act had no effect on the common law, by which it was alleged that Unitarianism was an indictable offence.

"It might with equal propriety be contended that nonconformity is still an offence at common law, notwithstanding the Toleration Act. What that Act did for Dissenters at large, the Trinity Bill has done for Unitarian Dissenters. Lord Mansfield's argument, in his celebrated speech in the House of Lords, in the case of Evans, is as applicable to the latter as the former: he contended, and the Lords unanimously concurred with him, that the Act, by *repealing the penalty, had abolished the crime.*

"The Act of 1779, for relieving Dissenting ministers from a subscription to the Thirty-nine Articles, was a virtual extension of legal toleration to Antitrinitarians, who were chiefly contemplated by it, and who reposed in security under its shelter, until the Trinity Bill (Act) converted what might have been called an indulgence into a right.

"On what principle the common law can be said to be against Unitarians, it is impossible to imagine. No one, however adverse to them, dares to charge them with the direct blasphemy of reviling Almighty God, or with the indirect blasphemy of casting abuse upon Jesus Christ. They can be convicted of blasphemy only by the schoolmen's definition of the crime, which is so loose that every religious error may be shewn to be involved in it, and every sect may use it against every other sect."

In this Appendix, Mr. Aspland thus alluded to the opinion said to have been given by Sir Samuel Romilly, that by the common law Unitarianism was still indictable:

"It is rumoured that Sir Samuel Romilly does not admit the correctness of the report. His general character makes this credible. There is no lawyer or statesman living from whom the public would less expect an intolerant sentiment. Whatever doctrines the interests of his clients may make it necessary for him to advance in his pleadings, every one is confident that both his judgment and his feelings are on the side of liberality."

Subsequently, Mr. Aspland possessed better evidence than mere rumour as to the personal sentiments of Sir Samuel Romilly, as the two following letters shew. They were found in Mr. Aspland's papers. Every objection to their being made public time has removed.

Sir Samuel Romilly to Dr. Charles Lloyd.

"Russell Square, Aug. 2, 1817.

"Dear Sir,—I am much obliged to you for calling my attention to the account given in the Monthly Repository* of what passed lately in the Court of Chancery relative to a chapel at Wolverhampton. The gentleman who has given an account of these proceedings is certainly mistaken in stating that I argued, that impugning the doctrine of the Trinity was an offence at common law originally, and has continued so after the repeal of the Acts. I maintained no such doctrine; and it was with great surprise and some indignation that I heard from Mr. Shadwell that there were some prosecutions now depending, which proceed upon the notion that there is such a common-law offence. All that I argued (and I cannot but think that it was necessary to the decision of the case) was, that a legacy for the purpose of propagating the doctrine of Unitarianism would not be established by the Court of Chancery, and to that proposition the Chancellor, as I understood him, assented. It was decided by Lord Hardwicke, and his decision has been acted upon by succeeding Chancellors, that legacies given by Jews for reading lectures on the Hebrew Law in their synagogues would not be established by the Court of Chancery; but there is a great difference between this and maintaining that a Jewish priest is indictable for teaching the Jewish law.

"I remain, dear Sir, with great respect and esteem, your most obedient servant,
SAMUEL ROMILLY."

"Russell Square, Aug. 10, 1817.

"Dear Sir,—There is nothing I wish less than to have it established that the opinion which, as counsel in the case of the Wolverhampton Chapel, I

---

* The report was communicated by Mr. Edgar Taylor, who was accidentally in the Court of Chancery on the opening of the case of Attorney-General *versus* Pearson, and whose sagacious mind at once perceived the long train of mischievous consequences which those proceedings might entail. He took very copious notes of the proceedings and communicated them to the Monthly Repository, where they will be found, Vol. XII. 132. 141.

expressed, is correct. It would, on the contrary, give me very great pleasure to find that I was mistaken. I am sorry, however, to say Mr. E. Taylor's arguments have not convinced me that I was.* He cannot understand how it can be maintained that the Court of Chancery will not administer a trust for Unitarian worship, unless Unitarianism be an offence indictable at common law. But surely, as a lawyer, he must know that there are many acts which are so illegal that courts of justice will give no countenance to them, although they do not amount to indictable offences. It is illegal to trade with an enemy's country during time of war, and courts of justice refuse on that ground to enforce contracts which arise out of such a trade; and yet no one imagines that a man could be indicted for engaging in such a trade, or for underwriting policies of insurance on goods or ships employed in it. I am, however, not at all disposed to enter into any argument in defence of my opinion. When I said that I thought the Chancellor assented to it, I alluded, not to any thing said by him in his judgment, but to his having nodded assent to the proposition at the time it was stated. I am very sorry that my argument should have been mistaken and therefore misstated; but it is a misfortune I would rather submit to than have this or my former letter published. Such a publication might lead to a controversy which would be to me a very odious one, if I had to maintain a doctrine which it would give me very sincere pleasure to see refuted.

"I remain, dear Sir, with great respect and esteem, yours, &c.,

S. ROMILLY."

The perusal of Mr. Aspland's "Inquiry into the Nature of the Sin of Blasphemy, and into the Propriety of regarding it as a Civil Offence," shortly after modified the opinions of Sir Samuel Romilly, who addressed the author in a letter which it is feared is now lost. The most distinct reference to it occurs in the following letter.

Rev. Robert Aspland to his Brother Isaac.

"Hackney Road (Monday), October 7, 1817.

"Dear Brother,—Mrs. Aspland and I had a very pleasant journey this summer. She went no further than the neighbourhood of Shrewsbury: I went forward to Chester and Liverpool, and from thence struck into North Wales, which I traversed as far as the Isle of Anglesea. From Carnarvon, I came through Merionethshire, by Bala, to Wrexham. I was exceedingly pleased with the grandeur of the scenery, far surpassing any thing which I had before witnessed. I ascended one mountain (Cader Idris), of which the ascent was five miles, and one half of that in the clouds.

---

* Mr. Taylor's views on the subject were printed in the Monthly Repository, XII. 535—547. What Sir Samuel Romilly received was probably a much less elaborate statement. The article in the Magazine is dated "September 10."

"At Shrewsbury I preached many times, and one sermon by desire of *all the denominations of Dissenters* who support the Lancasterian schools. This they have united in requesting me to print,* which I must do, to make some return for so much liberality.

"I think I sent you my sermons on *Blasphemy*. These have brought me a very handsome letter from Sir Samuel Romilly, who says I have satisfied him that blasphemy is not cognizable by human tribunals.

"My health is, I hope, better established, but I feel the necessity of taking great care of myself: so you will think when you learn that I am trying the effect of the disuse of the pipe, and have not actually tasted tobacco since Friday! Whatever be the result with regard to me, the *revenue* will deeply suffer; but this is a loss in which you and I shall not very deeply sympathize.

"Dear brother, yours affectionately,

ROBERT ASPLAND."

One or two other letters written during this year claim a place. That which follows relates to a series of doctrinal lectures preached at Parliament Court.†

Rev. Thomas Belsham to Rev. Robert Aspland.

"Essex Street, Feb. 20, 1817.

"My dear Sir,—I am so much out of the habit of such kind of services as those proposed to be performed at Parliament Court, that, much as I approve of them, I find myself quite unequal to undertaking any active part in them: otherwise I should not need the stimulus which you have had the goodness to apply to rouse me to exertion. My day of service is nearly over, and I must now plead the privilege of being a *miles emeritus*. I have no fear that the cause will suffer by the loss of my humble efforts. I have seen it advance and prosper when much better and abler instruments were withdrawn. And so will you. Mr. Fox's settlement in London is a most promising sign. And I have no doubt that the interests of truth and goodness will greatly prosper under your combined efforts. I could wish that I were young enough to co-operate with you. But all is ordered well: and I am satisfied that I have had it in my heart to diffuse the light and spirit of the gospel, and have been honoured with some success. May you and your fellow-labourers be blest

---

* It was published under the title, "The Virtuous Use of Talents enforced in reference to the Education of Poor Children." It had a considerable local circulation in Shrewsbury, and was afterwards reprinted by the author in the first volume of his Sermons, pp. 131—154, as a record of his sentiments on the important subject of popular education.

† In labours of this kind Mr. Aspland was at this period abundant, beyond what a prudent regard to health dictated. In addition to the weekly conferences at Hackney, he assisted, during this winter, in a weekly lecture at Worship Street, and in a course of Sunday-evening lectures at St. Thomas's, Southwark.

with far greater success; and may you long be spared to labour in the vineyard, and to train up others for the same honourable office!

"I am, dear Sir, very sincerely yours,

T. BELSHAM."

The next letter was written during a short absence from home in search of health.

Rev. Robert Aspland to Mrs. Aspland.

"Newport, Isle of Wight, June 9, 1817.

"My dear Sara,—I received your welcome letter yesterday, and rejoice that its contents are upon the whole so pleasing. The sight of your handwriting in this place serves to realize the thoughts of you which are suggested to me perpetually by so many scenes and so many persons. I often wish you were with me in the island, dear to you as well as to me by so many tender recollections. * * * I have a tolerable report to give of myself. The weather makes me prudent. I was driven into Newport on Friday by the wind and fog that have made the back of the island no longer endurable; and here, amongst friends, I have recruited my health and spirits. I preached twice yesterday, but I preached only, and I find no inconvenience from this small exertion. For my return I must reserve the history of my visits and the account of our friends. * * * Poor Goodier! his appearance excites fears more than hopes; though perhaps there is no great alteration in him since last summer. He is, I think, more reduced. I have not yet been able to learn Mr. Bloxam's opinion. R. A."

Rev. Thomas Belsham to Rev. Robert Aspland.

"Essex Street, Dec. 14, 1817.

"Dear Sir,—You are at liberty to make what use you please of my sermon for poor B.: but I would just suggest whether it might not be worth while to defer it till the following month, and, in the mean time, to obtain leave from Mr. Broadbent to prefix to the biographical account the engraving which is now preparing to be prefixed to our young friend's two sermons.

"I see in the Repository an angry query about Dr. Priestley's preaching other persons' sermons. The fact is, he made no more of a secret that he occasionally preached Dr. Enfield's and Mr. Lindsey's sermons, especially after his own had been destroyed at the riots, than Dr. Parr does of preaching Zollikofer's. He found it difficult to compose on trite, commonplace subjects, and, in general, he thought he could employ his time better. He would have laughed at the idea of branding such a report as a calumny.

"I am, dear Sir, very sincerely yours,

T. BELSHAM."

Towards the close of the year 1817, Mr. Aspland had an opportunity of publicly acting on the principle which he had deliberately adopted respecting the impropriety of treating Blasphemy as a civil offence. He had for some time been acquainted with Mr. William Hone, first as a bookseller, whose conversation shewed him to be far better acquainted with the contents of books than is common with men of his order, and afterwards as the publisher of a cheap weekly political journal which advocated Reform principles and exposed with much boldness the corruption of the Government of the day. In the crusade against the press commenced in that year by Sir William Garrow, the Attorney-General, and continued by his successor, Sir Samuel Shepherd, Mr. Hone was marked out for punishment, and three indictments, founded on *ex-officio* informations, were preferred against him for publishing certain "scandalous, irreligious, profane, impious and seditious libels." The publications thus characterized by the Attorney-General were in fact political squibs, in the shape of Parodies on the Church Catechism, the Lord's Prayer, the Ten Commandments, the Litany, and the Creed of St. Athanasius. Mr. Hone, immediately on discovering that these publications were offensive to the taste and feelings of religious readers, discontinued their publication, and, notwithstanding a pressing demand for them (the usual consequence of a Government prosecution), refused to sell another copy. But the Attorney-General had another object besides suppressing impiety, and the prosecution proceeded. In preparing for his defence, Mr. Hone, all but destitute and friendless, sought Mr. Aspland's help. It was given most freely. He felt it to be a sacred duty to carry out his own principles respecting charges of blasphemy, and also to protect a political victim endangered by a simulated zeal for religion on the part of his persecutors. By means of his numerous friends, the composition of the jury-panel was investigated. Mr. Hone was supplied with suggestions, illustrations and books necessary for his defence. No one can read the three arguments of William Hone without perceiving that he must have been largely helped by some one well versed in the curiosities of English theological literature. Mr. Aspland attended the Court of King's Bench at Guildhall, Dec. 18, the day of the first trial, and, taking his seat by his side, encouraged and aided Mr. Hone during the difficulties and anxieties of that eventful day. The line of defence adopted was, after detailing the circumstances attending the prosecution, to argue that parodies were no novelty; that they were as old as the invention of printing; that there had been numerous parodies on religious writings, none of which had been prosecuted; that a parody need not be regarded as designed to ridicule the thing parodied, but might be intended simply to convey ludicrous ideas relating to some other subject. He recited parodies by Martin Luther, Bishop Latimer, Dr. Boys, Dean of Canterbury, Dr. Burnet, Master of the Charter-house, and other distinguished divines, statesmen and scholars. He adduced with admirable effect parodies on sacred things recently published and received with applause by Government writers, and dwelt with energy on the fact, that one member of the Government, Mr. Canning, had made great use of Parody in holding up to ridicule and execration his political opponents. Again and again was this defence interrupted by the Attorney-General and by Mr. Justice Abbott: it was asserted that the production of other parodies, however objectionable, was no defence for him. For a time, every new portion of the defence was objected to, from either the bar or the bench; but in vain: the courage of the defendant was dauntless: each interruption increased his energy and resolution; he indignantly asked whether the Judge had "a right to demand the nature of his defence?" One parody adduced was especially pertinent, being on the Ten Commandments, and published by the friends of the Government to ridicule revolutionary politics. The Judge stopped its being read, denouncing it as " a wicked publication." The defendant's rejoinder was, "*It was on the right side* —that made all the difference." With remarkable presence of mind he thus converted every interruption into the means of strengthening his case. His speech in defence lasted nearly six hours, and was listened to with attention and surprise by a crowded bar, as well as by the people who thronged every avenue of the Court. During the whole of this time Mr. Aspland was busily engaged in finding the several passages that were needed, in noting down hints of arguments or illustrative facts, and to his ready and exact memory, the fruits of which on this occasion were very rapidly pencilled down in a bold and legible manuscript, Mr. Hone afterwards acknowledged that he was greatly indebted.* Mr. Justice Abbott in his charge to the jury stated

---

* The Rev. W. Stevens, of Maidstone, then a student at the Academy, was present on the occasion, and to his recollections the narrative above owes some of its facts. His letter on the subject concludes in these words: "The generous and manly conduct of your father produced in me the most thrilling delight. His support, I believe, was exceedingly welcome to Mr. Hone on that occasion. In speaking of it afterwards at your father's table, he said, that ' when on his

"that the parody for which the defendant was prosecuted was scandalous, irreligious and libellous;" but the jury, after an absence of less than a quarter of an hour, brought in a verdict of acquittal. Scarcely had the eager applause with which the verdict was received by the crowd died away, before it was announced that Mr. Hone would the next morning at nine o'clock be put on his trial on a second indictment for a parody on the Litany. Mr. Aspland regarded this as the idle threat of a baffled and angry official. Not imagining for a moment that the Government would run the risk of another defeat, he did not attend the second and third trials. But the persecuted man did not lack friends on these occasions; and although Lord Ellenborough, perhaps the most resolute and strong-willed Judge who had sate upon the bench during the last half-century, left a sick room to conduct the remaining trials, Mr. Hone pursued with increasing energy the same line of defence, successfully beating down every obstacle that was thrown in his way, and after speeches, on the second day of nearly seven hours, and on the third of upwards of eight hours, received from his juries verdicts of NOT GUILTY. Universally and loudly did the public opinion of England condemn these prosecutions. Had their result been different, the coarse party press then at the command of the Government would not have failed to raise odium against a minister of religion who had dared to appear in public as the friend of a man charged with blasphemy. In that case, doubtless, Mr. Aspland would have calmly endured the consequences of the faithful performance of duty.

---

first entrance into court that morning, and casting his eyes hastily around, he saw not an individual whom he could reckon as his friend, he was almost overpowered by his sense of loneliness and peril, till Mr. Aspland's voice reached his ear. But seeing him, he was comforted, and his courage instantly returned.'"

CHAPTER XXIII.

It is time to speak of Mr. Aspland's connection with an ancient and highly important Nonconformist Trust, of which he was a member more than thirty years, during twenty of which he took a very active part in the administration of its affairs.

Dr. Daniel Williams, the founder of the public Library in Redcross Street, London, which bears his name, was one of the most distinguished Dissenting ministers of his day. He was born at Wrexham, about the year 1644. Of his parentage and education little is known. But his studies began early, and were from the first preparatory for the Christian ministry. At the early age of nineteen, he was admitted a preacher among the Presbyterians. It shews the strength of his convictions that he deliberately cast in his lot amongst the Nonconformists at the very commencement of the persecution which lasted, with but short periods of intermission, from the passing of the Act of Uniformity to the Revolution of 1688. How earnest he was in the performance of his duties as a Christian minister, appears from a statement made by himself a few years before his death, that from his first entrance on the ministry he had not been obliged wholly to omit preaching more than five Lord's-days. This statement, considering the times of persecution through which he lived, is very remarkable. He preached for a short period in various places in England, but the times were unpropitious to a settlement. At Weston, the seat of Sir Thomas Wilbraham (whose lady was the friend and protector of many of the early Nonconformists), Mr. Williams was introduced to the Countess of Meath, and received from her an appointment to a chaplaincy in Ireland. He officiated for a time to the Presbyterian congregation in Drogheda, and thence he removed in 1667 to Dublin, where he was minister for twenty years to the congregation assembling in Wood Street. Driven from Ireland by the persecuting proceedings of the Government, in the last year of the reign of James II., he repaired to London. Here he at once rendered an important service to both civil and religious liberty, by withstanding, in the presence of some agents of the Court, those who would persuade the Dissenters of London to address the King on his dispensing with the penal laws. Mr. Williams argued that Charles II. had persecuted Dissenters rather for standing in the way of arbitrary power than for the exercise of their religion, and that now they could do nothing worse than declare for measures which would destroy the civil liberties of England. So clearly and strongly did he maintain his argument, that the motion for an address was rejected. Soon after the Revolution, he settled with a numerous congregation in Hand Alley, Bishopsgate Street. He habitually associated with the most eminent and more liberal ministers of London. Baxter held him in great esteem; and, during his decline, sometimes appointed him to be his substitute in preaching the Merchants' Lecture at Pinners' Hall. The acute Jeremiah White pronounced him to be "a man of the best natural parts in England." John Howe, Dr. Bates, Dr. Edmund Calamy and Matthew Henry, were his personal friends. In his religious opinions he was moderately orthodox. He disliked and resisted extreme Calvinism, and was denounced by the Independents as a Socinian. Some of his controversial writings led to a violent dispute between the Presbyterian and Independent ministers of London, and occasioned the disruption of the "happy union" which had been formed between the two bodies in 1691. Not content with attacking his orthodoxy, some of his Independent adversaries aspersed his morals. Mr. Williams appealed to the body of the Dissenting ministers to scrutinize his life and character. After a searching inquiry, protracted for several weeks, a committee, which had been appointed to investigate the charges, pronounced Mr. Williams "clear and innocent of all that was laid to his charge." In 1709, he received the diploma of a Doctor in Divinity from the University of Edinburgh and that of Glasgow. He was permitted to live through the dark and threatening days of Queen Anne, and had the happiness of presenting an address of congratulation to George I. on his peaceable accession to the throne. He died, after a short illness, Jan. 26, 1716, in the 73rd year of his age. He had been twice married, first to an Irish, afterwards to an English lady, and by each marriage had acquired a considerable fortune. During his life, he had used his "worldly estate" with moderation, that he might be the more useful to others after his death.* Dr. Calamy observes that the charitable uses to which he devoted the bulk of his estate were various in their kinds, and much calculated for the glory of God and the good of mankind; and had certain legal defects in his will been amended, the disposition of his property would have been incomparable. After providing for the settlement of his wife's jointure, and leaving a number of legacies to relations and friends, amongst whom were many ministers, it was directed that £150 should be paid to the Society for the Reformation of Manners; £100 for the education of youth in Dublin; £40 to the poor of Wood-Street congregation, Dublin; £50 to the poor of Hand-Alley congregation; £100 to poor French refugees; £20 to the poor of Shoreditch parish. To St. Thomas's Hospital and the workhouse in Bishopsgate Street, he gave the reversion of an estate in Cambridgeshire. To the Presbyterian meeting-house in Burnham, Essex, he gave his houses in that town. To the College of Glasgow, he left, for the purpose of educating certain students of South Britain, £100 and two estates in Hertfordshire and Essex. The sons of Presbyterian ministers, if equally eligible, are to be preferred by his Trustees as candidates for the bursaries. To the Society for propagating Christian Knowledge in Scotland, he gave £100 and an estate in Huntingdonshire. To the New-England Society, he left an estate in Essex, to provide religious instruction to the Negroes in the West Indies, and for the conversion of the American Indians. The Trustees appointed under the will were directed to open and support schools in certain towns of Wales, and in Chelmsford in Essex,—to maintain an itinerant preacher in Ireland,—to pay small annuities to the Academy at Carmarthen, and to the Presbyterian chapel at Wrexham,—to reprint and distribute, from time to time, the works of the Founder,—to preserve his Library for public use in a freehold edifice to be purchased or built for that purpose, and to appoint and remunerate a Librarian. The Trustees were directed to apply the surplus of his estate, in certain definite proportions, to the following objects:—the distribution of Bibles and Catechisms to the poor; to the relief of ministers' widows and poor ministers; to apprenticing poor children educated in the schools at Wrexham, &c.; to aiding students for the ministry; and to ministers in North and South Wales.

With the liberality which is the characteristic of the English Pres-

---

* See the terms of his will.

byterians, Dr. Williams laid down no creed for his Trustees or beneficiaries, and desired his Trustees to exercise their own judgment with respect to his will, and "to be the sole judges of what might be doubtfully or darkly expressed."

Twenty-three Trustees were appointed by Dr. Williams to carry his will into effect. They included several of the most eminent Presbyterians residing in London in 1711, when the will was signed, e.g. Rev. Matthew Henry, Rev. Thomas Reynolds, Rev. William Lorimer, Rev. Benjamin Robinson, Rev. Jeremy Smith, Dr. Joshua Oldfield, Dr. Edmund Calamy, Rev. William Tong, Rev. Z. Merrell, Dr. John Evans, Dr. William Harris, Rev. Isaac Bates, Rev. James Read, and Rev. George Smyth.

The long list of Trustees chosen to fill up vacancies, exhibits many honoured names. To mention only a few, there are, 1729, Drs. Newman, Wright, Grosvenor, Avery, Earl, Hughes and Thomas Hollis; 1738, Rev. Moses Lowman; 1739, Dr. Lawrence; 1744, Dr. Samuel Chandler; 1758, Dr. George Benson; 1761, Dr. Richard Price; 1762, Rev. Hugh Farmer and Dr. Kippis; 1770, Dr. Caleb Fleming; 1774, Dr. Abraham Rees; 1785, Rev. Hugh Worthington; and, 1794, Samuel Rogers.

Great difficulties were experienced by the first Trustees in carrying the Founder's will into effect. It was not till 1727 that they were able to begin the building of the Library. The sum allowed by the Court of Chancery for the edifice proved insufficient; and, after some delay, it was completed by means of the benefactions of the Trustees and their friends. The Trustees held their first meeting at the Library, Dec. 8, 1729. The spacious rooms contain the library of the Founder, also the collections of Dr. Bates* and Dr. William Harris, and large additions made by Rev. Mr. Davies, Rev. Thomas Rowe, and many others, and by the periodical votes and the donations of the Trustees. The entire collection is now supposed to contain about 17,000 volumes. The number of separate works is about 22,000, of which 9000 probably are pamphlets.† The present nett income of the estates is about £1516 per annum.

---

* Dr. Bates was a learned bibliographer, and his library abounded in rare and curious works. In the department of religious tracts, the Library at Redcross Street is particularly rich. The second volume of the Catalogue (pp. 438) is devoted exclusively to this department.

† Art. on Public Libraries, British Quarterly Review, August, 1847.

Dr. Williams's foundations have rendered large services to religion, learning and the cause of religious liberty. Many useful, and some distinguished ministers have been educated by the aid of his funds: Thomas Urwick, George Walker, Ebenezer Radcliffe and Newcome Cappe may be mentioned. The Library has been thrown open to all who have required to consult its treasures. A distinguished literary journal, not much given to find any thing praiseworthy in Nonconformist institutions, has thus expressed itself respecting the liberality of the Trustees: " No public library in England is so liberally conducted as this. Books are lent from it, at the discretion of the Trustees, to any part of the country. The Advocates Library at Edinburgh, and many upon the continent, offer the same accommodation to men of literary research; but in England this example of the Dissenters has not yet been followed."*

Another service rendered by Dr. Williams's foundations was eloquently expressed by Dr. James Lindsay in his Oration delivered on the occasion of the Centenary of the Founder's death:—"The house in which we are now assembled, built in compliance with our Founder's will, has become, through the liberality of the Trustees, the place of public business to the collective body of Dissenters in this great city;—a place in which noble stands have often been made against ecclesiastical usurpation; in which generous efforts have originated to promote the extension of religious privileges to men of all persuasions;—a central point, round which the friends of religious freedom in every part of Britain rally, and from which even recently a spirit has gone forth, by which the bigots and persecutors of another country are abashed, at least, if not finally overcome."†

It was on many accounts gratifying to Mr. Aspland to be called on to share the responsibilities of Dr. Williams's Trust. He was nominated by the Rev. Jeremiah Joyce, on the occasion of the removal of Rev. N. T. Heinekin from Brentford to Gainsborough, and took his

---

* Quarterly Review, Oct. 1813, p. 119.

† The reference was to the proceedings of the London Ministers, designed to stay the persecution of the French Protestants. The *Three Denominations* no longer meet in one body. The Presbyterians continue to meet in the Library at Redcross Street. The same privilege would have been freely granted to the other Two Denominations. But when they incorrectly styled themselves the Three Denominations, notwithstanding the separation and the recognition by the Crown of the Presbyterians as a separate body, the privilege ceased, and they have since assembled at the Congregational Library.

seat at the Board, June 24, 1811. The Chairman of the Board on that occasion was Rev. Thomas Belsham, who read to the newly-admitted Trustee the solemn concluding words of the Founder's will, in which he invokes the blessing of God upon its faithful execution, and entreats all concerned honestly and prudently and diligently to employ to those ends what he designed for the glory of God and the good of mankind. At the time of Mr. Aspland's admission, the Trust consisted of the following members:

Elected	*Clerical*	*Elected*	*Lay*
1774	Abraham Rees	1784	Edmund Calamy
1777	Thomas Tayler	1791	John Towgood
1785	Hugh Worthington		George Lewis
1787	James Lindsay	1793	John Wansey
1801	Thomas Belsham	1794	William Esdaile
1802	Jeremiah Joyce	1804	Swan Downer
1803	William Johnston	1805	Isaac Solly
1804	John Coates	1807	James Esdaile
1806	Joseph Barrett	1810	John Bentley
1807	James Pickbourn		Richard Holt
1809	El. Cogan	1810	John Wainewright
	Thomas Rees		*(Secretary)*.
1804	Thomas Morgan*		
	(Librarian).		

Amongst Mr. Aspland's associates in the Trust, there was no one with whom he was more frequently united, both in sentiment and action, than Dr. Thomas Rees. From that kind friend the Editor of

---

* The gentlemen afterwards associated with Mr. Aspland in the Trust were —

Elected	*Clerical*	*Elected*	*Lay*
1812	John Lane	1812	James Gibson
1814	Alex. Crombie, LL.D.		James Esdaile
1814	John Potticary	1815	Samuel Nicholson
1816	Arch. Barclay, LL.D.	1820	John Wansey
1819	Wm. Johnson Fox	1823	David Martineau
1820	John Stevenson Geary	1826	Edward Busk
1821	John Philip Malleson	1828	Joseph Yellowley
	John Jones, LL.D.	1829	Abraham Lincoln.
1825	David Davison, M.A.	1833	William Wansey
1827	John Scott Porter	1835	Isaac Solly Lister.
1830	Thomas Madge		
1831	James Yates, M.A.		
1832	Edward Tagart		
1833	George Kenrick		
1835	Joseph Hunter, F.S.A.		

this Memoir has received the following letter respecting the Trust and Mr. Aspland's share in its administration.

"Brixton, March 26, 1849.

"My dear Sir,—You will, I am sure, believe that no light consideration could deter me from complying with your request, to furnish some account of your excellent and revered father in his capacity of a Trustee of Dr. Williams's charities. There are, however, circumstances which render such an undertaking on my part a matter of some difficulty and delicacy. Those charities are under the management of more than twenty gentlemen of high character, all equally intent on the faithful discharge of their official duties. It might, on this account, be deemed somewhat invidious to select for special notice and commendation an individual member of the body, as having the appearance of disparaging the merits of his associates, and placing their services in an unfavourable contrast. But I need not fear a sinister interpretation of this kind being put upon my language. I estimate too highly the candour and generosity of my respected colleagues to believe them to be capable of taking offence at any terms of praise applied to the character and labours of an associate, who, while living, was held by them in high esteem, the value of whose co-operation they justly appreciated, and whose eminent services were, on frequent occasions, the subject of their eulogium.

"Mr. Aspland held his appointment for nearly forty years, having been admitted in 1811, two years subsequently to my own introduction into the Trust. He had at this time attained a position of great respectability, and established a high reputation, among the Presbyterian ministers of London, not alone by his professional services in the pulpit, but also by his active labours in religious and charitable institutions belonging to the Dissenters. The intellectual and moral qualities which had procured for him these distinctions, naturally recommended him to the favourable notice of Dr. Williams's Trustees, who gladly availed themselves of an early vacancy to introduce him into their ranks.

"Ardent in temper, and active from disposition and habit, Mr. Aspland was not a man to remain idle at his post. He promptly applied himself to learn the nature and the objects of the charge he had undertaken, and forthwith embarked with alacrity and zeal in the various labours it appeared to impose: and from this time forward, through the whole of his life, he was distinguished as one of the most assiduous and efficient members of the Trust.

"The extent and the value of Mr. Aspland's services cannot be fully understood and duly appreciated without a knowledge of the numerous and varied duties attached to the office of Trustee. A brief enumeration of the principal matters may furnish some notion of their nature and importance.

"The general business relating to Dr. Williams's charities comprehends, first, the charge and management of the property, chiefly landed estates, from which are derived the funds destined for their support; and, next, the application or appropriation of those funds to the benevolent objects they were appointed to promote. These objects comprise, among others, the maintenance of the public Library in Redcross Street—the education of divinity students in the University of Glasgow—the support of schools for the instruction of the children of the poor—the distribution of books on practical religion—the advancement of the Dissenting interest in Wales—the assistance of poor Dissenting ministers and the widows of such, &c., &c.

"The chief part of the business relating to these objects is transacted by the Trustees at large, at stated periodical meetings. But for the greater convenience and facility of disposing of matters of detail, much that relates to each department is referred to the management of standing committees. Whether, then, Mr. Aspland appeared at the general meetings or at those of any of the committees, on most of which he was appointed, he always occupied a prominent position as a regular, diligent and influential member.

"Numerous as were the claims on his time, from his professional engagements, or from requisitions to take a part in public proceedings in the Dissenting body, having reference to their civil rights or religious liberties, in which his assistance was frequently courted, he took his full share of the labours arising out of the several branches of the Trust. When questions arose as to the management of the property, he was generally present to join in the deliberations and to aid by his opinion and counsel; and on more than one occasion he was named one of a deputation to visit and examine the estates. Upon these deputations it was my happiness to be one of his associates; and I can bear my testimony to the admirable judgment and ability with which he discharged the duties of his mission.

"In the administration of the funds of the charity, the maintenance of the Library ranks among the objects of chief importance. Apart from the functions of the Librarian, which are distinct and weighty, the committee entrusted with its direction are charged with duties of considerable consequence. To them pertain the general superintendence of the Library, and the selection and purchase of books and manuscripts for its augmentation. In these occupations Mr. Aspland took deep interest and rendered great assistance. His studious habits, his varied erudition, and his extensive bibliographical knowledge, imparted great weight to his opinion and judgment in this department, and rendered his co-operation eminently valuable.

"A few years ago, the Library committee had to prepare a new Catalogue of the books. For the satisfactory accomplishment of this object, it was necessary that the entire collection should be carefully examined and collated. This labour was assigned, for convenience, to a small sub-committee, of whom Mr. Aspland was one; and his colleagues had the benefit of his presence and active co-operation through the whole of the troublesome task.

"The provision made by Dr. Williams for the education of divinity scholars at Glasgow, constitutes an important part of his charities. The selection of the students, and the determination of the qualifications for admission, rest with the Trustees. It has been their great aim to render these scholarships as serviceable as possible to the promotion of sound learning among those who are appointed to them, and they have with this view applied themselves with great care to fix the subjects and the books, and the measure of proficiency in the classical languages and the abstract sciences, as in their judgment the most proper to fit the applicant to enter with advantage on the College course, and to graduate with the highest credit and honour. Of the Glasgow College committee, on whom these important duties devolved, Mr. Aspland was long an active and efficient member. He took his share with his colleagues in the deliberations on the difficult question of the literary qualifications, and, while his health permitted, attended the examinations of the candidates for admission, intended to test their proficiency.

"The schools founded by Dr. Williams in Wales for the instruction of the children of the poor are comparatively humble institutions; but, in the state of education in the Principality, have been productive of much good. Mr. Aspland was a member of the committee having the more immediate charge of these seminaries. The object was one in which he felt a lively interest, and he took pleasure in watching over their management and promoting their efficiency. When the Trustees, in order to acquaint themselves with their actual condition, and to ascertain of what improvement they might be susceptible, appointed a deputation to visit and inspect them, Mr. Aspland was selected as one of the number. On this occasion I had the pleasure of being one of his associates, the other being our mutual friend Mr. James Esdaile. With that deference to his judgment and experience in such matters which was justly his due, we appointed him the Chairman of the deputation, and committed to him the chief labour of the examination of the scholars, and we had reason to be well pleased with the kindness and the efficiency with which he acquitted himself.

"It is scarcely necessary to descend into further details of the Trust business to shew with what zeal and fidelity Mr. Aspland discharged the duties of his office. It will suffice to add, that in all other matters under the administration of the managers, such as the selection of books on practical theology for distribution, the advancement of the Dissenting interest in Wales by the appointment of ministers to special services in particular localities, or in dispensing occasional assistance to poor ministers and ministers' widows, he was always ready to aid by his presence and his counsel, and to contribute his share of labour to accomplish to the utmost practicable extent the benevolent purposes contemplated by the founder of the Trust.

"In preparing this summary, I feel very sensibly that I have been able to convey but a very imperfect impression of the nature, extent and importance of Mr. Aspland's services in the administration of Dr. Williams's charities. Enough has, however, been said to render it apparent, that he devoted to them large portions of his time and energies; whilst his excellent understanding, his sound judgment and his philanthropic spirit, imparted to the whole singular value and efficiency.

"I cannot conclude this retrospect without expressing the gratification I experienced in being associated with my ever-esteemed and much-lamented friend in the discharge of common duties throughout the whole period of his connection with the Trust. During this long interval we were engaged in many important discussions in which differences of opinion might naturally occur; but on no occasion was the harmony of our feelings towards one another in the least degree disturbed, nor our friendly attachment—anterior in its origin to that of our professional career and official connection—ever for a single instant interrupted.

"Believe me to remain, my dear Sir, most truly yours,

THOMAS REES.

"*Rev. R. B. Aspland.*"

In the Centenary Oration already referred to, it was declared with great truth and with becoming pride, that "no Trust was ever discharged with more care, or applied with more disinterested fidelity to fulfil the intentions of the founder, than that of Dr. Williams."*

A circumstance may be mentioned in this connection which will illustrate the delicate sense of honour which actuated Mr. Aspland in the use of the patronage which belonged to the Trust. In the year 1819, his eldest son commenced the more public part of his education for the Christian ministry, and Glasgow was the University selected for him. There were more bursaries than one to be allotted that year by the Trustees, and his colleagues expressed their more than willingness to assign one to his son. He felt, however, an invincible reluctance to permit funds in the management of which he had a share to be applied to his own benefit, and he provided from his own means for his son's residence at

---

* Dr. Lindsay eloquently added, "If that Founder could have foreseen that men who were to be the ornaments of science as well as religion—the Chandlers and Kippises, the Prices and Priestleys, the Reeses and Belshams of the coming age, the future champions of that learning and freedom which he loved—if he could have foreseen that such men would have given their time and labour to promote the objects of his piety, it would have added one delightful feeling more to those which must have passed through his mind in contemplating the probable effects of his own beneficence."

Glasgow.* The self-denial was enhanced by the fact that at this period he had to bear the charge of educating seven or eight of his children.

To the purity of the administration of their office by the existing generation of Dr. Williams's Trustees and their immediate predecessors, remarkable testimony was lately borne by one in high legal station. In 1843, as one of the consequences of the decision, adverse to the Unitarians, of the suit respecting Lady Hewley's Trust, an information was filed against the Trustees of Dr. Williams by a solicitor who had been engaged for orthodox parties in the Hewley case. The suit was subsequently stayed by the order of Sir Frederick Pollock, the Attorney-General, in whose name the proceedings were necessarily taken. In 1846, the Attorney-General (Sir Frederick Thesiger) summoned to his chambers the counsel and solicitors of the Relators in the suit, and also the solicitor of the Trustees; and after listening to an argument protracted to a late hour at night, in which the respective law-agents contended for and against the renewal of the proceedings against the Trustees, he determined that his sanction as Attorney-General should be withdrawn from the Relators. The ground on which he gave his official protection to the Trustees was, that they had well and faithfully administered the Trust, and in all respects conformed to the wishes of the Founder. He did not think the suit, in the altered state of the law, a proper one, and refused to expose the charity to litigation and loss merely on account of the personal religious opinions of the Trustees.† Mr. Aspland did not live to receive this disinterested and significant testimony to the integrity of the Trust. The suit occasioned him some anxious hours during the last two years of his life, and he solaced himself during a portion of his long confinement to the house by studying whatever threw light on the principles and opinions of Dr. Daniel Williams, of the Trustees named in his will, and of their immediate successors.

One of the few rewards of his Trusteeship was the occasional society of his colleagues in office. Four times a year the Trustees, in accordance with the directions of their Founder, assembled round a table spread

---

* The same difficulty did not apply to his son's subsequent admission to the College at York. Then Mr. Aspland gratefully accepted the offer of the Trustees, conveyed to him in terms of marked kindness, to place his son as a student on the foundation.

† See the proceedings as reported in the *Record* and *Inquirer* newspapers, March, 1846.

with plain yet substantial hospitality. That frugal table had, however, attractions of the best kind;—knowledge and strong intellectual power generally, and sometimes eloquence and wit, seasoned the conversation of the guests. The party assembled in the principal room of the Library, which is hung round with portraits of Nonconformist worthies. Earlier in the century, before fashion had put aside all distinctions of costume, venerable divines in state-wigs and the other insignia of the clerical dress, and aged gentlemen in the becoming costume of a former generation, sat near the head of the table, and equalled, if they did not surpass, in dignity the figures which looked down upon them from the surrounding canvas. With stately grace did Dr. Abraham Rees preside over these simple banquets: his powers of conversation were great. On one side of him would sit Dr. Lindsay, on whom Nature had been prodigal in its gifts, and who to a noble person added the endowments of a powerful and cultivated mind. On the other side might be seen Mr. Belsham, whose manners were those of the gentleman, as his conversation was that of the scholar and the wit. Not unfrequently some interesting stranger, a scholar, or a traveller from abroad, or some valued friend of religious liberty—Dr. Parr, Mr. Everett, Mr. William Smith or Mr. G. W. Wood—was an invited guest.

From a manuscript book in Mr. Aspland's hand, dated 1821, are taken the following notes of a conversation, which may serve as a specimen of the table-talk of Dr. Williams's Library:

"*Jan. 11, 1821.—Dr. Rees* related the pleasant meetings of a Club which used to meet at the London Coffee-house, of which Dr. Franklin was a member. Every thing new in the Royal Society was there talked of. Dr. F. was the life of the Club; but when a stranger was introduced was always mute. On the breaking out of the American war, the Club became political: this lessened its usefulness; but the first news of proceedings in America were there to be learned.

"Dr. Franklin was exceedingly fond of the air-bath, i.e. of stripping himself and sitting in a strong current of air. Dr. Heberden once told him that he went beyond him in this way; for he not only sate unclothed in a draught, but took a pitcher of water and threw it up to the ceiling, and let it fall on his body.

"*Mr. Belsham.*—Dr. Franklin was sceptical. He told Dr. Priestley that he had never fairly studied the evidences of Christianity, and lamented that, owing to his having in early life been accustomed to hear Christianity ridiculed, he was never able to bring himself to study it seriously. Dr. Kippis and Dr. Harris always looked on Dr. F. with suspicion.

"*Dr. Rees.*—But Dr. Priestley idolized him. Dr. Kippis knew little of the world; Dr. Harris differed from Dr. F. in his politics. The truth lay between the two.

"*Dr. Rees* talked on his favourite subject of the safety of the *middle path*. He reminded Mr. Belsham that, in company with Dr. Price once, he (Mr. B.) had asserted that he was a middle man; upon which Dr. P. replied, 'If you be in the middle, I can point out one extreme; but where is the other?'

"*Mr. Le Breton* told of a late pleasantry at the Westminster school. There was a question (debated in Latin) concerning the morality of the Romans who killed Julius Cæsar, and it was said, 'Nec male fecerunt, nec bene fecerunt, sed *interfecerunt.*' What was the meaning of *inter* in this word? We had *medley* in a similar sense.

"*Mr. Belsham.*—*Chance-medley* is accidental homicide.

"*Dr. Rees* expatiated on his Arian views. He believed in the pre-existence of Christ—a distinguished spiritual being in a former state, perhaps this world, before the revolutions that preceded what is called the creation. The spiritual nature took the place of a human soul at generation. All souls pre-existed.

"*Mr. Belsham* would probably agree with the Dr. if he knew his meaning.

"Both Dr. Rees and Mr. Belsham eulogized Bishop Pearce as a commentator. His exposition of our Lord's saying to Mary, 'Touch me not,' was quoted with approbation. But Mr. Belsham said that Mr. Wakefield held the Bishop cheap as a biblical critic.

"*Dr. Rees* complained jocosely of the precipitancy of theological inquirers, who would not stop at the right point. *Mr. Belsham* replied, that he had been in the Dr.'s favourite *mean* for twenty years, which he thought quite long enough to remain in Arianism.

"Thomas Lord Lyttelton.—*Dr. T. Rees* inquired after the account of his death. *Mr. Belsham* was last week in company with a person who lived with him at the time of his death, which really took place as related. He had the day before made a brilliant speech in the House of Lords, and the excitement brought his brain into a morbid state. He was both superstitious and profligate.

"*Mr. Parkes.*—He had debauched two of his cousins.

"*Dr. Rees.*—He once told Dr. Priestley that they were agreed on the subject of a future life. The Dr. said, No; quite the contrary. His Lordship denied an hereafter; he believed in it on the testimony of Divine Revelation. Yes, said his Lordship, granting Divine Revelation, I believe in it too.

"On some observations of mine in censure of the *Morning Chronicle* and of *Mr. Perry's* degeneracy as a politician and writer, *Mr. Belsham* said, 'I was as bad as *Mr. Jekyll*, who had observed that he (Mr. J.) was a *Whig*, but not a *Perry-Whig.*'

"*Dr. Rees* recurred to the story of his having been forbidden, through Dr. Stanier Clarke, the librarian to Carlton House, to dedicate the Cyclopædia to the present King (see Mon. Repos. XV. 704), and of his having communicated with the Duke of Kent upon the subject, who expressed his conviction that his Majesty knew nothing of the matter—he, unlike his father, George III., being accustomed to leave matters to his secretaries—and promised that he would, on a fitting opportunity, mention the affair to the King. (The Duke attributed the prohibition to Clarke's bigotry; Dr. Rees attributes it to something personal growing out of the Cyclopædia.) The pretence of refusal was, that his Majesty must not be made responsible for the contents of so multifarious a work as the Cyclopædia; but on this the Duke of Kent remarked, that the plea was idle, for no one held even Dr. Rees, the editor, responsible for every article. The Dr. says he told the Duke that he should have liked to dedicate the work to him, but his (the Duke's) political opinions were so objectionable at Court. His Royal Highness assented, and stated that he should have been a candidate for the Presidency of the Royal Society, on the late vacancy by the death of Sir Joseph Banks, if he had not been enjoined to the contrary from Carlton House.

"At Library, Redcross Street, meeting of Book Committee, in conversation on brother F.'s plan of turning bookseller, *Dr. Rees* said that Dr. Chandler had been bookseller in London while minister at Peckham, and that he was in trade when he was chosen to the Old Jewry. He published his own answer to Collins, who used to frequent his shop."

Few men have through life more enjoyed the best pleasures of social intercourse than the subject of this Memoir. His powers of conversation were considerable; his animal spirits were seldom surpassed; he was quick in reading the character of a new associate, and equally happy in bringing out both its eccentric and its better qualities; he had humour himself and elicited it from others. In the not unimportant social art of story-telling he was sufficiently happy; and they that have listened with pleasure to his details of his early life, and his sketches of the religious world, will remember how racy was his style, and how successful he was in making his points. His happiest efforts in this way were over his pipe, of which he made almost a dramatic use, and tantalized the curiosity of his friends by a pause and an elaborate puff of tobacco whenever he approached the turning point of the story. If he occupied more than a proportionate share of the talk, it was usually freely granted to him by his associates. Of coxcombry and affectation and silliness he was markedly intolerant, and could in a very few minutes relieve a party from a tedious infliction of folly and vanity, by providing *a bridle for the ass, and a rod for the fool's back.*

If in his presence a corrupt sentiment was uttered, or a base action applauded, the offender was reminded of his transgression against good morals with such decision, yet with so much personal presence and dignity, that defence was commonly felt to be vain.

Mr. Aspland made little use of the opportunities which his vicinity to the metropolis and his social position afforded him, of entering into merely literary or political *coteries*. He had nothing of the now fashionable taste for *lionizing*. Unless he found in a companion intellectual, moral and social sympathies, he cared nothing for him as an object of any kind of celebrity. Although he had some literary friends whom he greatly valued, such as Anna Maria Porter, George Dyer, Mr. Rutt and Dr. Bowring, he did not think the habits of the literary class favourable to the cultivation of the finest moral qualities. In some instances which fell under his own personal observation, he saw that celebrity was fatal to religious sincerity, and that the admiration of the world darkened the moral vision and enfeebled the courage of men who in youth gave promise of better things.

It was once observed to the writer by a friend who often met Mr. Aspland in society, and in several circles, that he never saw him where he did not take and easily keep a foremost place. He might be surpassed by one in learning, by another in wit, by another in grace; yet his breadth of understanding, his well-stored memory and his habitual force of expression, always secured him respectful audience from the most gifted of his associates. At various periods of his life, he formed or united himself with several social clubs. One of these still exists, and bears very distinctly the impress of his ruling tastes. It deserves to be mentioned also on account of its contributions to Nonconformist literature, and the aid it has been enabled, during its existence of more than thirty years, to render to religious liberty.

The *Non-Con* Club was formed at his house in July, 1817. The object proposed by it is stated in the preamble of the minutes, written by his hand, to be, " to promote the great principles of Truth and Liberty as avowed and acted upon by the enlightened and liberal Nonconformists or Protestant Dissenters from the Church of England." He perceived in the signs of the times the approach of struggles, and he thought it well that the friends of liberal principles, on whose fellowship he could safely count, should be strengthened by more frequent intercourse, and by the interchange of their thoughts on passing events and their bearing on civil and religious liberty.—The rules of the Club were simple, aiming chiefly to secure to the members frequent meetings of a social kind and on an inexpensive plan, and prescribed that at each meeting an essay should be read "on some subject connected with Nonconformity." Each member presided in his turn, and was directed to give *verbatim* three standing toasts:—1, *The Memory of the Two Thousand;* 2, *John Milton;* and 3, *Civil and Religious Liberty all the World over.* The only members present at the formation of the Club were Mr. Aspland, Mr. Edgar Taylor, Rev. W. J. Fox, Mr. (now Sergeant) T. N. Talfourd and Mr. C. Richmond. The other original members were, Mr. (now Dr.) John Bowring, Dr. Morell, Dr. Thomas Rees, Mr. Richard Taylor, Mr. Smallfield, Mr. John Taylor and Mr. Samuel Parkes. They were afterwards joined, amongst others, by Dr. Barclay, Mr. M. D. Hill, Dr. Southwood Smith, Mr. Joseph Parkes, Rev. H. Acton, Rev. J. E. Bicheno, Mr. George Dyer, Dr. John Jones, Mr. Edward Taylor, Rev. D. Davison, Rev. J. Scott Porter, Rev. G. Roberts, Rev. John Coates, Rev. B. Mardon, Mr. James Yates, Mr. E. W. Field, Rev. E. Chapman, Rev. Geo. Kenrick, Rev. E. Tagart, Mr. Alderman Lawrence, Rev. Thomas Madge, Mr. H. C. Robinson, Mr. H. B. Fearon, Mr. Benj. Wood, M.P., Mr. John Dillon; and as honorary members, by Rev. W. Hincks, Rev. John Kenrick, Mr. (now Sir) Charles A. Elton and Mr. Walter Wilson. The formation of this Club was a very successful experiment. It furnished a friendly meeting-place for men well qualified by their principles and accomplishments to improve and adorn the social hour, and, as will be hereafter mentioned, it led to one or two not unimportant practical results. During the sitting of Parliament, Liberal Members of the House of Commons and distinguished foreigners were occasionally invited guests, and sometimes the discussions that ensued were interesting and important. For several years, in accordance with the original plan, essays were read by the members, and most of these were subsequently printed in the *Monthly Repository.* A list of the writers and their subjects is now subjoined. The series began, under the general title of "The Nonconformist," in Vol. XIII., and were stated to be the production of "gentlemen who had associated to promote inquiry into the literature and history of the Nonconformists."

1. Mr. Aspland—"A Vindication of the Two Thousand Ejected Ministers."

2. Dr. Bowring—"The Opinions of the Puritans respecting Civil and Religious Liberty."

3. Mr. W. J. Fox—" On the Conduct of the Quakers as distinguished from that of other Nonconformists in the Reign of Charles II."

4. Mr. S. Parkes—" On the General Prevalence of Superstition."

5. Dr. Thomas Rees—" Faustus Socinus and Francis David.'

6. Mr. Richmond—" The Cause of Nonconformity as connected with the Interests of General Literature."

7. Mr. Smallfield—" The Principles and Conduct of the Baptists respecting Civil and Religious Liberty."

8. Mr. Talfourd—" The Intolerance of the Dissenters usually denominated ' Orthodox,' as compared with that of the Established Churches."

9. Mr. Edgar Taylor—" Memoir of Wetstein."

10. Mr. Richard Taylor—" On High-church Infidels."

11. Dr. Bowring—" Sketch of the History and Literature of the Spanish Jews."

12. Mr. Aspland—" The Corporation and Test Acts."

13. Mr. W. J. Fox—" The controverted Clause in the 20th Article of the Church of England."

14. Mr. S. Parkes—" Life and Character of Hugh Peters, Chaplain to Oliver Cromwell and the Parliament."

15. Dr. T. Rees—" The Sentiments of the early Continental Reformers respecting Religious Liberty."

16. Mr. Talfourd—" The supposed Affinity of the Poetical Faculties with Arbitrary Power and Superstitious Faith."

17. Mr. Richmond—" On the Patronage of Religion by the Civil Power."

18. Mr. Edward Taylor—" On Mahometanism: its Church Establishment and Treatment of Nonconformists, particularly the Wahabites."

19. Dr. Bowring—" Ultra-Catholicism in France."

20. Mr. Aspland—" Inquiry into the Operation of Mr. Brougham's Education Bill as far as regards Protestant Dissenters."

21. Mr. Richard Taylor—" Inquiry respecting Private Property and the Authority and Perpetuity of the Apostolic Institution of a Community of Goods."

22. Mr. M. D. Hill—" On Freedom in Matters of Opinion."

23. Mr. Hincks—" The Old Crab-stock of Nonconformity."

24. Dr. T. Rees—" The Attempts that were made for the Reformation of Religion in Italy in the Seventeenth Century."

25. Mr. Richmond—"The existing Disabilities and Inconveniences which attach to Dissent from the Church of England."

26. Dr. Southwood Smith—"Plan of an Institution for acquiring and communicating an accurate Knowledge of the Scriptures without Expense."

27. Mr. Edgar Taylor—"Mahometan Influence on Christian Literature and Opinions."

28. Mr. Acton—"On the Maxim, that Christianity is Part and Parcel of the Law of the Land."

29. Mr. Walter Wilson—"On the Causes of the Decline of Nonconformity."

30. Mr. Richard Taylor—"On Religious Prosecutions."

31. Dr. Bowring—"State of Religion in Sweden."

32. Mr. Mardon—"The Principle of Subscription to Human Formularies of Faith."

CHAPTER XXIV.

A LARGE portion of the present Chapter must be devoted to a selection from Mr. Aspland's correspondence.

Rev. Thomas Belsham to Rev. Robert Aspland.

"Essex Street, Jan. 7, 1818.

"Dear Sir,—I enclose a few remarks upon my friend Heinekin's letter* in your last Repository; and having said my say, I mean now to take leave of the subject. The controversy lies in a nutshell; but the insurmountable obstacle is the want of authority from the New Testament, and the magical effect of the word Tradition. Upon this subject Catholics argue far more rationally than Protestants, who always assume, though they do not explicitly assert, the universal inspiration of the N. T. Let but each book be considered as a separate record, more or less perfect, and resting on its own specific evidence, and the spell is dissolved. All evidence will then be historical, or, if you please, traditional. Till this is done, we shall never appreciate the N. T. rationally or justly, nor value it according to its real and inestimable worth. But I am running into a dissertation instead of a letter.

"In your interesting memoir of Joyce you have fallen into an error—not, indeed, of any moment. He officiated and administered the Lord's Supper at Prince's Street the day when he underwent his painful and hazardous operation. When he returned home, Mr. Cline had been a short time in waiting for him.—With the best compliments of the season to yourself, Mrs. Aspland and your whole family circle, I am, dear Sir, very sincerely yours,

T. BELSHAM."

The severe and anxious duties which at this time occupied Mr. Aspland, as resident Tutor of the Unitarian Academy, as the Editor of two religious periodicals, and as the Secretary of the Unitarian Fund, in addition to those of the pulpit and the pastoral office, were excessive,

---

* Mr. Belsham's Plea for Infant Baptism was about this time the subject of much criticism in the Monthly Repository.

and in the end seriously impaired his health. During considerable portions of the years 1818 and 1819, he was disabled by serious illness. In ascending the mountain of Cader Idris, in the autumn of 1817, he had given himself a strain, of which at the time he made light, but the effects of which he felt to the close of his life in periodical visitations of acute local disease. His general health also for a time gave way, and he yielded to the urgent remonstrances of his medical advisers, so far as to contract the very wide circle of his public engagements. The financial condition of the Unitarian Academy, from the first unsatisfactory, had latterly become hopelessly bad. He felt it impossible to continue the struggle to maintain the institution, and after the session of 1818, the students did not return to Durham House. The Secretaryship of the Unitarian Fund, which he had held from the establishment of the Society in 1806, was also of necessity resigned,* and was undertaken by Rev. W. J. Fox, whose removal from Chichester to London, as successor to Mr. Vidler, had been earnestly promoted by Mr. Aspland, and had been hailed with general satisfaction by the friends of popular Unitarianism in London.

If pecuniary considerations had been allowed to sway him, he would at the same time have discontinued the *Monthly Repository*, the sale of which, after twelve years' struggle, was announced to be "not adequate to the expense, much less to the labour, required to conduct it reputably." The nation was now severely suffering from heavy taxation, the consequence of the costly war recently brought to a close. Periodical literature quickly feels the effects of hard times. But experience had increased his conviction of the importance to the Unitarian body of

---

* At the anniversary meeting held May 13, the following resolution was unanimously adopted: "That the members of this Society learn with deep regret that Mr. Aspland's ill health prevents his again accepting the office of Secretary. His important, laborious and continued services have entitled him to their warmest gratitude. They are convinced that the respectability, usefulness and permanence of the Unitarian Fund; its gradual progress; its present flourishing state; the removal of prejudices against its objects and means; the fitness of its plans, and the success of its endeavours, are mainly attributable to his zeal, prudence, ability and indefatigable exertion. It is their hope and prayer that his health may be perfectly re-established, and his valuable life long spared to his family and friends, the church of Christ, and society at large. And although his labours as Secretary of this Society be at present discontinued, they hope that he will continue to watch over its interests, and that he may continue to enjoy the reward of his disinterested exertions in its behalf by beholding the extensive diffusion of just and liberal sentiments of religion amongst the poor of this country."

a publication like the Monthly Repository, and indeed of " its necessity to enable them to co-operate in their various institutions and associations for common good," and, notwithstanding declining health, he made an earnest appeal to the denomination in behalf of the Magazine, anxious, at all events, to secure its continuance, even if he should find it necessary to resign the conduct of it into other hands. The appeal was answered with great liberality, and in the following year he was enabled to offer both it and the *Christian Reformer*, as successful and in a small degree profitable works, to his friend Mr. Rutt. The agreement to transfer the editorship and proprietorship of the two Magazines to that gentleman was all but completed, when, for some reasons not stated, it was suddenly put aside.—The following is one of many letters addressed to Mr. Aspland on the subject of the Monthly Repository.

Rev. John Yates to Rev. Robert Aspland.

"Dinglehead, near Liverpool, Jan. 21, 1818.

"My dear Sir,—It was with concern I learned from the Preface to the last volume of the Monthly Repository, that the work has not so extensive a sale as I expected. Some true friends of the cause here have made a point of speaking on the subject during the last fortnight, in consequence of which nearly forty additional copies will be ordered for Liverpool; and as Mr. Freme tells me there is an opportunity of a private conveyance, I write to inform you of this circumstance, that you may order a larger number of copies for January 1818 to be printed.

"I fear, my good friend, you will have the mortification to find that those who have displayed great zeal in words, as if there had been no honest, avowed and zealous Unitarians until they appeared, are not more steady, and more disposed to give their time and money and labour to the cause, than those who were always avowed Unitarians, but were chiefly distinguished in the world as the friends of religious liberty. All the facts at least that come to my knowledge confirm this sentiment in my mind, and particularly the subscriptions to the Repository.

"I fear you have more to do than your time and health can bear. Is it possible for you to get any help in collecting or writing what is practically interesting? If so, I should be glad to be one of any number to appropriate five guineas each to that object, to enable you to try that plan for the year during which you have engaged to continue the Repository. If the proposal be eligible to you, and yet no other person joins in the plan, you may (if you can get help by it) depend upon me for ten guineas.

"I have done nothing at present for the Christian Reformer, but I will be answerable for the sale of twenty copies more than have been sent to Liverpool.—With all good wishes and brotherly affection, I remain your faithful friend and servant, JOHN YATES."

Rev. Robert Aspland to his Brother Isaac.

"Hackney Road, March 7, 1818.

"Dear Brother,—You wonder, I dare say, at neither seeing me nor hearing from me. The truth is, I have had another serious fit of illness, from which I am scarcely recovered. And the weather is so unfavourable, that my recovery must yet be slow. In my state of weakness it would be unwise to face the damps of your neighbourhood, and therefore I fear that I must put off my visit until cuckoo time; though, at the same time, so desirous am I of being at Wicken, that, should the weather turn up marvellously fine next week, you must not be surprised at a sudden visit from me at the latter end of it.

"On one account I have been anxious to get to you—namely, that I might see our poor friend John Emons once more in this world. I think about him very frequently. Assure him of this; and say to him, from me, that I trust he can commit himself, with all his everlasting interests, to our merciful Father, the God and Father of our Lord Jesus Christ.

"I have just met with an account of one of our ancestors, John Aspland, who was given, it seems, to the sin of *sleeping in church*, and who was made to do penance for it. This was in the reign of Queen Elizabeth, in the year 1595. On Sunday, the 4th of June of that year, the said unfortunate sinner was obliged to stand forth in the middle aisle of his parish church of Witcham (Isle of Ely), after the reading of the gospel, and then and there in 'a loude voyce' to 'say and confesse as followeth—viz.,

"'Good neighbours, I acknowledge and confesse that I have offended Almighty God, and by my evil example you all, for that I have used to *sleepe* in the church, for which I am most harteley sorry; and I aske God and you all most hartey forgiveness for the same, promising, by God's helpe, never to offende hereafter in the like again.'

"I am afraid our unworthy ancestor, the aforesaid John Aspland, was given to good ale on Sundays. His descendants live in better times, and may sleep at church or meeting without molestation or public shame.

ROBERT ASPLAND."

His anxiety to see once more his humble friend John Emons, then like himself depressed by sickness, was repeatedly gratified. From the following letter, written some little time after this period, it would seem that the heart of this worthy old man yearned in his decline towards his friend at Hackney. The reader will notice the playful allusion to his having acted the part of a bishop.

Mr. John Emons to Rev. Robert Aspland.*

"My dear Friend,—I should like to have something to write to you about religion, but I find so little of it I do not know what to say. I go to hear the preachers in your brother's chapel;† but, alas! I find but little profit, except to discover a deal of ignorance. I go in hopes of finding grapes, but they almost always prove wild grapes. When I am hearing some of their discourses, I am fit to cry with the sons of the prophets—'Oh! thou man of God, there is death in the pot, for I cannot eat it.' It is true they pipe, but I cannot dance. They ofttimes strive to prove that Christ is God, but they are like John Bunyan's highway-menders—they mar instead of mend. Some of the hearers have said they had better let it alone, for they do more hurt than good. It hurts me, because I sit like a man handcuffed, and cannot defend my own cause. I hope when you come you will preach from those words where it is said, 'Thou hast well said, Master, for there is but one God.' Who knows but your smooth stone may be a means of slaying their boasted Goliah? I long to hear a good sound discourse. My heart pants for it, as the hart pants after the water-brook.

"Mr. Clack has preached at Wicken three or four times this summer, but he preaches at Mr. Lamon's, in his house. I had a letter from him a few days past, and he informs me his mother is very agreeable, and he thinks before it is long she will not be against his preaching in the meeting.

"My dear friend, I have sent you a few apples and grapes. It is but a small gift; but such as I have, I give unto you. That exceeds *other bishops* that give only their blessing.

"Your absence has sadly worn out my patience. I long to see you again. I have expected every time the last [*year?*] either that you would be taken from me, or I from you. But if it were so, I hope we should meet again to part no more.—I remain your old friend,

JOHN EMONS."

Rev. Robert Aspland to a near Relative.

"Nov. 7, 1818.

"You will have heard, before this reaches you, of the melancholy death of *Sir Samuel Romilly*, one of our best public men, if I ought not rather to say, the best. Poor man! hard study and intense grief upset his reason, and he was no longer master of his own actions. Deplorable as is the event, I entertain little concern as to the *manner* of it, except as it may furnish an

---

* The Editor has felt himself justified in correcting the orthography, and in one or two instances the grammar, of the original. This village blacksmith was no scholar, but he was something better—a truly wise and good man.

† The humble chapel which had been erected twenty years before for Robert Aspland, on his father's premises, was at this time kindly lent to some Methodist preachers.

occasion of triumph to mean and corrupt minds of the Government faction, and as it may be fatal to some weak minds as an example.

"I mentioned to you on my last visit, the subject of your *making a will:* let me again impress it upon you. Life is of all things, you know, least certain, and in the event of your dying intestate, there would be little provision for ——. I should, in your case, I think, give the house and business to ——, binding him to pay —— a fixed sum upon her coming of age, or by convenient instalments. Were your will made, you would be less alarmed at any sudden illness. I know your disposition to *put off* such things, and therefore *beg most seriously* that you would accomplish this most necessary work."

During the latter months of the year 1818, Mr. Aspland's health was sufficiently improved to enable him again to undertake public business. He had with much anxiety observed some symptoms of a growing disposition amongst "orthodox" Dissenters to dispute the right of Unitarians to the continued enjoyment of endowments handed down to them from Presbyterian ancestors. The opinions expressed on the state of the common law with respect to Unitarians, by judges and lawyers of eminence, did not diminish his anxiety. He conferred on the subject with Mr. Edgar Taylor, Mr. Richmond, Mr. Talfourd, with the other members of the Non-con Club, with the Committee of the Unitarian Fund, and with various friends in the provinces, and the result was a general opinion of the desirableness of forming a society for the protection of the civil rights of Unitarians. To such a society it was felt that the Unitarian body could most conveniently delegate the conduct of an application to Parliament for an alteration of the law which compelled Unitarians, on contracting marriage, to use a Trinitarian form of service. Mr. Belsham was of course, in an early stage of the business, consulted. His habitual distaste to popular combinations, and his jealousy (in itself most laudable, though on the present occasion, perhaps, unnecessarily aroused) of any possible encroachment on the independence of individual congregations, prevented his joining or aiding the projected organization.

Rev. Thomas Belsham to Rev. Robert Aspland.

"Essex Street, Nov. 14, 1818.

"My dear Sir,—Though I cannot approve of delegations, I think the method proposed of summoning respectable individuals to meet upon the subject of an application to Parliament for relief in the case of marriage, is highly judicious and expedient.* But would not our friend Mr. Christie be a far better chairman than Alderman Wood? To appoint Wood to conduct an application to Parliament, would be to bespeak a refusal. Mr. W. Smith should by all means be engaged to bring the business before the House. He is looked up to as a veteran senator.

"If I wished the Unitarians to become a powerful political sect, I should be a warm friend to that grand scheme of federal union, of which I heard so much in Lancashire. But as a friend to truth and liberty, which I think much impeded by such associations, I must dissent from them. And as I think our civil rights in no particular danger, a new society for their protection appears to me to be needless. Nor can I approve of any plans for separating Unitarians from their fellow-christians more than is absolutely necessary.

"We are the *salt* of the earth. But a lump of salt lying by itself will never fertilize the ground. It must be mixed and blended with the earth, in order to manure the soil and produce a copious harvest. I was brought up an Independent; and I am unwilling to bow to any authority beyond the limit of my own congregation. But these are the sentiments of an *old-fashioned* Unitarian; and we cannot expect that the new generation will always act upon our views: they must judge and act for themselves; and either way, I have no doubt that the great cause of truth and religion will go on prosperously; and that you may be long continued as an eminent instrument in the hand of Providence for the propagation of pure and uncorrupted Christianity, is the earnest wish and prayer of, dear Sir, yours very sincerely, T. BELSHAM."

Early in 1819, a meeting of Unitarians, convened by Mr. Fox, as Secretary of the Unitarian Fund, to consider the propriety of forming an "Association for protecting the Civil Rights of Unitarians," was held in London. In proposing to establish such a Society, Mr. Aspland argued that he was proposing no novelty, and pointed to the Deputies of the Three Denominations, the Protestant Society, the Friends' Committee of Sufferings, and the Committee of Privileges of the Wesleyan Methodists, as existing societies founded on the same principle. That it was expedient for Unitarians to unite in defending their civil rights, he argued from the general obloquy to which they were exposed, and

---

* In a letter addressed by Mr. Belsham to Mr. Aspland, the following year, in allusion to some exertions about to be made by the latter in promoting a reform of the Marriage Law, he wrote thus: "You are going abroad in a good cause, and I wish you good success and a good journey. I think you will probably live to see the marriage ceremony altered to your mind, for an alteration so reasonable cannot long fail of success."

the particular opinions recently expressed concerning their legal position. He alluded in these terms to the opinion of the late Sir Samuel Romilly: " In the discussion of the Wolverhampton case, a very unfavourable opinion had been expressed by that great man whose loss had recently occasioned so painful a shock. He declared this opinion in court; but besides the expression of opinion there, which might be attributed to the warmth of an advocate, he had in private letters since expressed a strong feeling of the insecurity of the basis on which the civil rights of Unitarians rest. I received a note from him not many months before his death, stating his deliberate opinion that Unitarians were not protected at law, and that no other course was open to them than an application to Parliament. He offered willingly to assist and support such an application, but observed that he was not very sanguine as to its success. There was therefore, in the opinion of this great man, a strong ground for action and exertion; and it appeared highly important to associate, with a view both to resist aggression, and to proceed, if necessary, to obtain security by legislative provisions. Nothing can be worse than uncertainty where liberty and property are concerned." He admitted that if no necessity existed for the proposed Association, it would be injurious, by appearing to separate the case of Unitarians from that of other Dissenters; but it was notorious there was no existing society would do what had been and might again be necessary. When Mr. Wright was under persecution, the Deputies were appealed to in vain. He dwelt on the disposition of reputed orthodox Dissenters to deprive Unitarians of their hereditary religious property, and urged that fact as a sufficient reason for the appointment of a standing committee, who should watch over the interests of the denomination, and be ready to act should any emergency arise. He shewed that the proposed Society need not interfere with any other, for no case would properly come within its jurisdiction which was not strictly Unitarian, or which would be within the scope of the Deputies or the Protestant Society. It could not make any separation between Unitarians and other Nonconformists. The question they really had to decide was, not whether such cases should be left to other associations, but whether they should be neglected and abandoned. On the subject of the desired extension of their privileges, he thus spoke: " I am thankful for what the Legislature, in compliance with public opinion, has already done; but if I say I am not contented, I only repeat Mr. William Smith's opinion, declared to Lord Liverpool on that nobleman's expressing a hope that Unitarians would be satisfied with the Trinity Bill: 'No, my Lord,' answered Mr. Smith, 'we shall not be satisfied while one disqualifying statute in matters of religion remains on the books.' This is my feeling also, and I therefore think the proposed Association very useful, not only to protect our rights, but to enlarge them, and those of every class of Dissenters; for in all general measures for that purpose, it would doubtless cheerfully concur with other societies." Mr. Aspland's arguments were seconded, in a speech of great ability and force, by Mr. Talfourd, and the meeting adopted the resolutions and constitution of the Society by an unanimous vote. The Secretaryship was undertaken by Mr. Edgar Taylor, and the important duties that devolved upon him were discharged, till nearly the close of his valuable life, with eminent ability and zeal.

A review of the hard struggles and important changes that took place in the five-and-twenty years that followed the establishment of the Unitarian Association, is the best vindication of the wisdom and foresight of its projectors. Sixteen or seventeen years of toil and repeated disappointment elapsed before the desired reform in the Marriage Law was achieved. During the greater part of that time Unitarians toiled alone, unhelped by other Nonconformists. But the fruit of their perseverance was shared at last equally by all the Dissenters of England, and none more rejoiced at this catholic result than the surviving projectors of the Unitarian Association. When the repeal of the Sacramental Test was sought, the Unitarian Association sent its representatives (and they proved efficient auxiliaries) to the United Committee, by which the great battle was fought and won for the Nonconformists of England. For many years the Unitarian Association took a large share of the responsibility and burthen of conducting the defence of the Hewley Trustees; but when the time came for an appeal to the Legislature for that protection, the necessity of which Sir Samuel Romilly saw a quarter of a century before, the existence of this Society did not obstruct, but aided, the formation of the more comprehensive body to which, under the name of the Presbyterian Union Committee, was entrusted the conduct of the Bill through Parliament. The apprehension that the Association must interfere with the independence of Unitarian congregations was in no degree realized.

In the year 1819, several prosecutions were instituted against persons for publishing and selling deistical and other irreligious books. One of the principal of these, R. Carlile, was tried and convicted before Chief

Justice Abbot, for publishing Paine's " Age of Reason." In his defence he pleaded that he was protected by the Trinity Bill, recently passed, which, he alleged, included Deists as well as Unitarians, whom he pronounced to be Deists under a cloak. The trial lasted three days, and attracted a great degree of public attention. A clerical correspondent of the *Times* newspaper, in commenting on Carlile's defence, asked the editor's opinion whether the repeal of the Act against the " Socinians" did not give this man some show of defence, and whether there were not some truth in his definition of a Socinian as a " Deist in a cloak"? The Clergyman disclaimed any desire to persecute a sect on account of their principles, but declared that the Act should have been allowed to continue on the Statute-book, because it would act as a barrier against infidelity, and because, if suffered to remain suspended as a sword over their heads, Socinians would be taught that the Legislature, though it did not punish, yet disapproved of their tenets. To the questions of the Clergyman, the editor of the *Times* expressed his opinion that " the Socinians ought to reply." Mr. Aspland immediately wrote two letters, which were inserted in the paper of the two following days. He stated that Unitarians had been so long accustomed to hard language from their theological opponents, that they could scarcely wonder at the Clergyman's readiness to accept of Mr. Carlile as an authority against them. The Chief Justice had declared his opinion respecting them not to be law, and no one, unless blinded by bigotry, would allow it to be moral truth. In the received sense of the term, Unitarians are not Deists, nor has their system any affinity with Deism. Unitarians, he thus argued, have been zealous defenders of Christianity. " Their ministers have always been accustomed to discuss and enforce zealously from the pulpit the evidences of Christianity. The work of Socinus that is best known is his Demonstration of the Truth of the Christian Religion. This book was translated into English, in 1731, by Combe, a dignitary of the Church of England, with a recommendatory Preface by Bishop Smallbrook, and a dedication to the then Queen. Several volumes of Dr. Priestley's works are devoted to the same subject; and I question whether any book be so well adapted to remove the prejudices and conciliate the affections of a sceptic of superior intellect, as his *Letters to a Philosophical Unbeliever*. And (not to multiply authorities, though many more names might be cited) who is it that is universally appealed to as (by way of distinction) the *Champion of Christianity?* Is it not Dr. Lardner?" The creed of the Unitarian is the

New Testament, interpreted by the best lights that biblical learning can supply. Christianity, he argued, was not the religion of a party, but of the universal church. Adducing the testimony of Mr. Charles Butler in his Life of Fenelon, as to what constituted the common Christianity received by all sects, he shewed that it was identical with Unitarianism. In confutation of Mr. Carlile's defence, Mr. Aspland remarked,—" His pleading the 53rd of the King (the Act for relieving those that do not believe the doctrine of the Trinity from certain pains and penalties) no more implicates them in his cause, than his appealing to the Toleration Act would have identified with himself the whole body of Protestant Dissenters. It is sufficiently clear that it protects the Unitarian Christian in the conscientious avowal of his opinions and observance of his worship; whether it have any collateral operation, it is not for him, but courts of law, to determine. But it is very strange that the Act should be considered, by either Mr. Carlile or the Clergyman, as commixing Deists and Unitarians; when the true state of the case is, that they were confounded in the 9th and 10th of William and Mary, but are separated by Mr. Smith's, which takes Unitarians from under the operation of the statute, but leaves all other persons contemplated by it in the precise condition in which they stood before."

The "Age of Reason" was first published when the statute now repealed was in full force. Unitarians shared the disgust felt by other Christians at its ribaldry and daring falsehoods. From their pens proceeded some of the earliest answers to it, and their societies have habitually distributed the defences of Christianity by Hartley, Clarke and Bishop Law. In commenting on the Clergyman's desire to evoke exploded *pains* and *penalties*, Mr. Aspland reminded him of the saying of his predecessor South, that Unitarians "were fitter to be crushed by the civil magistrate than to be merely confuted;" and of Dr. Jortin's comment on the saying—" Such is the true agonistic style or intolerant spirit; such the courage of a champion who challenges his adversary, and then calls upon the constable to come and help him." He quoted also Mr. Fox's remark, that "if the statutes were too bad to be put into practice, they ought not to be suffered to exist." After characterizing the alarm respecting the prevalence of Deism as extravagant, he thus expressed his disapprobation of religious prosecutions: "Nothing, in my humble judgment, can give even a momentary triumph to infidelity, unless it be the angry zeal of Christians in prosecuting its advocates, and placing them on the vantage-ground of suffering for their principles. This is, I am aware, an unpopular sentiment; but I trust I may be permitted to say, with the immortal Chillingworth, 'I have learned from ancient fathers of the church, that nothing is more against religion than to force religion.'" The Letters concluded with the quotation of a noble passage in behalf of free inquiry by Bishop Lowth, and by exposing the misnomer of styling Unitarians *Socinians*.

To these Letters the Clergyman offered no rejoinder, but kept a prudent silence.

In the pages of the Monthly Repository, Mr. Aspland, while he reprobated the prosecutions going on, and declared his conviction that the New Testament sanctioned no other proceeding against unbelievers than the use of argument, remonstrance and persuasion, and that there could be no religious liberty if men were denied the liberty of rejecting religion, felt himself called upon to express his disapprobation of Paine's mendacious and scurrilous book, and the absence of all sympathy with booksellers who braved the law merely for the sake of gain, and courted persecution as the means of notoriety and advancement in business.

By some who failed to observe the distinction between the case of an author publishing that which he believed to be truth, and that of a bookseller trading in a forbidden article, this censure of Carlile and his associates was resented as harsh and inconsistent with true liberality;* while there were not wanting men of unquestionable candour who entirely approved the course he had thought it right to pursue.

Rev. Thomas Belsham to Rev. Robert Aspland.

"Essex Street, Nov. 17, 1819.

"My dear Sir,—I have just been reading your admirable and seasonable Letters in the *Times*. I rejoice in their extensive circulation and the strong impression they have made, and wish it had been tenfold wider and greater.

"I have just received a letter from Dr. Parr,† in which he says, 'I am much pleased with Mr. Aspland's judicious and temperate reply to the clerical accuser.' And he wishes we would republish Bishop Lowth's celebrated

---

* Dr. Charles Lloyd published a letter of remonstrance, addressed to Mr. T. T. Clark, of Swakeleys, which he entitled, "*Monthly Repository Extraordinary*," &c.

† Dr. Parr paid to these Letters the remarkable compliment of reading them from his pulpit at Hatton, interspersing the reading with his own extempore comments. This singular substitute for a sermon was given, as the learned and eccentric Dr. afterwards explained, not to gratify a friend of the author of the Letters, who chanced on that Sunday to attend the church at Hatton, but to enlighten the ignorance of a "Birmingham bigot" whom the Dr., after the commencement of the service, observed amongst his audience.

Assize Sermon. Qu. Is there any such sermon? I strongly suspect that he means the Visitation Sermon from which you quote so pertinent a passage. What should you think of reprinting it, with a short preface suited to the times, and which you could so well draw up? But I will shew you what he says when I have the pleasure of meeting you at Mr. Le Breton's on Tuesday. I hope your sore throat is quite well. We all very much regretted your absence on Friday.—With compliments to the ladies, I am, dear Sir, very sincerely yours, T. BELSHAM."

Rev. Thomas Belsham to Rev. Robert Aspland.

"Essex Street, Nov. 26, 1820.

"My dear Sir,—I return your son's letter, with many thanks. I truly lament the death of that eminently learned man, Professor Young.* But what a highly privileged lot was his, to have life protracted to advanced age, in the full possession and exercise of his superior talents and powers, and then to be translated in a moment without any sense of pain! It is evident, however, that he felt something within which reminded him that death was at hand. I heard him say that J. Kenrick was the man best qualified to succeed Dugald Stewart. I am inclined to think that many will be of opinion that he would be the best successor to Professor Young. Dr. Rees told me of what passed at the Library, and Dr. Pett of what happened at the Mermaid. You should have had a Churchman in the chair, even if he were a blockhead. It is the artifice of the enemy to lay all blame upon the Unitarians. Is there mischief in the city, and a Unitarian hath not done it?

"The Professors† must be not a little mortified at the triumph of Jeffrey. As the students possess the power, I am glad they employed it so well. My sister joins in kind respects to you and the ladies, with, dear Sir, yours most sincerely, T. BELSHAM."

The political condition of England during the last years of George III. and the first years of the reign of George IV., was depressing to every patriotic mind. The Ministers were utterly indifferent to the constitutional liberties of the people; and the mingled severity and imbecility

---

* Professor Young died suddenly, while taking a warm bath, at Glasgow, Nov. 18, 1820. He had lectured that morning as usual; and in the junior Greek class, in illustrating the lesson of the day, he alluded more than once to death, as if the subject were irresistibly present to his mind. See Mon. Rep. XV. 682.

† A few days previously the students of Glasgow College had, very much against the wishes of the Professors, elected by a large majority Mr. Francis Jeffrey (now Lord Jeffrey) as Lord Rector. This office had been previously filled by generals, Tory placemen and obscure merchants. This election was the first of a series—including Thomas Campbell, Sir James Mackintosh, Sir Walter Scott, Lord John Russell, and more recently Mr. Macaulay—which have done honour to a literary and scientific corporation.

which characterized the administration of public affairs, made the rulers hateful to the mass of the people. As a counterpoise to the very general expressions of discontent, loyal addresses were got up by the supporters of the Government of the day, expressive of loyalty to the King, attachment to the Constitution, and utter abhorrence of the blasphemous and seditious doctrines alleged to have been industriously disseminated amongst the people. An address of this kind, got up at Hackney, was signed by some eminent Hebrew capitalists, who, unlike their sons and successors, were willing, at any cost of profession, to rank themselves amongst the friends of the powers that were. This circumstance led to the following note and letter:

Lord Holland to Rev. Robert Aspland.

"Lord Holland presents his best compliments to Mr. Aspland, and many apologies for the abruptness of this application. But he should feel much obliged to Mr. Aspland if he could inform him with certainty of the two following facts: first, if 'the Christian Religion' is named in the Loyal Address which has lately been signed at Hackney; and, secondly, if Mr. Rothschild and his partners have signed the Address which contains those words?

"Lord Holland is really ashamed of troubling Mr. Aspland so suddenly; but he is very desirous of ascertaining the fact before twelve o'clock; and Lord Holland has no acquaintance at Hackney who is likely to be able to ascertain the fact.

"Old Burlington Street, January 21, 1821."

"Old Burlington Street, Jan. 23.

"Dear Sir,—I ought to have thanked you ere this for your obliging attention to my note and for your enclosure, which I assure you diverted even the High-Churchmen of Oxford not a little.*

---

* Lord Holland, with that courage and respect for constitutional rights which marked his whole political course, attended a meeting of the Freeholders of Oxfordshire on January 22nd, and by his eloquence induced the meeting to put aside a very objectionable address which had been prepared by the "mock loyalists," as the *Times* newspaper termed them. The following passage in his speech, as reported by the *Times*, will shew the use made by Lord Holland of the information furnished him by Mr. Aspland.

"He was inclined to believe that many signed these addresses without reflecting on the importance of their signatures. As a proof of this, he hoped they would excuse him while he told them a London story, which, cockney like, he had just brought down with him. (A laugh.) There were two loyal declarations now circulating in the metropolis. (Here the noble lord drew copies of them from his pocket and commented on them.) The first was 'from the undersigned inhabitants of Hackney, which complained of the prevalence of blasphemy and sedition, as tending to subvert the faith of Christ.' In looking into the

"I shall, my dear Sir, be most ready and happy to attend to any suggestion from you on the subject of the Education Bill.

"Though a member of the Church of England, I am well aware of the strong tendency of all Establishments to accroach power to themselves, especially over those who are not of their communion, and who consequently ought to be entirely exempt from their interference or authority. For these reasons it is very desirable that the effect of any plan of Education should be well considered by the Dissenters; and I assure you I am disposed to resist any thing, even for so desirable an object as Education, which can in any way be considered as oppressive or vexatious to the Protestant Dissenters.

"I am, Sir, with many thanks, your obliged and obedient,

VASSALL HOLLAND.

"P. S.—I should prefer waiting till the Bill is in the House of Lords, or at least in Parliament, for I know by experience that when one's first impression of a measure of much detail is received from the shape in which it is first drawn up, one is apt, in discussing it in the future stages, to confound the provisions which remain with those that have been dropped or rejected in the course of it."

An explanation of Mr. Aspland's views and conduct in regard to the question of National Education as introduced into Parliament in 1821, is reserved for the next Chapter.

---

column of signatures, the second name he found was 'Zachariah Levi, Stamford Hill.' It first struck him that this gentleman might have been one of the worthy persons who go about, converted from the errors of Judaism to Christianity; but no, that was not the case. (Loud laughter.) The next name, however, was that of a Jew beyond all question; for it was that of M. N. Rothschild, the great Jew contractor, who comes forth in this time of peril to express his excessive dread of the prevalence of any opinion calculated to impair the stability of the pure Christian faith. (Peals of laughter for some time.) Mr. Rothschild's dread appeared most alarming; for in another loyal declaration, privately concocted among some merchants of London, there was this paragraph—'We declare it to be our firm and unalterable purpose to maintain our holy religion in all its purity.' To this declaration among the uncircumcised he (Lord Holland) again found Mr. Rothschild's name attached. (Loud laughter.) He begged not to be understood as lamenting that Jews mixed themselves up with Christians in asserting their opinions, for he, on the contrary, rather wished the Jews had more rights than they had, than that any they reasonably wished should be withheld from them. He merely stated this fact to shew the inconsiderate manner in which these addresses were got up and signed; and it was this that induced him to think that when the Jews and the Gentiles were all mixed up together, there was some little profit in the rear of all this expression of loyalty and Christian piety. The Jewish gentlemen could not have read these addresses when they signed them: that was his (Lord H.'s) opinion in charity, for he could not wantonly accuse any man of hypocrisy. In the language therefore to be found in that fine play of his late friend Mr. Sheridan, he would say with Moses in the School for Scandal, 'My principal is a Christian.' (Laughter.)"

The miserable and disgraceful proceedings consequent on the accession of George IV. and the return of his unhappy Queen to England, excited in Mr. Aspland's mind strong feelings of disgust and abhorrence. It is not necessary to describe particularly the part he, in common with nineteen-twentieths of the people of England, took to uphold the cause of a deeply-injured woman. In the following letter, written immediately after the death of Queen Caroline, there are some allusions to the subject.

Rev. Robert Aspland to Mrs. Aspland.

" Hackney, Aug. 17, 1821.

" My dear Wife,—My journey with the *twa* doctors was very agreeable, and we were all received with the usual hospitality of my good friend Ebr. Johnston. He expressed himself disappointed in not seeing you. Our public services went off pretty well, though the Wednesday was a continued heavy rain. The wet, exertion in preaching, or something, aggravated my rheumatic complaints, and brought them down into my throat, so that Friday and Saturday I was laid up; and Friday night was a sleepless one. However, I contrived to preach twice at Lewes on Sunday, and, thanks to a good constitution (under Providence), I was able on Monday morning to set out tramping with Richard and Edgar Taylor. We walked fourteen and rode eight miles, were literally starved upon a cross-road, and got to our friends, the Jansons, at Tunbridge Wells, in the evening, all fatigued, but myself bettered in point of health. Next morning, Edgar Taylor, frightened at our strong exertion and hard fare, left us by coach for the great city. Richard and I passed the day at the Wells, a good part of it spent walking in the rain. The evening allowed Mrs. Janson to accompany us in a little home excursion. Wednesday morning, Richard Taylor and I left the Wells and walked seven miles to breakfast at *Penshurst*, the ancient seat of the Sydneys. The road is a succession of beautiful scenery, and Penshurst is holy ground. We visited a Spanish chesnut planted on Sir Philip Sydney's birth, and by great good fortune we got down into the vault where that distinguished family lie in their resting-place. Our devotions (for such they were) were chiefly paid over *Algernon Sydney's* coffin, which we drew from its retirement in order to read the inscription. It is of stone. The corner of it was chipped off, though yet remaining in its place, and this (against the will of the guide whom we had over-persuaded to let us see the vault) I put in my pocket and brought home, as a memorial for our Sydney. Leaving Penshurst, we crossed the noble Kent hills and traversed Knowle Park, the seat of the now headless Dorset family, and so into the little known but exquisite vale of the Darrent, on which Dartford is situated, and which opens into the Thames a little below that town. In all we walked this day twenty-five miles. You may follow us on the map, and imagine us resting at night at Farningham, a pleasant village on the Maidstone road. Yesterday morning we walked to Erith, nine miles, to breakfast, and then took the Gravesend boat for London. After all this, I am quite well; rheumatism gone, and nothing personal to complain of.

"I say nothing personal, for I have suffered beyond expression for the poor *Queen*. I dare not give full vent to my feelings. No indignation, no loathing which I ever before remember, is an image of my present sentiments with regard to this low-minded * * Court. Feeling so much, I cannot attempt a funeral sermon. Our committee had met before my return, and resolved to allow me to put the pulpit in black. But this I will not do. Without a sermon, it would be preposterous; and, as Dr. Pett and I agreed this morning, no man ought to speak of the event in language less than treason. We might, let me say, have been mourners of a different description, for Brook and Lindsey were on the spot where the soldiers committed the murders.* They, thank God! escaped; but the scene has read them a lesson on a standing army which I hope they will never forget. R. A."

---

* At Cumberland Gate, on the occasion of the Queen's funeral. The authorities attempted to carry the remains of the persecuted Queen by back roads, so as to avoid the procession passing through the city. The people, roused with a chivalrous feeling of indignation, successfully resisted this intended indignity, but with the cost of a life or two.

CHAPTER XXV.

In the years 1820 and 1821, the attention of Parliament and of the country was directed to the subject of National Education. To Mr. Whitbread belongs the honour of having been the first to assert in Parliament the principle that Government was bound to provide the people with sufficient means of education. This was in 1807, in connection with a proposal to reform the Poor-law of England. In 1816, Mr. Brougham obtained a Select Committee to inquire into the existing provision for the education of the children of the poor in the Metropolis. In 1818, the Committee was revived, and with extended powers, including an inquiry into the education of the people of all England. The result of the inquiry was a Bill brought into Parliament by Mr. Brougham towards the close of the session 1820. On the understanding that it was not to be pressed during that session to its final stage, but that time should be given to the country to form and express its opinion on the merits of the plan, the Bill was allowed to be read a second time, was committed and reported with the blanks filled up.

The principal features of the plan thus submitted through Parliament to the consideration of the country were these. In order to the establishment of a public school, the proceedings must originate through a presentment on the part of the grand jury at the quarter sessions, or through a memorial signed by the resident officiating minister, or two justices, or five householders. The decision rested exclusively and finally with the justices at sessions. They might, if they saw fit, provide schools, not exceeding three in number, in any district. The salary of the schoolmaster to be not less than £20 or more than £30 per annum, exclusive of a house and garden. The salary and the cost of repairing the school buildings to be defrayed out of the parish rates. Schoolmasters under the proposed Act were to be not under twenty-four nor above forty years of age; to produce certificates as to their character, and to their being members of the Established Church, from the resident minister and two householders of their respective parishes. Parish clerks were declared eligible as schoolmasters, but the officiating minister of the district was ineligible. The choice of the schoolmaster to rest with the ratepayers, but the officiating minister to have a veto on the appointment. The schools to be visited by the ordinary, dean, chancellor or archdeacon. The visitor, where necessary, to have the power of removing or superannuating the schoolmaster. The ordinary to make an annual report of the state of the schools in his diocese, and the officiating minister at all times to have access to the schools of his own parish for the purpose of examining them. With him also rested the fixing of the rate of remuneration to be paid by the scholars, the hours of schooling, the times of vacation, and the appointment of assistant masters. Reading, writing and accounts, to be taught in each school. The Bible to be the only religious book taught. The minister's consent necessary to the introduction of any book in the school. The minister to have the power of directing the passages of Scripture to be taught by the master. The religious worship in the school to consist of Scripture extracts and the Lord's Prayer. The Church Catechism to be taught, and the scholars to attend the parish church. But the children of Dissenters might, by the direction of their parents, absent themselves from the church and the catechetical instruction, without being exposed to punishment, rebuke or admonition.

The Bill also included provisions for the regulation of old endowments, with a view of remedying defects in their constitution or management. As originally drawn and as explained by Mr. Brougham, it imposed upon the schoolmaster a Sacramental test; but Mr. Brougham, early in the discussion that ensued out of doors, expressed his willingness to abandon a clause which he found especially offensive to Protestant Dissenters.

On the merits of this scheme of national education, very different opinions were expressed by the leaders of the Dissenters. Dr. Shepherd (then Rev. William Shepherd), under the combined influence of an ardent zeal for the mental improvement of the great mass of the people, and of strong personal friendship for the author of the Bill, appeared publicly as its defender. As a proof that Mr. Brougham had no design to infringe upon the rights of Protestant Dissenters, he stated that, in an early stage of the plan, he had been consulted as to the regulations which were necessary for their protection, and that in reply he had informed Mr. Brougham that all that could properly be insisted on was exemption from the necessity of attending on the worship of the Established Church, and of learning any Catechism at variance with their several creeds. He thought it right, as the majority of the children and their parents would be members of the Church of England, that attendance on church should be imperative on all but the children of Dissenters. As it was necessary for the master to accompany the children to the parish church, it appeared to him a necessary provision that the master should be a member of the Church of England. The veto given to the officiating minister he thought practically unimportant, and no particular hardship upon Dissenters. To the Sacramental test originally intended to be imposed, Dr. Shepherd strongly objected; but that was abandoned before the author of the Bill received this expression of his opinions. For the sake of educating the mass of the people, Dr. Shepherd argued that Dissenters ought to be willing to make some sacrifices, but alleged that Mr. Brougham's Bill asked for no sacrifice whatever, save " of unreasonable jealousy and suspicion."

Others looked upon many of the details of the measure as objectionable, yet, in the hope of its receiving the needed amendments, gave it a general support. Some, in a generous zeal for education, were willing to take the Bill with all its faults, which they confessed to be great, rather than let legislation on this important subject be indefinitely postponed.

Mr. Aspland felt constrained to join the opponents of Mr. Brougham's Bill. In his place at Dr. Williams's Library, as one of the ministers of the Three Denominations, and previously at the Non-con Club, as well as through the press, he stated many grave objections to the Education Bill.* In zeal for the education of the people he was surpassed by none of his friends; but he was far from being satisfied that it was desirable that education should be *forced* by public authority. He observed that the most beneficial moral changes in society had been effected, in opposition even to political power, by private activity and benevolence. But even if the preliminary objection to the interference of the State were not insisted on, he argued that a measure designed for the benefit of the mass of the people would fail of success unless it

---

* See Monthly Repository for 1821, and " Inquiry into the Operation of Mr. Brougham's Bill, as far as regards the Protestant Dissenters. By a Nonconformist." 8vo. Pp. 23.

enlisted in its behalf popular sympathy. Mr. Brougham's scheme he regarded as essentially sectarian,—as avowedly and designedly framed and fitted for a single denomination,—as auxiliary in all its operations to the English hierarchy. In analyzing its details, he found many provisions which were injurious, directly or remotely, to Protestant Nonconformists.

That the power of appointing schools should rest exclusively with justices of the peace was unjust, considering that while Dissenters were generally excluded, the wealthier clergy were generally admitted to the bench. The effect would be, that in many instances it would depend upon the clergyman himself whether a school should be set up in his parish.

The regulations for the choice of the schoolmaster appeared to be framed not with a view to secure the fittest person, but to uphold clerical dignity and power. The choice was circumscribed by the exclusion of every Dissenter, every member of the Church of Scotland, and even of liberal Churchmen whose freedom of opinion was unpalatable to the parish incumbent. The Bill held out in this respect a premium to conformity, while it inflicted a penalty on nonconformity. The class of men whom the Bill invidiously selected and named as eligible, parish clerks, were often singularly unfit for the office of schoolmasters. The clerical veto and the exclusively clerical visitations were unjust violations of popular rights, devised to swell the patronage and increase the power of the clergy. The authority confided to the officiating minister to prescribe the passages of Scripture which the schoolmaster should teach, would in reality nullify the protection offered in other portions of the Bill to the children of Nonconformists. The eager proselytist need desire no other power. By a *cento* of unconnected texts strung together, the clergyman might artfully provide a system which no Roman Catholic, no Unitarian, no Protestant Dissenter, could allow his children to learn. However desirable the new arrangements for religious instruction to the young might appear to conscientious members of the Established Church, it was unjust to tax the whole community, consisting of a large proportion of Dissenters, for that in which they could have no share. The regulations for religious instruction would produce an undesirable and mischievous division of the pupils into the orthodox and favoured many, and the tolerated but despised few. Mr. Brougham's Parliamentary schools would never become schools for all. There would be no form in them for the children of

Jews, and few Roman Catholics would suffer their children to be taught religion by a Protestant parish clerk out of the authorized version of the Scriptures.

The answer given by Mr. Aspland to some portions of a plea for the Bill in the *Edinburgh Review*, attributed to Mr. Brougham, contains truths of no light importance to Protestant Dissenters.

"The Edinburgh Reviewer says that the Dissenters have been silent under greater encroachments upon their opinions and property; they did not oppose the grant of a large sum of money to the poor clergy, nor the vote of a million for the erection of new churches. But if they did not here oppose Government, a writer of less shrewdness than this might have guessed that the true reason was very different from their satisfaction in these measures. Let the Dissenters, however, learn a lesson of zeal and courage from such reproaches. Their silence, they perceive, is interpreted into acquiescence. It becomes a precedent; and if they ever afterwards speak out, they are charged with inconsistency and even with faction.

"To urge upon Dissenters, as the Reviewer does, the necessity of sacrifices for the public good, is in this case preposterous. To what are they to sacrifice, except to the complacency or ambition of the author of the Bill? They can give up only what regards their consciences; he has an easy surrender to make: his Bill is not essential to his own or others' happiness, and he may re-cast it so as to make it worthy of himself and of the great nation to whom it is proposed. The history of the sacrifices of the Dissenters is, in fact, the exposition of the loss of their liberty. By one concession they fastened the yoke of the Test Act upon their own necks and those of their children, and by another they lost, for a century at least, the only probable chance of their emancipation.

"Nothing would be more dangerous to the Dissenters than that the Legislature should presume upon their willingness to make concessions of conscience for the supposed public good. Were it allowed to proceed upon this principle—a very mistaken one, and one which no man could have adopted who knew the people to whom it relates—the present measure would speedily be followed by other and more fatal aggressions upon religious liberty."

The pamphlet from which this extract is taken was reviewed, together with some others directed against his Education Bill, by Mr. Brougham in the *Edinburgh Review* (Vol. XXXV. 214—257). Some of the objections were allowed to be weighty, and alterations in the Bill were suggested in order to remove them. The incurable evil of the plan was its professed and avowed connection with the Church Establishment. No alteration of details could remove the objections of

Dissenters founded on this principle. The Protestant Society and the General Body of Protestant Dissenting Ministers of the Three Denominations passed resolutions and agreed on petitions to Parliament against the scheme, and, in the session of 1821, Mr. Brougham dropped the Bill immediately after its first reading.

The proceedings connected with this abortive scheme of national education are worthy of attention, as shewing the tide-marks of religious liberty. That respect for the rights of conscience has advanced with great rapidity during the past quarter of a century, is shewn by the fate of the Education Bill more recently introduced by Sir James Graham, viewed side by side with that of Mr. Brougham. Both plans had the same fault of a too exclusive regard to the power and dignity of the clergy; but, compared with Mr. Brougham's Bill, that of Sir James Graham was almost harmless, yet it raised throughout the nation a storm of indignant opposition, before which the measure was instantly withdrawn. Had Mr. Brougham proposed in 1820 a Bill resembling that afterwards offered by the Government of Sir Robert Peel, there can be little doubt that the active opponents of it would have been found amongst the clergy rather than amongst the Nonconformists. The character and well-deserved fate of each Bill served to mark an era in the history of religious liberty in England. It may be confidently anticipated that one result of these successive failures in the attempt to bribe the clergy to become supporters of education by the offer of exclusive privileges and dignity, will be, that no sagacious English statesman will hereafter venture to propose a scheme of national education giving any obvious and unfair advantage to Churchmen or the clergy.

The increased power of Protestant Dissenters of the present day in vindicating their just rights, is no doubt in part the result of their larger numbers, and their admission to electoral, municipal and legislative privileges; but it must also in part be attributed to the watchful prudence and courage of the leaders of the Dissenters, in asserting, equally against friend and foe, the inalienable rights of conscience.

To one of the meetings of the London ministers, convened Feb. 14, 1821, to take Mr. Brougham's Bill into consideration, a painful and almost tragic interest attached, as it proved the death-scene of Dr. Jas. Lindsay, who had been for more than thirty-five years the pastor of the ancient Presbyterian congregation in Monkwell Street. Mr. Aspland was an eye-witness of this awful event, and continued, with a few others, to watch the corpse of his friend until the unmistakeable signs of death appeared.* He, in company with Mr. Belsham and others, was one of the pall-bearers on the occasion of the funeral at Bunhill Fields;

---

* The following narrative of the circumstances attending the death of Dr. Lindsay (the fullest published) was penned by Mr. Aspland. "On Wednesday, the 14th inst., the Dissenting Ministers of the Three Denominations had assembled to receive the Report of a Committee previously appointed to consider and watch the progress of Mr. Brougham's Education Bill. There were probably fifty in number. Dr. Rippon was in the chair. The business was opened by Dr. Rees, the chairman of the Committee, who related the substance of a conversation with which Mr. Brougham had favoured the Committee, we think the preceding day. He was followed by Mr. Innes, another member of the Committee, who corroborated Dr. Rees's statements and added other particulars. It being known that Dr. Lindsay differed in some degree from most of his brethren with regard to the magnitude of the evil involved in the Bill, there was now a general but friendly call upon the Doctor, who was also on the Committee, to explain his sentiments. This wish expressed by the Body, proceeded from that cordial respect which they universally entertained for him, and which his uniformly frank and courteous manners never for a moment permitted any difference of opinion to lessen. He rose and spoke with great ability, and with some animation, though not, in our judgment, with quite his usual energy, for about ten minutes. He did not defend Mr. Brougham's Bill, as has been reported, but maintained that some of its clauses were highly objectionable, and pledged himself to unite with his brethren in an honourable and candid opposition to them. He stated most clearly, however, that such, in his opinion, was the power of education over error and injustice, and even over whatever might be faulty in the plan of education itself, that he would rather have the Bill as it was than risk the postponement of a scheme of National Education to an indefinite period. At the same time, no one could have gone farther than he went in disclaiming all approbation of national religious establishments, and in asserting the principles of Nonconformity. He expressed a more than ordinary warmth of esteem for his brethren around him, and especially for the venerable Dr. Rees, who, he said, would have swayed his mind somewhat differently on the question, if he could have allowed himself to be determined by any authority whatever. He sate down, declaring that he would go with the meeting as far as he could, and that when he could go no further he would make no opposition, but cheerfully yield to the decision of the majority. Mr. Clayton then spoke for two or three minutes, and Dr. Waugh for about the same time. Something dropped by this last gentleman, led Dr. Rees to rise again to explain the *principle* of the Bill, which was not education simply, but education under ecclesiastical patronage. At this moment the eye of the writer met Dr. Lindsay's, and he assented by a decisive motion of the head to Dr. Rees's explanation, saying, without rising from his seat, ' Certainly, I admit it: that is the principle of the Bill.' These were his last words. After Dr. Rees had made one or two remarks, and Mr. Innes had thrown in an explanatory sentence, the Secretary, Dr. Morgan, was proceeding to read a series of resolutions proposed by the Committee to the adoption of the meeting, and had advanced to the fourth or fifth, when the attention of the persons around Dr. Lindsay was attracted by a sort of groan, three times repeated. They found him inclining forward on his walking-stick, and on lifting him up, perceived that he had been seized with a fit. A slight convulsive motion of the head and face was observed by the gentleman nearest to him. He

and, on the Sunday following, closed a sermon to his own congregation, on *The Excellence and Reward of Christian Integrity*, with the following address:

"The suddenness of Dr. LINDSAY's departure was awful, and gave a temporary shock to every feeling of the heart. Yet as an eye-witness of the mournful stroke, I now consider it as a most happy death. It was such a mode of dying as, in dependence on the Divine will, he had ventured amongst his more intimate friends to declare desirable. It was unattended (as far as spectators could judge) by the smallest sense of pain. The summons found the faithful servant of Christ at the post of duty. He fell in the arms of his brethren, who next to his family enjoyed his warmest affections; and he breathed his last in a place endeared to him by numberless associations of ideas, the very place that, had it been permitted us to choose, we should have selected for his closing scene. There seems a consistency in the order of Providence, that so public-spirited a life should terminate by a public death.

"Sudden dissolution is deprecated in the prayers of some churches, on the too rational presumption that all men are not at all times prepared for their final account. In this case, no one could entertain such a fear. Our departed brother had received a warning, if to his truly Christian mind any warning had been needful, in a long and severe illness, from which it appears he had but imperfectly recovered, and his character, always excellent, was ripened by his affliction, and his spirit was prepared for its translation to heaven.

"The mind of Dr. Lindsay was happily formed. His intellectual powers and his social affections were remarkably strong, and the purest moral and Christian principles put them in harmonious action. Every one knows that he was a just man and a good man; and every one feels that he was *great* by being just and good.

"There was in his whole character a pure and noble-minded simplicity. Never was human breast more free from sinister design, envy and suspicion. Never were manners more remote from art and affectation. In public and private he was the same man—warm-hearted, disinterested, open and generous.

---

was instantly carried into the inner library, and within five or six minutes medical aid was procured; but in vain: pulsation had ceased, and the spirit had fled. Till long after his death was matter of certainty he continued to be surrounded by his sorrowing brethren, one of whom, Dr. Waugh, offered up on the occasion a solemn and deeply impressive prayer to the Almighty.

"The shock of this calamity put an end to the business of the meeting; and as soon as the persons present could compose themselves sufficiently to recollect what had passed before their lamented brother's seizure, they congratulated each other that not the least deviation from urbanity or friendship had taken place in the conversation in which Dr. Lindsay had shared, and in fact, that no single expression had been uttered which even now any one of the speakers would have wished to retract or alter."

"The religious circle in which he moved and shone has had in it men of deeper learning, of more extensive knowledge, of more *brilliant* talents, and of greater opportunities of professional distinction; but it never possessed an individual who carried with him more completely the affections of all that approached him, who drew to himself without design or effort more respect and confidence, or whom a religious denomination would be more proud to put forth and say, 'He is one of us.'

"In any walk of literature or science, Dr. Lindsay might have been eminent. It may be regretted that circumstances over which he had no control prevented his being a benefactor to nations and ages. Yet he is not without a memorial upon earth. The present generation must be totally forgotten before his name will be lost to conversation; and his published Sermons will, if I mistake not, give him a lasting station amongst the superior English divines.

"Though brought up in a national religious Establishment, that of Scotland, Dr. Lindsay was a decided and zealous Protestant Dissenter. The rights of conscience in their greatest latitude were his favourite theme, in discoursing on which his fine countenance was lighted up with its brightest expression, and his hearty voice rose to its highest and most commanding tone.

"He was in the best, the Christian sense of the word, a patriot. He loved his country because he loved mankind. His zeal was ardent, but equable, for public morals and national freedom. His generosity of soul preserved him from political enmities, but it urged him to be the foremost to assert great moral principles, and to stand forward, even though he should stand alone, in the cause of innocence and justice and humanity and liberty.

"One subject of late engaged in a peculiar degree his thoughts and affections; I mean, the Education of the People. All other interests, those of patriotism, morals and religion, he considered to be involved in this. 'Give me,' he would say with his cordial warmth, 'Give me an educated population, and I care not what errors and delusions are abroad. They will be sooner or later scattered by the power of knowledge. This is in the hands of Providence the mighty instrument of reformation, and it will go on working until it subdue all opposition to the rights and peace and happiness of mankind, and prepare the way for the universal spread of the pure gospel of Christ.'

"This was, in fact, the substance of the last speech which he uttered—uttered, alas! with his dying voice. One would willingly take it as prophetic; and, for one's self, a better wish cannot be entertained than that in mature years, and even in age, there may be experienced the generous, the almost youthful enthusiasm of philanthropy which to the last moment animated and delighted this good man's bosom.

"To Protestant Dissenting ministers, a more encouraging spectacle cannot be exhibited than the history of their lamented and revered brother. He was scarcely a *popular* preacher, in the vulgar estimation of pulpit talents and services. He never canvassed for applause, nor ran about to gather fame. The attendants on his ministry were not the crowd. Yet his condition was such as a mitred head might envy. His hearers were personal friends. Every year proofs accumulated of their affection, and even of their devotion to his welfare. He had nothing more in this respect to desire. And, further, when death had finished his character, it appeared, perhaps to the surprise of some persons, that no man, no minister of the gospel, ever enjoyed a greater share of well-earned and rational popularity; not that noisy breath which goes before, but that steady respect and love which follow, exalted merit. His funeral obsequies, however mournful, were in one respect the triumph of integrity and charity, verifying the consolatory, animating truth, that notwithstanding the occasional prevalence of prejudice and bigotry, *The memory of the just is blessed.*"

The removal of Dr. Lindsay and the increasing years and infirmities of Dr. Abraham Rees and Mr. Belsham, were the occasion of Mr. Aspland's being called on to undertake a still larger share than hitherto in the administration of Dissenting trusts and the conduct of public business. From this time he appears to have acted a prominent part in the occasional meetings of the General Body of London Dissenting Ministers.

He had the satisfaction of preparing and submitting to them a series of resolutions on the subject of the severe Penal Laws which then stained the Statute-book of this country. The resolutions were adopted by an unanimous vote, and a Petition to Parliament was founded on them, praying for such a revision of the criminal code as would assimilate it more closely to the spirit of the Christian religion.*

Mr. Aspland never advocated the entire abolition of death-punishments, but he beheld with shame and grief the infliction of death for mere offences against the rights of property. His long-cherished opinion of the inexpediency and wickedness of capital punishments in all but cases of murder and extreme personal violence, were soon after this strengthened by a case which fell under his own notice, in which he had reasons for fearing that the irrevocable punishment of death was inflicted on one innocent of the crime of which he was convicted.

A man named Harris was tried and convicted at the Old Bailey, in November 1824, on the charge of robbing and attempting to drown, in a pond in the Hackney Fields, one Sarah Drew. The woman was the principal witness against him, and her identification of him as her assail-

---

* See Votes of House of Commons, May 23, 1821, and Mon. Rep. XVI. 372.

ant was unhesitating. From the report of the trial in the newspapers, Mr. Aspland, who was well acquainted with the spot where the robbery and assault were alleged to have been committed, felt some doubts about the truth of the story. He began to institute minute inquiries into the case, and found that, though the convict was by habit and repute a thief, and went amongst the fraternity of evil-doers by the slang name of *Kiddy Harris*, there were strong reasons for doubting his guilt in this particular instance. Mr. Aspland and the prisoner's attorney went together to Newgate, and conversed with Mr. Wontner, the jailer, and Mr. Cotton, the ordinary. Mr. Aspland had several interviews with the convict. He subsequently personally sifted all the evidence which the convict's family and associates offered in proof of his innocence. In this distasteful duty, the scene of which was a public-house in Brick Lane, near the haunts of a nest of thieves, he was assisted by an attorney's managing clerk, accustomed to criminal investigations. The case had its difficulties, and he was not without his doubts; but in the end saw reason to rest in his first impression of Harris's innocence. He drew up a memorial on the case, which he forwarded to the Home Secretary, Mr. Peel. The memorial was illustrated by a ground-plan of the Hackney Fields, which he had caused to be prepared after an exact admeasurement of the distances of the several points, and by comments on the discrepancies as to time and place in the evidence of the prosecutrix. Instead of entering into the investigation for himself, or referring it to the Judge before whom it was tried, the Secretary unfortunately referred the whole matter to the committing Magistrate. Mr. Aspland was more grieved than surprised to find this stipendiary officer, to whom the character and habits of Harris were known, impenetrable to every impression in favour of the convict. The Recorder's report was at length made, and Harris was ordered for execution. Mr. Aspland had a final interview with him in the condemned cell. The unhappy man was grateful for the exertions made in his behalf, and, while he acknowledged his habitual criminality, and described minutely the mode in which he had obtained a dishonest livelihood,* he solemnly declared his entire innocence of the crime for which he was doomed to die. The injustice of his doom seemed to exasperate his feelings, and he was incapable of calmly listening to religious instruction. He said

---

* His profession was that of a robber of carts, and such was the subdivision of labour amongst his fraternity, and the consequent feeling of *caste*, that he felt an indignity was put upon him by his being charged with a robbery of the person!

that he should be a murdered man, and that he should ascend the drop with a declaration to that effect. Mr. Aspland made every effort to obtain a reprieve. The day before the execution he was at Newgate, and believed that he had impressed one of the Sheriffs with his own view of the case. That gentleman left him with the promise that he would go at once to the Home Office, and do what he could to stay the execution. He was unhappily overruled by others, and his promise was unfulfilled. The event of this heart-sickening affair is thus briefly recorded in Mr. Aspland's diary:

"Monday, Feb. 21.—Engaged for last time in Harris's case, but did not see him. *All in vain. He was executed next morning, shrieking out murder!*"

For a time Mr. Aspland was able to keep in his sight, and retain some influence over, the widow and family of this hapless man. Familiarity with crime had not destroyed the maternal feelings in this woman's heart, and she expressed her deep anxiety for her eldest son, a fine youth sufficiently old to be open to the temptations of evil companions. According to her representations, it appeared as if his being the son of Kiddy Harris, who had suffered at Newgate, was a kind of distinction of him amongst their degraded neighbours, and led to his being noticed by the most daring thieves. Of the career and fate of this son of crime nothing is known.

It has been mentioned that Mr. Aspland was supported by the unanimous vote of the London Ministers in his resolutions on the Criminal Code. A very different result attended his attempt to persuade the same body, in the year 1823, to take into consideration the Penal Statutes affecting Religion, with the view of discountenancing the prosecutions against Unbelievers, which the Government of the day was then renewing.

It is little to the credit of the Ministers of the Three Denominations that they received with manifest impatience and dislike the following resolutions:

"That we feel ourselves called upon to repeat the declaration of our attachment to the principles of Religious Liberty, and our full conviction that the rights of Conscience are sacred, universal and inalienable.

"That we consider all penal statutes affecting Conscience, in matters purely spiritual,—that is to say, all statutes which make civil rights and privileges to be dependent upon the profession of a particular form of faith or the observance of a particular mode of worship, or which impose fine and imprisonment upon the avowal of opinions with regard to religion,—to be inconsistent with the liberal spirit of the British Constitution, directly repugnant to the merciful precepts of the Gospel, and an infringement of that Religious Liberty which the Sovereign Creator has granted to every human being as his birthright.

"And that, devoted as we are under the most solemn engagements to the profession and promotion of the Christian faith, with which we regard the best interests of mankind, for time and for eternity, to be indissolubly connected, and deploring as we do the abounding of Infidel principles and the unexampled circulation of Infidel publications, we cannot but regret, notwithstanding, the frequent appeal to the arm of the law for the violent suppression of sceptical works and for the punishment of unbelievers; being firmly persuaded that Christianity is able to stand in its own strength,—that inquiry and discussion have ever proved favourable to its sacred interests,—that the attempt to put down unbelief by force is so far from being effectual, that it begets a suspicion in the minds of the uninformed that Christians dare not trust the support of their faith to argument and evidence, and draws the sympathy of the populace towards the champions of Infidelity, who, if they were unmolested, would speedily sink into obscurity and contempt,—and that the infliction of civil pains and penalties upon the opposers of the Gospel is contrary to the injunctions of its exalted Founder, who has taught us that his kingdom is not of this world, and can be upheld only by argument and persuasion, and by the example of a charitable and merciful temper, and of a virtuous and holy life."

Mr. Aspland well knew that the principles thus boldly enunciated were unacceptable to some even amongst his own personal friends, but he was not the man to shrink from the advocacy of what he regarded as important truth because it was unpopular. He immediately took steps to secure a still more public and general assertion of the principle of religious liberty as applied to unbelievers in Christianity. He drew up and circulated through the country, for the signature of ministers and laymen of all denominations, an elaborate declaratory document, which, under the title of *The Christians' Petition to Parliament against the Prosecution of Unbelievers*,* attracted very considerable attention. It was signed by upwards of 2000 persons, including 98 ministers of religion. Amongst other distinguished names attached to the Petition were those of Dr. Parr, Mr. Roscoe and Mr. Charles Butler. It was, as might be expected, cordially approved by Lord Holland. By Sir James Mackintosh it was loudly applauded, not less for the purity and vigour of its style than for its wise and liberal sentiments. It was presented to the House of Commons on July 1, 1823, by Mr. Hume,

---

* This admirable document, which is too long for insertion here, will be found in the Mon. Rep. XVIII. 362—364.

and, a few days after, to the House of Lords by the Marquis of Lansdowne. In the Lower House it led to an interesting debate, in the course of which the principles advanced in the Petition were ably supported by Mr. Hume, Mr. William Smith and Mr. Ricardo, and opposed by Mr. Butterworth, Mr. Twiss, Mr. Wilberforce and Mr. Peel.

It was matter of gratifying reflection to Mr. Aspland that, on the Sunday when he introduced "the Christians' Petition" to his own congregation at Hackney, and stated to them the grounds on which he deemed it entitled to their support, he had Dr. Channing (then Mr. Channing) as a hearer. That distinguished man, it is well known, at the time expressed strong doubts of the expediency of the Petition. It has been conjectured that his sensitive Christian spirit was wounded by the gross attacks upon revealed religion then prevalent, and his piety was alarmed lest a plea against persecution should be misinterpreted into an apology for irreligion.*

But whatever doubts Dr. Channing felt when he was a worshiper at Hackney, further reflection, which possibly was stimulated by his listening on that occasion to the "Christians' Petition," convinced him that there could be no true religious liberty, if men were forbidden to question or deny religion itself. Soon after his return to America, he declared that the use of menace and reproach against unbelievers made Christianity unlovely and irrational, multiplied its foes, dimmed its brightest evidence, sapped its foundations and impaired its energy.† When, in 1834, Abner Kneeland was prosecuted for Atheism, the name first appended to a petition on his behalf, asserting the equal rights of Atheists to freedom of thought and speech with Christians, was that of Dr. Channing.

In 1821, Mr. Aspland first connected himself and the Gravel-Pit congregation with the Presbyterian Fund, of which he continued to the close of his life to be a trustee and manager. This institution ranks amongst the oldest and most important of the London Dissenting charities.‡ It was founded, immediately after the passing of the Act of

---

* See Mr. Aspland's Funeral Sermon for Dr. Channing, pp. 26, 27.

† Works, III. 328.

‡ For much valuable information on the subject of the Presbyterian Fund the Editor desires to make his grateful acknowledgments to Dr. Rees, who has long been its much-valued Secretary, and whose connection with the Board began as far back as the year 1813, when he became the minister of St. Thomas's chapel, Southwark, which from a very early period had made an annual contribution to the Fund.

Toleration, for the support of Protestant Dissenting worship, by contributing pecuniary assistance to small congregations and ministers of narrow incomes, and furnishing the means of education to students for the Christian ministry. It was instituted by the joint efforts and co-operation of the two denominations of Presbyterians and Independents during their celebrated, but very brief " Union." The funds were contributed, by both those religious bodies, by personal donations and congregational collections, and the Board of Managers was constituted of the ministers and certain lay members of the congregations thus contributing. In 1693, on the rupture of the union of the two denominations, the Independents withdrew from the management, and discontinued their pecuniary contributions. From this time, the charity was supported exclusively by the Presbyterian denomination, and hence obtained the designation of the *Presbyterian Fund*. The seceders afterwards established a somewhat similar charity of their own, which is denominated the *Congregational Fund Board*.

For a long series of years the Presbyterian Fund continued to be liberally supported by the principal Metropolitan congregations of that denomination, and the trustees and managers consisted of the ministers and certain lay members of those congregations, the rule being that every congregation contributing annually £40 should be entitled to nominate its minister and one lay gentleman to be manager, and to be allowed to nominate an extra lay manager for every £40 added to the annual contribution. It was remarkable that an important and opulent congregation like that assembling at the Gravel-Pit, Hackney, presided over by a succession of eminent and public-spirited ministers, such as George Smyth, Laugher, Price, Priestley and Belsham, had never contributed to this important Dissenting charity. The decline of several ancient Presbyterian congregations in London, and the consequent diminution of the resources of the Presbyterian Fund, made it important that the Hackney congregation should become contributors. Representations to this effect were made by Dr. Abraham Rees, then Secretary of the Fund, and Dr. Thomas Rees, to Mr. Aspland, who at once laid the matter before his congregation, and they without hesitation acceded to the proposal, and have from that time made the requisite annual collection.

One of the objects of the Fund is the maintenance of an academical institution in Wales for the education of students for the Christian ministry among Protestant Dissenters. In this institution, which is of great importance in connection with the Dissenting interest in the Principality, Mr. Aspland took a very lively interest, and on more than one occasion, when his health permitted, was appointed, in conjunction with Dr. Rees and others, one of the visitors to inspect the College at Carmarthen and examine the students.

The letters that immediately follow were written during journeys on behalf of the Presbyterian Board.

Rev. Robert Aspland to Miss Middleton.

"Caermarthen, Sunday Noon, July 6, 1823.

"My dear Anna,—My last was, I think, from Swansea. After writing it, I called on General Gifford, and was exceedingly pleased with him. He is anxious to promote a subscription, as a testimony of gratitude and respect and a provision, for Richard Wright. Are not the latter days come, when the lion is to lie down with the lamb?

"From Swansea we came next day (Wednesday) to this place, through Welsh villages which I cannot write and you could not read. Between the two places there is not much scenery, but the neighbourhood of both towns is highly interesting. South Wales, however, is hardly equal to my expectations; but I should add that we have not visited the most favourite spots, and that the weather has been extremely unpropitious. Yesterday, for instance, was from morning to night cold and wet.

"With the *living* scenery I have been highly amused, incessantly occupied, and upon the whole pleased. The good old Doctor is here in his glory, a bishop, full-wigged, amongst his clergy. Think of sixty parsons all pressing upon us!—two-thirds of them Trinitarians and Calvinists, but full of protestations of candour and of invitations to me, as well as the Doctor, to take their places of worship in our way home and to give them a word of exhortation. This is not *all* mercenary affection. I do believe that the Presbyterian Fund and Dr. Williams's Trust have saved Wales from the disease of bigotry, in its last stages at least. It was, you may believe, peculiarly gratifying to me to meet no less than twenty Unitarian ministers of the Principality, and these ranking amongst the best of our clergy for learning, talents and character, and above all, for independence. This I write in view of Aberguilly, the palace of the High-priest of Intolerance, the Bishop of St. David's, whom I look down upon while 'taking mine ease at mine inn,' the Ivy Bush, which is upon the bank of the beautiful river Torvy, upon which also Aberguilly stands.

"On Thursday, as the Caermarthen paper enclosed will tell you, was the Annual Assembly of the Welsh Divines, when six sermons, Welsh and English alternately, were preached to crowded congregations, the Doctor and I being the English preachers. The Examination of the Students took place in our august presence Friday and Saturday, on each of which days we dined publicly—so I may express myself on account of the large parties at dinner. This morning the Doctor has preached at the Presbyterian-Calvinistic place, I praying at the minister's request, Mr. Peter, our tutor, a prudent and hospitable Welsh divine. We have left them to Welsh preaching and communion. I have been invited to preach at the same place in the afternoon, but have declined. In the evening I am to hold forth at the *Dark Gate*, which is the ominous name of the Unitarian chapel."

Rev. Robert Aspland to Rev. R. Brook Aspland.

"Hackney, August 31, 1826.

"Dear Brook,—After parting with you yesterday week, we proceeded, as proposed, to Llanucklin, where we examined good Michael Jones's school, and then went on in a steady rain to Dolgelly. We had not been long here before the Stubbses arrived: they joined our dinner-party for the last time. In the evening we proceeded by Dinasmouthy, a desolate mountain and valley, to Malluid, a village with a comfortable inn, where we slept. On Wednesday, we went to Llanbrynmair to breakfast. Here the rain fell in torrents. We were obliged to take a chaise from the inn to the school, only a mile distant. We were repaid for our journey. With the school, with the chapel, with the state of the congregation, and above all with the minister, Mr. Roberts, we were abundantly satisfied. Llanbrynmair is the *see* of Welsh Congregational Dissent, and Roberts is the acknowledged bishop. Nowhere, I think, is Calvinism exhibited in so mild and unobjectionable a form. So great is Roberts's influence, that Methodism in either of its forms can hardly hold up its head in the district around him. His chapel, a very substantial, commodious and even handsome building, is in the midst of a wood! The original founders of it were driven to this spot as the only obtainable site; old *Sir Watkin* owning all the land between it and the village, and it being a rule with the Watkin family ('noble race of Shenkin!') not to allow any schism-shops on their domain. [It should be added, that through Roberts's influence and arguments the present Sir Watkin has broken through the rule, and granted him a lease of land for one of his affiliated chapels!] Near the chapel is a very good school-room, capable of containing, and containing actually on our visit, nearly 100 children. Both the chapel (holding upwards of 700 people) and the school-room were built by the congregation without foreign assistance, a remarkable thing among the ancient Britons! Opposite the chapel and beside the school-room is the parsonage-house, memorable as the birthplace of Dr. Rees, Llanbrynmair having been the residence of his father, *Lewis* (if I am not mistaken), who raised this and many other congregations, and was, in fact, the Dissenting apostle of North Wales. R. A."

This Chapter must close with the letters of two or three of Mr. Aspland's valued correspondents — Mrs. Cappe, Mr. Belsham and Mrs. Mary Hughes.

Mrs. Cappe to Rev. Robert Aspland.

"York, May 10, 1821.

"Dear Sir,—Having lately been much interested by the conclusion of Bishop Burnet's History of his Own Times, and still more by his Letter to Charles the Second, I have transcribed it for insertion in the Monthly Repository or the Christian Reformer, in whichsoever you think it would be most useful. How long will his *happy* restoration continue to be solemnly commemorated? I had yesterday a very interesting letter from Dr. Channing, of Massachusetts, who does me the favour of an occasional correspondence, and from whom, as well as from many others, I have great pleasure in hearing of the rapid improvement in knowledge, and especially in religious knowledge, taking place in that favoured district. Dr. C. is one of their first preachers, and not less eminent as an example of every Christian virtue. If you have not already seen it, I wish I could send you a sermon he published in December last, at Boston, entitled, 'Religion a Social Principle;' also a pamphlet by Andrews Norton, Dexter Professor of Sacred Literature in Cambridge, entitled, 'Thoughts on True and False Religion,' containing much originality and many very just, important and consolatory reflections. Dr. Channing speaks of him as 'one of their first scholars,' and as 'adding to learning great clearness and vigour of thought;' and this publication, as far as I am capable of judging, bears ample testimony to all this. I have also received an Address to the Massachusetts Peace Society on their Fifth Anniversary, by Hon. Josiah Quincey, and a copy for Mr. Fox, which Dr. C. has enclosed, under the idea, probably, of our being next-door neighbours. Will you be so good as to send it to him? How much do I wish to see these principles generally adopted by Unitarians, and advocated by writers in the Repository and Christian Reformer! My friends Mr. Welby and Mr. Kenrick have not yet seen these publications, having been absent at Halifax, at a meeting of ministers and Tract Society. I have not sealed the parcel for Mr. Fox, believing that my American friends would wish you to see it.—I am, with compliments to Mrs. Aspland, dear Sir, your sincere friend, C. CAPPE."

"York, May 29, 1821.

"Dear Sir,—As my neighbour Mr. J. Wilson is going to London, and kindly offers to take a letter or small parcel for me, I avail myself of the opportunity to congratulate you on seeing your name among the number of speakers at Freemasons' Hall on the British and Foreign School Society, and that you proposed four motions which were seconded and carried. The philanthropic Gazette, in which I saw this account, does not mention what was their purport, but I hope we shall be favoured with these particulars in the Repository or Christian Reformer of this month. I feel the greatest solicitude that Unitarians, who believe that holiness of life and devotedness to the will of God—'to visit the widow and fatherless in their affliction, and to keep themselves unspotted from the world'—is of the very essence of the gospel, should come prominently forward in every good word and work,—in advocating Bible Societies, British and Foreign School Societies, Religious Tract Societies, and I would add, *Peace Societies*, &c., of which it is our peculiar privilege at this day not merely to have seen the commencement, but to have witnessed their considerable progress. As I am unable to take an active part, but would gladly contribute the aged widow's mite, I am preparing a little work for the Tract Societies, consisting of the reflections formerly added to the Life of Christ, &c., referring to the respective narratives to which they relate as given in the Gospels themselves, by which means I hope it may be afforded sufficiently low to circulate more generally (if it should be approved) than the larger work. I will send you and Mr. Rutt and Mr. Eaton, &c., each a copy when it is completed, as I hope it will be in the course of the summer, for your approbation. I am very glad to hear that my friend Captain Thrush has consented to publish his little work. He is really an extraordinary and most exemplary character, and, what makes it most remarkable, I believe he was not personally acquainted with a single Unitarian till, by what is called *accident*, he met with our friend Mr. W. at Redcar. I hope Mr. Eaton is perfectly recovered: have the goodness to remember me kindly to him. I hope you received a small packet from me containing Bishop Burnet's Letter to Charles the Second, for whose happy restoration our city bells are at this moment ringing most joyfully!—With best compliments to Mrs. Aspland, I remain your truly obliged   C. CAPPE."

Rev. Thomas Belsham to Rev. Robert Aspland.

"Essex Street, July 12, 1822.

"My dear Sir,—Your son Theophilus gave us great pleasure on Sunday by reporting that you were so well, you intended to preach on the Sunday following. But Dr. Pett rather damped our satisfaction by telling us that you were indeed mending, but that he should not allow you to officiate at present. May you, my dear Sir, speedily be restored to health, and see many, many years of usefulness and comfort! I have, as you have heard, been laid aside for three Lord's-days by the loss of my voice, which I began to apprehend that I should never recover. But this would have been nothing, for it is time for me to withdraw from the field. Not so with respect to yourself and Mr. Fox: for such distinguished luminaries to be removed out of their place in the midst of life and usefulness, and when there are no successors to occupy their stations, would indeed be an awful visitation, which may God long avert!—for, indeed, it is not easy to conceive how a greater calamity can befal the Unitarian churches. But the cause is of God, and to him we may safely leave the protection of its advocates and heralds. He will never forsake either it or them.

"I cannot be sufficiently thankful that my health has been spared to finish my great and arduous but pleasing task. If I could have foreseen what I had to perform in the way of correcting, transcribing, re-composing and adding, no consideration on earth would have induced me to have undertaken the work. I should have thought it insanity. Thank God, I have finished it, to the best of my ability. But I should have been most thoroughly ashamed had it gone forth into the world in the crude, imperfect state in which it existed when I first consented to its publication. I may now cheerfully chant my *nunc dimittis*.

"You were down in my list for a copy of the octavo edition, but Mr. Wainewright informs me that he is sending you a copy of the quarto. I hope, therefore, that you will not think it a slight if I do not request your acceptance of another copy, as I shall avail myself of the circumstance to give a copy to some other of our brethren who may chance to want one and to whom it may be useful.

"I have lately heard from William Roberts, and wish I had an opportunity of shewing you the letter. He has lost his kind master, Mr. Harington; and now, at the age of fifty-four, broken in constitution, with a wife and six children, he has retired to a cottage which he has at Pursewaukum, near the chapel, to end his days in poverty and dependence. To add to his misfortunes, his eldest son, a boy of fourteen, has been turned out of the English school at Mersulipatan, where he was boarded, clothed and educated, because some Unitarian tracts which his father had given him were found in his possession. In this way, a Unitarian Christian is denied a privilege which is readily granted to Mahometans and Pagans!

"Would it not be advisable to form a Committee for the affairs of Madras alone, the object of which should be to secure an annuity to Roberts and to support the Unitarian congregation at Pursewaukum?—the proceedings of which Committee should be published in your Repository.

"With my best compliments to Mrs. Aspland and your whole family, I remain, dear Sir, most sincerely yours,

T. BELSHAM."

Mrs. Mary Hughes to Rev. Robert Aspland.

"Oct. 7, 1823.

"I seem to have heard very little from you, or concerning you and yours, for a long time past. My declining health rendered me anxious to get a small and probably a last composition* for the Christian Tract Society finished, that

---

* This was "An Address to the Teachers in Sunday-schools." It proved the last of the valuable series of tracts, nineteen in number, contributed to the Christian Tract Society. Her pure and benevolent life closed at Bristol, Dec. 14, 1824.

the labour already bestowed might not be quite thrown away; and as I have time and ability to do very little, that little occupied many days, and now I do not feel satisfied that it will be worth printing without some revisal; and my head being at this time pretty much *immersed in clouds*, I resolve to let it lie for two or three weeks, after which I shall perhaps be better able to judge of its merits and demerits: and should it want much mending, I fear I shall commit it to the flames rather than undertake it,—not, however, from idleness, but from a feeling of disability. Yet if you were to call upon me in a morning, or even spend an evening here, you would not perceive that any thing was the matter; for while my mind is excited, though far from being at ease, I converse exactly as usual. I am thankful for the ability to do this, and I do not think these exertions are hurtful to me.

"I laid this sheet aside to write a note to Miss Acland on a subject that you know lies near my heart. I heard yesterday that Mr. Clarkson was soon expected here, and I thought she might probably have an opportunity of conversing with him; in which case, I wished her to press him on the subject of having his most admirable pamphlet, published in two numbers of the Inquirer, on Freeing the Negroes, freely sold. I had just finished this, when Mr. Maurice came in, and I of course told him what I had been doing,—when he electrified me with saying, 'I have this moment parted with Mr. Clarkson: he is gone across the Square to Mr. Biddulph's, and will be at your door in a few minutes!' When Mr. M. had looked over my note, he said, 'Perhaps you would like to see him and prefer your own request.' You will not doubt that I eagerly caught at the proposal. He soon after rang our door-bell, and I had the delight of seeing him enter, of shaking hands, and for nearly half an hour conversing, with the *second* man of the present day (for I must hold our great Indian Reformer as the *first*)—a happiness which I could not have hoped for; but Mr. M., knowing my ardour in the *cause*, thought I had a claim upon it, and gave me that great indulgence. It was a real pleasure, for we instantly fell into most interesting conversation, and Mr. M. so contrived that C. spoke almost the whole time; and I had the satisfaction of finding that what I so earnestly wished with respect to the pamphlet was already resolved upon. I could have almost found in my heart to be angry with Mr. M. for actually *rising* from his seat and reminding Mr. C. that he had *three letters* to write, and other calls to make, before dinner. Even after this he continued to *sit*, and to give us more information for a minute or two, and every minute was a gain to me. To see before me and freely converse with a man in whose career of noble exertions I had taken so warm an interest years ago, in the days of my greatest enthusiasm! To do myself justice, I must say that, in all worthy causes, I am far from feeling any abatement of that enthusiasm. Small matters which in earlier life would have hurt or offended me, seem now as nothing—they do not occupy a second thought; but where right and wrong is concerned, either in principle or practice, my perceptions appear to myself to become more clear and my feelings *more acute* than formerly. This does not always add to my present happiness, but it spurs me on to all the exertions that are within my narrow reach.

"Oct. 8.—Mr. Clarkson had to hurry to Bath yesterday evening, and he returns here to a meeting this morning. I hope his influence will make a considerable impression, and that a petition of much more importance than the last will be in readiness for the next session of Parliament. Mr. Maurice told us that he has already travelled 1700 miles on the business! What a *providence* (I must term it) it is that on this new and grand effort being made, so many years after the first, that this great *apostle* in the cause should still have *health* and *faculties* equal to beginning another contest, which I fear will be nearly as arduous as the first! I trust he is to *see* a glorious *victory* achieved; and he may then depart not only in peace, but cheered with joyful anticipations of a *rich reward*, when he shall hereafter meet the thousands and *tens of thousands* who will rise up and call him blessed.

"I was most agreeably surprised when I gazed upon his fine intelligent and benevolent countenance; for our friend Mr. P * * many years ago, when I expressed a strong desire to see him, said, 'O, you would be disappointed in his appearance: he is a fat, commonplace-looking man.' How he could ever have thought so, seems wonderful."

CHAPTER XXVI.

During the whole of the spring of 1822, and during portions of the autumn of that year, Mr. Aspland was laid aside by severe illness. Violent palpitations and other irregularities of the circulation had before this time made his medical advisers apprehend the existence of organic disease. But the rapidity and apparent completeness of his recovery from successive attacks perplexed their judgment, and for a time disposed them to trace his sufferings to severe dyspepsia. The result, however, made it more than probable that at a very early period of his public life organic disease of the heart began its painful and ultimately fatal course.* By the strength of his constitution and his remarkable vivacity of spirits, he was enabled in the intervals of sickness to throw off the feelings and habits of the invalid, and to encounter an amount of toil which would have fatigued any one in the enjoyment of perfect health. His protracted studies in preparation for the pulpit, and the exciting duties of the Sunday, must have been highly injurious to him. Often he was prevented by the variety of his occupations from beginning the composition of his sermons till the Friday morning. The long sittings at his desk of the Friday and Saturday were often resumed early on the Sunday morning. Generally, in addition to two services (one of them of great length), there was a lecture to the young. In the evening of Sunday, his simple but not inhospitable table was commonly resorted to by a few friends, including several young men of

---

* As early as the year 1801, there were symptoms of an alarming character, although they were afterwards forgotten. On two occasions, it appears from letters written at the time, having retired to rest on Sunday night, his head shattered with the thinking, reading and speaking of the day, he awoke soon after midnight in a state of violent agitation, his limbs trembling and struggling, and his heart beating as if it would start from his breast.

great abilities, some of whom have since risen to professional eminence. Their conversation banished for the hour the sense of fatigue, and roused him to continued exertions of mind and voice. A disturbed, if not sleepless, night was the too frequent consequence of this protracted labour and excitement.

Early in the year already named, he tried the renovating effects of a visit to the sea-side and gentle horse exercise. His return to duty was, however, followed by aggravated symptoms, and he was advised by his medical friends to withdraw for several months to some retired village residence. It was the happiness (not unmingled with anxiety) of the writer to accompany him at this time for many weeks to a pleasant village in the county of Essex, to read with him many hours of every day, and to attend him in his slow but often not short forest rides. Never did his mind appear brighter than during this long sickness; and of mental depression the only apparent sign was the haggard, anxious look which is the index of disease. In consequence of the demand for supplies for the pulpits of Essex Street, Parliament Court and Jewin Street (the ministers of all which were at this time invalided), it was a difficult task to procure suitable preachers for the New Gravel-Pit congregation. In order to meet this difficulty and diminish the anxiety of their absent pastor, the congregation kindly resolved that they would, if necessary, conduct the religious service amongst themselves for a period of two months. This pledge was redeemed; and the knowledge that, happen what might, there would be a religious service, kept the congregation together in this time of difficulty. More than once the service was conducted by the venerable John Towill Rutt, who made use of the Forms of Prayer which he had formerly printed for a small congregation at Witham, in Essex, unprovided with a regular minister.

From the very few letters written at this period, only part of one is fit for the public eye.

Rev. Robert Aspland to his Brother Isaac.
"Chingford Green, Saturday, May 18, 1822.

"Dear Brother,—Being again banished from home on account of illness, and having a spare half hour, I sit down to give you a few lines. I had hoped that I was conquering my disorder, but it returned upon me with such violence this day week, that I was obliged to lie by on Sunday, and to resort to bloodletting and violent medicines. For the sake of quiet as well as of a purer air, I was advised to remove from Hackney; and hither Mrs. Aspland, Alfred and

I, with a maid-servant, came yesterday,—how long to stay, depends upon a higher Will than ours.

"This is a beautiful hamlet of the parish of Chingford, the most like Wicken of any little patch of houses that I have ever seen, but more private than even you are, and much more pleasant. We are at the foot of one of the highest and most delightful hills in this part of the county of Essex, which commands a view of London, Epping forest, the valley of the river Lea, and the upper grounds of Hertfordshire. East of us, within a furlong, is Epping forest; and at the distance of a mile and a half, is Woodford; and of two or three miles, Loughton. We are ten miles from town, and, as you see by my description, nearer to you by nearly all that distance. We have lodgings at a bettermost farm-house, and are, as far as we can judge thus early, as comfortable as we could hope in our circumstances to be. My horse is at lodgings, too; and according to the degree of my strength, I purpose, with his assistance, to explore the beautiful scenery of this interesting neighbourhood. Sometimes I shall ride *towards* you, and often visit you in thought and good wishes. You shall hear from time to time of my state.

"On Whit-Wednesday (the 29th inst.) is the anniversary of the Unitarian Fund. I am doomed to be absent from it, and so is my friend and neighbour *Fox*, the Secretary, and, unhappily, from the same cause. Before I fell ill the last time, I had procured as Chairman of the meeting, Mr. *Hammond*, of Fen Stanton, near St. Ives, who made such an admirable speech at the Huntingdon Reform County Meeting. He is an University man, a country gentleman, and zealously attached to the principles, both civil and religious, that we prize most highly.

"I am your affectionate Brother,

ROBERT ASPLAND."

He was enabled, August 18, 1822, to resume his pulpit duties, and selected for his subject, "Retirement, Self-communion and Devotion recommended from the Example of our Lord." The sermon, with a sequel, was afterwards printed, and forms Nos. XXI. and XXII. of the volume of "Sermons on various Subjects, chiefly Practical," published in 1833.

The adoption of Christianity by Rammohun Roy, and the conversion of a Baptist Missionary at Calcutta to the Unitarian doctrine, excited at this time great interest amongst English Unitarians. Mr. Ivimey, a Baptist minister of London, Secretary of the Baptist Missionary Society, published in the *Morning Chronicle* a petulant letter, in which he styled Unitarians "Socinians," Rammohun Roy "a Pagan," and Mr. Adam and his other converts "Pagan Unitarians." Mr. Aspland understood the motive, but did not admire the wisdom nor admit the justice, much less the charity, of this writer, in attempting to deprive the Christian religion of a witness so distinguished and impartial as Rammohun Roy. He felt it to be a duty publicly to remonstrate with Mr. Ivimey in the same journal in which the offensive letter appeared. In doing so he took the opportunity of communicating to the public the facts, as far as they were then known, respecting Rammohun Roy's Christianity.

Mr. Ivimey published a rejoinder, in which he vindicated the use of the term *Socinians* in preference to that of *Unitarians*, as necessary to avoid circumlocution, because the adoption of the latter name would imply that Trinitarians worship a plurality of Gods, whereas they are in reality Unitarians, worshiping one God in three persons. "To give the Socinians, then, this name exclusively, would be to grant them the very point which they seem desirous to assume, i. e. the point in debate."

In his second reply, Mr. Aspland confuted this argument in a way that scarcely admitted of an answer. In his first he had reminded Mr. Ivimey of the nickname *Anabaptists*, so long and so improperly fastened on the Baptists. Recurring to the term Baptist, Mr. Aspland observed, "This appellation is adopted by such Christians as practise baptism by immersion, on the personal profession of faith of the candidate; but the majority of the Christian world, who baptize infants by affusion, or sprinkling, might object, that for Anti-Pædo-Baptists to call themselves *Baptists*, is to beg the question; that this term implies that theirs is the only baptism; and that Pædo-Baptists are in truth as much Baptists as they. *This is the same argument as Mr. Ivimey's against the propriety of the name Unitarian; and whatever answer he would give in the one case, I should probably be willing to appropriate in the other.*"

In his rejoinder, Mr. Ivimey overlooked Mr. Aspland's positive claim for the Indian Reformer of the character and name of Christian, and represented his opponent as confounding Christianity with mere Theism. He sarcastically inquired whether, in the event of the Indian Reformer's visiting England and applying for admission to the Gravel-Pit congregation, he would "be received into full communion, merely on account of his agreeing with them in the doctrine of the Unity of God, notwithstanding he has not in his creed one sentiment *peculiar* to Christianity?" In penning this unfortunate sentence, the writer little foresaw that the Indian Reformer would visit England and receive a welcome, not merely at the Gravel-Pit and other Unitarian congregations, but also that he would sometimes attend the worship of "orthodox" churches, and be claimed by some of their ministers as one with them.

That Mr. Ivimey gained little glory in this controversy was probably the opinion of his biographer, Mr. George Pritchard, who makes in his Memoir no allusion to it.

The beginning of the year 1823 was darkened by the sudden removal of one of Mr. Aspland's most accomplished and valued Hackney friends, Dr. Samuel Pett. This estimable man was born in 1755, at Liskeard, in Cornwall. He studied first at the Liskeard Grammar School, and then at the Dissenting Academy at Daventry, where he had, amongst others, Mr. Cogan as a fellow-student and Mr. Belsham as a Tutor. He studied medicine at the University of Edinburgh, where he graduated in 1793. After practising for a short time as a physician at Plymouth, he removed into the neighbourhood of London, and in 1804 resumed at Hackney the practice of his profession, which he continued with advancing reputation until the day of his mortal sickness. "In performing one of the painful duties of his profession, he received a slight, and at the instant an imperceptible injury, which in the course of a few hours brought on a state of disease that baffled the power of medicine and the skill and assiduity of the most able and attentive medical friends." He expired on the evening of New-Year's Day, 1824. To a Dissenting minister it is a great privilege to have in his congregation men of thoughtful and cultivated minds. It was Mr. Aspland's privilege to have several of this description, whose presence stimulated the exercise of all his talents. For Dr. Pett he felt especial respect, as a man of superior intellect, extensive reading and varied knowledge. There was unbroken sympathy between them in moral sentiments and tastes, as well as in religious and political opinions. It was with deep emotion, and in the presence of an unusually large congregation, that, on the second Sunday in the year, Mr. Aspland delivered the funeral sermon, taking as his subject, "The Blessing pronounced by Christ on the Merciful" in Matthew xxv. 34—40. The sermon was printed and passed through two editions.

Mrs. Mary Hughes to Rev. Robert Aspland.

"Bristol, Feb. 2, 1823.

"* * I have to thank you for two letters, which did not indeed give me such intelligence as I could have wished to hear; but as events are not within the reach of our power, such as occur must be related. The death of the truly amiable and excellent Dr. Pett was indeed a lamentable event, and one for which his friends were so totally unprepared, that the blow fell with double weight. How well do I recollect his fine person and manners, and his great kindness to me when at Hackney! * * There is something peculiarly affecting in the recollection of the *last* time that you saw a friend from whom you are for this state finally separated. But what must have been your anxiety when you first apprehended danger!"

"Feb. 11.

"Four days ago, I had a nervous seizure which felt rather serious; and though I have been better since, it is more than probable that it will be soon succeeded by others, so that I think there would be some risk in giving many weeks' purchase for my life. I thankfully add that my mind is quite at ease. All events are in the hands of *Him* who ordereth all things *well.* Happily, I have little to do in the way of setting my worldly affairs in order; and for the rest, may I venture to adopt the words of an eloquent writer—'They who sleep in the bosom of a Father need not fear to be awakened.'

"We are delighted with the 'Pilgrimage of Helon,' and hope the whole will be given in an English dress. Why, but as the consequence of a heathenish education, should Attica be an object of enthusiastic interest to our youth, while Judæa excites no single thought? * * Once again, farewell. My most affectionate wishes attend you all.

M. HUGHES."

Rev. Robert Aspland to a Son—a Student.

"Hackney, Feb. 26, 1824.

"* * In your sermons* you must consult your own taste in the first instance, and afterwards the simplest and easiest writers. You will find great advantage in making sermons your Sunday reading; and amongst authors, I would name Tillotson, Atterbury, Farquhar and Enfield, as models. I would not have you aim at what is called eloquence. Be anxious only for solid thoughts, and put these into common English, and you will do well.

"* * A new curate is introduced at Essex Street, a Mr. ———, a convert from the Church, who has preached twice, and the first time very oddly. This gentleman is in orders, and has been for some time past doing duty in one of the churches at ———. He has come over to Unitarianism rather than to Unitarians. He is described as a High-churchman,† who has just liberality

---

* In a letter of an earlier date, he had touched on the same subject: "I read your essay at sermon-making with pleasure. It would be wrong to criticise a first attempt; but let me advise you in your next attempt to define a more precise *plan*, to avoid fineness and study simplicity, and to say no more than you really *have to say*, whatever be the number of pages occupied or unoccupied."

† This gentleman's Nonconformity, it is believed, soon came to an end.

enough to tolerate Dissenters. Mr. Belsham seems to make little progress. I am just going to dine with my venerable friend Dr. Rees, who is sometimes dying and sometimes the life and soul of a party. You will see a full account of the opening of Finsbury chapel in the Monthly Repository, drawn up by Southwood Smith. The chapel is still crowded, and Mr. Fox has the prospect of a numerous congregation. There is a notice of him, by Hazlitt, in the New Monthly, as a little body with a manly spirit, who is not so popular as Irving because he is not so big."

"April 21, 1824.

" * * You will see a good (full and correct) report of the debate on our Marriage Bill in the next Repository, drawn up by Mr. Edgar Taylor. The Archbishop of Canterbury made a speech for matter and manner quite worthy of the first minister of a Protestant Church. The Bishop of Chester's was a disgusting attempt to shew that words need not stand in a man's way. Our best speech altogether was from Lord Holland, who had the spirit of Fox upon him. We are most indebted, however, to the Marquis of Lansdowne, who is a sincere friend. He hopes for success, but apprehends a trick or two on the part of the old Chancellor."

"May 21, 1824.

" * * Our losing the Marriage Bill is not a matter of surprise. We are of course vexed, but I believe the Premier and Primate are as much chagrined as we. Hume, the Member, with whom I dined in a small party last week, tells me that there is great discord in the Cabinet, and that the old Chancellor is supported by the Duke of York, who begins to shine as the rising sun."

"Hackney, May 29, 1824.

" * * 'The Political Conduct of Milton' is not the easiest theme you could have chosen. I suppose you mean to vindicate him as Latin Secretary under the Commonwealth, and as the apologist of the High Court of Justice. You must take care that you are not betrayed into extravagance of doctrine or vehemence of language. *In medio tutissimus*, &c. The first thing you have to do is to look into Milton himself, his Defensio, &c. In the Sonnets and the Samson Agonistes you will find many lines and passages that will work up well in your essay. If you have Newton's edition of the Poems, you will see in some of the Notes the application of the poet's language to his own history. Newton's Life of Milton is tame, but should be consulted. The brief Life by Toland is better, but will not help you much. Hayley (Life of Milton, thin 4to) will serve you more, though, Whig as he was, he is but a timid defender. The best of all the Lives is Dr. Symmons's—a spirited vindication of the patriot-poet by a kindred spirit, though an Oxonian. You know Johnson's attack on the poet, and perhaps know that there is a special vindication of him, in reply to the snarling Jacobite critic, by Archdeacon Blackburne, printed in the Life of Thomas Hollis, in two vols. 4to, which is, of course, on your College shelves.

"Besides these works, you will have to look into the historians of the period: Hume, Clarendon, Macaulay, &c. Some of the Lives of contemporaries may also be serviceable, especially the Lives of Cromwell.

"To fortify Milton's case, you may refer to or quote Horace Walpole's judgment on the decapitation of Charles (I think, in his Noble and Royal Authors), and Mr. Fox's brief but comprehensive remarks upon the effect produced *abroad* by the proceedings of the Parliament of England, in the Introduction to his History of James.

"In an early volume of the Monthly Repository are gleanings from Milton's Prose Works, containing some of his most striking passages, which may save you some trouble: you may rely on their correctness.

"For your purpose, I know not that you need go further. An erudite paper is not expected on such an occasion, nor is it desirable that you should descend into biographical or historical minutiæ. Keep within moderate limits, for the sake of your auditors and of your own time (previously), and of your voice in the delivery. Seize a few great principles, and shew that you feel them to be principles, and great ones, by avoiding amplification. Your introduction should be cool, cautious, simple and perspicuous. The argument will be all the stronger for plain words. In your conclusion you may give the rein to imagination, or rather patriotic feeling. But from beginning to end, remember Milton was a serious and devout Christian, personally considered, and bring forward his religion and piety as the measure of his conduct and constant presumptions in his favour."

During the latter half of the year 1824, the Gravel-Pit chapel was closed, in order to receive extensive repairs (including an entirely new roof), which, notwithstanding its comparatively recent erection, were found absolutely necessary. The work to be done grew on the builder's hands as he proceeded, and, instead of weeks, months passed on before the renovated building was again ready for use. The cost of the alterations (about £1500) was provided with great liberality by the congregation, which was at this time in a very flourishing state. The temporary closing of the New Gravel-Pit meeting was the occasion of a liberal and truly kind offer from the Rev. Dr. J. Pye Smith, which the writer feels pleasure in thus publicly recording. Between this learned and excellent man and Mr. Aspland, notwithstanding the divergence of their theological views, friendly and even confidential intercourse, originating in meetings for the transaction of the business of the Three Denominations and the administration of Dissenting Charities, had long existed. Seeing the houseless condition of his neighbour's congregation, Dr. Smith generously offered him the use of the Old Gravel-Pit chapel, in the interval between the morning and afternoon service. Difficulties arose from the less liberal disposition of some of Dr. Smith's congregation, and the offer was in the end declined, with feelings of respect and gratitude for the intended neighbourly kindness.

Mr. Charles Butler to Rev. Robert Aspland.

"Lincoln's Inn, April 14, 1825.

"Dear Sir,—A letter which I have just received from Mr. Belsham, authorizes me to use his name in making this application to you, and to trouble you with the following request. I shall feel myself greatly obliged by your attending to it.

"Several years ago, I transcribed from some book the passage copied in the enclosed paper. A letter received by me informs me that 'Schism Guarded,' to which I have referred in it, was not written by Archbishop Usher, and that it was written by Archbishop Bramhall. I conjecture that I transcribed the passage from a work then before me, and cited 'Schism Guarded,' as containing sentiments corresponding with the passage which I transcribed; and I have a notion that I found the passage itself in 'The Principles and Practices of Moderate Divines.' This work is very rare; it is not in the Library of the British Museum; and I think I obtained the loan of it from the Dissenters' Library, through the interference of my most esteemed friend, Miss Lucy Aikin.

"Particular circumstances make me very desirous of ascertaining if the passage be in any work of Archbishop Usher's, and, if not, in what work it is to be found. I strongly think it is in some work of the Archbishop. His Grace was certainly a Calvinist, and might, therefore, wish for a latitudinarian explanation of the Thirty-nine Articles.

"If you can give me any information upon this head, I shall be greatly obliged to you for it. With the greatest respect, I have the honour to be your most obedient and most humble servant,

CHARLES BUTLER."

This was the very curious passage enclosed in Mr. Butler's letter:

"With Archbishop Usher,* they maintain that 'The Church of England did not define any of the questions as necessary to be believed, either *ex necessitate medii*, or *ex necessitate præcepti*, which is much less; but only bindeth her sons, for peace sake, not to oppose them.' 'We do not,' continues the learned Prelate, 'suffer any man to reject the Thirty-nine Articles of the

---

"* Schism Guarded, p. 396. See the Principles and Practice of Moderate Divines, p. 191."

Church of England at his pleasure; yet neither do we look upon them as essentials of saving faith, or legacies of Christ and his apostles; but in a mean, as pious opinions, fitted for the preservation of unity; neither do we oblige any man to believe them, but only not to contradict them."

On the same sheet are preserved the notes of Mr. Aspland's reply to Mr. Butler's inquiry:

"Totidem verbis in Stillingfleet's Rational Account of Grounds of Protestant Religion, p. 54, Vol. IV. of Works, fol. Stillingfleet quotes Bishop Bramhall's Schism Guarded, § 7, p. 396. And Replication to the Bishop of Chalcedon, p. 264.

"Bramhall maintains that the Apostles' Creed is 'a perfect rule and canon of faith, which comprehendeth all doctrinal points which are necessary for all Christians to salvation,' in Replication to Bp. of Chalcedon, p. 375, published with 'A Just Vindication of the Church of England,' 8vo, 1761.

"He also says in 'Replication,' p. 264, 'We do not hold our Thirty-nine Articles to be such necessary truths, *extra quam non est salus*, without which there is no salvation, nor enjoin ecclesiastick persons to swear unto them; but only to subscribe them as theological truths for the preservation of unity among us, and the extirpation of some growing errors.'

"Dr. Bennet, 'Essay on Thirty-nine Articles,' 8vo, 1715, quotes Mr. Butler's passages from 'Schism Guarded,' referring to § 1, ch. xi. p. 345, Dublin, 1676; and Ib. § 7, p. 400. Bennet contends that both Low and High Church subscribe the Articles with equal sincerity, and are fully persuaded that their subscription is not understood to profess a belief in them.—Essay, p. 438.

"He contends that Bramhall's words apply only to the laity.

"The Principles, &c., by Edward Fowler, Minister of Northill, Beds; afterwards D. D. and Bishop of Gloucester. He quotes the passages from Bramhall's 'Schism Guarded,' referring to him as Lord Primate of Ireland, and the late most Rev. and learned Archbishop of Armagh (p. 191). He says of moderate divines, that they profess heartily to subscribe the Thirty-nine Articles of our Church, taking that liberty in the interpretation of them that is allowed by the Church herself. Though it is most reasonable to presume that she requires subscription to them as to an instrument of peace only."

Dr. Abraham Rees, the venerable pastor of the Jewin-Street congregation and the editor of the Cyclopædia, died June 9, 1825, in the 82nd year of his age. By the will of Dr. Rees, the task of preaching his funeral sermon was assigned to Mr. Aspland, as the delivery of the funeral oration was to Dr. Thomas Rees.* The funeral took place at

---

* It is to be regretted that circumstances have hitherto prevented the publication by this gentleman of the Memoirs of the life of Dr. Rees and of his father,

Bunhill Fields, after the address had been delivered at the Old Jewry chapel in Jewin Street, over the body of the deceased pastor. The pall was borne by six ministers, of whom Mr. Aspland was one. The subject of the funeral sermon delivered on the following day from the pulpit of the deceased was, "The Reunion of the Wise and Good in a Future State." It has always appeared to the writer to be by far the best of the numerous funeral sermons published by its author, and it is probably not inferior to any of his pulpit compositions. It is within the writer's knowledge that it has ministered consolation to many persons grieving for the loss of friends.

Thus did the preacher sketch the life and character of his deceased friend:

"Dr. ABRAHAM REES was the son of the Rev. Lewis Rees, a Dissenting Minister who contributed during an almost unexampled length of active life to promote the cause of Nonconformity in North and South Wales, and whose praise is yet in all the churches of that Principality. His great-grandfather was a Welsh clergyman. By his mother's side he was collaterally descended from the celebrated Penry, who died a martyr to Nonconformity in the reign of Queen Elizabeth.

"Having received respectable grammar learning in his native country, with a view to the ministry, to which his father had devoted him from the birth, subject to the will of Providence, he was placed in an Academy for Dissenting Ministers conducted in this city by Dr. Jennings and Mr. (afterwards Dr.) Savage.* Here he made such proficiency, especially in the mathematics, that,

---

the Rev. Lewis Rees, of Lanbrynmair. Such a volume would have filled up many gaps in the history of English and especially London Nonconformity, and afforded much valuable matter for the biography of Dissenting ministers who have flourished during the past half century.

* At this Academy some of the most useful ministers of the last century were educated. Dr. Toulmin, in his Memoir of Dr. Jennings (Prot. Diss. Mag., Vol. V. 126) names Mr. Thomas and Dr. John Wright, of Bristol; Mr. Ralph, of Halifax; Dr. Caleb Evans; Drs. Rice, Harris and Samuel Wilton, of London; Dr. Cogan; Mr. Wood, of Leeds; Mr. Thomas Jervis, &c.

It is a very interesting fact that Dr. Rees, being a student at the Academy in the year 1760, was permitted by his Tutor to accompany the Dissenting Ministers when they presented the Address to George III. on his accession to the Throne. The Address was on that occasion read by Dr. Samuel Chandler, who was supported by 140 ministers. On the accession of George IV., in 1820, Dr. Abraham Rees, then the Father of the London Ministers, was selected as their representative and spokesman before the Throne. His venerable form, dignified carriage and manly elocution, would of themselves have bespoken respectful attention. The fact of Dr. Rees's having been present on a similar occasion sixty years previously, was made known to the King, and procured from him marked and repeated expressions of respect and kindness.

a vacancy occurring in that department of tuition, he was appointed by the Trustees of the institution to occupy it, before his regular term of study was completed. In this arduous situation he gave so much satisfaction, that he was soon after chosen to the more responsible office of resident Tutor, which he continued to hold for 23 years, to the credit of the Academy and the great advantage of the Dissenting cause. On his resignation the Academy was dissolved, which he always lamented as an event most injurious to the interests of the Dissenters, especially in and about this metropolis.

"For some time Dr. Rees officiated only as an occasional preacher. At length, in July, 1768, he was unanimously elected to succeed the Rev. Mr. Read as pastor of the Presbyterian congregation, St. Thomas's, Southwark; a connexion of which he was always accustomed to speak with pleasure. He remained in this situation 15 years, and the congregation flourished under his ministry. At the end of that term, he was invited to become minister of this congregation, then assembling in the Old Jewry in a place consecrated by the labours of a succession of eminently pious men, nearly the last of whom in the series was the highly-gifted and learned Dr. Chandler. From various causes, the congregation had much declined, and it was judged (wisely as appeared by the event), that Dr. Rees would revive the interest; and with this hope, and without any calculation of an increase of emolument, he accepted the invitation, and from 1783 to the period of his death continued to labour amongst you with unquestionable and increasing success.

"During a period of some years, he was engaged with his friend, the late Rev. Hugh Worthington, whose eloquence still reverberates in our ears, in delivering winter evening lectures at Salters' Hall, by means of which his usefulness and reputation as a preacher were much extended.

"For a short time he was connected as a Tutor with the Academical Institution at Hackney, which was set on foot with great liberality and high expectations, but by the operation of many adverse causes soon declined and fell, to the mortification of its patrons and the lasting regret of the liberal Dissenters.

"These public engagements our friend was fulfilling with a fidelity that will long be remembered with respect, at the same time that he was employed in literary undertakings of a magnitude sufficient to have absorbed the whole time and attention of a man of less vigour of mind, less constancy of purpose or less systematic perseverance. The works to which his name is affixed have earned for him great and richly-deserved celebrity at home and abroad. In acknowledgment of them he was honoured with academic titles by several learned bodies.

"From his station in the metropolis, his character and his talents, he was naturally connected with the various Dissenting Charities and Trusts established in London, and with some of them officially. His regularity, punctuality, sagacity and activity procured for him the confidence of his numerous associates in these establishments, and, what he valued still more, the gratitude of a great number of Dissenting Ministers, whom as well as their families by means of these connexions he was enabled to serve.

"To his native country, Wales, he was a great benefactor. The Dissenters of that part of the kingdom owe more to his unwearied attention to their interests than to any other individual that ever lived. His known zeal for his poorer brethren in the Welsh churches induced some generous persons, whose praise is not of men but of God, to place in his hands and at his discretion large pecuniary means for their relief. Heaven grant that these streams of Christian charity may not sink in his grave, but may still flow through some other channel for the refreshment of the laborious, but, in an earthly sense, ill-requited servants of the Most High God!

"I need not conceal that Dr. Rees was the principal distributor under His Majesty's Government of the Annual Parliamentary Bounty to indigent Dissenting Ministers; and if I were called upon to point out the most prominent excellence in his character, I should name his conscientious discharge of this delicate trust, in the administration of which he preserved on the one hand his independence, and on the other his affability and kindness.

"Our revered friend was a Protestant Dissenter from full and growing conviction. No man ever did more in the same space of time (and Heaven be praised that the term of his activity and influence was long!) for the promotion of our principles and of our credit in the eyes of the world. He guarded our institutions with jealousy; and he implored and conjured his associates, before many of whom I speak, to keep up the same watchfulness after his decease. In his occasional intercourse, as one of the representatives of the Body of Dissenting Ministers, with His Majesty's Court and Government, he was courteous, dignified, firm and upright. He was indeed a man qualified to speak with the enemy in the gate—though happily for the greater part of his time the prevailing sentiment of the successive administrations was friendly to the rights and privileges of the Dissenters.

"His character as a preacher it were needless to describe; it is engraven upon your hearts. He did not possess all the qualifications that the multitude most esteem in a preacher; his were sterling merits: sound and strong sense, a clearly-defined subject, well-digested thoughts, scriptural language, manly confidence in the affections of his auditory, and marked but sober earnestness. He practised no arts in the pulpit—on the contrary, he expressed his abhorrence of affectation, trick and meditated extravagance in a Christian Minister. His sound and practical and scriptural instructions were recommended and enforced by a person that commanded attention, and a deep sonorous voice that gave peculiar weight to his plain yet admirable style of composition.

"His theology he was wont to describe as the moderate scheme, lying between the extremes of opinion that prevail in the present day. Owning no human authority in religion, he yet avowed that he subscribed for the most part to the creed of the late Dr. Price, a truly good and great man, formed to be loved and admired, and to be had in everlasting remembrance. Our departed friend was equally anxious to secure in his religious system the supreme glory of God the Almighty Father, and to magnify the work, exalt the mediation, and honour the character, of the Saviour. With him, as with Dr. Price, religious worship was sacred to One Being, One Mind, One Person; and, as you learned yesterday, his views of the Divine government comprehended the final happiness of the whole intelligent creation.

"Though his own principles were fixed and steady, and in fact underwent little or no alteration for the last fifty years, he was of a catholic spirit towards all good men, to whom he gave with sincerity the right hand of fellowship.

"The character of Dr. Rees's mind was that of a sober thinker and logical reasoner. He possessed equal powers of comprehension and discrimination. His eye betokened his sagacity. He was quick in discerning men's foibles, and he sometimes laid them under tribute for the promotion of the objects of religious charity that lay near his heart.

"As a companion he was unrivalled. None that ever partook will forget his cheerful, cordial hospitality.

"I do not represent him, much as I revered him living, sincerely as I mourn him dead, and lasting as will be my remembrance of his talents and his virtues,—I do not represent him as a perfect man. He had doubtless his infirmities, but they were mere infirmities—and they were as few as I ever saw (for here I must speak my own opinion) in a man of the same natural robustness of mind, the same resolution, the same zeal, and the same anxiety for the great purposes to which his life and heart and soul and strength were devoted.

"The bodily weaknesses that were the consequences of extreme age, were no part of himself, and cannot be brought into the estimate of his character.

"His heart was always right. His Christian principles never forsook him. They had been the guide of his youth, and the distinction of his mature life, and they were the stay of his old age. His trust was fixed on the mercy of God through Christ, and he was not afraid to die. The expression of his eyes, and the posture of his hands, in his last moments, denoted that his mind was engaged in devotion after his tongue had ceased to perform its office. He sunk gradually into his last sleep, and the tenor of his life emboldens me to say, that he *died in the Lord.*

"Peace be to his ashes! Ever honoured be his name!"

Mr. Aspland completed at Midsummer 1825, the twentieth year of his ministry at Hackney. By the desire of the heads of the congregation, the occasion was celebrated by a social meeting, numerously attended, at which he and several of his personal friends, ministers and others, were the invited guests. Of this meeting no report was given;

for, as Editor of the Monthly Repository, he was never forward to admit articles into that work markedly complimentary to himself. But a document, prepared at this time, remains which will be read with interest on account of its autobiographical character. On the Sunday which closed the second decade of his pastorship at the Gravel-Pit, after a discourse on "Our Lord's Discretion as a Religious Teacher," he addressed his flock in these words:

"Indulge me now in a word or two in relation to a subject to which it may be expected by some that I should refer, but on which it is difficult to speak with propriety and delicacy;—I mean my pastoral connexion with this congregation. The present sabbath will complete the twentieth year of my ministry amongst you; but I know not that I should have ventured to take public notice of the circumstance, interesting as it is to my own feelings, if many of you had not, in the partiality of friendship, thought it worthy of observation.

"Sincerely do I bless God for the formation and continuance of a relation in which I have enjoyed much happiness, and have, I would hope, been in some small degree useful in the cause of Christian truth.

"To that cause, as far as I may have understood it, my public life has been humbly devoted: but if I have been able to render the least service to it, it is mainly owing to your sympathy and kindness and cordial support.

"In reviewing the ministry to which you have called me, I am sensible of many defects, but conscious also of some little change of mind and feeling, which I flatter myself has not lessened my power of usefulness.

"Let me freely say, then, that whilst my estimate of the value of the Christian religion, of the importance of free inquiry, and of the sacredness of the fundamental principle on which we associate, the unity in mind and person and the fatherly character of Almighty God, has been gradually rising, there are other points on which I find myself somewhat removed from my earlier thoughts and conclusions, though of these perhaps it would be more correct to say that I have altered my rules of thinking rather than my opinions.

"Concerning the person of Christ, I am compelled by the testimony of Scripture to believe that the Christian world is labouring under a great and hurtful misapprehension; but I confess that I look with growing reverence upon the character and attach increasing importance to the office of our Saviour; and that I am disposed to treat less dogmatically certain questions relating to the date of his existence and the mode of his birth.

"The view that I now take of man is higher than it once was. Without deciding upon the ever-disputed question, What is the mind of man? I frankly acknowledge that the tendencies of my thoughts are towards those that distinguish mind from matter, and that set up a spiritual as contradistinguished from the natural world. And with this veneration of man individually, my reverence of society has proportionally increased. The doctrine that there is a spirit in man, of higher being and nobler powers than that portion of him which is obvious to the senses, is of great and various influence. It gives a peculiar character to devotion as consisting in the communion of the mind of man with the spirit of God; and it represents in a pleasing light the state of the human being after death and the prospect of the world to come. In this view particularly wonderful and fearful is our make. I am consequently more desirous of union, as far as union is practicable, with my fellow-christians and fellow-creatures, and would rather lessen than aggravate the differences that prevail between us, making conformity the rule of life and nonconformity the exception.

" In fact, I am disposed to believe that as there is more virtue than vice in the world, so there is more truth than error in every church; and to conclude for this reason that some of our divisions are merely in words, and that most of them are enlarged beyond the requirements of truth, and much more of charity.

" When the occasion seems to call for it, you will bear me witness that I do not hesitate to assert what I consider to be truth or to expose what I believe to be serious error; but with my present views and feelings, I cannot make every sermon controversial, nor assume in the pulpit the tone and language of challenge, debate and defiance.

" Pardon this egotism. I have been reluctantly drawn into it; and I know not that I could with justice to you or myself have said less. A minister's usefulness depends upon his being thoroughly understood, and his congregation are entitled to an explicit statement of the leading principles of his faith and the general tendencies of his mind.

" Let us together commit ourselves to a merciful Providence. Some great and painful changes have taken place in our circle since we were brought into religious connexion—greater changes are certainly decreed—God Almighty grant us faith, that we may look back upon the past without repining, and forward to the future without dismay! May He condescend to bless us as a Christian people, that our profiting may appear to all, and that our union in outward ordinances may cherish the spirit of Christianity in our bosoms. May He keep us sound in faith, in charity, in patience. May He make peace within these walls and prosperity within all your dwellings. May He forgive all our imperfections and deliver us from all hurtful errors: may He carry on his own work among us: and under His gracious guidance and heavenly blessing, may we finally meet in the temple not made with hands, and mingle our voices in the universal chorus of praise to Him, the Creator, the Preserver, the Friend and the Father of all.—Amen and Amen."

The modification of taste and feeling (rather than change of opinion) indicated in this address, has probably been experienced by other men and in more denominations than one. In Mr. Aspland it was the necessary consequence of the growth of the Christian character and increased reverence for evangelical truth. By his accustomed hearers, the statement of his feelings, though listened to with deep attention, excited no surprise, and was rightly understood. By one or two accidental and less intelligent hearers, his meaning was misunderstood, and their reports of some change of opinion in the pastor of the Hackney congregation, magnified by popular exaggeration, occasioned the prevalence in more distant places of a rumour that he had returned to the orthodox views of his early life.*

Rev. Robert Aspland to Rev. Benjamin Mardon.

"Hackney, August 2, 1825.†

" My dear Sir,—The ridiculous report that has reached Maidstone, has been industriously circulated throughout the kingdom, and indeed—I know not why—some rumour of the kind has been afloat for many years. My orthodox brethren are determined to have me, but are rather injudicious in claiming me, as some of their own people may be induced by their silly representations to come over to me, since I will not go over to them.

"I suppose the present story has grown out of my preaching Dr. [Ab.] Rees's funeral sermon, and using in it (as is my custom) a little warmer language with regard to our Saviour than is common with some Unitarians: and, perhaps, too, out of my declaring in a sermon at home, on completing the 20th year of my ministry (which my congregation celebrated by a dinner), that *in the course of that time* my views had undergone some change—that I had left the *material* hypothesis which I once entertained—that I attached *less importance* to the question between the Arians and other Unitarians—and that I felt a *rising persuasion* of the *importance* of the *work* of our Lord, which I suppose is the case with most serious Christians as they advance in years. I know not, however, that on this subject I used on this occasion, or any other, stronger language than our venerable friend Belsham employs in the last No. of Repository.

" Your friendly interest in what concerns my name has led me to say thus much; more than I should say to some inquirers

---

* A similar rumour prevailed at the same time respecting Dr. Carpenter. At a prayer-meeting of an orthodox congregation in the West of England, thanksgiving was offered to God for having rescued these two ministers from soul-destroying errors. The willingness of the members of "orthodox" churches to credit such rumours respecting Unitarians of respectability and eminence, is in one point of view amiable. It shews the reluctance of their hearts to contemplate the doom of good men to the sufferings which are in their creed assigned as the inevitable penalty of errors retained to the close of life.

† This letter is taken from the Appendix of the Funeral Sermon preached at Worship Street by Rev. Benjamin Mardon.

"The part of the rumour that relates to my leaving the Gravel-Pit is, I suppose, an *inference* from the other part. I know of nothing that could remotely give it being.

"Thanks for your paper. Did not you send a similar one from Glasgow? You will be amused with a pamphlet on 1 John v. 7, by Dr. John Jones—just published—to prove the genuineness of the verse, and that its exclusion from the Epistle was the work of the Athanasians or Gnostics, to get rid of the strongest text in the New Testament for the *proper humanity* of Christ!

"Wishing you health, happiness and usefulness, I am, dear Sir, yours very truly,

ROBERT ASPLAND."

Of numerous public engagements which Mr. Aspland was about this time called upon to undertake, it is not thought necessary to make specific mention. But an exception must be made in favour of a pulpit duty which he undertook at Chester in the month of August, 1826, on the occasion of the ordination of his eldest son as the minister of the Presbyterian congregation in that ancient city. He was associated in this duty with Revds. J. G. Robberds and William Turner, Jun. (who conducted the devotional services), Dr. Shepherd, who delivered the sermon, and Mr. Joseph Swanwick, who delivered an address on behalf of the congregation to the minister-elect. On Mr. Aspland naturally devolved the duty of giving the Charge. The whole service was felt by all present to be singularly impressive, and at the request of the congregation was printed. A very friendly critic (understood to be Dr. Hutton), in reviewing it, observed, "It is difficult to conceive a Father placed in a situation more interesting, or more likely to try his feelings to the utmost. The minister of Christ, his own duties and responsibilities pressing upon his recollection, giving solemn charge to a brother minister, and that minister his own son, could not but have spoken from and to the heart. Mr. Aspland's standing in the church, his known devotedness to the cause of truth, and his intimate connexion with the young man whom he was addressing, must, as Mr. Swanwick justly observed, have given to his admonitions an especial authority and a peculiar grace."* The concise and detached counsels given in the concluding portion of the Charge embody the results of Mr. Aspland's large experience on the subject of the habits and means of usefulness of the Christian Minister. They will repay the thoughtful attention of both the student and the pastor.

---

* Mon. Repos. N.S. (1827) I. 108.

CHAPTER XXVII.

In the year 1825, the Unitarian Fund Society and the Unitarian Association were merged in a new and more comprehensive organization, which has since borne the name of the British and Foreign Unitarian Association. In the following year, the members of the Unitarian Book Society resolved to unite it with the Association. Experience had shewn that the conduct of distinct societies involved much practical inconvenience, and entailed unnecessary expense. It was hoped that a combination of the several societies would constitute both a point of union and centre of action, and would advance all the important objects for the promotion of which Unitarians had entered into association. The objects of the new Association were distributed over four departments: 1, Congregational and Missionary Affairs; 2, The Distribution of Books and Tracts; 3, The Promotion of Foreign Unitarianism; and 4, The Protection of the Civil Rights of Unitarians. Mr. Aspland yielded to the urgent wishes of the more zealous friends of the Society, and returned to his familiar post of Secretary. He continued to hold this office during the first five years of the existence of the new Association.

At the close of 1826, an important change took place in the conduct of the Monthly Repository. The cheerful prospects of the Unitarian Association induced its managers to believe that they could both extend the circulation of the Magazine, and make it the instrument of greater usefulness to the body, by taking it under their own control and management. A negociation was opened with Mr. Aspland through Mr. Edgar Taylor, which resulted in his transferring, at the end of the year, the property to the Unitarian Association. It was not without some painful emotions that he edited the last number of a work, which he had established and conducted for one-and-twenty years, and which had associated him in a long succession of literary labours with many learned and noble-minded men, some of whom had now passed on to their reward. He parted with the Magazine, cheered by the conviction that it had been "in some degree serviceable to the cause of Christian truth and freedom." He was certainly entitled to add, that "it had never been made the instrument of personal objects."*

The new series of the Magazine was conducted by the Committee of the Book Department of the Association, at the head of which was Dr. Rees. Notwithstanding the learning and varied talent enlisted in its behalf, the Monthly Repository did not, in its results, realize the eager anticipations of its friends; and at the end of the fourth volume its proprietorship was transferred to Rev. W. J. Fox. He continued to edit it until June, 1836; but, during the latter portion of his editorship, it put aside its theological character, and became almost exclusively a journal of literature and politics. It was next edited for a short time by Mr. R. H. Horne. An enlarged series commenced in 1837, under the conduct of Mr. Leigh Hunt, but was very soon discontinued.

The time has now arrived in this Memoir to speak of the measures taken to obtain the repeal of the Test and Corporation Acts, in originating and conducting which, Mr. Aspland took a conspicuous part. The often-repeated discussions, in and out of Parliament, on the subject of the Roman Catholic Disabilities, had evidently ripened the question of religious liberty, and prepared the popular mind for liberal measures of a far more comprehensive character than those which Mr. Fox and the other friends of freedom had unsuccessfully endeavoured to carry at the close of the 18th century.

The Corporation and Test Acts, passed in the infamous reign of Charles II., had continued, for more than 160 years, to disgrace the Statute-book; although for 83 years previously to 1828, Parliament had been accustomed to pass an annual Act of Indemnity† for the relief of those

---

* See the Preface to Monthly Repository, Vol. XXI. Mr. Richard Wright, than whom no one was better qualified to form an opinion on whatever affected Unitarianism in Great Britain, bore his testimony to the good effected by the first series of the Monthly Repository, in a "Survey" inserted in the closing No. of the work. "It has done much to promote scriptural knowledge, to expose error and superstition, and to promote candour and charity. For more than twenty years it has maintained its independent and liberal course, through good report and evil report, cherishing and promoting the glorious cause of pure and undefiled religion, and affording ready aid to all our public institutions, and to any of our churches when in trouble and difficulties, by lending its columns to their advocates."—Monthly Repository, XXI. 721.

† The history of the Indemnity Acts furnishes a singular comment on the merits of the early Dissenters and the ingratitude of those whom they benefited.

who had failed to comply with the provisions of the two Acts. The Corporation Act (Stat. 13 Car. II. St. 2, C. 1), passed in 1660, enacts that "no person can be legally elected to any office relating to the government of any city or corporation, unless, within a twelvemonth before, he has received the Sacrament of the Lord's Supper according to the rites of the Church of England," &c.* The Test Act (Stat. 25 Car. II. Cap. 2), passed in 1673, prescribed the taking of the Sacrament according to the rites of the Church of England, and a declaration against transubstantiation, as preliminary conditions to the enjoyment of any temporal office of trust. To the latter Act the Dissenters of the day, with "laudable disinterestedness,"† gave their support, seeing that the liberties of the country were perilled by a Popish heir-presumptive to the throne. Subsequently to the Revolution, William III., anxious for the restoration of all his Protestant subjects to their civil rights, expressed to Parliament his "hope that they would leave room for the admission of all Protestants willing and able to serve." George I. expressed his wish that the civil disabilities of Dissenters might cease; but was only able to modify their operation by a statute (5 Geo. I. C. 6), limiting the liability to prosecution to a period of six months, &c. George II. was said to be not less willing than his father to relieve his Protestant Dissenting subjects, to whom he was largely indebted for the defence of his throne against a rebellious Pretender. In 1736, Mr. Plumer's motion for the repeal of the obnoxious Acts was lost by a majority of 251 to 123. In 1739, the majority was 188 to 89. After an interval of forty-eight years, the question was renewed in Parliament

---

In 1745, when the throne of George II. was endangered by an alarming rebellion, armed associations of Dissenters were formed, and some leading men accepted of commissions from the King. Their patriotic loyalty exposed them to the penalties of the Test Act. The Government, "not insensible of its obligations to their active aid, in a moment of the utmost danger to the reigning family," instead of repealing the abominable laws which fixed a stigma upon the most loyal subjects of the crown, contented itself with passing an Act of Indemnity. An Act of the same kind was passed every year after, until the repeal of the Corporation and Test Acts did away with the imaginary offences, from the penalties of which Dissenters needed this left-handed protection.

* Blackstone (Commentaries, IV. 58), who describes these two Acts as bulwarks erected "to secure the Established Church against perils from Nonconformists of all denominations, Infidels, Turks, Jews, Heretics, Papists and Sectaries."

† Constitutional History of England, II. 532. Mr. Hallam praises the Nonconformists of 1673 in this matter, for "*much prudence* or laudable disinterestedness." We must demur to the prudence of conduct which fastened a servile yoke upon themselves and five generations of their descendants.

by Mr. Beaufoy, in 1787, when, after a debate of seven hours, the proposed repeal was lost by 178 against 100 votes. In 1789, the measure was again introduced and lost by a diminished majority of 124 against 104. The motion was renewed in 1790 by Mr. Fox; but was opposed by Mr. Pitt and all the influence of the Government, and the majority was swelled to 294 against 105 votes. In 1823 and 1824, there was a feeble agitation of the question; but it was not thought desirable to carry it into Parliament.

To the Non-Con Club belongs the merit of having originated the proceedings which led to a triumph of religious liberty as gratifying as it was unexpected. In the minutes of the Club, under the date Jan. 17, 1827,[*] there is this entry: "An interesting discussion took place as to the most effectual method of bringing the question of the repeal of the Test Laws before the public; and it being considered practicable to ensure a numerous general meeting of the London Dissenters under the auspices of forty or fifty leading names, the names of several gentlemen of the various denominations were noted down for that purpose."

The course contemplated was soon after taken by the Committee of the Deputies[†] for the several congregations of Protestant Dissenters of the Three Denominations, in and within twelve miles of London, appointed to protect their civil rights. At a meeting of this Committee, held March 9, 1827, a letter was read from the British and Foreign Unitarian Association, urging the Deputies to convene a general meeting to secure the co-operation of the several bodies of Protestant Dissenters in London. A similar letter was immediately after sent by the Board of Congregational Ministers. Before the close of the month, a meeting was held, at which were assembled the Committee of the Deputies, and representatives from the Protestant Society, the Unitarian Association, the Body of Ministers of the Three Denominations, and the Board of Congregational Ministers. The chair was taken by Mr. William Smith, the veteran Representative of Norwich, who had had the honour, in 1787, of being teller in the unsuccessful division on Mr.

---

[*] The members present were Rev. R. Aspland (Chairman), Rev. Dr. Barclay, Rev. D. Davison, Thomas Gibson, Esq., Mr. R. Hunter, Rev. J. S. Porter, Rev. Dr. Rees, Rev. Benjamin Mardon, Richard Taylor, Esq., Edward Taylor, Esq., and Christopher Richmond, Esq. (Secretary).

[†] This body was constituted in 1732, and the first assembly took place on the 29th of December in that year, Mr. Holden being Chairman. He was succeeded in 1736 by Dr. Benjamin Avery, who continued to preside over their proceedings for twenty-seven years.

Beaufoy's motion. Mr. Aspland appeared as one of the elected representatives of the Presbyterian Ministers of London, and had the great satisfaction, throughout these important proceedings, of being aided by a colleague of great experience and zeal unsurpassed, Dr. Thomas Rees. It was unanimously resolved to seek an early interview with several distinguished Members of both Houses of Parliament, in order to discuss and arrange with them the best mode of applying to Parliament for the repeal of the Corporation and Test Acts. The interview was without difficulty arranged, by the mediation of Mr. William Smith, and took place at Brown's Hotel, Palace Yard, April 6th. Lord Holland, never absent when religious liberty needed his services, took a very active share in the proceedings of the day. He was the only Peer present. The Liberal party of the House of Commons was suitably represented at this interesting conference by Lord John Russell, Lord Nugent, Mr. Marshall (recently elected on the ground of religious freedom as the Representative of the great county of York), Mr. Warburton, Mr. Spring Rice, the Hon. Robert John Smith (Bucks), Mr. Easthope, Mr. John Smith (Midhurst), and Mr. William Smith. All agreed that the Dissenters had too long withheld the prosecution of their just claim to equal civil rights, and recommended an immediate and a vigorous application to Parliament for relief. When the Members of Parliament had withdrawn, the Deputies and their associates passed an unanimous resolution, requesting Lord John Russell to move the House of Commons at such time as he might think proper during the session. With this request Lord Russell expressed a ready compliance. To conduct the proposed application to Parliament, an United Committee was formed, consisting of the Committee of Deputies, and delegates (not exceeding six in number) from each of the societies and bodies in London desirous of acting in unison. In addition to the bodies already named, the United Associated Presbytery of London sent delegates to the United Committee. But none were sent by the Society of Friends, by the Wesleyan Methodist Conference, and the Presbytery of the Scottish Church. In order to enlighten the public mind on the history of the question, and to awaken the dormant zeal of the Nonconformist body, it was resolved to prepare and publish a series of works advocating the claims of Dissenters. One of these, a periodical, entitled, "The Test-Act Reporter," which was extended to thirteen Nos. (including 516 pages), was entrusted to the editorial care of Mr. Aspland.

Mr. Edgar Taylor, the eminent legal adviser of the Unitarian Association, prepared a very able "Statement of the Case of the Protestant Dissenters under the Corporation and Test Acts," which was widely circulated, especially amongst Members of Parliament and the conductors of the public press. By the costly agency of the Quarterly Review, with which it was stitched up, it penetrated into college halls and libraries and country rectories; while by that of the Edinburgh Review and a variety of other periodicals, it found its way to persons of every class and denomination. Resolutions were passed and petitions signed, and all the other customary modes of carrying on the agitation of a public question, were put into active operation. In the preparation of these documents, Mr. Aspland took an active share. The General Body of Ministers adopted without alteration the draft of a petition which he had prepared. It is inserted in the Test-Act Reporter (pp. 30, 31), and may be read with advantage, as containing, in a very brief compass, a comprehensive statement of the case of the Protestant Dissenters, expressed in a perfectly English style, combining strength with purity.

While all this preparation for an active campaign was going on, Lord Liverpool, the Premier of a compact and powerful, but not very popular Administration, was struck down by what proved a fatal illness. The death, a few months previously, of the Duke of York, had inflicted a heavy blow on the High-church and Tory party. To this party, the Premiership of Mr. Canning, resisted unsuccessfully by secret treachery and open hostility, was the source of bitter mortification. The brief session of Parliament which followed the construction of Mr. Canning's Government, gave little promise of any great measure like the repeal of the Test and Corporation Acts being carried. Party feuds were exasperated by the personal rancour of some of the leading opponents of the new Administration. The leading Whigs, notwithstanding the haughty remonstrance and protest of Lord Grey, gave Mr. Canning an almost enthusiastic support. If the Dissenters did not altogether share the confidence felt by their representatives in Parliament, it was easily explained by their surprise and regret at Mr. Canning's declaration of his purpose to oppose, at least for a time, the repeal of the Test Act.

Rev. Robert Aspland to Rev. R. Brook Aspland.

"Hackney, May 17, 1827.

"Dear Brook,—There is no *division* amongst the London ministers on the Corporation and Test Acts. We are proceeding in spite of Canning's threatened hostility. But he is trying through Brougham to put us to sleep: he will, however, try in vain. We are to have a little Parliament on Tuesday morning, consisting of some *half-hundred* Members of both Houses, and our General Committee. The object of the meeting is to impress Peers and Commoners with our feelings, and to agree with them upon the extent to which we shall go this session."

The conference was long and earnest. It was attended by Lords Holland, King, Althorp, Milton, J. Russell, Ebrington, Clifton, George Cavendish and Nugent; by Mr. Brougham, Mr. Byng, Mr. Sykes, Mr. J. Wood, Sir Robert Wilson, Mr. John Smith, Hon. R. Smith, Mr. A. Dawson, and many others. By the majority of these distinguished men an opinion was expressed that the active prosecution of efforts to obtain the repeal that session was inexpedient. From this counsel Lord John Russell and Mr. John Smith explicitly dissented, the latter gentleman expressing his conviction that the Dissenters would, by retreat at such a moment, abandon victory when it was in their sight. The United Committee subsequently met and agreed, by a majority of votes, that Lord John Russell should be requested to postpone the intended motion until the following session. Mr. Aspland had expressed more than doubts on the wisdom of this course; and his friends Dr. Rees and Mr. Bowring, and some others, spoke and voted with him in the minority. It was the unanimous opinion of the Committee, that the Dissenters should every where proceed with their petitions, and forward them for presentation to Parliament.

Early in June, Lord John Russell announced in the House of Commons, on the occasion of presenting various petitions for the repeal of the Test Acts, the course which, in deference to the recorded opinion of the United Committee, had been decided upon. Alluding to the recent change in the Administration, he said, " Upon that event many of the Dissenters, feeling, as it were by instinct, that a Ministry was formed more favourable to religious liberty than any which had existed during the thirty-seven years in which this question had slept, doubted whether it were fair, and whether it were politic, to force such a Ministry to an immediate expression of opinion upon this important subject. *Others, with whom I agreed, did think that the present was a favourable time for the discussion.*" He added, that though he felt himself bound to obey the instructions of the United Committee, he had received various intimations from individuals that in their opinion the majority of the Dissenters wished the question to be pressed.

The death of Mr. Canning, immediately after the termination of the session, struck the friends of liberal opinions in England with consternation and grief. In their inability to forecast coming changes, they feared that the removal of this brilliant advocate of Catholic Emancipation had deferred to a far distant day the triumph of religious liberty. Dissenters shared the common grief at Mr. Canning's untimely removal. They had previously been satisfied that his declared hostility to their claims had escaped from him hastily in the irritation of debate, that he had no settled purpose of opposition to their just demands, and indulged the hope that, when firmly seated in power, he would give his assent to all measures necessary to the relief of conscience.

Had Mr. Canning's life been protracted, it is probable that the relief of Protestant Dissenters would have been postponed. It was generally, but most erroneously, supposed that the Protestant Dissenters were irreconcilably opposed to the admission of Roman Catholics to civil privileges. Not only Mr. Canning, but many Liberal Members of Parliament, indulged the fear that if the Dissenters were first admitted to the full enjoyment of the Constitution, they would afterwards prove bitter opponents of similar concessions to the Roman Catholics. This fear shewed want of acquaintance with the recent rapid growth of liberal opinions amongst the Dissenters, and also indicated an inability to estimate the power of a great principle, like that of religious liberty, to force honest minds, however unwilling at first, to receive and apply it in its full extent.

Lord Goderich's feeble Administration, which followed, fell to pieces before Parliament met, and a new, and, as it was at the time supposed, *Tory* Administration was formed by the Duke of Wellington.

The apparent darkening of the political horizon increased the energy of the Dissenters in making fit preparations for what they believed was to be only the first of a series of struggles to be continued from year to year. At a special meeting of the General Body of the Ministers of London, Mr. Aspland proposed an Address to Protestant Dissenting Ministers throughout the United Kingdom, and to the religious public in general, on the subject of the scandal thrown upon Christianity by the Test and Corporation Laws, and the gross perversion of the Lord's Supper in making it a mere civil or political test. In not one of the numerous documents and publications of the time was this, the religious part of the argument, more earnestly stated and discussed; and the fact that this Address,* penned by an Unitarian minister, was

---

* The "Address" deeply moved the feelings of one of the most eminent and

adopted, nay, received by acclamation, by a very numerous assemblage of ministers, nine-tenths of whom held Orthodox opinions, ought to be regarded as a proof that, in spite of all the divisions of the Christian church, there is a common Christianity which all alike revere, and which might be made the basis of a closer union than has ever yet existed amongst the sects of Christendom.

Notwithstanding the altered relations of parties, there were still here and there doubters and objectors in the Nonconformist ranks, who alleged that the time for action was not come, or that the course pursued was not the best. An extract from Mr. Aspland's Diary at the beginning of 1828, will shew that there were some difficulties in the path of the United Committee besides those created by Tories and High-churchmen. The gentleman referred to was one of great and deserved influence in public life, but one in whom the "native hue of resolution" had given way to age and that habitual despondency which was the result of a life of unsuccessful opposition.

"I spoke my mind very freely to ——— as to his constant clogging our cause with doubts and fears, and endeavouring, against the sense of our best Parliamentary friends, to keep us back. He avowed (as I told him I had predicted of him, as he must remember, last year) that this was not a fit time—in one sense, less fit than last session; that we were wrong in petitioning, especially the Lords; that we should wait for a strong Whig Administration, who would grant us our claims quietly. Against this I argued and protested, all the other gentlemen being in great measure with me. I told him I would rather not have our question carried than that it should be smuggled through. The benefit of it would consist in its coming as a matter of open right, a concession to justice and liberty. I anticipated a long struggle, but the sooner we began the nearer would be the victory. Parliament and the country, and even the Dissenters, wanted discussion to enlighten them. No Ministry would ever volunteer to give us our rights, and perhaps the Whigs least of all, who do not need the charge of being Dissenters to make them odious. And though we cannot *force* our question, we must make a show of strength to have it seriously considered by the Legislature and the Court. The aged Member pleaded his experience," &c.

---

learned ministers of the Independent body, who was present at Dr. Williams's Library when it was brought forward, and who a few hours afterwards addressed to Mr. Aspland a letter of respect and affection, and made the reverent feeling evidenced in the Address the ground of an appeal to him to re-consider his theological system. It is much to be regretted that this letter, in one view most creditable to the Christian sympathies of its author, and Mr. Aspland's reply, have not been preserved.

As soon as Parliament met, the Committee were occupied from day to day in making the necessary preparations. On Mr. Aspland it devolved, in company with a small deputation, to wait on the principal Members of the Liberal party. The Diary mentions visits to Lord Holland, Lord John Russell, Mr. John Smith, Mr. Spring Rice, Lord Milton, Lord Nugent, Mr. Baring, Sir Robert Wilson, Lord Normanby, Mr. Brownlow, Sir Francis Burdett, Mr. Abercrombie, Mr. Hume, Mr. Onslow, Mr. Benett, Sir James Mackintosh, Mr. Ward and Sir John Newport. There are traces of Mr. Aspland's intention to make a note respecting each of these visits: it was, however, owing to the great press of work at this time, only partially fulfilled.

"The United Committee having appointed a Deputation, consisting of the Chairman (Mr. W. Smith, M.P.), Mr. Henry Waymouth (Deputy Chairman), Mr. Busk, Dr. Browne, Mr. Robert Winter (the Secretary) and myself, we went up, Saturday morning, January 5, by appointment, to Mr. John Smith, M.P., in Grosvenor Square. He received us with great affability, and we had a good deal of free talk. His own family, he says, which is generally divided in politics, is united on this point. He contemplates a very respectable division in the House of Commons. He approves of our petitions, and is for our going on heartily. He evidently *hopes* to see a Whig Administration. The Whigs he thinks are committed to us. 'I should like to see how Spring Rice,' he remarked, 'would look one in the face if he were not to support the motion.' Appealing to Mr. W. Smith and me, he said there was a strong prejudice against the Unitarians which he could not understand. On Christmas-day, the clergyman whom he attended had, on consulting with him, omitted the Athanasian Creed, which he (J. S.) declared he abhorred."

"January 7.—We called this morning by appointment on Lord Holland, at 10, Berkeley Square. He was, as usual, very courteous, frank and warm in our cause. He readily undertook the question in the House of Lords; approved of our petitioning both Houses, but recommended not to *move* in the Lords unless we should go through the Commons. He anticipates a strong majority against us in his own House. I read to him part of Bishop of Peterborough's (Marsh's) Charge, just published, in which the Bishop predicts that if Dissenters are put on a level with the Church, they will soon cast an eye upon her *good things*. He laughed heartily and said that was the question, particularly in Ireland.

"I consulted with him about the petition of General Body of Dissenting Ministers, which I am to send to him, with a note explanatory of the party from whom it comes. He will present it the same night that Lord John Russell presents it in the Commons."

On Sunday, January 27, 1828, Mr. Aspland addressed the Gravel-Pit congregation in these terms:*

"It is not my design, nor can it be necessary, to go fully into the history, or to examine minutely the provisions, of the Corporation and Test Acts. Publications are daily issuing from the press which give full information concerning these oppressive laws; and the Petition prepared for your signature, which will be read at the close of the service, states fully, and I believe correctly, our principal objections to them. The stress of the grievance is this: that, under heavy and ruinous penalties, they forbid any one to hold any office in any corporation, or any place of trust and emolument under his Majesty, who shall not, in one case within one year before, and in the other within three months after entering upon such place or office, have taken the Sacrament of the Lord's Supper according to the rites of the Church of England.

"The clause in the Corporation Act requiring the Sacramental Test, was not an original part of the Bill, but was introduced in its passage through Parliament. It could scarcely have been designed against the Presbyterians, then the principal body of Dissenters, since it is well known that the majority of them, agreeing in the propriety of a National Church, if it were but the true Church, and holding the same doctrines as are taught in the Church of England, did not scruple occasional conformity.

"The Test Act was passed in an agitated period to exclude Roman Catholics from places under a Government which was justly suspected of a leaning to Popery. It was strangely approved and helped forward by the Nonconformists, who were willing to exclude some of their own body from honour and influence, if by so doing they could keep out the Papists, as the Roman Catholics were then termed. They relied upon a secret understanding that after a time they should have relief in this and other matters. The engagement was not kept, and the result was, like that of many other compromises of principle, that the fetters forged for another class of persons, were suffered to press heavily upon those that helped to make them.

"With regard to Roman Catholics, the Test Act was most absurd; for the reason assigned for shutting them out was their dangerous principles, such as that oaths may be dispensed with by the priest, and that faith is not to be kept with heretics, and yet the Test was of no avail whatever except as the Catholics were men of honour and conscience.

"In truth, all tests of opinions and all religious tests of civil merit or demerit, are bad both in principle and effect; they suppose infallibility in the imposers,

---

* The petition from the Hackney congregation was presented to the House, Feb. 4, by Mr. John Smith, who observed that the statement of their case did the petitioners great credit. The petition itself was printed in Christian Reformer (12mo), XIV. 52—57.

and they are a temptation to hypocrisy on the part of those on whom they are imposed. They let in men of no principle, and shut out only the conscientious.

"The Test Act has become a greater grievance to Dissenters than its framers could ever have contemplated; the weight of it being in proportion to the greatness of the country and the extent of its revenue.

"Acts of Indemnity are yearly passed which are vulgarly supposed to protect Dissenters; but in truth they do not touch the case of conscientious Dissenters, they merely prolong the time in which conformity will be available. There are many exclusions by the Test Act which these Acts cannot possibly reach. And what a situation is the Dissenter placed in, that he must plead his indemnity for not having done what he considers a sinful deed, that is, prostituted the Lord's Supper to worldly ends!

"The oppressive operation of the Test Laws is incalculable. Dissenters in a certain rank of life meet it every where. But the insult is still greater than the injury. And the indirect influence of these laws of exclusion is diffused through our Universities, our legal and mercantile associations, and our still more private circles.

"England is almost the only civilized country in which a very large proportion of her population lies under disabilities with regard to the public service, and this without any colourable pretence from the character of the excluded party. There was a time when the services of the Dissenters were generally acknowledged in bringing about the Revolution of 1688, in contributing to the settlement of the present reigning family on the throne, and in defending the crown of the Brunswick dynasty against two well-nigh successful rebellions. And the present generation of Dissenters cannot yield to any of their countrymen in any of the talents, qualities and habits, that constitute useful, honourable and virtuous citizenship.

"We ask not for power or place. All we seek is, not to be pronounced unworthy of power or place; not to be disqualified for serving our country as if we were criminals. As we are the occasion, under Providence, of our children being Nonconformists, we are bound to take every constitutional step to prevent their suffering in their civil relation by the performance of their religious duty. This is no political struggle. We act under religious motives and with Christian views. We wish to remove from our common faith the opprobrium of countenancing persecution, and of using one of its own most solemn ordinances for the purposes of oppression. We are not actuated on this occasion by hostility to the Established Church, for the Test Laws are of no advantage to her; but, on the contrary, impose a painful burthen on her pious ministers, and make her a party to her own degradation in the abuse of the Lord's Supper. We entertain no factious schemes, no sectarian wishes; what we seek for ourselves, we ask and are ready to give to all; we claim not indemnity, not indulgence, but liberty. Liberty of conscience is every man's birthright, and in proportion as our beloved country extends and guards this sacred right, the grant of God to man in his creation, will she unite her children in the bonds of peace, secure all her righteous laws and strengthen all her just institutions, increase her wealth and extend her influence, and thus draw down the blessing of Almighty God, the rule of whose all-perfect government it is to bless nations by means of their own wisdom, justice and charity."

On the 26th of February, the long-anticipated discussion took place in the House of Commons. In a speech worthy of himself and the occasion, Lord John Russell moved for a Committee of the whole House, "to consider so much of the Test and Corporation Acts as disqualified Protestant Dissenters from holding corporate and other offices." He said that he approached the question with a kind of awe which, were it not for circumstances of an alleviating nature, would amount to absolute despair, from the remembrance that the last time it was pressed upon the notice of the House it was introduced by the eloquence and argument of Mr. Fox. But he rejoiced to know that during the thirty-eight years which had elapsed since Mr. Fox's unsuccessful attempt, public opinion had been gradually advancing. He then proceeded to state the principle on which he founded his motion. It was that broad principle which had been asserted in the greater part of the petitions presented on this subject to the House—"that every man ought to have the liberty of forming his religious opinion from the impressions made on his own mind; that having formed that opinion, he ought to be at liberty to entertain it freely, to maintain it without interference, and to worship his God in his own manner, without any restriction or reservation whatever; and that any penalty or disqualification imposed upon him, is of the nature of persecution, and is an offence to God and an injury to man." He gave a very lucid history of the two Acts, and shewed that the circumstances under which they had been passed had ceased to exist. He exposed the hardship which the Acts inflicted on a class of loyal and deserving citizens. He shewed that they were at variance not only with the practice existing in Scotland and Ireland, but also with the course pursued in every civilized nation of Europe. He concluded with an eloquent description (almost prophetic) of what the Duke of Wellington might do to attach the Protestant Dissenters to the Constitution of their country, to render them contented and happy, and to make them willing to bear their just proportions of the burthens of the State. "The illustrious person now at the head of his Majesty's councils,—he, the preserver of Portugal, the deliverer of Spain, the conqueror at Waterloo,—that great personage, entitled as he is to the thanks and gratitude of the country, standing in the singular position that he does, commanding the patronage of the Church and the patronage of the State, having an army of 110,000 men attached to him from long service and command,—I had almost said, having at his command the power of the Sovereign,—even he, Sir, great as is his power, and extensive as is his patronage, must modify his opinions and fashion his actions to the age in which he lives. Great as have been his conquests and his services, to the spirit of the age in which he lives he must bow. He must look to the signs of the times; and if so, he must perceive the necessity of granting those rights which the Protestant Dissenters have demanded year after year—rights which may be retarded, but cannot be long withheld."—The motion was seconded by Mr. John Smith, who remarked, in the course of a long and able speech, that so far from censuring, he could not help respecting and applauding, the conduct of those Dissenters, whether Baptists or Unitarians, who preferred poverty and obscurity to burthening their consciences by complying with a form to which their opinions were averse. Hypocrites in religion might dispense with the form as well as the substance, when it suited their convenience to do so; and it was the curse of a country which enacted such laws to make hypocrites by Acts of Parliament. But the men who, in defiance of such laws and the penalties they threatened, and the poverty they entailed, stood firm to their conscientious opinions, instead of being objectionable, were " worthy of all acceptation," and were much more worthy of employment than those who were capable of courting it by the surrender of their principles.—Mr. Marshall and Mr. George Wilbraham followed on the same side. Amongst many admirable speeches spoken that night, there was not one closer in argument or finer in spirit than that of Mr. Wilbraham. After describing very beautifully the Lord's Supper, he said, " I would ask whether it is consistent with the principles of our holy religion to make that ceremony, which ought to be the bond of human charity, the symbol of religious difference and defiance? Whether it is pious to make the most holy rite which can take place between man and his Creator, a mere scaffold by which he is to climb to high situations in this world, a mere stepping-stone to the fulfilment of projects of avarice and ambition? I would ask, in the language of one of our poets, whether it is right

> " 'To make the symbol of atoning grace
> An office key, a picklock to a place?'"

Sir Robert Inglis opposed the motion, arguing that tests were necessary to the existence of an Establishment; that this implied preference, and preference implied exclusion. He was answered by Mr. Fergusson. The motion was also supported in speeches of great power by Lord Althorp, Lord Milton and Mr. Brougham. On behalf of the Government it was resisted by Mr. Huskisson, who, however, said not one word to vindicate civil exclusion by a religious test, and by Mr. Peel, whose chief defence of the law as it stood was, that it was inoperative, and that the grievance of which Dissenters complained was rather theoretical than practical. An eight hours' debate was closed by a feeble speech from Lord Palmerston, who said he could not consent to remove from Dissenters an imaginary grievance, while the real inflictions which pressed upon the Roman Catholics remained unrepealed.

In this important debate, the argument and the earnestness were entirely on one side; and, to the surprise and joy of the Dissenters, the vote confirmed the argument. At one o'clock in the morning the House divided, when there appeared—Ayes, 237; Noes, 193;—thus shewing a majority of 44 votes for going into Committee.*

The full extent of the victory gained was made manifest by the proceedings of the House of Commons when it went into Committee, on Thursday, February 28. Mr. Peel admitted, with a slight reservation, that " the vote of the other night was perfectly decisive;" but asked for delay, to consider the subject in all its bearings and consult with his colleagues. Lord John Russell declined to postpone his resolution, which was for a repeal of so much of the Act of the 13th and 25th Car. II. and 16th of George II. as " called upon all Protestant Dissenters to subscribe to certain formulæ and take the Sacrament of the Lord's Supper." The resolution was carried without a division. Mr. Christopher Richmond was immediately instructed by the United Committee to prepare a Bill founded on this resolution of the House of Commons, which was with the least delay introduced by Lord John Russell and read a first time. The second reading was fixed for Friday,

---

* Mr. Aspland was a deeply interested auditor of this debate, being seated under the gallery, where he had the privilege of conversing from time to time with Sir James Mackintosh and other distinguished friends of religious liberty. He often spoke of the enthusiastic joy with which the result of the division was hailed. On leaving the House, his arm was seized by Mr. Spring Rice (Lord Monteagle), who, with his hat off, continued to cheer until he had reached the other side of Palace Yard. The cheering was heard at Charing Cross.

March 14. Acting on a suggestion previously offered by Sir Thomas Acland, Mr. Sturges Bourne on this occasion proposed that, in lieu of the Sacramental Test, Dissenters should, on entering office, make a Declaration to the effect that they would not use the power or influence of their office to the injury of the Established Church. The proposed Declaration was at once resisted by some of the supporters of the Bill as unnecessary and nugatory, but it soon appeared that its adoption was necessary to secure the support of the Government and consequent safety of the Bill. The United Committee agreed to a series of resolutions, proposed by Mr. Aspland, protesting against the Declaration as unnecessary and unreasonable, but intimating that they were prepared to acquiesce in it rather than peril the loss of the Bill. At the same time, the Committee resolved, and took measures for their feeling being understood in Parliament, that they regarded the Declaration as not intended to bind the declarant, being a Protestant, to abstain from that free expression of his opinions, as an individual, and from those measures for the maintenance and support of his own faith and worship, in the use of which he was already protected by the law.

The Bill passed the House of Commons without further obstruction, and was immediately read a first time in the House of Lords. The second reading was, on the 17th of April, moved by Lord Holland, in a speech which Mr. Aspland characterized as "irresistible in argument, ingenious in illustration, and abounding in humorous quotation and anecdote." The Archbishop of York and the Bishops of Lincoln, Durham and Chester, declared their approbation of the measure, subject to revision in the Committee. Lord Winchelsea called for an addition to the Declaration, to test the orthodoxy of the declarant and to ensure the rejection of Unitarians, whom he denounced as infidels. Lord Eldon from his heart and soul said "Not Content" to the Bill, because he could not consent to give up the Constitution of the country, and to sacrifice it as well as the Established Church. The Duke of Wellington declared that the Bill now received the support and concurrence of his Government, on the ground that it secured the religious peace of the country, and that the amendments introduced in it afforded ample security to the Church. Under the quieting influence of the Duke's declaration, the second reading passed without a division.* In the Committee, Lord Eldon moved that an Oath should

---

* "April 17. Second reading of Corporation and Test Act Bill in H. of Lords. I was admitted on an order from *Lord Eldon*. Lord Holland's speech great. The Bishops' pretty good. Duke of Wellington for peace! No division."—*Diary*.

be substituted for the Declaration. Thirty-two Peers voted for, and one hundred against, the amendment. Various other injurious alterations of the Bill were proposed by Lord Eldon and his friends; but the watchful vigilance of Lords Holland, Lansdowne and Grey, and the firmness of the Duke of Wellington, caused their rejection by large majorities. One alteration, very lamentable in its effects, was made in the form of the Declaration. Lord Harewood, in a speech on the Bill going into Committee, expressed his wish that a clause should be inserted in the Declaration, from which it might appear that the person taking it believed in the Christian religion. He did not expect additional security from the Declaration, but he wished it to be so worded for the credit of Parliament. The suggestion accorded with the feelings of many Peers and Bishops, and, on the motion of the Bishop of Landaff, a clause was added to the Declaration—"on the true faith of a Christian." Lord Holland spoke and voted and protested in the Journals of the House* against the addition. The United Committee publicly recorded their regret that the Declaration should be converted into any thing like a profession of religious faith (however general) as a qualification for civil office.†

The Bill as amended finally passed the Lords without a division, Lord Holland expressing on the occasion gratitude to the House and congratulation to the country. The amendments of the Lords were discussed and agreed to by the Commons on the 2nd of May. Lord John Russell explained that a person declaring "on the true faith of a Christian," could only be understood to mean on the faith of that community of Christians to which he belonged; and Mr. Brougham and other Members expressed the opinion that the Declaration had been made much worse in the other House of Parliament. The Royal Assent was given to the Act on May 9, 1828. It came into immediate operation, and relieved a numerous and most deserving portion of the King's subjects from a degrading stigma, and opened to Nonconformists a path of honourable ambition, which many have since trodden to the great advantage of their country. Regarded in itself and its immediate consequences, the Repeal Act was most memorable, and

---

* Hansard, XIX. 49.

† Could they have foreseen that this clause would be the means of excluding Jews for several years from important civil privileges, and would be nearly the last relic of the days of persecution to be defended by High-church bigotry, it is to be hoped that they would have resisted it at every stage of the Bill, even at the hazard of postponing relief from their own disabilities.

formed an important era in the history of religious liberty. But regarded, as it properly may be, as the first of a long series of wise and liberal changes which have been going on in the same direction to the present day, and which have produced more benignant results than the legislation of any period of equal duration in the history of Great Britain, the Repeal Act becomes a national era, to which it may without exaggeration be anticipated that the future historian will point as deserving the grateful admiration of posterity.

It was a fortunate circumstance that during the continuance of this important struggle Mr. Aspland enjoyed unusual health, and was able to devote his whole strength to the cause to which he gave his whole heart.*

It was determined to celebrate the great triumph of religious liberty by a Commemoration Dinner.† The Duke of Sussex consented to preside, making the single condition that the meeting should recognize the equal claim of the Roman Catholic to the liberty now conceded to the Protestant Dissenter. This gratifying festival was held on the 18th of June, at Freemasons' Hall, was attended by four hundred noblemen and gentlemen, and in respect to the talents of the speakers, the high tone maintained through a meeting which lasted seven hours and a half, and the rapturous enthusiasm of all present, was probably never surpassed. The only ministers of religion who took part in the proceedings of the Commemoration Dinner were two gentlemen who had been fellow-students at college, afterwards near neighbours for seventeen years and friends for thirty years—Dr. Cox and the subject of this Memoir. Dr. Cox proposed the health of *The Archbishops and Bishops and other Members of the Established Church who liberally promoted the restoration of the Protestant Dissenters to their Constitutional Rights.* Mr. Aspland had the honour of replying to a toast given by the Chair-

---

* How varied were his labours may be seen in the Minutes of the United Committee, preserved in the Test-Act Reporter. For services in not less than five departments he received the respectful acknowledgment of the United Committee previous to their breaking up (see Test-Act Reporter, pp. 483, 484). It may be added that the Committee expended during their proceedings about £3000, of which two-thirds were defrayed by the deputies of the London congregations, and the remaining one-third was discharged by the Protestant Society for the Protection of Religious Liberty.

† The list of stewards (133 in number), of various denominations and residing in widely-separated districts, is a remarkable document. It would not be easy to form a list of the same number of private gentlemen, that should comprise a greater amount of intelligence and well-deserved influence.

man—*The Protestant Dissenting Ministers, the worthy successors of the ever-memorable Two Thousand who sacrificed interest to conscience.*

The toast was acknowledged in a speech which must have a place in this Memoir:

"May it please your Royal Highness, at the request of the managers of this Meeting, I rise to acknowledge the honour you have done to myself and my brethren, the Protestant Dissenting Ministers, by the toast so kindly given from the Chair, and so cordially cheered by the company.

"Sir, we are a humble class of men, but we may be allowed some share of Christian pride on the present occasion, and we do feel proud that we are met to celebrate the triumph of those great principles to which we and our fathers have been devoted; in the promotion of which we have employed our small portion of talents; and for the sake of which we should have been ready, I trust, to meet privations and sufferings at the call of conscience.

"Sir, you have done us honour by uniting us with the ever-memorable two thousand,—men who made a noble sacrifice of all that is dearest in this life to the great cause of truth and freedom. We cannot pretend, Sir, to their profound and varied learning, to their unspotted and exemplary manners, and to their exquisite sense of religious honour; but we do share with them, and every Dissenting minister would consider himself calumniated if it were not admitted that he did share with them, in their ardent love of liberty, civil and religious liberty,—England's distinction, and England's happiness.

"Sir, when I speak with veneration of the ever-memorable two thousand ministers who cheerfully renounced the highest interests and honours which the Church of England could confer, in order to maintain the integrity and purity of their consciences, I am not aware that I am moved by any sectarian feelings; for I look with veneration also upon those ministers of the National Church who, in the time of the Commonwealth, made equal sacrifices to their religious convictions; and I may answer, I am sure, for my Protestant Dissenting brethren, and the ministers and Protestant Dissenters in the room will bear me out in saying, that we look back with veneration likewise to the ministers of the Roman Catholic Religion who, in times when reason, justice and mercy were trampled under foot, and when they were regarded as traitors because they were true to their religion, gave up every thing to their consciences, mistaken consciences, it may be,—(but who am I, to say mistaken? They were conscious of their innocence, and felt assurance in their faith, and their own was the only conscience that could guide them)—to conscience they surrendered every thing valuable in life, and even life itself, giving to their faith the surest pledge of their sincerity,—their dying testimony (cheers). I say then, Sir, I have no sectarian feelings when I rejoice in the tribute of respect which you have paid to the memory of the two thousand Ejected Ministers: I could select two thousand names from the clergy of the Church of England.

and two thousand from the Roman Catholic clergy, that have exhibited the same fearless and self-denying devotion to their honest sense of religion, and I would say, that the six thousand should be equally held in reverence and honour as a noble army of confessors and martyrs (cheers). For, Sir, allow me to say that I regard such tried examples of the integrity that never flinches, and the conscience that nothing worldly can overcome, as a nation's wealth: no matter where the examples are found—they dignify human nature and exalt our country; and but for men of this character, England would not have obtained the liberty in which she so justly rejoices, nor would she have had the present august Family to govern her, a Family honoured by being called to the throne in order to preserve the liberties of the people. It appears to me that a Meeting like this reads a lesson of incalculable benefit to youth, when it holds out to admiration religious integrity under any form; and I am persuaded your Royal Highness will agree with me in saying, that nothing could have been more eloquent or more wise, and nothing more Christian, than the declaration of a learned and gifted prelate in his place in the House of Lords, who, when the Dissenting Claims were brought before their Lordships in 1779, said, in words never to be erased from my mind, 'I am not afraid, my Lords, of men of scrupulous consciences; but I will tell you whom I am afraid of,—and they are the men that believe every thing, that subscribe every thing, and that vote for every thing.'

"I will not detain your Royal Highness and the company long, but my mind is so full, my heart is so full upon the present occasion, that I cannot sit down without saying a word or two upon another topic. It is not often that we Dissenting ministers have the honour and the privilege of speaking to persons of the rank and importance of those whom I am now addressing; and therefore I take this opportunity of expressing my earnest wish that right honourable Lords and honourable Members of the House of Commons would bear in mind, that whatever the Dissenters may want, and whatever Dissenting ministers may want, there is one thing they do possess; they know the history of their fathers, their sainted fathers; they know the principles of the Constitution of England, and they regard themselves as having been mainly instrumental in placing the present illustrious Family, of which your Royal Highness is so distinguished a member, upon the Throne (cheers). Sir, it is our boast that our fathers were mainly instrumental in that which I must ever consider a happy and glorious event: and let no member of that august House ever feel astonishment or surprise if the Dissenters, who took so active and responsible a part in their settlement in this country upon the principles of freedom, should still profess and support the same principles, even if,—a supposition I dare hardly entertain,—even if, in some inauspicious moment, any member of that House should seem to forget them.

"You cannot be surprised, Sir, that Dissenting ministers hail the event that we are met to celebrate, for they know and feel that it is but the harbinger of good things to come: they regard it as a pledge to the country on the part of the legislature and the government, that hereafter measures of conciliation, and not of coercion, shall be pursued with regard to conscience;—and let those measures be pursued, and what grandeur, what happiness, is there to which England may not attain!

"Allow me, Sir, to express one hope; I express it not for myself, but for my children and my children's children; and I know that I express the hope and feeling of my brethren in the ministry, and of the Protestant Dissenters generally; it is, that the repeal of the Sacramental Test is an earnest of the repeal of other tests not enacted by the government, but by corporations, and learned corporations; it is, that our country, our beloved country, our mother country, which has dealt rather hardly with us Dissenting children, which has allowed us hitherto only the crumbs of learning that have fallen from her table, will, by and by, open her bosom, her maternal bosom, and receive us to her cordial embraces; and that hereafter we Dissenters shall have our fair portion of the children's bread (cheers).*

"In conclusion, allow me to say, Sir, that we Dissenting ministers have been accustomed to watch the signs of the times, as is natural to those who have been inured to storms and perils; and we have observed, as you, Sir, must have observed, with infinite pleasure, that the course of legislation in this great kingdom, for the last quarter of a century, has been all in one line, and that the straight-forward path of justice; and we can hardly doubt, we can have no doubt, that things will go on,—under that ever-adorable and merciful Providence which, amidst the commotion and confusion of human affairs, causes all things to work together for good,—to greater and greater perfection, and that the government of this country will be still more paternal and still more

---

* Sir Francis Burdett thus alluded, in a speech delivered on the same evening, to this topic: "I listened with pleasure to the Reverend Gentleman who spoke with a liberality and good sense that did him honour, at the same time that he lamented the ungenerous policy which withholds any source of education from the Dissenters of England. He said, with a modesty I admired, that they had been only allowed to pick up the crumbs;—I think that Reverend Gentleman showed he had not fed upon crumbs, but that he had been nurtured with the choicest food which the feast of learning could produce. Gentlemen, I did listen to that learned, and politic, and Christian, and eloquent address, with a delight I have scarcely words to express; and I must confess that if no other good result had come from this meeting but that of eliciting such sentiments from those Dissenters, who have expressed themselves with so much liberality and talent, (efforts which it seems to me only a diffidence and modesty not justified by their powerful talents and powerful minds can prevent being more frequently exhibited,) that result would alone be a most important one; and I am sure that the more we can call them forth, the more we can produce them before the public, the more will this great cause gain as well as their character triumph; the more will religious liberty be advanced, and the firmer may we entertain the hope that its ultimate triumph will be soon attained."

Christian. But let me not be mistaken; when I speak of a Christian government, God forbid that I should be thought to express a wish that the government should ally itself to a sect, that it should be Protestant as opposed to the Catholics, or Church of England as opposed to Dissenters. What I mean is—judging from the past and looking at all the auguries of the times—that the future government of this country, the best and the greatest country on the face of the earth, will and must be the government *of* the people, and *for* the people. Sir, let the course of government in this country be, as it has been under the present happy reign, and as I am certain it will continue to be, wise and beneficent, and then the three great religious divisions of the country,—the members of the Church of England, the members of the Roman Catholic Church, the old church, let my Dissenting brethren remember, the church of our fathers, and the members of the various Dissenting churches,—instead of consisting of so many opposing establishments, and reckoning any one's gain another's loss, will be bound together in the bond of peace and charity, and form that triple cord that cannot be broken; in the strength of which, our Rulers (to use the words of that great man whose language has been quoted with so much felicity, and whose prose is poetry, and whom I may here quote with peculiar propriety, because he was not only an ardent lover of his country, but also a Nonconformist,—I mean John Milton) 'may be able to steer the tall and goodly vessel of the Commonwealth through all the gusts and tides of the world's mutability' (repeated cheers)."*

Mr. Charles Butler to Rev. Robert Aspland.

"Lincoln's Inn, June 19, 1828.

"Dear Sir,—I have often corresponded with you, but never had the pleasure of seeing you till yesterday, at the Dinner to celebrate the Repeal of the Sacramental Test.

"This dinner I shall never forget. The speeches pronounced at it on civil and religious liberty, the power of argument, the impressive appeals to the heart, the noble sentiments of real Christianity, and, above all, the generous feelings towards the Roman Catholics, with which they abounded, will never escape my memory or my gratitude.

"You were pre-eminently great. I hung upon every word you spoke. When you mentioned, with so much sympathy, the poor Roman Catholic priests who have suffered for conscientious principles, I was lost in admiration of your real liberality of mind and fearless disdain of prejudice. May my country abound with such as you! This assuredly is wishing her a great good.

---

* When, at half-past one in the morning, the Duke of Sussex vacated the chair, he proceeded to the distant part of the room where Mr. Aspland was, and taking him by the hand in his accustomed frank and hearty manner, said, "I thank you, Mr. Aspland, for the lecture which you have read my family, but I wish you to remember that I at least have not deserved it."

"I have advocated the Catholic cause since 1778, the year in which the first Bill for the relief of the Catholics was brought into Parliament. I had great pleasure yesterday in thinking that I had uniformly advocated it on principles applicable to the case of all religious dissidents from the Church of the State. Early in life I met with 'Locke's First Letter on Toleration,' which, you know, comprises all that is to be found in his subsequent Letters. His doctrine of religious liberty became mine, and I have undeviatingly adhered to it. The sanguinary code of Queen Elizabeth—the Court of High Commission—the Episcopalian persecution in Scotland—the ejection of the Presbyterian ministers by the Act of Uniformity—the proceedings in Oates's plot—the scanty measure of religious liberty doled out in the Act of Toleration,—I have frequently and loudly lamented and reprobated. As frequently and as loudly have I lamented and reprobated the Inquisition—the Marian persecution—the massacre on St. Bartholomew's day—the revocation of the Edict of Nantes—the expatriation of the Jews and Moriscoes from Spain—and the niggard toleration yet shewn to Protestants in some Catholic countries on the continent. I perfectly agree with Father Persons, in his 'Judgment of a Catholic Englishman,' that 'neither breathing nor the use of common ayre is more due unto man, or common to all, than ought to be the liberty of conscience to Christian men: whereby eche one liveth to God and to himselfe; and without which he struggleth with the torment of a continued lingering death.'

"In my 'History of the English Catholics,' I have recorded Mr. Fox's having said to me, that 'I should not meet with so many real friends to civil and religious liberty as I seemed to expect.' What a stride has the glorious cause taken since his death! What a spring did it take yesterday! But never, never should our obligations to Mr. Fox be forgotten. He took up our cause while it lay shivering on the ground, and, to use the words of Gray,

'Oped its young eye to bear the blaze of greatness.'

"In fact, religious liberty was his favourite theme; and when he dwelt upon it, his periods rolled with more than his ordinary magnificence. How greatly did his nephew yesterday bring the uncle before all of us who remembered him! I have great pleasure to say that, when the Catholic Relief Bill was pending in 1791, Mr. Pitt exerted all his powers in our cause. You know what favourites we were with Mr. Burke—how Mr. Wyndham spoke of us—that a wish for our emancipation was the last word uttered by Mr. Grattan. What men were these! How great is their authority!

"I am sure that yesterday, whenever the Duke of Wellington's great and glorious victory at Waterloo, and our hopes of him, were mentioned, it brought to your mind the oration for Marcellus, in which Cicero shews so admirably how greatly a general shares his triumphs with his officers and his soldiers, but that a deed of clemency is all his own. Should not his Grace, should not his Grace's friends, sometimes think of this?

"I had the pleasure of sitting next to our common friend, Dr. Thomas Rees. May God bless you both! Though we now pray in different churches, may we, and all who joined us yesterday, meet in the celestial tabernacle, and sing the praises of the Almighty, and bless his holy name through all eternity!

"Excuse my taking this liberty, and believe me, with the most heartfelt thanks to you and your friends for your celestial deed of yesterday,

"Your and their most obliged and most obedient servant,

CHARLES BUTLER."

Rev. Robert Aspland to Mr. Charles Butler.

"Hackney, Tuesday, June 24, 1828.

"My dear Sir,—I thought nothing could have added to my enjoyment in connection with the meeting of Wednesday last, but you have, by your generous expression of approbation, not only renewed, but also heightened my pleasure. Accept my thanks for your too flattering encomium; you magnify far too much my humble services to our common cause of liberty; but you do not overrate my zeal for the restoration of my Roman Catholic brethren to their ancient and unalienable rights of conscience.

"It was, my dear Sir, a proud thing for us, who have ever maintained the civil right to religious liberty, to see on Wednesday such an assemblage of our Dissenting brethren, the most important in every respect which I have known, declaring with uncontrollable enthusiasm their sympathy with the still oppressed Catholics. Be assured that an impulse was given on that day to the Dissenting mind, which must, in its effects, be favourable to your particular question.

"I say Amen to your pious and heavenly wishes. There are bigots every where, and 'in many things we offend all.' I was brought up to think every evil of persons of your profession; but your books of piety soon disabused my mind and heart, and I have never read without high gratification your Martyrologies, abounding with so many examples of heroic Christianity. I can now delight in the hope of meeting Roman Catholics of all ages and countries in the Heavenly Father's mansions; and my joy is yet greater from knowing that multitudes of them breathe the same hope with regard to us, whom they cannot but regard as mistaken brethren.

"May the spirit of Charity be poured out upon all denominations, and may Christians prove their relationship towards their Divine Master, by manifesting the same mind 'that was in him.'

"I take the liberty to send with this, a copy (I fear hastily transcribed by some young clerk) of our Unitarian Association resolutions, one of which, relating to the Roman Catholics, I have already had the honour of transmitting to Mr. Blount.

"The bearer of this is my son Sydney, who is training up for the profession of the law, in the office of my friends Taylor and Roscoe, and who is desirous of the honour of seeing one so distinguished as yourself in your profession, in literature, and in the defence of liberty.

"I remain, dear Sir, your much obliged friend and devoted servant,

ROBERT ASPLAND."*

Lord Holland to Rev. Robert Aspland.

"Holland House, June 20, 1828.

"Dear Sir,—I have been prevailed upon, against my better judgment, to revise my speech,† on moving the repeal of the Test Acts, for the Parliamentary Debates, and the editor has sent me some copies paged and sewed up separately. I shall be flattered by your accepting one in remembrance of our communications and intercourse on this interesting and important question, and I have ventured to enclose one.

"If you ever come to this side of London, it would gratify me extremely to see you at Holland House, and to have an opportunity of thanking you, *vivâ voce*, for many personal as well as public favours, fresh and of older date, for which I feel myself very sensibly your obliged

VASSALL HOLLAND.

"P. S. I generally breakfast between half-past ten and eleven o'clock, and if you can call in any morning at that hour, shall be happy to see you."

This long Chapter must contain one further extract from the Diary:

"Saturday, June 28.—Breakfasted at Holland House. Present, Lord and Lady Holland, Sir James Mackintosh and Mr. Allen. The conversation was very interesting. In allusion to part of my speech at Freemasons' Hall, he talked of the doors of the Universities being thrown open to Dissenters; how it was to be done, by by-laws or Act of Parliament? I told him my own case

---

* This letter is taken verbatim from the *Catholic Journal*, June 28, 1828, in which it was, at Mr. Butler's *earnest* request, printed. The Editor, referring to the Commemoration dinner, says (June 21), "The effusions—we cannot call them speeches—of Lord John Russell and Lord Holland—names never now to be separated from the cause of religious liberty—of Mr. Brougham, Mr. Denman and Sir Francis Burdett;—above all, that beautiful discourse of the Rev. Mr. Aspland—beautiful, almost divine, in its spirit of charity, are already in every part of the country; and if they do not finally expel from it every impulse of bigotry, there is no authority in wisdom, no virtue in persuasion, no influence in example."

† The speech, as revised, was printed in Christian Reformer (12mo), XIV. 277, 308.

—sent from the neighbourhood of Cambridge to Aberdeen—and he cried out 'Abominable!' He confirmed the report of the King's personal hostility to the late repeal, and said he almost exacted a pledge from Ministers to oppose it. He told me that he had an offer of coming into the Ministry with Mr. Canning, but refused on account of his pledges to Dissenters. Lady Holland admitted me after breakfast to her drawing-room, and shewed me the box Napoleon sent to her, with a few lines in his own handwriting, a little before his death,—indeed, the last exertion of his pen,—and inquired where she might send me an engraving of it."

CHAPTER XXVIII.

The repeal of the Test and Corporation Acts was the certain harbinger of the repeal of the Catholic disabilities. During the close of the year 1828, and the early part of the following year, the agitation of the question of Catholic Emancipation shook society in England, and especially the religious portion of it, to its very centre. In common with the whole Unitarian denomination, Mr. Aspland felt that he was bound by moral obligations which had derived new force from the admission of Protestant Dissenters to their civil rights, to labour with his whole strength for the acquisition of the same advantages for the Roman Catholics of England and Ireland. Immediately after the celebration at Freemasons' Hall, he was summoned to attend a meeting at the Duke of Norfolk's, in St. James's Square, consisting of gentlemen professing various forms of religion, to consult on the expediency of forming an association for the advancement of religious liberty. Mr. Charles Butler, Mr. Blount, Col. Stonor, Mr. Isaac Lyon Goldsmid, Mr. Montefiore, Mr. John Bowring and Rev. W. J. Fox, were present, but no practical details respecting the proposed association were then agreed upon; and before another meeting could be got together, it was apparent that the object of their solicitude was virtually secured.

Upon the subject of the admission of Roman Catholics to equal political rights with their Protestant fellow-subjects, public opinion was so nearly divided, that great importance attached to the course taken at this crisis by the Protestant Dissenters. Happily for their reputation as Christian men, their conduct, with some few exceptions, did not belie the pledges virtually given on their behalf by their representatives at the Repeal festival. Mr. Aspland had the advantage of the counsel of several of the leaders of the Liberal party, as to the mode in which most service could be rendered to the cause of religious liberty. It is regretted that a copy of the letter which gave occasion to the following interesting reply has not been preserved.

Lord John Russell to Rev. Robert Aspland.

"Woburn Abbey, Oct. 9, 1828.

"Sir,—Although I think there is no one more capable than yourself of deciding on the best mode of proceeding towards our common object, yet I will not hesitate a moment in giving you my best judgment upon the subject. The Irish Roman Catholics are demanding loudly that an insult upon their faith should no longer be the test of fitness for civil office and legislative functions. The Brunswick Clubs as loudly require that this test should remain. The Government profess neutrality. They dislike violence on the one side as well as the other. They have no line of their own, or common object, but to preserve peace. Such is the state of the country and the Ministry.

"When the Catholics last year proposed uniting with the Dissenters, I earnestly advised the Dissenters against it. Policy apart, I thought it wrong to come to Parliament with a partnership of grievances, differing in motive, nature and extent. But now the case is altered. The Protestant Dissenters are among those who enjoy a monopoly of civil rights as against the Catholic. Will they, ought they to remain silent under such circumstances? While intolerant men proclaim their narrow principles, will not they assert their noble and beautiful principles?

"Now to your questions. I think you ought not to petition *totidem verbis* for the Roman Catholic, but for the removal of all remaining oaths which require a declaration of religious opinion as a qualification for the enjoyment of civil rights. The last resolution of the Dissenting Ministers of the Three Denominations upon this head seems to me excellent. This form has the advantage of not adding to the clamour on one side or the other; it appears, on the contrary, a solemn record of a grave opinion on a question which distracts the country.

"I think this should be done by congregations, unless where, from other circumstances, larger bodies happen to be brought together. Petitions to the Legislature might be agreed upon, similar to several, I may say many, presented last year from Churchmen, praying generally for the removal of all religious disabilities. You may find several examples among the printed Petitions of the House of Commons. The time of petitioning should not be long before the meeting of Parliament.

"Likewise, where a general meeting is called for purposes of intolerance, in counties or towns, the friends of religious liberty ought to attend, and protest against such a purpose.

"Such a course, depend upon it, would not be unpalatable to Government. The Brunswick Clubs and Newcastle Letters are greatly so, and they would like a counterpoise. Besides, you know that on the Roman Catholic question itself the Cabinet is equally divided. The Unitarians, I know, are too firm in their principles to be shaken from their high ground of freedom by the intemperance of the Irish leaders. They know that discontent and contention are, to use a phrase of Bishop Hoadly, only 'the desperate effects of religious intolerance.'

"I may perhaps state in so many words, though I have already implied it, that I am sure nothing can be more false than the suggestion lately made, that the Duke of Wellington wishes for a public expression of illiberal feeling. Besides, your opinions are not of yesterday or to-day; they are eternal, and should be universal.

"With every feeling of regard, I remain, your faithful Servant,

J. Russell."

The advice given by Lord John Russell was followed by several public bodies in whose counsels Mr. Aspland had a share. The Committee of the Unitarian Association met, Dec. 11, 1828, and passed a resolution to the effect, "That entire and unrestricted liberty of religious faith and worship is the right of every human being, and that this right is violated by the establishment of any religious test of fitness for civil office." The Unitarian congregations throughout the kingdom were recommended to petition Parliament for the abolition of all religious penalties and civil disabilities. The United Committee which had conducted the application to Parliament for the repeal of the Test and Corporation Acts, met for the last time on Monday, Dec. 15, 1828, and worthily closed their important and successful labours by expressing their desire "for the entire abolition of all laws interfering with the rights of conscience, and attaching civil disabilities to religious faith and worship."

Still, it was matter of notoriety that a small minority of Dissenting ministers in London were resolved to oppose to the last Catholic Emancipation. Under the influence of a fanatical hatred of Popery, they were unable to see the inconsistency of such a proceeding on the part of Protestant Dissenters, themselves but recently admitted to the free exercise of all their civil rights. The General Body of Protestant Dissenting Ministers of London met on January 20, 1829, at Dr. Williams's Library, to consider the expediency of issuing a declaration of their earnest desire for the repeal of all remaining persecuting statutes. Mr. Aspland had the honourable duty assigned to him of moving the resolutions suitable to the occasion, which, in addition to the assertion of the general principle of religious liberty, expressed loyal confidence in the wisdom and conciliatory spirit of the Legislature and of his Majesty's Government, and asserted the expediency of petitioning Parliament for the adoption of measures that would unite all the subjects of the realm in the enjoyment of equal religious liberty. His address to his reverend brethren on this occasion made a deep impression. A critic far from friendly* admitted that it was "powerfully argumentative" and "truly eloquent." The motion was seconded by Dr. Robert Winter, the esteemed minister of the Independent congregation of New Court, Carey Street, who professed his approbation of "every word to which his friend had given such eloquent utterance," and was able to add that he himself had published similar sentiments thirty years previously. The discussion that followed was shared, amongst others, by Mr. Aspland's former tutor, Rev. Joseph Hughes, who zealously supported the resolutions, and commended in terms sufficiently handsome the address of the mover. An opponent appeared in the person of the Rev. Joseph Ivimey, the pastor of the Baptist congregation of Eagle Street, who maintained that it was unsafe to entrust Roman Catholics with political power, and that the withholding of it was no detriment to their religious liberty, and moved an amendment declaring it inexpedient for the Body of Ministers to publish resolutions or present petitions to Parliament on the subject of the Catholic claims. Mr. Aspland replied in a tone of good-humoured irony, and reminded the mover of the amendment that it was something new in English religious history to see a Baptist upholding persecution. The debate, after an adjournment of a week, and an unsuccessful attempt to evade the matter of it by moving the previous question, ended in the adoption of the resolutions by a very large majority. Lord Holland presented the petition to the Lords, and Lord J. Russell that to the Commons; and both introduced it with remarks in illustration of the respectful attention to which they considered it entitled. The honourable mention made by Lord Holland of the Dissenting Ministers of London, should never be forgotten: "It was true that this body was not invested with any legal authority; it had no corporate seal, no legal corporate existence; it received no actual official emolument; it held no official situation; it had no authority over others, no claim even to any authority, except that derived from the piety, the virtue, the great learning, of many of its members. He was sure that they themselves would be the last men to assume any authority they did not legally possess; but he might say for them, besides that authority which they possessed, and their own virtues, that they were persons who had long been recognized by the Government, and that they were the descendants of those men who had separately negociated, through the medium of the illustrious Locke,

---

* Rev. Joseph Ivimey.

with the Government, for that Toleration Act which was the corner-stone of that great edifice he hoped now to see completed."

The efforts of the friends of religious liberty were crowned with success, and early in the session of 1829, Catholic Emancipation was registered in the statutes of Great Britain and Ireland. Fervently did Mr. Aspland utter the language of congratulation on this auspicious event, both from the pulpit and the press.

The debate at Dr. Williams's Library led to a singular publication, which, however little it may be entitled to notice by its own merits, must be mentioned on account of its connection with circumstances not unimportant in the history of religious parties. Mr. Ivimey, while smarting under his defeat, published an angry pamphlet,* in which he indulged in many despicable personalities against the mover of the resolutions which he had unsuccessfully resisted, reproached the orthodox ministers for the "Socinian spirit" which he alleged animated the General Body, asserted that the Congregational and Particular Baptist denominations were dishonoured by ranging themselves under leaders who were publicly known as oppugners of the doctrines of the gospel, and invited the orthodox Dissenters to unite with him in a Chancery suit to expel the Socinians from the administration of Dr. Williams's Trust. Many of his orthodox brethren felt that they were disgraced by this effusion of bigotry; and on the motion of an Independent minister, seconded by an "orthodox" Presbyterian, the pamphlet was referred, at the adjourned meeting of ministers, to the consideration of a Committee of Privilege. Beyond a short article in the "Christian Reformer,"† Mr. Aspland took no notice of Mr. Ivimey's attack. The imputation of being under *Socinian* influence rankled in the minds of some orthodox members of the Body, and combined with other circumstances to produce a result of some importance to the Three Denomi-

---

* "Dr. Williams's Library, and the Debate on the Roman Catholic Claims, Jan. 20, 1829; with the History of the Adjourned Meeting on the 27th. To which is added, Extracts from 'The Manchester Socinian Controversy;' Laws relative to Dissenting Trusts; a True Copy of the last Will and Testament of the late Rev. Daniel Williams, D.D., first published in 1717; and Papers relating to the late Daniel Williams, D.D., and the Trust established by his Will. The whole intended to shew the Necessity of an immediate Separation between the Trinitarian and Socinian Members of the General Body of Dissenting Ministers in London, and as an Appeal to the Evangelical Dissenters throughout the Kingdom to support, by their Pecuniary Contributions, a Suit in Chancery to recover the Library, &c., from the Socinians. With an Engraving of Dr. Williams's Library, Red-cross Street. By Joseph Ivimey. London—Wightman and Cramp. 1829."

† Entitled, "The Bigot Abroad," Vol. XIII. 191.

nations, which will be hereafter described. An immediate result of Mr. Ivimey's allegation was the publication, by a writer of greater power and somewhat better spirit, of a Letter to Lord Holland,* describing the nature of the union which bound together the Ministers of the Three Denominations, and opposing as false and calumnious, "both as regarded the history of the Petition agreed to on Jan. 27th, and all other matters in which the Dissenting Ministers act as a body, the representation that Unitarians were their leaders, and that the orthodox Dissenters could not, or would not, resist the measures and influence of the Unitarian party among them." In commenting on this Letter, an able writer in the Monthly Repository remarked, that it was satisfactory to find that the honour of originating and carrying the Petition was worth contesting with the Unitarians. "But the plain fact is, that it was moved by an Unitarian minister and carried by Unitarian votes. But for the 'one-seventh' who 'by mere numerical force could do nothing,' the six-sevenths *would* have done nothing, and the Petition would have been extinguished by the previous question. The Unitarians alone unanimously supported the Petition. It was only for them to have stood neutral, or to have divided, or to have absented themselves, in the same proportion as the Trinitarians, and the cause of Intolerance would, even in the feebleness of dissolution, have gained a victory where it ought only to have encountered the most deadly hostility. It would better become our orthodox brethren, instead of being so sensitive about Unitarian influence, to come manfully forward, and render honour where honour is due, for the preservation of Dissent from a stain so foul and indelible."†

During the years 1828 and 1829, Mr. Aspland lost some valued friends, of most of whom mention has been repeatedly made in this Memoir.

On January 30, 1828, died at Hackney Fields, the Rev. James Holt,‡ who for the eleven years subsequent to his retirement from the exercise of the Christian ministry, had been a member of the Gravel-

---

* The title of this pamphlet was—"A Letter to the Right Hon. Lord Holland, occasioned by the Petition from the General Body of the Dissenting Ministers of London, for the Relief of the Roman Catholics: with Strictures on a Petition of an opposite nature, from some Dissenting Ministers, and other Remarks occasioned by recent Circumstances. By a Member of the General Body. London—Holdsworth and Ball. 1829."

† Monthly Repository (1829), Vol. III., N. S., p. 430.

‡ See Mr. Aspland's obituary memoir of Mr. Holt in Christian Reformer (12mo), Vol. XIII. 125.

Pit congregation. He was brought up as a member of the Church of England, but during his apprenticeship to an engraver in London he adopted the sentiments of the Calvinistic Methodists. Subsequently he joined the Independents, and having his attention directed to the Christian ministry, he entered himself a student at the Independent Academy at Homerton. After a series of ministerial engagements amongst the Independents, his opinions underwent great modification, and he successively ministered to Presbyterian societies at Plymouth Dock, Dartmouth, Crediton and Cirencester. In his sixty-second year, he retired to Hackney, where the amiable simplicity of his character procured him the respect of a limited circle of friends. He had acquired a moderate property by marriage with a lady of Dartmouth, who died suddenly in 1806. His habits were always simple and strictly economical, and he anxiously consulted Mr. Aspland how he could appropriate the accumulations of his life so as best to serve the cause of Unitarianism, in which he felt a deep and growing interest. By the advice of his pastor, he founded by will a trust for the education of students for the Unitarian ministry. Dr. Thomas Rees and Mr. Samuel Hart were associated with Mr. Aspland in the execution of this simple but useful trust, which has already assisted in the education of several highly-valued Unitarian ministers. Mr. Holt was interred in the burial-ground of the Gravel-Pit chapel, and by his own desire it was recorded on his tomb, that "after ten years' earnest, incessant inquiry, he became a decided Unitarian, and continued so invariably until death."

Early in the next year he followed to the grave (over which he spoke the funeral address) his old friend, Mr. Benjamin Flower, who died at Dalston, February 17th, 1829, and was buried at Forster's Street, near Harlow. In an interesting obituary memoir inserted in the Christian Reformer (XV. 98), Mr. Aspland thus characterized this eccentric but fearless and upright man:

"His temperament was constitutionally warm, and this led him to an occasional fervour, and even severity of language, which was sometimes misunderstood: the writer ventures, however, from an intimacy of thirty years, to say, that never was there a human being who made more conscience of truth, or was more desirous of extending to others the ample liberty which he claimed for himself. He was quick-sighted to what appeared to him to be religious hypocrisy or political servility, and he was no doubt sometimes mistaken in his suspicions, and sometimes immoderate in his accusations; but his errors leaned to the side of truth and liberty."

On the 16th of April in the same year, he attended, at Worship Street, the funeral of Mr. David Eaton, the Rev. Benjamin Mardon officiating at the service. On the following Sunday, in fulfilment of the dying request of his friend, Mr. Aspland preached at Worship Street the funeral sermon, and subsequently printed in the Christian Reformer the biographical sketch of Mr. Eaton's life and character with which the discourse concluded.*

In its next blow, death struck still nearer to his heart, and brought suddenly to the grave, on the 9th of July, 1829, his half-brother, Mr. Isaac Aspland, of Wicken. He keenly felt every family bereavement. His diary shews that he noted to the close of life, with tender sorrow, the anniversary of the death of his parents, and generally on those sacred days avoided or declined all festive engagements. He mourned most sincerely the loss of his brother, in whom uprightness and strength of principle were united with a singular degree of good-nature.

Rev. Robert Aspland to Mrs. Aspland.

"Wicken, July 14, 1829.

"My dear Sara,—I sit down in this once more gloomy house to fulfil my promise. For your satisfaction, let me begin with saying that I am quite well, and that, notwithstanding the sorrowful scene before me, I have had no return of my complaint.

"One comfort there is to us, and that is, the extraordinary sympathy of the whole village and neighbourhood. William Seaber, who met me at Newmarket on Sunday, and who had been that morning as well as before at Wicken, told me that 'there was not a dry eye in the place;' and this was no figure. Every one I have met was in tears; and at the funeral yesterday the whole village was assembled, and many persons from the neighbourhood, and all appeared greatly moved. The suddenness of the event has contributed to this deep impression, but much is owing to poor Isaac's good qualities, which made him an universal favourite. None of us had any conception until now how much he was esteemed and beloved.

"I find it difficult to bring my mind to the reality of the sad change. Several times I have found myself calculating and planning on the supposition of Isaac's being here. Those that five days ago saw him moving about, and heard his good-humoured voice, are still less able than myself to realize the melancholy fact: they one and all say, 'It can't be; it is a dream.'

"I found the widow, Mary and Isaac in such sorrow and distress as I have rarely, if ever, witnessed. Their grief went at once to my heart. My coming,

---

* Christian Reformer (12mo), XV. 227.

however, has been a relief, and I hope and trust, under the blessing of the Father of mercies, that it will contribute to the composure at least of my poor mourning friends. All the family followed the corpse; and trying as the effort was to Mrs. Aspland and Mary, it has, I have no doubt, done them good; it seemed as if the open grave were a vein through which the bitterness of grief was discharged.

"Another trying duty remains, the burden of which will lie heavy upon *me*; I refer to the funeral sermon. This is to be preached at Wicken on Sunday afternoon. A great concourse of people is expected, and my good friend John Emons is at this time arranging for the use of some commodious barn in the village. Our service is to begin at three o'clock, at which time you and the dear family at Hackney will, I am sure, be with us in spirit. Methodists and Church-people are equally anxious about this service, and have volunteered to shut up both church and meeting on the occasion.

"Your ever affectionate husband,
ROBERT ASPLAND."

The arrangements made by his good friend John Emons for this funeral service, proved inadequate to the accommodation of the large concourse of people who flocked into the village on the Sunday afternoon.* From 1 Cor. xv. 26, he addressed an audience composed of persons of every variety of faith professed in that part of Cambridgeshire, and although he asserted explicitly the doctrine of universal final salvation, he appeared to carry with him the approbation and sympathy of his audience.

Before the close of the year died the successor and biographer of Lindsey, and the friend and vindicator of Priestley, the Rev. Thomas Belsham. For more than a quarter of a century, notwithstanding occasional and wide differences of opinion, Mr. Aspland had been permitted to enjoy the confidence and friendship of this learned and able and high-minded man. He was buried on Friday, November 20th, at Bunhill Fields, in the tomb of the confessor whose virtues he has recorded in one of the most instructive religious biographies in the English language.†

---

* A large barn at the entrance of the village was the place of meeting, and a market-cart the temporary pulpit. The place was not only filled, but the audience in front of the building exceeded in number that within. The afternoon was fine, and the pulpit was fixed at the threshold of the barn. The scene has been described to the writer as remarkably impressive, notwithstanding the rudeness of the place of meeting.

† Mr. Belsham published his Memoirs of Mr. Lindsey in 1812. It is greatly to be regretted that Mr. Belsham's Life was not written with the fulness of per-

By the desire of Mr. Belsham, Mr. Aspland officiated at the grave. In the address to Mr. Belsham's mourning friends, he reminded them that the spot around which they were gathered was " consecrated to Christian friendship."*

" Distinguished as this place of tombs is by the virtuous names of those that inhabit its melancholy abodes, there is not a sepulchre in this sacred ground that contains more honoured ashes than that which is now open before me. The memory of THEOPHILUS LINDSEY is fragrant in this Christian assembly, and we are now about to lay beside him his friend, his successor in the pastoral office, his fellow-labourer in the cause of divine truth, and his affectionate biographer. Amiable and venerable were they in their lives, and, agreeably to their mutual wishes and pledges, in death they are not divided."

After a brief narrative of the leading events in Mr. Belsham's life, the address closed with this sketch of his character:

" When Dr. Priestley left his native land, he publicly confided to Mr. Belsham the defence of Unitarianism. Our friend and brother modestly but resolvedly accepted the charge as from the hand of Providence. During many years he was the incessant, the unwearied, and, may I not add, the successful advocate of divine truth. 'Being dead, he yet speaketh,' and his various works will long live to attest his learning, his laboriousness, his zeal, his fearless devotion to pure Christianity, and his benevolent anxiety for the moral and spiritual interests of his fellow-creatures.

" As a writer, our departed friend was distinguished by the clearness of his conceptions and the perspicuity of his style. He possessed beyond most authors the happy art of simplifying a difficult subject, and of making even abstract and metaphysical propositions intelligible to the unlearned reader. There were occasions on which he did not disdain the ornaments of composition; and passages might be quoted from his writings as examples of felicity of diction, and of a chaste but fervid imagination.

" In the pulpit, there was in our friend the dignity that belongs to manly simplicity. He practised no arts in preaching. There was an interesting repose in his manner. A distinct enunciation, and a clear and steady tone of voice, allowed the hearer to receive calmly and to meditate freely upon the matter of discourse.

" Mr. Belsham professed to follow Dr. Hartley as a metaphysician, and,

---

sonal knowledge and other qualities that characterized the Memoirs of Lindsey. How admirable Mr. Belsham's correspondence was, the readers of this Memoir have had opportunities of judging. Is it too late to hope that it may yet be collected and published?

* It had been agreed upon in the life-time of Mr. and Mrs. Lindsey and Mr. Belsham, that their remains should rest in the same grave.

with few exceptions, he adopted and maintained the theological system of Dr. Priestley. As an expounder of these masterly writers, and a commentator on their best works, he is beyond all praise.

"From the decisions of his own powerful mind, as well as from early connections, Mr. Belsham was the consistent and zealous friend of civil and religious liberty; and he lived through a period when the patriotism of every public man was severely tried.

"With remarkable decision and boldness of mind, especially as a theologian, our departed friend united the greatest gentleness and courtesy. Persons knowing him only as a controversial writer, often expressed their surprise and delight on first feeling the attraction of his urbanity of manners. His native kindness of heart imparted a pleasantness to his countenance and voice in the social circle. His sympathies were quick, and many were the occasions when he could not conceal in public the tenderness of his feelings. He was unostentatious in his virtues; but I have reason to believe that his private charities were answerable to the known generosity of his heart."

The members of the Gravel-Pit congregation, holding in respectful and grateful remembrance Mr. Belsham's pastoral labours at Hackney from 1794 to 1805, requested Mr. Aspland to preach a sermon on the occasion of his death. He selected the appropriate subject of *Courage and Confidence in the Cause of Christian Truth;* and the discourse was afterwards, at the request of his hearers, printed.

While death was thus thinning the ranks of his friends and religious coadjutors, Mr. Aspland was consoled by the conviction that Providence would, in every emergency, raise up champions equal to the defence of truth and righteousness. He was deeply interested in the important struggle for religious freedom made by the Remonstrant Synod of Ulster; and when the Rev. Henry Montgomery, the intrepid and successful leader of the upright band of Non-subscribing ministers in the North of Ireland, visited England in the beginning of the year 1829, Mr. Aspland incited a number of "the friends of religious liberty," including Calvinists, Episcopalians, Roman Catholics and Unitarians, to welcome him at a public entertainment.* The meeting was remarkably successful, and, being timed at a most critical period, answered a more

---

* Of this interesting meeting a brief report appeared in the Monthly Repository (N.S.), III. 141—148. Mr. Aspland expressed, in a very glowing speech, his admiration of Mr. Montgomery and the estimable body of men with whom he was associated in the defence of the rights of conscience, from amongst whom he especially selected Mr. Porter, whose integrity of conscience had proved itself invulnerable, and who had shewn himself ready to sacrifice every thing for truth and liberty.

important end even than the well-deserved recognition of Mr. Montgomery's public services.

He had, shortly after, the satisfaction of still further strengthening the bonds of union between the friends of Unitarianism in England and Ireland. Reference is made to this circumstance in the following letter, addressed to the writer, by Rev. William Hamilton Drummond, D.D.

"Dublin, Sept. 5, 1849.

"Dear Sir,—As every occurrence recalling the memory of your excellent father may form an item in the Memoirs with which the Christian Reformer is enriching its pages, you may not deem it altogether uninteresting to learn that I have in my possession three letters of his addressed to me, bearing date June 27, 1828, May 1 and May 11, 1829. The first contains a copy of a resolution of the British and Foreign Unitarian Association, to ask Dr. D. to preach their anniversary sermon, * * * 'in order to testify their sympathy with him, and to draw into closer union the Unitarians of Great Britain and Ireland.' It then proceeds to state that 'a measure had been urged on the Committee by several correspondents in Ireland, which might be found useful—viz., a visit to that country on the part of some of their most respected members—that such a visit might lay the foundation of intercourse and united exertion by the Unitarians of both islands.' Though no regular plan was then devised or matured for carrying out the design thus suggested, there has not ceased, ever since, to be a cordial fraternal intercourse between the brethren. We in Ireland have profited much, and I confidently trust shall continue to profit more and more, by the visits, the preaching, the writings and friendly correspondence of English Unitarians.

"In a subsequent letter he says, 'I am pleased with the account of your present engagements.* Your Archbishop (Magee) is quite *au fait* at epithets; but I have heard my Lord Holland apply one to his Grace, founded upon his evidence before the House of Lords, in the Irish Inquiry Committee, which neither you nor I would consent to provoke by our conduct for archiepiscopal honours and emoluments. The point of the evidence in question was, as you may recollect, the Athanasian Creed.

"'We cannot regret that your time in London will be somewhat shortened by your visit to Bristol, since we are assured that both you and Dr. Carpenter will be mutually delighted by your interview, and that you cannot meet each other without strengthening one another's hands and hearts for our common cause, which, saving Dr. Magee's authority, I must continue to believe to be the strong and immoveable cause of Christian truth and divine wisdom.'

---

* Dr. Drummond was at this time engaged in the composition of two letters of rebuke to Archbishop Magee, who had contemptuously styled Unitarianism a "feeble and conceited heresy."

"These extracts, though other documents were wanting, would suffice to shew Mr. Aspland's earnest zeal to promote the cause of Unitarian Christianity both at home and abroad, and his firm belief that it *is* ' the strong and immoveable cause of Christian truth and divine wisdom.' With a heartfelt conviction of the same belief, I remain, dear Sir, very faithfully yours,

W. H. DRUMMOND."

In the autumn of 1828, Mr. Aspland visited some of the principal Unitarian congregations of the North-west of England, as a deputation from the Unitarian Association. On this mission he preached at Northampton, Liverpool, Manchester, Bolton, Chowbent, Dukinfield, Hyde, Chester and Warrington.* At Manchester he was the guest of Mr. G. W. Wood and Rev. J. G. Robberds, and at Liverpool of Mr. Freme and Mr. Ashton Yates. At the house of the last-named gentleman he had the pleasure of meeting a distinguished member of the Jewish sect, well known to the public by his enlightened mind and generous spirit, and since distinguished by a mark of his Sovereign's favour. This gentleman, together with his daughter, had been a hearer of Mr. Aspland, a day or two before, at Paradise-Street Chapel. On that occasion the xith chapter of Paul's Epistle to the Romans was read in the introductory service; and the sermon, founded on the concluding words of Peter's first sermon to the Jews at Jerusalem (Acts ii. 39) was a cheering statement of the prospects of the human race, founded on the providence and immutable perfections of God.† His candid Hebrew auditors, at that time little accustomed to the mode and forms of Christian worship, listened to the preacher with gratified attention, and the elder of them took the opportunity, at Mr. Yates's table, of expressing his sense

---

* At each of these places a collection was made in aid of the Association, and in several of them the names of annual subscribers were obtained. The following table will shew what were Mr. Aspland's labours, and with what immediate success they were rewarded:

Date	Place	£	s	d
Sept. 21.	Northampton	10	0	0
Oct. 12.	Liverpool—Paradise-Street Chapel	39	3	0
,, 19.	Morning—Manchester, Cross-Street	28	14	0
,, ,,	Afternoon—Bolton	10	9	6
,, 21.	Chowbent	5	16	4
,, 26.	Morning—Manchester—Mosley-St. Chapel	16	4	2
,, ,,	Afternoon—Dukinfield	20	0	0
,, ,,	Evening—Manchester—Greengate Chapel	11	15	3
,, 28.	Hyde	12	12	0
Nov. 2.	Chester	40	0	0
,, 5.	Warrington	11	0	0

† The sermon is printed in the volume published in 1833.

of the liberality of spirit which pervaded the service. He added, that "he was especially struck, as coming from a Christian teacher, with the generous and hopeful spirit evinced towards the people of Israel in the *shorter sermon*." Being asked to explain his meaning, he referred to the preacher's declaration, that "God had not cast away his ancient people, but that all Israel should be saved." Mr. Aspland then explained that what he had listened to as a shorter sermon was, in fact, part of a letter of Paul to the Romans, and that he welcomed with inexpressible delight, and infinitely more than he should any compliment personal to himself, this unconscious testimony from an intelligent and candid Hebrew to the liberality and love towards the Hebrew race of a Christian apostle.

In 1829, Mr. Aspland, for the first and only time, visited Paris, in order to fetch home a daughter, who had been finishing her school education there. He stopped several weeks in that interesting capital. The extracts now offered from letters written in and respecting Paris, while they may amuse by their earnest admiration of almost every thing French, disclose the keenness and accuracy of his perception of the tendency of national events in that country, which was on the eve of another revolution.

Rev. Robert Aspland to Mrs. Aspland.

"Paris, Sept. 21, 1829.

"My dear Wife,—I am more and more pleased with Paris. Six months would scarcely be enough to get a thorough knowledge of it and its environs. The English appear to me to know little or nothing of the French. They are certainly far above us in many important respects. I have been disappointed in nothing, and agreeably surprised in almost every thing. Caroline is afraid I should become a Frenchman. She is home-sick, and cherishes all her English prejudices. So, probably, should I, if I were shut up for months in a *pension*.

"M. Babinet and I have met and are meeting. He appears to greater advantage at home than he did at London, pleased as we were with him there. He has sent for his mother-in-law from the country to give me a dinner *chez lui*, on Thursday. Last night he introduced me to a *soirée* at the house of M. L. Aimé Martin, one of the literati of France. There I met Count Lainé, pair de France, and several distinguished men. Madame Aimé Martin was the wife of St. Pierre, the beautiful writer, and I was introduced to a daughter of St. Pierre's, by a former wife, as the *Virginie* of the pretty story which you recollect. She accepts the distinction. She is the wife of the Commandant of Paris. The Madame, a fine woman, with little or no appearance of *age*, and with much wit and *philosophy*, kept my French and English on the stretch for two hours. She inquired after *ma femme*. I told her you had been a reader and admirer of St. Pierre, and she has sent you a copy of Paul and Virginie inscribed with her *hommage*. I was complimented, I assure you, on my *French*, and flattered in a variety of ways.

ROBERT ASPLAND."

Rev. Robert Aspland to Mrs. Aspland.

" My dear Sara,—Since I wrote this morning, I have been to l'Institut, and seen (I cannot say assisted at) one of its *seances*. The only individual whom I could make out was *Cuvier*. They are fine creatures here. I had only to announce myself at the doors as an English *man of letters* (I suppose there is nothing wrong or vain in this description), and was instantly admitted to the sitting and to the library, where there is a statue of Voltaire which I shall never forget.

"Leaving the Institut, I sought out *Gregoire, l'ancien Eveque*. It took me a long time to find him. A priest and professor whom I accidentally met assisted me, and though close by him, did not know whether he was in Paris or in heaven or——he did not say the rest. The ex-bishop was delighted to receive me. He is a beautiful character. I was introduced to his sitting and bed-room. Over the bed was a figure of the Crucifixion. You may imagine him all you have ever conceived *Fenelon* to be. He took care to apprize me both of his orthodoxy and his philanthropy. I hope to see him again.

R. A."

Rev. Robert Aspland to his daughter Ellen.

" Hackney, Oct. 20, 1829.

" * * I am a complete *convert* to France. Almost every thing was better than I expected. The English, at least at home, appear to me to be unjust to the French, with regard to their character and their institutions. In both, in the latter especially, they are, in some respects, far before us. Caroline, however, will allow nothing of this. I assure you that my Gallic predilections expose me to a constant and hot fire amongst all my acquaintances. Paris is truly a fine city—its churches, its palaces, its gardens and its fountains, never fail to recreate an unprejudiced English eye. Every thing seems to be accommodated to public enjoyment, and strangers are treated as a privileged class. The people are proverbially temperate and well-behaved. I observed little of the levity here attributed to the French character. I should rather say it was marked by sobriety, and even seriousness. But then it must be remembered that this is a critical moment—politics engross every mind. The eagerness for the journals is wonderful, and the whole nation seem bent upon the preservation of the liberty assured to them by the Charter. My opinion is that the people will triumph over the Government: should the Court be obstinate, that fine country, and with it all Europe, may be involved (which Heaven forbid!) in the horrors of war.

"I was fortunate in some of my French introductions. A M. Babinet, a Professor in one of the Colleges, had been over here just before my visit, on a sort of Unitarian mission. In him I found a useful guide, a delightful companion, and an active, zealous friend. He introduced me to some of the literati, and, amongst others, to M. Aimé Martin. * * * I met also Viscount Lainé, one of the peers of France, the joint leader, with Chateaubriand, of the liberals in the Upper Chamber. He is a venerable man, and the utmost confidence is reposed in him by the friends of liberty. Upon the political will probably depend the *religious* condition of France for the next century. Unitarianism, if I do not deceive myself, is upon the point of breaking out; the better sort of minds are disgusted equally with the Roman Catholic absurdity and foolery and with the heartlessness and dreariness of scepticism. They will not become Protestants, but they must be, sooner or later, *Catholic Unitarians*—a new denomination, in which I sometimes amuse myself by thinking that mankind will at length find all that they covet for the understanding, imagination and affections.

"There are still good and steady Roman Catholics in Paris. By some of these, through the kindness of Mr. C. Butler, I was welcomed as an old friend. I had two delightful interviews with Bishop Gregoire, whose fine face and noble mien and fascinating manners I shall never forget. We conversed a good while upon the French Revolution, in which he was one of the actors, and one of the few whose hands were never stained with cruelty. He still boasts of being a *republican*, and is quite content with the state of persecution in which his political integrity has placed him for the last thirty years. You may suppose that my recollection of the great and strange events that have occurred in France within the period just mentioned increased not a little the intenseness of my feelings on looking around me. I gazed till I forgot myself on some of the epochs and buildings celebrated for good or ill deeds. One constant feeling of regret with me, I confess, was that NAPOLEON was no longer visible. Without him, France, and especially Paris, sometimes appeared to me as a mighty body without a soul. It is well, you will say, that this sheet is not to pass through the scrutinies of the Bourbon; and perhaps my political heresy may be bolder than would be tolerated in many English circles. My excuse must be that of Bishop Gregoire—'I cannot see with any eyes but my own.'"*

---

* Soon after his return home, Mr. Aspland communicated to the Unitarian public (though without his name) some of his impressions respecting Paris and the French. The article will be found in the Monthly Repository, N.S., Vol. III. p. 777.

CHAPTER XXIX.

George the Fourth died at Windsor, June 26, 1830. There was little in the personal character of this sensual, fickle and heartless monarch, that a minister of religion could commend. During the life of the King, Mr. Aspland had not shrunk from expressing disapprobation of his immorality, and especially of his cruelty to his unhappy Queen. But he did not think the time of the monarch's death the most suitable for dwelling on his faults. By a large portion of the public press the memory of the King was held up to execration within a few hours of his death. Some who had habitually palliated his follies, and treated him in the height of his power with servile adulation, joined in the common censure. In accordance with the custom established at the Gravel-Pit meeting-house, of noticing from the pulpit those events that exercised any serious influence on the national welfare, Mr. Aspland preached, on the 4th of July, from Isaiah xiv. 18, on Royal Mortality. He touched with a gentle hand on the faults of the departed King, and dwelt with discrimination on the character of his reign, as the following extracts will shew:

"It is neither my duty nor my wish to enter upon a close review of the character of the deceased King, or of the measures of his reign. We are, probably, incompetent as yet to form and pronounce a just judgment. They that come after us will be able to do this coolly, and therefore usefully; although in the history of all individuals, whether high or low in social rank, there are doubtless many events which will not be fully understood until the day when the secrets of all hearts shall be disclosed.

"Open transgressions of the law of God, acknowledged and enforced by the common sense of mankind, admit of no defence, whoever is the transgressor: yet equity as well as candour demands that some allowance should be made for those whose condition exposes them to peculiar temptations. In the case of princes, it ought never to be forgotten that the institutions of society, established or acquiesced in by the people, place them in a position which is peculiarly disadvantageous in a moral point of view. We force them by our laws into an unnatural condition, and then, somewhat unreasonably, expect them to resist the strong temptations which that condition calls up around them. Whilst we endeavour to guard society against what we may consider evil in their example, it behoves us to look at their faults with some commiseration, and to give ample praise to all their virtues.

"Happily, the personal character of princes is of less moment than it once was to the peace and happiness of nations. In communities that are only partially free and enlightened, they are subject in no small degree to public opinion; and under the influence of the spirit of modern times, a nation, united in its sentiments, will not long wish and seek in vain for any social improvement.

"The reign of his late Majesty, including the period of the Regency, during which he exercised the Royal functions, will be distinguished in the annals of our country to the end of time. No people ever gained, in the same number of years, more of what is called military glory; and the time is, I fear, very far distant when such glory will cease to dazzle the eyes of mankind. A war, almost unexampled both in its duration and the extent of its ravages, was brought to a triumphant conclusion; and an Enemy, the greatest warrior and hero of late ages, was subdued and humbled and held in the condition of a captive. The ultimate effect of this war, though eminently successful, upon the finances and the commerce of the kingdom, cannot even now be distinctly foreseen. The enormous expenditure with which it was carried on, has for a long period embarrassed and perplexed all the operations of trade and agriculture; and the difficulties and distresses of the nation will probably continue and may possibly increase. Nor ought we to repine at such visitations of Divine Providence. The derangement of the social frame is the natural result, may we not say the just punishment, of war; and the judgments of Heaven will prove mercies if by them the nations be taught righteousness, and be brought to resolve that they will neither learn nor endure war any longer.

"In other respects, the reign which is just closed may be pronounced glorious, in a sense in which even a Christian philanthropist cannot dispute the propriety of the term glory. It has been distinguished by many great discoveries and useful inventions. Philosophy and Science have made splendid advances. Education has been wonderfully extended, and the cultivation of literature has been pursued with unprecedented ardour. Humanity has triumphed in numberless reforms in favour of the unhappy victims of vice and crime, and Charity has waved her peaceful banners over many a new establishment dedicated to Mercy.

"Above all other auspicious features of the reign of George the Fourth, let it not be overlooked in this place that it has been signally honoured by the achievements of Religious Liberty. The Unitarian, the Protestant Dissenter, the Roman Catholic, whatever be his judgment of particular measures of the late King's government, cannot reflect without deep gratitude that under it his civil and political condition has been unspeakably improved, that penal statutes and exclusive, degrading tests have been abolished, and that a considerable approach has been made towards that religious equality which is the only sure cement of national concord, and which is equally called for by the true policy of nations and by the spirit of the gospel of Christ.

"The reign is over; the King sleeps with his fathers; and, in a Christian sense, I say, without any invidious reservation, Peace be to his memory!"

The Ministers of the Three Denominations met on the 17th of July to agree upon suitable Addresses on the accession of William IV. and Queen Adelaide. The Addresses agreed upon* were prepared by Mr. Aspland. By the courtesy of the ministers, the office of presenting the Address on the occasion of an accession had always devolved on one of the Presbyterian denomination. In 1689, Dr. William Bates, of Hackney, presented to King William and Queen Mary the joint Address of the Presbyterians and Independents. In 1702, Dr. Daniel Williams presented to Queen Anne the Address of the Three Denominations, who then appeared in union at Court for the first time. In 1714, Dr. Williams, attended by nearly one hundred ministers, presented the Address to George I. In 1727, Rev. (afterwards Dr.) John Evans presented the Address to George II., and Dr. Edmund Calamy that to

---

* A letter to the writer, dated July 22, 1830, gives an account of the proceedings at this meeting, which shews how kindly a spirit then prevailed between Baptists, Presbyterians and Independents, at least amongst the leaders of these denominations. As soon as the meeting was constituted, the venerable Dr. Rippon, patting Mr. Aspland on the shoulder, said—"Come, come, my good boy, you have something for us; you are always ready." The drafts of Addresses were ultimately placed on the table by Rev. W. J. Fox, Dr. J. P. Smith and Mr. Aspland. Those of the two latter were read by their authors to the meeting. Dr. Smith's was to the Queen, and alluded in considerable detail to the lives and characters of her ancestors, and urged her to imitate their example in upholding religion and the Protestant faith. It was remarked that Addresses to a Queen were usually brief and general; that, as Queen of England, her Majesty occupied a position of higher dignity than any German ancestors could give her; and that it was desirable to avoid the appearance, however remote, of preaching at her Majesty in the Address. With his usual candour and good temper, Dr. Smith admitted the force of some of these criticisms. After the Addresses of Mr. Aspland were read, Mr. Fox begged to withdraw his, as Mr. A. had forestalled every topic on which he had touched. Dr. Rippon asked leave to move that Dr. Smith give him, for his own private reading, a copy of the Address, and thereupon Mr. Aspland jocularly moved that Dr. Smith's draft be an Address to Dr. Rippon; and the ministers pleasantly closed the business by unanimously adopting the Addresses of Mr. Aspland.

Queen Caroline. In 1760, Dr. Samuel Chandler, attended by one hundred and forty ministers, presented the Address to George III.; and, as already stated, in 1820, Dr. Abraham Rees, supported by eighty-nine ministers, presented the Address to George IV. The exclusive possession of the post of honour by the Presbyterians, doubtless originated in their superior numbers and influence. Reversed as the proportion in numbers had now become, the retention of this privilege by the Presbyterian body could no longer be justified. They had therefore announced their purpose, previously to the presentation to William IV., to assert the right which ancient custom, confirmed by express resolution, gave them, once more, and then to relinquish it, and concur in the regular rotation of precedence of the Three Denominations. This was regarded as a becoming concession by the majority of the other denominations, and acknowledged as such by them in a vote (not, however, unanimous) of thanks.

On this occasion, the honour of being the spokesman for the Three Denominations was awarded to Mr. Aspland. The ceremony took place on the 28th of July. Ninety-five ministers attended. In accordance with ancient custom, they were received by the King *upon the Throne,*—a distinction enjoyed only by the City of London, the two Universities, the London clergy, and the Dissenting ministers when they appear as a body. When they appear by deputation, they are received in the Royal Closet. With much dignity of manner, Mr. Aspland presented the Addresses and received the Answers.* In an interval between the presentation of the two Addresses, the King, little accustomed to the straitness of Court ceremonial, gave way to the feelings which the occasion had excited, and, in addition to the prepared Reply, addressed the ministers in a little extempore speech, which, if not felicitous in diction, evinced his good and amiable feelings. Dr. Thomas Rees was presented as Secretary of the General Body of Ministers, and by him the ministers individually were presented to the King.

The official distinction conferred upon Dr. Rees and Mr. Aspland, did not escape the evil eye of fanatics and bigots of different denominations. The *Record*, a newspaper devoted to the interests of the Evangelical Church party, sounded the alarm, and bewailed the appearance at Court of " the Arian, the Socinian, the members of the God-denying

---

* These documents will be found in the Christian Reformer, Vol. XVI. pp. 334—336, 377, 378.

apostacy," not merely in the company of "the avowed champions of the faith," but as their "heads and representatives." The editor concluded several columns of gross reviling by calling "on the orthodox Dissenters of London to wipe away from them this deep stigma on their character as men of consistency and men of God." The cry was immediately echoed by Mr. G. C. Smith, a person commonly known in the religious world of London as *Boatswain Smith*, the Editor of the Soldiers' and Sailors' Magazine. He made his first appeal against the "Socinian representation at the Throne" at an "open-air service," in the presence of nearly two thousand persons. He next called a public meeting at the London Tavern, at which resolutions were proposed, 1, denouncing the latitudinarian liberality of the day; 2, declaratory of the orthodoxy of the doctrines of the Trinity, Atonement, &c.; 3, stating that Unitarians or Socinians, denying these orthodox doctrines, though entitled to civil and religious liberty, ought to be left to co-operate with those who hold the same sentiments; 4, disavowing on the part of the meeting that they were represented at or "conducted to the Throne" "by the Socinian minister who read the Address to King William IV. and to Queen Adelaide, and the Socinian *or Arian* minister who introduced the deputation to the Court;" 5, deploring that in this Address of the Three Denominations, read to the King by a Socinian minister, the name of Jesus Christ and his glorious atonement were not once mentioned, and attributing the omission* to "the distressing union of Socinians, or Unitarians, with the Trinitarians;" 6, contrasting the Address with that presented by the Society of Friends, and the several Replies given by the Monarch to the two bodies; 7 to 10, acknowledging the services of the *Record* and the *Evangelical Magazine*, and of several orthodox ministers, in raising their voice against all future union with Socinians and Unitarians; and 11, asserting it to be the imperative duty of every Trinitarian minister to withdraw *in toto* from a union with Socinian ministers.

Other meetings were held—by Mr. Ivimey and his friends in London, and by the orthodox Presbyterians of North Shields—at which similar resolutions were passed. Insignificant as these demonstrations at the time appeared, and discountenanced as they were by many Dissenters of respectable station and influence, they served to call into action a

---

* In this detection of heresy in the Address, the Boatswain surpassed the writer in the Record, who commended it as breathing "the language of pious desire as well for the eternal as for the temporal interests of the new monarch."

coarse and fanatical bigotry amongst the mass of the orthodox Dissenters of the metropolis, which, if secretly disapproved by their best leaders, was too strong to be openly resisted by them, and at no distant day, as we shall presently see, led to a serious and permanent division of the Three Denominations.

From this petty agitation Mr. Aspland turned, not without deep disgust. He did not, however, allow the anonymous invectives with which the press of the orthodox Dissenters teemed, to alter his conduct or affect his feelings towards the gentlemen with whom he was accustomed to act, and who were at this time forward in disclaiming all participation in and approval of the agitation of Messrs. Smith and Ivimey.

The outburst of the French Revolution, in July 1830, occasioned by the ordinances of Charles X. destroying the liberty of the press in France and annihilating the Chamber of Deputies, awakened in the minds of all lovers of liberty the most enthusiastic hopes. To this and the preceding topic the following animated letter alludes.

Rev. Robert Aspland to Rev. R. Brook Aspland.

"Hackney, Aug. 27, 1830.

"Dear Brook,—* * * We seem to have lived an age since we last met; so many, and some such glorious events have intervened. This French Revolution absorbs my whole mind and exhausts my joy. I am ready to say, 'It is the Lord's doing, and it is marvellous in our eyes.' 'A nation has been born in a day.' The sublime spectacle is always before me, and by night as well as by day; and I really sometimes fear that I am about to awake from a delightful dream. To keep myself sober, I am taking the alterative of *Burke's Reflections*, but the dose fails. I cannot find this man's prophetic wisdom, and I am profane enough to laugh at his sublimities and pathetics. He was indeed a gay sophister (to borrow a word of his coinage) and a gorgeous declaimer; but there my praise, at least, terminates.

"The Cambridgeshire election* would have been a great matter but for this, which makes every thing else little. Our friend Fyson did himself great credit by his manly conduct and his vigilant activity. Our two Members are

---

* At the general election which had just taken place, very great changes had been made in the representation of the kingdom. In the county of Cambridge, of which Mr. Aspland was a freeholder, Lord Charles Manners was displaced by Mr. Adeane, an improvement in effecting which Mr. Aspland actively assisted. He was the means of calling together and organizing an important Liberal Committee in London, and had the gratification of going to the poll with nearly all the freeholders of his native village, who, together with the freeholders of Fordham, headed by his valued friend Mr. Fyson, secured the election of the independent candidate as the colleague of Lord Francis Godolphin Osborne.

not quite third-rate men, but they have excluded a fourth-rate, though one in the foremost rank of servility and corruption. What think you of Lord Francis Osborne's describing the French Revolution as *a contest between two princes;* and then, by way of *contrast* (in the parrot-prate of the small technical Whigs), referring to *our Revolution* of 1688! Is it nature or education that so often makes the son of a lord almost a fool? The Duke of Bedford disgraced himself in Cambridgeshire by *forcing* his tenants—making two hundred votes or more—to vote for the two old Members,—Lord Charles, the inveterate enemy of freedom and never-failing supporter of Ministerial profligacy, one of them!

"I know not that I have any thing to tell of the visit to the Throne beyond what is public. We were certainly received graciously, and were all pleased with the Royal personages; the more pleased, because they did not thrust their royalty in our faces. The King made a little extempore speech to us, which set Sir Robert Peel quivering: the purport was, that he would neither make nor admit distinctions between his people on account of religion, and that *all should go to heaven* (he promised as much) in their own way. My orthodox brethren treated me during the whole day with studied kindness. Some thirty of us, chiefly Independents and Baptists, dined together afterwards, my post being the chair. The thirty included most of the *heads* (I was going to say *hearts* also) of the Three Denominations; and you may judge of our spirit by the unanimous resolution that was passed, that I should form the plan of an annual dinner of the Ministers, for the sake of keeping up a spirit of kind fellowship. The report of this may have whetted the bigotry of the London Tavern fanatics. But your mother craves a little space, and I can only sign myself, Your affectionate father,

ROBERT ASPLAND."

Rev. Robert Aspland to his Daughter Ellen.

"Hackney, Dec. 2, 1830.

"My dear Ellen,—* * * You are, I know, politician enough to rejoice in the late changes abroad and at home. The Revolution in France I was, you are aware, quite prepared for; but, with all my admiration of the sense and virtue of the French people, I could not expect so thorough, and at the same time so temperate, a national reform. My only fears now regard the despots around that fine country; but, mark my words! should they dare to coalesce once more against the independence and liberty of France, *thrones* in Europe will be valued precisely at their worth as *fire-wood.*

"I can scarcely believe that I have lived to see an English Administration formed on the basis of parliamentary reform, retrenchment and peace, the King himself being the adviser of these great and saving measures. To some individuals of the new Government I have no great liking; but I respect the talent of the Ministry, and I confide in their patriotism, because the leaders are sound men, and all of them would lose more than they could gain by treachery to the people.

"'The spreading insurrection of the labouring poor is truly alarming. All must condemn violent and tumultuary proceedings; but much is to be said for the unhappy people. They have been ground down to the lowest degree of suffering, and they might all have perished by inches without commiseration from the aristocracy. They have made themselves heard and seen; and the Government, the landlord and the parson, must for their own sakes attend to their complaints. I met Mr. Adeane, our new Cambridgeshire Member, this morning, who tells me that he is summoned into the country to assist in putting down a plotted movement at Cambridge on Saturday. There has been one dreadful fire in the county, and I feel much for our friends there.

"Aunt Anna will, I expect, put into the parcel a few copies of my Wareham sermon,* which may suffice to explain to the public what our *ism* is.

"With sincere affection, dear Ellen, your father,

R. ASPLAND."

In the year 1831, the arrival in England of Rajah Rammohun Roy, who exhibited the rare and striking spectacle of a Brahmin of Hindoostan, who had worked himself out of the darkness of Heathenism into Theism, and through Theism to Christianity, excited in many religious circles of the country the deepest interest. To the Unitarians it was a delightful confirmation of the scriptural character of their opinions, that so able and impartial an inquirer had found in Christianity the doctrines in the profession of which they were united. Mr. Aspland was gratified by many opportunities of intercourse with this distinguished Oriental Reformer, and has recorded his admiration of his intellectual energies, moral qualities, dignified aspect, courteous manners, candid judgment and liberal views. One of the first sentiments which the Rajah expressed to Mr. Aspland, when visiting him at Hackney soon after his arrival in London, was his astonishment to find so much bigotry amongst the majority of Christians towards the Unitarians. He said that it too much resembled the rancorous feelings of his idola-

---

* On Wednesday, Sept. 29, 1830, Mr. Aspland had preached at Wareham, Dorsetshire, a sermon on the occasion of opening there a new chapel, dedicated to the worship of the One God the Father. At the request of the congregation, the sermon was printed, under the title, "The Religious Belief of Unitarian Christians truly stated, and vindicated from Popular Misrepresentation." The sermon is valuable as a very precise statement of the points wherein Unitarians agree and differ. It has passed through two large editions. On the Sunday previous to the opening at Wareham, Mr. Aspland preached to his old friends at Newport, and the journey thence into Dorsetshire, in the company of Rev. Edmund Kell and other friends, was particularly agreeable.

trous countrymen against those that renounced their false gods. The Rajah attended the meeting of the Unitarian Association; and in the name of the Society and of his Unitarian brethren of England, Mr. Aspland, who filled the chair on that memorable day, welcomed the advent of their distinguished guest. In the simple address which the Rajah delivered on that occasion, he distinctly avowed himself a believer in the One God, and in almost all the doctrines of Unitarians, and declared his conviction that scripture seconded the system of Unitarian Christianity, and that common sense was on its side.

The gratification afforded to his European friends by the visit of Rammohun Roy, was purchased at a costly price. In little more than two years after his arrival, his noble form was struck by disease; and he died, Sept. 27, 1833, after a short illness, at Stapleton Grove, near Bristol. In most of the Unitarian pulpits of England was mournful reference made to the Rajah's death. At Hackney, where he had been an occasional worshiper, the sad event led Mr. Aspland to discourse on *the Future Accession of Good Men of all Climes to Christianity, and their Final Congregation in Heaven*, and to offer a brief sketch of the life and character of the deceased Rajah,* which concludes in these terms:

---

* It was not Mr. Aspland's intention or wish in the first instance to print this sermon. He considered the sermon of Dr. Carpenter to be the proper funereal tribute to the memory of the Rajah. To his surprise, a London bookseller put out, without authority, an edition of the sermon preached at Hackney, from notes taken at the delivery. This publication proved to be mean and illiterate; and he first used the powers which the law gave him for the suppression of the pirated edition, and then felt there was no alternative but to print the sermon, with illustrative notes, in a suitable form and manner.—The writer has looked carefully, though with little success, through Mr. Aspland's papers, in the hope of finding letters from Rammohun Roy, suitable for insertion in this Memoir. The letter which follows was given by the gentleman to whom it was addressed, to Mr. Aspland for publication, but it is believed that it has not hitherto appeared in print.

Rajah Rammohun Roy to Mr. William Alexander, of Yarmouth.

"5, Cumberland Terrace, Regent's Park, July 16, 1831.

"My dear Sir,—Our mutual friend Dr. Bowring has communicated to me your long letter to his address, which I have read with interest, as it completely recals the recollection of our former correspondence.

"I do not wonder that you should have felt surprise at my silence for some years, the cause of which can only be fully appreciated by those who knew the troubles in which I was involved. They were such that I entirely neglected my correspondence with Persia, England, America and every part of the world, as is well known to my friends in various quarters who complained of my neglect of their communications. However, I thank the Supreme Author and Ruler of the universe that, by a firm reliance on His goodness and overruling providence,

"Centuries may intervene before his equal in all respects shall rise up in Hindoostan, so bright a light shining in so dark a place. He is a memorable example to the world of what an individual may accomplish by firmness of purpose, diligence, perseverance, fortitude, disinterestedness and candour, in the acquirement of truth, amidst the greatest disadvantages, and the diffusion of truth, amidst opposition and reproach. Would that they could be warned by his example, who, with all the opportunities of improvement around them, neither inquire nor think, neither instruct nor are instructed, lay down no error and acquire no truth, and, except as far as self-interest prompts, meditate no one good service to their fellow-creatures.

"The name of Rammohun Roy will endure as long as the history of religious truth. It is already, in part, and will hereafter be generally cherished in both hemispheres, in that which is distinguished by his birth, and in this, which will, it is now probable, have the boast of keeping his honoured relics: *here*, he will be celebrated for breaking the first link of the long chain which has pressed down the heart of his country to the dust; *at home*, when India shall stretch out her hands to the true God, he will be revered as the first of her Reformers and Philanthropists."—Pp. 25, 26.

The introduction of the Reform Bill and the subsequent appeal of the King's government to the country in its behalf, excited in Mr. Aspland's mind gratitude and patriotic hope. The change of opinion which he had lived to see, was wonderful and delightful. When

---

which brings good out of evil, I have been enabled to survive and overcome these severe afflictions, and to learn from them lessons of resignation to the Divine Will, of humility and distrust of human strength, and the vain and transitory nature of all worldly affairs. 'Whom the Lord loveth he chasteneth.' By temporal calamities we are taught to withdraw the heart from things which are perishable, and to fix it upon those which are eternal.

"Since my arrival in England, I have enjoyed an opportunity of seeing a very great number of our religious friends, and have reaped the highest gratification from associating with them in public and in private, at their social parties and in their public assemblies. I have attended the different places of worship with benefit and instruction. I rejoice to find that true religion is so well appreciated, and in its purest form so fully attended, by so large a portion of the most intelligent and respectable part of the community. But in a free country like this, the institutions of which are every day making further advances towards perfection, truth must prevail over error, rational piety over bigotry, and the light of reason must ultimately dispel the clouds of superstition.

"Owing to my indisposition, I was unable to answer your letter earlier, and express my gratitude for all the kind interest you have taken on my behalf. On my tour to the country, if I find it possible to take Yarmouth in my way, it will afford me infinite gratification to call upon you at your residence. In the mean time, wishing you speedy restoration to your usual strength, and every success in life, I remain, with regard and esteem, my dear Sir, yours most obediently,

RAMMOHUN ROY."

he first visited London, he saw the cells in the Tower in which Horne Tooke, Mr. Joyce and others, were confined, awaiting their trial under a charge of high treason, their crime in reality being their earnest efforts to procure a searching reform of Parliament; and now he had the gratification of aiding the Ministers of the King and a large majority of the people of England in carrying a great measure of legislative reform, in some particulars more extensive than the Reformers of the 18th century had in their most sanguine hours ventured to propose.

On the Sunday following the coronation of King William and Queen Adelaide, he gave expression to the gratitude and joy which warmed his heart, in a sermon on *Christian Patriotism*. This he afterwards published, with the further title of *The Wishes and Prayers of Britons for their Country in the Present Crisis*. It was the only sermon published on the occasion, in addition to the official discourse delivered at the august ceremonial by the Bishop of London. A friendly critic dwelt with satisfaction on " the approach towards an identity of principle in these two discourses, delivered as they were by such very different persons and to such very different auditors."* The spirit of Mr. Aspland's discourse will appear from one of the introductory passages.

" The coronation of a king, always an imposing spectacle, is in this case the more impressive to the nation, in that the August Personage who is called by Divine Providence to fill the throne, has distinguished himself, beyond almost all his predecessors, by an immediate and spontaneous attention to the wants and wishes of his people, and has summoned around him servants who have been long honoured for their public integrity, and have pledged themselves by the whole of their past lives to measures which have for their object the reformation of the frame of government, so as to adapt it to the altered and improved condition of the age, the healing of discontents and the union of all classes of men in the enjoyment of common laws and equal rights, the lessening of the public burdens, the preservation of peace and the cultivation of amicable intercourse with all nations, the diffusion of useful knowledge, and the promotion of the national industry and wealth. They who behold with indifference a mere state-ceremonial, or smile at a pageantry which in the lapse of time, and the growth of reason, may have lost much of its meaning and all its fitness, must still feel that there is moral grandeur in the exhibition of the Ruler of one of the most powerful, rich and refined nations of the earth, entering with sincerity and solemnity, and before the face of the whole people, into a covenant to reign legally, uprightly and beneficially, and appealing to Heaven to witness his vows, and to ratify his obligations, and to send down a

---

* Monthly Repository, N. S., V. 726.

blessing upon them, a common blessing to himself and the people committed to his charge. Amidst such a scene, a sympathy with both King and People is as rational, amiable and Christian, as it is natural; and the Christian minister who is most careful to exclude from the pulpit all political topics that engender or irritate party feeling, may consistently recognize, share and endeavour to improve, the universal sentiment."—Pp. 2, 3.

In the spring of 1832, Mr. Aspland lost, in Mr. Christopher Richmond, a valued and an accomplished friend. In the minutes of the Non-Con Club he inscribed this memorial of him:

"The Club are anxious to record on their minutes their gratitude to their late lamented Treasurer, Christopher Richmond, Esq., and their sincere and lasting respect for his memory.

"In connection with the members of this Club his deportment was always courteous and friendly: he entered fully and zealously into the purpose entertained by the Club from the beginning of maintaining cordial amity amongst the members as the means of promoting their higher object of serving, as occasions present themselves, the great and holy cause of Freedom.

"He was always ready, notwithstanding an habitual retiringness, the result of modesty, to give his professional services in aid of any of the public measures contemplated or assisted by the Club.

"Cheerfully did he co-operate, as far as his labours could be useful, with the legal advisers of our Roman Catholic brethren, in facilitating the measure of their Emancipation.

"The Protestant Dissenters naturally looked to his sound and cool-judging mind for aid in the difficulties which beset the legislative provision for the abolition of the Sacramental Test, commonly described as the Repeal of the Corporation and Test Acts, and the published minutes of their proceedings shew and will testify to posterity with what care and devotion he watched and promoted this long-delayed act of justice, the carrying of which he, in common with all the members of this Club, hailed as one of the most memorable triumphs of truth and freedom over sophistry, bigotry and intolerance, and as the sure harbinger of the reforms necessary to make rights and duties reciprocal and equal, and to establish the British Government on the principles of common sense and sound morals—in other words, on the public good.

"To him the Unitarians of England are indebted, jointly with some others who yet live to serve their generation, for various plans of relief from the odious and oppressive Marriage Service, prescribed by the Liturgy of the Church of England, any one of which would have been available to its righteous object, if the intolerant spirit and exclusive purposes of certain individuals in the House of Lords, had not led them to find out objections to every particular measure in order to frustrate altogether the deliverance of an obnoxious sect from oppression. The course of public events has at length wrought what wisdom and charity failed to effect, and in a Reformed Parliament the claims of the Established Church to harass and tax persons who renounce its communion on their entering into that social state upon which the Almighty has pronounced his blessing, will be undoubtedly silenced for ever, and that not only with regard to Unitarians, whose case is the most trying, but also in reference to the whole body of Protestant Dissenters,—another memorable proof that resistance to an equitable demand only causes the demand to be enlarged, and rouses a spirit which instantly overwhelms interested and bigoted opposition; and whenever this further triumph of religious liberty shall be gained, the name of Richmond will be inscribed on the banner of victory.

"Our departed friend's last thoughts and feelings in public matters were excited by the Reform Bill, now happily the law of the land and in satisfactory operation. In this he saw, as it is hoped and believed survivors will find, a new era for England of good government, peace and prosperity and public virtue.

"In a word, he has left an example of the usefulness which may be attained, and of the posthumous respect which may be treasured up, by a love of truth and freedom, consistently professed and perseveringly acted upon; by the application of talents through even a short life to a good and noble end; and by the cultivation of those social virtues which heighten men's powers and sanctify their pursuits.

"While, therefore, we lament the loss of such a friend and coadjutor, we take leave of him with satisfaction in his character and unfeigned respect for his memory,—resolving to persevere in the same course which has justly entitled him to this inadequate but sincere eulogium on his unspotted and honoured name."

The Gravel-Pit congregation, at their annual meeting held towards the close of 1831, passed an unanimous resolution requesting their pastor to print a volume of his Discourses, as a permanent record of his instructions from the pulpit. He gratefully acceded to their wishes, and published, in the beginning of 1833, a volume of "Sermons on Various Subjects, chiefly Practical." It was naturally dedicated to the members of his flock, and contains an expression of his warm sense of the courtesy and kindness which he had experienced from them during the whole period of his ministry, now extended to nearly twenty-eight years.

The merits of the volume were described, with equal discrimination and kindness, by the Rev. John Kentish, in the following terms:

"This is a *consecrated* memorial of the reciprocal affection of the Pastor and the Flock; and also of his Theological knowledge, vigorous and discriminating sense, comprehensive thought, and power of seeing beneath the surface, and of conveying sound instruction in language at once terse, perspicuous, appropriate and energetic. His person and voice and distinct elocution commanded regard: yet these alone would not have procured for him the favour of his well-informed audiences; not apart from the intrinsically good qualities of his sermons. I scarcely know the modern discourses that equal them for a wide compass of ideas. Every topic has justice done to it. We meet with nothing superficial. In point of exactness of definition, accurate reasoning, judicious scriptural exposition, and natural and copious applications, they remind me of the sermons of our good old English Preachers, at the end of the seventeenth and the beginning of the eighteenth century. Indeed, those great masters of the Pulpit were favourite authors with Mr. Aspland. Without being their servile imitator, he improved his own compositions by his study of theirs."—Christ. Ref. (1846), pp. 104, 105.

Mr. James Taylor to Rev. Robert Aspland.

"Philadelphia, April 8, 1833.

"My good Friend,—Let me begin by congratulating you on the removal of your son to Bristol, where he is associated with Dr. Carpenter, one of the best and most amiable of men. You know the circumstances of my introduction to, and personal intercourse with him. I often look back on it with peculiar satisfaction. Judging from the impression made on my own mind in relation to the Doctor, it seems to me that inestimable *moral* benefit cannot fail to accrue from a ministerial connection with one of so excellent a frame of mind. It is like enjoying a foretaste of heaven. Perhaps I write the more feelingly on such a topic, because it is our happiness to have one of the best of human beings for our minister. I have just finished a letter for Mr. Smallfield, to which I would refer, in preference to a repetition of its contents. Dr. Channing is here, and although very weak, yet in better health and much better spirits than when here eleven years ago; he has also different *feelings*; since that period his mind took a spring, and one natural consequence has been, a much more liberal spirit is now apparent in him. Mr. Henry Ware was also at our church yesterday; he too is in feeble health, though on the recovery. Neither of them could preach; both expressed high gratification in the largeness of the congregation, and the pulpit performances of our minister. A society so well suited, and so thoroughly convinced of this, can furnish no matter for detail; besides, Mr. Sill is able to answer every friendly inquiry relative to our ecclesiastical state.

"There is trouble among the Presbyterians; and, from some late indications, it would seem as if, at no distant day, old-fashioned orthodoxy would meet with little favour in the General Assembly. Then, too, there is the Andover Creed, in which the eternal Sonship of Jesus is not recognized; and the New-Haven divinity, which hardly amounts to semi-orthodoxy. As a specimen of the manner in which the two classes of Presbyterians treat each other, the debates in the Philadelphia Presbytery might be referred to; so great was the hostility of the two parties, that the last General Assembly recommended such a division of that Presbytery as would put an end to contention. Accordingly, the Presbytery was divided; but when the Synod met, the roll of the second Presbytery of Philadelphia was not called, and the members from that Presbytery were not allowed to take their seats; thus, the proceedings of the General Assembly were nullified. So much for harmony. Both parties are narrow-minded; the liberality of the new school extending only to those of similar views and feelings with themselves. During the sitting of the Presbytery some time ago, a Mr. M'Calla made some pretty strong insinuations against the orthodoxy of Mr. Barnes, another minister in this city; and, for the purpose of shewing that heresy did not always manifest itself, related the following story:—Two of our brethren, entire strangers in this city, being desirous of hearing Dr. M'Cauley, made diligent inquiry respecting the appearance and position of his church, when they were truly informed that it was almost at the corner of two streets, and had a marble front. Not paying sufficient attention to the names of these streets, and happening to go up Locust Street as high as Tenth Street, they found a building answering the above description, and entered the church, when they were strongly prepossessed in favour of the preacher, from the unction of his prayers, the beauty of his language, and the eloquence of his manner. On returning to their lodgings, they gave expression to their feelings, and were not a little astonished when told that they had been listening to Mr. Furness, a Unitarian minister. At this moment, Mr. Barnes said, 'I hope the brother does not mean to say that I preach like Mr. Furness.' 'O no!' rejoined M'Calla, 'I only meant to say that Mr. Furness can preach like a good Presbyterian.'

"The recent conduct of the dominant party in South Carolina, and the modern theories respecting what are called 'State rights,' augur ill, both as respects the practicability and permanency of republican governments. I wish that the question of nullification had been boldly met. The tariff was merely a pretext, and at some future and probably not distant day, we may have to contend with more than one State. The habits and views of the slave-holding and free States are so dissimilar and discordant, that we ought to look forward to a separation, and I know not that an amicable separation would be prejudicial to the latter; though I greatly doubt if the slaves in 'the *nation* of South Carolina,'—the black population of which constitutes the majority,—could be held in subjection to their masters; for, in case of disunion, the facilities for reclaiming them would no longer be granted by the free States.

"I am also somewhat sceptical as to the immense benefits that are expected from your reformed Parliament. In other words, I doubt whether the reformation is not more partial and nominal than thorough and real. It would seem as if there was little regard to economy, and little consideration for the middle classes. The salary of the Speaker of the House of Commons might have been reduced one-half. He receives more than the President of the United States, though between the duties of the two stations there is a vast disparity. The projected reform of the Church will still leave *Lord* and Legislative Bishops; but, if report speaks truth, some of our Unitarian friends must shut their mouths; for a Dissenting minister in the House of Commons would be as far removed from his proper sphere as an Episcopal Bishop in the House of Peers. The Church revenues belong to the nation, and ought to be applied to public purposes. Our American Bishops work hard and often fare badly; but, being zealous and disinterested, they enjoy the confidence of Episcopalians generally, and the respect of the community at large. Wherever the population is sufficiently numerous, ministers are adequately supported. None are enriched by their profession in our most prosperous communities; but their compensation enables them to support their families in great comfort, without resorting to any other means of adding to their incomes. On this account, the connection between minister and people is much more intimate than in English large towns. As for London congregations, constituted as they usually are, the minister can be known and regarded only as a preacher.

"The schism between 'the Friends' is likely to continue. A controversy is going on between the Roman Catholics and Presbyterians, both here and at New York. It must be rather up-hill work to sustain the Protestant principle of the sufficiency of Holy Scripture, and at the same time to justify the requisition of a subscription to 'the Confession of Faith,' &c. The discussion here has arrived at an interesting point,—the Roman Catholic having accused the Presbyterian writer of having made garbled quotations, and misrepresented the meaning of Latin authors. He has, therefore, proposed to meet his opponent, to submit the matter to a sworn interpreter, and to abide by his translation and award,—engaging to make a public and ample apology, if it shall appear that these accusations are false or unfounded.

"It was gratifying to learn, through Miss Leishman, that I was held in remembrance last New-Year's day. I am often present with you in spirit. A few days ago, Dr. Channing mentioned the text and subject of your sermon when he accompanied you to your chapel, and spoke of the sermon in terms truly pleasing to me. I can also with great truth inform you, that you stand high in the estimation of Mr. Henry Ware, himself of a kindred spirit with Dr. Carpenter. Unless you visit us, it is not likely that you will ever see either of these gentlemen again. I therefore write with the greater freedom. Our ministers, one after another, visit England; but you all seem immoveably fixed in the little island. How it would rejoice my heart to shake you by the hand, and shew you some of the hospitalities of Philadelphia! At any rate, accept my earnest wishes for your present welfare, your continued usefulness, and eternal happiness. "Yours most affectionately,

JAMES TAYLOR."

In the course of this year, Mr. Aspland's early and affectionate friend, John Emons, of Wicken, died, in his 86th year.

Rev. Robert Aspland to Mrs. Emons.

"Hackney, August 31, 1833.

"My dear Mrs. Emons,—It has pleased Divine Providence to call to another world my long and highly-esteemed friend, your husband. This event is in the course of nature. Our departed friend was spared beyond the common age of man; and we must remember, with gratitude to the Supreme Disposer, that his life was as happy as this imperfect state allows human life to be. At the same time, we cannot part with friends with whom we have been for the greater portion of our days intimately or tenderly connected, without feeling a pang at heart. If I feel this, how much stronger must you, a widow, and your now fatherless daughters feel it?

"I was from a child, as you well know, in habits of close friendship with Mr. Emons. My earlier summers were made more interesting to me by his society. He was in some things my guide and instructor. In religion, our minds advanced side by side, and step for step. His thorough acquaintance with his Bible, and his searching thoughts on all scriptural subjects, made him an invaluable companion to a young inquirer after Divine Truth. I shall ever remember him with affectionate regard; and to the latest moment of my life it will be a comfort to me to reflect that I may, on some occasions, have been able to assist his active and powerful mind, and to add to the number of his enjoyments.

"It gives me great pleasure to learn that my venerable friend was permitted to leave the world without much bodily suffering, and especially that his faculties were bright to the last, that his mind was serene, that he was able to express his satisfaction and happiness, and that with nearly his last breath he bore his testimony to those views of Christian truth which for a great part of his life he had courageously professed. 'Being dead, he yet speaketh,' and I hope and pray that his neighbours, and, above all, his family, may continue to hear his dying voice.

"You, my much-esteemed friend, have the consolation of knowing that he, of whom you are bereaved, endeavoured to live the life of the just; that he lamented those imperfections which are common to man; that he wished to resemble that Saviour whom he devoutly loved; and that he worshiped the Ever-Blessed God and Father with heart and soul and mind and strength. And, knowing this, you cannot sorrow as those that have no hope. He is, doubtless, gone to his rest in Paradise; and may and ought we not to regard the serene and cloudless setting of his sun as an earnest of its rising again in a glorious morning?

"At first, I felt a strong desire to be present at the funeral, and to offer my services towards improving the mournful event; but, in the state of my health at that time, I found, upon consideration, that the task would have been too painful for me, associated as it would have been with many other melancholy recollections. Wicken now appears to me as a place of tombs. Let a few more changes take place, and I shall feel an interest in the village chiefly on account of them that sleep.

"My absence on this occasion was of less consequence, as you had so pious, judicious and tender-hearted a friend with you as Mr. Clack. He has supplied me with the substance of his sermon, which is all that I could wish. The conclusion of it, relating to the character of our deceased friend, I have caused to be printed in the Obituary of the Christian Reformer for the present month; and I have added some further remarks of my own in the number following. Such an extraordinary moral character as your dear husband's ought to be known and remembered beyond the circle of his family and intimate friends.

"Wishing for yourself Christian peace and happiness until you rejoin the departed, in a better world, and praying that all his and your children may be followers of him in so far as he was a follower of Christ,

"I remain, my dear friend, yours, in true and lasting sympathy,

ROBERT ASPLAND."

CHAPTER XXX.

The point at which this Memoir has arrived makes it expedient to gather together, and present in one view, the long-continued, often disappointed, but at last successful, efforts to obtain for the Unitarians relief from the marriage service of the Church of England, which, until the first of August, 1837, was obligatory on all persons (except Jews and Quakers) contracting marriage in England and Wales.

In the eye of the law, prior at least to Lord Hardwicke's Act (26 Geo. II., c. 33), marriage was regarded as a civil contract. On the passing of that law, the Protestant Dissenters slumbered, and allowed the right they previously possessed (which, however, it must be admitted they rarely exercised), of celebrating marriages in the face of their own congregations, to be taken from them. To the mass of Protestant Dissenters, a century ago, a Trinitarian marriage service was not unacceptable. To Unitarians, however, the service in the Book of Common Prayer was, from the first, distasteful and oppressive; but it was not till the year 1819, that any vigorous and combined attempt was made to obtain relief from the burthen.

There were great difficulties in the way. The Bishops and the Government, it was foreseen, would look with little favour on any measure interfering with the usages and emoluments of the Established Church. The Unitarians, besides, were not agreed as to the best way of remedying the evil. Some were for a return to the old law and practice, and opposed any plan which involved the necessity of a religious service, whether in a church of the Establishment or a Dissenting meeting-house. Another, and perhaps the greater portion of the Unitarian body, in their earnest desire to be freed from the necessity of using a Trinitarian form of service, were prepared to acquiesce in almost any change of the law which would effect this one object. After much discussion, the Committee of the Unitarian Association adopted the draft of a Bill, drawn up by Mr. Christopher Richmond, by which clergymen officiating at the marriage of Protestant Dissenters were authorized and required, on receiving a written notice from one or both of the contracting parties, to use only that portion of the service which begins with the words, " I require and charge you both," and ends with the words, " thereto I give thee my troth." The practical effect of this enactment (had it passed) would have been to do away with the devotional part of the marriage service, when used by Dissenters.

The Bill was introduced into the House of Commons by Mr. William Smith, June 16, 1819. The Government did not oppose it; and Mr. Wilberforce, while he professed approbation of its object, expressed his aversion to any thing that would encourage the idea that marriage was simply a civil contract, and not a divine ordinance. On the part of the Church of England, Dr. Phillimore expressed his fears that the marriage service might, if the Bill were to pass into a law, lose in the eyes of members of the Church some of that reverence with which it had hitherto been regarded, and that the clergy might feel conscientious scruples in performing a ceremony stripped of its religious character. Sir James Mackintosh remarked in reply, that the way to degrade the religious service of the Church was to compel its use by those who disbelieved the doctrine it expressed. In opposition to the other objection, he maintained that the clergy must fulfil the duties imposed on them by the Legislature, for the Establishment was simply the creature of civil policy.—Owing to the advanced period of the session, the Bill was not carried beyond the second reading. Nor was the measure more fortunate on its introduction a second and a third time. Dr. Stoddart, an eminent civilian, suggested another mode of relief; and, in conformity with his advice, a Bill was offered to the House of Lords, in 1823, by which the liberty of solemnizing marriages according to their own religious forms was conceded to Dissenters, provided they complied with the preliminary forms in use by the Church, and subsequently registered the marriage in the parish books. This plan was evidently an improvement on that first suggested. On June 12, the measure was debated in the House of Lords, on the motion of the Marquess of Lansdowne for the second reading of the Bill. Lord Chancellor Eldon energetically opposed it on two grounds: first, that it would open the door to irregular marriages; and next, that it was intolerable that the clergy of the Established Church should be made parties to the acts of Dissenters, and compelled to sanction those of " the worst sects of congregationists." Lord Liverpool confessed that the object and argument of the Bill were unanswerable, but objected to some of its details. The Archbishop of Canterbury expressed infinite alarm at any attempt to alter the Liturgy of the Church to meet doctrinal objections, but said no man exceeded him in respect for religious scruples and feelings. He added that the Church of England was a tolerant Church, and disclaimed all pretension to infallibility. Although the Archbishop and the Premier voted for the Bill going into Committee, the Chancellor's opposition prevailed, and the Bill was lost by a majority of six votes. In the session of 1824, it was resolved to limit the application for relief to Unitarians. There seemed to be a better prospect of success for a Bill framed on this principle than for a more comprehensive measure. Notwithstanding the previous efforts of the Unitarian Association in behalf of all classes of Dissenters, little or no assistance had been rendered by other Nonconformist societies. The Bill founded on Dr. Stoddart's suggestion, but narrowed in its application to Unitarian Dissenters, was twice keenly debated in the House of Lords. On the first occasion it passed the second reading by the narrow majority of 2, but on the second the Bill was lost by a majority of 39 votes. Each debate was adorned by a speech from Lord Holland in his finest style. The closeness of argument, the keenness of satire, the brilliancy of wit, the accurate and extensive knowledge of these noble addresses, are set off by a simplicity and vigour of style that remind us of his distinguished relative, Charles James Fox. Amongst the episcopal opponents of the Bill, the foremost was Dr. Law, the Bishop of Chester, who affected to question the reality of Unitarian scruples against the marriage service of the Church of England. Numerous as, in the course of his parliamentary life, were the rebukes which Lord Holland gave to members of the episcopal bench, not one was better deserved or more unanswerable than that given by him on this occasion to Bishop Law. Alluding to the strange contrast which his sentiments exhibited to those of his distinguished father (the liberal Bishop of Carlisle), Lord Holland said he should certainly wonder at his conduct if he looked less at *ex quo natus* than *quibuscum vixit*.*

In 1825, a new Bill was introduced by Mr. W. Smith into the House of Commons, the provisions of which secured a registration of Unitarian

---

* Very full reports of these two admirable speeches will be found in the Monthly Repository, Vol. XIX. pp. 249 and 309.

marriages independently of the clergy of the Established Church. This Bill passed through every stage in the Lower House without a division, but was lost in the Lords by a majority of 4. The Lord Chancellor, in this debate, laid down his favourite doctrine, that the Trinity Bill did not protect Unitarians from the operation of the common law.* Dr. Blomfield, then newly created Bishop of Chester, assisted the Lord Chancellor in destroying the Bill.

In 1827, when the matter was again introduced into Parliament, Mr. Canning, the Premier, and Lord Lyndhurst, the Chancellor, were both favourable to the relief of Unitarians from a Trinitarian form of marriage service. The Bill passed the Commons, and in the Lords forced itself (notwithstanding renewed opposition from Lord Eldon) into Committee by a majority of 7 votes—the numbers being, for going into Committee, 61; against, 54.

In Committee the opposition were sufficiently powerful to mutilate and disfigure the Bill, and to such a degree, that its promoters felt little anxiety to carry it forward, and it was never proposed for a third reading. It now became evident that without the active assistance of the Government, there was little probability of any measure, granting effectual relief, being passed. This conviction led to a series of anxious, and at first unproductive, conferences with the successive heads of the Administration.

Soon after his accession to office, the Duke of Wellington promised a favourable consideration to the claims of the Unitarian body; but so large a portion of the session was occupied with the debates on the Repeal of the Test and Corporation Acts, that it was not thought expedient to attempt, during the session of 1828, any alteration in the marriage law. In 1829, the Catholic Relief Bill occupied almost exclusive attention. Then followed a series of excited sessions consequent on the dissolution of the Tory Ministry and the struggles for reform in Parliament.

In 1834, the general subject of the grievances of Dissenters was extensively agitated throughout the country. In the "Case of the Pro-

---

* In consequence of this, a long and most ably argued petition was immediately drawn up (it is believed by Mr. Aspland), and presented to both Houses of Parliament, on the legal position of Unitarians, and praying that a full and efficient inquiry might take place into the law as affecting Unitarians, and that, if necessary, further protection might be given them. See Monthly Repository, XX. 382.

testant Dissenters" put forth by the United Committee, one of the grievances alleged was "compulsory conformity to the rites and ceremonies of the Established Church in the celebration of marriage." But, except as to the general statement of the grievance, the Dissenters were far from being united in sentiment. The Deputies passed a resolution, and forwarded it to the Government, demanding a recognition of the principle that marriage was simply a civil contract. When the United Committee, however, debated the subject, and saw the consequences of this principle, they declined to sanction the resolution of the Deputies.

If Dissenters were perplexed by the difficulties of the subject, not less so was Lord Grey's Government. On the meeting of Parliament, Lord John Russell intimated that the other demands of the Dissenters were under consideration, but that it was his purpose to introduce a Bill for the regulation of Dissenters' marriages. The Marriage Bill which redeemed this promise was designed for the benefit of all classes of Nonconformists, but was cumbrous and generally unsatisfactory to Dissenters. It left in the hands of the clergy the publication of banns, but threw upon Dissenting ministers the entire responsibility of registering the marriage. Dissenting ministers, previous to solemnizing marriages, were, according to the provisions of this Bill, to procure a licence; but the granting such licence was not made obligatory on the Bishop. It is scarcely necessary to say, that no denomination of Dissenters shewed any anxiety for the passing of a measure the beneficial designs of which might be obstructed in any diocese by a Bishop hostile to the religious liberty of Dissenters; and the session closed without relief from the grievance of Church marriages.

The session of 1835 found Sir Robert Peel the leader of the Administration in the Lower House of Parliament. He, too, proposed a Marriage Bill. It was, in fact, a revival of the Bill of 1827, as it left the Lords' Committee. That Bill was professedly for the relief of Unitarians alone—this was offered as a boon to all classes of Dissenters. It provided for the marriage of Dissenters (the fact of *both* parties being such to be previously declared on oath) by the civil magistrate, after fourteen days' notice. The magistrate was to give certificates of the contract, one of which he was to send to the clergyman of the parish, for entry in a parochial register. The magistrate was authorized to receive a fee from the contracting parties, five-sevenths of which he was to hand over to the parish clergyman. This measure was received with considerable favour in the House of Commons, but it found little or none out of doors.*

Sir Robert Peel's enforced resignation of office caused this Bill to share the fate of its numerous predecessors.

In 1836, the long-agitated question was brought to a successful termination by two Bills, introduced by the Government of Lord Melbourne, for securing a general registration of births, deaths and marriages, and for legalizing the marriages of Protestant Dissenters, either in their own licensed meeting-houses, or in the office of a superintendent registrar. These wise and important measures were passed with little difficulty, although some clauses were inserted by the Lords into the Marriage Bill, which made that measure less convenient and less acceptable to the Dissenters. The new Marriage Act was certainly a bold, though not a perfect measure. It retained the old principle of marriage being a civil contract, yet it facilitated the addition, by all who desired it, of a religious service, and thus removed from the body of Protestant Dissenters the stigma of slighting religion in the marriage contract. It greatly surpassed all preceding attempts at legislation, and not least in this, that it provided no compensation to the clergy for the fees of which it was the means of depriving them. In all the proceedings, from first to last, connected with this great reform, Mr. Aspland took a large share. What labour, what anxiety, what sickness of heart springing from hope deferred, they involved, is now known but to few. Firmness, patience and courageous perseverance were qualities absolutely necessary in those who sought reforms, whether civil or ecclesiastical, during the first thirty years of this century. But Mr. Aspland and his fellow-labourers had the wisdom to perceive, that, though often defeated, their cause was gaining ground; that repeated discussion was lowering the pretensions of ecclesiastical domination, and instructing the mind, both of Parliament and the public, in the principles of religious liberty. To the Unitarians these discussions proved eminently serviceable, and there can be little doubt that they laid the foundation, in the mind of Sir

---

* Immediately after its proposal by Sir Robert Peel, Mr. Aspland expressed his opinion of it, in a letter to his son, thus:—"Were it to pass in its present shape, it would fix the brand of a *caste* upon the Dissenters, and would divide them into two new sects, the church-married and the justice-married. What do you think of our genteel lasses going up to Worship Street or Bow Street, and being sworn before his worship, in the presence of a crowd of disorderlies, as to their taking a certain gentleman for a husband, after a fortnight's publicity, according to the meeting-house fashion!"

Robert Peel and other statesmen, of those just and liberal sentiments which led to the passing of the Dissenters' Chapels Bill. If the Unitarians* bore the heat and burthen of this struggle, the immediate fruits of which were shared by many who entered the field only at the eleventh hour, the former afterwards were benefited, independently and in spite of the opposition of the eleventh-hour men.

The highest praise in the conduct of the Marriage Bill is unquestionably due to the late Mr. Edgar Taylor, whose legal knowledge and acuteness, whose great personal influence and untiring zeal, contributed greatly to the success of the efforts of the Unitarian Association. Previous mention has been made of the services in the same cause of Mr. Christopher Richmond.

Mr. Aspland, as Secretary of the British and Foreign Unitarian Association, issued a circular Address of advice to the Unitarian Ministers of England and Wales, on the requirements of the Marriage and Registration Acts, and subsequently submitted to the Presbyterian ministers of London a Form of Service for contracting marriage, which was approved by that body, and has since been in general use amongst the Unitarians. Its peculiar merit is, that it retains the best portions of the marriage service in the Book of Common Prayer, the solemn beauty of which has impressed the minds of many successive generations, and that its additions to that service are solemn, dignified and tender.

It is now proper to record the circumstances preceding and attending the dissolution of the Three Denominations, which had from the time of the Revolution of 1688 acted together with tolerable, if not unbroken unanimity. Already in this Memoir there have been intimations of outbreaks of angry bigotry against Unitarians, when acting as members and for the benefit of the general body of Dissenters. These outbreaks were at first confined chiefly to the illiterate and fanatical members of the Independent and Baptist denominations, but more particularly of the former. In private intercourse with their Presbyterian brethren, these attacks were disowned and censured by many of the leading "orthodox" ministers. The Wolverhampton and the Hewley suits, having for their object to dispossess Trustees on the ground of their Unitarianism, increased the feelings of distrust on the part of the English Presbyterians of the fair dealing of their orthodox coadjutors, and inflamed the doctrinal antipathy of the other two denominations

---

* Including in this term the Freethinking Christians and the General Baptists.

against the Unitarians. The institutions conducted jointly by the Three Denominations became agitated by the symptoms of an approaching struggle. In the Widows' Fund, as early as 1830, the rise of bigotry was seen in a proposal to remove the annual sermon from the chapel in Jewin Street. In the affairs of the Orphan Working School, orthodox bigotry enjoyed a full triumph. That excellent institution had from the first been supported by the joint contributions of the Three Denominations. A religious service, for the benefit of the children, had been conducted from 1760 to 1834, in the chapel of the institution, amicably and usefully, by the ministers of the Three Denominations. It was now, however, resolved to exclude from this religious service the Unitarian members of the body. To effect this, it was at first proposed to dismantle the chapel, in order to enlarge the establishment, and convert it into a dormitory. But eventually the measure was carried, against the votes and protest of a third of the Governors, upon the avowed plea that there could be no union with, no toleration of, services which the "majority regarded as destructive to salvation."*

But the crowning act of exclusion was one effected by the Body of Ministers. For seven years Dr. Thomas Rees had filled the office of Secretary to the United Body, and had discharged the duties of his office with such propriety and ability as to receive again and again the thanks of the body. He was now set aside; and there was no attempt made to conceal the fact that this was done solely on religious grounds, and that the "orthodox" majority did not choose to be represented by a Secretary whose doctrinal views were not consonant with their own.

This proceeding was regarded as a violation of the principle of equal religious liberty on which the union of the Three Denominations had been originally based. The engagement and understanding on the formation of the union was, that the bodies should not call in question, or interfere with, each other's religious opinions and doctrines. To have passed over the conduct of the majority in this case, would have been to invite further insult, and eventually the proscription of the Unitarian members of the body. Further union with men who had thus betrayed the first principles of religious liberty was, if practicable, highly inexpedient. The Presbyterian Ministers of London and its vicinity

---

* At the meeting at which the decision was come to, Mr. Aspland expressed his deep regret at the division that prevailed in the charity, which he pronounced to be "discreditable to them as Christians, and most hurtful to them as Protestant Dissenters."

met on March 4, 1836, at Dr. Williams's Library, to consider the course which it behoved them to adopt. A strong feeling pervaded the body that the crisis demanded prompt and decisive measures, for the assertion of its independence and the preservation of its rights and privileges. It was resolved by the votes of a very large majority to dissolve the union, so far as they, the Presbyterians, were concerned, and to claim for themselves the independent exercise of the privileges which hitherto they had enjoyed as a portion of the general body. The resolutions passed at this meeting, after recapitulating the terms of the original union, and the various acts by which those terms had been violated, proceeded to state—

"That, contemplating these proceedings and various indications of the disposition of the majority of the members of the United Body of Ministers, we cannot entertain a doubt that it is the wish and purpose of such majority eventually to exclude the Presbyterian body from the union, or to make its relative position such as no religious body, alive to its own dignity, could consent to occupy.

"That, therefore, we feel it to be an imperative though painful duty,—imposed upon us equally by regard to our own character as Protestant Dissenting Ministers, who hold it to be one of the inalienable rights of conscience, that no man shall, without his own consent, be answerable to another for his honest judgment upon the sense of the Holy Scriptures, by respect for the memory of those that went before us and laid the foundation of our freedom, and by regard to the welfare of those that shall come after us,—to withdraw as a body from an union, the compact of which has been violated, and in which we can see no prospect of equal and peaceful co-operation, or of real and effective service to the interests of religious liberty."

This important document,* which was prepared and moved by Mr. Aspland, concluded by disavowing all angry and hostile feelings, and by tendering to the other two denominations sincere wishes for their usefulness in the cause of freedom, truth and virtue.

On the following day, the Presbyterian Deputies met and passed resolutions of a similar character. Dr. Rees, Mr. Aspland and Mr. Madge, waited immediately on Lord Melbourne and Lord John Russell, to state and explain the withdrawment of the English Presbyterians from the two other bodies of Protestant Dissenting Ministers.

In addition to the causes of division now stated, considerable political disagreement developed itself amongst the English Dissenters soon

---

* See the Christian Reformer, N. S. (1836), pp. 276, 277.

after the meeting of the Reformed Parliament. In enumerating the grievances from which they asked and expected a Liberal Administration to free them, the English Presbyterians, and with them many of the other denominations, confined themselves to practical points—such as Church-rates, compulsory Church Marriages, &c.; whilst others included in their statement the existence of a State Church, and asked for the expulsion of the Bishops from the House of Lords, and the severance of the Church from the State. The course of the latter party was equally embarrassing to Dissenters and to their friends in the Administration. It was beheld by Mr. Aspland and many others in the Unitarian body with deep regret. He saw at once with what a powerful weapon these impracticable politicians were arming the clergy, and that the influence and power of the Church would be greatly and most undesirably increased by this insane attack upon its very existence. Upon all these topics the extracts that follow, from his Diary and letters, will shew what were Mr. Aspland's opinions and feelings.

"Feb. 4, 1833.—There is a stir upon the Marriage question. The Independents are striving to be considered by Ministers as *the Dissenters*, and have had separate conferences, the result of which they will not disclose. We shall have to explain to Government their insidious measures, which are not approved by the best of their own body. The subject is before the general body at Redcross Street. Some are for a dash—others of us are for consulting the interests and wishes of the Reform Government."

"March 12.—To town, to a meeting of the body at the Library, to choose twelve delegates to United Committee. Independents trickish. I left early, on account of an engagement. Afterwards, the young members carried vote by ballot. I had every Presbyterian vote; but Dr. Winter,* the Chairman, was thrown overboard by his own brethren!"

"May 25.—With a deputation of United Committee of Dissenters to Earl Grey, at Downing Street, consisting of Mr. Waymouth, W. Smith, Dr. J. B.

---

* Dr. Winter, the grandson of the celebrated Thomas Bradbury, died August 9, 1833. Mr. Aspland entertained great respect for Dr. Winter, whom he described, in an obituary notice, as "a truly upright, honourable and amiable man," and as "exempt from bigotry and sectarian zeal and extravagance." Alluding to the incident noted above, Mr. Aspland assigned as the cause of the strange slight put upon this venerable minister, to "his being an advocate of the union, and the real and friendly union, of the *Three* Denominations. But if his liberality, untainted by insincerity, were not accordant with the sentiments and purposes of many of his own denomination, it was properly appreciated, and is respectfully and gratefully remembered, by others whose good opinion he was accustomed to consider a testimony to his having manifested 'the spirit of Christianity.'"

Brown, T. Wilson, Dr. Newman, &c. We were courteously received, and obtained general promises with regard to parochial assessments on places of worship, the marriage law, &c. We were with Earl Grey, who was alone, three quarters of an hour."

"May 26, Whit-Sunday.—In the evening, I preached at Little Portland Street. Mr. Tagart, the minister, had preached in the morning, and now read prayers. My sermon from Philipp. iii. 3. Very large and attentive congregation. A good company of divines present, also Rammohun Roy and Mr. Agar, the patron of the chapel. The building spacious, commodious and elegant."

"May 28.—My good old friend John Marsom died, in his 88th year. The funeral at Worship Street, June 3. I met the corpse there and officiated. Address and prayer extempore. Fifty or sixty persons present."

"June 13.—Mr. Edgar Taylor and I visited Lord Holland this morning, at Great Burlington Street, where we had an hour of his delightful conversation. Topics, the Unitarian Marriage Bill, with other Dissenting topics—also the Ministers, the Tories, the Bishops, &c."

Rev. Robert Aspland to Rev. R. Brook Aspland.

"Hackney, Feb. 19, 1834.

" * * * Sydney will have told you of our successful meeting yesterday.* I shall propose on Friday, when we have the first committee meeting, to set on foot a periodical, called the English Presbyterian Reporter, to contain letters from the journals, &c., in defence of our body.

"We are all in merry confusion, having got up a party and provided coaches, &c., to go to the *Oratorio* to-night, and being this afternoon informed that the pious Bishop of London has forbidden the profane performance.

"With Mr. Edgar Taylor, I saw Lord Holland confidentially the other day. We had a pleasant morning chat with him. He says Lord Grey and the Cabinet are not a little displeased at the conduct of the violent party amongst us. But for Lord H.'s representations with regard to some of us, the Cabinet would have thrown us off and left us to shift for ourselves. Lord H. has requested a note from me, explaining the views and designs of the *Moderates*, to be shewn to his Cabinet brethren."

"March 4, 1834.

" * * * On Saturday I wrote confidentially to Lord HOLLAND, on the subject of Dissenters' views and expectations. A pretty long letter from him, received this morning, is highly satisfactory. He says my letter arrived quite opportunely. He shewed it to Lord Grey, 'who was much pleased with it:' 'it has done good, and softened many angry impressions.' I expressed my dissatisfaction with the proposed Marriage Bill, and hinted that *the hand of*

---

* To establish the English Presbyterian Association.

the Church was in it: his Lordship expresses himself 'a little disappointed that the Bill is not entirely approved of' by me, and declares that the Church has no hand in it—any amendment of reasonable Dissenters is welcomed. But he fears 'the finger of the Church will be more busy (in the House of Lords) in spoiling this, or any other Bill of the sort, than it has been in framing it.' He almost says the Bishops are *sulky*.

"While I assured Lord Holland the Cabinet might rely upon the mass of the Dissenters, I ventured to *advise* that Ministers should make some *demonstration* of an intention to relieve Dissenters in other matters besides marriage. He says he is 'very glad' I mentioned *Church-rates*, and *assures* me that Government will make more than a 'demonstration' on this point, and will, in fact, do what 'will prove satisfactory to every reasonable Dissenter.' He is 'pretty confident' that in due time our wishes, with regard to the Universities, will be accomplished. Of the '*Reformer*' which I sent him he says, 'Many thanks for your periodical work. I have read many articles in it with great pleasure.'

"I see by the papers that Lord Grey took my advice,* and made a *demonstration* in our favour last night. What *he said* (explained by Lord H.'s letter, without its being referred to) may be made use of as you please.

"You should have good care that your *Dissenters'* meeting is a respectable one, and called with rational as well as honest views, before you commit yourself to it.

"Lord Holland recommended to me, as I do to you, 'Second Travels of an Irish Gentleman in Search,' &c., 2 vols. The writer outdoes Tom Moore in humour, and floors him in argument. He has been said to be Archbishop *Whately*. Lord H. says No. Whoever he be, he is of the Whately or liberal school; one of us, in fact, with some *Paley* expedients for climbing over Church-of-England difficulties."

"March 17, 1834.

"I was summoned to the *United Committee* (but read *dis*-united) to-day, and refused to attend. Hypocrisy written on certain faces warns me away from the sight. The state of the Dissenters is deplorable. No common understanding, no confidence, disowned almost by the Government. * * In such a condition, men that value sterling principle, and entertain a sense of honour, have no other course than to keep aloof. Meantime, we have contrived, by our violence and folly, to force into union the hostile parties within the Church, and to strengthen the Conservative party; though I think we have done another thing, and that is, to shew the sane portion of the old Church of England that the Unitarians, the descendants from, or connections of, the old English Presbyterians, are not, as their red-hot divines taught them, the rancorous enemies of the Establishment.

---

* "This, on reading it, sounds big, but I am content to let the expression stand.

"Poor Sir Jas. Mackintosh's book on the 'Revolution' is out (4to, 3 guineas). He has fallen into sad hands. An introductory Memoir, made up from his own writings, seems designed to lower him in *moral* rank. This comes of his *mortgaging* his talents and posthumous fame to the London booksellers!"

" May 26.—Introduced Dr. Tuckerman and Hon. Mr. Phillips to Lord Holland, at Holland House. Our interview lasted an hour and a half. Lord H. in better health than usual, and cheerful, notwithstanding the distractions in the Cabinet.

" July 9.—Lord Grey's Ministry expired, after three years and a half's duration! But only Lord Grey and Lord Althorp have yet (the 10th) sent in their resignations. An anxious political week.

" — 15.—Lord Melbourne Premier. Lord Althorp to be brought back. Attended Aged Ministers' Society at King's Head. The ministers present, on the suggestion of Dr. J. P. Smith, signed a requisition for a general meeting of the Body, to express *gratitude*, &c., to Lord Grey, on resigning office. Signers, Dr. Smith, Dr. Humphrys, Dr. Collyer, Dr. Newman, Messrs. Russell, Yockney and R. A.

" Aug. 18.—Dr. J. P. Smith called, to read to me his proposed resolution in the Body to-morrow, in honour of Earl Grey.

" — 19.—Meeting of Body to-day at Library, to consider of complimentary resolution to Lord Grey. I exceedingly regretted that, through indisposition, I could not be present. *The motion was opposed, and withdrawn.*

Rev. Robert Aspland to Rev. John Kenrick.

"Hackney, March 20, 1835.

" My dear Sir,—Permit me to thank you most cordially for your communication of last month. You will have seen that I ventured to give it a *heading*, as for a new *department* in the work. This I did, relying partly upon your kind offer of continental intelligence. I almost envy you the faculty of being at home amidst the German literati. If you have any thing for me this month, it will be in time by the 25th; and may I request that you will address me here, and always leave the postman and me to settle the account.

" Are you not amused with the simplicity of the reformed and reforming House, in hailing with such applause Sir Robert's Dissenting Marriage Bill? It is an artful though clumsy measure. The Dissenters cannot accept it, and the great Unpaid would not work it if they did; but the end is answered by our having liberty of conscience offered us, at the price of civil degradation, and by the Premier's having to boast, notwithstanding our perverseness, that he has redeemed one of his pledges!

" You will see in next No. of C. R. a full report, from short-hand writer's notes, of the Vice-Chancellor's Judgment,—a wretched though mischievous effusion of intolerance. It makes Unitarians outlaws, and strips us of all our public property, and incapacitates us for every religious trust. This, of course, is not to be borne. We shall appeal; but we want a general fund for the protection of the whole body, and the Presbyterian Association is about to make an effort to raise one, so as to be able to meet every case of legal persecution promptly, boldly, and with the most effective instruments. I trust we shall have the sympathies and the assistance of our body throughout the kingdom.

"It seems that the Judge's bench is to be turned into a pulpit. Every day gives us some new forensic sermon. The Judgment in the Methodist cause is ludicrous. I see to-day symptoms of the Chancellor's correcting the Vice's orthodox propensities. This latter has now before him the case of a worthy man whom I know, Michael Jones, of Llanuchllyn, who, though a good Independent, is ejected by an Antinomian gang because he is moderately Calvinistic, and holds the *passive-power* scheme of the late Dr. Williams, of Rotherham. He, poor fellow! will, I expect, be decreed to be wanting in Vice-Chancery soundness of theological faith. How long will this official foolery be suffered to harass and plunder the liberal Dissenters, *of all creeds?*

"But I am trespassing upon time which you devote to higher authorities and better things than the Vice-Chancellor and his Greek-law, and hasten to subscribe myself,

"Your much obliged and obedient friend and servant,

ROBERT ASPLAND."

"March 26.—At Waredraper's nursery grounds, for shrubs and plants for the G. P. ground. A stranger pointed me out as 'the man that says there is no Christ.' *I reprimanded him for being out without a keeper.*"

"April 8.—Peel and Wellington Ministry out. At the Orphan Working School dinner, sate between Mr. Baines, M. P., and Mr. Clay, our Member for the Tower Hamlets. Both had come down from the House, where Sir Robert Peel had just announced his resignation. Lord Brougham was in the chair. He spoke much and long, but feebly. He bewailed being a *Lord*, and losing, under the call of public duty, his real power. He recognized me and offered his hand."

"April 11.—Dr. Rees wrote me word that he had received notice of intention to oppose his re-election as Secretary of the General Body of Ministers, at the annual meeting at the Library on Tuesday next, on account of opinions, and to put up Mr. Geo. Clayton in his place. I wrote on the subject to the following ministers—Messrs. Geary, Means, Squier, Yates, Dr. Barclay, Wood, Hunter, Madge, Tagart, Kenrick, Davison, Dr. Newman, T. Russell, J. Coates, J. Clayton, Dr. J. P. Smith, Le Breton and Cogan."

"April 14.—Annual meeting of body at Library. Attempt of intolerants to exclude Dr. Rees from the office of Secretary. Mr. Barrett in the chair. I spoke freely. Discussion adjourned."

"April 28.—At adjourned meeting of body, the intolerants voted Dr. Rees *out* of Secretaryship, and George Clayton *in*, by a great majority. Not above half a dozen Independents and Baptists stood by us. Hints were thrown out of something further."

Rev. Robert Aspland to Rev R. Brook Aspland.

"Hackney, May 6, 1835.

"Dear Brook,—We are making a great effort in the Presbyterian Association to raise a fund to enable us to meet the enemy in the gate. We have issued a circular appeal to the country, and are forming ourselves into parties for canvassing our richer friends throughout the kingdom.* Mr. G. W. Wood has undertaken Lancashire; Mr. Mardon and I may scour Kent; and Richard Taylor and I propose to run down to Chichester, Portsmouth and Isle of Wight. I shall be disappointed if we do not get £2000 or £3000.

"The Association is, I assure you, not inactive. We are carrying the Wolverhampton case, by appeal, to the House of Lords; and we have taken a bold step (but tell only Dr. Carpenter and Mr. Palmer, and enjoin secrecy upon them for the present) with regard to the Lady Hewley case. Agreeably to the hint thrown out in last number of the C. R., we have procured from some of the beneficiaries of the charity a *remonstrance* to the Lords Commissioners of the Great Seal, and we ourselves as a society have sent resolutions to the *Attorney-General*, pointing out the illegality of the course agreed to be pursued relative to the ex-Chancellor's judgment. We shall not, I hope, be sent to Newgate.

"The orthodox here wax worse and worse. The Body of Ministers have refused to re-elect Dr. Rees to their Secretaryship, avowing openly their opinion of his unfitness, on account of his religious creed, and have chosen Geo. Clayton, who, much to my surprise and to the chagrin of his brother John, my neighbour and acquaintance, has suffered himself to be used as a tool by the bigots. These sons of liberty have thrown out pretty plain hints that they mean to purge the body, and to throw us off as so much peccant matter. We shall have, I take it, to expose their machinations, and to appeal from them to the Government and the people."

"May 12, 1835.— * * * The Unitarian Association have, at my instance, determined on a new plan at the annual meeting. After the Sermon, the Committee's Report is to be read to the congregation, and four gentlemen are to be requested to address the audience on topics of their own selection connected with the meeting,—the whole to be considered as part of the *service*, and to be concluded devotionally. Afterwards, the subscribers are to

---

* In furtherance of this object, Mr. Aspland during this summer visited Bristol, Bath, Bridgewater, Exeter, Plymouth, Crediton, Moreton Hampstead, Collumpton, Taunton, Gloucester, preaching at most of these places, and inviting contributions to the fund for the defence of English Presbyterian rights. Other members of Mr. Aspland's family visited, for the same object, many of the congregations in the Eastern and Northern and North-Western counties.

form their meeting for business. The four gentlemen are Dr. Carpenter, Mr. G. W. Wood, Mr. Abraham Clarke and myself. Mr. Yates retires from the Secretaryship, and I am reluctantly drawn to consent to take the office."

"Aug. 1.—A *prophet* called to deliver a message *from above;* but I told him I could not receive it, and shewed him the door. He gave his name ———; a tradesman-looking man of 55."

"Sept. 18.— * * * There is to be a celebration of the Tricentenary of the English Bible on the first Sunday in October. This may be a good opportunity for preaching upon the *principle,* as opposed to what are called the *principles* of the Reformation; upon the evil as well as the good of the event; upon the incompleteness of the reform, and of the inconsistency of those who with the same breath cry up the Reformation and vilify sincere Reformers."

"March 15, 1836.

"The great matter now is our Presbyterian secession. I penned the Ministers' resolutions, Edgar Taylor the Deputies'. We have been nearly unanimous, i. e. we liberals. Three Scottish Secession men, brimful of orthodoxy—Broadfoot, Young and Redpath—*protest* and assert themselves to be the *Presbyterian Body of Ministers*. The claim is allowed, of course, by the Independents and Baptists, in order to keep together *Three Denominations,* for the sake of the privilege of access to the Throne. But we *ex*pose and *op*pose this, I hope to the satisfaction of his Majesty's Government. You saw, no doubt, the *news* of our deputation to Lord Melbourne. We were received most courteously, and I believe we made the right impression. Lord John Russell was with us part of the time. To him I addressed some strong remarks on the *political* conduct of our opponents. We are to see Lord Holland to-morrow; and the result will be, I doubt not, that the Government will not acknowledge any *Presbyterian* body but ourselves, and will receive the several bodies separately and with equal privileges.

"The orthodox are surprised and astounded. They never dreamt of our striking so sudden and decisive a blow. They flattered themselves with the success of various schemes for extinguishing us gradually. Their present hope of setting up the Scotchmen in our place must be far from agreeable to them, except as a piece of resentment, for these are the folk that will every where trip up the heels of the Independents, if they succeed in courts of law against the English Presbyterians.

"We are expecting Lord Cottenham's judgment on the Wolverhampton case, and some of us do not despair. In the worst event, we shall go to the Lords, as we shall probably with the Hewley suit."

The letter which follows was addressed to an eminent Independent minister, with whom Mr. Aspland had been in the habit of acting in a variety of public trusts, and for whom he entertained, to the close of life, respect and affection. Of the painful and discreditable proceedings connected with the Orphan School, to which the letter refers with well-deserved indignation, a report will be found in the Christian Reformer (N. S.), Vol. III. p. 203.

Rev. Robert Aspland to ⸺⸺.

"Mare Street, April 9, 1836.

"My dear Sir,—It was not till this morning, after a long search, that I found your letter, which I send to you, that you may copy it, or use it otherwise, at your discretion. I must, however, request its being returned, at your convenience, as it is my justification for a statement repeatedly made by me, that some of the most liberal and important members of the Congregational denomination could no longer, as heretofore, satisfy themselves in the union of the Three Denominations.

"I did not answer the letter, my dear Sir, because I felt that I should have imposed upon you a long discussion, and that any answer must have been, in fact, an assertion and defence of the first principle of Protestantism, not to say of Protestant Dissent. You do not see it, but the invariable argument, nay, the very 'term,' of the 'orthodox,' is an assumption of *infallibility*. Our neighbour *H*⸺ takes up the admitted principle when he denounces you as a 'blind guide.'

"But if I do not take care I shall commit the error of plunging into controversy, which I mean to avoid. I have to thank you for a kind note relating to the Orphan Working School. This is a painful subject. The conduct of some of your leading men in this affair has given us *Presbyterians* (for such, allow me to say, we are, and such we purpose to be) a stronger feeling of disgust than I ever remember to have seen produced by any wantonness of any majority. Often have we exclaimed, 'Would that we had to do with men of the world, actuated by *a sense of honour*, rather than with men who, laying claim to a divinely-inspired personal holiness, violate the first principles of honesty, avow the violation, and laugh in the faces of the injured, esteeming their complaining a mark of their *simplicity*.' At the last court, we were less shocked at Mr. B⸺'s appearing to give the signal to the mob below, and at Mr. T⸺'s joining in, if not leading, the *hissings* against us, than with Dr. B⸺'s grave insult, that because we professed unbounded liberality, we ought to allow the Calvinistic party to drive us out of the temple. Nay, for one, I was not more disgusted when, at a former court, Mr. W⸺, high in the Evangelical ranks, cried out, while I was urging the iniquity of receiving our subscriptions and depriving us of the rights legally appertaining to them—'We like Socinian money!' an exclamation received by the patron of Evangelical Dissent, sitting by him, with a laugh, which in its manner indicated what I will not put down on paper, with regard to both the person and what he considered his cause.

"I envy not the majority their triumph; much rather would I be wronged than bear about the consciousness of wilful injury. Nay, we have—I speak from experience—some reason to rejoice in our maltreatment. It has drawn the ties of union closer amongst our people, and increased their attachment to a system of divine truth which includes, as essential to it, moral justice and social charity.

"If the Independents mean that we should regard them as *practically* Christian men, they will yet devise some scheme by which we may separate from them without suffering the 'spoiling of our goods.'

"I write in *confidence*, and therefore very freely; and here, as between us, let the matter drop.

"We are to meet, I learn, on Wednesday, in consequence of the removal of our poor friend Coates; and on that and all other occasions I hope to be regarded, my dear Sir, as

"Yours, with high esteem,
ROBERT ASPLAND."

Rev. Robert Aspland to Rev. R. Brook Aspland.

"July 22, 1836.

"We (Edgar Taylor and myself) were with Lord Plunkett on Tuesday, by appointment, on our Presbyterian question. He received us frankly, affably, and even cordially, and went freely with us into legal and more general points. His judgment as well as sympathy is wholly with us. He evidently *wonders* at *Shadwell* and *Copley* law. We are working with a quarto pamphlet, entitled, 'Memorial and Statement.' A copy will be sent to each member of the Cabinet, the law officers, &c. I will take care that a copy finds its way to Bristol, with the understanding that it falls into none but *clean hands*.

"I am just out of an affliction, sitting for another portrait. If the three now in the family go down to another generation, I shall be regarded, I think, as 'three persons under one name.'"

The accession of Queen Victoria, in 1837, led to the preparation of loyal Addresses by various public bodies, and amongst the rest, by the Presbyterian Ministers of London. There was considerable speculation, and some anxiety, as to the mode in which the Address would be received by the Sovereign. In itself, it was of little consequence whether an Address from certain of her Presbyterian subjects was received by the Queen on the Throne or in the Closet; but the decision on this point became important when viewed as the test of the civil equality, or otherwise, of the Presbyterians with the other two denominations. The correspondence which follows will shew that the efforts made to save the independence and uphold the dignity of the Presbyterian body were crowned with perfect success.

Rev. R. Aspland to the Right Honourable Lord Holland.

"Hackney, July 7, 1837.

"My Lord,—Permit me to put into your hands a copy of an Address to her Majesty upon her happy accession, agreed upon by the Body of *Presbyterian Ministers*.

" It will now be for her Majesty's Government to decide in what manner the Presbyterian body, in its separate capacity, shall be received at Court. We cannot believe that a Liberal Administration will acknowledge another body (if body it may be called), consisting only of two or three *Scottish* Ministers, to be the Body of *English* Presbyterian Ministers in and near London. We were *driven* out from the other bodies by bigotry; we now stand upon our independence; and we hope and trust we shall not lose any civil privilege by our retiring in our corporate capacity to save ourselves from persecution and insult. We ask no more than to be received at Court in the same manner as the other two denominations, and I am persuaded your Lordship will concede that we ought not to ask less.—I am, my Lord, your much obliged and very obedient servant,

ROBERT ASPLAND."

Right Hon. Lord Holland to Rev. Robert Aspland.

" July 8.

" Dear Sir,—Many thanks for the copy of your excellent Address. With respect to the manner of presenting it, I am not at present authorized to give you any positive answer, not having hitherto spoken on the subject to Lord Melbourne, Lord John Russell, or any of my colleagues; and if there is any question of form and etiquette affecting it, it would perhaps be improper as well as premature in me to give any individual, much more official, opinion on the subject.

"As to my private wishes on the subject, I think you are not likely to mistake them; but one cannot disguise from oneself that if the privilege granted to a joint body is extended to any in their separate capacity, it will be natural for other bodies, especially those who are composed of very large numbers, to apply to be admitted to a similar privilege; and that objection urged to such admission which rests on *special* grounds, will be ungracious and invidious. However, it will be for us to consider whether that be really any great inconvenience, or, if it be, whether there is no method of obviating or avoiding it, without refusing the Body of Presbyterian Ministers in and near London the access to the Throne which they have hitherto enjoyed.

" If you have any thing to suggest on the subject, I will thank you to furnish me with it in confidence and in good time; as whenever or wherever it is discussed, I should like to be ready with every example and every argument that is likely to obviate any scruples or difficulties that may be felt to the reception on the Throne of one separate and distinct sect.—Yours,

VASSALL HOLLAND."

In reply, Mr. Aspland furnished Lord Holland with a statement, of which the following are the most important parts:

"The Presbyterian Body of Ministers separated itself from the Independents and Baptists, in consequence of repeated and offensive violations of the principle of the union (i. e. non-interference with regard to religious opinions), and of the known determination of the leaders of the majority to introduce laws by which its independence, and even existence, would have been ultimately, though gradually, destroyed.

"The separation was unanimous in the Presbyterian body, with the exception of three Scottish ministers (of whom one is since dead); so that the Presbyterian body is entire, and (it is humbly suggested) entitled to the same rights and privileges as it enjoyed in conjunction with the Two other bodies.

"The attempt of the Two other bodies to pass themselves off as the *Three* Denominations, on account of their having two Scottish Presbyterians amongst them, would be ridiculous, if it were not fraudful and injurious with regard to the Presbyterian body, and an imposition upon the public.

"On other occasions, the Independents especially have denied that these Scottish ministers can be fairly denominated *English* Presbyterians. When, lately, these Scottish ministers came down upon the *Hewley spoil*, taken from the Unitarians by the Independents, Mr. Thomas Wilson, the relator in the suit for the Independents and their acknowledged patron, made *affidavit* that the aforesaid ministers were never regarded or termed *English* Presbyterians; and further, that the Unitarians are the only *body* of English Presbyterians existing. In conformity with this, a rich Protestant Dissenting charity, called the 'Widows' Fund,' founded by and for the Three Denominations, has been again and again declared, by votes of the governors and subscribers, not applicable to the widows of Scottish ministers located in England, on the express ground of such ministers not being, in any honest sense of the denomination, *English* Presbyterians.

"Before the union of the Three Denominations, each denomination had separately the privilege of addressing the Sovereign, and of receiving an answer; though in what precise form (i. e. whether upon the Throne, or in the Closet) does not appear. By retiring from the union, the Presbyterian body conceives itself to be in precisely the same position, relatively to the Government, as it was before the union was formed.

"On the accession of his late lamented Majesty, the Quakers were, for the first time, received upon the Throne; and the Quakers are about the same in numbers, and in the proportion of their body in London to those in the country, as the English Presbyterians.

"The Presbyterian Ministers in and about London, though comparatively few, are virtually the representatives of the English Presbyterians at large, comprising many numerous and wealthy congregations, whose members are in various important towns the active strength of the Liberal party, and the leading supporters of her Majesty's present Government: four-fifths of the Protestant Dissenting Members of Parliament are from this body.

"The Presbyterian body does not expect her Majesty's Ministers to adjudicate between it and the Two other denominations; but it relies upon the justice and impartiality of the Government to place it upon an equality with those denominations, as far as regards reception at Court."

Dr. Rees, as Secretary of the Presbyterian Body, had in the mean time applied to Lord John Russell, the Home Secretary, and stated the grounds on which they asked access to the Throne and the Closet in their separate capacity. He stated, and proved to the satisfaction of the Home Secretary, that the Presbyterians had presented Addresses and been received on the Throne before their union with the other denominations. The production of two or three Addresses, and the replies to them, presented in this manner in the reigns of Charles II. and James II., settled the question, equally to the satisfaction of the Government and the Presbyterian Body.

Right Hon. Lord Holland to Rev. Robert Aspland.

"July 14.

"My dear Sir,—I believe it is decided that your Address will be received on the Throne. I am very glad of this.—Believe me ever truly yours,

VASSALL HOLLAND."

On the 21st of July, the Presbyterian Ministers of London and its vicinity were received by Queen Victoria, surrounded by her splendid Court, her venerable uncle, the Duke of Sussex, standing to the right of the Throne. The Address was read by Mr. Aspland. One passage of it appeared particularly to move the Queen—that in which reference was made to the Duke of Kent, "whose virtues endeared him to the British people, and to no portion of them more than the Protestant Dissenters," and also to the Duchess of Kent, by whose enlightened counsels, and moral and religious instruction, the Queen's early years had been nurtured.

On the same day the Presbyterian Ministers presented, at Buckingham Palace, an Address to the Duchess of Kent. Mr. Aspland was again the speaker. The Address alluded to the virtues and the premature death of the Duke of Kent, and to the faithful discharge by the Duchess of the momentous trust which had devolved on her, in the education of her illustrious Daughter.

The reply of the Duchess was singularly beautiful, and bespoke the feelings of a happy Mother.*

On the following day, Mr. Aspland, Dr. Rees, Mr. Tagart and Mr. Barrett, as a deputation from the Presbyterian Ministers, waited on the Queen Dowager at Bushy Park, with an Address of condolence. Queen Adelaide was deeply affected, both in receiving and replying to the Address. The presentation of this Address was probably the more welcome, from the omission of a similar mark of respect and sympathy on the part of the other Two denominations.

In respect to the painful struggle which this chapter of the Memoir has described, it only remains to add, that the reader must not suppose that his energy and abundant labours at this period indicate Mr. Aspland's possession of health and strength. During a large portion of this time, sickness and languor were his portion; and in the intervals of his public appearances, his family often beheld him prostrate in strength, and struggling painfully but resolutely with the distressing symptoms of organic disease.

---

* The Addresses and Replies will be found in the Christian Reformer (N. S.), IV. 562—566. The former have been much admired for the judicious selection of topics and simple but dignified style. They were drawn up by Mr. Aspland.

CHAPTER XXXI.

It is necessary to carry the Memoir back to the year 1834. The *Monthly Repository*, now chiefly devoted to politics, literature and the fine arts, had ceased to possess the confidence of the Unitarian body, and was no longer regarded as a suitable channel for the expression of their religious views. To afford the Unitarian denomination the ampler means of communicating with each other on their common cause, Mr. Aspland enlarged the *Christian Reformer* from the *duodecimo* to the *octavo* size. The New Series began in 1834, and terminated at the close of its eleventh year. Its early volumes are perhaps as valuable as any of the long series issued by its Editor. Its success, considerable at first, soon diminished, chiefly in consequence of the establishment of other Unitarian periodical works. When the competition demanded increased exertion to sustain the *Christian Reformer*, the Editor was so enfeebled by sickness as to be able to do little beyond correcting the proofs.

Rev. Robert Aspland to Rev. Robert Wallace.

"Hackney, Jan. 24, 1834.

"My dear Sir,—I duly received your two letters, and thank you heartily for them. They will both do honour to the Christian Reformer. The 'Inquiry into the Distinction of Sects'* is a novel topic, and has a direct bearing upon our faith as Unitarians. 'Pamphilus' † I had read with much pleasure in the 'Globe,' though I knew not to whom we were indebted for so much sound criticism and just remonstrance. I quite agree with you in your estimate of the Improved Version, and have always thought that, however well intended, it has done us great harm, and put our cause back perhaps a quarter of a century. * * Although, after what you have said, I must not be urgent with you for help in the Review department, there is one book, a thin octavo

---

* See the very interesting series of papers on the Distinction of Sects in the Apostolic Age, C. R., N. S., I. 94, 208, 284, 371, 455, 531.

† "Critical Remarks on the Improved Version," I. 185.

volume, with which I am disposed to tempt you, viz., 'The Arians of the Fourth Century; by J. H. Newman, M. A., Fellow of Oriel College.' It is a curiosity. There is some ingenuity and some learning, but quite enough paradox and high-church presumption, and even *papism*, to keep a reviewer alive. A few remarks upon it would be an amusement to you. The work is, I see, cried up by the jog-trot supporters of orthodoxy in the old Church of England.

"* * * With less of sanguine expectation than when I commenced Editor, eight-and-twenty years ago, I am yet disposed to think the prospects of the Reformer highly encouraging. The juncture is favourable. Without some such work, at this period of persecution from the 'Evangelicals' of every breed, we should scarcely be able to make a good and common stand in self-defence. And I am inclined to believe that the times may lead more than Unitarians to look into the only theological periodical which dares 'speak free.' * *

The same motive—a sense of duty in helping to resist a common danger—which induced Mr. Aspland to resume extensive editorial duties, also influenced him, in the year 1835, in deference to the wishes of the Committee of the Unitarian Association, to put on once more the harness as Secretary.

Mr. Aspland sometimes happily availed himself of local circumstances to impress important truths on the minds of his neighbours. An occasion of this sort happened in the spring of 1836. Two publicans in the village of Hackney died at the same time. Before they were buried, the feelings of their friends were outraged by the appearance of a scandalous "religious" placard—headed, in black characters, "A Warning Voice"—in which the deceased persons were spoken of as already in torment, and the like fate was threatened to survivors who should tread in their footsteps. Whether the publicans had been better or worse than the average of their order, is unknown. Their friends and acquaintance were naturally very indignant at this outrage, and solicited a highly-intelligent young man resident in the village to draw up something in reply. He mentioned the circumstances to Mr. Aspland. His sympathy and indignation were roused, and in less than half an hour the following counter-placard was sent to the printer.

"Another Warning Voice!

"When a neighbour is removed by Death, survivors are naturally led to serious reflection, and such as possess 'the same mind that was in Christ Jesus,' 'weep with them that weep,' and do what in them lies to 'comfort those that mourn.'

"But what must be thought of the head or heart of that man who on the sudden and untimely death of neighbours dares to pronounce their eternal doom, and harrows up the feelings of bereaved families by representing that the deceased are gone to perdition?

"Let the author of the abominable placard, headed 'A Warning Voice,' examine himself by the rules laid down by our Saviour, and he will find that he is wanting in piety as well as common humanity; that he invades the office of the Lord Jesus by setting up for a Judge of Souls; and that he is in danger of falling under the Divine sentence, '*He shall have judgment without mercy that hath shewed no mercy.*'

"Vain is all the talk about the 'Bible' and the 'Sabbath,' if Charity and Mercy be trampled under foot, as they have been by this anonymous accuser of departed fellow-creatures. 'Pure and undefiled Religion is this—to visit the fatherless and widows in their affliction,' in order to lighten grief and impart consolation: it is, on the other hand, daring impiety, if indeed it be not madness, to deal damnation round a neighbourhood, and to scatter firebrands, arrows and death.

"The merciless utterer of the 'Warning Voice' is himself warned, that though he may escape the visitation of the law of his country, he is amenable to the law of God, which condemns all that are 'full of malignity,' 'despiteful, proud, boasters,' 'without natural affection, implacable, unmerciful.'

"'*An Hypocrite with his mouth destroyeth his neighbour; but a man of Understanding holdeth his peace.*'"

The counter-placard was extensively distributed through the parish, excited much attention, and procured for the unknown writer loud expressions of approbation. A friend to whom the writer is indebted for this fact remarks, "I remember telling Mr. Aspland at the time, it was the most useful sermon he had ever preached; and now, looking back, I am still disposed to think it was so."

He interested himself warmly, in the year 1836, in plans for the improvement of the psalmody in his congregation. Although not possessed of any musical skill, Mr. Aspland was fond of sacred music, and took great care each Sunday to select for the choir of the Gravel-Pit, tunes suitable in feeling and expression to the hymns chosen. It was always his habit to attend with much exactness to the minutiæ of religious worship. He thought it not unimportant, when practicable, to make the prayers, the selections from the Scriptures, the hymns and the tunes, in unison with the subject or spirit of the discourse. The experience of thirty years led him to desire, in common with many of his hearers, the introduction of an organ into the chapel. There were some prejudices to overcome. The following statement of his views on the subject of psalmody, and instrumental music in aid of it, submitted to the congregational committee, was very serviceable in calming opposition and inducing the congregation to procure an organ.

"July 6, 1836.

"Mr. Aspland, in the discharge of a public duty, brought the state of the Psalmody at the Gravel-Pit before the Committee. This he did on the complaint and at the instance of many members of the congregation, and particularly the heads of some of the largest families. In fact, the singing has for some time ceased to answer the end of psalmody, and has been disreputable to the Gravel-Pit congregation. There can be no *sacred music* where there is *no music at all*.

"Mr. Aspland took the opinion of Mr. *Edward Taylor*, a warm friend of the congregation, and one of the best composers of sacred music, and one of the most accomplished vocalists of the age, and laid it before the Committee. His opinion, formed upon the known circumstances of the congregation, is in favour of an organ.

"Having done thus much, Mr. Aspland left and leaves the matter entirely in the hands of the congregation. He declined taking the chair at the last meeting, though formally voted into it, and forbore mingling in the discussion. He has used no influence with any one voter, nor will he use any, even in his own family. He will acquiesce in the decision of the congregation, whatever it be, giving every member equal credit for being swayed in his vote by a pure Christian regard to the best interests of the congregation; and he has no doubt that all the members of the congregation will acquiesce equally in whatever may appear to be the decided sense of the congregation. The case is not one of principle, but of arrangement and detail, depending very much upon taste and habit. Here, any heat of temper or angry language, whether in the majority or minority, would be strangely out of place.

"Mr. Aspland has no hesitation in stating that, persuaded as he is of the hopelessness of good vocal music *alone*, he is, subject to the wishes of the congregation, in favour of an organ,—not to supersede, but to lead and assist, the human voice. He has known the instrument so played, simply and devotionally, as to *increase* as well as *improve* the singing, and to encourage the younger part of the congregation to cultivate and exercise publicly this delightful part of worship. An organ may be abused, but so may any *tune*. Some of the old Dissenters called all divine music worldly, though they could not read David's Psalms without being admonished of the use of instrumental music in the service of the One True God, or the history of the Temple (first or second), without learning that singing to various instruments, one resembling at least the organ, was the common practice, approved by the *prophets*, and having virtually the Divine sanction.

"Our LORD reproved what he found faulty in the religious services of his countrymen, but he certainly did not blame them for the music of the Temple service, which he carefully frequented, though it is matter of history that that music was partly instrumental.

"The Christian church in all its branches (with one or two small exceptions) has ever used and delighted in sacred music, both instrumental and vocal. It is no novelty amongst Unitarian societies. There is scarcely one of any consideration, out of London, which has not introduced it, some for the best part of a century; and it is generally believed, if it may not be said *known*, in such societies, that the music has been among the aids, perhaps causes, of prosperity.

"These reasons may not satisfy every reader that an organ is necessary, but they may possibly convince him that Christians may take different views of this subject, as a practical one, without losing aught of their mutual respect and kind affection, or of their zeal for the welfare of their common church."

In the autumn of this year he had the gratification of visiting Bristol, and attending, first an interesting meeting of the Western Unitarian Society,* and then of the British and Foreign Scientific Association. During the week of this meeting, the 24th of August, Bartholomew-day, was celebrated at Bristol by the Non-Con Club, of whom the principal members were then assembled in that city; and they were joined at a social meeting, over which Mr. Aspland presided, by many friends of the Lewin's Mead and other Unitarian congregations. On the Sunday previous, a congregation brilliant from its numbers and the literary and philosophical attainments of many who were present, listened at Lewin's Mead with rapt attention to the discourses of Mr. Aspland † in the morning, and Mr. Madge in the evening. In addition to the various sources of gratification afforded by the more public engagements, he enjoyed in private intercourse, during this happy visit, the society of Dr. Carpenter, Mr. Wellbeloved, Mr. Kenrick, Mr. Acton and many other eminent men.

In the month of September in this year died the venerable Unitarian missionary (whose name has been frequently mentioned in this Memoir), Richard Wright.

Rev. Robert Aspland to Rev. R. Brook Aspland.

"Hackney, Sept. 25, 1836.

"Dear Brook,—I had heard of the decease of my excellent friend, before

---

* At this meeting, a vote was passed of gratitude to Mr. Aspland, Mr. Edgar Taylor and their fellow-labourers, for their "indefatigable and very able services" to the English Presbyterians.

† The subject was Scepticism. The sermon is the first in the posthumous volume of Discourses.

yours arrived in the afternoon of yesterday, from Dr. Davies, who was at Boston on Sunday last. Mr. G. Roberts had received an invitation to officiate at the funeral.

"I know not that I can tell you any thing of our good friend which you do not know, or with which you may not refresh your memory by looking into his 'Missionary Life,' which is no doubt in your library. His great merit was to have educated himself, and to have acquired, amidst ministerial labours and the hard duties of a common schoolmaster, a store of various useful knowledge. He rose from a very humble rank, and was, I think, apprenticed to a village blacksmith. As generally happens in such characters, he owed every thing to a mother of strong mind, fixed character and habitual piety. With so many disadvantages of education, person and dialect, no man ever rose so high or did so much good in the same department of intellectual exertion.

"His moral qualities were admirable. With a few and comparatively small defects, and these the result of his original position in society, he had many and great virtues,—probity, diligence, punctuality, perseverance, united with warm affections, gratitude, love of country, and steady and ardent devotion. I had often occasion to observe and to admire his independence of mind and high sense of honour. His character was sometimes tried in the furnace of affliction, and was always brightened in the process. Our acquaintance was of long standing, and for many years growing; our friendship confidential. He did not conceal from me even what he knew to be his weaknesses. I feel at this moment, when I am writing of him historically, that I have few friends left, out of my own family, who have as strong a hold upon my affections. His departure, retired and silent as he has been for some years, will excite wide and deep regret in our denomination; for though we may have advocates of much more learning, and pleaders of a higher and more powerful style of eloquence, there is no one whose name after death will be pronounced with purer esteem and warmer gratitude than that of RICHARD WRIGHT.

"I am pleased with the fact of his *good* letter to the congregation at Lutton having appeared in the last No. of C. R., and with the thought that his seeing it there may have cheered the few last days of his mortal existence with the persuasion, which I know he delighted to cherish, that I was gratified with the exertions of his pen, and that I honoured his character as an advocate and monitor in the cause of virtue and true religion."

On the occasion of the celebration, in October, 1835, of the Third Centenary of the printing of the first entire version in English of the Holy Scriptures, Mr. Aspland preached, and at the unanimous request of his congregation published, three sermons on the English Bible and the Reformation. These discourses contain a condensed narrative of the history of the translation of the Scriptures into the English tongue, of the Protestant Reformation, and the matters in debate between the Churches of Rome and England, including an estimate of the advantages and disadvantages of the Reformation, and of what remains to be done for the complete restoration of pure Christianity. Incidentally, several biographical sketches are introduced of Socinus, Erasmus and Grotius. The passages relating to the two latter (pp. 48—50) give them a far higher place, as actual though not professed Reformers, than has been customary amongst Protestant writers. As to both, but particularly as to Erasmus, his judgment was subsequently confirmed by that of Mr. Hallam, expressed in his invaluable History of Literature.*

Rev. James Taylor to Rev. Robert Aspland.

"Philadelphia, April 20, 1837.

"My dear Sir,— * * * As Mr. Wood† can give much information in its details, I will only advert to general facts. It is matter of regret to those of us who are plain, old-fashioned Unitarians, that, among several Unitarian young preachers, various notions are held, which appear to us not only unscriptural, but calculated, though not intended, to destroy all faith in the divine origin and truth of Christianity. Thus, one attempts to shew that the prophecies in the Old Testament quoted in the N. T., and applied to him by apostles who actually heard their Master's expositions and applications of them to himself, have no reference to him. Another attempts to explain the

---

* Of Erasmus, Mr. Aspland remarked, " His not joining the Reformation has been generally regretted and even blamed by Protestants, but I cannot help thinking that his very liberality of soul prevented his union with men who, while in the integrity of their hearts they thought they were serving Christ, were, as he thought, and as we now think, degrading a beautiful moral system into a mere collection of articles of faith, and overthrowing a despotism, venerable at least for its antiquity and universality, in order to set up another quite as galling, and more degrading and vexatious, from its being the despotism of individual over individual, and the despotism of a party stunning the ears of the world with shouts of liberty."—P. 49.

Mr. Hallam, after mentioning the Colloquies of Erasmus, so full of pungent remarks against the observances of the Romish Church, proceeds to say—" But about the time of this very publication, we find Erasmus growing by degrees more averse to the radical innovations of Luther. He has been severely blamed for this by most Protestants. * * * But it is to be remembered, that he did not by any means espouse all the opinions either of Luther or Zwingle; that he was disgusted at the virulent language too common among the Reformers, and at the outrages committed by the populace; * * *and that if he had gone among the Reformers, he must either have concealed his real opinions more than he had hitherto done, or lived as Melancthon did afterwards, the victim of calumny and oppression."—Literature of Europe, I. 490, 491.

† Rev. Samuel Wood, then on a visit to Philadelphia, and introduced to Mr. Taylor by Mr. Aspland.

process, and speculates on the cause, of his miracles, alias *wonders;* carefully keeping out of view his repeated appeals to his mighty works in proof of his mission from God, and his peculiar character and office as the Messiah. A third professes to have discovered that his personal character was *miraculously* formed, using that term not as wonderful merely, but in its popular sense; and these talk largely and confidently of new discoveries yet to be made of what our Lord really was, discoveries not predicated on what is recorded by the four evangelists, but the results of investigation and study by men well educated, though as destitute of a divine commission as the most illiterate and vulgar class. This is not all. There are among our junior preachers a goodly number who affect to talk of the philosophy of Christianity, and who have a strange hankering after what they call spiritualization. Professing to enlighten, to me they appear to be 'darkening counsel by words without knowledge.' In the desire of attracting notice, such men imagine that their object will be best and most speedily attained by striking out into something which they regard as a new and untrodden path: with such, the great and proper object of a Christian minister is little, if at all considered. * * *

" Your orthodox brethren, as might have been expected, now that the Test and Corporation Laws are abrogated, shew the cloven foot. They will no longer keep measures with the Unitarians. Will not the Scotch Presbyterians steal a successful march on you? You were right in withdrawing from the English orthodox Dissenters. Although among orthodox bodies there are individuals who are of liberal views and Christian feelings, generally speaking, yet, taken collectively, they are pretty uniform in their doings. The discipline of party is so powerfully administered, that the timid are overawed and the moderate silenced.—You doubtless hear of our political state. The government, having annihilated the former Bank of the United States, and being at actual war with the mercantile classes, has greatly aggravated and will wantonly protract the existing embarrassments; yet this is a *popular* government, emanating from the people—the majority of whom possess neither intellect, character nor property. In a word, the mob rule. Beware, in your efforts to obtain a redress of real grievances, that the right of suffrage is sufficiently guarded; else you may suffer as we suffer.—How zealous his Grace of Canterbury and his Lordship of London have shewn themselves for the preservation of the Church, and for the edification of the common people! This zeal would be less equivocal, had it been manifested and acted on before the Church Reform Bill was brought forward by the administration, and if it were not so closely connected with the continuance of the present extravagant incomes of the superior clergy. As for the Bishop of Exeter, by openly setting decorum at defiance, it is to be presumed that he exhibited himself in his true character. How unlike the never-to-be-forgotten and universally-esteemed Bishop White! In 1814, when, in consequence of a rise of almost 50 per cent. on nearly every article, it was proposed to advance his and the other ministers' salaries, he entreated that the motion might be withdrawn, saying, that himself and his brethren ought to bear their proportion of the burden, and not to tax the congregation, who were alike suffering by the existing state of things. Bishop White was not rich, his salary was moderate, and several were dependent on him. Could there be a more striking contrast? Had *he* been one of your hierarchy, he would at an early day have taken the lead in any proper scheme of Church Reform: of his benevolent concern for others and entire disinterestedness, the instances are numerous.

"I am, very truly, your friend,

JAMES TAYLOR."

Rt. Hon. Lord Holland to Rev. Robert Aspland.

"May 1, 1837.

"My dear Sir,—I shall have great pleasure in presenting your petition to the House of Lords,* and still greater in seeing you any morning, between twelve and two (say Wednesday), that you find it most convenient to come so far. The delusion or misrepresentation about the Church-rate Bill, in spreading which the clergy really exceeded all their former practices, is, I think, gradually subsiding, and the moderation and good sense of the later petitions from the Dissenters have mainly tended to dispel it.

"I think, with equal forbearance and firmness, they may very reasonably hope to effect some beneficial reform in the Universities; but in that, as in all other things, they must abstain from putting forth premises more large than are necessary to attain their immediate and practicable conclusions.—Yours,

VASSALL HOLLAND."

Towards the close of the year 1837, the distributors of the Parliamentary Grant resolved to recommend Dr. Thomas Rees to the Government as the principal receiver—a compliment fully earned by a long series of public services rendered by that gentleman to the Protestant Dissenters of England and Wales, and a significant proof that the previous rejection of him by the majority of the ministers of the Three Denominations as their Secretary, was the effect, not of personal dislike, but of party injustice. It was with sincere gratification that Mr. Aspland found himself united with Dr. J. P. Smith, the representative of the Independent, and Dr. Cox of the Baptist denomination, as a deputation to Lord Melbourne and Mr. Spring Rice, Chancellor of the Exchequer, to announce and obtain the ratification of this appointment. They had at Downing Street that hearty reception which the Premier so well knew how to give, and were immediately assured that

---

* A petition from the parish of Hackney for the abolition of Church-rates.

the nomination of Dr. Rees was perfectly acceptable to the Government.

The greater part of the year 1838 was passed by Mr. Aspland in bodily suffering and comparative seclusion. There were some circumstances which rendered the privation of the means of public usefulness particularly painful. He had observed with anxiety the rise, in some of the younger ministers of his denomination, of a spirit of dissatisfaction with the institutions and opinions established and generally current amongst Unitarians. He hoped that a friendly discussion might lead to a better mutual understanding, and to the formation of a stronger bond of union amongst the several Unitarian congregations than had previously existed. With this view, it was resolved by the Committee of the Unitarian Association to call an Aggregate Meeting of Unitarians, to be held in London at Whitsuntide, to consult on common interests, and especially on a closer and more effective union. When the meeting took place, Mr. Aspland was laid aside by illness. He had hoped much from this Unitarian council, and had contemplated taking an active part in its proceedings. In a letter addressed to Mr. Travers, the Chairman, he lamented his disappointment, and thus proceeded to describe the objects of the assembly and the spirit which ought to animate its proceedings:

"The Meeting, my dear Sir, has grown out of the condition of our body. As a denomination we are in a *crisis*,—but many are in my view the indications of Divine Providence that the coming change will be for the better. The dissatisfaction felt by many in our actual state, is less a confession of our weakness than an acknowledgment of our capacity, and a recognition of a higher duty than has yet been *practically* admitted. And the fierce spirit of hostility that rages against us on every side,—so strange and unexpected, and so inconsistent with the intelligence and improvement of our age and country in almost every thing else,—is, in one sense, an admission of our power; and *our power* can consist only in character, in reason and in 'the sword of the spirit, which is the word of God.'

"You meet, my dear Sir, as brethren; no individual, no party of individuals, having authority above the rest. Yours will be a friendly conference rather than a debate, and consequently there will be no 'striving for mastery,' nor any triumph of a majority over a minority. You will take into view, not the peculiar opinions and feelings of individuals, or the condition and prospects of this or that congregation, but the manifest wants and powers and duties of the whole denomination. By unreserved communication, by frank and generous counsel, by fraternal advice, by the expression of Christian sympathy, and by the tender of needed help,—all will be edified, and even he whose opinion or plan may not be adopted or generally approved will go away blessing God that he has been present at one of the few ecclesiastical assemblies since the days of the Apostles, in which spiritual dominion has been neither claimed nor allowed,—in which, in fact, the first and most eager feeling and declaration of the whole assembly have been on behalf of the sacred rights of every private conscience."

His anticipations were not fulfilled. A great practical error was committed in providing for the guidance of the meeting no well-defined line of discussion. Imprudences of speech incidental to debate, provoked retaliatory remarks equally mischievous. Some appeared to apprehend an invasion by their brethren on their intellectual liberty, or by an ecclesiastical confederation on their congregational independence. Many were startled and pained by the assertion that the bond which held Unitarians together was merely the negation of orthodoxy. Distrust and mutual misunderstanding were the immediate effects of this unfortunate Aggregate Meeting.

To no one in the Unitarian body was this result more painful than to Mr. Aspland. His Diary contains traces of a feeling of rising impatience at his own inability of action. Thus,

"1838, June 24.—This is now the fourth Sunday that I have been *silent*, the whole indeed of this month, and I seem as far as ever from the pulpit. But let me remember my last text and subject—'The will of the Lord be done.'"

His ordinary medical adviser expressed his desire of a second opinion on the case: that of Dr. Bright was taken, who prescribed active medical treatment and long-continued rest.

Rev. Robert Aspland to Rev. Dr. Rees.

"Woodford Wells, Friday, August 3rd, 1838.

"My dear Sir,—I am forbidden to write *a needless* line, but under this description I can scarcely bring a short letter to you.

"You must have been surprised at my *breaking down* so suddenly and entirely. The truth is, that the *gout* was only a symptom of a crisis in my constitution. I have long been a sufferer, to a degree which I cannot now describe or even look back upon, from disorder in the organ of the heart. For years, I may say, I studied to conceal the complaint, revealing it at home only when it was necessary to explain something said, or something not done. When I was driven, at length, to take unreserved medical advice, it was found that my life hung upon a thread. In this condition I gave myself wholly up to my advisers, and am here in seclusion and quiet, undergoing a course of mercurial medicine. The *effect* is hardly yet apparent, though my general health is decidedly improved, and my feelings, which I hope are a true barometer, are much more comfortable. Could I regain anything like a healthy or even regular pulsation, I should consider myself on the eve of restoration to the ordinary habits of life. But I bless the Author and Disposer of our days, I am not anxious, or, I hope, impatient. Hitherto, I have found it no effort to say, 'His will be done.'

"I duly estimate your kindness in offering for my sake to put on again the pulpit harness on Sunday morning, which, after so long a period of total freedom, must, I fear, be irksome to you. But I rejoice in the persuasion that the task will be lightened by the consciousness that you are serving and giving relief to an *old friend*.

"My friends at Hackney have most kindly taken the pulpit out of my hands; but I cannot help asking you to administer the *Lord's Supper* on Sunday morning. * * * There having been no observance of the Sacrament last month, I fear its further discontinuance may break up the really good habit of the congregation with regard to this most beneficial ordinance. * * *

"I see in the Morning Chronicle an advertisement *against* the Government from the *Three* Denominations. Should not Mr. Bischoff vindicate the *Presbyterians* from this continued misrepresentation? Pray think of this.

"Present my kindest regards to Mrs. Rees, and believe me, my dear Sir, your obliged and faithful friend, ROBERT ASPLAND."

The removal by death of his aged friend Mr. William Sturch, the author of "Apeleutherus," and a zealous friend of liberty, occasioned the following letter.

Rev. Robert Aspland to Mrs. Sturch.

"Woodford Wells, Sept. 18th, 1838.

"My dear Madam,—I cannot reconcile it to my feelings to let the late solemn event pass by, without assuring you and your family of my sincere condolence. Mr. Sturch's venerable age and long increasing infirmities must have prepared you for his departure; but it is not possible to see the grave close upon so much intelligence, virtue and goodness, without deep affliction; and to you and his children, who alone knew his worth, the pang of separation (with all the alleviations supplied by a kind Providence) has been, I am sure, severely trying.

"Yet I need not remind you, my dear Madam, that you have a source of consolation in the character of him over whom you are called to mourn. While his eminent powers of mind and stores of knowledge commanded universal respect, the tenor of his long life excited habitual esteem and confidence. I never knew a person who with so much true independence of mind united so many of the better qualities of the heart. In public and in private life he discharged well and truly all the duties which his excellent and well-regulated understanding acknowledged.

"To that Supreme Benevolence which he habitually recognized and adored, his family and friends may resign his spirit, satisfied that in all the future dispensations of the Merciful Disposer, it must be well with one who in his temper and habits was a practical disciple of our Great Example in all righteousness and charity.

"I write from a retirement into which I have been driven by a malady, the issue of which is yet uncertain. My seclusion enables me to review the past, and amidst my varied feelings none is stronger than the hope that in the world to come, whenever I am summoned to it, I may not be found unworthy of the society of those departed friends whom I have been accustomed to delight in as the wise and good,—and amongst these the image of your deceased husband always rises up pleasingly to my view.

" Sincerely sympathizing with you and the members of your family, I am, my dear Madam, your obliged and affectionate Christian friend and servant,
ROBERT ASPLAND."

At the close of a retirement of six months, Mr. Aspland expressed the desire to return to public duty. Dr. Bright remonstrated, telling him, "if he entered the pulpit, he could not ensure his leaving it alive." He answered, "that it was better to die in harness than to lead a life of inactivity."

On the 2nd of December he re-entered the pulpit at the Gravel-Pit, and preached from Ps. xciv. 19, his subject being—*Piety a Resource in Trouble*. Though he spoke for nearly an hour, he sustained no inconvenience from the effort beyond one or two sensations of faintness.

In 1839, he projected and carried into execution the publication of a series of Tracts "designed to vindicate Religious and Christian Liberty." They were, with one exception, not original, but reprints of Tracts by Milton, Thomas Gordon, Charles Fox, Dr. George Campbell, Hoadly, Bishop Hare, Sir Michael Foster, Hales and Sir Matthew Hale. The original Tract was a very ingenious essay, by a physician of some eminence in the capital of Scotland, "On the Proper Conduct of Religious Education," &c.

Mr. Aspland also composed and published at this time, a Catechism and Prayers for the Young. The former continues to be extensively used, and is a very instructive manual of scriptural and religious knowledge. In the early years of his ministry, Mr. Aspland objected to catechetical instruction of the young in their religious and moral duty, probably from his recollection of the abuse of this mode of instruction in "orthodox" churches, and of the way in which in his early years he himself had been taxed beyond his capacity by the Assembly's Catechism. A larger experience, however, shewed him the expediency, if not the necessity, of teaching children the lessons of Divine wisdom *authoritatively*, of fixing them by repetition in the memory, and of furnishing them with a standard to which in after life they might refer. It was his apprehension that the younger members of Unitarian families were sometimes left untaught, from the fear of teaching them any thing which in the progress of their minds they might have to unlearn.

In the course of this year he officiated at the opening of the new chapel at Dukinfield. His sermon was preached from Mark xi. 17—*My house shall be called the house of prayer for all nations.* * He went through the fatigues of the several services and private meetings consequent on this occasion with a degree of animation and power that astonished those who knew the state of his health. His countenance was, when he began, pallid, and his once remarkably erect frame was somewhat bowed by days and nights of pain; but as he warmed in his subject, a stranger would scarcely have supposed that the earnest, clear and sonorous elocution which kept his attention untired for more than an hour, was that of an enfeebled invalid, conscious that his life hung upon almost a thread. From Dukinfield he proceeded into Yorkshire, where he took part in the ordination of Rev. Frederick Hornblower as the pastor of the Lydgate congregation. In this service he was associated with the Rev. Charles Wicksteed, Rev. W. Turner, Jun., Rev. R. Brook Aspland, and Mr. Sidney Morehouse as the representative of the Lydgate congregation. Mr. Wicksteed delivered the charge to the young minister, and Mr. Aspland preached the sermon to the congregation, his subject being (Luke x. 21, 23, 24)†—*Our Lord's Joy in contemplating the Result of his benevolent Mission, an Example of rejoicing in the Progress and final Triumph of Divine Truth.* From Lydgate he proceeded to Leeds, where he was the guest of the Rev. Charles Wicksteed. To the pen of that valued friend the writer is indebted for the interesting sequel to this Chapter.

Rev. Charles Wicksteed to Rev. R. Brook Aspland.

"Leeds, Nov. 8, 1849.

"My dear Friend,—You ask me to recal some of the circumstances attending your Father's visit to Leeds in September 1840, and in making this request

---

* In explaining the remarkable transaction of Christ's driving the buyers and sellers out of the temple, he followed Joseph Mede and Bishop Hurd, and treated it not merely as an assertion of his authority as the Messiah, but as a prophetic declaration of the catholic spirit and far-spread triumphs of the gospel.

† It is No. XIX. in the posthumous volume of Discourses.

you invite me to undertake a very easy and agreeable task. The circumstances of that visit are vividly impressed upon my memory, and I shall be happy if in recalling them I can reciprocate to yourself and others any portion of that interest which I have felt while reading the successive chapters of the instructive biography in which you are engaged.

"It was, I think, at the opening of the new chapel at Dukinfield that Mr. Aspland arranged to pay a visit to the North. On that occasion some of the congregation at Lydgate applied to him to take a part in the ordination services of Mr. F. Hornblower; and finding that public duty would bring him thus far on his way to Leeds, I ventured to request that he would honour me by spending a few days under my roof, and afford my congregation the benefit of his services on the Sunday. It was in your study that this interview took place, and I remember your Father's searching gaze when I spoke to him, and the frank cordiality with which (this scrutiny over) he accepted the invitation. About that time, some little alienation had arisen, partly from real, partly from imaginary causes, between your Father, and the school of Unitarians whom he might be considered to represent, and some of the younger ministers of our body. A new periodical had a few years previously been commenced in Lancashire, occupying, as he conceived, the same ground and aiming at the same general object as the Magazines which he had conducted for so long a time and with so untiring an energy. A disposition was manifesting itself to undervalue some of those central denominational institutions which he had, from a conviction of their great importance, devoted so much time and effort to establish; and much was said about the age of controversy —that is, as he regarded it, of earnest and open defence of scriptural truth— being past. Added to this, a reaction was manifesting itself in many minds against some of the distinguishing principles of the philosophy of Locke and Priestley, and a mode of discussing several theological questions was arising which appeared to him to have the danger, without the explicitness, of scepticism. These things had given him considerable pain. Some of them he regarded as diversions from that cause to which it had been the labour of his life to give unity and strength; and in others he saw nothing but an unsettling shallowness and mysticism. These are the trials which every generation, in a moving and advancing country, almost always inflicts upon its older men. The young forget the things that are behind, and press forward to those that are before,—feeling after newer things, and hoping to find truer. It is just what, amid similar doubts and fears, their predecessors had done before them. Thus a new set of views and aims grow up, in which the older men, having in some instances tested them and found them wanting, feel no confidence, and with which, in other instances, a characteristic indisposition to open afresh questions in their minds already settled, and a preference of stability and repose, prevents them from feeling any active sympathy. This sober equipoise and still maturity of thought has no charm for the earlier periods of life, which are usually only captivated by something extravagant in view or exaggerated in character. The older men in consequence regard the younger as rash and unripe, and the younger men regard the older as stationary and dogmatic. Thus, with an equal honesty of purpose, it may be, and an equal love of truth on both sides, a certain want of sympathy and mutual trust arises among men of the same time and the same church.

"I think your Father had felt this very deeply. He feared that a generation was arising that was forgetting the past, with its noble struggles and its successful labours; and some of the younger men, with a strong personal and traditional respect for him, were perhaps disposed too much to look upon him as a landmark of the past, a sign of where the waters of life in the last generation had subsided. In all this there was some exaggeration on both sides; an exaggeration which the absence of full, frequent and friendly intercourse rather tended to increase. Your Father's visit, therefore, to the North, after so many years, and on an occasion so peculiarly interesting to him, to yourself, and to a numerous Christian community, was looked upon with very lively interest. Many men embraced with eagerness the opportunity, by gathering round him on that occasion, to shew that they had not forgotten or ceased to appreciate the spirit and manliness with which he had fought the battles of Christian Truth and Civil Liberty; and he on his part, I think, felt a cordial joy in this sympathy, and was but too happy to bel'eve that his younger brethren were, after all, more sincerely attached to that household of faith which he himself so dearly loved, than he had been daring to hope.

"The day of the opening of your new chapel I need not recal to your mind, nor the visit to Lydgate in which you took a part. But you lost sight of Mr. Aspland after this, and I can supply the wanting link. On the Sunday following his arrival in Leeds, he preached, to large congregations in Millhill chapel, two excellent sermons, which appear in the posthumous volume of his Discourses. The subject of the sermon in the morning was, 'The conscientious and liberal Man a Servant of Christ, a Benefactor to his Species, and an Heir of the Divine Blessing.' In the evening, he took for his subject the fifteenth chapter of Luke, on the Prodigal Son; the whole of which he wished to read out as the text of his sermon, and in substitution for the regular lesson. I am not sure whether he did this, or whether, as I rather think, he yielded to my wish, that the lesson should be read in its proper place; but it has amused me since to remember that in this difference it was not the older man that was the more conservative of usage. This sermon was listened to with the deepest interest, and was, in truth, a most beautiful and impressive one. All the features of the narrative were brought out with the utmost feeling and tact; and there was a cautious solemnity in the application of the doctrine of forgiveness, which, while it detracted nothing from the prevailing tenderness of the sermon, prevented the possibility of too loose or indulgent an interpretation of it. He was under the medical advice of his son at the time of this visit, but no trace of illness could be detected in the vigour and animation of his services; and some of the older members of the congregation, acquaintances of his own, remarking this to him, he compared himself to the race-horse that could not be reined in, but, when once upon the course, thought of nothing but the goal.

"But it was not only on subjects of the highest importance that his heart was active. Every thing human about him seemed to engage a portion of his regards. The two great objects of general interest in Leeds, were the vast cloth-hall and the unparalleled flax-mill of the Messrs. Marshall, at that time newly erected. Over both of these I had the pleasure of conducting him. On the Monday, a friend had placed his carriage at our disposal, and we were to have gone together to visit the birth-place of Priestley, but the weather was very unfavourable, and he, I am sorry to say, was far from well. During the few days he spent with us, some members of the congregation came to see him at my house, and others he visited in their own. One family in the country, with whom he spent the interval between the two services on Sunday, drew towards them his especial regards. Their kindness, uprightness and simplicity, quite won his heart. In reference to all these visits, he did not seem to feel as an ordinary guest, pleased with the attentions paid him, but more as one who was filled with hope and gladness at the sight of a sound religious stock, in whose hands the interests of truth and virtue might be safe. In our own family and household he took no less interest, making friends with our baby-child with a boisterous mirth that was always amply repaid by herself. Whatever the subject on which we were engaged, he always turned away from it on her admission into the room to give her a full and *magnificent* greeting. Each evening, as the engagements of the day closed in, we drew our chairs to the fire, and talked sometimes far into the night. He had manifestly an earnest and serious interest in my ministerial labours and position, the topics of my study, and the course of my inquiries. He not only listened with great consideration to many statements which I made to him of views which I was disposed to form, or of difficulties which obstructed my path, but in some instances avowed that he had felt the same, and in others suggested qualifying considerations to which his larger experience and fuller knowledge had led him to attach importance. But all this was done not only with a respectful kindness, but, considering our relative age and standing, I could not but think with a singular modesty and delicacy of feeling. It was with an unfeigned sorrow that my wife and I parted with him. I assure you it seemed that day as if a glad presence had departed from the house. With this visit I believe he was much pleased:* indeed, I think I may use a stronger expression, and

---

* In confirmation of this opinion, it is but just to give an extract or two from one of Mr. Aspland's letters, dated "Blenheim Square, Leeds, Monday, Sept. 14, 1840:"

"Our good friend W. met me at the coach, and brought me to this pleasant

say that with this visit I believe he was much *comforted*. He saw that the good old cause was the cause we had at heart still, and felt more satisfied with the prospects of the future than he had sometimes been before. As for myself, the renewal of intercourse, after a separation of some years, with one who had never omitted an opportunity of kindness to myself or any member of my family,* was exceedingly gratifying: and I have been in the habit since, of linking his visit to Leeds with one that he paid to Shrewsbury some five-and-twenty years previously, when he preached the sermons for the Lancasterian schools in that town, and was, I think, my father's guest, and when there was a certain impression of radiance and animation, which still clings to my memory, as part of my childish associations with the preacher and the service.

"I do not know whether these recollections may appear to you too trifling or too personal to interest others, but in that case they may be returned to my own bosom, where they have a place among my memories of intercourse with departed friends, from which they are not likely to be removed.

"I remain, my dear friend, very sincerely yours,

CHARLES WICKSTEED."

---

and hospitable house, into which I was cordially welcomed by his amiable wife, and in which I have been much entertained with their interesting and lovely babe. We went in the evening to Chapel-town, Mr. B.'s. The large family of the B.'s are all agreeable, and Mr. and Mrs. B. unaffectedly hospitable—all sound English Presbyterians. * * *

"I am glad that I came hither on many accounts, particularly as I might never otherwise have known all my host's excellences of head and heart. He is in an important station."

* "It is with pleasure that I avail myself of this opportunity of mentioning what a kind and friendly interest Mr. Aspland took in the arrangements necessary to be made for commencing my career as a student at Glasgow, and what valuable advice he afterwards gave me, on the completion of my course at that University, for the conduct in private of my theological studies. He favoured me with a long communication (which, I regret to say, in the lapse of nearly twenty years, has been now mislaid), containing an outline of a course of study, with the names of the best authors to be consulted, on critical theology, on pastoral duties, and on personal religious culture. I have reason to believe, from intercourse with many, both of his immediate students and of others in whom he only took a general interest as a Christian minister, that this considerate and active kindness was during his life extended to a large number of young men preparing for this sacred calling, on whom the expression of a friendly interest in their prospects and pursuits exercises a cheering and encouraging influence that older men do not at all times realize."

CHAPTER XXXII.

Few public events affected Mr. Aspland with so deep a feeling of regret as the death of Lord Holland, who expired, after a short illness, Oct. 22, 1840, aged 67. In common with thousands, he had admired this distinguished man for the inflexible consistency and unsullied purity of his public life, and especially for his generous devotion to religious liberty, of which the English Presbyterians had received many proofs. But Mr. Aspland had the melancholy privilege of mingling personal with public recollections and regrets, and remembered "the venerable and benignant countenance and the cordial voice" which had more than once bid him welcome to Holland House; the "frank politeness which at once relieved all his embarrassment;" that "constant flow of conversation, so natural, so animated, so various, so rich with observation and anecdote;" that "wit which never gave a wound;" and above all, that "goodness of heart which appeared in every look and accent, and gave additional value to every talent and acquirement."*

The body of Presbyterian Ministers of London met on November 3, and recorded, in a resolution drawn up by Mr. Aspland, their grief at the death of Lord Holland, and their profound respect for his memory.† Two days after, the *Non-Con* Club, at his suggestion, adopted the following resolution:

"That we are eager to seize the occasion of our first meeting after the decease of Lord Holland, to record our heartfelt respect for his memory, and our deep concern at the loss which the country, and in particular the Nonconformists of all denominations, have sustained by this melancholy event;

---

* Mr. Macaulay's beautiful tribute to the memory of Lord Holland in Edinburgh Review, No. CXLVIII.

† See Christian Reformer (1840), p. 820.

and to express our admiration of his mind and character as a statesman, formed upon the model of his illustrious uncle, Charles James Fox, like whom he was devoted to the 'good old cause' for which Algernon Sydney died, and was distinguished in particular by his just perception and cordial love of liberty, civil and religious, and his almost intuitive abhorrence of every form and degree of bigotry, intolerance and persecution."*

Early in the following year, death removed three venerable men who had been united for more than half a century in the bonds of common literary tastes and religious sentiments and cordial friendship. During more than thirty-five years, Mr. Aspland had enjoyed very friendly intercourse with all of them. William Frend, the Unitarian confessor of Jesus' College, Cambridge, died Feb. 21, in the 84th year of his age. To the Monthly Repository he was an early and a tolerably constant contributor. To him it was indebted during many of its early years for a series of political articles, written in the manly spirit of a disciple of Charles James Fox. At a time when a large portion of the daily and periodical press of England was tainted with servility and political corruption, and disgraced by its warlike spirit, his fearless remarks on passing events and the sentiments of public men, were very serviceable to civil liberty and peace.

March 2, died, in his 86th year, George Dyer, the friend and biographer of Robert Robinson, and, like him, distinguished by simplicity and purity of character.

On the day following died, in the 81st year of his age, John Towill Rutt,† one of the biographers of Gilbert Wakefield, and the editor of the works of Priestley. In him Mr. Aspland lost an indefatigable fellow-labourer and a warmly-attached friend, to whom during a large portion of his ministry at Hackney he had stood in the pastoral rela-

---

* Minutes of the Club.

† "In early boyhood he was placed under the care of the Rev. Dr. Toulmin, of Taunton, with whom he remained until of a proper age to be admitted as a scholar of St. Paul's School. At that ancient establishment he manifested ability of no common order, and was even more distinguished by that love of learning and ardent desire for intellectual improvement which characterized his long life, than for the talent which he displayed. This quality, and the excellent powers of his mind and character, made such an impression upon Dr. Roberts, the head master, who took an especial interest in his welfare, that he strongly urged upon his father the propriety of his sending his son to one of the English Universities, where those powers would be more fully called into exercise; with which, however, his father's religious scruples (he being a strict Nonconformist) would not permit him to comply."—*Memorials of John Towill Rutt*, printed for private circulation.

tion. The distinguished son-in-law of Mr. Rutt, Mr. Justice Talfourd, truly says, "To the Unitarian periodical works, the 'Monthly Repository' and the 'Christian Reformer,' he was for many years a constant contributor, gratifying his desire to promote what he believed to be the cause of truth, and neither obtaining nor desiring any other recompence." But, in truth, Mr. Rutt had been more than a contributor to the *Monthly Repository;* occasionally, during the absence or disability through illness of the Editor, he was its conductor; and at one time an arrangement was all but completed by which he would have formally and permanently undertaken the editorial duties. Within a very few days of his death, Mr. Aspland received from him the following brief but characteristic note.

J. T. Rutt, Esq., to Rev. Robert Aspland.

"Bexley, 25 Feb., '41.

"My dear Sir,—I learned in town, yesterday, that after, I fear, 'wearisome nights' and days of much *corporeal* affliction, Frend had left the world, and left a brother octogenarian a warning, by which I ought to improve.

"You will, no doubt, give your readers a memoir of Frend, and I write a line in haste to say that I have his Academica (including an account of his family) much at your service, should you not possess it. With our kind regards to yourself and family, yours,

J. T. RUTT."

The year 1841 was marked by that alternation of severe and depressing illnesses and remarkable recoveries, which characterized the last ten years of Mr. Aspland's life. But with each attack the suffering was protracted, and the hope of rallying grew weaker. He was enabled to preach, on the first Sunday in May, his annual sermon to the young; and delivered one of the three interesting sermons, printed in the posthumous volume, entitled, "Counsels of Experience; or, Lessons that we Learn as we Advance in Life."* Before the end of the month he was again disabled, and had the mortification of spending in a sick chamber the Whitsun week, in which the anniversary meeting of the Unitarian Association was held at Hackney. His resignation of the office of Secretary was received with expressions of deep regret, and "thanks for his long and inestimable services." A zealous and able successor was found in the Rev. Edward Tagart.

A few extracts from the Diary belong to this year:

"June 20, Sunday.—I got out, after nearly a month's confinement from

---

* Sermon XXIV., p. 443.

abscess and gout. I found myself very lame and feeble. Sate in the pulpit on a stool made on purpose. Great relief, but much fatigued.

"June 22.—Parliament prorogued for dissolution. A worse Parliament cannot be; a world of treachery and faction.

" — 28.—The elections begin to kindle one's anxiety. Sleep broken. Two Liberals (of whom my friend Benjamin Wood is one) returned, without opposition, for Southwark.

" — 29.—Newspapers late. Reports *not satisfactory* from the country. City of London election; news from hour to hour by Messrs. J. Clennell, E. Ford and C. Green, &c.; at first, all right—then going wrong—next better (the one o'clock poll)—and afterwards worse and worse.

" — 30.—This morning, doubtful if Lord John Russell be in; if not, the Tories have three Members! Disastrous reports from the country. N. B. Wood and Russell *in* with two Tories!

" July 1.—Election for Tower Hamlets. I went in a carriage to poll at noon at the Mermaid. I was kindly received by several gentlemen, and was introduced to and had pleasant conversation with Colonel Fox, who recollected meeting me at Holland House. Clay and Fox triumphant. Hackney did its duty. Accounts from the country still bad. All of us in the election fever. N. B. The excitement of going up to the poll was bodily distressing.

" — 4, Sunday.—*Anniversary of my personal settlement at the Gravel-Pit, thirty-six years ago!*"

In the autumn his strength was wonderfully recruited, and he spent a month in Cheshire, Liverpool, North Wales and Leicestershire; preached the charity sermons at Dukinfield; preached before the Cheshire Presbyterian Association at Hyde;* and attended and spoke at the business meeting as a Deputation from the Unitarian Association; and on his homeward journey preached at Leicester, where a part of his family was settled.

During his visit to Dukinfield, he was called upon to fulfil the pleasant duty of officiating at the marriage of his youngest son. It was the only occasion of his performing this office for a member of his own family, and the mingled dignity and tenderness with which he delivered the address, made a deep impression on the assembled congregation. The visits which he paid during this tour to several of his children, were, both to himself and them, the source of the most lively pleasure. Friends, looking at his animated countenance, and listening to his earnest and deeply interesting conversation, the stream of which flowed on from morning to night, vainly hoped that his health was

---

* On "The Unlawful Arts of Controversy." Printed both separately by the Association and in the posthumous volume, Sermon IV., p. 64.

re-established, and that he was about to enjoy a green and vigorous old age.

The letter which follows, while it shews the undiminished interest he took in the Unitarian Association, will put on record his sentiments on some of the practical details of its administration:

Rev. Robert Aspland to Rev. Charles Wicksteed.

"Hackney, Dec. 14, 1841.

"My dear Sir,—I respect your scruples, but I do not think they need stand in the way of your acceptance of the office of our preacher. By accepting, you commit yourself to no more than the general principle of the Association, and not at all to the details of management. That is a proper subject for discussion, and will, it is probable, be discussed at the meeting for business, the day before the meeting for worship. You might, if you thought proper, without the least inconsistency, give notice to the Committee in your very letter of acceptance (on which you see I reckon) that at the business meeting you intend to raise that question.

"We went fully, I remember, into the subject at the time to which you refer, and came to the conclusion that we could not reduce our establishment, as we are booksellers and publishers to a pretty large extent, without injury to the Association; but that, having machinery capable of much more than our actual work, we ought to bring up our business to our capacity. In that, I cannot say that we have succeeded, but we have at any rate made the effort.

"A central metropolitan office is found advantageous, if not necessary, to all our religious societies; and I think it may be shewn that *indirectly*, more perhaps than directly, our office has been of great use to our cause.

"A paid Secretary is absolutely necessary to relieve the Hon. Sec. of mere mechanical drudgery, and he is besides the manager of our Book department, which, though of small account in our Reports and figures, as compared with the great popular societies, is, I am confident, of great use and importance in the circulation of our works, and consequently in the diffusion of our opinions.

"The Committee are to meet on Monday, the 20th inst., to determine this and other matters, and I should be happy to lay before them then your final answer; *happy*, that is to say, if it be favourable; for we should all be grievously mortified at your refusal, especially as we have ventured to talk of you, out of doors, as our public advocate.

"I might have said that at the time to which I have referred, there was a complaint also from *Norwich* of the disproportionate expenditure of our establishment, in consequence of which Mr. Dowson, of that place, was invited to come up and discuss the matter with the Committee, which he did, and was so far satisfied as to continue down to the present time a liberal supporter and active friend of the Association.

"I am afraid that, if I were now to revisit Leeds, I should complain more of fires being out than of smoke from the factory chimneys. These are indeed serious times. Would it not almost appear that Divine Providence is bringing the people to their senses by means of sufferings?

"Present my kindest respects to your lady, and believe me, my dear Sir, your friend and brother, ROBERT ASPLAND."

Rev. Robert Aspland to Rev. R. Brook Aspland.

"Hackney, Jan. 31, 1842.

"Dear Brook,—I am happy to say that I was in the pulpit yesterday morning, and am not further damaged than by fatigue.

"The heads of the congregation met numerously yesterday to offer me the relief of an assistant. The meeting was, I learn, very harmonious, and towards me respectful, affectionate and liberal. I know not yet the exact resolutions passed, but I believe the choice of a help will be referred to me. This I shall in some sense regret: it will place me in a state of great difficulty."

"1842. March 16.—Finished reading again Sir James Mackintosh's Vindiciæ Gallicæ—loose and declamatory, but germs of wisdom and eloquence. Some *almost* noble passages. M. afraid of Burke while answering him. His future political change (if so it can be called) might have been foreseen in this popular and somewhat splendid book. Led to re-peruse the above work by our reading *Memoirs* of Mackintosh by his son (2 vols. 8vo); and the reading of both led me irresistibly to Burke's Reflections.

"March 16.—I was so incensed at Peel's proposal of an INCOME TAX, that I drew up in my own name a short but strong Petition against the proposal to the House of Commons—first draft being, without erasure or alteration, sent off. W—— took it to the House of Commons for Sir Wm. Clay, but, he being away at the Levee, brought it back, and I sent it by post.

"April 9.—The Presbyterian Body to the Throne. The Addresses (three) on the birth of the Prince of Wales, read by Mr. Madge,* were drawn up by me.

---

* "It had been at first resolved that Mr. Aspland, who had so ably discharged the same duty on several preceding occasions, should appear at the head of this deputation, and present all the Addresses; but, to their great concern, a severe attack of indisposition deprived them of his valuable services." Dr. Rees's account in Christian Reformer (8vo Series), Vol. IX. p. 310, where the Addresses and Replies are given. In 1840, Mr. Aspland had the honour of reading the Addresses on the escape of the Queen from assassination attempted by Oxford. On that occasion the Court was held solely for the purpose of receiving the Addresses of the Dissenting Ministers,—a circumstance without a precedent in the history of the English Court. Mr. Aspland, no incompetent judge on such a point, was accustomed to speak with enthusiasm of the beautiful elocution of Queen Victoria in reading the Replies to Addresses on the Thone. See Christ. Ref., Vol. VII. p. 622.

"April 11.—Reading Life of Bishop (Calcutta) Middleton, by Le Bas, 2 vols. 8vo,—a heavy book. The Bishop a good and practical man, but a dull hero. His opinion important that *missions* to the East Indies will succeed at first only among Europeans and the half or no-cast people,—that education and civilization are the only means to be looked to for Christianizing India. The Bishop saw *Rammohun Roy* several times, and pronounces him a Deist,—not even, he (the Bishop) *fears*, ' a Socinian.'

" May 1.—Preached annual sermon to the Young, on conformity to the world. Sorely tried in the pulpit and at the Sacrament.

" — 26.—Mr. S. Cotton brought me from Messrs. Haslam and Bischoff, Gurney's Report of the Judges' vivâ-voce answers to the Lords' questions in the Hewley Appeal. Seven only delivered their opinions. Mr. Justice Maule only for appellants (the Unitarians) *throughout;* the six others more or less adverse, amongst whom pre-eminently were Erskine (son of the great forensic orator), and Baron Gurney, so many years a Baptist communicant (himself dipped on confession) at Maze Pond, and afterwards a worshiper, &c. at the Antitrinitarian meeting-house, Old Jewry. Most of the seven declared that improper evidence,—amongst the rest, Dr. Pye Smith's, of which I told him on his calling here on the 27th,—had been admitted. *All agreed that Unitarians do not now lie under common-law disabilities.*"

In the summer of this year, he was happily enabled once more to visit the scattered members of his family at their several homes. While in Leicestershire, he visited the Monastery of St. Bernard's.

" July 25, Monday.—We went through Mount Sorrel and near to Loughborough, and then through several villages to Charnwood Forest, wild and desolate, but great part of it enclosed and under the plough—crops pretty good, and not so late as might have been expected. Much rock, slate and granite, reminding me of Dartmoor. After many inquiries, some fruitless, we arrived by an almost impassable road at the Monastery, St. Bernard's, on Mount Vernon, near, if not in the parish of, Whittick, where is a Catholic chapel of three years standing, the date of the Monastery. The brotherhood is of the Cistercian order, or Trappists. The number of monks is twenty-four, half lay brothers. We were received by Father Edmund, who led us into a neat refreshment-room, supplied us with bread and butter, water and beer, according to the hospitable usage of the establishment, and waited upon us with plates, &c., assisted by an evil-looking, Moor-like lay brother. Father Edmund was exceedingly affable, attentive, playfully so to the children, and even gallant to the ladies. He shewed us an illuminated Service Book, a MS. of the order of several hundred years: there were a few other devotional books in the room, and prints of religious houses and of St. Bernard, the patron, and other Saints. On learning who and what I was, he gave me his family history—his name M——, from Hackney. * * * He also proposed to introduce me to the Superior, the Prior, Father ——, whose family name is Palmer. This gentleman was very courteous and communicative, apparently a simple devotee. Both accompanied us to the chapel, and the Superior took me to the garden and explained every thing that I seemed to wish to understand. My impression from him was, that the discipline of these Trappists is not so insupportably severe as the rules of the order would lead us to suppose. He explained his motives for joining the brotherhood, 'to be with God—only with God.' Several of the monks were in the fields and garden at work. The farm, as yet small, is made from the wild rocky heath, by dint of labour and by virtue of manure, and is extending every year. The crops were good, and the garden appeared productive. The products of the garden are for the table of the monks, who lament the loss of their house and grounds near Nantes, in France, whence they were driven by the Revolution of 1830, as far as I understood, by the Republican mob, not by any ordonnance of Louis Philippe or of the barricade government. Even Napoleon had tolerated the Trappists and other monkish orders, only limiting the number of each brotherhood to twenty. The first French Revolution drove these drones from France, who flew to England and settled at Lulworth, Dorsetshire, under the patronage and on the estate of Mr. Weld. They had returned to France, and now talk of their twenty acres of garden there, and the sumptuous dessert they enjoyed. The Prior told me, for instance, he had as many as a dozen of the finest peaches in the world on his plate at one time. The Trappists are allowed the beverage of the country in which they are, whether wine, cider or beer. The last-named drink was of the quality of table ale. The bread was black, from wheat and barley, the wheat from their own crop of last year being now nearly exhausted by their charity to the poor around them. Their butter from their own dairy, which was set before us, was sweet and good. They have this at their meals as well as cheese. They are not restricted as to quantity. Their breakfast, or rather their dinner of rice milk, at 10 a.m., and their supper at 6 p.m., are their only meals. They have of course an infirmary, where every one goes when indisposed, and here they have (if, I presume, recommended by a medical man) meat, eggs, wine, and whatever good things are at hand. The medical attendant, a Catholic, lives at Whittick. One of the brothers is so much of a doctor as to bleed. The more common complaint, as I learned from F. Edmund, is *indigestion*. They have seven services, founded, the Prior told me, upon the Psalmist's 'seven times a day,' viz. 2 a.m., 6, 9, 12, 5, and some two other hours, but these are all short. On Sunday mornings there is a sermon, which is attended by the people of the neighbourhood. They use the *Athanasian Creed*, except on Festivals, for which there is a special service, contrary to the usage of the Church of England. Each monk sleeps on a mattress of straw, with pillow of the same. The cowl serves for night-cap. I inquired, but could learn little, about their library or scholarship. F. Edmund seemed inclined to boast of a correspondence which one of the brethren of superior talents had entered into with a neighbouring clergyman, who, on a visit to Mount Vernon, had attacked F. Edmund with ensnaring questions. The controversy was said to be going on.

"One of our party observed a youth in a smock frock and correspondent dress, and inquired who he was, and whether he was sent to the monastery for education? The answer was, that he was sent to *retard* his education, he being so sharp a boy as to outrun and discourage his brothers.

"There are numerous visitors in the season. We saw, probably, not less than fifty.

"The poor in the neighbourhood are fed from the monastery, and the monks are sent for to their bed-sides in sickness and death. Many of the neighbouring poor die Roman Catholics. F. Edmund shrewdly and voluntarily observed, that there was influence in meat and drink to the poor, not without a reflection upon the neighbouring clergy, who are fattening upon the tithes.

"Both F. Edmund and the Prior spoke to me unreservedly and triumphantly of the prevalence of the Roman Catholic faith in England, and of the probable speedy return of England, &c., to the Catholic Church. The present building of the monastery is very confined. A new monastic house is nearly finished close by, more spacious and convenient. Here is to be a new and imposing church, with a steeple of wide dimensions. No money is taken by the monks; but there is a poor-box, which appeared, from the sound of the silver we put in it, to be well filled to-day. This monastery must have been built, and be kept up, at great expense. The fathers spoke only by hints of their funds, which, I imagine, are partly derived from France, and partly by subscriptions of the faithful. The General of the order, to whom implicit obedience is rendered, resides at Rome.

"The Catholic nobility and gentry of England probably subscribe to this and other monasteries as means of faith propagation."

From Leicester he proceeded into Cheshire, where he purposed to assist at the marriage of his third son; but the outbreak of the workpeople in the manufacturing districts in that memorable year, disconcerted all his plans. To a spectator from a distance, an ordinary trade "turn-out" is sufficiently alarming, exhibiting society in a state of chaos, and for a time putting every thing that is good and civilizing in abeyance, and giving prominence to the worst and most malignant features of human nature. The rising of 1842 was, however, far more serious than an ordinary "turn-out," and was a widely-organized conspiracy on the part of the work-people of every class to prevent, by the influence of fear, the downward tendency of wages, occasioned by diminished capital and contracted demand. Some of the entries in the

Diary, recording amongst other things the beginning of this outbreak, which he had the opportunity of observing, are worth preserving.

"Aug. 6, Saturday.—To the *Quiet Shepherd* amongst the hills. On our way, passed through a long procession of the first *turn-outs* from Messrs. Bayley's mill, Stalybridge, consisting of men and boys, women and girls, walking two and two, and apparently commanded by leaders. The men were quiet, but gave us hard looks and sneers and derisive bows; the women were more garrulous, and called out to us; but we could hear and understand little, except that they wished us to know that our dress and the carriage were an offence.

" — 7, Sunday.—I preached at Dukinfield from Ps. cxxxiii. 1. Great agitation amongst the people, whose stare to-day indicated some movement. All the talk is of this. The bad news arrived of judgment in the Lords in the Hewley case against the Unitarians. I expected a modified decision, and was much moved by the judgment, which will be a heavy blow to us, followed, as it no doubt will be, by other adverse proceedings.

" — 8, Monday.—The agitation and tumult growing. Miss L —— came to Alfred's to sleep for security. All our dinner engagements for several days forwards put off by ourselves and our friends. The procession of malcontents, some carrying bludgeons, &c., down Dukinfield-hill to Ashton, really alarming.

" — 9.—All agitation! I was eye-witness to 'the madness of the people.' We were in a sort imprisoned at Alfred's all day. The tumult prevailing without; various rumours, all alarming. We resolved to hasten to Liverpool, and wrote accordingly, and began to pack up.

" — 10.—Reports as to difficulty and danger of travelling very threatening. To Manchester; that town apparently quiet; but we heard of tumults and saw soldiers. We felt relieved on reaching Lindsey's quiet house at Liverpool this evening.

" — 28.—(At Dukinfield again.) Much conversation on state of things here with —— (*a manufacturer*). He feels the turn-out every way, but maintains that education has done much for the common people, and that there is a large body of thinking, sound-judging and right-feeling people among them, who do not appear wanting in moral courage. It does not tell much for the people, however, that, according to his own statement, their wages at the last and reduced scale, before the turn-out, averaged, for man, woman and child, 10s. each individual per week.* He says that, for every person employed, there must be reckoned one unemployed, so that the allotment for each in a family, including babes, will be 5s. per head, which, where there are several in a family, would be a sufficiency, but for want of economy, &c.

---

* Similar testimony was given on oath at the special assize at Liverpool, before Lord Abinger, who tried, with passionate and almost brutal severity, many of the insurgents and conspirators.

"Aug. 29.—— —— (*a workman*) came by invitation this evening to chat with me. He gave me his interesting religious history, explained the state of parties (religious and political) in this neighbourhood, and stated his views, as a workman, of the present turn-out. He divides the blame between *some* of the masters, who by a trick as to machinery and hands have undersold others, and the men. He considers Chartism and political disaffection generally to have been the cause of the organized rising. He considers education to have done great good, in proportion to its extent, but laments that few are really well-informed, and fewer still have courage to act up to their knowledge.

"Joanna Southcott's followers still exist here, divided into three parties, *Southcotians, Israelites* and *Nazarenes*. Some men of property, he says, are in the *second* class. Of the more wealthy early disciples of Joanna, some have gone back to the Church of England, and some are now of no religion.

"—31.—Returned home from Lancashire and Cheshire, after an absence of six weeks, during which we have had remarkably fine weather, good and improving health, and experienced abundant kindness from our children and friends, and found all well at home. God be praised!"

Rev. Robert Aspland to Rev. R. Brook Aspland.

"Liverpool, August 11, 1842.

"Dear Brook,—I duly received the second edition of the *Guardian*, and have read with more concern than surprise of the outrages yesterday at Manchester. The report of these confirms my suspicion of an *organized* rising, and my apprehension of more serious mischief. Pray relieve our anxiety by a daily note until the storm seem to be overpast."

To this was appended this playful note to his daughter-in-law:

"Dear Jane,—Should Brook be upon his *march with the rebels* all day to-morrow, I look to you to be penwoman for him and us, and to relate the circumstances of his arrest or enlistment, and the temper in which he bears his captivity!—Your loving father, R. A."

"Liverpool, August 15.

"We rejoice to learn that you are yet safe. But the state of things is so gloomy and threatening, that we all think I had better give up all thought of going to Knutsford. I may be obliged to return home sooner than I intended, in order to avoid the abominable Income-tax penalty, for I do not see how I can fill up the papers here; i. e. if the monarch people will leave any of the great roads open to the metropolis.

"As far, too, as we can judge, it seems better that you should remain at home to meet emergencies, especially as you can scarcely now hope to have the accommodation of a private carriage. Brother Green can perform the ceremony and fasten the knot as well as we; and our absence, however mortifying, will be explained to all by the troubles of the neighbourhood.

"I hope and trust the young couple will suffer no greater inconvenience than *a change of ministry*.

"On Saturday, Mr. Jevons and Mr. John Robberds came and secured me for yesterday morning at the Park. I preached accordingly at the cosey old chapel, and suffer no inconvenience to-day. Lindsey and I dined at Mr. Jevons's, and drank tea at Mr. Thomas Jevons's. We had a delightful promenade in the afternoon beside the grounds of my late esteemed friend, John Freme; the pleasure, however, a little dashed, as to myself, by the feeling that the hospitable house was no longer accessible. Such is the price to be paid for living to any degree of age."

"Sunday, Sept. 4.—We had a visit to-day from Mrs. S——, formerly Miss Benwell, of Battersea. She was eager to renew our acquaintance, commenced when I was at Battersea under Joseph Hughes, in the year 1797 or 1798. She reminded me of many incidents which I had forgotten. I did not think that in my early youth, and my own comparatively humble condition, I was an object of so much attention to her (as her recollections prove), placed as she then was in the midst of affluence, and with gay and golden prospects before her. She attended the morning service and joined in the Sacrament, and left us in the afternoon. Her visit was extremely agreeable to us all."

Rev. Robert Aspland to Rev. R. Brook Aspland.

"Hackney, Oct. 18, 1842.

"Dear Brook,—You will be afflicted to hear that our admirable friend Fearon is no more.* He breathed his last yesterday afternoon. The event was wholly unexpected by the family. Henry has written to me, requesting that I would apprize you of the bereavement, and remind you of your engagement to officiate at the funeral. * * *

"Our friend's departure must have been sudden. I had a long note from him on Saturday, written on Friday, in his usual or rather best manner. In answer to a question of mine, he told me that he approved of the reasoning of the Morning Chronicle against the 'Ashburton Treaty,' and avowed that he had had a hand in the controversy.

"Alas, what shadows we are! Blessed be God, we are allowed to hope for a more substantial and enduring life!

"Your affectionate father,

ROBERT ASPLAND."

---

* Mr. H. B. Fearon, of London and Hampstead, the author of "Narrative of a Journey through the Eastern and Western States of America," and "Thoughts on Materialism." He was a man of fine intellectual powers, warmed with the purest patriotism, and always ready for every friendly and generous action. Two years before this, he and Mr. Aspland had taken a week's tour together in Kent. Both were invalids. The unreserved communication of experience and feelings that then took place, was to both the subject of pleasant recollection to the close of life.

The death of Dr. Channing, October 2, 1842, excited in both worlds the profoundest regret. At a special meeting of the Unitarian Association Committee, convened to pay some token of respect to his memory, Mr. Aspland attended and drew up the resolutions, which were proposed by himself, Dr. Hutton and Mr. Tagart. From the pulpit Mr. Aspland delivered a discourse, in which he essayed to delineate the character of Dr. Channing " as a writer, philanthropist and divine." The portrait is drawn with freedom, and shade, as well as light, is admitted into the picture. Allusion is made to the depreciatory estimate of Priestley, once published by Channing, and afterwards silently omitted in the republication of the tract. When preaching to the Gravel-Pit congregation, it would have been an instance of defective moral taste or courage not to have introduced this subject, even at the cost of expressing disapprobation of Channing's slight to the memory of a great and good man.

Rev. Robert Aspland to Rev. R. Brook Aspland.

"Hackney, Dec. 6, 1842.

"Dear Brook,—My sermon is at length out. It will not satisfy—it may offend—certain of Channing's idolators. I am not sorry, however, to have had an opportunity of asserting his merits with some discrimination, and of shewing that Dr. Priestley is not by all of us abandoned to be trodden under foot.

"I have received the funeral services on the occasion by Gannett and Ellis: they are very good—very interesting—Gannett's especially, as giving a little personal history. They say (at least one of them says, I think both), that he was more highly extolled, and praised in a more unqualified manner, here than at home.

"I must not, however, dismiss the subject without saying that Channing was good, eminently good, and in some respects truly great."

The defenceless legal position of the English Presbyterians had, ever since the final decision of the Hewley suit, anxiously occupied the mind of Mr. Aspland; and frequent and long were the consultations, personal and by letter, which he held with Mr. G. W. Wood, and other leading friends in England and Ireland. The way was full of peril, and a single false step might be irreparably injurious to the Presbyterian body. It will be seen that, to the protection of their rights, he devoted nearly all the remainder of his strength and life.

Rev. Robert Aspland to Rev. R. Brook Aspland.

"Hackney, Jan. 12, 1843.

"Dear Brook,—I have at length succeeded in forming an English Presbyterian Union, on a large scale and better plan than heretofore. I got the Unitarian Association Committee to originate the matter. The first meeting of ministers and lay representatives of congregations, &c., was held December 29, at the Association-rooms; the second at Dr. Williams's Library, on Tuesday last. We were upwards of seventy, unanimous and in a right spirit. We chose a confidential Committee of about a dozen, with full powers, and an adequate purse made up in the room. This Committee will meet on Tuesday; and we shall soon, I presume, be in communication with the Government and our friends in Parliament—our object being legislative protection.

"I am, and have been for some time, in frequent and confidential correspondence with Mr. G. W. Wood, who will, I hope, soon join us. You are perhaps aware that in the summer he and a few others went up to Sir Robert Peel and the Attorney-General, and obtained a promise that no new bill should be filed against us pending the Hewley suit. The suit being at an end, we must look for something more, the event having thrown down all our fences, and exposed us to inroads from our enemies. The opinion of almost all our professional friends is, that, according to the law as now declared, all our foundations before 1813 are endangered—say even the Gravel-Pit and also Dukinfield, you having built on a Trinitarian foundation, as the law ('the perfection of reason') will have it. Whether we shall obtain protection, remains to be seen. The Irish brethren have been up with petitions to the Castle. Their case is somewhat different from ours, suits having been commenced as to some places and threatened as to many others

"Mr. J. Ashton Yates was our chairman at the first meeting; Mr. B. Wood, M. P. for Southwark, at the other. The latter gentleman is a valuable coadjutor, not merely from his station, but also from his mild manners, uniform good sense and business habits. * * *

"You refer to the review of the sermon on Channing. It is curious that Harriet Martineau writes to me that all I have said of Channing in relation to Dr. Priestley is true and right. I have also seen a letter of Lucy Aikin's, a friend and constant correspondent of Channing's, in which she says that in one of his *last* letters to her he expressed surprise and gratitude at the favour of the English Unitarians towards him after his 'attack' upon Dr. Priestley, and his sorrow that he had ever written the offensive note.

"Yours ever affectionately, R. ASPLAND."

"Feb. 26, 1843.

"* * * The Attorney-General will not suffer any information to be filed in his name against us without consulting with us, nor, as I understand, till the question of legislative protection be settled.

"George Matthews has given us printed, and through Mr. S. Cotton verbal, notice of an attack upon Red-cross Street; and we have reason to believe several informations against chapels are being prepared.

"Yet we are not discouraged. I have seen, as part of a deputation, Lord John Russell and the Marquis of Lansdowne, who are, as we reckoned upon, cordial friends. Since I was laid aside, my brethren have been with Lord Cottenham and the Solicitor-General, whose language is all that we could desire."

"March 30.—To Manchester Buildings. Thence, with Mr. G. W. Wood, Mr. E. Field and Mr. J. A. Yates, to the Lord Chancellor, in House of Lords. He was courteous, and informed us he had drawn up clauses of a Bill for our *protection* to be submitted to the Cabinet.

"April 12.—A Bill of relief is actually *before the Cabinet*. It will not do; but we do not despair of getting a measure adopted which will be satisfactory, at least as regards chapels and their endowments. The authorities impose silence upon us for a time, in order that their course may not be obstructed by bigotry and fanaticism. As soon as our tongues are loosed, we will speak out to the whole country.

" — 21.—Died the good Duke of Sussex, aged 70.*

---

* Mr. Aspland gratified his respect and affection for this fine-hearted and clear-headed British Prince, by a funeral discourse, preached at the Gravel-Pit, April 30, 1843, from Rom. ii. 10. The character of the Duke, as drawn by him on this occasion, was inserted in the Christian Reformer, X. 333. The Duke availed himself of several opportunities, subsequent to the Test-Act dinner, of marking his good-will to Mr. Aspland. At a public dinner of the St. Patrick's charity-school, which, at the request of Mr. Charles Butler, Mr. A. attended, the Duke, in proposing his health, alluded to the speech at the Test-Act dinner, saying, that from the moment he heard it, he had "put down Mr. Aspland *in his book* as a friend." That this was no mere courtly phrase was evidenced by the very remarkable interest which the Duke took in the volume of Discourses published by Mr. A. in 1833. The copy belonging to the Duke was purchased, at the sale of his library, by Mr. Richard Cogan. It appears to have been most carefully read and re-read; there is scarcely a page without one or more marginal notes in the Duke's manuscript. On the margin of the contents are marked dates and places, such as "Newstead Abbey," "Holkham" and "Oak Hill," as if it had been made a travelling companion. On the title-page is written, "Presented to me by the Author, a most excellent, valuable and intellectual man." The sermon (No. VI., p. 93) entitled, "True Religion as opposed to Superstition," appears, from the marginal notes, to have attracted especial attention. At p. 110, opposite to a passage describing the superstitious and irreligious nature of popular notions of "saving religion," is written—*This is very strikingly put*. At p. 300, beneath some remarks on the consequences of public transgressions, war, conquest and luxury, is written—*Hear, ye kings!* At p. 298, where, in illustration of the truth that ordinary calamities are not judgments, the preacher remarks, that sudden death may equally seize the blasphemer uttering an oath, and the servant of God pleading the cause of truth and righteousness, there is this marginal note—*True, but how different the death; the former at war with his fellow-creature, the latter in peace with all the world.* In the sermon (No. XII.) against long-continued resentments, reference is made to the evening sacrifice of the Jews, beneath which this very appropriate note is written—*The Jews now, as previous to the Christian era, began their supper of the Sabbath by blessing a cup of wine,*

"April 28.—Deputation Committee—Messrs. G. W. Wood, B. Wood, Jas. Esdaile and myself—to Sir James Graham, at Home Office, at one. Most satisfactory interview. Sir James understands the question, and is apparently with us, and will move the Cabinet, and promises we shall have an assurance from the Government in about a week.

"May 1.—The deputation from the Presbyterian Union (consisting of Mr. G. W. Wood, S. Smith, E. Field and myself) went to Lord Stanley, at the Colonial Office, by appointment, at three o'clock. He received us very courteously, admitted that we were entitled to relief, but stated his difficulties. We set him right on some points and gave him information on others, and left him under the persuasion that his influence in the Cabinet will be in our favour.

"— 27.—To Mr. E. Field's, where the Deputation Committee and the associated lawyers discussed the Bill framed, on the Attorney-General's suggestions, for our relief. Agreed to it."

The crisis at which the Unitarian Association held its anniversary this year, gave to the proceedings unwonted interest. The preacher was Dr. Montgomery. Mr. Aspland was happily enabled to attend and take part in both the morning and evening meeting. Not soon will his friends forget the energy, never in the days of his youth surpassed, with which he addressed the Unitarians whom he saw assembled from many parts of the country. At the evening meeting, he alluded to the proceedings recently commenced against himself and others who were present, as trustees of Dr. Williams's estates. As the only record of a determination which he had made not to answer inquiries from a court of law into his religious opinions, insertion must be given to the conclusion of his evening speech.

"It is well known to most of this company, that several gentlemen here round the table, who are of the number of trustees of Dr. Williams' Library, in Red-cross Street, have been obliged to enter their appearances to submit before the Chancellor to interrogatories, and undergo indignities of the extent and measure of which we ourselves had no conception. I am quite justified, Mr. Chairman, and ladies and gentlemen, in bringing this matter before you in the present anniversary meeting, because one of the interrogatories we are called on to answer is this, whether we are attached to a certain society, called the Unitarian Association, and whether we have read the books and tracts of the society, and whether those tracts and books are not contrary to

---

which was passed round the table, and called the cup of brotherly love or good fellowship. Many of the notes indicate that the Duke entirely dissented from the orthodox faith. This has been satisfactorily shewn by Mr. Richard Cogan, in his very interesting paper in the Christian Reformer (1845, p. 813), entitled, "Heterodoxy of H. R. H. the late Duke of Sussex," the proofs being drawn from autograph annotations on Hay's "Religio Philosophi."

the doctrine of the Trinity, the Athanasian Creed and the doctrine of Original Sin. Sir, there are many other interrogatories which we are called upon to answer, but for one I have made up my mind. According to my present judgment, I will answer none of their interrogatories. In civil matters I will go as far as any man on the face of the earth in yielding obedience to the powers that be; but in matters of conscience, in questions as to my faith, I mean to be silent. I will not give a reason of the hope that is in me on compulsion. Sir, what may be the fate of this suit now commenced, or what may be the fate of us, the individual trustees, of whom several are now around me, I know not; probably several will join me in refusing to give any answer to the interrogatories touching our personal faith, and if they do, we may be sent by an order from the Vice-Chancellor of England to reside for a time in lodgings provided for us by the state in the Queen's Bench. Should we be carried there, I know we shall carry with us the sympathies and the affections of not only the best people of our own denomination, but of the best people of England. I believe they will not dare to proceed to such an extremity; but let them :—from our prison walls we will speak to the people, and we shall speak, I am persuaded, with a more commanding voice than they have ever yet heard from us."

The hopes which the friendly disposition of the Government had inspired were not to be realized in the session of 1843.

" July 4.—The Lord Chancellor fixed five o'clock p.m. at the House of Lords for seeing our deputation. After attending and waiting some time for the Chancellor, we were obliged, unless we would have been contented with five minutes, to ask for another appointment, which was fixed for tomorrow, Lincoln's-Inn Hall, one o'clock. We went into the House of Lords with our two Members of Parliament (Mr. G. W. Wood and Mr. B. Wood), and had a conference with Lord Cottenham in the outer-room. He was surprised nothing was done; seemed to suspect intentions, &c.; thought we might as well soon see Lord Brougham; and advised us to press the Government, the session of Parliament being so nearly at an end.

" — 5.—Mr. G. W. Wood, Mr. B. Wood, Mr. E. Field and myself, met in Lincoln's-Inn Hall, and were introduced at one o'clock to the Chancellor in his private room. He began by saying he could do nothing for us; he had the North of Ireland upon him — 800,000 (!) of the Irish Presbyterians opposing us. We said the Irish case was different from ours. He asked, would we take a Bill for England? We said we must be content with what we could get. He expressed a willingness to give us the first clause of the Bill as settled by the Attorney-General, that clause protecting such endowments as Hackney and Essex Street. We urged more, and, in spite of his private secretary (Perry), he appeared to give way a little, upon further information as to our case. The great point was, however, that he consented and promised to confer with Lord Cottenham, and allowed us to say as much to Lord C.

"We then agreed to get an interview for two or three of us with Lord C. immediately, and Field and I retired to Sydney's chambers, where we three agreed upon the draft of an address to his Lordship, giving him thanks for his past good services, and authority to act for us,—explaining the points on which we were most anxious.

"July 18.—To Mr. G. W. Wood's. Proceeded (Mr. G. W. W., Mr. B. Wood, Mr. E. Field) to Grafton Street, Lord Brougham's, where Mr. Duckworth (Master in Chancery) joined us. We all went to House of Lords. Lord Brougham received us at first very coldly; but, upon being urged, went in more than once to the Chancellor, sitting on appeals, and at last engaged to urge our Bill, as now pared down. We got a copy engrossed and carried to him in the House of Lords.

" — 25.—Deputation by appointment at Sir Robert Peel's house, Whitehall; present, Messrs. G. W. Wood, T. Thornely, B. Wood, E. Field, J. Esdaile and myself. Sir Robert gave us an hour; his tone desponding. Ireland the difficulty. We came away with the impression that we should have no Bill this session. But Sir Robert engaged to speak to the Law officers and Irish members. He suggests an amicable settlement between the two contending parties in Ireland, Dr. Cooke's and Dr. Montgomery's.

"Aug. 8.—The English deputation and the Irish deputation waited by appointment on the English Attorney-General (Sir Frederick Pollock) at his chambers, King's Bench Walk, where the Irish Attorney-General (Hon. T. B. C. Smith) met us. Sir F. P. undertook not to file any informations against our chapels during the recess of Parliament, without first laying the case before us and hearing our answer. The Hon. T. B. C. S. undertook not to file any new information without consulting and receiving instructions from the Government here; he could not undertake to stay pending suits.

" — 16.—To town, to the Library. In my absence Dr. Montgomery called to take leave. He explained only that, after conferences and communications with Sir Robert Peel, Lord Brougham, &c., he was going home with a light heart."

Some friends there were, acquainted with the secret and deeply-important transactions described in these extracts from the Diary, who did not participate in the strong conviction felt by Mr. Wood, Dr. Montgomery and Mr. Aspland, that the Government had acted with perfect good faith; that circumstances altogether unforeseen had prevented the realization of the hopes which they had in the early part of the session encouraged; and that, notwithstanding the present disappointment, a good foundation was laid for legislative protection of Presbyterian trusts in the following session.

The fruit of these long and anxious negociations was the Dissenters' Chapels Bill, introduced and carried in 1844, in the face of an organized and uncompromising opposition, in which were combined all the fanatics in and out of the Established Church in England and Ireland. The fierce temper displayed by the "religious world," in both countries, against the Bill, proved that Sir Robert Peel and the Lord Chancellor acted most prudently in not attempting to legislate on the subject at the close of a session. Had the urgency of their Presbyterian suitors induced them to make the attempt in 1843, not only must they have failed then, but it is not improbable that the Bill of 1844 would not have been proposed, or, if proposed, not carried.

Rev. Robert Aspland to Rev. R. Brook Aspland.

"Hackney, Aug. 3, 1843.

"Dear Brook,—I have been nearly worn out with this negociation with the Government. We are wrecked on the Irish coast, but not through any fault of the State pilots, except perhaps Sir Robert's characteristic indecision. An attempt is being made, through the influence of the Government, to settle the dispute between the Irish parties, with a view to a legislative measure of relief for both countries next session. Meantime, we hope for, and have little or no doubt of, the Attorney-General's protection of our *chapels* and their endowments during the interval.

"The Williams's Trust suit will, I suppose, sleep during the long vacation.

"A circular will soon be sent from the Committee to our brethren at large, which will in substance assure our friends that we consider ourselves standing better now than at the beginning of the session of Parliament.

"I have been writing in the midst of a thunder-storm (from 2 to 3 o'clock p.m.), following and accompanied by torrents of rain. The weather is certainly threatening. From various parts I hear of a general and fatal blight upon the wheat crop. A bad harvest is only wanting to make the cup of public distress overflow, and almost ensure national ruin."

"August 11, 1843.

"* * * I am amused with your account of A——'s studies. Are you not afraid of the theology, or rather demonology, of John Bunyan? I remember, when a child, being frightened out of my wits by a vision of the imaginative Tinker's Beelzebub.

"We have seen the Attorney-General for England, and the same officer for Ireland; and though we must not talk of a *pledge* or a positive promise, we are authorized to say to our brethren, *Fear nothing at present.*"

Mr. Aspland spent the greater part of the month of September in Devonshire, and was sufficiently well to preach before the Devon and Cornwall Unitarian Association at Colyton. He was the guest of two friends, to whom he was very warmly attached, Rev. M. L. Yeates, of Collumpton, and his old pupil, Rev. John Smethurst, of Moreton-Hampstead. A letter of reminiscences of this visit, from the last-named friend, is now before the writer; and one or two passages are transcribed, as exhibiting Mr. Aspland in both a social and a pensive mood.

"Your Father reached Collumpton in the latter part of the first week of September, and on the Monday following I joined him there, at the house of my good and much-lamented friend Mr. Yeates. The day after, we were joined by Mr. Odgers, of Plymouth; and on the Wednesday we all went to Colyton, where your Father preached a most eloquent sermon, and spoke with much energy at the dinner. All the day, particularly on our way back to Collumpton, he appeared to be in as good and high spirits as ever I saw him. * * * It was evening when we reached my house at Moreton. Though in good spirits, he seemed fatigued with the ride. When he was sitting down, just on the spot where I am now writing, he looked at me and said, 'Smethurst, I feel I shall not live much longer.' I think these were his exact words—and he immediately added in a cheerful voice, 'that gives me no uneasiness.' * * * We went together one day to Haytor Rocks. The scene from them is perhaps the finest in the West of England. They are about eight miles from Moreton, and the road is not good, but your Father seemed to enjoy the ride. The last two or three miles are on an open down at a great elevation, and as the day was remarkably fine, we had a splendid view over the South Hams, and as far as the Coast. Whether it was the high ground, or the clear pure air we found there, I know not, but I never witnessed such a change in any one as in your Father on that occasion. It seemed as if he had cast from him a load. He breathed freely and spoke with an animation which surprised Mr. Yeates and myself. * * * I never heard him more eloquent than he was on some subjects which started up in conversation on that day. Mr. Yeates was perfectly astonished, and many times afterwards did he mention our being at Haytor Rocks as one of the most interesting events of his life. Your Father, I have reason to believe, had most pleasing reminiscences of that day's excursion; for in several notes which I had from him during the following winter, there was always some playful and pleasant allusion to the Haytor Giants, as he styled the rocks. Alas! I suppose that must have been the last rural excursion that he enjoyed."

Besides preaching in the pulpits of his friends at Collumpton and Moreton, he spent one Sunday at Exeter, and preached in George's Meeting. This was a melancholy day and a most depressing duty. A few weeks before he had been in correspondence with his friend, the Rev. Henry Acton, with whom he had planned interviews and journeys during this visit to the West. In the interval, Mr. Acton, though in the prime of life, had been struck down by paralysis, and, after languishing six days, died. With his own anticipations of a not distant dismissal, it will be understood how sorrowful were Mr. Aspland's emotions when occupying the pulpit which his late friend had adorned for twenty years. After the service, he had an interview in the vestry with the bereaved family,—a widow and six children. In recording it, he speaks of it as "a distressing scene." Of the solitariness and sadness of that day at Exeter, Mr. Aspland often afterwards spoke and wrote.

CHAPTER XXXIII.

Within a week or two of his return home, Mr. Aspland was painfully shocked by the sudden death of Mr. G. W. Wood, M.P. Under any circumstances he would have deplored this event, as a serious loss to the English Presbyterian denomination, for no layman of the present age devoted so much time, influence and talent, to the promotion of their interests as Mr. Wood. Mr. Aspland had enjoyed peculiar opportunities of appreciating his services in defending the property and religious liberty of the Unitarians: he had observed in conferences with the members of the Government, to which politically he was opposed, the confidence reposed in Mr. Wood by the Prime Minister and his colleagues, as a prudent, able and honourable man. Remembering the perilous condition of the chapels and trusts of the English and Irish Unitarians, Mr. Aspland might well pronounce the death of Mr. Wood at this crisis an "irreparable loss" to the religious body "whose true and lasting welfare was near his heart, whose vital interests he ably maintained, and whom he represented before the Government and the Parliament with truth and dignity."*

Mr. Aspland naturally regarded the removal of his contemporary, associate and friend, as a memento of his own not distant summons. He remembered that during the anxious and sometimes toilsome labours in which they had been during the year associated, they had often compared the symptoms of their several cases, and come to the conclusion that both were suffering from the same complaint. Any one seeing them together in 1843, and observing Mr. Wood's robust and upright form, and his countenance unmarked by that anxious expression which is the frequent symptom of chronic disease, would not have anticipated that Mr. Aspland would be the survivor.

---

* Obituary in the Christian Reformer (N. S.), X. 729.

On the Sunday (October 8) following Mr. Wood's death, Mr. Aspland went to meeting fatigued and dejected. The day was hot. He attempted to stand during the delivery of the sermon, which was an earnest dissuasive against delays in religion. The heat, anxiety and emotion occasioned by the subject, brought on faintness and difficulty of breathing, and he was obliged to close the service abruptly. The duties of the Sunday were subsequently to this matter of great anxiety both to himself and his friends. The assistance of Dr. Thomas Sadler was secured by the congregation in the month of November. This engagement was the source of satisfaction and comfort to Mr. Aspland to the close of his life; and the hours which the young minister passed in the library at Hackney Grove, conversing on pastoral duties and reading aloud to the invalid, were improving to one and interesting to both.

Of the bodily sufferings which, with but few intervals of ease and comfort, darkened the two last years of his life, there is no necessity for a minute description. A few extracts from his Diary and Letters will serve to shew that they were most severe, and in what spirit they were endured.

"1843. Nov. 4.—After a comfortless day went to bed gasping, and after trying to lie down, was convulsed with spasmodic affection of the organs of respiration for two or three hours in the middle of the night. I took ether, &c. Towards morning I got some hard sleep; awoke in the morning exhausted.

"— 5, Sunday.—I had given notice of a sermon this morning on *The present State of the Religious World as to Persecution*. I began the sermon days ago, but indisposition prevented my doing much at it. My state this morning kept me of course a prisoner.

"Dec. 3.—Quite disabled from going out. Such sabbaths are wearisome and humbling; but I have preached to others patience and resignation!

"— 31, Sunday.—Preached from 1 Tim. iv. 10, 'We trust in the living God.'*

"Thus ends another year! God be praised for all his mercies!

"1844. Jan. 7, Sunday.—Preached from Mark xiii. 32—*Futurity known to God only*.

"— 23.—My *birthday*, 62. 'What is your life?' My state of health does not justify me in reckoning upon the return of the day; but I trust I am prepared to say, 'The will of the Lord be done!'

---

* This instructive and deeply-devotional discourse was, at the writer's request, printed in the *Christian Reformer* (N. S. Vol. I., 1845, pp. 9—16). It abounds in touching allusions to his own state and prospects, and to the removal of those who had gone before "to the house appointed for all living."

"Feb. 3.—*Anniversary of my dear mother's death;* also of the birth (a year ago) of Mary's* infant."

The intervals between the paroxysms of his complaint were still marked by much hopefulness and even vivacity of spirits. He took great delight in the company of his grandchildren, and eagerly inquired from the distant members of his family for *nursery news*, and made the indications of their opening minds and characters, as reported to him, the subject of frequent conversation. Of the playfulness of his talk during these intervals of ease, little idea can be given to strangers. The following notes, written to a lady, a much-esteemed member of his congregation, shew that he could still write with playfulness and ease. There is reference in one of them to a remark, strangely attributed to him, expressive of contempt for female writers.

Rev. Robert Aspland to Miss Wood.

"Grove, Hackney, Jan. 31, 1844.

"Dear Miss Wood,—I perceive with regret that your article of Review, kindly sent from the country, is left out of present No. of C. R. It was allotted with others for the No., and during the paroxysm of my late illness postponed to others which better *fitted in*. You may reckon upon seeing it next month, and I beg to say once for all, that any notices of any of the publications of your very estimable friends the *Howitts*, in whose sad affliction I sincerely sympathize, will be acceptable,—with one only condition,—brevity.

"Whilst I write smoothly to you, how *rough* could I be with your sister Sarah—the popular Tale-writer—for not sending me a copy of the 'Tests of Time'! I have got it, notwithstanding; and for her great sin she may expect the utmost severity of criticism! Do punish by alarming her.

"I have written above of my *late illness*. Thanks to a good Providence, through Dr. Bright's and Mr. Hacon's means, I can use this language. So improved am I, that I calculate (D. v.) on delivering next Sunday morning the second of two sermons on *Superstition*, of which the first was delivered last Sunday fortnight.

"I hope your family has re-assembled in goodly number and promising health,—in good spirits I am sure they are, as they ought to be.

"Our reports from the Isle of Wight are various from day to day; when best, we *rejoice with trembling!*

"Our united regards to your whole family, even including the *authoress*, and believe me to be your very sincere and now old friend,

ROBERT ASPLAND."

---

* His youngest daughter, the wife of Mr. Henry Ridge, now seriously ill at Ventnor, where she had been advised by her medical friends to winter.

"Grove, Hackney, Feb. 6, 1844.

"My dear Miss Wood,—Accept my thanks for your note in reply, which reached me only by the last post yesternight. I grieve at the melancholy report of Mrs. Wood's state. You have, I trust, the consolation that no glimpses of consciousness afflict her, by shewing her the decay of her mind. In such privations and troubles we have but one plain duty—submission.

"Thank your sister for her frankness, but tell her that the reported speech is to me a mystery. I should feel humbled by giving a serious contradiction to a misrepresentation so absurd, and charging me with a sentiment so illiberal and barbarous. We read perpetually, and with satisfaction and sometimes with delight, female authors, homebred and foreign. The misconception may have arisen (though how, none of *us* can explain) from my laughing occasionally at *very fine* writers, of *both sexes*, aspiring to be *transcendental and sublime*, especially when they are vehemently bepraised and held up as models for admiration and patterns to be copied.

"I can say no more, but my sincere regard for your sister, and my cordial approval of her literary labours, would not let me say less.

"I was out on Sunday morning, riding to and fro, and accompanied my friend Mr. Young* to a mid-day charitable meeting in town yesterday; and, though I feel the effects of both the exertions, am not aware that I am damaged by them in my general health.

"My feebleness is the sole reason of my not calling upon you. When you or any of your sisters are in this neighbourhood, pray call, if only to shew that you do not pass by my door as that of a woman or pen-woman hater.

"Kindest regards and best wishes to you all, in which Mrs. A. and Miss Middleton (here you have our whole present family) join, and believe me yours very truly and affectionately, ROBERT ASPLAND."

The sermon referred to in the first of these notes was delivered on February 4, and was the last he was permitted to preach. It was one of two discourses, originally composed many years previously, on the history and consequences of Superstition. Both discourses, as now delivered, were enriched by many additional passages, suggested by his recent reading or by the aspect of the times. Two or three of these passages, as the last which he wrote for and delivered from the pulpit, will be read by his friends with melancholy interest:

"The religion of Mahomed combined in strange alliance some of the first

---

* The writer cannot allow the name of Mr. James Young, his father's friend during the whole of his ministry at Hackney, and his zealous associate in many good works, to pass without an expression of respect and gratitude. To Mr. Young's kindness Mr. Aspland was especially indebted during his long sickness for many friendly and gratifying attentions.

principles of the Hebrew and Christian systems with the fierce superstition of the Heathen wanderers of the great desert. The vital essence of it was implicit faith and ferocious energy. Death, slavery, tribute to unbelievers, were the glad-tidings of the Arabian Prophet. To the idolaters indeed, or those who acknowledged no special revelation, one alternative only was proposed, conversion or the sword. The people of the Book, as they are termed in the Koran,—or four sects of Christians, Jews, Magians and Sabians,—were favoured in being permitted to redeem their adherence to their ancient law, by the payment of tribute and other marks of humiliation and servitude.*

"Melancholy is the reflection that the history of the Christian church for ages is the same dark tale of brutal intolerance, differing only in the actors,— accompanied and encouraged by superstition as gross as that of Mahometans and Pagans. The degree of the superstition invariably marked the height to which the waves of persecution rose: as *that* fell, *these* subsided. The recent attempt to bring back into the church certain exploded superstitions, has been signalized by the revival of the principle that it is the duty of the civil power to coerce heresy and punish heretics. On the other side, the sentiment of fear pervading the minds of sects which have renounced outward superstition, has produced to some extent the same effect,—leading them into unsocial habits and intolerant judgments,—into the condemnation of such as differ from them, and the prediction, if not the imprecation, of eternal Divine judgments upon their heads on account of their opinions. With both these parties the worst and most fatal error and heresy is to think favourably and speak charitably of all mankind, and to believe and avow that there is ample shelter in the mercy of the Heavenly Father for all his sincere, though mistaken children, of every faith and worship."

"The tides and currents of public opinion are ruled by general laws. Ebb and flow, action and re-action, are as sure as day and night, light and shade. The prevalent enthusiasm succeeded a state of indifference, and is causing the return of superstition. A party has sprung up in the National Church which is desirous of going back, and of restoring exploded dogmas and obsolete observances. It is sought to exalt the Church above the State,—in other words, to recover the lost power of the Priesthood, of whose divine right the sacramental and other awful mysteries are so many proofs and tokens. The novelty has for a time and to a degree succeeded, partly owing, it must be confessed, to the high character of some of the leaders of the movement, shewn by their readiness to make sacrifices for conscience' sake. But that it will ultimately prevail, no one can fear who is not ready to admit that the intel-

---

* "Hallam, Mid. Ages, II. 167 (8vo, 3rd ed., 1822).

lectual exertions of ages may be wholly fruitless,—that the human mind has come to a stop,—that the great and glorious principles of the Christian revelation may be again hidden under the veil of human authority,—and that society, which in every thing else is seeking and demanding more light and liberty, will re-plunge into the darkness of barbarous times, rivet the yoke of bondage upon its own neck, and bow down in utter prostration of spirit before the least formidable order of the usurpers of human rights and divine prerogatives.

"If we may judge of the future by the past history of the church, this theological epidemic will, after it has done its work, go off, not however without weakening many Christian minds and destroying some,—giving way to some other intellectual process in its turn,—the final result being sterner inquiry, better defined truth and more resolute freedom."

The words of exhortation which closed his ministry of more than forty years, were very characteristic of one of the great objects of all his preaching and writing:

"Hear, in conclusion, the language of the great Apostle of us Gentiles, the pure language of the gospel, designed to oppose and rebuke all superstition whatever,—*I will that men* PRAY EVERYWHERE, *lifting up* HOLY HANDS, WITHOUT WRATH AND DOUBTING,—without *doubting* their share in the Father's love and their right and privilege to approach the Father's throne,—without *wrath* against any of their fellow-christians and fellow-men, who, in the integrity and charity of their hearts and the uprightness and purity of their lives, claim the same relationship to God, and exercise the same privilege and right, though it may be with forms to them strange and in tongues to them unknown."

These last words were uttered with an energy* which left a strong impression on his hearers, some of whom were not without the fear that the voice to which they had been so long accustomed would not be often again heard within the walls of the Gravel-Pit meeting.

When Parliament met, the anxieties respecting legislative protection to English and Irish Presbyterian chapels and trusts were renewed. He was enabled to take his share in some of the preliminary arrangements for the Parliamentary campaign, but was denied the privilege of sharing in the toil of the arduous and gloriously successful struggle.

Rev. Robert Aspland to Rev. R. Brook Aspland.

"Hackney, Feb. 9, 1844.

"Dear Brook,—I am in correspondence with Mr. William Rayner Wood.

---

* "I sate and got through pretty well, voice clearing and strengthening as I went on."—*Diary.*

I tell him that we want some Member of Parliament* to take his father's place as representative of the Lancashire, Yorkshire and Cheshire Unitarians. We have chosen Mr. Benjamin Wood as our spokesman for London. My unfortunate illness has been a hindrance to our movement. Should I recover the power of locomotion, my first feeble efforts will be in this direction. * * * We shall gladly co-operate with any gentlemen Lancashire and Cheshire may appoint, be they few or many; but we must not interfere with each other's organization."

"Feb. 13, 1844.

"I have little to say more, except that I have explained pretty fully to Mr. W. R. Wood our general plan and my particular views. He will, I hope, understand from my last to him that your body must act for itself, and that we propose no more than to co-operate with whomsoever you may appoint as your representatives in London. You will always bear in mind that deputations to *Ministers* are strong in proportion to the number of Members of Parliament they contain.

"We are about to call a meeting of our select committee, to determine upon the plan of the campaign; and I wish you to send me by *to-morrow night's post* the names and addresses (if already unknown) of your representatives, that they may be forthwith summoned to the council, which may be held as early as Saturday, certainly not much later.

"Have you heard of Dewey's famous Lecture at the Lyceum, New York, on American Manners and Morals? I have, in a New York paper of the middle of last month, an account of it, which will be made use of in next Christian Reformer. It is a masculine production.

"We had further accounts yesterday—from various quarters—of the Ventnor invalid; upon the whole, good. The babe is said to be getting on marvellously in body and mind. How I should enjoy seeing all the grandchildren in one game of romps!

"The bright and joyous H. Hutton preached a sermon at G. P., Sunday morning, which delighted everybody: he was also *great* in the evening, and had a *monster* congregation.

"This weather is against me, but I bear up. We had a thick (the ladies—learned—call it *dense*) fog this morning, with the thermometer outside my window at 26! The sun is now (half-past three, p. m.) out, though feeble; the fog is (to use a *Yankee* term corresponding to that above) *sparse*, and the instrument is at 36!

"Thanks to a good Providence, we have weathered two-thirds and the

---

* With what indefatigable zeal this want was supplied by Mr. Mark Philips, M. P., and how efficiently he was supported by Mr. Thomas Thornely, M. P., is admiringly and gratefully remembered by every Unitarian of England and Ireland.

worst portion of the winter, and may (to-morrow being Valentine's, or, as we were taught in Cambridgeshire, the *hedge-row pairing* day) look forward to the 'singing of birds,' so pleasant to the wisest of men in the Old Book.

"I must not add more (having written several letters, and having one or two more to write) than that, with love to Jane and the 'offsprings,' and to Alfred and Maria and their ditto,—I am, your affectionate Father,

ROBERT ASPLAND."

"Feb. 15, 1844.

"I received your welcome *valentine* this morning. Your appointment* surprises, but of course pleases me, on many accounts. I have this day written to Mr. Benjamin Wood and Mr. E. Field to summon the Committees, including yours, the names of whose members I have announced, for Tuesday next, the 20th instant."

On the very day of this last note, Mr. Aspland received the sad news of the illness and disability, through paralysis, of Mr. B. Wood. Of the English Presbyterians who had in the previous session taken part in the confidential negotiations with the Government so well conducted by Mr. G. W. Wood, Mr. E. W. Field was almost the only one now left capable of resuming the responsible office. He entered on the important work with energy and talent never surpassed, and, assisted by a most efficient Committee, including many Members of Parliament and representatives from various parts of England and Ireland, had the satisfaction, after a struggle of several months' duration, to see the Unitarians of England and Ireland protected by the Dissenters' Chapels Act.

From his sick chamber, Mr. Aspland watched with deep and constantly increasing interest the progress of the struggle. When the Bill had passed the Lords, and had reached the stage of its second reading in the House of Commons (June 6), he was in a state of great debility. A member of his family, whose privilege it was to be present at the very memorable debate of that evening—in which Sir Wm. Follett, Mr. Gladstone, Mr. Macaulay, Mr. Sheil, Lord John Russell and Sir Robert Peel took part—carried to Hackney, two hours after midnight, the gratifying intelligence of the result of the debate in a majority for the Bill of 190 votes. As soon as he reached the house, he was summoned to the bed-side of the invalid, who heard the tidings with joy, and thanked God for the protection granted in the hour of need. The success acted

---

* As one of a deputation from the Lancashire and Cheshire Presbyterian Association.

like a charm. Never was the power of mind over the weakness of the body more strikingly displayed. He rose at once from his bed, dressed, and hastened to his library; and during the hour that preceded and followed the sunrise on that beautiful summer's morning, he listened with untired ear to the recollections of the glorious debate, commenting, as the narrative proceeded, on the arguments used by the several speakers, in tones, the strength and energy of which was a gratifying sound to the assembled members of his family.

Habitually resigned as he was to his state of seclusion, there were still seasons when he keenly felt his inability to engage in public and ministerial labours. For many years it had been his practice to address the younger portion of his flock on the first Sunday in May. On the previous year he had addressed them, in a sermon of great power, on *The Sense of Duty the rightful governing Principle of Human Life.** Although now incapable of entering the pulpit, he was unwilling that the annual sermon should be given up, and at his particular request it was undertaken by his son, and an announcement was given that the sick pastor would send a written address to the young persons of his flock. During the whole of the week he was worse than usual—in fact, gasping for breath, and quite disabled from writing. On Sunday morning, May 5, he sent for his son to his sick room, and said to him,

" Explain to my young friends why I cannot address them, as I wished and intended.

" Tell them that one object I had in view was to assure them most solemnly, that during my retirement from the pulpit I have been reviewing the opinions I have held and supported there, and that I am more and more satisfied they are (generally speaking) the principles of the pure gospel, and principles that will live and influence and bless the world.

" Tell them that it is the result of my careful experience, that *early* piety is a great blessing, and that piety that is not early is rarely perfect. It is a preservative in the midst of evil, a motive to all good, and a support in all trouble.

" Tell them that I am more and more convinced of the supreme importance of the religion of Jesus Christ, by which I mean the plain gospel as set forth in the four Gospels and the Acts of the Apostles.

---

* This discourse was the last pulpit composition which his broken health permitted him to finish. It is the last sermon in the posthumous volume, pp. 463—482.

It is my earnest desire and prayer that they may adhere to this pure plain gospel, in opposition to superstition on the one side, and pretended philosophy on the other, which consists only in swelling words of vanity.

"Tell them that, in my view, the only way to keep up piety in the young is by attendance on religious ordinances, by reading the Scriptures seriously and carefully, and by the exercise of personal devotion.

"Tell them that my experience agrees with that of all who have gone before me, that no one can know the value of revealed religion till he has tried it in all the changes of human life, and that in the advanced period of life it is found to be indispensable. The hope of immortality is necessary for man, and there is no ground for that hope but in the gospel of Jesus Christ.

"Tell them also that my wishes and prayers are with them and for them, for time and for eternity."

This pastoral message and blessing was spoken as rapidly as his son could take it down in short-hand, without a moment's hesitation, and without the recal or alteration of a word.*

As the year advanced and drew towards its close, all hope of his recovery departed. He sustained an unexpected and severe loss in the illness and death of Mr. Hacon, who for many years had been not less his kind personal friend than his skilful medical attendant. He was a man of masculine understanding,—quite superior to the little arts by which in some cases, despite the want of talent, professional popularity is achieved,—and was uncompromising in his opinions on both religion and politics. Mr. Aspland greatly enjoyed his visits, and the more so that medical topics entered very sparingly into the conversation that ensued.†

---

* During the preceding week he had given another remarkable proof of his power of rapid and correct dictation. A petition from the Gravel-Pit congregation in favour of the Dissenters' Chapels Bill was brought to him for his signature. He thought it did not sufficiently bring out the peculiar features of the case of the congregation, and though too ill at the time to use the pen, he dictated, without a single pause beyond that which the writer needed, the very comprehensive and well-expressed petition presented to the Lords, May 2, by the Marquis of Lansdowne, and which will be found in the Presbyterian Reporter, pp. 177, 178.

† Mr. Hacon appreciated the mental strength of his patient, and treated him with perfect candour when speaking of the progress of his disease. The writer can never forget a conversation with his father on this point. After the morning service one Sunday in May, he said very calmly to his son—"Mr. Hacon has

The continued illness and evident decline of his youngest daughter was a great trial to Mr. Aspland's affectionate heart. Though residing in the same village, each was too much reduced in strength to be able to visit the other. The members of the family, and especially the young children of the dying mother, daily passed between the sick rooms of the two sufferers, and carried messages of affection and comfort. But the sense of inevitable separation for this life was to both keenly distressing, and was a foretaste of the bitterness of death. The following letter is almost sacred in its character, and is surrendered to the public eye only under a sense of duty, exhibiting as it does the strong piety and warm affection of a sorrowful father.

Rev. Robert Aspland to Mrs. Henry Ridge.

"Grove, Nov. 24, 1844.

"My very dear Mary,—You have heard, and I am sure with much satisfaction, that I am apparently recovering, after having long been, in my own opinion and that of my various medical attendants, at death's door. Having had so many relapses and such new attacks of disease in divers forms, I dare not be sanguine in my hopes, but I think the probability is that I may be spared a little longer for the benefit of my family and congregation.

"I am yet so feeble, that I cannot extend my movements beyond my two rooms; it would be imprudent, and might be dangerous, to attempt to go up and down stairs. This cuts me off from the possibility of seeing you at present, and it wrings my heart, my dearest Mary, to hear of your extreme weakness and suffering without being able to drop into your ear any balm of consolation. I am therefore obliged to content myself with the poor and cold substitute of a few written words.

"I can speak to you, my dear child, as one who has been in extremity and

---

been sitting with me. He has told me that he fears that water is forming in my chest. I asked him, if that were the case, whether my dismissal must not be a very painful struggle? He answered, that 'in all probability it would.' I thanked him for the frankness of his communication, and told him I was prepared for all."

Subsequently to Mr. Hacon's fatal illness, Mr. Aspland was attended with affectionate vigilance by his son-in-law, Mr. Michael Harris. It is impossible for the writer to refrain from expressing in this place the gratitude felt by all the members of Mr. Aspland's family towards Dr. Bright and Dr. Southwood Smith, both of whom, notwithstanding the heavy demands on their time and professional skill, were ever ready to come over to Hackney to visit him, and who, with that generosity which is often found in combination with the highest professional attainments, would never allow their attendance to be regarded otherwise than as friendly visits.

tried danger; my comfort always was, as yours, I trust, is, that we are in the hands of a merciful Father, who doth not afflict or grieve us without a benevolent purpose. Let us exercise faith in the Divine goodness, and try to imitate the resignation and submission of the Son of Man, our heaven-exalted brother, the best beloved of the sons of God, and we shall be accepted, notwithstanding our imperfections, and in sorrow and trouble there will be laid and felt underneath us the Everlasting Arm. The gospel promise is not only of forgiveness and redemption in the world to come, but of help and mercy in the present world: no temptation, no trial befals us, but what is common to man, and He that lays on the affliction, will make a way to escape or give strength to suffer, without losing confidence in our Saviour and in his and our God and Father.

"You have seen and experienced enough, dear Mary, to learn that there is no unalloyed happiness on earth; our very pleasures are dashed with pains, to make them suitable to our mortal condition. Happy is it for us that we learn from the teaching and the example of Jesus, the doctrine of life and immortality,—and that we are allowed to indulge the blissful hope of the re-union of parents and children and endeared friends, and their junction with all the wise and good in a state infinitely beyond the clouds and shadows of time and sense.

"Cultivate, I beseech you, even in your darkest moments, these enlivening thoughts and joyful expectations; give yourself up, whether for life or death, to the Father in heaven; trust all that you love,—your husband, children and family,—to the never-failing Providence of Him who is Love, who hath said that he will keep that which you commit to him to the day of merciful restitution.

"My prayers ascend for you, with those for myself and all our dear friends, to the Throne of the Heavenly Grace. May the Lord God Almighty keep and save and bless you! May He alleviate, if it seem not fit to his Infinite Wisdom to remove your affliction! May He, according to his fatherly promise, make all your bed in your sickness, an earnest of comfort and joy above all present conception for ever and ever!

"I am, my very dear Mary,

"Your ever affectionate and sympathizing Father,

ROBERT ASPLAND."

Towards the close of the year Mr. Aspland made preparations for transferring the conduct of the *Christian Reformer* to the hands of another. He had now been engaged as the Editor of an Unitarian Magazine for thirty-nine years, during twelve of which (viz. from 1815 to 1826) he had superintended the publication of two volumes annually,

making the total number of periodical volumes edited by him fifty-one.*
It was a comforting reflection to him, on reviewing his work, that he
could "lay down his office without self-condemnation for a single sentence written by his pen." In the Address in which he took a Farewell of his readers, he felt it to be his duty to the religious denomination in whose service he had spent his strength, to vindicate himself,
and the great and good men in whose steps he had trod, from the
charge of neglecting the *spirit* of revelation by a too exclusive regard
to the *letter* of Scripture. The passage is worthy of attention, as his
deliberate and final judgment on some of the matters in controversy
between what may be called the *scriptural* and the *philosophical* school
of Unitarians.

"At a time when so many are eager in pulling up and removing ancient landmarks, it may be necessary to explain, that in using the term Unitarian the Editor means bonâ fide to denote a form of real Christianity—the system of doctrine, as to its great outlines, maintained, in some instances with many privations and sufferings, by Biddle, Milton, Locke, Emlyn, Newton, Lardner, (Dr.) Taylor, Price, Priestley, Lindsey, Belsham and Carpenter. These are names not to be ashamed of. They are referred to, not as authorities, but as guides. They did not rest in the *letter* of Scripture, but through this they attained to its *spirit*. Their faith in the gospel was genuine and strong. They honoured and obeyed Jesus, as the Messiah, believing equally his doctrines and his miracles, and especially the peculiarly Christian miracle of his resurrection from the dead to immortality. And their testimony has always

---

* In relation to his printer, Mr. Aspland was most careful and exact in the performance of duties, which, unfortunately, are very often neglected by literary men. The testimony of Mr. Charles Green on this point is given in a letter recently received by the writer:

"He was about the best active writer for the press I have ever been acquainted with,—his MS. so plain, and all the niceties of punctuation, &c. attended to so carefully. Whatever he did, he did well. In reference to anything, trifling or important, his dislike of slovenliness was perhaps exceeded only by his hatred of deception—one of the most marked traits of his character. Careful himself, he would tolerate no carelessness in others; and a *foul* proof was rarely returned without a word or two of reproof to both compositor and reader—not offensively, yet very significantly given. He was an admirable proof-reader; the smallest defect caught his eye and received the correction of his pen. Many pleasant, improving hours I have passed in his study—his eye and pen sometimes engaged on articles for the current No., whilst tongue and ear were given to me. He could gossip—so well!—but his was never *idle* gossip. Increased intercourse with the world, and with men of various shades of opinion, has only served to raise my estimate of your Father's character, both intellectually and moral. So few do I find who seem to me to make any very near approach to him!"

been felt to be powerful in behalf of both the truth and the sense of Divine Revelation."

Immediately after the publication of this Address, his dwelling became a house of mourning, through the death, long foreseen, of his youngest daughter. The bereavement was probably the more keenly felt from the circumstance, that, with only one exception (that of an infant born in the Isle of Wight, which lived but a few hours), all his children reached maturity, and that for more than forty years death had not struck any one living under his roof.

Rev. Robert Aspland to Rev. R. Brook Aspland.

"Hackney, Wednesday, Dec. 4, 1844.

"Dear Brook,—The sad event broke upon us at last suddenly. All, blessed be God! was composure and peace. She died with one of her hands locked in Henry's—the hand was not even contracted by death—and her parting breath was not distinguishable.

"She last smiled on her dear babe on Monday.

"Your letter, and a later one from Alfred, as well as one previously of paternal comfort from me, occupied, and pleasantly, her latest thoughts. * * *

"I am glad the Farewell is so candidly received, and that so many of our brethren express themselves in so friendly and sympathizing a manner. Mr. Kentish's note would be a cordial to a fainting heart."*

During the year of continued weakness, and frequently acute suffering, that followed, little occurred on which a biographer can dwell. His patience and fortitude were fully equal to his trials. The entries in the Diary become less frequent and are more brief, and the manuscript occasionally exhibits the feebleness of the writer. He again records, Feb. 3, the anniversary of his mother's death, and adds, " I could think of nothing else." " May 25, Sunday.—Alas! another silent and wearisome sabbath! I am severely tried; but let me ever remember that it is the Sovereign will, and that I am in the Supreme hand of the All-Merciful." The date of the last entry is December 1: " Upon the whole, better." He had now been a close prisoner to the house since August 11. His strength was entirely gone, but his mind,

---

* The letter contains many particulars respecting the intended funeral. Mr. Aspland did not hold funereal ceremonies cheap; in fact, he paid great attention to them. In the case of his daughter, deprived as he was of the power of following her remains to their last resting-place, it seemed to comfort him to enter minutely into all the arrangements of the funeral.

happily, was for the most part clear and bright to the last.* In early life he had entertained great fear of death, thinking that the parting of body and soul involved a distressing struggle. But now Death had no terrors for him. On the last Saturday of the year he grew perceptibly worse. Now and then, for a few minutes, his mind wandered. His sight began to fail. He spoke to the beloved ones about him with calmness and perfect resignation of his approaching end, and in a few emphatic words declared his unfailing faith in God's mercy, the truth of the gospel and man's immortal destiny.

On the Sunday and Monday there were moments when his strength seemed about to rally. He watched with apparently deep interest the symptoms of approaching death, and asked if the failure of the sight were common to dying persons. He got up for a short time on Monday (Dec. 29), and, remembering a box of Brosely pipes which his eldest grandson had sent him some little time previously, but of which he had made no use, he asked for one, observing, "What will that poor lad say if I go out of the world without having used any of his present?" Soon after midnight he fell into a tranquil slumber, from which he woke about two o'clock, and immediately breathed his last.

In death his countenance was placid, and his lofty and massive forehead seemed still noble.†

The members of the Gravel-Pit congregation prepared for the reception of his remains a vault in the burial-ground, which had been in times past his daily walk, and in the planting of every tree and shrub of which he had had a voice. A site was selected for his grave in the centre of the south portion of the ground, being that which, in one of his visits to the place, he had indicated as the spot where he should wish to lie.

The funeral obsequies, on Tuesday, Jan. 6, were attended by nearly all the members of the Gravel-Pit congregation, and by the Unitarian ministers of London and its vicinity. As the long funeral train passed through the village of Hackney, it was observed that many of the

---

* He continued to read the Christian Reformer in the proof-sheets, and the whole of the number which was published the day after his death had been read and revised by him. The last articles contributed by him were the brief but just and forcible obituaries of Sir William Follett and Earl Grey, inserted in the August No., p. 595.

† On a post-mortem examination, the heart was discovered to be enlarged to twice its normal size, shewing the working of severe and long-continued disease in that vital organ.

houses, inhabited by persons of different religious denominations, were closed in token of respect to his memory. The funeral service was conducted by Dr. Thomas Rees, and the funeral sermon, on the following Sunday, was preached by Rev. Thomas Madge,—both of whom discharged these painful offices of friendship with affectionate reverence for the memory of their departed fellow-labourer.* The tomb has the following inscription:

SACRED
TO THE MEMORY OF
THE REV. ROBERT ASPLAND,
WHO WAS BORN AT WICKEN, IN THE COUNTY OF CAMBRIDGE,
JANUARY 23, 1782,
AND DIED AT HACKNEY, DECEMBER 30, 1845,
HAVING BEEN PASTOR OF THIS CONGREGATION FOR MORE THAN
FORTY YEARS.

It would not be becoming in the writer of this Memoir to attempt a formal delineation of the intellectual and moral character of his Father. It has been his desire to furnish the reader with ample materials for correct judgment on this subject. An able and faithful Tribute to the Memory of Mr. Aspland appeared in the pages of the *Christian Reformer* (1846, Vol. II. pp. 103—108), from the pen of the Rev. John Kentish, some portions of which are here inserted.

"Mr. Aspland filled, during many years, a situation of such importance, and filled it so well, that his memory claims a tribute of grateful respect from those who knew the value of his character. His virtues —private, domestic, social—aided the effect of his public labours. * * * I had the satisfaction of hearing one of his probationary sermons" (at Hackney in 1805). "For its matter, style, arrangement and delivery, it was of high merit, and gave promise of his solid usefulness and reputation. The choice, assuredly, reflected eminent credit on those who made it, and on its object. It is seldom that a minister so young has possessed qualifications so substantial. But Mr. A.'s settlement at Hackney, and the approbation which he continued to meet with from his hearers, did him signal honour, for another reason. He persevered in reading and in thought, and abated nothing of his diligence. Had he remitted it, he could never have attained to worthy distinction, nor

---

* The event of Mr. Aspland's death was noticed in very many pulpits of the Unitarian body, and brief tributes to his memory appeared in several of the London and Provincial newspapers, and in the Unitarian periodicals, both English and American.

have produced the beneficial effects which followed on his ministry. It was only by the assiduous cultivation and exercise of his powers, that he could be welcomed as the fit successor of Mayo, Smith* and Laugher†—of Price and Priestley and Belsham.

"Such was the nature of his situation, that he would be summoned to take a leading part among the Dissenters of London and its vicinity. For this, too, he was admirably fitted.

"To all his new engagements, Mr. Aspland devoted himself with earnestness and deliberation. His first concern was to fulfil his ministry. In performing the services of the House of Prayer, he appeared to great advantage. He conducted the public worship appropriately and effectively; with a strict regard to its general ends, and to varying circumstances and seasons. What the tenor of his sermons was—and what were their characteristic recommendations—will, I think, be best judged of from a volume of them which he published in 1833, at the request and expense of his stated auditors. This is a *consecrated* memorial of the reciprocal affection of the Pastor and the Flock; and also of his Theological knowledge, vigorous and discriminating sense, comprehensive thought, and power of seeing beneath the surface, and of conveying sound instruction in language at once terse, perspicuous, appropriate and energetic. His person and voice and distinct elocution commanded regard: yet these alone would not have procured for him the favour of his well-informed audiences; not apart from the intrinsically good qualities of his sermons. I scarcely know the modern discourses that equal them for a wide compass of ideas. Every topic has justice done to it. We meet with nothing superficial. In point of exactness of definition, accurate reasoning, judicious Scriptural exposition, and natural and copious applications, they remind me of the sermons of our good old English Preachers, at the end of the seventeenth and the beginning of the eighteenth century. Indeed, those great masters of the Pulpit were favourite authors with Mr. Aspland. Without being their servile imitator, he improved his own compositions by his study of theirs.

"Persons who know anything of the Protestant Dissenters of the

---

* "The Rev. George Smith. See his Funeral Sermon, by Dr. S. Chandler. In many striking features, Mr. Aspland's character bore a resemblance to *his*; and so did some parts of his personal history.

† "The Rev. Timothy Laugher, a fellow-student and intimate friend of Dr. Kippis, who has recorded his virtues in a Funeral Discourse.

Metropolis and its neighbourhood, cannot need to be informed that the ministers, together with some members of their respective congregations, execute important charitable trusts, and share in the management of several voluntary associations. The just and beneficial discharge of these offices must require punctuality and method, a competent acquaintance with the world and human nature, quick perception, judicious zeal and firm decision. Such were Mr. Aspland's habits and attainments. He was, in the best sense of the words, 'a man of business;' observant of its forms, for the sake of maintaining its spirit and advancing its purposes—yet observant of them with a truly liberal temper. At the same time, he was a ready, correct and powerful speaker: nor did he less excel in promptly framing the resolutions and other documents which emanate from public bodies.

" His talents, standing and address, gave him a favourable—nor unfrequently, a confidential—introduction to persons of high rank and office; especially to noble and honourable members of the Legislature, whose political attachments harmonized with his own.*

" Of his successive publications, my limits do not permit me to speak in detail: all are greatly creditable to him as a writer, and manifest his strong intellect, sound principles and valuable aims.

" The work for which this article is designed, had its origin in his public spirit, and mainly owes its success to his superintendence as its Editor. Here, then, it were unpardonable to be silent on his merits in that capacity. The undertaking was almost new: his manner of carrying it out, was absolutely such. Nothing had existed among us that was entirely the prototype of the Monthly Repository, &c. &c. Early in the eighteenth century, and nearly to the middle of it, excellent *Occasional* Papers had been printed, in the defence of Freedom, Spiritual and Civil.† More recently, Non-subscribing Dissenters had witnessed, and in some feeble degree encouraged, a series of volumes devoted exclusively to Theological and Scriptural Criticism.‡ An attempt had even been made to circulate something like a useful and attractive *Miscellany* among our body. These endeavours failed. Mr.

---

* " His admirable Discourse, on occasion of the death of C. J. Fox, cannot be forgotten. Mr. A. was deliberately the advocate of the Free *Constitution* of his country; and intent upon the reparation, not the demolition, of the fabric.

† " Other papers besides the *Occasional*, and of the same character, marked this period: let a general reference to them suffice.

‡ "I have particularly in view the *Theological Repository*, and the *Commentaries and Essays*.

Aspland's had a happier issue. The Monthly Publication which I have referred to, has virtually been edited by himself, or under his auspices, through forty years. With a slight change of title, size and series, it has been the same in its principles and objects [*alter et idem*]: and, with a short interval, which circumstances made unavoidable, (and which I, for one, short as it was, shall always regret,) it has continued in his hands—his property and welcome care. There are few examples of a single and individual Editor of such a work, possessing it so long —none of a better fulfilment of such delicate and arduous functions. I call them so, on account of the miscellaneous character of the publication, and of the various tastes of its readers.

"It was Mr. A.'s purpose to render it a Miscellany at once of Theology and Literature. In glancing at the series of volumes, I perceive constant proofs of the Editor's ability and judgment. He guards against bringing himself unnecessarily before his readers. It is only at fitting times that he comes forward. Whenever he does this, we find him writing so well and pertinently, that we are desirous of his writing more. The truth is, that his editorial authority and influence were the greater and the more beneficial for his comparative silence. He would not allow of his pages being diverted from their legitimate design; and among works of its class, THIS has obtained a very satisfactory reputation. Its bearing and good effects on the progress of principles involving Man's dearest interests, will be acknowledged.

"The period at which Mr. Aspland lived, was exciting. Throughout his public course, grave questions were agitated: they regarded Education, the alliance of Church and State, penal and disabling Statutes, vexatious claims, threatened encroachments and spoliation. As to all of them, he thought for himself, and fearlessly avowed the result of his thoughts; eloquently pleading, in the spirit of equal Freedom, for the rights of Conscience and Mankind. In what he did, and in what he refrained from doing, he was alike wise, manly and independent. It is with especial pleasure that I look back on his timely and effectual resistance to certain attempts at Parliamentary interference with the Education of the People.

"In an early part of his life, he proved his attachment to Locke's*

---

* " He had been ardently desirous of seeing a monument to Locke erected, by public subscription, in St. Paul's Cathedral. This is still to be wished: but I should rejoice yet more in the increased circulation of Locke's Works, and, most

name and writings. His love of them grew with his growth. Yet he survived to witness no small injustice done to Locke in the house of his friends!

"Like that illustrious man, he was an unwavering believer in *historical* Christianity; in Christianity as it rests on miraculous attestation. 'One was his Master, even Christ:' but, in taking HIM as the Master, he deemed it essential to investigate the claims which Christ himself has urged.

"It were almost superfluous to add that Mr. Aspland, from the beginning to the end of his ministry, was a Christian Unitarian. Why, and in what sense, he was such—why, and how supremely, he valued 'this doctrine according to godliness'—and in how excellent a way he laboured for its defence and its diffusion—let his writings and his life declare.

"I have already referred to his stores of Theological knowledge. He was familiar with it, in almost every branch. With the best Theology of the best times of his own country he was particularly conversant. There was no man to whom, in this walk of study, his friends could have applied more safely and advantageously. His reading here included not merely polemical and practical Divinity, but, moreover, Ecclesiastical History and Dissenting Antiquities and Biography.

"How affectionate Mr. Aspland was in his family, and how kind and hospitable to his friends, I shall only intimate. As 'the heart knoweth its own bitterness,' so its best joys are secret. In his HOME, his personal sufferings—continued and severe as they were—would have been less felt by him, if he had not also felt for those who watched incessantly at his couch, and marked, with mingled hope and apprehension, the vicissitudes of his disease. Not exempted from these and other heavy trials, he experienced, nevertheless, singular domestic happiness: and richly did he merit, and, in return, most largely communicate, it. Mournfully pleasing remembrances and cheering anticipations are the privilege of those of his survivors whom he most loved, and of all who once took sweet counsel together with him, and walked to the House of God in company, and shared in his generous regards, and were blessed with his instructions and example.

"Of that EXAMPLE let his brethren, and most of all his younger

---

of all, in the growing influence of his grand principles of Religion, Philosophy and Government. We are unjust to the present and the coming generation, if we disregard the past.

brethren, in the ministry, be mindful. Let them recollect that, notwithstanding his superior native talents, his constitutional ardour, and his social temper, he gave himself to *reading*, meditation and prayer, and was thence enabled to be eminently respectable and useful in his public services. I repeat, that unless he had been at once diligent and wise, he might have sunk into one of the characters, from which he turned with intuitive distaste—into either an empty speculatist or a voluble declaimer."

To this Tribute the only additions which the writer wishes to add are from friends who enjoyed the pulpit instructions of Mr. Aspland for a long series of years. The first is an extract from the diary of a lady.

"The Sunday week succeeding to our marriage we took the Sacrament together at Mr. Aspland's chapel, and from that period to the present* have been constant attendants,—where we have found increasing pleasure, satisfaction, and, I trust, profit; for so ought it to have been, since to his duties as a minister he has been ever faithful, probing the secret recesses of the heart that he might purify and amend, and endeavouring to build up his people in their most holy faith.

"The best of his time and talents have always been devoted to his pulpit duties, as his most solid, instructive and delightful sermons well attest. They have been the production of an intellect, I believe, far above the common standard, enlarged by extensive reading, and doubtless by *deep meditation;* as who of all his hearers but must acknowledge his deep insight into the human heart—who but at times must have been startled at the image portrayed in his mirror? He would treat as beautifully and usefully of *the joy with which a stranger intermeddleth not*, as of *the bitterness which the heart only knoweth.* He would lay bare for our instruction the little world within,—its sins, its frailties, its holy aspirations and good affections. In his pulpit discourses he had but one end in view, and from this he never turned aside to render himself what is termed a popular preacher. The simile, the metaphor, were never employed merely to adorn the style and attract the ears of the multitude, but simply to illustrate and bring home his meaning; and it was seldom the great truths he taught required aught but his plain, forcible and nervous language to illustrate or adorn them.

"Thus happily placed for the performance of Christian worship, our Sundays became a day of *delightful recreation*, and were ever looked forward to as such; and the young who in process of time have grown up to accompany us, have equally participated in our enjoyment."

---

* The interval being twenty-two years.

The next is an extract from a letter addressed to the writer, detailing the circumstances of the death of an aged friend who had been many years a member of the Gravel-Pit congregation.

"He died quite quietly and with scarcely a struggle, and was conscious and collected to the last. During his illness a circumstance occurred which will perhaps give you some pleasure. He himself seemed never to entertain the idea of recovery, and had from the first considered this his last illness. But he was neither excited nor depressed by this. He was throughout perfectly calm and happy, and one morning called my mother to his bedside, and pointing to a portrait which hung in his room of your Father, said, 'I have been looking at Mr. Aspland's portrait, and thinking that I can never be sufficiently grateful to God that I have had the privilege of sitting under him for so many years, and of learning from him those comforting doctrines of Unitarianism which I now feel so consoling and so great a support to me at the close of my life.' These were nearly his words, and wholly their effect."

APPENDIX.

LIST OF THE PUBLICATIONS OF THE REV. R. ASPLAND.

1. Divine Judgments on Guilty Nations, their Causes and Effects considered, in a Discourse delivered at Newport, in the Isle of Wight. With a Preface and Notes by Benjamin Flower. 8vo. Cambridge, 1804.

2. Reflections upon the Liberal Spirit of the Apostles and the Benevolent Design of the Christian Ministry: a Discourse delivered on Sunday, July 7, 1805, before the Unitarian Congregation, Hackney, upon occasion of entering on the Pastoral Office. 8vo. Harlow, 1805.

3. The Fall of Eminent Men in Critical Periods a National Calamity: a Sermon on occasion of the Death of the Right Hon. Charles James Fox. 8vo. London, 1806.

4. The Duty and Reward of sacrificing Temporal Interests on the Altar of Truth, exemplified in the Character of Abraham: a Sermon, at Hackney, on the Death of the Rev. Theophilus Lindsey, M. A. 8vo. London, 1808.

5. An Oration delivered on Monday, October 16, 1809, on laying the First Stone of the New Gravel-Pit Meeting-house in Paradise Field, Hackney. 8vo. Harlow, 1809.

6. Bigotry and Intolerance defeated; or an Account of the Prosecution of Mr. John Gisburne, Unitarian Minister of Soham, Cambridgeshire; with an Exposure and Correction of the Defects and Mistakes of Mr. Andrew Fuller's Narrative of that Affair. 8vo. Harlow, 1810. (A second edition, 12mo, 1811.)

7. A Selection of Psalms and Hymns for Unitarian Worship. 18mo. London, 1810. (Various other editions.)

8. A Vindication of Unitarian Worship: a Sermon preached on Sunday, Nov. 4, 1810, on occasion of the Opening of the New Gravel-Pit Meeting-house, Hackney. 8vo. London, 1810.

9. The Beneficial Influence of Christianity on the Character and Condition of the Female Sex: a Sermon preached at the Rev. Dr. Rees's Meeting-house, Jewin Street, Aldersgate Street, on Wednesday, April 8, 1812, in

behalf of the Society for the Relief of the Necessitous Widows and Fatherless Children of Protestant Dissenting Ministers. 8vo. Hackney, 1812.

10. A Vindication of Religious Liberty: a Sermon preached at Bridport, on Wednesday, June 17, 1812, before the Western Unitarian Society. 12mo. Hackney, 1812.

11. A Plea for Unitarian Dissenters, in a Letter of Expostulation to the Rev. H. H. Norris, M.A., on that Part of his late Work against the Hackney Auxiliary Bible Society which relates to Unitarians. 8vo. Hackney, 1813. (A second edition, 12mo, 1815.)

12. British Pulpit Eloquence: a Selection of Sermons, in Chronological Order, from the Works of the most eminent Divines of Great Britain, during the Seventeenth and Eighteenth Centuries; with Biographical and Critical Notices. Vol. I. 8vo. London, 1814.

13. Three Sermons.—I. The Unitarian Christian's Appeal to his Fellow-christians on the Christian Name. II. The Apostles' Creed concerning the One God and the Man Christ Jesus. III. The inseparable Connexion between the Unity and the Benevolence of God. 12mo. London, 1814. (A second edition, with a Vindication of Religious Liberty prefixed. 12mo. London, 1816.)

14. The Power of Truth: a Sermon preached before the Unitarian Society for promoting Christian Knowledge, at Essex-Street Chapel, on Thursday, April 13, 1815. 8vo. London, 1815.

15. The Tendency of the Human Condition to Improvement, and its ultimate Perfection in Heaven: a Sermon preached before the Unitarian Church, Hackney, on Sunday Morning, Feb. 18, 1816, on occasion of the lamented Death of Mr. James Hennell. 8vo. London, 1816.

16. Resignation to the Will of God, illustrated and enforced by the Example of Jesus Christ: a Sermon preached at the Unitarian Chapel, Reading, Berks, on Sunday Evening, March 24, 1816, on occasion of the Death of Mr. James Drover. With an Appendix, containing some Thoughts on the Supports and Consolations which the Unitarian System furnishes in Seasons of Affliction and Trouble, and especially in the Hour of Death. 8vo. London, 1816.

17. The Memory of the Righteous: a Sermon preached before the Unitarian Church, Hackney, Sunday Morning, Feb. 2, 1817, on occasion of the lamented Death of Ed. Longdon Mackmurdo, Esq., who departed this Life January 23, 1817, in the Sixty-first Year of his Age. 8vo. Hackney, 1817.

18. An Inquiry into the Nature of the Sin of Blasphemy, and into the Propriety of regarding it as a Civil Offence: in Three Sermons delivered before the Unitarian Church, Hackney, on the Sunday Mornings of July 13, 20 and 27, 1817; with Notes, and an Appendix on the present State of the Law with respect to Unitarians. 8vo. London, 1817.

19. The virtuous Use of Talents enforced, in reference to the Education of

Poor Children: a Sermon preached at the High-Street Chapel in Shrewsbury, on Sunday, September 14, 1817, on behalf of the Royal Lancasterian School established in that Town. 8vo. Shrewsbury, 1817.

20. A Funeral Sermon preached on Wednesday, November 19, 1817, the Day of the Interment of Her late R. H. the Princess Charlotte of Wales, before the Unitarian Church, Hackney. 8vo. London, 1817.

21. Inquiry into the Operation of Mr. Brougham's Education Bill, as far as regards the Protestant Dissenters. By a Nonconformist. 8vo. London, 1821.

22. An Attempt to ascertain the Import of the Title "Son of Man" commonly assumed by our Lord: a Sermon preached before several Unitarian Associations, and printed at their request. 12mo. London, 1821. (A second edition, 12mo. London, 1826.)

23. The Character of Jesus Christ an Evidence of his Divine Mission: a Sermon preached at the Gravel-Pit Meeting, Hackney, and at Lewin's Mead, Bristol. 12mo. London, 1821. (A second edition, 12mo, 1826.)

24. The Blessing pronounced by Christ on the Merciful: a Sermon preached at the New Gravel-Pit Meeting-house, Hackney, on the Morning of Sunday, January 12, 1823, on occasion of the much-lamented Death of Samuel Pett, Esq., M.D., of Clapton, who departed this Life on the 1st of January, in the 58th Year of his Age. 8vo. London, 1823.

25. The Apostle Paul's Confession of Heresy: a Sermon preached before the Sussex Unitarian Association at Brighton, on Wednesday, August 27, and on the Opening of the New Unitarian Chapel at Hanley, Staffordshire, on Wednesday, Nov. 19th, 1823. 12mo. London, 1824.

26. A Summary of the Theological Controversies which of late Years have agitated the City of Geneva. By M. J. J. Chenevière. Translated from the original French. 8vo. London, 1824.

27. The Re-union of the Wise and Good in a Future State: a Sermon on occasion of the Death of the Rev. Abraham Rees, D.D., F.R.S., F.L.S., &c., who departed this Life on the 9th of June, in the Eighty-second Year of his Age: to which is added the Address delivered over the Body, by Thomas Rees, LL.D., F.S.A. 8vo. London, 1825. (A second edition, 8vo. London, 1825.)

28. Causes of the slow Progress of Christian Truth: a Discourse delivered before the Western Unitarian Society, in the Conigree Meeting-house, Trowbridge, Wilts, on Wednesday, July 13, 1825. 12mo. London, 1825.

29. Two Sermons preached in the Chapel in Lewin's Mead, Bristol, on the Morning and Evening of Sunday, Oct. 16, 1825.—I. On the Future State of the Righteous, occasioned by the Death of Mrs. Mary Rowe.—II. On Numbering our Days, suggested by a recent unusual Mortality in the Congregation. 8vo. London, 1825.

30. The Charge at the Ordination of the Rev. R. Brook Aspland, M.A.,

in the Chapel, Crook's Lane, Chester, on Wednesday, Aug. 9, 1826. 8vo. Chester, 1826.

31. Elton *versus* Elton, or Mr. Elton's "Second Thoughts" answered by his First: being Remarks on his Reasons for returning to the Church of England. (Extracted from the Christian Reformer.) 12mo. London, 1828.

32. The Religious Belief of Unitarian Christians truly stated and vindicated from Popular Misrepresentation: a Sermon preached Sept. 29, 1830, at the Opening of the New Chapel, Wareham, Dorsetshire, dedicated to the Worship of the One God, the Father. 8vo. London, 1831. (A second edition, 8vo. London, 1831.)

33. Christian Patriotism; or the Wishes and Prayers of Britons for their Country in the present Crisis: a Sermon preached Sept. 11, 1831, being the Sunday after the Coronation of H. M. King Wm. the Fourth. 8vo. London, 1831.

34. The Divine Dispensations a Series of Moral Discipline: a Sermon preached at Bath, July, 18, 1832, before the Society of Unitarian Christians established in the West of England for promoting Christian Knowledge and the Practice of Virtue by the distribution of Books. 8vo. Hackney, 1832.

35. Sermons on various Subjects, chiefly Practical. 8vo. London, 1833.

36. The Future Accession of Good Men of all Climes to Christianity, and their final Congregation in Heaven: a Sermon on occasion of the lamented Death of the Rajah Rammohun Roy, preached at the New Gravel-Pit Meeting, Hackney, on Sunday, October 6th, 1833; with a Biographical Sketch of the distinguished Oriental Reformer. Second edition, 8vo. London, 1833.

37. The English Bible and the Reformation: the Substance of Three Sermons preached at the New Gravel-Pit Meeting-house, Hackney, on Sunday Mornings, Oct. 4, 11 and 18, 1835, in celebration of the Third Centenary of the Printing of the first entire Version in English of the Holy Scriptures. 8vo. Hackney, 1835.

38. Richard Baxter's last Religious Sentiments. 8vo. London, 1836.

39. Form of Solemnization of Matrimony agreed upon by the Presbyterian Body of Ministers in and near London, Dec. 20, 1836. 8vo. London, 1837.

40. The Beauty and Excellence of Christian Morality: a Sermon for the Young, delivered at the New Gravel-Pit Meeting-house, Hackney, May 6, 1838. 12mo. London, 1838.

41. A Catechism for Children, designed to teach the First Principles of the Christian Religion and the Plain and Great Moral Duties. 18mo. London, 1840. (Second edition, 1843; third edition, 1848.)

42. Prayers to be used with and by Children, in Families and Schools. 18mo. London, 1840.

43. Tracts for the People, designed to vindicate Religious and Christian Liberty. 12mo. London, 1840.

44. An Attempt to delineate the Character of the Rev. William Ellery

Channing, D.D., of Boston, in the United States of America, lately deceased, as a Writer, Philanthropist and Divine; in a Sermon preached at the New Gravel-Pit Meeting-house, Hackney, on Sunday, November 13, 1842. With an Appendix, consisting of Extracts from Dr. Channing's Works, and Notes. 8vo. London, 1842.

45. The Monthly Repository of Theology and General Literature. 21 vols. 8vo. London, 1806—1826.

46. The Christian Reformer; or New Evangelical Miscellany. 19 vols. 12mo. London, 1815—1833.

47. The Christian Reformer; or Unitarian Magazine and Review. 11 vols. 8vo. London, 1834—1844.

48. The Presbyterian Reporter; being a Register of Parliamentary Proceedings and Public Documents relating to the Dissenting Chapels' and Endowments' Bill for the Protection of the Presbyterians in England and Ireland, not subscribing to Articles of Christian Faith of Human Compilation.

Mr. Aspland also superintended the publication of the following works:

49. The Scripture Account of the Attributes and Worship of God, and of the Character and Offices of Jesus Christ. 12mo. Hackney, 1816.

50. The Geneva Catechism; entitled Catechism, or Instruction on the Christian Religion prepared by the Pastors of Geneva, for the use of the Swiss and French Protestant Churches. Translated from the French. Second edition. 12mo. London, 1824.

Posthumous.

51. Sermons on various Subjects, chiefly Practical. 8vo. London, 1847.

52. The Evidence for the Truth of Christianity not impaired by the Lapse of Time: Three Sermons preached at the New Gravel-Pit Chapel, Hackney. 8vo. London, 1847.

53. Counsels and Cautions to the Young: being Three Sermons addressed to the Younger Members of the New Gravel-Pit Congregation, Hackney. 8vo. London, 1847.

54. A Caution against the unlawful, immoral and unchristian Arts of Controversy. A Sermon preached at the Ancient Presbyterian Chapel of Gee Cross, on Wednesday, Sept. 1, 1841, before the Cheshire Presbyterian Association. 8vo. London, 1847.

ORIGINAL LETTERS ILLUSTRATIVE OF THE MEMOIR.

[The letters which follow were not discovered by the Editor in time to be inserted in their proper place.]

Rev. Joshua Toulmin, D.D., to Rev. Robert Aspland.

No. I.

Taunton, May 12, 1803.

Dear Sir,—It is, methinks, truly a long time since I had the pleasure of any communications from you. I have to regret that your "earnest desire of writing" should yield to "checks" and "avocations." Correspondence, like devotion, seems necessary to preserve the sentiments of friendship and to fan affection, as that is to keep alive piety.

I will deem it a pleasing incident for me that the "Life of Biddle," falling in your way, should remind you of its author, who is gratified and encouraged by the approbation and encomiums with which you honour this piece of biography.

It will not lower your idea of its utility, nor, I hope, give you an unfavourable idea of the vanity of the biographer, if I transcribe what was said of it by so great and good a Prelate as the late Lord Primate of Ireland, Archbishop Newcome, in a letter with which he honoured me, November 8, 1790:

"The Life of Biddle forms a curious part of the history of theological opinions and of theological rancour. It does you as much honour to publish it, as it did my very worthy and learned friend, Dr. George Benson, to revive the story of Calvin and Servetus."

By the way, what a contrast there is in the views men entertain of the same action! I have heard some one said that it was the Devil who put it into Dr. Benson's head to publish the case of Servetus!

If I mistake not, your Unitarian meeting was fixed for the first Wednesday in June; but I conceive that, in that case, it must be changed and postponed to, perhaps, the following week, for on *that* day will be held the General Assembly in Worship Street. When I received yours, I could not entertain the distant hope of being with you. But circumstances have arisen to make it possible. I thought that, several weeks back, I should have been in London to attend the progress of a Bill through Parliament relative to our Navigation. This business has been postponed, and on the point of being given up, but is now resumed, and will, I believe, be carried on; and I am likely to set off for Town next Monday. Should it so happen that my public business should be finished before your meeting is held, and should that be held so as to fall in with the time of my leaving Town, and I could take the Isle of Wight on my return, then I might enjoy the pleasure of making one among you. But there are so many chances against this concurrence of circumstances, that I cannot build my hopes on it. I shall, however, hear of your meeting when I am in Town, and know the time of it.

Your idea of an extensive Association meets my approbation, but how it is practicable I doubt. I may, perhaps, have the pleasure of seeing Mr. Silver, and of knowing his sentiments. He is a young gentleman, and young men are vigorous, active and sanguine.

Have you cultivated the acquaintance of Mr. Dalton? If you should not have frequent intercourses with him, you will, however, find no difficulty in conveying to him my respects, and my request that, if he has done with the three volumes of "Essays and Letters," he would avail himself of any opportunity that may offer to transmit them to me, to the care of Mr. Stower, Printer, Charles Street, Hatton Garden.

Mr. Stower, several months back, said that the impression of my Portsmouth Sermon was sold, and that there was a demand for it. He wished me to reprint it. I demurred on it. I knew not whether all the copies taken by your Society were disposed of. I doubted whether the demand would indemnify the press. The Western Unitarian Society has wished for a new impression of my Sermon on the word "Mystery," and engaged to take 100 copies. If I render them at four-pence each, that will not cover the expenses of so small an impression as 250. Will your Society take off any?

I beg my kind respects to Messrs. Cookes and their ladies, especially Mr. and Mrs. Thomas Cooke, my hosts, Mr. Kirkpatrick, Mrs. Aspland, and all friends. With sincere regards and esteem, I am, dear Sir, your faithful friend and servant,

J. TOULMIN.

No. II.

Birmingham, New Hall Street, Dec. 24, 1805.

Dear Sir,—Indeed I blush to think how long I have been in your debt. The first cause is, that as there was a friendly message in it to the amiable Mrs. * * *, I sent it to her; she soon after fell into that state of mind which has, in its issue, deprived us of all intercourses with her, and your letter has never been returned to me. When I see Mr. * * *, I forget to inquire after it. Soon after it was written, your plans for life underwent a great and unexpected change, on the final result of which I sincerely congratulate you. May many years of usefulness and respectability, to an unusual degree, answer your most sanguine hopes and fervent prayers! I soon procured your inauguration Sermon, which I have read with singular pleasure, as a very fair specimen of the accuracy of your judgment, the powers of your mind, and the liberality of your spirit, in each view doing you no little honour. My worthy colleague bestows on it his approbation and praise, which is never prostituted to partiality, and is always valuable because it is always judicious.

The change of connections which we have made is singular; I hope it will advance our felicity and usefulness. It does, I trust, credit to the temper of our respective circles, that our *Anabaptistical errors,* as some would call them, are no bar to the acceptableness of our ministry among them. Such instances will, I would promise myself, contribute to wear away prejudice against our sentiments, and leave the minds of many more open to inquiry and conviction. I can have but a few years before me for life and service; but it was of importance, I conceived, and even a duty, to avail myself of an opening, unsought and unexpected, offering to heighten my comforts and to enlarge my usefulness. My settlement here, I *think* I may say, was and has been of no small service to unite and settle a large and most respectable, but which had been a discordant, society. Your period of life opens to you the prospect of many years of very useful service in one of the first situations among us. Your mind feels an ardour congenial to the importance of your post.

But it is time that I thank you for not being displeased with my delay and silence, and for favouring me with another letter while a former lay unnoticed.

I am glad that the Theological Magazine is to be continued, and in an improved form, and I promise great advantage to it from its being under your conduct. From my readiness on former occasions, it may be supposed that I shall not be backward to contribute my assistance, such as it is, on this, though I fear it will not often rise above mediocre. You are mistaken in imagining that I have many papers by me; I must prepare what I may communicate. At present I have, also, too many irons in the fire. My attention is now engaged by a detached biographical piece, Memoirs of my excellent predecessor, Mr. Samuel Bourn. My History of Taunton calls for the Supplement to complete it; and much do I wish to set about the Continuation of Neal in good earnest. However, I shall be gratified if I can now and then supply an article worthy a place in your miscellany. I am disposed to promise you three biographical ones, which it has been long in my intention to draw up,—viz., for February, a sketch of the life of Mr. Cardale; of Mr. William Foot for March; and Dr. Foster for April. As I have finished the preceding sentence, I am disposed to correct myself, and to say that I will begin with Dr. Robertson, " the Father," as Mr. Lindsey calls him, " of Unitarian Nonconformity in our day," and then take the others in succession. To these it occurs to my thoughts to add Dr. Caleb Fleming. I will communicate your wishes to our friend Mr. Hamper. Mr. Kentish desires his best respects, but he *promises* nothing; yet I doubt not that you will have him for an occasional correspondent. May I recommend it to you to apply to Mr. William Turner, of Newcastle, Mr. Bretland, of Exeter, through Mr. Manning to Mr. Merivale, of Exeter, for any papers of his excellent father, and to Mr. Hazlitt, of Wem.

I have not heard from my good son, the Judge, since he has been in his new station. The uncertainty of the communication and the distance preclude any dependence, and almost any expectations, from that quarter.

I shall be glad to receive your Prospectus. A number and any packet at the beginning of the month may be forwarded to me in Mr. Belcher's parcels from Crosby or Ostell.

I beg my kind compliments to Mrs. Aspland. I am, with great esteem, my dear Sir, yours truly and affectionately,

JOSHUA TOULMIN.

No. III.

Birmingham, November 6, 1809.

Dear Sir,—I have not yet made my thanks, which I now sincerely and cordially tender, for the kind hospitalities and attentions received from Mrs. Aspland and yourself on my late visit to Hackney. I want time to furnish several articles for the Repository, especially a Memoir of Crellius, the Son, to correct the account of his death too confidently, if not exultingly, expressed in the Eclectic Review for September or August.

I enclose a small article. I am glad the day of Jubilee is gone by. The Committee of the New Meeting voted that it was not their wish to have the doors opened for worship. I had conveyed to them, not an absolute refusal of my services in the pulpit, but my sense of serious and great difficulties, in every view of the subject, and submitted to their consideration the propriety and probable consequences of Dissenting congregations taking any notice of the interference of others pointing out the time and occasions of having their worship. There had been a respectful request to all the ministers in the town to preach, from the High and Low Bailiff, at a town meeting held in a very *informal* manner. After this, assiduous endeavours were used to call all the congregation together to propose a religious service. The measure succeeded. It was determined to have service; but *I* was not asked to conduct it, in consequence of the manner in which I had delivered my sentiments on the subject. A dependence was entertained of my colleague's complying with a request to conduct the services of the day; but, when he was applied to, he absolutely declined to do it. This created a perplexity. Mr. Corrie was not easily found. At last he was met with, and came and read the Episcopal Prayer and a sermon of Bishop Hoadly on the Accession of Queen Anne. The collection amounted to £44. 11s. Too much ill-humour, I am told, has been shewn on this affair, of which I myself was not the object. A majority of Mr. Kell's congregation voted for service. On the day they collected £7 odd, and on the next Sunday morning it was made up to somewhat more than £11. There was no service at Mr. Brewer's place, nor at Mr. Bennet's, a Lady Huntingdon's chapel. Both Mr. Morgan's and Carr's Lane were open. Good Mr. James Scott preached both at Stourbridge and Cradley. Friend Bransby was reluctantly prevailed on to preach. His text was, " They shouted, God save the King!" His sermon, it is reported, was a *lamentation* on the reign. Mr. Shattock shut his doors. There was no service at Mr. Field's in Warwick, nor at Mr. Emans' in Coventry. They both, at express invitation, went to hear and dine with Dr. Parr, who preached an hour and fifteen minutes. Mr. E. writes to me, "The Doctor's discourse was full of sound Whig sentiments, and steered equally clear of commendation as of censure. The matter was not well arranged; but there were a number of luminous passages in it. The whole was expressed and delivered with his accustomed emphasis and energy. He gave us a history of the Service appointed for the Accession, and of the several changes that have been made in it, and spoke in the highest terms of, and repeated with the greatest fervour, the Prayer for Unity, which was first added to it upon the Accession of George the First."

William Smith, Esq., M.P.,* to Rev. Robert Aspland.

No. I.

Parndon House, Essex, Dec. 27, 1812.

Dear Sir,—You must be perfectly convinced that my feelings on the subject you mention are always the same. I should have been happy to have brought it forward last year, because the time appeared favourable; and I am convinced that if I had not been unavoidably impeded by the events of the day, we should have had a good chance of success. How far anything resembling a similar spirit may prevail in the ensuing session, I cannot at present foresee; but rather fear that the hostility which High-Churchmen seem to be preparing against the Catholics, may be extended to all farther concessions of every kind to any class of religionists. Their hostility, however, will no otherwise affect or deter me, than as it may be likely to produce effect in practice; for so far from having given up either this or any other point for which we have yet to contend, when Lord Liverpool and Lord Harrowby, after the passing of the last Bill, said to me, "Well, we hope you will be contented now," I immediately replied, "Yes, *till next year*—but you know we have farther claims:" and I shall unquestionably be ready to bring them forward, if it should generally be deemed advisable. Whether petitions will forward us or not, must, I think, also depend on the apparent temper of the day. I suppose the petitioners would derive no assistance from the Methodists; but this you can ascertain with more facility than I can. Your hint respecting the 10 Anne is valuable to me: I may have known, but had quite forgotten it.

I am, dear Sir, your faithful, humble servant,

WILLIAM SMITH.

No. II.†

Seymour Street, June 8, 1827.

Dear Sir,—I am neither displeased nor do I wonder at the earnestness of your

---

* Endorsed thus—"In answer to an inquiry concerning his motion of Repeal of 9 William and Mary."

† "In reply to a communication of the resolutions of Unitarian Association, June 6, on Marriage Bill."

Unitarian Committee respecting the delay of the Marriage Bill, nor at their very probable suspicions that it may have been *unnecessarily* delayed. I only wish that they knew a little more by experience, what Lord Stowell some years ago most piteously lamented to me, how high among "the miseries of human life" stands the task of carrying through Parliament (especially late) a Bill, neither a measure of Government, nor of Opposition, nor of private interest, nor of general acceptance. Every one of these favoured descriptions shove it aside—it is put off without mercy; and one is often obliged to wait day after day for a favourable opportunity, till midnight or past, as I did last Friday, and then postpone, almost indefinitely. To add to all this, which is the common lot, and therefore no legitimate subject of complaint, our Bill is allowed by every one in principle, but objected to by scores in detail—one person to one point, and another to another, and often directly in each other's teeth; and I, who want to carry my point, not merely to swagger and make a noise, am compelled to hear all with patience and endeavour to make my hat fit every head. This I have been at, incessantly, for some weeks, making appointments with Mr. Peel, the Solicitor-General, the Oxford University Member, and other gentlemen (some kept and others not), till at last I *hope* I have drawn the affair to a close, and fashioned it into a PASS-able shape. This I thought NECESSARY, well knowing that, though all *appeared* fair, it had a host of secret enemies who only wanted a leader to start up and, with a joint effort, turn it out of doors. The great obstacle is the objections of the clergymen to perform even the shadow of a religious office differing from the established ritual, and especially for semi-deistical sectarians,—so that, to use the Solicitor-General's own words, "I must pass *by* the Church, not through it." By negotiation I hope to secure the *support* of these men, instead of rousing their opposition, which will almost to a certainty carry us through the Commons, and gain the *assistance* of the Bishop of Chester in the Lords,—a matter of considerable importance.

You are at perfect liberty to shew this to any friends.

I am, dear Sir, very truly yours,

WILLIAM SMITH.

In addition to all the rest, Mr. E. Taylor's illness has cut off all the help I looked for.

Mr. John Scott* to Rev. Robert Aspland.

3, Maida Place, Edgeware Road, December 30, 1812.

Dear Sir,—When I had the pleasure of seeing you, years ago, at my father's

---

* An able writer on literary and political topics, known in London first as the editor of the *Champion* newspaper, a journal in which Mr. Justice Talfourd and many other literary men essayed their youthful powers. He was afterwards editor of the *London Magazine*, and fell in a political duel.

house at Aberdeen, it did not seem very likely that I should ever be engaged in discharging the duties of a political writer. Yet it is even so—and I believe you are aware of the fact. At the desire of a gentleman in Lincolnshire, the Stamford News has been occasionally, I think, introduced to your notice, which paper I have conducted since its establishment. Of what has befallen its proprietor, in consequence of our attempts to expose the brutality and impolicy of the mode of punishment adopted in the army, public report has doubtless informed you. The publication, however, so far from being injured by coming in contact with the arm of power, has thriven so much, that we are encouraged to render it the basis of a London journal, the plan of which I now beg to lay before you. I have taken the liberty of forwarding you twelve copies of the Country paper, containing the prospectus of the London one. If you can do me a service, by introducing these to persons not unlikely to patronize the intended work, I am tempted to think that our previous acquaintance, and, I hope I may add, approbation of the political sentiments which it is our aim to enforce, will incline you so to do. I also add a couple of papers in which you will find a report of the proceedings of the very respectable meeting at Boston that assembled to congratulate Mr. Drakard on his liberation from confinement.

Although I have not until now had an opportunity of craving leave to renew our acquaintance, yet I have not been unobserving of those efforts in behalf of freedom of thought and action which you have at different times made with so much credit to your character. When I have seen your different publications, I have ever recollected with pleasure that at one time I knew the author, and benefited by his conversation. I have recently paid a visit to my friends in Aberdeen, all of whom had heard of the successful progress you have made by the impetus of talent, of which they well remembered the dawn, and expressed much satisfaction in consequence.

I will be very happy to call on you at Hackney any day you may be at leisure; and, begging you to excuse my intruding on you with the papers, I subscribe myself, your sincere friend and servant,

J. SCOTT.

William Hone to Rev. Robert Aspland.

No. I.

King's Bench Prison, June 28, 1817.

Sir,—I had the pleasure of receiving from you lists of my Juries, with remarks and intimations of much value, were it not that these Juries are abandoned. You will perceive by my register that I protested against them, which protest produced a letter from Mr. Litchfield, Solicitor to the Treasury, "consenting to waive the said nominations in consequence of the said notice, and further consenting that a fresh appointment shall be made by the Master of the Crown Office." I much incline to persuade myself that the prosecutions against me will be abandoned altogether; if they are not, I will furnish you with the fresh lists as soon as nominated.

I take this opportunity of saying that *(in the mean time)* I shall be greatly obliged by suggestions, hints, &c., for my defence. Surely I have seen a Sermon by Bishop Latimer, which he preached, I think before Edward VI., with a pack of cards in the pulpit—have you it, or can you procure it for me? What good History is there of the Common Prayer, shewing how its various portions originated, and what are peculiarly questionable? Where can I see Bishop Clayton's (Clogher?) Speech in the Irish House of Lords against the Athanasian Creed, somewhere about 1750? When did Earl Stanhope move to reform our statutes by repealing enactments against witches feeding the devil with beef, &c.? I want much of this kind of lore, which I dearly love, and think I can make good use of on my trials. Redcross-Street Library perhaps has things of great use to me. There were numerous Parodies against the Dissenters in Charles's time—can you get me the loan of any? James's Conferences with the Scots Commissioners at Hampton Court would be of much use to me; the orthodox monarch punned and quibbled and joked mightily, if I remember right. Has not Swift some Parodies? Surely he wrote one on the Nicene Creed against Walpole.

You may be surprised that I should put these questions to you at so late an hour. I assure you I am greatly at sea for want of materials. Abundance of well-meaning people call on me and talk of their good wishes for me, but few, *very* few, have rendered me any *real* service. I am wholly helpless here. I have books to be sure, but not such as help me to what I want, and what I should find if I were out and could rummage in a few collections similar to yours or the late Samuel Palmer's, or amongst black-letter collectors' stores. I sadly want hints, &c.

I have hastily trespassed upon you thus far. Will you excuse the liberty of my saying that I believe you will do me what service you have in your power.

I am, Sir, with great respect, your most obedient servant,

W. HONE.

No. II.

45, Ludgate Hill, November 20, 1818.

Dear Sir,—When I was about preparing a Prospectus of my Trials for insertion in the reviews and magazines of the ensuing month, I was seized with blood on my brain, which laid me by. With the assistance, however, of Dr. Birkbeck and a good apothecary, I am recovering fast, but remain very weak after blistering, cupping and a lowering regimen. I have never felt well since my trials, and perhaps never shall, as I have had no rest—no peace.

Your health I hope has improved, so as to enable you to lecture in the Borough, where I purposed hearing you; but this affair ends it, I fear. You will perhaps be able to notice the enclosed in the Monthly Repository. I do not ask this as a favour from *you*. I have *had* favour and countenance from you which I shall never forget, because under circumstances the most momentous in my life, nor ever cease to acknowledge, because, with the exception of yourself and at the most two others, I was literally deserted.

My head is very weak.

I am, dear Sir, your faithful servant,

W. HONE.

No. III.

Ludgate Hill, December 21, 1822.

My dear Sir,—* * * Really I know not what sort of a master of the revels I shall be on New-year's-day. As the time approaches, my fears increase. I am neither juvenile nor inventive, and surely shall be a lord of *mis*rule if I am forced into office. I can neither sing, dance nor play music; even the bladder and string refuse harmony to the touch of my fingers; cows in spring-time leap more gracefully; and, as to songs, " I know nothing nor won't be learned." These are fearful thoughts, and let them be thought on by the young folks.

Yesterday was the last of the three days in the calendar, on the first of which, in 1817, you encouraged me by your presence " to the height of that *great* argument" that, in its consequences, enables me to hold a pen to-day in acknowledgment of your unlooked-for support then. There is a gratitude that words do not exist to express, and mine is of it.

I am, my dear Sir, with affectionate respect, yours faithfully,

W. HONE.

INDEX.

Aberdeen, journey to, in 1799, 75. Professors in, 1799, 78.
Academy, Unitarian, 298, 303—330.
Acton, Rev. H., 284, 583.
Adams', John, syllabus, &c., 372.
Advice to students of divinity, 43.
Aggregate meeting of Unitarians, 555.
Aikin, Rev. John, 184.
Aikin, Edmund, 229.
Allchin, Mr., 192.
Amory, Thomas, 184.
Anniversary preachers before Unitarian Fund, 283.
Arian ministers in London, 1791, 185.
Aspland, Isaac, of Downham, 1.
Aspland, Isaac, of Wicken, 9, 99, 107, 497.
Aspland, John, of Soham, 6.
Aspland, Robert, Sen., of Wicken, 2, 5, 121, 123, 125, 146, 150.
Aspland, Rev. R., his birth, 3—an early politician, 5—school at Soham, 6—at Islington, 7—at Highgate, 9—at Hackney, 9—baptized, 15—visits Rev. T. Thomas, 18—recommended to the Ward Trustees, 19—assists in Mr. Thomas's schools, 21—becomes acquainted with the Middletons, 22—his theological reading, 26—admitted to Ward's Foundation, 30—studies at Battersea under Mr. Hughes, 32—heretical tendencies, 34—begins to preach, 41—enters the Bristol academy, 47—leaves Bristol, 66—his orthodoxy suspected, 70—preaches at Wicken, 71—his orthodoxy further declines, 73—goes to Aberdeen, 73—enters Marischal College, 78—changes in his religious views, 80—89—mental struggles, 90—leaves Aberdeen, 91—employments at Wicken, 92—ceases to be a member of the Devonshire-Square church, 95—resigns the Ward exhibition, 96—accepts an offer to engage in trade, 97—is disgusted with trade, 102—104—is invited to preach at Newport, 104—accepts the pastoral office there, 107—marries, 108—is dismissed by the Devonshire-Square church, 108—is ordained at Newport, 111—joins in establishing the Southern Unitarian Society, 112—begins school-keeping, 113—plans at Newport, 114—reflections on the birth of a son, 120—letter on future punishment, 120—abandons Arianism, 123—taste for gardening, 126—loses his first-born child, 127—preaches and publishes a fast sermon, 134—becomes a contributor to the Universal Theological Magazine, 140—is invited to remove to Norton, 144—accepts the invitation, 145—is invited at the same time to Warminster, 146—illness and death of his father, 146—farewell sermon at Newport, 156—is invited to preach as a candidate at Hackney, 165, 171—removes to Norton, 168—preaches on probation, 173—is invited to become the pastor, 173—preaches and publishes his initiatory sermon, 174, 175—is invited to become afternoon preacher at Newington Green, also at Worship Street, 177—early difficulties at Hackney, 177—preaches a funeral sermon for Charles James Fox, 181—establishes the Monthly Repository, 189—with Mr. Eaton establishes the Unitarian Fund, 194—establishes religious conferences at Hackney, 199—gives lectures to the younger members of his flock, 202—gives evidence respecting the Nottingham election, 203—preaches and prints a funeral sermon for Rev. Theophilus Lindsey, 206—preaches at Soham, 208—attends the assizes at Cambridge, 209, 225—controversy with Mr. Fuller on the Soham business, 211—215—extracts from his diary,

216—236—lays the foundation-stone of the New Gravel-Pit chapel, 231—establishes the Christian Tract Society, 249—last sermon at the Old Gravel-Pit, 254—opening of New meeting, 255—makes a selection of Hymns, 257—joins in the opposition to Lord Sidmouth's Bill, 262—sermon on the Trinity Bill, 278—preaches before the Widows' Fund, 296—letter to Rev. S. Webley, 298—founds and conducts the Unitarian Academy, 303—330—lectures on preaching, 320—converts an Atheist, 331—visits Hanwood, 341—illness at Liverpool, 343—publishes his Plea for Unitarian Dissenters, 347—publishes Three Sermons, 351—British Pulpit Eloquence, 353—establishes the Christian Reformer, 356—preaches on the peace in 1814, 357—illness and death of his mother, 361—365—preaches the funeral sermon for Rev. W. Vidler, 368—preaches and publishes sermons on Blasphemy, 380—is elected on Williams's Trust, 393—powers of conversation, 402—forms the Non-Con Club, 403—advocates the establishment of the Unitarian Association, 413—letters on Carlile's prosecution, 416—opposes Brougham's Education Bill, 426—exerts himself to save a capital convict, 433—draws up the Christians' Petition, 436—severe illness, 446—defends Rammohun Roy and rebukes Mr. Ivimey, 448—preaches the funeral sermon for Dr. Abraham Rees, 455—completes the twentieth year of his ministry at Hackney, 459—takes part in an ordination at Chester, 463—agitates for the repeal of the Test and Corporation Acts, 465—speech at the Commemoration Dinner, 482—correspondence with Mr. Charles Butler, 485—488—advocates Catholic Emancipation, 490—officiates at the funeral of the Rev. Thomas Belsham, 499—journey on behalf of the Unitarian Association, 502—visits Paris, 503—prepares and presents an address to William IV., 508—preaches a sermon on the coronation of William IV., 516—publishes a volume of Sermons, 518—assists in obtaining the Marriage Bill, 524—530—composes Form of Marriage, 530—presents addresses to Queen Victoria and Queen Adelaide, 544—enlarges the Christian Reformer, 546—serious illness, 556—returns to public duty, 558—opens the chapel at Dukinfield, &c., 559—visits Cheshire and Yorkshire, 559—563—preaches funeral sermon for Dr. Channing, 576—forms an English Presbyterian Union, 576—speech at the Unitarian Association, 579—last visit to Devonshire, 583—mourns the death of Mr. G. W. Wood, 585—preaches his last sermon, 588—address to the young, 593—illness and death of his youngest daughter, 595—598—closes his editorial labours, 596—decline and death, 598, 599—list of his publications, 607.

Aspland, Mrs., 110, 130, 147, 148, 150, 191.
Aspland, William, of Wicken, 101.

Badcock, Mr., 184.
Baptisms at Maze Pond, &c., 29—at Newport, 110.
Baptist Assembly, 122.
Barbauld, Rev. R., 190, 218.
Baron, Rev. Thomas, 43.
Battersea, academy at, 32.
Bellingham, the assassin, 272.
Belsham, Rev. Thomas, 12, 119, 127, 128, 141, 143, 145, 155, 162, 165, 172, 185, 198, 204, 206, 259, 263, 265—269, 270, 274, 278, 305, 306, 314, 349, 360, 376, 384, 385, 407, 412, 418, 419, 442, 498—500.
Bogue and Bennett, Messrs., 97.
Boyle, Mr., 100.
Brekell, Mr., 184.
Bretland, Mr., 184.
Bright, Dr., 556, 558, 595.
Brighton Unitarian chapel, 276.
Bristol Academy, 48. Its students in 1798, 50.
Bristol Education Society, 49.
Broadbent, Rev. T. B., 313.
Brook, Hannah, 3.
Brougham's Education Bill, 424.
Brown, Principal, 86.
Browne, Rev. Theophilus, 129.
Burdett, Sir Francis, 254, 484.
Butcher, Rev. Edmund, 185, 284.
Butler, Mr. Charles, 436, 454, 485, 487.
Button, Mr. William, 139.

Calder, Dr., 184.
Cambridge assizes, 209, 225.
Canning, Mr., 469, 470, 471.
Cant terms, 141.
Cappe, Rev. N., 184, 190.
Cappe, Mrs., 190, 333, 371, 441.
Cardale, Rev. P., 184.
Carlile's, Richard, trials, 415.
Carmarthen academy, 439.
Carpenter, Rev. Benjamin, 184.
Carpenter, Dr., 191, 249, 282, 462.
Catechism and Prayers for the Young, 558.
Catholic disabilities, repeal of, 490.
Channing, Dr., 437, 441, 521, 576.
Chillingworth, 354.

Christian Miscellany, 186.
Christian Reformer, 356, 546.
Christian Tract Society, 249, 337.
Christians' petition, 436.
Christie, Mr. John, 174, 191.
Christie, Mr. William, 241.
Clark, Rev. S., 184, 191.
Clarke, Rev. Richard, 106.
Clarke, Abraham, 112.
Clarkson, Mr., 444.
Cogan, Dr., 119, 333.
Cogan, Rev. E., 217.
Coke, Dr., 261.
Coles, Rev. Thomas, 77.
Commemoration dinner, 481.
Commentaries and Essays, 184.
Conferences, religious, at Hackney, 199, 217—225.
Congregational Fund Board, 438.
Conversations, notes of, 400.
Convicts for transportation, 122.
Cooke, Mr. Thomas, 106, 112, 117.
Cooper, Mr. Alexander, 98.
Cooper, Rev. Thomas, 322.
Corporation and Test Acts, 465.
Corresponding Society, London, 273.
Cox, Rev. Dr., 50, 71, 126, 167. His letter of reminiscences, 67.
Cox, Dr., of Fishponds, 160.
Crompton, Dr., 203.

Dalton, Rev. Thomas, 112, 613.
David, Rev. Job, 49, 159, 184, 192.
Deacon, Mr., of Leicester, 167.
Debates on repeal of Test and Corporation Acts, 476—481.
Declaration in the Test Repeal Act, 480.
Defoe's Review, 186.
Deputies, committee of London, 467.
Devonshire Square, Baptist church at, 13, 27, 94—96, 108.
Dewhurst, Rev. John, 308—311.
Dissenters' Chapels Bill, 582, 592.
Doctrine of future punishment, 120, 125.
Drummond, Dr. W. H., 501.
Dudley charity sermon, 228.
Dukinfield, 559, 567, 573.
Dunton's Athenian Gazette, 186.
Dyer, Mr. George, 176, 565.

Eaton, Mr. David, 191, 192, 497.
Eddowes, Mr. Ralph, 245.
Edwards, Rev. John, 165.
Emons, John, 4, 41, 102, 123, 126, 165, 410, 411, 522.
English Presbyterian Reporter, 534.
Erasmus, 552.
Essex-Street chapel, 162, 165.
Evans, Dr. John, 28, 103, 111, 112, 185, 191.
Evanson, Mr., 184.
Expository preaching, 115.
Eyre, Rev. John, 10, 15, 16.

Fast-day, 1803, 134. Sermons, character of, 137.
Fearon, Mr., 575.
Flower, Mr. Benjamin, 6, 46, 126, 137, 138, 139, 142, 151, 191, 221, 240, 253, 257, 496.
Flower, Mrs., 142, 221, 252.
Foljambe, Mr., 184.
Forbes, Mr., 78, 79.
Foster, Mr. John, 31, 32, 33, 34, 159, 160, 161.
Foster, Thomas, the Unitarian Quaker, 234.
Fox's, Charles James, death, 179. His character, 180.
French Revolution of 1830, 511.
Frend, Mr. W., 253, 565.
Fry, Rev. Richard, 239.
Fullagar, Rev. John, 111.
Fuller, Rev. Andrew, 3, 5, 14, 15, 26, 36, 76, 123, 140, 145, 207—215, 226, 227, 275, 363.
Fyson, Robert, 37, 38, 41, 81, 149.

Gambier, Mr. J. E., 191.
Garnham, Mr., 184.
George IV., 506.
Gill, Mr., of Gainsborough, 184.
Gillyat, a schoolmaster at Islington, 7, 73.
Gisburne, Rev. John, of Soham, 207, 215, 222.
Godwin, Mr., 131.
Goldsmidt, Sir L., anecdote of, 502.
Goodier, Rev. Benjamin, 159, 322, 328.
Gravel-Pit congregation, Hackney, 165, 172, 175, 199, 220, 223, 231, 235, 254—256, 257, 259, 437, 447, 450, 474, 518, 548, 557, 569.
Green, Mr. Charles, 597.
Gregoire, Abbé, 504, 505.
Grey, Earl, 204, 534, 535.
Grundy, Rev. J., 254, 284.
Gunning's, Miss, "Farmer's Boy," 130.

Hacon, Mr., 595.
Hall, Rev. Robert, 19, 20, 27, 45, 51, 72, 73, 125, 134, 138, 139.
Hallam, Mr., 552.
Hardy, Thomas, 74, 373.
Harries, Rev. Edward, 335.
Harris, Mr. Michael, 595.
Harris, the convict, case of, 433.
Harvest, disastrous, of 1799, 76.
Harvey, Mr. D. W., 196.
Haynes's, Hopton, Scriptural Account, 356.
Hazlitt, Mr., of Maidstone, 184.
Hewley suit, 576.
Holden, Rev. L., 191.
Holland, Lord, 181, 204, 205, 371, 378, 420, 421, 470, 473, 479, 480, 488, 493, 501, 534, 536, 542, 543, 544, 551, 564.

Holland, Rev. John, 190, 282.
Holt, Rev. James, 495.
Hone, William, trial of, 386. Letters from, 618.
Hooker, Richard, 354.
Horncastle, 228.
Horsfield, Rev. T. W., 322, 329.
Houghton, Mr., of Norwich, 228, 230.
Hoxton academy, 456.
Hughes, Rev. Joseph, 18, 30, 31, 39, 40.
Hughes, Rev. William, 159.
Hughes, Mrs. Mary, 249, 335, 338, 443, 450.
Huntingdon, William, S. S., 11.

Income-tax, 1804, 143.
Indemnity Acts, 465.
Isle of Wight, apprehensions of invasion, 132, 142.
Ivimey, Mr., 97, 448, 493, 494, 510.

James, Mr. Isaac, 88.
Jeffrey, Mr., 419.
Johns, Rev. William, 327, 328.
Jones, Rev. Daniel, 192.
Joyce, Rev. Jeremiah, 8, 192, 312, 366, 407.
Joyce, Mr. Joshua, 366.
Jubilee, celebration of, 239.

Kell, Rev. Edmund, 159.
Kenrick, Rev. Timothy, death of, 145.
Kenrick, Rev. John, 191, 419, 536.
Kent, Duchess of, 544.
Kentish, Rev. John, 13, 137, 173, 191, 192, 198, 206, 217, 281, 284, 518, 600.
Kidd, Professor, 78, 79.

Lancaster, Joseph, 229.
Lardner, Dr., 224.
Law, Bishop, 277.
Lectures to the young at Hackney, 202, 218.
Lewis, Mr. G., 185.
Library, the, 186.
Lillie, Rev. W., 184.
Lindsay, Dr. James, 185, 204, 228, 429.
Lindsey, Rev. Theophilus, 162, 183, 184, 193, 198, 205.
Lindsey, Mrs., 193, 207.
Liverpool, persecution at, 375.
Lloyd, Dr. Charles, 238, 382, 418.
Lord's Supper, administration of, 115.
Lyons, Rev. James, 283, 287, 291.

Mackay, Mr., of Belfast, 184.
Madge, Rev. Thomas, 192.
Mardon, Rev. B., 462.
Marron, M., 370, 371.
Marsom, Mr. John, 47, 75, 111, 124, 142, 146, 173, 184, 191, 195, 534.
Mason, Dr., of New York, 248.
Medley, Rev. Samuel, 35.

Meeke, Rev. J. C., 322.
Merivale, Mr., 184.
Methodists, Wesleyan, 262.
Middleton, Joshua, 22.
Middleton, Miss, 191.
Middleton, Miss Anna, 110.
Middleton, Mr. Jesse, 120.
Middleton, Mr. John, 22.
Middleton, Rev. Erasmus, 22.
Middleton, Sara, 47, 53, 55, 57, 60, 62, 64, 65, 72, 80, 82, 90, 92, 108.
Mills, Rev. John, 111.
Milton, John, 452.
Milton, Lord, 204.
Ministers of the Three Denominations, meetings of, 435, 492, 495.
Monastery of St. Bernard's, 570.
Montgomery, Dr. Henry, 500.
Monthly Repository, 189, 464—writers in Vol. I., 191, 546.
Morell, Dr. John, 315.
Mott, Rev. William, 106.
Mottershead, Mr., 184.
Mower, Mr., of Woodseats, 170.

Nayler, Mr. Benjamin, 168.
Newport congregation, 105, 107, 109, 114, 159—ordination at, 111—conferences at, 124—fears of invasion, 132, 143.
Nicklin, Rev. Thomas, 101.
Non-Con Club, 403, 467, 517, 550, 564.
Nonconformist, the, in Monthly Repository, 404.
Norris, Rev. H. H., 200, 344.
Norton in Derbyshire, 162, 168.
Norton Hall, 168.
Nottingham election, 1807, 203.

Occasional Papers, 186.
O'Flanagan, Patrick (a pasquinade), 345.
Old Whig, 186.
Oration on laying foundation of the Gravel-Pit chapel, 232.
Ordination service at Newport, 111, 112—at Chester, 463—at Lydgate, 559.
Organ, on the use of an, 549.
Orphan Working School, 531, 540.
Outrage on the Danish fleet, 220.

Palmer, Mr., of Macclesfield, 184.
Palmer, Rev. S., 190, 233, 350.
Paris, visit to, 503.
Parkes, Mr. S., 218.
Parker, Rev. S., 192.
Parliamentary grant, 554.
Parr, Dr., 418, 436.
Peace of 1801, 118.
Penal laws, 433.
Perceval, Mr., 259, 272.
Periodical literature of the Presbyterians, 186.

Persecution of French Protestants, 370.
Pett, Dr., 450.
Philosophical Society at Newport, 116, 154.
Pickbourn, Rev. James, 196.
Pitt's, Mr., triple assessment, 36.
Placard to rebuke fanaticism, 547.
Platts, Mr., of Boston, 228.
Plea for Unitarian Dissenters, 347.
Porter, Anna Maria, 25, 72.
Porter, Jane, 25.
Porter, Rev. Edward, of Highgate, 9.
Potticary, Rev. John, 106, 154, 156.
Preachers, 1735—1812, before the Widows' Fund, 294.
Presbyterian congregations, changes of doctrine in, 183.
Presbyterian deputies, 522.
Presbyterian Fund, 437.
Presbyterian ministers of London, 531, 541, 564.
Price, Dr., 175, 184.
Priestley, Dr., 175, 184.
Protestant Dissenters' Magazine, 186.
Psalmody, on, 548.

Quarles's "Historie of Samson," 163.
Queen Caroline's death, 422.
"Queen's Book," the, 146.

Rammohun Roy, 448, 513—515.
Rees, Dr. Abraham, 185, 204, 433, 439, 440, 455.
Rees, Dr. Thomas, 283, 395—398, 437, 531, 537, 554, 556.
Reform Act, 515.
Reformation, tricentenary of the, 551.
Reid, Mr. W. H., 191.
Review of the year 1809, 234.
Revolution of 1688, 151.
Revolution Society at Newport, 116.
Ricardo, David, 234.
Richards, Rev. W., 191.
Richmond, Mr. C., 517.
Ridge, Mrs. Henry, 595.
Riots in London, 8.
Rippon, Dr., 137, 508.
Roberts, Mr., of Llanbrynmair, 440.
Robertson, Rev. James, 379.
Robinson, Mr. H. C., 191.
Robinson, Robert, 4, 23.
Romilly, Sir Samuel, 371, 379, 382, 383, 411.
Ronalds, Mr. Francis, 166, 171.
Roscoe, Mr., 436.
Russell, Lord John, 468, 470, 476, 491.
Rutt, Mr. J. T., 170, 173, 178, 191, 233, 565.
Ryland, Dr., 14, 48, 53, 56, 60, 88.

Saunders, Rev. Samuel, 32.
Scott, Rev. Russell, 111, 112.
Scott, Mr., of Ipswich, 184.

Scott, Mr. John, 617.
Severn, Rev. W., 191.
Shadwell, Mr., 379.
Shepherd, Dr., on the Education Bill, 425.
Shore, Mr., of Meersbrook, 143, 144, 169, 171, 176.
Sidmouth's, Lord, Bill, 259.
Simpson, Rev. John, 195.
Sitch, Mr. J., 109.
Smethurst, Rev. John, 317, 322, 583.
Smith, Dr. J. P., 155, 233, 453, 508.
Smith, Boatswain, 510.
Smith, William, M.P., 112, 144, 263, 274, 276, 616.
Society for promoting the Knowledge of the Scriptures, 184.
Soham, town of, 4, 5, 207, 221.
Southern Unitarian Society, 112, 122, 128, 129, 140.
Spurrell, Mr. J., 190, 191.
Stapleton, French prison at, 53.
Stevens, Rev. William, 159, 318, 387.
Stuart, Professor, 78, 83, 88, 89.
Students at the Unitarian academy, 322.
Sturch, Mr. W., 557.
Sussex, Duke of, 481, 485, 578.
Sutton, Archbishop, 277.

Taylor, Mr. James, of Philadelphia, 244, 519, 552.
Taylor, Bishop Jeremy, 355.
Test-Act Reporter, 468.
Thanksgiving-day, 1802, 121—of 1814, 357.
Theological Repository and its contributors, 184.
Thomas, Rev. Timothy, 13, 18, 21, 26, 27, 45, 70, 73, 80, 83, 93, 94, 95, 109.
Thomas, Rev. Joshua, 21.
Thompson, Rev. Josiah, 20, 21, 236.
Three Denominations of London Ministers, 492, 495, 508. Dissolution of, 530—545.
Thrush, Captain, 442.
Tingcombe, Rev. John, 159.
Toleration Act, attempts to amend, 259, 273.
Toulmin, Dr., 110, 111, 112, 123, 129, 191, 237—240, 612.
Toulmin, Rev. Henry, 184.
Townshend, Rev. J., 191.
Tracts for the People, 558.
Travelling in 1800, 107.
Trinity Bill, 276.
Trustees, Dr. Williams's, 394.
Turner, Rev. W., 190, 191.
Turn-out of work-people, 572.
Tutchin, Mr., an ejected minister, 105.
Twining, Rev. Thomas, 106.

Unitarian Association established, 413
    British and Foreign, 464, 502, 568.

Unitarian academy, 298, 303—330, 408.
Unitarian Committee, resolution of, 492.
Unitarian Fund, 196, 253, 281—292.
Unitarian Marriage Bills, 524—530.
Unitarian Society, 184.
United Committee of Protestant Dissenters, 468, 472, 473, 535.
Universal Theological Magazine, 139, 140, 145, 156, 188, 189.
Universalists' Miscellany, 187.

Vice-Chancellor Shadwell's judgment, 536.
Victoria, Queen, 541.
Vidler, Rev. William, 139, 141, 145, 187, 195, 220, 367.

Wakefield, Gilbert, 184.
Walker, Rev. George, 184.
Wallace, Rev. Robert, 546.
Ward, Dr. James, 18. His Foundation, 18, 19, 96.
Wareham, opening of the Unitarian chapel at, 513.
Warwick Tract Society, 228.
Waters, Mr., of Ashburton, 184.
Watts, Rev. Gabriel, 105.
Webley, Rev. S., of Wedmore, 297.
Wellbeloved, Rev. C., 137, 192, 193.
Western Unitarian Society, 550.

Wiche, Rev. G., 184.
Wicken, village of, 1, 5, 41, 45, 71, 125.
Widows' Fund, 293.
White, Bishop of Philadelphia, 248, 553.
Wicksteed, Rev. Charles, 559, 568.
Willetts, Mr., of Newcastle, 184.
Williams, Dr. Daniel, and his Trusts, 389, 439, 579, 582.
Williams, Dr., of Sydenham, 184.
Winder, Mr. Henry, 291.
Winter, Dr. Robert, 159, 533.
Winterbotham, Rev. W., 35.
Wolverhampton chapel, case of the, 378.
Wood, Mr. G. W., M.P., 577, 584, 585.
Wood, Mr. W. R., 590.
Wood, Mr. B., M.P., 592.
Wood, Rev. William, of Leeds, 173.
Wood, Miss, 587, 588.
Worship-Street Baptist chapel, 47, 103.
Worthington, Rev. Hugh, 186, 297.
Wright, Rev. Richard, 137, 188, 284, 465, 550.
Wright, Mr. John, of Liverpool, 375.
Wright, Dr. John, 184.
Wyvill, Rev. C., 252.

Yates, Rev. John, 409.
York General Baptists, 193.
Young, Professor, 419.
Young, Mr. James, 588.

ERRATA.

Page 7, line 6 from the bottom, for "who was," read, who had been.*
— 105, note, line 3 from the bottom, for "Uniformity," read, Toleration.
— 192, note, line 4 from the bottom, for "Rev." read, Mr.

* Dr. Davies resigned the office of Tutor at Homerton at Midsummer, 1787.

www.ingramcontent.com/pod-product-compliance
Lightning Source LLC
Chambersburg PA
CBHW081837230426
43669CB00018B/2734